Rise of the PHOENIX

Other Books by Useni Eugene Perkins

SOCIOLOGY

Explosion of Chicago's Black Street Gangs: 1900 to the Present
Harvesting New Generations: The Positive Development of Black Youth
Home is a Dirty Street: The Social Oppression of Black Children

POETRY

An Apology to my African Brother
Black is Beautiful
Midnight Blues in the Afternoon
Silhouette
The West Wall
We Have Been There Before: A Poetic Narrative Through Black History
Memories and Images: Selected Poems
Bikabi: Peace & Harmony
Poetry from the Masters: Black Arts Movement
edited by Useni Eugene Perkins

CHILDREN'S

Afrocentric Self Inventory and Discovery Workbook for African American Youth
Black Fairy and Other Plays
Hey Black Child: Poems for Black Children.
Urban Quartet: Realities Facing Today's Youth (Plays)

WORKBOOKS

Achieving Your True Potential: A Workbook for Black Youth
Sankofa Male Responsibility Curriculum
Sankofa Developmental and Educational Manual for Fathers

Rise of the PHOENIX

VOICES FROM CHICAGO'S BLACK STRUGGLE, 1960-1975

EDITED BY

Useni Eugene Perkins

FOREWORD BY JULIEANNA L. RICHARDSON

Chicago

Third World Press Foundation
Publishers since 1967
Chicago

First Edition
Printed in the United States of America

Library of Congress Control Number
2017953363

ISBN 13
978-0-88378-306-1

22 21 20 19 18 17   6 5 4 3 2 1

Cover photo of The Wall of Respect by Roy Lewis

In memory of the following Freedom Fighters who shared their stories with us before joining our Ancestors:

Hannibal Tirus Afrik

Dr. Donn Bailey

Gwendolyn Brooks

Dr. Margaret G. Burroughs

Kelan Phil Cohran

Henry English

Okoro Harold Johnson

Theodis Leonard

Robert Lucas

Lu Palmer

Milele Cheryl Simms

Dr. Barbara Sizemore

Nahaz Rodgers

Theodore Ward

Mayor Harold Washington

And to the many, many other ancestors who also struggled to help Black Chicago achieve self-determination, self-reliance and equality.

Contents

Section One: Cultural Arts and Black Awareness

Section Two: Institution Building and Community Advocacy

Section Three: Political Awareness

Section Four: Educational Advocacy and Reform

Section Five: "Les Enfants" of Chicago's Black Struggle

Section Six: Epilogue

Appendix

Contributors

FOREWORD

Julieanna L. Richardson

When I was approached by Useni Eugene Perkins to write the foreword for this book, *Rise of the Phoenix: Voices from Chicago's Black Struggle 1960-1975,* I accepted so with great honor. The request came from one of Chicago's treasures—a respected poet, playwright and community activist. I first learned of Mr. Perkins when I was a young college student studying theatre at a time when black voices were so rare. That was eight years before I moved to Chicago in 1980 as a young lawyer-determined to represent black artists and art organizations. My law firm introduced me to Val Gray Ward and Frances Ward of Kuumba Theatre, and the Chicago community opened me up to an avalanche of blackness. It was in the words of Trinity United Church of Christ's Reverend Jeremiah Wright "unashamedly black." It was also bold, passionate and committed. It is this Chicago community that I would fall in love with and call my home. It is this community, sometimes frankly, that I miss today.

The period of 1960 to1975 is a seminal period in Chicago's and American history and deserving for the spotlight that this book shines on it. It is important because Chicago played a critical leadership role in the Civil Rights and Black Power movements and to not have this role acknowledged and studied by scholars and historians would be the ultimate tragedy. I have spent the past twelve years working on *The HistoryMakers,* a 501 (c) (3) nonprofit organization, an organization I founded to create the largest repository of African American video oral history interviews. As of this writing, our archive houses 9,000 hours of African American videotaped first person narratives. My project, like this book, is based on the premise that it is important to document the life, culture and contributions of African Americans through the words and memories of those who lived the history they so passionately speak of and to fill in the missing historical record. Very little is known of this period. Too often Chicago's contributions are overshadowed and have been too little studied for the importance that they represent to the historical canon. The question is why? In some accounts, those who made the history have passed away and so tragically have their libraries of knowledge. In other cases, people were too busy creating history to document it and, finally, there are those who fear or distrust that the telling of their stories will result in their misuse or distortion, not thinking of what loss this is to society in general and to current and future generations in particular.

Too often our community has imposed upon itself the burden of reinventing itself every generation bereft of its historical memory. The question is why, and so I applaud wholeheartedly those who stepped forward to tell their stories. For within their stories lie our stories, our history and our sense of agency.

During the fifteen year period covered by *Rise of the Phoenix*, Chicago's black community could be best described as a tempest in the tea pot. It no longer wanted to be contained, told what to do or restricted. It had tired of kitchenette apartments, restrictive covenants, segregation, unfair hiring practices, unequal pay and poor living conditions. It had found its "blackness" and was gleeful in the finding. The focus was on Africa, Pan-Africanism and connecting those African descendants with their Motherland. There was a certain energy that permeated the air. The commitment to change and to social and civic action could be found almost everywhere. Those who were trying to keep the status quo were often forced to step aside and, most importantly, move out of the way. This change and how it came to be is documented here. Some of it was planned, some organic and chaotic, and some efforts failed. But the importance lies in the efforts of those who were valiant and defiant manner.

As you read these pages, you will learn or be reminded through the writings of sociologist and cultural leader Carol Adams about the group called Catalyst—change agents who contributed to the political, educational and social fabric of the city. They took on WTTW, the elections of Mayor Richard Hatcher and Chicago alderman Fred Hubbard, and the seating of blacks on the board of the United Way. Composed of historians, scholars and writers like Lerone Bennett, Anderson Thompson and Charles Houston, as well as advertising agency owner Vince Culler and founder Charles Ross, the Catalyst's motto was "We Don't Stop. We Won't Stop." So was the case with the Coordinating Council of Community Organizations (CCCO) led by the legendary Al Raby, who would serve as its spokesperson. CCCO invited Dr. Martin Luther King, Jr. to Chicago to lead a march in the racially segregated Marquette Park—an experience that would cause Dr. King to refer to Chicago as one of the most segregated places in America. CCCO would activate others into action like Robert Starks, a young college student who would also become active with the Chicago Friends of SNCC. CCCO would also take on housing and school desegregation issues as well. This is why the essays written by community activist/teachers Theodis Leonard, Sr. and Hannibal Afrik provide important context. From white flight to the Willis Wagons that resulted in shortened school days and substandard conditions for minority students, these two committed teachers provide an important historical context with their descriptions of freedom days, parental schools, closed campuses, the role of truant officers and school policy committees. They tell of their efforts to instill a sense of pride in students who had been abandoned by the system; one such student was Dwight McKee, who provides historical context of growing up in Memphis where he saw few whites and moving to Chicago where he saw no whites. He also speaks of the veil that separated the South and West side communities, the empowerment of gangs along with the emergence of Jeff Fort, Herb Kent's role in tempering gang violence and the role of students in pushing for change. While one is heartened by the change that Gwendolyn Brooks made in the life of writer Ellis Cose, though he did not realize it at the time (being young and unaware), one cannot help but wonder and be saddened by the description of the positive changes at Fenger High School with the SOUL program and how they have disappeared 40 years later.

We also learn of the importance of 1968 with the assassination of Reverend Martin Luther King, the contentious Democratic Convention and the role of Mayor Richard J. Daley, the election of President Richard Nixon, the continued emergence of the Black Power Movement and the riots that erupted across the United States. Reverend Jesse Jackson and Operation Breadbasket played a pivotal role in all that happened.

While the names of Reverend Jackson, Al Raby, Reverend Clay Evans, Bill Berry, Reverends Claude and Addie Wyatt are better known, in this book, you will also learn about important but lesser known names like Victor Adams, Sharron Matthews, Harold Charles, Bobby Wright, Roy Stell, Arleen Hunter, Dorothy Roberson, Betty Randallto to name a few.

In the area of post-secondary education, we learn of the beginnings of Malcolm X College, Olive Harvey College and the Center for Inner City Studies and its Communiversity as well as the influence of Chicago Teachers College (now Chicago State University). Their contributions to the Chicago community have been significant and wide spread. One has to ponder what Chicago and Chicago's black community would have been without them. Central to this discussion are the difference between urban studies and inner city studies as well as the creation and emergence of an African-centered curriculum. The creation and influence of UFOMI (United Afrikans For One Motherland, International) and the *Afrika Must Unite Magazine* under the leadership Ruwa Chiri is also told so poignantly by Sarudzayi Sevanhu.

Furthermore, this time of social upheaval was balanced by the creation of new cultural icons and cultural institutions giving forth new images and new identities.

Kuumba Theatre, ETA Theatre, DuSable Museum, Third World Press, the African Heritage Ensemble and many, many more were active educating the community and providing a cultural renaissance that still begs to be studied and given its proper place in history.

This is ultimately what Useni Eugene Perkins has done and begs us to continue. This is a start...an important start. Without him taking this important step forward, this period and its importance could have faded from view. Read on and see how you can learn or if you were part of this important period, add to the historical record. In time, many will call this a critically important period in Chicago's history. For this we owe Useni Eugene Perkins and Third World Press a debt of gratitude.

PREFACE

When perusing the many books written on the Civil Rights Movement and to a lesser degree the Black Power Movement, Chicago is seldom given the space and recognition it deserves. Aside from acknowledging the brutal 1955 Money, Mississippi murder of fourteen-year-old Chicagoan Emmett Till as a major precursor to these movements, as well as Dr. Martin Luther King Jr.'s compromised Freedom Movement and the assassination of Chairman Fred Hampton of the Chicago Black Panther Party, Chicago's role in these movements become a mere footnote in history. Yet when you critically review the period from 1960 to 1975, when these movements were most active, a discernable person can see the major role Chicago played in each. I found this gross omission to be unacceptable. In this regard, I sought out to tell the story of the role Black Chicago actually played in what many considered to be one of the most important periods in American history. To accomplish this task, I felt the story could best be told by those who were actively involved in Chicago's Black struggle from 1960 to 1975. Also, because I make no claim to be a historian, this format would best be suited for my experience as a social practitioner, writer and activist. When I shared my thoughts about this project with Haki R. Madhubuti, publisher of Third World Press, he encouraged me to pursue it. With this incentive, I proceeded to identify people who lived in Chicago from 1960 to 1975 and had some involvement in Chicago's Black struggle during that period. Because of the diversity of this struggle, it was important that the people I asked to participate in this project represented a broad cross-section of the Black community.

To assist me in identifying people to participate in this project, I consulted with Bennett Johnson, Vice President of Third World Press, and Rev John Porter, both veterans of Chicago's Black struggle. A list of people was identified and asked to write a paper about their experiences and perceptions of Chicago's Black struggle from 1960 to 1975. Of the fifty-four people whom we asked, forty-one favorably responded. Unfortunately, among those who did submit papers, nine have made their transition before the book was completed. Also, there were several prominent activists, from that period, whom I would have liked to have participated but chose not to, while from others I received no response. Also, to insure that the book captured the voices of some people who were difficult to contact or had made their transition, we extracted statements or interviews they had made during 1960 to 1975 from the *Black Express Newspaper* (Courtesy of Vivian Harsh Collection) and the *Black Books Bulletin* (Courtesy of Third World Press).

The editing of these papers was minimal because I felt it was important that each voice be recorded as it was originally written. As the editor, I did not want to impose my judgment or personal opinion on any of the narratives. However, if there was a pronounced discrepancy in a narrative, I would discuss it with the author and reach a mutual agreement.

I am grateful to all who contributed papers to this project and believe they provide a representative, if not definitive, commentary on the important events that took place during Chicago's Black struggle from 1960-1975. As you will discern, these events are told from many perspectives and describe the personal observations and experiences that influenced these writers to participate in the struggle to change Chicago's longtime image of being the most segregated city in America to one which provide equal opportunities to all of its citizens.

These events are listed under the following five sections that corresponds to their primary focus, although some do overlap. Section One: Cultural Arts and Black Awareness – Papers that delineated how the arts and culture contributed to the ideological and cultural foundation of the struggle. Section Two: Institution Building and Community Advocacy – Papers that delineate the role community organizations, alliances and institutions played as advocates in the struggle.

Section Three: Political Awareness – Papers that delineate the role politics played in shaping the strategy and political dynamics of the struggle. Section Four: Educational Advocacy and Reform – Papers that delineate efforts to improve the quality of education for Black students that best serve the needs and interest of the Black community. Section Five: Les Enfants of Chicago's Black Struggle – Papers that delineate what influenced the younger generation of that period to become involved in the Black struggle.

To have a labor of love come to fruition is most gratifying. Although the completion of this book took longer than I anticipated, the passion I had for it never withered. With a sense of humility and appreciation, I'm indebted to many for helping to make this book possible. First, I would like to give thanks to the God I serve for helping me to make it through several health challenges I had during the development of this book. I'm especially thankful to my brother-in-struggle and publisher, Haki Madhubuti, for maintaining confidence in me and sharing my vision to capture the spirit of Chicago's Black struggle from1960 to 1975. Despite the bleak economic climate that publishers faced, he never wavered in his commitment to publish the book. Also, Bennett Johnson continued to provide support and counsel during times when I needed help to keep things in focus. Also, as she has done with my other books published by Third World Press, Gwendolyn Mitchell, the senior editor, provided candid suggestions and excellent editorial help. Additionally, I would like to thank Denise Borel Billups for her meticulous formatting of the manuscript and graphic design and Brittany Green, intern from Chicago State University for additional proofing. I also would like to acknowledge my wife Sharon Diane, daughter Julia Evalyn, son Russell Patrice, sister-in-law Thelma, niece Marian, nephew Louverture and my ancestors: parents, Marion and Eva, brothers, Robert and Toussaint, Margaret G. Burroughs, teachers, Ms. Berry, Ms. Gray, Ms. Proctor and my spiritual mentor Paul Robeson for their support during my life journey.

Finally, it is my hope that this book will influence others to do more extensive research and writings on Chicago's Black Struggle, so that the present and future generations will have an accurate recorded history of the sacrifices made in our protracted struggle to correct many of the injustices that still resonate in what Carl Sandburg boasted as "The city with the big shoulders."

A Luta Continua
Useni Eugene Perkins

INTRODUCTION

The Genesis of Chicago's Black Struggle

The Black struggle in Chicago for equality, self-determination and self-reliance from 1960 to 1975 cannot be fully comprehended without having some knowledge of the continuum of struggle that preceded it. The very essence of struggle during any one period in history is ultimately influenced by past events that serve as a blueprint for future generations. The Black struggle that emanated in Chicago from 1960 to 1975 would never have taken place had it not adhered to this principle. When viewed from a continuum of struggle, we can identify a cascade of events that led to this important and turbulent period.

There were four historic events prior to 1960 that became the prologue for the Civil Rights and Black Power movements. The first was the historic May 17, 1954 ruling of the *U.S. Supreme Court in Brown v. Board of Education,* which was cited by Supreme Court Justice Warren "That in the field of public education the doctrine of 'separate but equal' has no place." This ruling was an affront to the advocates of white supremacy and only **widened** the racial divide between white and Black Americans. The second event was the August 28, 1955 brutal murder of young Chicagoan Emmett Till in Money, Mississippi by white vigilantes. After three days, Till's brutalized body was found in the Tallahatchie River and later brought to rest at Roberts Temple in Chicago before thousands of mournful onlookers. His courageous mother, Mamie E. Bradley, asked for her son's casket to remain open so all the world could witness this dastardly act of racial violence.

The third event was the December 1, 1955 arrest of NAACP volunteer worker Rosa Parks who was arrested for refusing to yield her seat to a white man on a Montgomery, Alabama bus. Her arrest drew national attention and ushered in the arrival of Dr. Martin Luther King Jr., who became president of the Montgomery Improvement Association, which led a successful bus boycott for one year. The fourth event occurred in September 1957 at Central High School in Little Rock, Arkansas when nine Black students were recruited to enroll in the previously all-white school. Oval Faubus, governor of Arkansas, ordered the Arkansas National Guard to turn the students back on the first day of classes while a crowd of angry whites jeered their approval. To counter this order, President Dwight Eisenhower federalized the National Guard to ensure the safety of the "Little Rock Nine." These events and others that followed made it poignantly evident that the struggle for equality, self-determination and self-reliance would constitute a movement of Black resistance yet to be seen in America. Like the majestic Phoenix bird of Kemetic (Egyptian) mythology, Black Americans began to rise from the epochs of social, political and economic ashes of racial injustice that denied them full rights as American citizens. Now they were poised and regenerated to confront the vestiges of discrimination and racism with new resolve and determination. The Phoenix bird had risen again and Black Chicago would never again be the same.

This overview does not profess to be a comprehensive narrative of Chicago's Black Struggle from its genesis to 1960. It does; however, acknowledge some of the historical highlights that led to the Civil Rights and Black Power movements of the sixties. It also acknowledges that the infamous Trans-Atlantic Slave Trade resulted in the displacement of enslaved Africans throughout America. Although, this overview is focused primarily on Blacks who settled in Chicago. The events which took place in Chicago from 1960 to 1975 were, therefore, intricately linked with the national (and international) Civil Rights and Black movements, which left an indelible mark on American history.

Jean Baptiste Pointe DuSable: The Father of Chicago's Black Struggle

In chronicling the struggle of Blacks who first settled in the region we now call Chicago, it is inevitable that we begin with Jean Baptiste Pointe DuSable. Although there may have been other Blacks who ventured into this region before DuSable, there exists no substantive evidence to confirm this possibility. It is, therefore, reasonable to assume that the struggle for Black equality, self-determination and self-reliance began when DuSable, a man of African descent, set foot in the Northwest Territory around 1770. At that time, the area where DuSable settled was called Eschikagau. It was given this name by the Pottawatomie Indians because the land had the smell of onions. Later, the area was renamed Chicagou and in 1804 became known as Chicago.

It is inconceivable to postulate **that** when he arrived in the Northwest Territory, DuSable did not encounter many formidable challenges. As a lone Black man, he no doubt had come into contact with the various adverse entities that were trying to control this region. Despite his entrepreneur skills, diplomatic attributes and frontier savvy, DuSable, nonetheless, was a Black man struggling to survive in a region inhabited by several Indian tribes (Pottawatomie and Ottawa) and occupied by armies from the imperialistic countries of

England and France. But because of his unobtrusive demeanor, he received little opposition from the Native Americans who welcomed him as a man of integrity and sincerity. This can be substantiated by the fact that he became a trusted friend of the Pottawatomie tribe and married a Pottawatomie woman. This marriage was later consummated in a Catholic church, which provides some insight about his religious beliefs. Also, it is speculated by some that DuSable was enstooled as a chief among the Pottawatomie people.

However, his encounters with the British and French were undoubtedly less cordial. As advocates of slavery, it was highly unlikely that either country would extend unbridled hospitality to a Black man. Among the few documents that do exist regarding the activities of DuSable, one suggest he favored the French. This suggestion stems from the time he was arrested by the British because of his cordial relationship with the French which they considered to be "treasonable intercourse with the enemy." After his arrest, he was taken to Fort Michilimacknac where he was held for several months. A report made by the fort's commander, Colonel Arent Schuyler de Peyster, acknowledges that DuSable was "a handsome Negro, well-educated and settled at Eschikaguy, but much in the French interest." The irony of his imprisonment was that after he was released, the British employed him for a brief period.

Prior to 1779, the British and French had engaged in a war to control the Northwest Territory during the French and Indian war. The British eventually won this war and was awarded all of the French held territory east of the Mississippi River, as decreed by the 1763 Treaty of Paris. However, during this period the American colonies had withdrawn from England and in 1776 began the Revolutionary War. When the Revolutionary War was over, the French attempted to gain back the land they had lost to the British during the French and Indian War. Thus, when DuSable arrived in the region, the British, French and colonists all wanted to gain and maintain control over the Northwest Territory. For DuSable to survive, prosper and build a successful trading post during this turbulent period was indeed a remarkable achievement. In so doing, it can rightfully be said that he was the first non-Indian to settle in Chicago, but also was the first Black Chicagoan to engage in the struggle to achieve equality, self-determination and self-reliance. Although it is generally believed that Jean Baptiste Pointe DuSable was born in Haiti of Haitian and French parentage, there exists no authentic documentation to verify this belief. The primary reasons his lineage has been linked to this parentage is due to his name, his possible mulatto appearance, and the fact that he was considered to be well-educated, which could have resulted from him attending school in France. It was also believed that he lived for a brief period in New Orleans where he met Jacques Clemorgan (also a man of unknown origin), who later traveled with him to St. Louis, Missouri. However, it was not inconceivable that he also could have been a fugitive slave who learned some of his skills from other enslaved

Africans in New Orleans. Since New Orleans was a major port on the Mississippi River for exporting cotton, sugarcane and furs, it was more than likely DuSable developed his skills there before going to St Louis. St Louis is where we can actually begin to authenticate DuSable's presence due to documents that have been traced to him regarding several business transactions.

After spending some time in the St. Louis area, DuSable travelled to Eschikagou where he used his skills as a fur trader, cooper, husbandman and miller to establish a major trading post near the Eschikagou River, which eventually grew into a lodging house, bakery, dairy, smokehouse, with a large stable. Lerone Bennet, Jr., the imminent historian makes the following statement about DuSable's arrival in Chicago. "In the fullness of time, DuSable's dream became the flesh of other men's legends. His seed–the original settlement–became a forest of concrete and steel. The canoes that stopped at his door gave way to locomotives and ships, his trading posts became mail-order houses and department stores, his workshop factories and mills. White men came from Ireland and Germany, and Sweden and Black men came from everywhere to sit in the wind of his dream. But only a handful knew Chicago's deepest and best-kept secret: its father was an African-American." As indicated earlier, he married a Potawatomi woman named Catherine, who bore him two children, Jean and Suzanne. He and his family remained in Eschikagou for approximately sixteen years until he sold his holdings to a French trader named Joseph Le Maia, who later sold the trading post to a Canadian named John Kinzie. It is believed that he and his family moved to Peoria, Illinois and then to St. Louis, Missouri where he died around 1818. The legacy of Jean Baptist Pointe DuSable is one of an extraordinary man whose determination, courage and entrepreneurial vision left roots in early Chicago that enabled it to blossom into a major industrial and commercial city. In his seminal book, *Black Chicago's First Century,* sociologist and historian Christopher Reed affirms DuSable's indisputable influence on early Chicago when he states: "The city's historically recognized founder, Jean Baptiste Pointe DuSable, personified the concept of agency or the exertion of personal power or influence."

What impact this influence had on Blacks, who gradually began to migrate to Chicago after DuSable's departure, cannot be verified with a plethora of recorded documents. Yet, from the threads of information that do exist and the relics of oral tradition, certain assumptions can be made. Reed also cites in his exhaustive research that a few Blacks of West African descent lived in Chicago in 1830. As a budding frontier town, Reed called Chicago a "city of refuge" that also attracted a diverse population of "half-breeds," representing a mixture of many ethnic groups. Also, DuSable's pioneering business ventures undoubtedly inspired other Blacks who later settled in Chicago to become entrepreneurs. Some of these early Black entrepreneurs were Lewis Isabel, who started a barber shop in

1838; Abrose Jackson, who opened the first Black owned restaurant in the early forties; John Jones, who opened a tailor shop; and Harry Knight, who owned Chicago's largest stable in 1852.

The first formal, recorded census of Chicago in 1850 indicated that the Black population in Chicago was less than two percent. We can assume that the small number of Blacks who did populate Chicago prior to 1850 were probably, like DuSable, acclimated to frontier living. Then too, it was quite likely that some were fugitive slaves who had fled the antebellum south to find refuge in a less threatening environment. It was also conceivable, because of their small numbers, that Blacks were able to intermingle with the larger white population with little tension. However, as more Blacks began to populate Chicago after the 1850s, the scourge of white racism began to lift its veil of prejudice to reveal its true feelings toward Blacks.

Illinois, a Free State Cloaked in White Supremacy

Illinois was considered to be a free state, as constituted by the Missouri Compromise of 1820, that separated free states from slave states. Nonetheless, the ethos of slavery germinated within its boundaries.

One of the staunchest critics of Illinois' defacto form of segregation was Elijah Lovejoy, a free Black man. After a brief career as a reporter in St Louis, Lovejoy attended the Theological Seminary in Princeton before returning to St Louis as editor of the St Louis Observer. His editorials against slavery drew the wrath of segregationists and he eventually moved to Alton, Illinois and continued his strident attacks against slavery. On November 7, 1837, a mob of segregationists confronted him at a warehouse where he had concealed his press. When he refused to acquiesce to their demands, one of the segregationists shot him. The assassination of Elijah Lovejoy sent a clear message to abolitionists that slavery in Illinois was still sanctioned by some die-hard whites. This warning became increasingly more evident after the enactment of the Fugitive Slave Law in 1850, which sanctioned the right of slave owners to retrieve their runaway slaves. Greater credibility was given to this law in 1857, when the Supreme Court ruled in its infamous Dred Scott Decision that Blacks were not entitled to the same rights under the Constitution as whites. Despite the fact these social doctrines had a deleterious effect on Black Chicagoans, they continued to persevere due to their unrelenting determination to be free. For example, the Quinn Chapel African Methodist Episcopal Church, founded in 1844 and acknowledged as Chicago's first Black institution, was a major depot in the Illinois Underground Railroad. Led by four women, known as the "Big Four," Quinn Chapel A.M.E. assisted many fugitive slaves in reaching

Canada. Also called the Mother Institution, it helped to birth other Black institutions, the most notable ones being Bethel A.M.E. Church (1862) and Provident Hospital (1891).

In fact, because Chicago provided a temporary haven for fugitive enslaved Africans, pro-slavers dubbed it "a nigger loving city." Free Black Chicagoans publicly displayed their support of the Underground Railroad in words and deeds. One account of their contempt for slavery was reported in the *Chicago Daily Journal*, when two hundred armed Black Chicagoans confronted the police, who had sanctioned the return of three fugitive enslaved Africans to their slave masters.

However, the most daunting issue that permeated Black Chicago during the early 1850s was the question of slavery. The southern states were determined to preserve the institution of slavery at any cost and some were threatening to secede from the union if necessary. Conversely, most of the northern states, though opposed to slavery, vacillated in their efforts to address this pending national crisis. Thus, the stage was being set for what was to become a pivotal period in American history—the events that fueled the Civil War. Illinois played a prominent role in this horrific war because Abraham Lincoln, who now lived in Illinois, was campaigning to be the Republican Party's nominee for president of the United States. In a series of famous debates with state senator Stephen A. Douglas, who was seeking the Democratic Party's nomination for president, Lincoln proved he was a formidable debater to the much heralded Douglas. Eventually, Lincoln won his party's nomination for president but Douglas lost to John C. Breckinridge because of the split between northern Democrats and Southern Democrats. Lincoln prevailed over Breckinridge in a close election and became America's 16th president.

Although Lincoln often claimed he opposed slavery, he only moderately addressed this issue and instead, focused on preserving the union. His position on slavery could best be summarized in a statement he made to Horace Greely, a white abolitionist, in 1862 when he stated: "If I could save the union without freeing any slave, I would do it; and if I could save it by freeing some and leaving others alone, I would also do that. What I do about slavery, and the colored race, I do because it helps save the Union." Indeed, Lincoln equivocated over slavery throughout his life and left a legacy that is romantically pristine, grossly controversial and steeped in Machiavellianism.

During the Civil War, Black Chicagoans were eager to fight for the union. Their enthusiasm was motivated by two factors: (1) That they could help abolish slavery and (2) That they would earn full citizenship for their service. When President Lincoln finally approved the enlistment of Blacks in the Union army, Black Chicagoans were well represented. Black recruits from Chicago helped to form the 29th Regiment. The deeds of this regiment were auspicious and Reed cites two events that substantiates its momentous record: its engagements at Petersburg and Appomattox in 1865, both which played major roles in the Confederacy's demise. Reed also cites that the 29th Illinois lost 234 men during its encounters with the Confederate army. But outstanding services to the Union failed to provide Black Chicagoans the entitlements they rightfully deserved. When they returned to Chicago after this calamitous and divisive war, their status as second class citizens had not changed.

As already noted, the Blacks who settled in Chicago were a determined and stubborn group **who** refused to acquiesce to white racism. Indeed, they understood that as the great orator and abolitionist Frederick Douglass stated, "There is no progress without struggle." This quote, taken from Douglass' prophetic speech at the West India Emancipation in 1857, became a constant reminder to Black Chicagoans that racial justice could never be achieved without agitation and advocacy.

Lincoln's presidency did little, if any, to reduce the racial tension that continued to resonate in Chicago. Even though Chicago had a strong abolitionist movement, it could not neutralize even the subtlest of racial disparities that kept Blacks from being full beneficiaries of the American Dream. Nonetheless, Black Chicagoans refused to be paralyzed by the social and political injustices that threatened the progress they had achieved. The most devastating threat to this progress, **were** the Black Laws enacted by the Illinois State Legislature in 1848. These discriminatory laws denied Black immigration, forbade a black to testify in a case involving any white, and denied Blacks voting rights and opportunities to be jurors. If not for the persistent courage of John Jones, Cook County's first elected Black official, these racist laws may have gone unabated for many more years. Elected as a Cook County Commissioner in 1871, Jones authored a persuasive document titled "The Black Laws of Illinois, Why They Should Be Repealed" in 1864, which eventually led the Illinois Legislature to abolish the Black Laws. Jones continued his advocacy for racial justice, helped to desegregate the school system, and was the first Black appointed to the school board. Even though the Black Laws had been repealed, other forms of racial injustices continued to stymie Blacks from achieving racial parity.

Blacks Seek Chicago as the "Promised Land"

As America approached the twentieth century, Chicago was becoming a magnet for Blacks who were seeking relief from the economic and social ills spurned by southern repression and injustice. The promises that came with the Reconstruction Era (1865-1877) eventually dissipated and southern Blacks once again found themselves in a quagmire of overt discrimination and racism. The South had instituted a system of neo-slavery and the lynching of Black men and women was being executed without fear of federal reprisal.

Southern Blacks also believed that Chicago would afford them opportunities denied them in the South. For many southern Blacks, Chicago became analogous to the "promised land" that awaited the ancient Israelites in the Old Testament. In fact some Blacks, who came to Chicago during this period, believed Chicago was "the land of milk and honey" that God promised to Moses. Indeed, through the advocacy and courageous deeds of a determined Black community, Black Chicagoans did live in an environment where the sanctions fostered by racism were less overt than in the South. Even though this was true, Chicago was far from being a Camelotic haven for Black people.

Instead, the rigorous demands associated with urban life, provided these southern Blacks with a new set of formidable challenges. But Black Chicagoans, like Blacks throughout America, were accustomed to mounting resistance against social injustices and were not about to abnegate this cherished legacy. Despite being denied their full rights as citizens, Black Chicagoans were making some achievements. To their dismay, these achievements could not be exhibited at the 1893 World's Columbian Exposition held in Chicago because the exposition excluded Black Americans from exhibiting on its major fair grounds. Nonetheless, Black Chicagoans did leave an impressionable image on the thousands, many from Africa and the Caribbean, who attended this international event. Also, the exclusion of Black Americans did not go unchallenged. A document titled, "The Reason Why the Colored American is Not In the World's Columbian Exposition," co-authored by Ferdinand L. Barnett and Ida B. Wells, was fiercely critical of this exclusion. To placate some of its critics, the exposition provided a Haitian pavilion which drew mixed reactions and a debate between Frederick Douglas and Ida B. Wells about its purpose and relevancy. Despite these problems, Black leaders of many persuasions did have an opportunity to speak in forums and seminars outside of the major fair grounds. Among those who did participate were James Weldon Johnson, Benjamin Turner, Booker T. Washington and the charismatic Frederick Douglas, who gave a rousing speech at the opening session of the National Colored Men's Protection Association.

The U.S. Census Report for 1900 reveals that Chicago's Black population increased to over thirty thousand (approximately two percent of the city's total) as the result of Chicago's first great Black migration. But because of Chicago's rigid lines of racial discrimination, Blacks were largely restricted to reside in the Black Belt, which later expanded and became known as Bronzeville. The boundaries that contained the Black Belt were enforced by Chicago's restrictive housing covenants that earned it the dubious distinction of being the most segregated city in America. The racial implications of these covenants were far reaching and also applied to public parks and beaches. One incident that reflected this defacto policy took place on Sunday, July 27, 1919 at the 29th Street beach. On this infamous day a Black youth, Eugene Williams, was beaten and stoned to death by white hoodlums because they believed he crossed an imaginary line that separated whites from Blacks. These covenants were not just confined to housing but also to the public. A few Blacks at the beach, who had observed this brutal incident, retaliated and Chicago joined a litany of other cities during the "Red Summer" **which was** plagued by race riots.

It was well-documented by the Chicago Commission on Race Relations that whites not only used the riot to terrorize the Black community, but also as a means to further the racial divide between whites and Blacks. The Ku Klux Klan saw this racial divide as an opportunity to bring its doctrine of white supremacy to Chicago. From 1920 to 1927, the Ku Klux Klan publicly promoted its racist doctrine and earned the reputation of being the largest Klan in any northern city. Although its public hostilities toward Blacks subsided after 1927, the residue of its racist doctrine continued to resonate in many of Chicago's political, economic and social institutions. As Dr. Martin Luther King Jr. was to learn during his Freedom Movement in the sixties, discrimination and racism were more entrenched in Chicago than in the segregated hamlets of the Confederate South.

In 1871 Chicago's first "Great Fire" decimated much of the city's property and growing economy. Although many Blacks also suffered from this urban catastrophe, Professor Reed postulates they were more resilient than whites in recovering from the trauma that resulted after this tragedy. No doubt the hardships and tribulations Blacks endured from slavery allowed them to better cope with such a devastating event. However, Chicago's second "Great Fire" in 1874 had a greater debilitating effect on Blacks because of the **high** number of fatalities and loss of property that it precipitated.

But what had become the hallmark of Black Chicagoans, their tenacity and fortitude to overcome the most severe of crisis, helped them to recover from these disasters and began what Reed calls "The Gilded Age."

The Gilded Age

The Gilded Age heralded in a new generation of Blacks who, although still disproportionately anchored in poverty, began to have a marked influence in certain spheres of Chicago life. Also, their loyalty to America remained steadfast despite the ever present vestiges of white racism.

In 1915, Oscar DePriest became Chicago's first Black alderman after being elected to the Cook County Board in 1904. Other milestones in Black achievement included Emma Ann Reynolds, the first Black woman to graduate from Northwestern University in 1895; Maurice Curtis, the first member of Cook County Hospital staff; Dr. Daniel Hale Williams, who performed the first successful heart surgery at Provident Hospital in 1893; and the indomitable Ida B. Wells, who crusaded against lynching and advocated for women's rights. Also, Robert S. Abbott founded the *Chicago Defender* in 1905 and journalist Claude Barnett founded the *Associated Negro Press* in 1919. In addition to these individual achievements, Black Chicago had developed a network of Black organizations—political, cultural, and civic—that were addressing the myriad of social and economic ills that kept a disproportionate number of Blacks in poverty. Black women played a major role in many of these organizations, especially those that targeted educational and social disparities. In this regard, we can call them "race women" as a counter part to the "race men" who were unapologetic in displaying their loyalty to uplifting Black people from the social and economic bondage of neo-slavery.

When America declared war against Spain in 1898 (after blaming it for the explosion that damaged the battleship Maine in the Havana Harbor of Cuba), Black Chicagoans once again were given an opportunity to prove their mettle. In 1898 the Illinois Legislature approved the formation of the 8th Illinois Regiment, the first all-black regiment to be headed by Black officers. The military lineage of the 8th Illinois Regiment could be traced to the 8th and 10th cavalries that was comprised of the famous Buffalo Soldiers, who fought so valiantly during the American-Indian wars. To head this historic regiment, an intensive search was made to find someone who *could* live up to the high standards expected of its commanding officer. After months of screening, lobbying and political shenanigans, Colonel John Marshall, a person with limited military experience, was selected to head the 8th Regiment. Aside from his clout from local politicians, he was known as a stern disciplinarian and an ardent advocate for racial pride.

Although some Blacks, including Ida B. Wells, felt that Blacks should not participate in this questionable war, many Black men eagerly enlisted in the 8th Regiment. They were mustered into duty on July 21, 1898 at Camp Tanner in Springfield, Illinois. After its deployment to Cuba, the 8th Regiment engaged in limited combat but received many accolades for its provost duties. For many Black Chicagoans, enlistment in the military continued to be one option they believed would help them gain first class citizenship.

When America entered World War I, Black men from Chicago were once again eager to show their mettle. However, since many were denied enlistment at some recruiting stations, it took the Selective Service Act of 1917 to ensure that Blacks would serve in the Armed Forces. In addition to the Black men who were drafted during World War I, some participated as National Guardsmen from the 8th Illinois Regiment. When the 8th Illinois arrived in France it was renamed the 370th Regiment and bared the uniform of the French 59th Division. Under its new name, the 8th Illinois was cited for its outstanding service in Hindenburg, Paris and fought with the French 59th Division in Belgium, which led to the climax of World War I. For their valor in combat, sixty-eight Black Chicagoans received the Croix de Gueve and twenty-one were awarded the Distinguished Service Cross, America's second highest military honor. Of the 2,500 Black Chicagoans who served in World War I, only 1,260 returned.

Chicago's Black Renaissance

Like the previous wars that Black Chicagoans fought to demonstrate their loyalty to America, it did little to improve their status when they returned to Chicago. Regardless of the social, economic and political injustices it faced, the Black community continued to expand and by 1925 over one hundred thousand Blacks resided in what St. Claire Drake and Horace Cayton called Black Metropolis, the name given to their comprehensive study of Black Chicagoans published in 1945. Drake and Cayton acknowledged that "[the years] from 1924 to 1929 were no doubt the most prosperous ones the Negro community in Chicago had ever experienced." This prosperity was reflected along South Parkway and Michigan Boulevards where many of Chicago's Black elite lived. Concomitant with this prosperity was the development of several Black owned insurance companies, two banks and a host of other businesses ranging from so-called "mom and pop stores" to fashionable entertainment venues.

Bronzeville was emerging as a self-contained community and populated by Blacks from a variety of professions as well as blue collar workers from the steel mills, garment district, railroad and Chicago's thriving stock yards. Naturally this prosperity did not fare too well with white Chicagoans and Chicago's restricted housing covenant was rigorously enforced to prevent Blacks from moving to predominantly white communities. Black Chicago was also emerging as one of America's most progressive, self-reliant communities and became the catalyst for attracting many national Black organizations and Black leaders of various political and ideological persuasions. By 1920, the National Association for the Advancement of Colored People and the Urban League had both established themselves as strong advocates of social injustice for Black Chicagoans. Additionally, the *Chicago Defender* and the *Chicago Conservator* remained steadfast in their journalistic vigilance against all forms of white oppression. Among the nationally recognized Black leaders who frequented Black Chicago were Booker T. Washington, W.E.B. DuBois and Marcus Garvey. In fact, Garvey's United Negro Improvement Association (UNIA) had a membership of approximately seven thousand in the early l920s. Despite the fact the UNIA found a home in Chicago, Garvey spent limited time there due to Robert Sengstack's (founder of the *Chicago Defender*) less than cordial acceptance of him. Despite Harlem's more publicized and glamorous image, Black Chicago was on the verge of starting a renaissance that would equal or surpass America's fabled Black community.

In 1920 Black Chicagoans numbered approximately 110,000 and were five percent of Chicago's population. Two years before the Great Depression in 1930, Black Chicagoans numbered 230,000. Blacks continued to migrate to Chicago despite a weakened economy and fewer job opportunities. The proverbial saying "If you couldn't make it in Chicago—you couldn't make it anywhere," probably was the incentive why many continued to come to Chicago regardless of the depression. The Great Depression had stymied America's economic growth and caused the national unemployment rate to reach an unprecedented high of twenty percent. As could be expected, Blacks were disproportionately affected by these economic collapses, but managed to maintain a marginal subsistence due to their historical resilience to survive under the most adverse conditions.

To address this deepening economic crisis, President Franklin Delano Roosevelt enacted the Works Progress Administration (WPA) legislature, which gradually led America back to economic normalcy, although Blacks remained disproportionately indigent compared to the white population. During this period, Black Chicagoans were not to be denied their efficacy for creative and artistic expression. This was particularly true of Chicago's budding Black artist movement, which began to flourish in 1932 after the decline of the Harlem Renaissance. Arna Bontemps, a product of the Harlem Renaissance, stated, "Chicago was the center of the second phase of Negro literary awakening." Novelist Willard Motley, in an article titled "Negro Art in Chicago," spoke about how the Federal Art Program provided opportunities for Black artists to develop their crafts. He mentions Charles White, Elizabeth Catlett, Eldzier Cortor, Bernard Goss and Charles Davis as being among the vanguard of Black artists who resided in Chicago. In her book, *The Chicago Black Renaissance and Women Activism,* Anne Meis Knupfere acknowledges the scope of this movement when she stated "Chicago Black writers and artists created a cultural and political front during the Chicago Black Renaissance." During this period Black artists were forging a new and viable creative paradigm that Darlene Hines collaborates in her introduction to BLACK CHICAGO RENAISSANCE when she states, "In synchronic ways, the artistic community provided new representations of black humanity and articulated the pride, hope, humor, dreams, desires, frustrations, anger and beauty in the lives of everyday black people." Bronzeville was also becoming a Mecca for black artists and was the founding home of the DuSable Museum of African American History, originally named the Ebony Museum of History.

Across the street from this pioneering institution was the South Side Art Center, which was a major venue for Black artists to join in fellowship and display their works. In proximity to these two institutions was the Abraham Lincoln Centre where some of Langston Hughes and Theodore Ward's plays were performed. It also served as the venue where St. Claire Drake and Horace Cayton wrote their classic study of Black Chicagoans, titled *Black*

Metropolis. In addition, two of America's most important Black writers, Richard Wright and Gwendolyn Brooks, lived in Bronzeville after leaving Jackson, Mississippi and Topeka, Kansas respectively.

Wright's potent novel, *Native Son*, electrified the literary establishment and became the generic novel on Black life in Chicago. It was also the first Black book to be selected as book of the month. Brooks also achieved a first when she was awarded a Pulitzer Prize for her engrossing volume of poetry titled *Anne Allen* in 1950. Also, Brook's only published novel, *Maude Martha*, provides a candid and sobering story of a young lady who lived in Chicago's Bronzeville. It should be noted that while Richard Wright departed to France, Gwendolyn Brooks remained in Bronzeville and became a mentor and role model to many young poets of the Black Arts Movement. Other Black writers like Margaret Walker, Alton Bland, Frank Marshall Davis, Frank London Brown and Alice Browning, helped Chicago's Black community to be a nurturing environment for the Black writers who were to follow in the sixties. While some historians have attempted to cast an ominous shadow of Communism on the Chicago Arts Renaissance, they failed to discredit the major role Black artists and activists played in helping to make Black Chicago a major cultural metropolis. This is not to disclaim the **influence** Communism had on some of them, but to place this influence within the context of artistic freedom to express their disenchantment with the hypercritical principles of a democratic society.

The fact that Chicago had become a major cultural center for Black art and culture was evident in it being selected to host the American Negro Exposition in 1940. This historic event was to showcase in the various artistic genres the progress made by Blacks since **their** emancipation from slavery. As Adam Green elaborates in his book, *Selling the Race, Culture, Community, and Black Chicago,* this was a colossal challenge to those responsible for its implementation. To undertake this task, Truman Gibson Jr., a highly respected attorney, headed a team of distinguished Black notables who were assigned the collective responsible for making it happen. After much internal conflict, controversy and financial woes, the exposition opened on July 4th at the Chicago Coliseum. The outcome of the American Negro Exposition drew a wide range of divergent views. Some felt it lacked the artistic verve and opulence deserving of such a momentous occasion. Others believed its core principles were compromised to appease Chicago's growing Black bourgeoisie population.

Struggle for Political Empowerment

When Japan attacked Pearl Harbor on December 7, 1941, Blacks were once again inducted in the military to serve their country of citizenship that continued to deny them the same entitlements and justice afforded to whites. Black Chicagoans who served in this horrific war returned to Chicago with a greater thirst for freedom, but quickly learned that service to one's country was not equated with equal opportunity and justice. Irrespective of Chicago's inherent but subtle discriminatory practices, Black Chicagoans were beginning to fill positions that, heretofore, were exclusively reserved for whites. In principle, they were becoming a sterling example of what Blacks could achieve if they would mobilize their collective resources under a common cause that would benefit all Black Chicagoans.

But true to the doctrine of "divide and conquer," that has historically kept oppressed people in a state of confusion and mistrust, the political potential of Black Chicago failed to materialize. Since politics are critical to a people's ascension to equality, self-determination and self-reliance, the guardians of City Hall proceeded to follow the despotic leadership of Mayor Richard J. Daley. Chicago's Black communities became replicas of Southern plantations with many Black politicians and clergymen serving as their overseers. This pattern of urban neo-slavery was maintained, with little opposition, from the mid-forties to the early sixties. Congressman William Dawson, a staunch supporter of Mayor Daley, played a major role in ensuing that the Black Community conformed to Daley's antebellum platitudes.

During his unprecedented reign, Mayor Daley ruled Chicago as though he had been ordained by God, and controlled a political machine that few cities could rival. In their exhaustive bibliography of Mayor Daley, *American Pharaoh,* Adam Cohen and Elizabeth Taylor graphically describe how he rose from an altar boy to become a five term mayor and Chicago's most powerful politician. Indeed, in his role as "Pharaoh," he became a major voice in the national Democratic Party and was a strong ally of the Kennedy clan before and after the election of John F. Kennedy's brief presidency.

Much of Mayor Daley's power came from his ability to accommodate white ethnic groups, while patronizing many Black leaders to support his political dynasty. Thus, many Black leaders, regardless of their personal achievements, performed their perfunctory duties like robots. Daley's political machine operated under the principle of quid pro quo that became the moral standard for measuring one's loyalty to the Democratic Party. However, loyalty to the Democratic Party did not translate into empowerment for Black Chicagoans. On the contrary, it generally resulted in the containment of Black Chicagoans from mobilizing a collective and assertive effort that could seriously challenge the Daley machine. This pronouncement was not intended to discredit the laudable efforts of those

Black Chicagoans whose passion for self-determination, self-reliance and equality could never be co-opted. If it were not for their relentless opposition, Mayor Daley would have literally controlled every life-affirming institution in the Black community.

Many of his cronies were indicted for various nefarious acts within the city government during the growth of a Black labor movement, deflection from the Machine by a few Black politicians, a failing public school system, the expansion of violent street groups, legal challenges to Chicago's restricted housing covenant, deterioration of many Black communities, accounts of police brutality against citizens, and finally the corrosion of public housing. However, Mayor Daley remained an imposing political force until he died of a heart attack on December 19, 1976. Also, to Daley's credit, when it was in his interest to placate Black leaders, he supported causes that may not have been consistent with his personal views. An example of this patronizing occurred in 1956 when he hosted an inter-racial official dinner at the Sheraton Blacksone hotel in honor of Prime Minister Kwame Nkrumah of Ghana, who later became its first president. Claude A. Barnett, the distinguished editor of the Associated Negro Press, was the master of ceremonies. Also, in attendance at this auspicious event was his beautiful wife Etta Moten Barnett and other Black luminaries, such as Truman K. Gibson Jr., Rev Archibald J. Carey Jr., Mrs. Edith Sampson, former US alternate delegate Dr. Theodore K. Lawless, an African-American dermatologist, medical researcher, philanthropist, and one of Daley's staunchest supporters, Rev. J. H. Jackson, president of the National Baptist Convention. During his speech Prime Minister Nkrumah declared, "If Ghana is free and others are not free, I would not count myself as being free and freedom will not be complete...and if we Africans are liberated, we will not be free until self-respect and honor are accorded men of color everywhere."Whether or not these words were intended to embarrass Mayor Daley may be questionable, but their substance were quite evident.

Undeniably, Black Chicagoans never surrendered their relentless passion to achieve self determination, self-reliance and equality. They had crossed too many "hills and valleys" during their protracted struggle since Jean Baptiste Pointe DuSable first settled in Chicago, and were destined to pass it on to future generations. The contributors in this book represent some of the voices that are heirs to this destiny.

REFERENCES

Reed, Christopher R. Black *Chicago's First Century*. University of Missouri Press. 2005
Travis, Dempsey J. *An Autobiography of Black Chicago*. Urban Research Press. 1981
Travis, Dempsey J. *An Autobiography of Black Politics*. Urban Research Press. 1987
Doliner, Brian (Ed). *The Negro in Illinois: The WPA Papers*. University of Illinois Press. 2013
Carson, Clayborne (Ed). *Civil Rights Chronicle: The African Americans Struggle for Freedom*. Legacy Press. 2003
Green, Adam. Selling the Race. University of Chicago Press. 2007
Lemann, Nicholas. *The Promised Land*. Alfred A. Knopf. 1991
Hines, Darlene. (Ed). *The Black Chicago Renaissance*. University of Northwestern Press. 2012
Campbell, *Tom Fighting Slavery In Chicago*, Ampersand, Inc, 2009
Perkins, Useni Eugene, *Home is A Dirty Street: Social Oppression of Black Children*, Third World Press, 1976

SECTION ONE
CULTURAL ARTS AND BLACK AWARENESS

"The artist must take sides. He must elect to fight for freedom or slavery. I have made my choice. I had no alternate."

Paul Robeson

AFFIRMING THE TRADITION, TRANSCENDING THE CONDITION

Abena Joan Brown

"When I look back at the history of the cultural arts movement, I'm reminded that W.E.B. DuBois told us back in the 20s that the Negro Arts movement should be by the Negro people, for the Negro people, about the Negro people and near the Negro people. And I think, in the evolution of our culture paradigms, most of us have taken to heart that maybe the movement should be by, it should be for , it should be about, but the near has rarely been seriously considered. We have failed, historically, to internalize W.E.B's maxim in our cultural forms so that African Americans could really benefit from the awakening and mirror image of ourselves. To do so would lead to the development of institutions for the transmission of our own values, our traditions, our lifestyles—the things that important to us as a people.

ETA Creative Arts Foundation, Inc. emerged out of such a consciousness which was developed with others in the Chicago movement of the 60s. We began to understand that culture is the vehicle which drives all people across the planet. We understood that once we are very clear about our own identity, our values, our traditions, our world class history as a people, certain fundamental questions about not only who we are, but what we should be doing would be answered. How do we build a future while we are on the planet and how do we move beyond that to leave something for the next generation.

In this quest, I went back to some of the ancient and historical cultural paradigms. I went back to our Cultural historians to discover that, indeed, integration in the cultural arts was as much a fallacy as it had been in every other sphere of our lives. Meaning that the most talented among us, the most competent among us, the most competent among us had, most often, fled our neighborhoods, rather than use our talents and skills within the context of community – or "near" the Negro people.

And, over 25 years, this has been a wonderful, wonderful work. As a community based institution, one of things which has endeared ETA to the Black community is that we are in the neighborhood as a demonstrated commitment to it. People are pleased that they don't have to go "clear 'cross town" to see themselves in our stories which are mirror images of our possibilities ....to see and be a part of those stories which resonate in our hearts and minds.

The institutional growth of ETA Creative Foundation has been quite phenomenal. A fact sheet which is incorporated in this document will attest to our many accomplishments, structurally and organizationally. As part of this growth and the recognition for the future is a priority, we began to think about preservation of our artistic integrity.

While we had been very fortunate to find the work that expresses our mission, we began to ask, "how can we make sure that this work will continue, that there will always be a flow of producible work." In any given year, ETA would receive 60 or 70 plays, but as we read the plays, finding those which were affirming, triumphant, transcendent with character never or seldom seen was like finding a pearl.

Looking at these results led to our understanding of a simple fact: If the theater is, indeed, a collaborative process, which it is; if it is a place where stories are told, which it is; and if it is a place where we want "our story" to be told, in the first voice; then the griot—the playwright must be encouraged; developed if you will. We decided that ETA must aggressively find these griots and bring them into the collaborative process of the theater. We also knew the most writers sit off in a room somewhere and just say, "Well, I think I'll write a play". They might very well feel compelled to write a play. But, most of what we were getting suggested that the writer was not necessarily thinking about the theater, but, rather writing something for movie or television production... something that would "sell." And, in so doing, many writers were copying things they saw on television—that which was selling – and thought it was really us – Black people. This is not a comment about Black writers and "selling" because writers, like all of us want a venue for their work. But, ETA wanted to encourage more writers to tell stories for the theater. The writers' frustration and reluctance is understandable since we don't have enough theaters with the structure and financial foundation to produce work; others don't want to take a chance on new writers. The need to fill those seats drives many to the tried and true... to the validated.

So we decided to bring the writers into collaboration with ETA... have them come and work with the producer, with the artistic staff, with the business staff, with the technical staff, the designers, with the Director; then, maybe, that vision becomes a collective one to make the play come out in its best possible form and, as a result, fill the seats.

The other concern was that even with all the remarkable work done during the 60s, a "school of thought" about what African American Theater could and should be had not been concretized and/ or generally accepted among the African American theater community. Within the context of ETA's overall mission and long range objectives, we were interested in developing a comprehensive context for our production choices to guide those who succeeded the current leadership. Moreover, because ETA also has a commitment to the field, we wanted also to insure a flow of producible work, not only for ETA but all African American stages, in particular and by so doing contribute to the theatre at large.

It was hoped that a network could be encouraged, so that new writers would have a venue for their work around the country and at the same time, new classics for the stage would be created and validated by such efforts.

With this larger concern, a panel of nationally known theater practitioners and patrons were called together in series of dialogues in the PDI (Playwrights Discovery/Development Initiative), from which emerged the paradigm for the call to writers.

We know that this work, which is still in progress, is important. We now more firmly than ever believe that the Cultural paradigm is the basis of it all. And, once we get that straight, we will know how to make decisions (in our own best interest) in every area of our lives. We are pleased to share this document with you... It is a call, and we pray for your response, to enlarge upon this vision to make it one which will serve us all in the present and for generations to come.

As President/Producer of ETA Creative Arts Foundation, I am deeply appreciative and thankful for the time and effort put in by the esteemed panel who have worked in the vineyards to bring clarity and vision to the PDI. To have the opportunity to work with such formidable minds, hearts and spirits, has enlarged upon my being. The response of the griots attest to the hunger out there to have a serious consideration of them as special beings in bringing authentic, valid projections of us a people to ourselves. I also, on behalf of the Board of Directors, Staff and other volunteers also want to thank the Chicago Community Trust, the Mayor, Morris Kaplan Foundation and AT&T for their generous support of the PDI program."

[Reprinted from Playwrights Discovery/Development Initiative by ETA Creative Performing Arts Foundation, Inc,. 1971]

THE IDEATION OF BLACKNESS: RE-CENTERING A WORLD ORDER

Iva E. Carruthers

"...all of you, your children, their chil dren, their children after them and genera tions after them again and again, all will be victims till the way is found again, till the return of our way, the way."

—Ayi Kwei Armah, *2000 Seasons*

Along the journey I have come to appreciate more and more the wisdom of the African proverb, "An invasion of an army can be resisted but an invasion of ideas can't be resisted."

The essence and power of the ideas that were birthed out of Chicago during this seminal period, 1960-75 ought be memorialized and understood for what they were—the invasion of ideas that have opened up and transformed the spaces of discourse, visioning and action of Pan-Africanism. The invasion of ideas deeply embedded in the consciousness and commitments of a new generation of African youth will continue to bear fruit as long as we remember that transformation begins with a vision and ideas for change, bolstered by intention and attention to commitment and resources to effect the change.

Between the period of 1960 and 1975, Chicago was an epicenter of African centered thought in quest for "the way." "The way" begins with what I frame as the ideation of Blackness to re-center a world order. Chicago was an epicenter not only in the embryonic stages of ideation of African centered thought, but in the intersection of where ideation was manifested as practical efforts of institutionalization. Intellectual and ideological liberation spawned independent re-centering of race analyses and innovative models of praxis. These ideations and models of praxis, where belief met action, fragile as they were, resulted in an unequivocal and irrefutable paradigm shift in the development of Pan-African thought and networks across the world. This article contributes to the collective attestation of this seismic paradigm shift, which impacted virtually every community and institutional expression possible, including the cultural arts, education, politics, the economy, religion, media and the family.

While many know that a shift in ideation occurred, few know the extent to which Chicago was not only at the epicenter of that shift, but that there was deep and intentional efforts to create, connect and sustain think tanks and intellectual networks that would give birth to a global 20th century Pan-African movement.

"I'm Black and I'm proud" became more than a James Brown song, but a people's mantra! And, African centered thought became more than a response to external societal rejection, but an independent act of reclamation for the minds and hearts of the people.

This period of reclamation is truly epitomized in the image and meaning of "the Sankofa Bird." "Sankofa" is a word in the Twi language of Ghana that translates as "Go back and get it;" (san - to return; ko - to go; fa - to fetch, to seek and take). The Asante Adinkra symbol of a bird has its head turned backwards taking an egg off its back, or is otherwise represented by a heart shape. In its fullest meaning, Sankofa is a call of reclamation of the past in order to understand the present and help shape the future for the good of the community. This period of reclamation was but a continuation and strengthening of 19th century Pan African movements, and has indeed laid a solid foundation for the 21st century movement and challenges of liberation for people of African descent the world over. To be sure, reparatory justice and reparations are essential means to that end. This period of reclamation continues to guide the way back through, the way of the past, in the context of the present, to create the future.

Like many others, I was privileged to be a part of this transformative movement as an activist scholar and (scholarvist). I was positioned to be a part of this transformative movement as a sister woman and womanist sister. I was poised to be a participant witness and witness co-creator of this transformative movement. This reflection of remembrance offers some historical markers, celebratory moments, and cautionary instruction as guideposts for the heirs of the legacy.

During this early period of the 1970s, the ideation of Blackness or Afrocentricity, with a goal to create an intentional counter narrative and networks of counter ideological warriors, was deeply rooted in Chicago. *Africana: The Encyclopedia of the African and African American Experience* declares that "Molefi Kete Asante first coined the term Afrocentrism in 1976, although it has its roots in Pan-Africanism" (p. 45).

The fact is that scholar activists in Chicago, members of the Association of African Historians published The Afrocentric World Review in 1973. Though *Africana: The Encyclopedia of the African and African American Experience* does not even include nor name John Henrik Clarke or Cheikh Anta Diop as influential thinkers of this period, not to mention many other scholars doing global Pan African ideation and institutional development. It was in Chicago and often in my house, that such visioning and strategic planning was occurring, resulting in a plethora of activities and institutions which would intersect and fortify the movement. Specifically, it was in the home of me and Jacob Carruthers that the ideation of the Afrocentric World Review and "Afrocentricity" as a construct to initiate a paradigm shift was planned over time with many consultations and conversations. There were many who were engaged but the intellectual and spiritual capital of persons such as Dr. Anderson Thompson, Dr. Harold Pates, Jake Beason, Bernetta Bush, Dr. Bobby Wright, Dr. Clifton Washington, Lorenzo Martin and Dr. Conrad Worrill should be acknowledged and were critical. There were three elder scholars from New York who were at the center of Chicago's movement: John H. Clarke, John Jackson (Clarke's mentor) and Yosef ben-Jochannan. And, Ralph Crowder of Minneapolis was a great contributor and archivist. Audio tapes of these gatherings exist. The aim of the Afrocentric World Review was:

> "Developing an ethnic awareness and racial consciousness no longer based solely on victim analysis, class exploitation or colonial subjugation, but, one that aims toward the establishment of Black goals and objectives that point the way to our forefathers' dreams: A World Wide African Community...a New African Frame of Reference...founded on Black ideas, rather than the ideas of non-Blacks...a methodological directive necessitates, among other things, Black studies about non-Blacks...ideas and objectives which truly represent the interest of the bulk of scattered African people, wherever they now exist in the world."
>
> **[p. 1, 2. Volume 1 Number 1, Winter 1973]**

The dedicatory pages of the Afrocentric World Review included the words of Edward Wilmot Blyden (1832 -1912)

> "We need some African power, some great center of the race where our physical, pecuniary, and intellectual strength may be collected...we must establish and maintain the various institutions."

This 19th century declaration by a father of Pan Africanism guided the thinkers and workers of the Chicago movement. And though there are many meta narratives of this period to be lifted up, I want to lift up four herein that may otherwise be overlooked: (1) the intentionality and attention to language and constructs (2) the intentionality and attention to collective and cooperative models of institutional building (3) the positive inclusion and role of women in the leadership and activity as scholar activists and (4) the strategic and successful outreach across geographical, experiential and language barriers that resulted in a nexus of global Pan African think tanks and activists that has only matured over the years.

Intentionality and Attention to Language and Constructs

The Center for Inner City Studies, Northeastern Illinois University, became a crucible of academic and intellectual warfare as well as a home for the "Communiversity" and the Association for African Historians. This nexus between the academy and community embraced an intentional paradigm shift of ideas, as called forth by Jacob Carruthers and Anderson Thompson.

Jacob Carruthers penned a seminal piece on the "Science of Oppression," arguing for deconstructing white western scientific methodologies as non-universal and objective.

> What has stood in the way of using collective wisdom in the past is the influence of outside allies and foreign ideas which has been more directive than informative –a condition that must be radically altered. ...the foreign influences have refuted our collective wisdom, and all to our disadvantage. Needless to say, this absurdity was primarily the responsibility of the educated component of our people who accepted the outsider's knowledge too uncritically.
>
> **[p. 5 Science and Oppression 1972 Northeastern Illinois University Center for Inner City Studies]**

Anderson Thompson called for:

> The creation of Afrikan historiography challenges contemporary Afrikan thinkers to understand that ideas are weapons of warfare and that Blacks have historically been instruments in our own destruction in this kind of struggle. We must also understand that many of our best ideological warriors are servants of the enemy, and many of our best and most creative Black minds have been immobilized for they don't know (or are unwilling to acknowledge) that there is a race war going on. (Anderson Thompson, *Black Books Bulletin,* 1975)

During a five year period, Jacob and I made multiple visits and research trips to Haiti. We unearthed a trajectory of reflection upon the facts, principles and consequences of the Haitian revolution on world order, then and now. And, our research and visits to Africa in 1972, 1973 and 1975 would lead to a direct introduction and connection to Carlos Moore and Cheikh Anta Diop. It was Dr. Carlos Moore, living in exile in Senegal, who served as the major liaison to me, Jake and Dr. Cheikh Anta Diop. That relationship led to my student group being welcomed by Dr. Diop and subsequent student study groups visiting with him.

And most significantly, it should be noted that Dr. John Henrik Clarke was most responsible for getting the works of Dr. Diop translated into English. He convinced Lawrence Hill Publishers to engage Mercer Cook for the translation of *African Origins of Civilization: Myth or Reality,* released in 1974.

The strategic and subsequential connections to the particular research of Cheikh A. Diop and Theopile Obenga would ultimately result in the reciprocal translations of many manuscripts and study tour partnerships. The reclamation of the Kemitic Studies and Mdw Ntr as a foundational Pan African system of thought to inform "the way," opened new pathways to understand the African origins of civilization, not just as a lesson in history, but moreover as a basis to ultimately argue for a prophetic and contemporary vision for a Confederation of African States.

Linguistic analysis from Mdw Ntr to comparisons with traditional African languages, e.g. Wolof would inform "the way" and affirm the premise that western language cannot always convey the deep meaning of African philosophical and metaphysical understandings of the human experience; thus, language, proverbial declarations, iconic and symbolic ideations informed the methodological approaches to historiography and institutional development.

All of the above would make a formidable contribution to the development of Black Studies programs and a reclamation of Egyptology from the total hegemony of western scholarship (including the U of Chicago Oriental Institute). Clearly, this was a watershed moment in the development of Pan-African Afrocentric networks and metanoic energy of global researchers which exist today.

Intentionality and Attention to Collective and Cooperative Models of Institutional Building

Akin to an ideational paradigm shift, there was a parallel shift from more traditional approaches to institutional and organizational building during this period. Notably, in response to what was being (re)discovered about "the way," there was intentional attention to exploring models of collective and collaborative leadership, cooperative and resource sharing. There were many models of such developments in the areas of the arts, education and political action and advocacy. Specifically, I was instrumental in the founding of Jiandaa, a 75 acre camp and educational center for children, as well as Edward Wilmot Blyden Center for Creative Development, a K-8th grade full time institution that became a charter member of the Council of Black Institutions (CIBI). Both of these institutions were founded on principles of family cooperatives, male female equity in leadership and execution and principles of "not equal giving but equal sacrifice" and "unity without uniformity." They, like many of the institutional expressions which emerged during this period, embraced principles of the Nguzo Saba.

The lessons from the farm/camp, Jiandaa, affirmed the value of fostering a connection to the land as a source of creation and sustainability of life. Young people were required and responsive to the challenges of creating community from growing, storing and preparing of food, to building of shelters, lessons in safety and security and interdependence, while developing one's particular gifts. The lessons from the farm/camp affirmed the possibility to create alternative ways of living in community that was counter to rugged individualism, violence and disdain for education. The lesson from the Edward Wilmot Blyden Center for Creative Development was that independent schools, full time or as Saturday schools, were essential to creating a way and passing on necessary lessons to the next generations.

Graduating several 8th grade classes, students from Blyden Center were ultimately merged into programs of The Center for New Horizons and the Institute for Positive Education. They were forerunners and models of educational praxis for schools in a variety of settings, including churches, and they became models of opportunity and challenge for the dynamics of failing public schools, costs to sustain private schools and ultimately the charter school movement.

Both of these institutions evidenced the African proverb, "Until the lion can write his own stories, the hunter will always be the hero."

The Positive Inclusion and Role of Women in the Leadership and Activity as Scholar Activists

A leopard is chasing us, and you are asking me, "Is it a male or a female?"

African Proverb

During this period, questions of black male and female relationships and family dynamics surfaced as issues of internal and external examination. No question, this was being driven by several factors. External forces of feminism were engendering self-reflection, collective examination and choices by black women relative to the question of the nature of the struggle–against whom and what?

Racism, sexism and/or homosexism? Internal forces of appropriating or misappropriating African models of family norms. Male female relationships posed another set of dynamics. Polygamy, male dominance and gender and sexual norms related to homophobia were too points of tension.

During this period, as student movements on college campuses were occurring, including Black Studies movements, the inflammatory situation at Cornell University erupted in an internal crisis between black male and female coeds, with accusations of violent and dehumanizing treatment of black women by black men under the justification of adopting and returning to the ways of African tradition. As a graduate student at Northwestern University at the time, I was one of the sister consultants asked to come meet with the students at Cornell to help assess and work through the crisis.

During this period, black women experienced and confronted black male sexism in all its forms. However, most saw the expressions of white feminism as an extension of white male dominated culture as more problematic. For sure, clarity was embodied in the proclamation of womanism. I, for example, was accused by *Ms. Magazine* as being the most racist sociologist in the nation for an article I published lifting up this issue.

What I can attest to is that my personal experiences of Black male sexism in my contexts, were minimal and inconsequential to my autonomy and the collective outputs of Black women. The ideation of oneness, partnership and harmony were embraced in the context of historical analysis, i.e. with us from the very beginning of African creation. And today, are still reflected in African ontological views of vital forces which are principles of male and female forces/energy in all things and people. Eurocentric philosophy tends to articulate this in terms of principles of opposites, hierarchy and tension. However, the more appropriate and concise formulation of these African ideas are embodied in the principles of appositional unity, mutuality and interdependence as characteristics of Africanity in Black families. I argued that this was especially true for families navigating the myriad assaults and consequences upon Black families in the trail of the diasporic Euro-American slave trade system.

It is upon this foundation of African appositional unity and mutuality that the female and male principles were evident in the general social organization of African life and most specifically in the efforts at institutional building in Chicago during this period. One could research the many couples who were exhibiting "appositional unity," acknowledging differences between male and female, but not making those differences inherently hierarchal and oppressive, but rather complementary and synergistic. One such couple who should be celebrated was Jorga and Lou Palmer. They made storytelling and journalistic and media institutional development that were "enough to make a Negro turn Black."

The divide and tensions were possibly greater between those who were single and married with the implications for extramarital liaisons, as well as those whose spouses, whether male or female, were or were not interested in "the way" or the movement over and above struggles of power between the sexes.

The Development of a Nexus of Global Pan African Think Tanks and Activist Networks

During this period, the intersectionality of travels, along with ideations, activities and networks represented by me and Jake Carruthers, Hoyt Fuller and Lerone Bennett Jr. (*Negro Digest*), Carlos Moore, Thomson Elkin Sithole, Haki and Safisha Madubuti (Third World Press)) were particularly fruitful in the development of institutional linkages between certain thought leaders and activists in the Chicago epicenter and those on the African continent, and later Brazil and Melanesia.

Divine destiny and personal interactions set the stage for strategic and successful outreach across geographical, experiential and language barriers that created and/or strengthened a nexus of global Pan African think tanks and activists that has only matured over the years. Activities and people associated with The Pan African Festac (Hoyt Fuller and Lerone Bennett Jr.); South African expatriates in the U.S., other parts of Africa and Europe (Sithole); capacity to translate multiple languages and move between continents (Carlos Moore); capacity to publish (Haki and Safisha); and opportunity to travel, meet and facilitate institutional and organizational connections (Jake and Iva) had domino and deep impact. The point important to note is that a collective cooperative agenda, matched by opportunities to have global and personal interactions, can go a long way to change the trajectory and power of a few to be armed with the invasion of ideas.

> If your vision is for a year plant wheat, if you vision is for a decade plant trees, and if your vision is for a lifetime plant people. (African Proverb)

Aye Kwei Armah warns us that we must:

> Come again upon the way....the way is not the rule of men. The way is never women ruling men. The way is reciprocity. The way is not barrenness. Nor is the way this heedless fecundity. The way is not blind productivity. The way is creation knowing its purpose, wise in the withholding of itself from snares, from destroyers...

Our beloved mother and mentor to many during this period as well as co-founder of the DuSable Museum of African American History, Dr. Margaret Burroughs, left us with the work we must do for our children as the essence of Sankofa:

> I must find the truth of heritage for myself and pass it on to them.
> In years to come, I believe because I have armed them with the truth,
> my children and their children's children will venerate me.

For it is the truth that will make us free!

(Last stanza of *What Shall I Tell My Children Who Are Black* 1999)

A Luta Continua!

THE NEW VOICES SING OF BLACK CULTURAL POWER

Useni Eugene Perkins

Listen, and you will hear the new voices of black culture in Chicago.

On a Sunday afternoon at the Abraham Lincoln center, 700 E. Oakwood, Black musicians experiment with exciting sounds which can better capture the feelings of their people.

In the Louis Theater at 35th Street and Michigan, four black actors take to the stage to rehearse a new three-act play by a young playwright, who has depicted contemporary Afro-American life.

Not far away at the Afro Arts Theater, 3947 S. Drexel, a singing group entertains an audience with music that recaptures the legacy of West African chants, Charleston Street Cries, and St. Louis blues, while a tall black Cleopatra leads dancers in elegant maneuvers.

In a small room of the Afro-American Museum of History, 3806 S. Michigan, a group of black writers meet. A poet stands, wearing a full natural and begins reading lines which move like the agonizing harmony of a John Coltrane solo.

Across the street, at the South Side Community Art Center, where black photographers and artists are developing their talents, a group of black school children try with pencils and sketch pads to re-create the styles of an African art exhibit.

Who are these people and organizations responsible for the awakening of black culture? They are many; but each one is motivated by the desire to articulate and express their culture through their own life style and experience.

Perhaps not since the days of the Harlem Renaissance in the 1930s has there been such interest in the cultural development of black people. Black artists today are concerned with what poet-playwright LeRoi Jones calls, "Art for people's sake."

Amidst the social changes evolving in Chicago, it is clear that the city's black people are demanding cultural—as well as economic and political—power.

One organization that has become a catalyst to this reemergence is the Organization of Black American Culture (OBAC), a group of black artists who came together to foster a greater appreciation of black culture, and to provide a better climate for the development of a black aesthetic. They have formed workshops in writing, drama and art to help black artists develop their ideas and talents.

The now famous Wall of Respect at 43rd Street and Langley, with its mural of black people, is one of OBAC's most impressive achievements. The most durable of its workshops has been the writer's group, under the direction of Hoyt Fuller, editor of *Negro Digest*.

Outstanding in this group is 25-year-old Don L. Lee whose honest and powerful poetry has made him a favorite of the black community. His work speaks directly to black people, dealing with life from a black man's perspective.

He has already had two successful volumes of poems published, *Think Black* and *Black Pride* and a third volume, *Don't Cry, Scream,* will soon be published by the Broadside Press in Detroit.

Don currently is a black writer-in-residence at Cornell University and is on the editorial staff of Black Expression, a journal of literature and art.

Other poets fostered in the OBAC workshop include Jewel Latimore, a student at Wilson Junior College who also has published two books of poems, *Images in Black* and *Black Essence;* Carolyn M. Rodgers, a young teacher whose first volume of poetry, *Paper Soul,* was recently released; and Sigemonde Kharlos Wimberli, associate editor of Lawndale's West Side Torch newspaper, whose *Ghetto Scenes* expresses the mood of his community in graphic, first-hand detail.

Ruwa Chiri, a Rhodesian student now attending the Illinois Institute of Technology, has a "down-to-earth" style perhaps best expressed in his widely read poem, "Sixteen: South Street."

Those who ask why there is a need for black poetry might do well to read this passage from a poem by Countee Cullen, one of the leading writers of the Harlem Renaissance:

> Yet do I marvel at this curious thing;
> To make a poet black and bid him sing!

Although the poets are receiving considerable attention, there are many other talented writers who are contributing to this movement. Foremost among them are Mike Cook, a recent winner of a short story contest sponsored by Gwendolyn Brooks; James Cunningham, author of a soon-to-be-published critique on James Baldwin; Cecil M. Brown, who has been featured in *Negro Digest*; and David Llorens, staff writer for *Ebony Magazine*. Many of these writers are encouraged by Fuller and Miss Brooks, Pulitzer Prize winner in poetry and newly appointed Poet Laureate of Illinois.

Richard Wright's 1930s novel, *Native Son*, grew out of Chicago to become a classic statement on the black man's plight in a hostile white society. It is not in the least sophomoric to say that a similar classic could emanate from the talent of one of these young black writers.

A popular gathering place for black writers is the Ellis Book Store on 6447 Cottage Grove, which features the most extensive collection of black literature in Chicago. Curtis Ellis, the owner, encourages black writers and has held autograph receptions for many of them.

A number of publication ventures are also under development by black writers, including the Free Black Press and the Third World Press, both of which are serving as new vehicles for black writers. There is also a fine magazine called *Kenyatta* and two newspapers, *Tazama Uhuru and Documents*, geared primarily for the black community.

The summer edition of The Drama Review devoted its entire space this year (1968) to the present status of black theater. Edited by the gifted playwright, Ed Bullins, the edition attempted to cover the black theater movement in America. Although the Chicago black theater scene is conspicuously absent in the report, there is now some effort being made to develop a meaningful theater. One of the men working in this field is Theodore Ward, who has set up shop in the Louis Theater on 35th Street and Michigan, a former movie house. Ward, director and founder of the South Side Center for Performing Arts and a veteran playwright, started this theater in September 1967. After great difficulty and hectic fund-raising problems, he finally opened with a production of his own play, *Our Lan'*, a two-act drama about the black man's struggle to gain economic independence during the Reconstruction period. The play did not attract large audiences, but Ward still hopes the community will eventually support the theater. Ward is trying to create a cultural center which "is devoted to the training of Negro youths and adults in theater craftsmanship, as well as providing an outlet for Negro drama which expresses some vital part of Negro life and spirit."

The theater's current production is Ronald Milner's penetrating contemporary drama, *Whose Got His Own.*

Since its opening in December, 1967, the Afro Arts Theater, another converted movie house, has been the brightest cultural development in the black community. Each weekend it features an array of talent that includes Afro-American dancers, singing groups, drama, movies, and music by The Pharaohs, formerly called the Artistic Heritage Ensemble.

As a community theater, the Afro Arts is a significant institution because it encompasses the types of programs which are both relevant and inspirational to the black community. The development of similar theaters is greatly needed.

If a black theater is to survive, it must not be bound to the value systems of the white power structure. A true black community theater must feature programs within the framework of its peoples' experience, making every effort to polarize existing resources—

actors, musicians, playwrights and directors—from the community itself.

The Chicago Park District has many skillful black drama instructors. However, there is an obvious lack of black-oriented plays being produced in the district's drama program, which is tied in with the values of the white establishment.

One drama instructor with long tenure in the Park District is Harold Johnson, the director at the Stateway Garden Homes. But like other black instructors, he has had to implement his art apart from the district's paternalism.

Some of his credits include a production of *Raisin in the Sun* and *Psalms of Protest*, which he helped write.

Harold states, "A black theater must be completely controlled by black people and attempt to unmask the aberrations and stereotypes created by the white media." He believes that black talent should be promoted by black people and is one of the architects of Ebony Talent and Productions Inc., a group formed to seek opportunities for black performers.

Dramatist Val Gray Ward has, through her abundance of talent and perseverance, been able to achieve some amount of recognition. Called the "voice of the black writer," she is endowed with a deep sensitivity and understanding of her people.

Mrs. Ward is able to interpret, in a variety of moods, the fundamental meanings from the material she recites. This past summer, she participated in a pilot project of the Chicago Office of Economic Opportunity to bring drama to the black community, taking a mobile stage into the heart of the ghetto to perform Douglas Turner Ward's one-act plays, *Happy Ending* and *Day of Absence*.

A total black theater has yet to be achieved in Chicago, but the development of such a theater is inevitable. For as writers continue to seek creative ways to express the black experience, it appears certain that the theater must be the focal point.

Ever since the '20s, when King Oliver and his Creole Jazz Band brought their New Orleans sound to Chicago, the city has maintained some facsimile of a musical tradition. Even though the roots planted by these musicians have either been transplanted or diluted, the black community has managed to preserve some of their legacy.

The work of our contemporary musicians takes place in scattered spots throughout the community and creates scenes of excitement for the people who come to hear the new sound.

Composer and arranger Richard Abrams moves his slender body as he directs his group in music filled, with the beat of bongo drums and the blare of brass instruments. The sound is painful, powerful and exciting. It is the kind of energetic music that has become familiar with the Association for the Advancement of Creative Musicians.

At the White Elephant Pub Club, 911 S. Kedzie, a popular night spot in Lawndale, President Abrams and members of his AACM often play a series of weekend concerts.

Founded in 1965, the AACM was organized to provide opportunities for creative musicians to display their talents in concert setting. Based at the Abraham Lincoln Center, its primary concern is, as composer, arranger and Abrams states, "to expose and showcase original music of its members and to conduct a free training program for young aspiring musicians." The AACM is a vital part of the black cultural movement.

The non-profit Chicago Community Music Foundation is designed to provide music opportunities for inner-city youths who are interested in developing musical skills. Charles Walton, tireless co-director of the Foundation, states, "By exposing children to music at an early age, we are able to help them form disciplines which can be transferred to other activities."

The foundation was started in 1962 and now serves more than 200 children and presents many concerts throughout the year to showcase the talents of its young members.

Phil Cohran and his Artistic Heritage Ensemble are known in the city's black community for their concerts. Many of them performed this past summer under sponsorship of the Illinois Arts Council. Dressed in red dashiki and spotless white pants, Cohran entrances the youngsters with the playing of his "frankie phone," or African thumb piano. Hundreds of black people turn out to hear the effervescent music produced by his group.

Other groups such as Odell Brown and the Organizers, the Paul Weston Trio and Troy Robinson Combo have continued to maintain the rich musical heritage first nourished by the soil of Africa.

Historically, Chicago has been a budding center for black artists. Charles White, Eldzier Cortor, Margaret Burroughs, Richard Hunt, Bernard Goss, Archibald Motley, and Marion Perkins are a few of the outstanding artists whose talents were nurtured within the boundaries of Bronzeville's (black community).

But the incentives of many black artists have never been fully realized because in Chicago, they still have to confront social barriers not posed to the white artist.

In 1965 a Black Arts Colony was formed on 31st Street, near Dr. Martin Luther King Jr. Dr., to bring black artists together and to promote greater interest among black people in buying art. The venture, started by William McBride, Frank Sheppard, Howard Mallory, Jose Williams, Art Tyler and Ben and Mary Daniels, never quite achieved its goal. But ironically, the death of the colony did not come from lack of support, but instead, was caused by the heavy machinery of urban renewal.

One gallery owned by a black artist is the C. Rodger Wilson Studio and Gallery at 1458 E. 53d Street and has been open for many years.

Another black-operated gallery is the Arts Gallery and Studio located at 7032 Stony Island, the only black distributor of art material in Chicago.

The East Shore Galleries, at 2541 E. 75th Street, is one of the newer art galleries that hopes to provide more outlets for black artists. Owner Joyce Bowen, has hopes of maintaining a gallery which will host shows, exhibitions, lectures, concerts and other programs.

The South Side Community Art Center, 3841 S. Michigan, an institution of long standing, still maintains the most popular gallery for exhibiting black artists. At present, despite financial problems, it has workshops in writing, still photography, drawings, etchings and drama for youths and adults.

Behind the Art Center is a two-story coach house, where Douglas Williams, its director and a talented sculptor, lives with his wife and two children.

Douglas, who was also director of the much-acclaimed On the Beach summer cultural program in 1968, is a relentless worker who usually can be found in his overcrowded workshop.

A graduate of the Art Institute, Douglas develops forms in what he calls, "their natural or primitive state." He has already had two one-man shows and has been widely exhibited throughout the Chicago area.

Ramon Price, a mild-spoken man, has been a supporter of young black artists for many years. An accomplished artist, he is head of the art department at Du Sable High School and a board member of the Art Center. He is a meticulous artist whose sensitive etchings of black people have gained him many admirers.

The name Conservative Vice Lords may seem to be a misrepresentation to those who remember when this group once roamed the streets of Lawndale. But today, these young adults are trying to project a new image by becoming involved in community cultural programs. An example of this is illustrated in a newly formed program sponsored by the Illinois Sequicentennial Commission in conjunction with the Museum of Contemporary Art to help the CVL's establish an art gallery and studio on W. 16th Street.

The project has already had an impact on the community. Among its early achievements, is a mural of photography done by photographer Roy Lewis, which is beginning to receive the type of acclaim given to the Wall of Respect. Jackie Hetherington, the director of the Lawndale Art Project, is encouraged by the support it is receiving and feels the gallery will provide a significant service to the community.

Jeff Donaldson, an artist who is an active participant in the black arts movement, is a leader of the Coalition of Black Revolutionary Artists (COBRA). COBRA has yet to make its sting felt, but it has the velocity and creative talent to achieve whatever it sets out to do.

No mention of black artists would be representative of this movement without listing Rodger Wilson, Sylvester Britton, William Walker, Edward Christmas, Herman King, Sherman Beck, Thomas Ingram, Anna McCullough, Robert Wooley and Robert Jones. And we should not overlook those people who have been dedicated to the cause long before this re-emergence. Some of these people are F. H. Hammurabi, director of the House of Knowledge, a cultural educational agency on the South Side; Ishmael Flores, director of the Afro-American Heritage Assn.; Christine Johnson, author and educator; and Margaret Burroughs, founder and director of the Museum of Afro-American History. This list of artists in Chicago's black community is brief, as it can only begin to describe the personalities and the accomplishments of the men and women working in the new black culture.

But a few obvious factors do emerge from even a short survey of the field: The black artists in Chicago are determined to be recognized, and from this determination they are developing a sense of creativity and power that will provide their movement with a stronger foundation from which to grow.

But perhaps most significantly is the fact that much of the movement's impetus is being generated by community groups. The Lawndale Cultural Development Project is one such group providing programs to develop talent and create cultural opportunities. Another community group has obtained a two-story brick building located at 3309 Monroe. The House of Umoja ("unity" in Swahili) provides a number of cultural programs and serves as an educational center. On the South Side, a coalition of black students have organized the Umoja Black Student Center, which offers programs in black history, African languages, and black awareness.

Through these programs and many others, black people are, for the first time, beginning to see the beauty in their own culture. They no longer want the cultural standards of white America imposed upon them. Instead, black people are realizing they have a cultural heritage, which not only better represents their life experiences, but is, indeed, black and beautiful.

[Reprinted from "The new voices sing of black cultural power" in Chicago Daily News, *December 7, 1968]*

THE CHALLENGE OF BLACKNESS: MEDIA WHITE

Lerone Bennett, Jr.

The Urban Crisis is a reflection of our failure to create a single social community in America. And since the creation of community is a primary responsibility of communicators, the urban crisis is a direct challenge to media representatives. From a social standpoint, a community is a body of people sharing common expectations and common obligations. A real community is based on reciprocity of emotions and relations among individuals sharing a common vision of the possibilities and potentialities of man. But the basic fact in race relations in America today is that black and white Americans do not live and act within the perspective of the same community or the same communications channel.Mass media in America reflect that general reality. In fact, it is impossible to speak of mass media in America without adding the specification of white or black mass media. It is impossible to speak of general publications when these are edited for white or black publics.

This is a fundamental fact of life and of communications in America: divided publics and divided communities. If we grapple with the implications of this fact, we will realize that white-oriented media cannot solve the race problem in America because white-oriented media are part of the race problem. They reflect the interests, values, and aspirations of white people. In this case, at least, McLuhan is *right: The medium is the message, and the message is that white is right.*

Let us begin there. And let us realize that the Black Rebellion is a rejection of that message and of media and institutions which project that message. Let us realize also that the Black Rebellion is a revelation, a message, and a medium. Like all rebellions, the Black Rebellion is a way of revealing reality. Like all rebellions, the Black Rebellion is a medium which reveals in depth and detail the reality men are living. And one confronts the very real problems of white-oriented media in confronting the fact that the Black Rebellion is a medium of truth which has revealed the reality of white-oriented media and the publics they serve.

The reality we are living is divided into white and black realities. So-called general media are white and are servants of white reality. They stand in an adversary relationship with the black community. They find themselves in the difficult position of reporting a court case to which they are parties. And until white-oriented media resolve the contradictions of their existence, it will not be meaningful or useful to talk about the technical problems of reporting the content.

I will have little to say here about the technical aspects, of the problem—how to cover a rebellion, how much space to give to this or that spokesman. These are technical problems, and the problem is structural, not technical. Stated bluntly, the problem is that the men who control media have not yet decided that they want to pay the price of democracy. Until that decision is made, it is useless to waste time talking about the implementation of the decision.

In my opinion, the structural contradictions of white media are rooted in the structural contradictions of American society. As a result of these contradictions, we have been hampered at home and abroad by a journalism of surprise and sudden catastrophes rather than a journalism of depth and development and involvement. By and large, American journalism reflects the bias of middle-class white scholarship which is weighted heavily against radical change. At a recent meeting of the American Sociological Association, Dr. Dan Dodson underlined this fact and asked: "Could not a good case be made that the behavioral scientist's major function is to provide the rationalizations on which the contemporary order rests? Is not the role of the historian fundamentally that of providing the rationalizations as to why the power order deserves to be in the dominant positions it holds?" Dr. Dodson added: "At the middle of the last century the theologians were called on to provide the rationalizations as to why the power order could not get creativeness from some people. Thus was born the theory of infant damnation. By the end of the century the psychologists had emerged with status, hence they-provided a new and secular version of infant damnation, which is the low I.Q. Very rapidly ... we sociologists are providing our version of infant damnation which is low social class. Thus it goes. If one reads the literature of 'validated hypotheses' about those who are outside the power order, he is impressed with the endless clichés of 'low I.Q.,' 'low social class,' 'weak ego strength,' 'lack of father image with which to relate,' 'inability to forego immediate pleasure for long-range goals,' 'matriarchal domination,' 'cultural deprivation.'. One comes to the conclusion that if the little man ever succeeds in making his outreach and up reach to full selfhood, his first job will be to beat down the mythologies the behavioral scientists have created about him."

These mythologies permeate all the institutions of American society, including the press. As a result, we are being smothered by extremists of the middle—extremists of the status quo. Nothing indicates this more clearly than the response to the Black Rebellion, the embodiment of the black masses' outreach to full selfhood and manhood. The development and the implications of this movement make up one of the most important stories in contemporary history. Yet, by and large, it has not been told in all its depth and dimensions in white-oriented media. More than anything else, the Black Rebellion is the black man's response to the pervasive influence of white racism in every American institution, including the press.

It is impossible for people to communicate if they are not speaking from the same agenda. In this country we are not speaking from the same agenda. We are not even speaking the same language. The gaps and distortions in the reporting of the Black Rebellion are reflections of the general in¬ability of media to deal creatively with social change. The Kerner Commission emphasized this fact by accusing white media of failing to communicate the urgency of the problem to white Americans and by failing to include black Americans in their vision of America. The Commission very properly suggested the hiring of additional black reporters. White editors and reporters should also read Negro-oriented publications on both the national and local levels.

But, beyond all that, there is a need for white-oriented media to integrate their vision, their control, and their management. In other words, we face the need, not for just a new reporter here, or a new story there, but for fundamental change in the spirit permeating white-oriented media. We face the need for white-oriented media to transcend the limitations of whiteness.

To cite only one example: It is unfortunate that only one black columnist is syndicated nationally by white media. As a result, the interpretation of the news is as white as Snow White. We are told, of course, that media are neutral, but it is a strange neutrality which trumpets the viewpoints of scores of right-wing columnists and a handful of white liberal columnists and ignores articulate black spokesmen like Charles Hamilton, Vincent Harding, Ossie Davis, Hoyt Fuller, or any one of a number of brilliant black men I can name.

A new vision would integrate reporting and interpretation. A new vision would stop studying the South Side of Chicago and start studying the North Side of Chicago. A new vision would come to grips with white racism and with the institutions—political, economic, and religious institutions—which perpetuate racism in this society.

It is not enough today to run a few articles preaching the cloudy rhetoric of brotherhood. It is time now to take on the institutional roots of racism—and the institutional roots are in the white community.

Like most black people, I am tired of white people studying the black community. The libraries of this country are weighed down with studies of the South Side of Chicago, but I do not know of a single book dealing with the North Side of Chicago from a racial perspective. The race problem in America is a white problem, not a black problem.

The race problem in Chicago is in the North Side of Chicago, and the problems will not be solved until media confront the problems of the North Side of Chicago. It will not be solved until media ask themselves some dangerous questions about the values of ordinary whites and the interests of powerful white institutions.

An article on this subject in the *New York Post* referred to the marches by the late Martin Luther King Jr., through the Gage Park area of Chicago. Pete Hamill visited the neighborhood and wrote:

> This was the way the Hollywood Hustlers used to put their cardboard America together, in a time more innocent than ours.
>
> Children played in the streets, or burbled from baby carriages. Young boys mowed lawns which still smelled sweetly from the morning rains. Housewives pushed strollers to the grocery stores, or drove the family cars to the supermarkets. A man on vacation nailed a brass numeral to his front door. A lot of people seemed to be polishing cars with an almost reverent devotion. Gage Park on Monday afternoon seemed as innocuous as any place where Doris Day lived on film.
>
> But underneath, past the front doors of those two-story houses, in the secret places behind those lawns and those automobiles and those smiling children, Gage Park was like a tray of summer worms. By the time the thing that is crawling through Gage Park has hooked its last inhabitant, that neighborhood is almost certainly going to murder someone. It is going to murder someone because of the accident of color. It is going to murder someone over the combination of wood, metal and concrete which the inhabitants fondly describe as their property.

That same animal is crawling through the Gage Parks of New York and California and Nebraska. That animal is the biggest news story in this country. If we do not confront it soon, an unspeakably horrible disaster is going to happen here.

I believe media can communicate the depth of this problem. American mass media can sell almost anything. Isn't it strange that media cannot sell the idea of a color-blind America? We can sell detergent, but we cannot sell the Declaration of Independence. Is it possible that we believe in the detergent and do not believe in the Declaration of Independence? We can make a man hate himself because he doesn't have the right model car, we can make a woman tremble for fear of bad breath or dishpan hands, but we make it possible for men and women to love themselves while violating all the precepts of Christianity and the Declaration of Independence.

In short, there has never been a total effort on the part of the cultural apparatus to teach Americans to live together. I believe the urgencies of the hour make it necessary for media to embark on such a crusade. We dare not think that we can solve this problem by occasional articles urging whites to take a Negro to dinner. To deal with this problem, we must dig down to our sacred mythologies, including the mythologies which separate the private and public sectors.

As a result of decades of miseducation by all media, including the press, white Americans have completely unrealistic ideas about the private and public sectors. And it will not be possible to solve this problem until the media assume responsibility for educating Americans on public investments and social development. Consider, for example, the hue and cry in the public press over the pennies America doles out to indigent blacks. Yet there is silence about the incredible waste of our public resources and the billions poured into gimmickry and gadgets.

The Negro-oriented media also feel the pressure of social change. The Black Rebellion is a total revolution, and every institution in the black community is bending to the winds of change. Black media are becoming more militant, more black. To borrow a phrase from LeRoi Jones, it seems likely that they will be blacker tomorrow. There is a new tide of black consciousness in the black community. Black readers are more assertive, more demanding, more militant. They are demanding more information about themselves and their struggle. As a result, new media are springing up across the country, and established media are expanding their formats to satisfy new demands. This trend defines our situation. For as long as so-called general media reflect a white reality, there will be a need for media oriented to the full dimensions of the excluded Negro personality.

More than one hundred years ago, the first editorial of the first Negro newspaper, *Freedom's Journal,* said: "Too long have others spoken for us. We want to speak for ourselves." Black people still want to speak for themselves. It may be, as Ralph Ellison has said, that they speak for whites, too.

In the larger sense; therefore, the urban crisis is a magnificent opportunity for all Americans. It is an opportunity for white America to become America. It is an opportunity for white media to become media. It is an opportunity for media to return to the fundamental principle of journalism—which is, in the words of the Black Rebellion, to tell it like it is.

Permission granted by Lerone Bennett Jr. Reprinted from The Challenge of Blackness, *Johnson Publishing Co. Chicago Position paper, Conference, "The Media and the Cities," University of Chicago Center for Urban Studies, May, 1968.*

ARTISTIC IMAGERY AS A FACTOR IN THE POLITICS OF SOCIALIZATION AND AFRICAN LIBERATION DURING THE 1960S AND BEYOND

Harold Pates

As I reflect upon the impact that the 1960s had on African-American imagery and identity, I recall a rebirth of African consciousness, a proud acceptance of our ancestral countenance. Our color and our contours were some of the elements that motivated a musical and visual focus for many of the artistic creations that achieved lasting value. As contrasted with the fifties, the forties and the thirties, the sixties gave birth to a Black Power consciousness that was translated through the intellects and talents of a Black populace, which had acknowledged the results of the resistance struggle of the past, and the Civil Rights marches and organizations. There was a realization that the underlying political principle of social integration and equality, for which the civil rights movement had so gallantly struggled, could become socially operative only if African-Americans continued to submit to the dominance of whites in their institutions and subject their own cultural imperatives to the incidental.

Historically, our ancestral African countenance, color and contours, were the foundations upon which: day-to-day personal shame, family rejection and embarrassment, disdain, or in more colloquial terms, the material from which much street corner "signifying" and comedy were derived. We, as African-American people, had essentially been de-Africanized. The sixties jolted us into a wholesome transformation and political maturity that facilitated an African-American cultural renaissance that produced revolutionary music, visual art, literature, oratory and dignity.

During the forties and fifties, our carefree acceptance of everything that was European as the universal standard by which societal value was determined, had effectively guaranteed and reinforced the continuum of African-American oppression. Although we were not yet integrated, "Europeaness" was a value and condition for acceptable appearance, travel destinations, how to think, behave and talk and in some instances, how to sing. To be a "European Negro" was, to a great extent, the ultimate aspiration among many African-Americans. Although a European Negro is a political aberration, as a symbol of a double consciousness, it was demonstrative of an enslaved spirit that was comfortable with white authority.

The general psycho-social transformation of African-American people that occurred during the sixties was revolutionary. When compared to the previous three decades during which there was greater African-American cultural tolerance of all aspects of white supremacy. This transformation resulted in a consciousness that projected African-Americans into a period of self-criticism and self-realization, as they subjected themselves to the previously unexamined acceptance of Euro-American methods of marketing racist values and beliefs.

It was this new consciousness that gave new meaning to the African-American countenance, color and contours. In Chicago, the "Negro" theater became the "Afro-Arts" theater. In New York, the Black Theater Alliance emerged. The "Last Poets," along with other conscious Black poets, created their own unique rhyme and meter that corresponded to the rhythms of the African drums and the new jazz music. All were espousing poetic revolutions with an uncompromising defiance. Both the visual artist and the jazz musician began to manifest a significantly more Africanized spirituality. That spirituality characterized the appearance, the discourse, and in many instances the diets and the courtships of the new genre of artist. To engage in this time of critical self-examination required conscious African-Americans to purge themselves of the western white way, in order to experience an African rebirth. The artist intensified the search for those things African as reference points for the creation of environments, features and characteristics for the African imagery that was to be recreated. A new architecture and design emerged as they were reflected in the artistic jewelry being sold by African-American entrepreneurs in the outdoor markets.

The most concrete element in programming and marketing white supremacy values into the colonized peoples of the world has been the blond, blue-eyed, white face, a noticeable effect of Hollywood culture. The fact that a cosmetic industry developed product lines that produced African feature medication was confirmation that the western standard of beauty, the image of a white God, had dominated the minds and spirit of African-Americans to the extent that the African ancestral countenance was repugnant to those who possessed it. The more prominent the African countenance, the more profound the curse.

The conscious artist of the sixties imposed the African countenance upon African people and both "Black and African" became marketable and beautiful. The wearing of the natural hairstyle was accompanied by the abandonment of the skin whiteners and bleaching creams. The artists boldly and confidently represented Africa's beauty in sculpture, on canvas, in drawings and with photographs.

In Chicago, the teachings of Phil Cohran with the African Heritage Ensemble and his francophone, along with the imagery and music of Rashaan Roland Kirk, Miles Davis, Sonny Rollins, Pharaoh Sanders, Yusef Lateef, John Coltrane and others, accompanied the paintings of Jeff Donaldson, Murray de Pillars, Katon Mitchell, Calvin Jones, Bill Walker and other visual artists. Formations such as the Coalition of Black American Artists were being created, and "walls of respect" were being painted in Black communities around the country. The blue-eyed, white European imagery had been purged as the Black artist brought aesthetic balance and normalcy back to African-Americans who, because of the effectiveness of western methods of "educating" and inculcating white supremacy, could hardly tolerate the sight of themselves.

Historically, the European rape of African slaves and the result, miscegenation, contributed to the color caste distinctions within the slave families and populations, i.e., the acceptance of the mulatto slave progeny of the master as being on a socially higher level than the darker skinned slave. Thus, during slavery and reconstruction, white image supremacy became systemic and "Negroes" who were Black became the pariahs in all western colonial and post slavery societies. This condition prevailed until the sixties. Elijah Mohammed and his followers referenced the Black man as the original man, which ignited a cautious respect among some "Negroes." Many African-Americans preferred to be identified as colored or "Negro." During the three decades preceding the sixties, "Negroes" were relatively comfortable just being colored and having the white supremacy managers also manage integration.

During the sixties the symbiosis between the masses of the people and the artists created James Brown, whose "volcanic explosion" declared, "Say it Loud, I'm Black and I'm Proud." The larva of this eruption flowed into the national Black communities; into the minds, hearts and limbs of Black children as they internalized James Brown's declaration. Those who had been endowed with dark skin had achieved a higher level of social esteem to the extent that many lighter skinned African-Americans began to experience a sensitive social discomfort. The artists' paintings imposed the Black face, with its African features, upon the populace as Nina Simone reminded African-Americans that there was glory in being Black as she sang, "To Be Young Gifted and Black." The artists of the sixties contributed an artistic therapy to African-Americans that sowed the seeds for greater unity, and a healthy identity as African people.

The African physical contours or physique have generally been distinguishable from non-African peoples and has substantially been the subject of great mystery to Europeans. This is particularly noticeable in much of the post reconstruction literature that formed the basis for some of the early 20th century elementary school reading. Books and academic literature, the contours of the lips, the nose, the eyes, the woman's breasts, hips and thighs, and even the hair were mimicked in the early black-faced minstrel shows. This ridicule continued throughout the thirties, forties, and fifties in the movie industry to the extent that this imagery had great influence on African-Americans' self-esteem, as they tolerated their own physical contours.

During the sixties the visual artist emphasized the African nose, lips and hips. It was emphasized to the extent that grandmothers of the past were reluctant to recommend to their daughters that they should squeeze their progeny's noses, so that instead, the noses would assume a more aquiline contour. The corset was abandoned as African-American women achieved greater comfort with their hips and breasts being integral to the black and beautiful imagery of the sixties.

Natural became both a style and an imposing revolutionary statement. The style was represented in the visual arts and also worn by many of the musical "doo wop" groups, such as the Four Tops and the Temptations. While more African-Americans wore the natural as a style and not as a symbol of a revolutionary, visual artists' depiction of the natural, along with the recharacterization of the African physiognomy, had indeed achieved a revolutionary level of unashamed social acceptance in the Black world.

The Africans' natural resistance to subliminal strategies of oppression and slavery was given heightened illumination by the artists of the sixties. The Africans' greater acceptance of his brothers and sisters, worldwide in contemporary discourse, can be attributed to the African-Americans' rebirth during the sixties, and the resounding of those rebirth pains that were heard and acknowledged worldwide. "Wherever we are, we are African."

Note from contributor, Harold Pate: I'd like to acknowledge the contributions made by my friends and colleagues, Dr. Anderson Thompson, Judge Bernetta Bush and Ms. Loren Cress Love, to the substance of this work.

REFLECTIONS ON THE 1960S—A PERSONAL NARRATIVE

Francis Ward

The decade of the 1960s is arguably the most misinterpreted and misunderstood time period in American history. These raucous, volatile and tempestuous ten years have been widely and inaccurately stereotyped as only a time of violence, disorder, unbridled sex and drug use. Right wing conservatives have almost unanimously condemned the sixties as a time of riots and lawlessness—the critical turning point when American moral and religious values were totally corrupted. The favorite conservative line is, "Everything went wrong in the sixties." Wholesome American children turned away from "traditional family values," argue the conservatives, to become nomadic hippies with an endemic disrespect for law and authority. Institutions like schools, churches, universities, civic and fraternal organizations—once the bulwark of a presumably stable American society—all of a sudden became infected with and corrupted by a strange pathology called "liberalism."

Without doubt, the sixties was a time of unrest and social upheaval when some fundamental assumptions about American society were questioned and challenged. But the right wing conservatives, who make the kinds of arguments cited above, are totally wrong in their understanding and interpretation of why these events happened, and their meaning. American society was never as stable and serene as the conservatives said then and say now. There were always tensions—between whites and blacks, rich and poor, liberal and conservative, conservative and progressive radicals, and within many families. American institutions weren't corrupted by liberalism, but by pervasive racism and sexism that permeated every fabric of American life.

But it was easy to argue a false serenity, as the conservatives have done, because the news media failed to consistently report problems and tensions that bubbled below the surface. Community leaders and opinion-makers, for the most part, remained silent about the ills and problems in American life. Television, the dominant medium of mass communication and entertainment during the 1950s, was totally absent of any tensions and controversy. Also, the Hollywood film industry for decades had churned out films, which slavishly upheld the myth that all was right and good in America. During the 1950s, films like *The Wild One* with Marlon Brando and *The Man With the Golden Arm* with Frank Sinatra began to probe beneath the surface to reveal problems of violence and drug use; however, such films were the exception, not the norm.

Sparked by the Civil Rights revolution, the 1960s did become a turning point when the country was finally forced to face problems, which for decades had been swept under the rug and largely ignored. It's most important to remember that the sixties is still the subject of intense debate, analysis, interpretation and disagreement. Fundamental questions still remain unanswered: How should the sixties be understood and remembered? What is the legacy?

Traditionally missing from most analyses of the 1960s are the positive changes that occurred within black America. Without a doubt, this decade produced the greatest advancements ever in civil rights. The landmark Civil Rights Act of 1964 and Voting Rights Act of 1965 brought about fundamental changes, perhaps the most important of which was the beginning of the end of legalized racial segregation. The first in a sustained wave of black elected officials emerged in the sixties with the election of black mayors in Gary, Indiana (Richard Hatcher) and Cleveland, Ohio (Carl Stokes), both in 1967. The most successful (certainly not the first) black-owned recording company—Motown Records in Detroit—emerged during the 1960s. The Motown sound and its string of successful artists—from the Temptations to the Supremes—revolutionized American music and popular culture. Also without doubt, the success of the black Civil Rights Movement of the 1960s was the motive force behind similar movements, which later evolved to defend and redefine the rights of women, gays and lesbians, Hispanics and the disabled.

Before proceeding further, it's necessary to take a moment to dispel a long-held myth. The Civil Rights Movement did not begin in the 1950s when Dr. Martin Luther King, Jr. headed the Montgomery, Alabama bus boycott and later founded the Southern Christian Leadership Conference. The movement of the 1950s and 1960s was preceded by a long, sustained string of events going back almost two hundred years. The first slave revolts of the 1700s were surely the earliest stages of the Civil Rights Movement. The Abolitionist fight against slavery leading up to the Civil War, 1861-1865, was also a key phase of the Civil Rights Movement.

The events following the Civil War—ratification of the Thirteenth, Fourteenth, and Fifteenth Amendments to the Constitution, Reconstruction, the rise of the Ku Klux Klan as the most famous homegrown American terrorist organization, and the systematic disenfranchisement of black Americans, especially in the South—all were critical parts in the chain of events we now define as the Civil Rights Movement. Finally, the oldest Civil Rights organization in America, the NAACP, was founded in February 1909, twenty years before Martin Luther King, Jr. was born.

Largely forgotten by white America, but enormously valued by black America, was the black consciousness movement of the 1960s. This was a wide-ranging amalgam of black writers, poets, visual artists, singers, musicians, actors and academics who were influenced by the ideas of black solidarity and identity that emerged during the sixties. Black consciousness was heavily influenced by the teachings and writings of Marcus Garvey, founder of the Back to Africa Movement of the 1920s; Malcolm X; and scholar/activists such as the late John Henrik Clarke, for many years a professor at Hunter College in New York City. The sixties and beyond became the greatest period of black artistic and literary creativity in American history, surpassing the period of the Harlem Renaissance of the 1920s.

Black consciousness spawned a great number of organizations which shared common themes of black pride and solidarity, black empowerment, resistance to white racism, and identification with Africa as the Motherland of people of African descent worldwide. One such organization was the Kuumba Players, founded in the spring of 1968 in our home on the South Side of Chicago by my wife, Val Ward. Val selected the name Kuumba (pronounced Koo-UMM-bah) because of its African roots. In the Kiswahili language of East Africa, Kuumba means "to create," and is also translated as "creativity." In the Mshona language in Zimbabwe, Kuumba means to build creatively with one's hands. In the Wolof language, spoken widely in several West African nations, Kuumba is often used as the first name of a woman.

Val envisioned Kuumba as a unique arts and theater organization. The name was later changed to the Kuumba Workshop, and a few years later to Kuumba Theatre. It would produce a season of plays every year with the goal of teaching and entertaining. From the very beginning, Val and those she gathered around her—myself, our children, and friends who shared a similar vision—believed passionately that art rooted in the black experience had to do more than simply entertain. The art should also strive to teach some important lessons—about life, about self, relations and others, about community, values, attitudes, institutions, society, culture, politics and other subjects. In 1972, the Kuumba Theatre incorporated the dual teaching/entertaining role as one of the twelve principles upon which Kuumba would base its artistic productions and other arts-related activities. The twelve principles are outlined at the end of this article. We knew these ideas were a radical departure from traditional concepts of art and theatre, but that's precisely what Val wanted.

I came to Chicago in late December 1964 to work for *Jet* magazine, a weekly newsmagazine with a predominantly black national readership. Jet's sister publication was *Ebony,* a monthly feature magazine with the largest predominantly black readership in the world. Both magazines are still owned and published by Johnson Publishing Company in Chicago.

When the Kuumba Players was founded in 1968, I had become a general-assignment reporter with the *Chicago Sun-Times,* today one of two mainstream white daily newspapers (the other is the *Chicago Tribune*) published in Chicago. The black-owned *Chicago Defender* was a third daily paper, thought it never rivaled the *Sun Times* or *Tribune* in circulation or reader influence. From July 1969 to January 1978—about eight and a half years—I was a national correspondent in the Midwest (Chicago) bureau of the *Los Angeles Times.*

From the beginning and throughout the history of the Kuumba Theatre, Val and I shared a division of labor. She was the artistic director who selected the plays, sometimes directing and starring in them. She was the main public face of the Kuumba Theatre. I handled the management and administrative responsibilities—keeping the records; raising the money, mostly through writing proposals for grants; directing hired staff; doing publicity; and writing checks to pay the actors and sometimes musicians. Val was paid (when money was available, and sometimes it wasn't) and I was not paid. Operating the Kuumba Theatre was a labor of love for both of us, done out of the commitment to its principles, never for the money. Had money been the prime motivation, Kuumba wouldn't have lasted beyond 1968.

I had to carefully balance my responsibilities to Kuumba after hours with my role as a reporter during the day. I never wrote articles or reviews about Kuumba, although I occasionally used my contacts in the media to get publicity for Kuumba. But I never co-mingled the two roles. Should I have done otherwise? Should I have used my position as a media professional to advance the cause of the Kuumba Theatre and other organizations whose causes I believed in? I sometimes ponder such questions, but I felt at the time I had the professional responsibility to remain neutral as a reporter and not allow my journalism to be influenced (at least not consciously) by my partisan beliefs. I still think this was the right decision. For years I firmly believed in the anti-apartheid movement that was very active in Chicago and other cities to isolate and weaken the white minority racist government in South Africa. But I never became actively involved with anti-apartheid organizations, though I did indirectly support anti-apartheid causes through the Kuumba Theatre.

The years from 1968 to 1975—the period covered in this article—were mainly a period of growth and development for Kuumba. Its greatest successes at its home base in Chicago and with touring productions came after 1975, which is beyond the scope of this article. Kuumba didn't have much money, but it did have a loyal core of actors and musicians.

During its first seven years Kuumba performed a number of plays not well known in the mainstream, but which we felt an obligation to do, since these black playwrights would most likely get exposure only through an organization like Kuumba. It also became a strong public advocate on certain issues, like its criticism of the trend in black exploitation films of the early seventies. During these formative years Kuumba did plays on weekends at different locations, the most important of which was the South Side Art Center, 3831 South Michigan Avenue. We only did the works of black writers.

Kuumba was a pioneer in developing the theory and practice of the ritual form of live, spontaneous theater. The essential components of ritual theater are improvisation and audience involvement. Kuumba added a third element—teaching some important lessons, like opposition to drug use and violence against others. The challenge to the actor was to capture the power of the spoken word and transmit that feeling to the audience. Rituals eliminated the separation of actors and audience. At times, actors in Kuumba rituals did most of the performance while mingling directly with audience members. Some ritual performances were done with formal sets, lighting and sound. But there were also performances (no admission) in bars and taverns, on playgrounds, in prisons with inmates as the audience. But the feeling and commitment were always there.

The most powerful example of ritual theater done by the Kuumba Theatre was a play called *Destruction or Unity?* Val gave it this name because two of the most vital options facing black Americans at the time were unity, based on common goals and ideals, or self-hatred and destruction from crime, drug use and declining family life. The full production combined blues, jazz and gospel music, interpretive dance and dramatic poetry. It could be done as a full-length production or in shorter excerpts.

Destruction or Unity? was performed at the Krannert Center for the Performing Arts on the campus of the University of Illinois at Champaign-Urbana on April 25, 1970. It was on the same bill with *The Life of Harriet Tubman*, a work that I wrote based on the life of the famous nineteenth century freedom fighter. Val played the lead role of Harriet Tubman. Val also produced and directed *Destruction or Unity?* This was during the academic year September 1969-May 1970 when Val was director of the African American Cultural Program at the U of I.

The most memorable performance of *Destruction or Unity?* was done at the St. James United Methodist Church, 4611 South Ellis Avenue on Chicago's South Side on November 22, 1970. A second performance was done at the church on December 13, 1970, sponsored by Black Methodists for Church Renewal. This was one of the many groups of blacks within major white religious denominations during the 1960s and 1970s, who were searching for a new sense of meaning and identity.

During the winter of 1970 and most of 1971, excerpts of *Destruction or Unity?* were done on weekends at the South Side Art Center. *Chicago Courier* gave this description of a scene from the ritual: "There is hellfire and damnation preaching. A sister bolts from the audience and begins to 'testify' and her testimony is black poetry, written by the likes of Don L. Lee, Imamu Amiri Baraka and Johari Amini. A brother tells what it's like to read a 'really good, black poem,' and a child talks about the death of five black children in Birmingham. All the while the audience says 'Amen' and forgets that it is a play. The audience becomes part of the experience, because the experience is them."[1]

The ritual was done on the same bill with *Contribution*, a one-act play by Ted Shine about black family life. *The Bulletin*, a South Side Chicago weekly newspaper, said, "*Contribution* plays tribute to an aging but noble black grandmother who, despite her years and outward humility, teaches an object lesson to an arrogant, immature grandson in the meaning of militancy and the art of survival."[2]

Another short play done by Kuumba during the early 1970s was *The Leader* by Joseph White. This was a satire on the leadership style of black ministers. The *Chicago Defender* offered this description on April 8, 1971: "An explosive play, *The Leader* examines black leadership in the Civil Rights Movement, opened in Chicago this weekend. The Joseph White drama was presented by the Kuumba Workshop at the South Side Community Art Center. *The Leader* is a one-act ritual written in the early 1960s that depicts a strutting, arrogant, vain and corrupt Rev. Abraham Lincoln Brown who, though revered by ecstatic, unquestioning followers, becomes totally insensitive to their needs and aspirations, and allows himself to be victimized by a whimsical, treacherous white mistress, Cora...Written at the time of the sit-ins and freedom rides throughout the South, the work questions not only the ease with which a licentious white woman corrupts a Black minister, but the extent to which the drive for Black liberation has been set back by the personal ambitions of its leadership."[3]

The Kuumba Theatre also experimented with taking versions of its rituals for live, on-the-spot performances in locations where you usually don't find live drama—in bars, taverns, on playgrounds and prisons. Val's idea was to take the live drama to wherever people were willing to watch and listen. Former *Chicago Sun-Times* columnist Ellis Cose described one such setting. "For several hours on Christmas Eve [Dec. 24, 1970], members of a black theater workshop read black poetry to patrons of two South Side lounges, in what they called bringing 'live black theater to the people.' The artists were members of the Kuumba Workshop, an organization conceived nearly two years ago as a vehicle for black artists of all kinds to showcase their talents while at the same time conveying a positive message about blackness to their overwhelmingly black audience."[4]

In 1971 Kuumba issued a strong denunciation of the hit film *Sweet Sweetback's Badass Song*, which was produced and directed by Melvin Van Peebles, who also played the main character, Sweetback. The criticism seemed strange and unwarranted to some blacks since this was probably the first time a film made by a black producer with mostly black characters had bucked the traditional Hollywood system of distribution and made a lot of money. *Sweetback's* storyline is simple. A black stud who performs in a peep show kills a white policeman and spends the rest of the time being chased by other white cops all over Los Angeles, and then from L.A. to the Mexican border. Sweetback successfully eludes the cops and escapes to Mexico.

Kuumba's criticism was based on the film's overwhelmingly negative images. Our arguments were summarized in a ten-page position paper we issued. The hero is a hustler and stud with no redeeming qualities, except that it takes him less than a minute to seduce and have sex with every woman he meets. The other black characters in the film were Sweetback's friends from the peep show. The white police officers were all pathological racists with not an ounce of tolerance or understanding. The film received an X rating because the explicit sex and nudity were every bit as palpable as in any other X-rated film. It opens with a nude prostitute having sex with a small boy who later grows into the man Sweetback.

The main goal of *Sweet Sweetback* was like all of the other blaxsploitation films of that era, the illusory black "victory" over the white oppressor. The film's supporters loved it because Sweetback beat the system and won. He killed four white cops and got away.

The following year—1972—Kuumba issued another position paper highly critical of another blaxsploitation film, *Super Fly,* about a flamboyant cocaine dealer in Harlem named Priest, played by Ron O'Neal. The film cleverly supports the use of cocaine. Every time Priest does something successful, like score with his girlfriend or get some money, he's seen sniffing coke. The connection is unmistakable. Priest also sports a gaudy pimpmobile and wears all of the stylish fashions of the time, a flashy lifestyle built on his success as a coke dealer.

Priest says he wants to make one more big score (sale of cocaine) to earn enough money to retire from the business. But the corrupt white police commander to whom Priest has paid protection money all these years threatens to kill Priest if he quits.

The climactic scene at the end of the film shows Priest defying the police commander, getting into his pimpmobile and driving away in victory. I remember sitting in a downtown Chicago theater full of underage kids (who weren't supposed to see this R-rated film) and hearing the deafening roar go on for nearly ten minutes. For them, Super Fly getting away was black "victory" over the white oppressor.

The following are the first three of ten points summarized in the Kuumba position paper against *Super Fly*:

1. The film advocates using dope—the biggest most destructive killer of black people in the country.
2. It never deals with the deadly consequences of dope dealing, which is sweeping black communities like a ravaging plague.

3. It glorifies the hustler as a hero—another in a long succession of such films which glorify and distort the image and influence of black hustlers, studs and pimps.

In 1973 the Kuumba Theatre had a long run of its most financially successful play up to that time, *The Image Makers,* a satire of blaxsploitation films that was written by Useni Eugene Perkins. The play showed how the messages and images in these films were clearly crafted and delivered to black audiences throughout the country by white creators in a Hollywood film industry bent only on making money. The overriding message of *The Image Makers* was that blacks had to take control and reshape their own images and messages, or remain captives of a system of exploitation and enslavement. The play was very popular with audiences and sparked considerable audience discussion after each performance. Since its earliest beginnings, Kuumba had engaged its audiences in discussion of every show. *The Image Makers* was also very consistent with the public positions Kuumba took in opposition to films like Super Fly and *Sweetback*. We opened the play at the South Side Art Center in 1973, but continued the run in 1974 when Kuumba moved to a larger space at 2222 South Michigan Avenue, in a building that we found out later was once home to gangsters of the 1920s. In January 1977 Kuumba performed *The Image Makers* as its entry in the World Festival of Black and African Arts (FESTAC) in Lagos, Nigeria.

Kuumba Liberation Awards

For four consecutive years, 1972, 1973, 1974, and 1975, the Kuumba Theatre held an awards program in which it presented awards to people whom Kuumba felt had made exemplary contributions to the black freedom struggle. Typically, three or four awardees were cited in each program. These programs helped to solidify Kuumba's reputation as more than just a theater group. We were about theater as an instrument for liberation and renewal, but Kuumba wanted to make a statement beyond its live drama. We felt compelled to bring public notice to serious, principled people whom we regarded as "unheralded heroes" in the freedom struggle. Space won't permit naming every awardee, but this short list should make the point:

1. 1972: Hoyt W. Fuller, then editor of *Black World* magazine.
2. 1973: Dudley Randell, founder of Broadside Press in Detroit, and Haki R. Madhubuti (formerly Don L. Lee), founder of Third World Press in Chicago. Though small publishing companies, Broadside and Third

World pioneered in publishing the works of many black poets and writers when few publishing outlets were open to them at the time.

3. 1974: Sterling Brown, a longtime distinguished professor of English at Howard University in Washington, D.C.
4. 1975: Hayward C. Brown, a member of the Fayette County (Tennessee) Civic and Welfare League, which established the famed Tent City in Fayette County on behalf of blacks who had fought for civil rights.

In December 1969, three years before the Liberation Awards, the Kuumba Theatre organized a national tribute to the late Gwendolyn Brooks at the old Afro-Arts Theatre on the South Side. Poets and writers from around the nation wrote special tributes to Gwen (a longtime personal friend to me and Val, and foremost financial supporter of Kuumba for many years). The poems and essays in honor of Gwendolyn Brooks were incorporated in a book, *To Gwen, With Love,* which was published by Johnson Publishing Company in 1970.

Some Lessons Learned—Not to be Forgotten

During my years as reporter and executive with the Kuumba Theatre, I became involved in, or was a witness, to some complex situations which are useful to repeat now because they provide valuable lessons. One situation that comes to mind occurred in the early 1970s just after the Kuumba Theatre had filed the first of what were to become yearly grant applications to the National Endowment for the Arts, the main federal agency that funds arts organizations and programs, and the Illinois Arts Council. Val and I began to hear rumors that Kuumba had "sold out" to get money from white funding sources. As with almost every rumor, nobody could trace the source. As days and weeks passed, the rumors became more prevalent with the persistent theme: white money means white control. Val and I had to explain to Kuumba members and friends that the grant applications didn't amount to selling out and there wasn't the slightest evidence anybody could point to that the content of Kuumba's plays and programs were affected in any way.

The rumors were based on the false notion that if you took any money from whites, you had to subject yourself to their control. The rumors gradually subsided. Nobody ever stepped up and confronted me or Val about the white money, but some of those we believed were responsible for the rumors today take lots of money from white sources. That's because they have since learned the lesson we clearly understood thirty-five years ago.

> **Lesson #1:** Taking money from whites doesn't mean you've sold out and compromised your principles. In no way does white money automatically mean white control.

Those who compromise their principles for money don't have strong principles in the first place. All money comes with some kind of strings attached. The NEA and IAC never attempted to dictate the kind of art Kuumba would represent. Both did require extensive reports on how the money was spent—standard practice with nay funding source, black or white, and totally legitimate.

Closely related to lesson one was what happened with the launch of a new magazine in the late 1970s—*First World: An International Journal of Black Thought*. The idea for the magazine came about after the late John H. Johnson, owner of Johnson Publishing Company, had discontinued publication of *Black World* magazine in 1976.

Black World and its editor, the late Hoyt W. Fuller, were strong friends of the black consciousness movement. *Black World* was the only publishing outlet for many of the black poets and writers who could never get published in the mainstream white press.

Many of us felt a great loss with the demise of *Black World*. Val and I became involved with a group of friends and supporters of Hoyt Fuller who wanted to launch a new magazine to replace *Black World,* but with greater editorial freedom. The launch effort had problems from the start, but a rigid and inflexible opposition to any connections to whites made the task far more difficult. The majority of the *First World* friends adamantly opposed any grant applications to white funding sources. The reasons were the same as with Kuumba years earlier—white money meant white control. Also, I wanted to do a story for the *L.A. Times* on the effort to launch a new national magazine, but the same opponents would have none of it. They argued fiercely that the white establishment press would only distort the truth.

First World magazine published its first edition in 1978. Publication was sporadic and inconsistent after that. Most of those involved in the launch effort, however well-meaning, had no idea of the enormous cost of publishing, let alone distributing, a national magazine.

In the summer of 1981, Hoyt Fuller dropped dead of a heart attack in downtown Atlanta, his hometown. He had moved to College Park just outside of Atlanta after leaving Chicago, and his home also served as office for *First World*. The magazine hung on briefly after Hoyt's death, but eventually folded. It would be wrong to say the magazine would have succeeded had we sought and received money from white funding sources. I'm not sure of that. But I am sure that a bad situation was made immeasurably worse by an irrational and wholly unfounded fear that even the smallest support from whites would automatically translate into white control.

Lesson #2: Be confident enough in your goals and methods to dispel any fear of outside control.

Also closely related to lesson two was the unspoken but unmistakable suspicion of me as a reporter for the white establishment press. Though they were too polite to say it, the real reason most *First World* friends didn't like the idea of an *L.A. Times* story was because they mistrusted me. This was nothing new for me. For years, I had encountered other blacks who were reluctant to candidly speak at meetings "because the white press is here with us." The root cause was a widespread mistrust of all white institutions, including the white establishment news media. I always understood this. What I never understood was the absence of similar mistrust of other blacks who also worked in white establishment institutions, like the YWCA, the Chicago school board, and the University of Chicago.

I believe I eventually overcame most of the suspicions because I did many good stories on issues crucial to the black community. Also, the work Val and I did at the Kuumba Theatre spoke for itself, regardless of ties to the white establishment.

Lesson #3: Never judge anyone's loyalty or commitment based solely on where he or she works.

The Kuumba Theatre's Twelve Principles of Art

Adopted in 1972

1. We are an African people, bound together as a worldwide African family by race, ancestry, culture and common oppression.
2. Black art and black life are inseparable. Our art is not fantasy and must be rooted in the historic experiences of African people. It is the recreation and interpretation of black life.
3. Black art must be functional. To entertain is not enough. It must teach some valuable lessons or leave some important messages with its readers, listeners or viewers.
4. Black art must deal honestly and fully with every aspect of the black condition, past and present.
5. Black art must present positive images of African people, and if not, say something relevant to them about their condition while presenting negative images. At no time should it ever reinforce self-hatred or white-inflicted stereotypes.

6. Black art must clearly show the social, political, economic and cultural contexts of any realities it treats. It is not enough to simply show a particular black reality. Our art must tell why it exists, its effects and offer necessary alternatives.
7. Black art must relate to all black people, not just the middle class or intellectuals.
8. We reject, totally and eternally, the sterile Western concept of "art for art's sake." There is no such thing and never has been. "All art reflects the value system from which it comes," says Ron Karenga.
9. There is a direct and lasting relationship between black art and politics. Black artists have a fundamental and permanent responsibility to be involved in and contribute significantly to the liberation struggle.
10. Black artists not only owe an equitable portion of their time and talent to the black community, but also their earnings.
11. Black art and artists must be fully supported and judged by black people.
12. Black artists must be rooted in the black community and totally involved in its activities and struggles.

CITATIONS

1. "Kuumba is Art for Black Folk," by Helen H. King. *The Chicago Courier*, Feb. 20, 1971, page 1.
The Chicago Courier was one of many weekly newspapers with a primarily black readership.
2. "New Black Theater Here," (writer not named). *The Bulletin—a South Side Chicago weekly newspaper*, Nov. 4, 1970, page 10.
3. "Kuumba Workshop Premieres 'The Leader,'" (writer not named). *Chicago Daily Defender*, April 8, 1972, page 15.
4. "Black Art Conveys Pride in Blackness," a column by Ellis Cose. *Chicago Sun-Times*, Jan. 8, 1971, page 56.

IMAGE MAKING: KUUMBA WORKSHOP AND BLACK LIBERATION THEATRE

D. Soyini Madison

Part One: Initial Queries

I.

I would like to begin by recounting two demands of the international Black Power Movement (mid-1960s to mid-1970s) and what has come to be known as her sister: The Black Arts Movement: one was the demand for human dignity and the other was the demand for liberation. The first, individual and internal: I am a human being; the second, social and worldly: people inhabiting freedom.

This demand to be human and to be free was a mind, hand, and heart endeavor: It required learning, labor, and love. It required a Pan African Revolution. Those dispossessed of whatever those possessions were: their bodies, their land, their histories, languages, memories, their ancient stories and their dignity became at this moment and time embodiments of imagined change—change both deadly and beautiful.

II.

The question becomes, what performative processes and what collective action were required to become a liberated human being: "If another world is possible" how did these possibilities come into fruition for a movement dismissed by some as mere gestures of narrow nationalism—as essentialist, short lived and artistically sophomoric. While for others it has been hailed as "A time like no other" a revolution that still haunts us and of which we are still indebted. In order to understand what it meant to be a liberated human being and the collective action required, we couldn't ignore the pan-Africanist philosophies that undergirded the Movement. I often turn to the words of the post-colonial political philosopher and the first president of Ghana Kwame Nkrumah: "practice without thought is blind and thought without practice is empty." There is alchemy of combined thought and action where body and mind, where thinking and doing, culminate in an ETHICS of action. In the academy, we are too familiar with the theory/ practice coupling and divide; I am not dragging up these old tensions. Instead I want to make a point about a particular time and space where the question of ethics brings to light something new and where reflection and reason provide insight, then urgency, into the responsibility and moral imperative of action—this was the post-colonial struggle and reality. And black people born in the USA who were "in the movement" identified as African people. Within that temporality, we learn that thoughts stand still, stagnant and weightless, without the materiality of action. Action gives our thoughts materiality to be seen, heard, felt, through the senses, but, moreover, action makes manifest the labors of thoughts, acknowledging the very labor of thinking, no longer as internal and empty (perhaps lonely, painful) but culminating in a shared action. Nkrumah's pan-Africanist positionality asserts that thoughts need action, but it can never be one-sided: action needs thought, so that we do not blow ourselves and the world to bits in the blind reverie of revolution. Action without thought leaves us vulnerable; it can too quickly turn action into action for actions sake alone—dogma, fundamentalism, and binaries can be momentarily liberating, perhaps necessary—but after some time they become dead-end short cuts to thinking. For Nkrumah's pan-Africanist vision, time worn fundamentalism became anti-thought.

III.

In this path to the liberated human being where collective action constitutes reciprocal processes of thought, feeling, and practice, the lacuna now forming is the question of Culture—of culture and political economy. Another post-colonial, political philosopher, Amilcar Cabral reflects how Pan-Africanist thought, before the dawn of neo-liberalism, re-envisioned Marxist notions of mode of production into an Africanist cultural paradigm that influenced how the Black Arts Movement not only articulated connections between culture and political economy, but how a "cultural revolution" was not without economic consequence as it relates to black poverty.

Cabral writes "*...The brain behind Nazi propaganda, heard culture being discussed, he brought out his revolver. That shows that the Nazis—who were and are the most tragic expression of imperialism and of its thirst for domination—even if they were all degenerates like Hitler, had a clear idea of the value of culture as a factor of resistance.*" (260)

For Cabral, whatever may be the material aspects of domination, it can be maintained only by the permanent, organized repression of the cultural life of the people concerned.

For every society, for every group of people, considered as an evolving entity, the level of the productive forces indicates the stage of development of the society and of each of its components in relation to nature and its capacity to act or to react in relation to nature. It indicates and conditions, the type of material relationships (expressed objectively or subjectively which exists among various elements or groups constituting the society in question.) Cabral writes that Culture is perhaps, the product of this history just as the flower is the product of a plant.

For these African political theorists the fundamental characteristic of a culture is the highly dependent and reciprocal nature of its linkages with the social and economic reality of the environment with the level of productive forces and the mode of production of the society, which created it. (263)

IV.

The Case Study. These brief and introductory queries serve as a kind of lens out of which to examine a rather short play, during a rather short period of time, in what Jamaica Kinkaid might call a small place: the United States of America.

It is 1973—Chicago, Ill. The Play is the *Image Makers*. The playwright is Useni Eugene Perkins. The theatre company is The Kuumba Workshop AND all of this is within the overarching temporality of the Chicago Black Arts Movement, and the grander temporality of pan-Africanism and the Black Arts Movement.

The words of Francis Ward, Administrative Director of the Kuumba Workshop and husband of Kuumba's founder and director, Val Gray Ward, describes the times both in Chicago and across the black diaspora.

"Nobody who lived through the decade of the 1960s will ever forget that era, regardless of his or her political persuasion. Whether you like or disapproved of the tempo of the times, you could never forget the fire, the ferment, the combativeness, and the sudden new aggressiveness of a people, long characterized by their passivity. The rapid changes and turn of events made a few years seem like a lifetime....Kuumba was born out of this ferment, this swirling milieu of frenzied action and reaction. When Val Gray Ward called together some friends in the spring of 1968 to found a new instrument for artistic, political change, what eventually took shape was an organization dedicated to creating quality black art, defined and legitimized by black people....The driving force behind the first series of meetings was the determined quest to create black-controlled arts and cultural organization that could consolidate the ideas of the 1960s and become a living, viable, sustaining institution thereafter. What Val and her friends sought to initiate was an institution that could capture the spirit of the times, and also establish itself on an unshakable foundation of principle and truth....the highest calling of the black artist is service to his or her community...black art and black life are inseparable/we must clean up, create, build...this became Kuumba's slogan this is what Kuumba means..."

The guiding principles of Kuumba reflected the guiding principles of the Black Arts Movement. I enumerate them here:

- To excavate hidden histories of Blackness
- To honor a self-determined blackness: Art to, for, and from Black People
- To create new forms—An unceasingly Inventive art of alternative designs; symbols; mythologies;
- To commit to an Aesthetic of Ethics—A politics and value of black communitarianism: consciousness and action

These tenets were in keeping with Amari Baraka's Revolutionary Theatre: To honor, in Baraka's words "....the imagination (from image, magi, magician, as a "practical vector from the soul. It stores all data, and can be called on to solve all our "problems." The imagination is the projection of ourselves past our sense of ourselves as "things"—the imagination as image is all possibility, because from the image, the initial circumscribed energy, any use (idea) is possible. And so begins that image's use in the world. Possibility is what moves us. Force. Spirit. Feeling."

And "swirling" around Kuumba Workshop's force, spirit and feeling were specific temporalities—Watershed Moments—historical ghosts of past, present, and future:

- During the early 1960s Chicago was the home of Elijah Muhammad and the Black Muslims—they were a commanding force in black communities across the city with their beliefs of black separatism, self-determination, economic independence, and racial pride.
- **1965 Dr. Martin Luther King Jr.'s** open-housing march occurred in the violently segregated white Southwest Side on Chicago becoming infamous when King stated that he had never seen so much hate displayed, not even in the heart of Mississippi
- **June 1966 brought the Freedom Rally**, becoming another testament to black organizing when over 100,000 protestors occupied Chicago's Soldier's Field—to voice a freedom agenda—one of them being to end the War in Viet Nam

- **1968 Democratic Convention** where televised images of protesters being beaten bloody, tear gassed, dragged through downtown streets of Chicago and thrown in police wagons—the same year marking the Chicago Riots, after the assassination of Dr. King, that lasted over two days and stretched 28 blocks
- **Dec 1969 Deputy Chairman** of the Illinois Black Panther Party, Fred Hampton, one of the most eloquent orators of the time, who organized a truce among street gangs; initiated a free breakfast program; organized communities across the city on principals of class consciousness and building multi-racial coalitions was brutally assassinated by the states attorney's office under the sanction of the Chicago police department and the FBI in the middle of the night while he was sleeping in his bed.

V.
THE PLAY:

Kuumba Workshop Presents The Image Makers

SLIDE 1 {Val and Francis} Val Gray Ward tells me on May 3, 2013:
"It was a winter evening in 1977 and we had just ended rehearsal. We were coming out the building when two cars of white men pulled up, two of them jumped out of the cars and told us to stand against the wall and put our hands up—Francis said they had revolvers—they were calling us all kinds of bad names, it was awful, they told us we were not going to do that play—they are stopping the play—they were cursing and calling us terrible names, calling us Niggers and we were not going to do that nigger play… I said we are going to do the play and we are going to do whatever play we want to do and there is nothing you can do about it—we are not scared of you. They said they were the police—I said I'm going to call the police on you! These are our streets -- I starting shouting and fussing and cussing in bigger form than all them put together. I said Nobody is scared of you on this street…. I remember they got in their cars cussing and calling us niggers and drove off."

SLIDE 2 {the Image Makers Program} The play they were rehearsing for—the play the white men in the cars wanted to scare them into not performing—was *The Image Makers*, a provocative performance that had been highly reviewed by both black and white progressive media when it first premiered in 1973 years before the threatening incident with the white men on the street. When Kuumba first opened Image Makers audiences came from across the country, uncommon for a small black community theatre. Kuumba was in rehearsals that night to revive it in preparation for a trip to Lagos, Nigeria where the company had been invited to perform the play at FESTAC 1977. **[The second Black World/African Festival of Art and Culture—a 29 day celebration of black culture that drew approximately 20,00 artists and scholars from 56 countries—Kuumba filled the hall and received a standing ovation]**

The play centers on a plan to save the economically declining movie industry by pandering to the untapped market of black theatergoers by creating black super heroes. They have a formula that will turn ordinary black people into "Super" Negroes overnight. They will use technology to create super black people and save the industry. The character Uncle Tom **[SLIDE 3. UNCLE TOM]** is invited in to meet **[SLIDE 4. WHITE FACES]** **[SLIDE 5. MR. HOLLYWOOD]** Mr. Hollywood, The Minister of Finance, The Minister of Propaganda and Dr. Frankenstein, **[SLIDE 6. DR FRANKENSTEIN]** **[SLIDE 7. DR. FRANKENSTEIN]** and their messenger and playful delight, Miss America **[SLIDE 8. MISS AMERICA]**. While shuffling and grinning, Mr. Hollywood gives Uncle Tom his assignment: "We want you to go into the ghetto and bring back four of your people. We are looking for certain types. We need a pimp, a dope pusher, a real cool cat, and a person who would like to be somebody else." Tom goes into the ghetto and with promises of big money he brings back all four. They each drink Dr. Frankenstein's magic formula and we see them change before our eyes into Sweetback, Superfly, Shaft, and Blackcula **[SLIDE 9. SLIDE OF SUPERFLY]** This grand and spectacular Blaxploitation film gets underway and when a question is raised about scripts, Mr. Hollywood replies "the scripts are unimportant. We'll write most of them during production—they don't need to make sense. As long as the audience sees these Supper Negroes doing super things they will be satisfied. Sweetback bursts on the stage running to his theme song and with the help of flashing lights Sweetback runs back and forth across the stage, falling down/getting up, losing his breath/catching his breath, getting caught /getting away and then he's gone. As one critic stated: "Although the running only lasts a few minutes, we have the impression that we have seen the entire film, and in terms of the message it had for black people—we have." Next comes Blackula, **[SLIDE 9. BLACKULA]** then Shaft, then Superfly. Each in turn demonstrating that in about a minute they can recreate the entirety of the films, while the director-producer-cameraman is right there recording it all and counting millions."

Another critic writes: By this time, the fact black people are being used and exploited is open and apparent and the need to see a change in the play's reality becomes a need to see a change in the world. Who makes our images and their motivations for doing so are clear. What is not clear is what we will do about it." The play offers a response.

In the next scene, we see a group of militants in a planning session. **[SLIDE 10.MILITANTS]** We learn that the movie industry is pouring all its money into another film this time it will be a gigantic production involving all the super star Negroes plus hundreds of extras and starring none other than good old Uncle Tom. The movie will run for eight hours to give the super Negroes time to show all of their super moves. But when the filming starts we see the militants have arranged to also be a part of the cast. Instead of following the plan the militants take over and systematically eliminate all the white characters in the movie industry. However, the Super Negroes are given the opportunity for redemption and although Uncle Tom is also given a chance to change he just cannot bring himself to do it. So he has to be eliminated too. The play ends with idea that "Uncle Tom" was the one image where the system prevailed.

The End.

As we address the theme of this conference, a few excerpts from critics of the time are insightful:

Chicago Tribune–Nov, 2 1973 by Linda Winer—: "Kuumba Workshop says that it creates theater by and for black people and for black people only. Then it fails, I say. I sat in the makeshift auditorium up three floors at the South Side Community Art Center, 3831 S. Michigan Ave and found The Image Makers a pertinent, credible and [yes] entertaining Saturday evening of political theatre for people with a last name like Winer. Not just because I hunger for good political theater in a city almost barren of any that are consciously so—more because this one is worth it!

Chicago Reader–1973 By John Lanahan—I'll admit political theater does have its limitations and that if it is badly done it can be wretched. When it is well done, however, as is the Image Makers it glorifies the refusal of the human animal to be bullied into categorization and oppression. In a decade plagued by bored relativism, the Image Makers espouses a faith in man's ability to change the present, and sounds and outraged but insistent note of hope for the future. It's nice to see a show nowadays that really believes it.

VI.
In conclusion

Thought/Practice; Culture/Economy; Revolutionary Theatre and Collective Action: What Kuumba and Image Makers Does, Now/Then

Transracial performances may be traced to the 1600s but what becomes of them within the temporality of the BAM and a black community theatre in Chicago?

- First, It is a historic moment, of grand proportions, that can be further examined in contemporary studies of whiteface, theatrical spectacle that generally examines how white supremacy, privilege, and purity are contested and restaged (Faedra Chatard Carpenter) to unestle taken for granted/common sense and troubled realities of whiteness, particularly in contestation with non-whiteness.
- Second, Image Makers not only worked toward the de-privileging of white power by privileging it surfaces—making it hyper-visible, comic, and strange but it put whiteness in the room within a particular temporality to control, dismantle and repurpose its hopes, dreams and strategies
- **Third. IMAGE MAKERS inspires a serious re-visioning of the re-visioning of Uncle Tom. The black journalist Clarence Page remind us** "Josiah Henson revealed how complicated the cruel and peculiar institution of slavery could be. Separated from his family as a young boy when he was sold as property in an estate sale, Henson was a loyal servant until he learned he might be sold again. In 1830, he escaped to Canada and founded a settlement, a trade school and a lumber business, while also helping other slaves to escape.

When he returned after the war, a free man, to his former owners, the lady of the house is said to have told him in surprise, "Why, Sir, you're a gentleman now." Josiah Henson's autobiography, "Truth Is Stranger Than Fiction," became a best seller and helped Harriet Beecher Stowe recreate the day-to-day life of slaves for what would be her own bestseller, a book that enflamed the abolitionist movement.

Abraham Lincoln might in 1862, might have said "So you're the little woman who wrote the book that started this great war!" But, in 1973 and 2013 Uncle Tom, in other words "is a prickly American paradox." Uncle Tom is not simply an insult for many Black People, but a traitor, a person without a soul, the epitome of all that is vile and violent in the historical terrors that rage against black life.

While Stowe's Uncle Tom was cast as a heroic figure that encouraged two long-suffering slave women to escape and then undergoes a fatal beating because he would not betray them or his Christian faith, his image was destroyed, just as the Uncle Tom in the Kuumba performance, then by courage and now by cowardice. The Image Makers' Tom might ultimately be the vendetta for Stowe's noble Tom—killing off the minstrel legacy and the Image from the ghastly buffoon "Tom Shows. This may not be the intent, but Image Makers further complicate the palimpsest and traces of the worn over Tom figure and his destruction at the end of the play: Which Tom is being destroyed? The implications for dignity and what it means to be black and fully human abound in the moment of Tom's death.

- Fourth. Image Makers Then/Now performed the political economy of Culture—the linkages among culture, economic forces, desire, art, poverty, persuasion, personhood, and liberation culminated in the robust staging and penetrating rhetoric of comic seriousness and parody writ large. Image Makers performed how Black artists and critics worried that the powerful economies of Blaxploitation films found renewed fodder for black cultural distortion by reverting and erasing the labor of the hard won anti-stereotype work, of black cultural produces, by riveting the liberatory "black is beautiful" back onto itself with distorted gusto and buffoonish Technicolor to make stereotypical images anew. One critic noted (Ed Guerroro) it was a project in the "containment of insurgent black political aspirations." I would obviously add cultural as well.
- Fifth. Image Makers reminds us "Now/Then" that Blaxploitation may have been (may be) Formulaic as the pimp, gangster, cool dude or sexy female counterparts violently acted revenge fantasies against bad white people, but as evidenced by box office sales many black people loved them and some are classics. Across the black film boom from 1970 through 1973 there were 91 productions—47 considered models of the Blaxploitation formula (Marshall Hyatt 1989, 244-245 and James P. Murray 1973b) pp.35 and 36

I will close with a brief excerpt from an oral history interview conducted on November 19, 2012 with Useni Eugene Perkins:

> "Today, as I look back on all that I have done and all the struggles of the Black Chicago and Black Arts movement—I'm aware we did not remedy all the problems of those time, perhaps we even created a few, but what is most important to me now, what is most urgent to me at this moment, is the future—I believe all the cultural work that we do now must be for the future. It must be for our Children. Because this is the chronic state of which we live."

(Presented at the International Performing Studies Conference at Stanford University June 2, 2013.)

THE 1960S FOR ME

Okoro Harold Johnson

The 1960s was a dynamic period of turmoil and change. Not only in regard to the Civil Rights struggle of Dr. Martin Luther King Jr. and others, but also for the arts and theater. My history and background are in the theater. Abena Joan Brown and I were drama students at Roosevelt University in 1949. We sat around for a year waiting to be cast in a play, but there were no roles for butlers and maids, so we were not cast in anything. We went out into the community and became members of Drama Incorporated, a community group headed by Miss Lillian Thompkins. She instilled in us that Blacks needed their own theaters and buildings. That was the inspiration for organizing Ebony Talent Associates, which eventually became Entertainment Arts Foundation.

My teaching experience in theater began at Stateway Gardens Housing Projects in 1957. I taught there all during the 1960s. In four years I was able to elevate a group of people, (many of whom had never seen a play,) to the production of *A Raisin in the Sun* by Lorraine Hansberry, which was selected as the first Black play to be presented at the Chicago Park District's Theater on the Lake at Fullerton and the Outer Drive.

The sixties was a great period for Black theater. In addition to Lorraine Hansberry's *Raisin,* Ossie Davis' *Purlie Victorious,* LeRoi Jones' *Dutchman,* James Baldwin's *The Amen Corner,* Ed Bullins' *In the Wine Time,* Charles Gordone's *No Place to be Somebody,* and Lonne Elder's *Ceremonies in Dark Old Men* were among the new Black plays of the sixties.

Oscar Brown Jr. was Chicago's most prolific playwright of the sixties. With his ill-fortuned Kicks & Co., he also wrote and produced such plays as *Joy 66, Summer in the City, Big Time Buck White* and *Opportunity Please Knock.*

A part of my theatrical experience of the sixties was working with Oscar and several of his productions. However, my greatest experience then, was my directorial involvement in the TV series *Bird of the Iron Feather,* which was Chicago's first soap opera. It was produced in 1969 by WTTW television, Chicago's Public Broadcasting Station. The production was financed by a $600,000 grant from the Ford Foundation. Its chief writer was Richard Durham, former national editor of the *Chicago Defender* and *Muhammed Speaks* newspapers. Mr. Durham was also the Peabody Award winner for the CBS radio series *Destination Freedom,* for which he wrote fifty-four half-hour episodes. The production was first conceived of as having two white directors who were currently employed at WTTW, Peter Strand and Lou Abraham, and it was to be written by college students. However, because of the involvement of The Coalition for United Community Action, a community rights organization headed by Reverend C.T. Vivian and the Catalyst, many changes were negotiated. The first was when I became the first black television director in the city of Chicago.

This began when Mr. Durham informed me that the WTTW program was forthcoming. Since there were no Black televisions directors in Chicago, he suggested that I enroll in a program for African Americans at WGBH in Boston. I took the six-week program and was awarded a certificate stating that I was a qualified television director.

With this certificate and fifteen years of experience directing theater, I applied for the job as director of the upcoming yet unnamed black television series. I was immediately told that they had their directors and had no plans to hire anyone else. The question came up as to how could you do a black TV program without any blacks involved in the production. I was told that they would hire me as a drama coach but not as a director. I responded that I was a qualified TV director and that was the job I wanted. The fight was on and after many weeks of bitter negotiating, not only for the directing job but several other demands like live music and Richard Durham as chief writer, I was to sign the contract on Wednesday. However, my wife's mother died in Birmingham and I had to go to the funeral on Wednesday, so I told them I would sign the contract on the following Monday. When I came back ready to sign the contract, Clarence McIntosh, the only black employee at WTTW, had gone to New York and hired Leroy Inman to take the drama coach job and I was out completely. This move was to fulfill the need for a black face in the production, but not a black director.

This was where the community organizations came in. The Coalition's reaction to this was to mount a more aggressive and strategic strategy. The Coalition had been working with the Blackstone Rangers in the fight for construction jobs in the Loop and decided to take a busload of them to the next negotiating session. With the Rangers, we closed the station down, locked the doors, cut off all the telephone communication and said, "NOW LET'S NEGOTIATE."

Ed Morris, the station's manger, came out pleading, "Harold, Harold, what do you want us to do?" We had a list of eleven demands; my name as director was on top. One of them was to hire Richard Durham at a 2,500 dollars per script salary rather than the 450 dollars that the station had offered. We also demanded that WTTW hire RIchard Muhal Abrams as musical director and to place a black person in every aspect of production. If there were none qualified, train them. The question came up—what to do with Leroy Inman, the person they had brought in from New York? We answered to hire him as a director, too, which allowed for two black and two white directors. Inman was also qualified as a director.

Then the question came up as to who would acquaint me with the WTTW system. A short training period was necessary. It had to be one of the two white directors. Peter Strand outright refused the task. There had to be at least four directors to carry the load so we allowed Strand to stay on. Lou Abraham, a Jewish director, enthusiastically took on the job. We were ready to go with Richard Durham as chief writer. However, there was a problem with the salary of 450 dollars a script offered to Durham. In Boston the writers were paid 2,500 dollars a script. We demanded the same amount for Durham, and got it. WTTW wanted to use recorded music rather than live music to further save money. We again demanded live music and got Muhal Richard Abrahams as musical director and Oscar Brown, Jr. to sing the theme song which was written by Mark Durham, Richard's son.

Richard Durham conceived the title *Bird of the Iron Feather* from a speech by Frederick Douglass in 1847, depicting the sons and daughters of slaves who were unable to fly to freedom. They were the bird for the hunter's gun, a bird of iron feathers.

I was told that after my training period they would tell me when I was ready to direct a show. Knowing the attitude of the station, I told them that I would tell *them* when I was ready. That is what happened. After a month of training, I selected the script, "The Funeral," which was the opening episode, featuring Yolanda Bryant and David McKnight, both of whom I had worked with in the past. The story line was the funeral of the lead character, Jonah Rhodes, the policeman that the story was based on. Everything after that was a flashback.

Everyone in the station expected me to fall on my face. I found this out because they left the sound system open throughout the station. When I zipped through the episode without any retakes, someone who had been listening yelled out, "WOW HAROLD, THAT WAS FANTASTIC."

Ed Morris, the station manager, congratulated me on a fine job. I turned around to shake the hand of Lou Abraham, the person who had trained me, but he refused to shake my hand and said, "Don't you ever come into the studio when I'm directing again."

I was flabbergasted; I asked Ed Morris what this was all about.

He said, "Don't you know? Step outside the director's booth and I will tell you. What you just did in a month was what it has taken Abraham fifteen years to do, and you just did it better. Something that he never expected of a Black man."

I said, "Well, I'll be damned." I had never experienced such an attitude.

Abraham came out and repeated the statement, "Don't you come into my studio."

I said, "You can kiss my ass. I'm a director now. I can go anywhere in this building I want to."

I directed three additional episodes, "Themes for Unfinished Faces," "The Contract Buyer" and "His Story or Mine." *Bird* first aired on January 19, 1970 and ran for seven weeks with twenty-four half-hour episodes, playing Monday, Tuesday and Wednesday nights at 7:30 p.m. Black audiences loved it and could not wait for the show to come on. White audiences and bourgeois blacks were confused and disturbed by the ghetto images and language portrayed in the series. However, it won two Emmys. The program ended in March of 1970.

Very significantly, the year following *Bird*, 1971, was the year that all radio and television stations in Chicago had to apply for license renewal by the Interstate Commerce Commission. In their applications, they had to prove that they equally and legally conducted their business with fairness to all groups and races in their listening area. *Bird of the Iron Feather* proved no television station in the city was in compliance; therefore, we formed an organization to challenge the license of every radio and television station unless, they hired blacks in front of and behind the cameras. The organization was named Taking Care of Business (TCB). We brought in personnel from Washington, D.C. who were familiar with the procedure and won the case.

I'm sure that many black employees of radio and television today do not know what made it possible to do their jobs today. As a result of the fight for *Bird of The Iron Feather*, we had won another fight for the rights of black people.

Additional Commentary on the 1960s

Another historical incident that occurred in the dynamic sixties was the assassination of Fred Hampton, chairman of the Illinois chapter of the Black Panther Party, on December 4, 1969. WTTW became indirectly involved with this situation. The night of the shooting, I was working late at the station. I saw the police, led by Cook County, Illinois State's Attorney Edward Hanrahan, laying out a large number of rifles and handguns on a table in preparation for a television presentation. I later found out that the presentation was related to the Fred Hampton murder. The implication of this was that these were the many weapons confiscated from the Fred Hampton's home. This charade was run later that night on WTTW. It was later revealed that only one shot was fired from the Hampton house and only one gun was retrieved. Nearly one hundred shots were fired into the house. It was also later revealed that, after the raid, police put two more shots into Hampton's head and said, "Now he's good and dead." This was the turbulent sixties.

HOW OBAC WAS BORN: A PERSONAL MEMOIR

Abdul Alkalimat aka Gerald McWorter

The origin of the Organization of Black American Culture (OBAC) is a story rooted in the lives of specific people, the life of a city, and dynamic relationships that spanned different generations. OBAC was founded by three people in 1967: Conrad Kent Rivers (1933-1968), Hoyt Fuller (1923-1981), and Gerald McWorter (1942). Chicago gave rise to one of the most important local expressions of the national Black consciousness and Black arts movement. OBAC is part of this story, the life of an innovative and vibrant movement toward a new Black aesthetic that emerged in virtually every city in the country. OBAC represented continuity with the past, reflected the present, and set the stage for much of what was yet to develop.

I was born in the famous Chicago Cabrini-Green projects to working-class parents. My father was a steel worker and my mother was a clerical worker; neither had graduated from high school. However, my father came from a family sired by a paternal ancestor, who in 1819 had purchased his freedom in Kentucky and moved to Illinois in 1831. His legal property rights were defined by a special act of the Illinois State Legislature in 1837. My maternal ancestry was rooted in the struggles of the labor movement.

My mother's brother, Otto, and his wife, Eleanor, were full-time progressive activists from the National Negro Congress and the Steel Workers Organizing Committee, who had turned all of us kids onto W.E.B. DuBois and Paul Robeson. I especially remember them giving me a record about the Underground Railroad, and a book about great Black people called *Thirteen Against the Odds*. My father's older sister, Thelma, was part of the black arts scene in Chicago during the thirties and forties. Her house was full of original paintings and traditional African sculptures. My background influences were strong in Black culture and working-class politics. Like most Black families, the McWorter clan sacrificed for education. My family got its first degree from the University of Chicago in 1914, and I found myself studying toward a Ph.D. in sociology at this same university in the 1960s.

During the summer of 1962, I was working at the downtown post office as a weekend sub (that was when the hours varied to your individual taste and the money was good). I lived in the far South Side community called Chatham and rode the Cottage Grove bus to 63rd Street, where I transferred to the El (rapid transit train) to go downtown. One day while standing and reading a book (Ashley Montagu, *The Natural Superiority of Women*) on a very crowded bus someone tapped me on the shoulder and said, "I know Ashley Montagu." That is how I first met Conrad Kent Rivers and from that point our friendship was on.

Conrad was about ten years older, but he was advanced for his age and therefore seemed much older. Conrad had great teachers and was well-educated. He was from Philadelphia and had been close to Langston Hughes, virtually a protégée. Another influence was Casper Jordan, a librarian in Ohio. There was also an uncle in Atlanta, a brilliant literary critic who I got drunk with in Pascal's Motor Hotel in Atlanta while he quoted Black songs from known poets and unknown ones, including the greatest white muse William Shakespeare.

Conrad and I rode the bus and the El to the post office, where he worked as well. We went through the assignment station after punching in and got assigned to the same place. We talked all day—I found a mentor, and he found an energetic student. Our relationship developed quickly. He opened the door for me to the world of Black literature. He taught me what he knew, and I challenged him and drove him to discipline and self-renewal like every good student should. That summer, I read all of Wright, Ellison, and Baldwin, in addition to Chester Himes, and all of the major poets of the Harlem Renaissance. We used to ride down the street in his green Thunderbird convertible reciting Black poetry. I remember once pulling up in front of a bus stop, and reciting the great Claude McKay sonnet, "If We Must Die," to people waiting for the bus. I was singing and they were amused and bewildered. As we sped away through a red light, everyone smiled, laughed, and waved goodbye. I was in love with Blackness and they somehow knew that what was happening was a good thing.

Conrad introduced me to Hoyt Fuller. He was a sophisticated world-class literary figure—an editor, a journalist, and itinerant critic of injustice and immorality from a Black perspective. Most importantly, Hoyt was concerned about listening to and assisting the young. Although I was one of the few isolated Blacks at the University of Chicago, Hoyt joined Conrad in providing me with a rare form of Black mentorship. In return, I was helpful to them by being their resident angry theoretician from the current youthful sixties scene.

Hoyt seemed to have been where intellectuals of his generation wanted to go. He had been an expatriate in Europe and Africa. He achieved professional excellence in mainstream journalism, both Black and white. And he was in the process of building the premiere Black journal of the 1960s—*Negro Digest/Black World*. He published most of us, many for the first time, and he reported on the relevant artistic and literary trends. Indeed, he was our Alain Locke (*Phylon*), Charles Johnson (*Opportunity*), or DuBois (*Crisis*) because he dared to publish new and innovative work. He'd go beyond a normal editor's mandate by sometimes publishing us not for the work submitted, but to encourage us so we would persevere and create work beyond what we might otherwise have achieved. He was the impresario par excellence to the Black arts literature of the 1960s. The OBAC Writers Workshop became what it did because of Hoyt Fuller.

Hoyt, Conrad, and I would meet in Hoyt's apartment, where scotch and water flowed in his oversized glasses. He lived in a South Side high rise near the lake, in an apartment filled with books and art from all over the Black world, as well as some of the best from world culture in general. Hoyt was not a narrow person, and he was adamant about fighting in the interest of Black people.

Sometimes we were joined by others. I remember once when Ronald Fair, the novelist and sculptor, joined us in a heated debate. It is interesting to note now that the meeting ended just short of physical violence, as Conrad and Ronald verbally fought over their respective views of Hemmingway's craft, its relevance to their work, and Black writing in general. We have yet to have a full discussion of the intellectual and technical issues that fueled the debates of the 1960s. At that point I understood some of the issues, but felt that the Rivers-Fair debate was an agenda item plaguing an older set, and that we of the sixties had other more pressing issues to deal with.

Out of these many varied discussions, we were able to reach a common view that a positive Black consciousness (image of self and the world) was essential, and that we should and could do something about it. We named ourselves the Chicago Committee for the Arts, and planned a public meeting at the South Side Community Arts Center: the only WPA cultural project still going strong. We had a program of three people—Arna Bontemps (poet/historian/librarian), Margaret Danner (poet), and Terry Callier (poet/musician).

Hoyt summed it up this way:

> Miss Danner, whose poetry long had reflected the now fashionable "Black is beautiful" philosophy, represented the venerable. Mr. Callier, a rising and as yet "undiscovered" star, represented that which is ever new in simple untarnished Black talent; and Mr. Bontemps, a national treasure, was Black literary history on the hoof, a virtual walking encyclopedia of the past half century of literary labors among Black people. It was a stimulating Sunday afternoon. *Negro Digest*, July 1968, pg. 92.

We began to network and build the group. The key to expanding the group was aimed toward the activists of the current scene. I pulled in Jeff Donaldson, a high school art teacher at my former school Marshall High (later a professor of art and Dean at

Howard University), and a mutual friend Bennett Johnson, a politico and publisher with a commitment to cultural advancement of the community. I also pulled in one of my rare close Black friends from the University of Chicago, Joe Simpson, then a Ph.D. candidate in psycho-pharmacology (Joe is now doing cancer related research after getting a medical degree). He became the secretary of OBAC and coordinator of the community workshop programs. Diana Slaughter, now at the University of Pennsylvania, was my other running buddy.

Another friend pulled in was the Attorney E. Duke McNeil. We used to meet above his record store on 47th Street, just west of King Drive (then South Parkway). Also, Donald Smith (Center for Inner City Studies, then later at Bernard Baruch College in New York City), George Ricks (musicologist with the Board of Education), and Ronald Dunham, a printer. There were few sisters involved at this point.

As the group was developing, we needed a name. The name the Organization of Black American Culture (OBAC) was developed during a phone conversation between Jeff Donaldson and myself. We were both interested in Africa and had a working relationship for several years, which included working together on his 1964 book of sketches with commentary, *The Civil Rights Yearbook*. The key was that the acronym had "OBA" as its root, which was Yoruba (a Nigerian language) for royal, chief, or leader: the role we envisioned for our organization. Shortly afterwards, Jeff designed the OBAC logo. Our creativity and inspired interaction reflected the positive vibes of the period, the organization, and friends and colleagues who worked together and made history.

Chicago had always had exciting community level arts activity. So when OBAC formed and began to expand, it did so with other organizations that already existed. The best example was the Association for the Advancement of Creative Musicians (AACM), formed in 1965. OBAC built a working relationship with the AACM, especially with then leader Muhal Richard Abrams, during the same period OBAC went to 43rd Street to paint "The Wall." AACM went to 43rd Street to play their vanguard sounds—Joseph Jarman, Roscoe Mitchell, Christopher Gaddy, Charles Clark, and others. It was a different business plan for the blues joint—the herb tea and orange juice crowd. In some areas, OBAC recruited people who left to establish independent organizations. For example, in drama, Val Gray-Ward was on the OBAC council, but later left to form what became the Kuumba drama workshop. The three main workshops of OBAC were the writers' workshop, the visual arts workshop, and the community workshop.

One of the interesting aspects of this process was that a school of Chicago Street photography had emerged. They were part of OBAC and that gave them an insider's position to document the history. They froze our images in creative arts of political culture—

Billy Abernathy, Bobby Sengstacke, Roy Lewis, Onegua, Ed Christmas, and others. They were magical in capturing images of fundamental human reality in the everyday motion of the African American people. They made us look timeless.

After forming and consolidating a leadership group, we decided to organize a public program in order to introduce ourselves to the community. We planned a general program to be held in the auditorium of the Center for Inner City Studies. Ann Smith, then involved in speech and theatre at Northeastern Illinois University and now at the University of Illinois, joined to direct us and pull the program together. This program was quite a spectacular event. Each member of the leadership spoke and explained their area of expertise and responsibility. The key artistic moment was the inspiring poetry recital by Amos Mor, who was at that time, the reigning underground Black Poet Laureate in Chicago. I chaired the program, and presented the general theoretical statement. It was the best example of DuBois' talented tenth of the Chicago Black arts scene—a Black style noblesse oblige set all the way.

But after two-thirds of the program, there was tension between the rational/conceptual and the emotional/experiential aspects. There was theory and there was demonstration, but tension existed because both aspects had not yet been brought together. I was an "egghead" not associated with the expressive. Sherri Scott had been in the program as a hip be-bop inspired singer/dancer who turned everyone on. This was also the period of Aretha Franklin's great spiritual power of feeling and rhythm. The tension reached a high point as someone put on Aretha and Sherri began to dance. The OBAC leadership turned to me and demanded I join her. As chairperson of the organization, it was up to me to demonstrate that we had the commitment to overcome ourselves and bring the two aspects of our organization into one dynamic union. I was embarrassed for a moment, hesitant because my dancing skills were weak (not from religious taboo, just too much library and parental control after dark). As she danced on, I leaped to my feet and began to get down, Afro-boo-ga-loo. The Black U of C "egghead" had soul, and OBAC's introduction to the community threatened mainstream assimilation with the inspired cultural dynamic of Black people getting down.

The summer of 1967 was really quite an experience—it was what James Foreman had called "the high tide of resistance." The three OBAC workshops got off to a whirlwind start, and OBAC became known on the national scene almost immediately. Jeff Donaldson led the visual arts workshop through an amazing process of collective action in creating the first public mural of the movement, "The Wall of Respect." The wall was jazz, a collective product inspired by tradition, guided by the politics of Black art, and created by gifted, creative art-makers. Hoyt led the writers' workshop and patiently guided the initial discussions in which one topic dominated—what is Black writing? What is the Black aesthetic? And Joe Simpson led discussions and hosted speakers from other cities in exploring the meaning of art and cultural innovation in the larger social setting of the fight for Black liberation.

The summer of 1967 was key for two other reasons—the Newark Black Power Conference and my departure from Chicago. Hoyt and I co-chaired the workshop on the professions (see Floyd Barbour, ed., *The Black Power Revolt*). It was a critical time because we had the responsibility of defining OBAC's ideological orientation. My ideological position (yet to fully emerge) was suggested by a slogan in my report to the final plenary—"We must not only help to develop revolutionary professionals, but we must develop professional revolutionaries!" The conference was a turning point as we were all being confronted by the vicious repressive powers of the U.S. in putting down urban rebellions all over the country. I kept hearing Amiri Baraka's mandate about Black art: *We want poems that shoot guns*. Our theories must lead to practice. I took my commitment to Black people seriously, so I followed my commitment—in the fall of 1967—from the University of Chicago and the chairmanship of OBAC to Fisk University.

I changed my name in 1969, two years after leaving Chicago. I had left Fisk to join Vincent Harding, Stephen Henderson, A.B. Spellman, Clyde Taylor and Larry Rushing to found the Institute of the Black World in Atlanta. Kofi Wangara (Harold Lawrence) joined our department of history and sociology at Spellman and Vincent was our chair. It was an identity moment. Kofi translated McWorter into IBN Alkalimat, "the son of word." I defined my role as a Black Studies scholar activist. He helped me choose Abdul Hakimu, "servant of knowledge." I found language, comfort, and security in this Ki Swahili/Arabic framework. My full name means "servant of knowledge, the son of word," but to my oldest relative, Alberta McWorter Ewing who is (105), I am still little Gerry.

ARTIST IN FOCUS: INTERVIEW WITH TED WARD

Useni Eugene Perkins

Ted Ward is a small man, in physical dimensions, but his profile as a gifted playwright is of enormous proportion. Although his contribution to drama cannot be denied, the name of Ted Ward has yet to gain its rightful place in American Theatre. He is very much alive; however, still the rebel, the critic, the cynic and the craftsman who continues to gnaw at the contradictions in America with unrelenting energy.

Ted Ward lives in Chicago. His career spans the post Harlem Renaissance, the Federal Government Writer's Project, the McCarthy "Witch Hunts" and now, the Black Arts Movement. Born in 1908 in Thibodaux, Louisiana, he began his writing career after working at various odd jobs. His interest in writing took him to the University of Wisconsin, where he won the Zona Gale Fellowship in Creative Writing for two consecutive years. After leaving the University of Wisconsin, he joined the John Reed Writer's Club. While a member of this group, he wrote his first play, *Sick and Tired*. The play won him second place in a contest sponsored by a labor organization, and it was apparent that a significant playwright had emerged.

Ted Ward's next play and perhaps his most controversial, *Big White Fog,* was performed by the Federal Theater Guild at Chicago's Great Northern Theater. *Big White Fog* dealt with a decade in the life of a Black family that was caught up in the midst of poverty, racism and the Marcus Garvey Movement. Although it was acclaimed a success, it closed after ten weeks. Ted Ward was determined to bring Black drama to the stage and went to New York where he helped found the Negro Playwright Company in 1940. In New York, *Big White Fog* was again put into production, but this time it failed to equal the success it had achieved in Chicago. In 1946 his best-known play, *Our Lan'*, lasted for only five weeks. Ted Ward had written one of the first plays that truly depicted the spirit of the Black man's struggle to win his freedom during the Reconstruction Period.

Ted Ward was never interested in mimicking the white man's version of Black people. He refused to use his craft to reinforce this racist and distorted view of Black life. Instead, he held steadfastly to his convictions, knowing full well that such a position was inimical to the interest of White America. And as was true of other Black writers who have repudiated the status quo, he was branded a deviant. But Ted Ward never relinquished his dream to build a true Black Theatre, and in 1967 organized the South Side Art Center of the Performing Arts at the Louis Theater in Chicago. The SSACPP opened with *Our Lan'* and it ran for nearly a year with little support from the press or the affluent Black community. The Louis Theater closed in 1969 after providing Chicago with some of the most significant Black drama it had seen in years.

Chicago was once again fortunate to have the privilege of seeing a premiere of a Ted Ward play, *The Daubers*. Written in 1952, it opened with X-Bag on February 15, 1974, at the Parkway Community House.

After the most stimulating interview printed here, Ted Ward continued to talk about a number of issues which, unfortunately, were not recorded. However, hopefully, when his autobiography is published, we will get a deeper insight into the conscious of this profound man.

Ted Ward is more than a playwright, he is a production.

The following interview was made at the home of Ted Ward. It was an informal occasion, but one which this interviewer will always remember.

PERKINS: We'll begin the interview with this question: Ted, How do you feel about your play, *The Daubers,* having its premier in Chicago? At least, it is my understanding that the play has never been performed before.

WARD: Well, there's two questions involved. One is that it's never been done because it's never been released—that is the first question. The second question is that I am primarily interested in the development of X-Bag (Experimental Black Actors Guild). It seems to be moving toward a very solid creation of a great cultural need in Chicago. So, I gave them the play and I'm looking forward to the production as an experiment for myself, really.

PERKINS: Would you care to comment on the theme of the play?

WARD: Fundamentally, what the play has to say is that under our system of education we assume that if we can complete our education, accept the principles of democracy and maybe the puritan ethic, that we have a pattern for success in life; and normally, I think most of us who achieve an education and find themselves fairly well secure, assume that all the masses of people have to do is follow their example. They don't realize that perhaps it is accidental, to a large extent, that they have escaped the limitations imposed by the pressing class above them to prevent the emergence of the masses. So, what I am saying is that there is a matter of absolute social responsibility. If we have leadership, if we have people who do the right thing, who live according to our idea of social progress and advancement, they have to be involved; they cannot escape the ghetto. It permeates the total atmosphere in which they have to live to survive.

PERKINS: Would you say that the same situation exist today among many so-called Black bourgeois, or Black middle-class—this kind of attitude that you have articulated?

WARD: Of course, it does. It definitely does. It isn't that you wish to condemn the middle class. I mean that we have seen expressions by them, like the marches under Dr. King; we know that these people are not totally apathetic. But the point of it is, that their goal—their idea of achievement—is individualistic and as a result of it they spend their time in these individualistic pursuits. I am not satisfied with the Negro middle class. Why should I be? The Negro middle class is emulating the white middle class and they don't realize how deeply they are involved with this kind of emulation. They don't realize because, after all, there is a struggle for survival to get a decent place to live, and so on and so forth, and they feel that this is an individual problem.

PERKINS: It seems to me that you are talking about something that Carter G. Woodson referred to in the *Miseducation of the Negro* that those who do get educated are still miseducated; and so consequently, they act out those roles which may not be consistent with the needs of the black masses.

WARD: That is right. This is a definite thing. This is true of all people—the underprivileged people of any society—whether you mention them as middle class or not. The whole education system, the whole structure of the state is designed to maintain the status quo.

PERKINS: You talked about the X-Bag—black experimental actors—and your desire to help them develop more of a viable theater because you see certain potentials in this group. I was wondering, what are your general feelings about Black theater in Chicago?

WARD: I've had some bitter experiences on that level. We tend to ape the white man, and we tend to look over our shoulders askance to see "how am I doing," so to speak. And so, as a result of it, since theater is at a distance from us, and for good reason, we are not involved really in theater as a weapon for our own culture and development in our progress as a people in the middle of a society. And as a result of it, we do not have—and it is a disgrace that this society does not have—a competent theater. We have many other problems behind this; the financial thing, the question of who's going to patronize it. We've seen Negroes now that are flooding the Loop because of the new tendency in the movie industry. But, if you examine the content of these movies, you have to admit they are inimical to the interest of the Negro people because they are being fed on the basis of so-called myths, or a creation of a myth, Negro heroes who turn out to be nothing but either pimps, dope peddlers, or fly-by-night hustlers. There is nothing constructive about this. It almost looks like Hollywood has reverted tactically to just a new guise for the old mammy tradition, the old ignorant, lazy, shiftless Negro; but the content is fundamentally the same—to teach white people to disrespect you and to teach you that you don't belong. I mean it's degrading. Most of these pictures are definitely degrading and in the long range they cannot be profitable to the Negro people.

PERKINS: Do you feel that a true Black theater can, in some small way, counteract some of the negative images that are being developed in the movie industry?

WARD: The whole history of the theater indicates that cultural institutions ought to be really devoted to the simple interest of common man. In other words, it should reflect some vital aspect of the life of the people in a given community, you see. Otherwise, how do people learn? All right, there are all kinds of forces that prohibit the emergence of the Negro. One of the primary ones, of course, is the Negro himself in that he has not recognized the importance of Negro theater.

PERKINS: Do you feel that there has been any significant improvements in black theater since the early fifties?

WARD: It's a mixture. You've had one or two fairly decent things; but in the main, Negro theatre seems to be, such as it is today, the same old appeasement of white taste. We don't realize it but just as Bert Williams and George Walker and others had to blacken their faces and come out telling coon jokes against their own people because they wanted to make a living. The Negro today is shrewd enough to realize that if he wants to get some loot, he's got to be able to cater to an audience that will supply him with that loot. The general feeling is that if he rides black pride, you see, and the revolutionary pulses among Negro people—even if he distorts it by showing a gangster accomplishing and doing—that he can make money off of his own people.

PERKINS: Wouldn't you agree that you do have young black playwrights today who seem to be more politically conscious of the very things that you are talking about—who are not allowing themselves to fall prey to this type of white mentality; who are trying to make some honest statement in terms of the black tradition in this country?

WARD: Well, yes. That is in a certain sense true. The question is on one hand, the so-called black esthetics and on the other, the tendency toward modernism—which is alien to the whole life and tradition of the Negro people. It's not easy to break these two things down—but when a people assume that a new esthetic becomes, let's say, scatological in their language, they've already alienated a vast majority of the public. It seems that they're being courageous, progressive—but I think the truth is they haven't understood what Frantz Fanon was talking about when he wrote about the necessity of the rejection of the morality of the West. I think that we have to understand that what is involved here is a question of human communication and the validity of the problems that are raised. This is what I see. While I cannot give you any sound generalization as to the position of the young Negro writer, what I'm encouraged by is that so many of them are writing. They'll come to it one of these days.

PERKINS: Many of your better known plays seem to be of a historical nature. I'm referring to *Big White Fog* and *Our Lan'*; would you care to comment on this?

WARD: Well, yes. I would say this—if you are generally interested in the progress of the people, and the need for solidarity, you have to go back to find out if there is any basis for such an outlook on your part. So, as I began writing *Big White Fog,* it was not a historical play. It had to do with the actual situation of the Negro in the midst of the Depression. Many different outlooks, but all of them really stemming out of manufactured white people as to what the Negro could do for himself and the achievement of his freedom. And so, the Negro came North in this great Hegira [migration] seeking freedom and happiness. But he is astounded to find that it wasn't here; and so he didn't know what to do about it. So we had streams like Marcus Garvey, we had the NAACP with its pronouncements, the Urban League and so on and so forth. None of them seemed to be valid in the sense that they could actually bring about the relief that the Negro is seeking.

PERKINS: Which group do you think came closest to doing this?

WARD: This is a question that needs thorough analysis. But Garvey had the spirit and it seemed to me that in one sense it was an answer; but it was an incredible answer in this respect: that he failed to recognize the fact that the Negro was an exploited, oppressed minority.

PERKINS: You don't think he recognized this?

WARD: I think not. He felt that on the will of the morale of the Negro people and their dissatisfaction with the life in which they lived in America that this thing is possible. In this very day the prominent Negro couldn't get off the boat anywhere in Africa without the approval of the imperialist. Even W.E.B DuBois was refused admittance to Africa at one time. And certainly this was true of many Negroes who sought to go to Africa—just on a social basis or in order to get some historical truth on Pan Africanism and what not.

PERKINS: Your play, *The Big White Fog,* had pretty good success here in Chicago where it premiered. When it was done in New York, it wasn't received as well.

WARD: Well, there are two things that happened. One was that you had the signing of the Nazi-Soviet Pact, so there was a revolt on the part of the American intellectual as a class against communism. Second, this play was associated in a sense with the Negro's struggle for democracy and had one element in it which was very positive and pertinent. It was that whites, as well as Negroes, went to the rescue of this family to prevent this eviction. The father is killed in it, but it was assumed that what the play was saying was that the only output of the Negro was white and black unity under communism, which wasn't true. But what the play was depicting was the different outlooks which the Negro couldn't see because it constituted a big white fog—you know, that obscured any possibility under the prevailing circumstances for finding a way out. So the New York critics attacked the play, but the play was a definite success in Chicago.

PERKINS: Other than *Our Lan'*, I can't recall any of your plays being done in recent years. If this is true, are there reasons for this?

WARD: In late years, in the last ten years, my plays are beginning to be done. It was assumed that because *Big White Fog* was attacked, and then again *Our LAN'* was supposed to have failed on Broadway, that either I must be anti-American or that I couldn't write. This was basic to the whole thing. So, if the white frowns—I was talking about this a moment ago—the Negro tends to look over his shoulder. He has not yet developed, in the main, the sense of judgment as to what is essential about a certain play. What does it have to say, he has not yet developed that kind of critical faculty in general in America. He listens to what pleases the ear; what he assumes to be the truth. But you see, a play, if it is of any count at all, it's a result of a gift—the gift of a peculiar type of mind which is a poetic mind; the ability to take the seemingly unrelated phenomena of the world around it and bring it into something authentic so that people can really grasp it. And this is why the theater has always been regarded as dangerous. Now, this has been known, you see. We've had censorship and so on to guard against this.

PERKINS: Are you saying that perhaps your plays were censored because of political reasons?

WARD: I think ultimately, yes. Not at first…not at first. Now, *Our Lan'*, for instance, told the truth about Reconstruction. This is taboo in America; we still don't want the truth about Reconstruction.

PERKINS: Do you feel it's possible or likely that Chicago can support a theater institution like the Negro Ensemble Company? I know that on various occasions you have attempted to start your own theater institution.

WARD: Well unfortunately in America, unless you go strictly commercial, you need foundation help and we do not have foundations of our own that are capable of giving anybody $800,000 as was done with the Negro Ensemble Company in New York. If you apply for funds—any size—there is a complete investigation of what you want to do and so on and so forth. You put up a theater, if you happen to get it, where in the first year you'll probably do one Negro play and all the rest are European imports. Now, evidently, this wasn't satisfactory enough to the foundation that gave the original support because they're [Negro Ensemble] on their own now—I understand.

PERKINS: Not totally, they're still getting foundation support.

WARD: Well, you know that people have to eat; you know actors—and there is the question of the unions, stage hands and others. In that sense, I think that the community theater idea is a sound one. This is where we can get off the boat. But if we keep waiting for a seat… to have the right seats and the right decorations and the right—how shall I put it—people from downtown coming to see us, if we cease that and begin to concentrate on the theater as such and its benefits, to ourselves and our children, then theater offers one of the most exciting forms of entertainment in the world. And, it's also one of the most productive in the sense that men do get ideas. A child in a peanut gallery can pick up ideas that will last him for a lifetime.

PERKINS: Don't you think that some black groups in Chicago, like Kuumba Liberators, X-Bag, that you've identified already, and Ebony Talent, are a few black groups that are community based, who are trying to develop that kind of a theater?

WARD: I welcome… I welcome… I welcome these different organizations in their attempt. But I hope to see an amalgamation of forces of these groups into one significant organization. Now this is very difficult because people want to eat and they can't afford to pay their actors. So, it's a vocational as far as the actors and people who contribute to the theater are concerned. For instance, why should I give X-Bag a play that's never been done; and I know it's an original and it may arouse public attention? Why should I give it to them…is because of the fact I realize the need for this kind of material. I'm not saying that *The Daubers* is going to be a success—nobody can predict that—but I think it's important enough to give it to them.

PERKINS: I agree with you when you mentioned that there's a need for black groups to come together, some kind of consortium, some kind of amalgamation, so that we can draw from all of their sources…

WARD: They should be able to exchange their personnel.

PERKINS: I think that the time is right for something like this. I think what is missing is someone of your stature to sort of provide leadership which has been missing…someone who may be neutral and can provide a perspective of theater, which some people do not have right now.

WARD: I may be known as a writer, but there are factors in there that I have no control over. A man needs to know management; he needs to know how to play politics; that is diplomatic. In other words, he needs to be able to mobilize people and give them direction.

PERKINS: But, you have theater wisdom.

WARD: All right, I have a certain amount of it. But if you listen to what I've said it shows that I also feel very confused about the general situation in America. I have no answers to the problems. I tried years ago to summarize my views and what I discovered was we don't have a public that is ready for it. So, it means gradual acquisition of the public, of developing a core of people who find theater worthwhile to themselves and will consistently come out and support it.

PERKINS: Could you name a few black plays which you have seen in the last five years which you feel merit special praise?

WARD: Being a playwright, this is a ticklish question to me. I don't want to knock anything that I've seen; I don't want to go overboard on any praises. It's very difficult. I've tried to figure out which of the things that I felt were really worthy—but there is a mixture there. There is a mixture in a sense that I can't totally say that we have developed playwrights... theater, as such, that is competent; and a playwright who is devoted to the basic interest of his people in the sense that he does not distort his meaning for the sake of the public or acquiring an audience.

PERKINS: So what you're saying to me is the serious playwright is going to have to be more committed; he's going to study more; he's going to really have to put it on the line as it is if meaningful plays are to emerge from the Black playwright.

WARD: You see, it begins with a philosophic position—that's one thing. But he needs a technique and he's throwing technique out like a baby with the bath water; and this is an unfortunate thing. It's a hard process to learn no matter what the art form is. It's a very difficult thing to put together, a mosaic that tells a certain thing and can attract an audience. And, we're not...we're too concerned with sloganizing, rather than going to the heart presenting a picture; whereas, the meaning is absolutely clear and nobody can escape it.

PERKINS: White critics seem to categorize most black plays as being too political and filled with polemics to be considered as serious theater. What are your feelings about these allegations?

WARD: The white man, you see... if you want to write a white play, he'll accept it. But anything that raises perspective, dignity or forthrightness on the part of a Negro is inimical to the white man. He's prone to feel that he's superior to begin with and so he's qualified to judge you—and he's not, you see. He knows nothing, really, about you because he's never been exposed to Black culture. What he has seen is the same old stereotypes and clichés and his superior attitude that what you are saying doesn't really amount to much. Secondly, you have no right to say it the way you say it because you don't follow the pattern of what he wants. Pat him on the back and he is great.

PERKINS: Do you feel that the black esthetic is sufficiently defined for black critics to properly evaluate black plays?

WARD: As I understand the word *esthetic* it has nothing to do with race—nothing to do with race. It is a development that is inherent to a certain country, of cultural traditions, of its way of life. So, as a result of it, the Chinese theater might look different from Japanese theater; Japanese theater might look different from an American theater, or an English theater. You see, that's a matter of not content, as such, because you might find a capitalist play out of Japan; and you might find a revolutionary play out of China; you might find a struggle of the Negro people in America. Esthetics to me means the capacity to tell it in the way your people can understand it. It is not a matter of language in the sense that you are going to use a four-letter word to show that a person is angry about a certain situation... the thing to do is to develop the situation so that everybody can see that this is either wrong or that he has a right to be hostile toward it. That's the act on the stage. In other words, to dramatize the thing in itself; and this you cannot get away from in any esthetics.

PERKINS: I'm still confused about whether or not you are saying that there is a black esthetic, or that the black esthetic has become so much a part of the American culture that there can't be an area of cultural development, cultural expression, which is uniquely black in terms of the African heritage and the Black experience.

WARD: We have manifestation and a creative spirit in music, for instance; the white man hasn't been able to copy it—the best he can do is follow it. We live a special way of life; so would a nationalist government somewhere else—living a special way of life. But this is not a matter of esthetics; this is simply craftsmanship.

PERKINS: What plays are you working on now?

WARD: I'm not working on a play at the moment; I'm doing an autobiography. I have some work that I want to do, you see. One of the interesting things about this production, *The Daubers*, is that it gave me a chance to look at my work. I would like to have that happen over and over again with plays of mine, but the opportunity doesn't exist. Interestingly enough, for instance you mentioned *Big White Fog*—Macmillan publishers is bringing out *Big White Fog* in mid-February. For 35 years this play was lost. That's right; and I can show you a letter from the editor who says that it is one of the great plays of the century. Why didn't the Negro know something about that? Why didn't he even try to do the play?

PERKINS: The black masses didn't get a chance to really make decisions on the play because it was not exposed enough to the black masses.

WARD: That's part of the whole question of cultural control, as to whether or not you get to your people. You see there is the money angle on one hand, and the other, is whether the white man has praised it.

PERKINS: I understand, Ted, that you have a number of plays that would sort of chronicle the black man's history, experience, in this country from let's say, the twenties up to the present.

WARD: No, that isn't true. You see, without a theater you can't equally grow. You write things and you put them in a drawer, but you have no test. You have to have an audience... that's the only way you know...

PERKINS: But you have written plays that span that period of time. Where are those plays and what's happening to them?

WARD: There's a batch of plays right there (points to a stack of plays on a shelf).

PERKINS: That's what I'm referring to.

WARD: Well, the point of it is, I'm in no position to evaluate them except from the angle that I did what I have tried to do and I didn't have...you see, I didn't have the opportunity. For instance, Henrik Ibsen would go down to the sea and he would spend at least two years on every one of his major plays. I had my family, so I had to rush to try to find, to get a production in order to be able to eat and so I couldn't devote that kind of time. So, I can't say that my plays are all good. They satisfy me only from one angle in that I said what I wanted to say, but I didn't say it well. I needed more work to get it into this form where it actually belonged. Just like this play [*The Daubers*], I learned just in the first week of rehearsals that there were weaknesses in it, and I rewrote those spots. The theater is a collaborative thing. The artist and the actor and the director, they have to come together. I don't say it is a great play, but at least I learned something by just having the possibility of doing it and if I had to write the play over again, I probably wouldn't write it the way I have written it. That's because of certain angles of growth on my part and certain impinging of the society situation upon me as an individual.

PERKINS: You say that you are writing your autobiography. Is there some play that you have in your mind that you hope to write or that you have been writing?

WARD: I shouldn't say this, but I started John Brown in 1948 and I have never satisfied myself with it. And one of the peculiar things about it is I lost the manuscript in a screening production. All I have is an original research on the play and a first draft which is not complete. And I think, too, that maybe John Brown wasn't proper for a play. I might still do the play—I don't know, because I think he was a white man who personified the essence of democracy in the relation to the Negro people. He was morally consistent and he had the breadth of knowledge to see what the political and social situation was in this country.

PERKINS: What advice would you give to a young person who is trying to become a playwright?

WARD: First, to try to understand what his craft is...what consists of craft. I take it for granted that if he really wants to become a playwright, he already has his heart on certain positive values and his outlook is not just that he wants to make himself some money. In other words, if he's interested in the life of his people, and the improvement of that life, or improvement of human society, and so as a result of it, if he concentrates on his craft, he will learn that there are definitive laws which underlie human understanding—receptivity. As I've said, it's where you're going. Are you a liar? Do you actually attempt to predict truth about human life in your time? Take the person who would write a play and ignore the existence of China and ignore the existence of the Soviet Union. Don't you know that he's not being objective? He is lying...because if people are going to make a judgment, they've got to make a judgment in reference to these things. I'm not saying he should advocate communism.

PERKINS: He may be uninformed, too.

WARD: The point of it is, there are too many means of communication today...

PERKINS: So, what you're saying is that he should not be uninformed.

WARD: He's got to learn all the time, you see; but it doesn't mean he's going to sprawl out everything that comes along...He has a basic pattern, too, of what is acceptable, in a sense, and what he should investigate and find out whether he's been wrong about this or wrong about that or whether he's right about this. For instance, one play isn't going to condemn him for life. He'll write another play because no matter what problems he touches, there are different aspects to them...and a different set of characters are going to approach them in a different way, and not as puppets that he just dangles on a string—but they are going to live.

(Interview – January 26, 1973)

ALLEY B: THE CREATION OF THE WALL OF RESPECT

William Walker

It was all happening
At 43rd and Langley ...Called a Fast Track...
Fast Track for the dealers...
Fast Track for the whores...
Fast track for the pimps...
Yes... Fast Track for the boosters...
For the walking stores...

Yes ...43rd and Langley Street...
Where fools dare not tread...
Yes... 43rd and Langley Street...
Where people would roll up their car windows...
And lock their doors...
When driving through the area...
Yes... 43rd and Langley Street...
Where rafielding was truly the Code...

Yes...43rd and Langley Street...
Where Fathers and Mothers...
Had little... or no influence...on their children...

Yes ... 43rd and Langley Street...
Where killers and stick up men would be honored...

Yes...43rd and Langley Street...
Where we... The artists from OBA-Ci...
Would dare go...

Yes....
The artists would go to 43rd and Langley Street ...
Where most people would not go...
Yes... we... The artists from OBA-Ci...
Would go to 43rd and Langley Street
Where Distrust...Self-hatred...
Self-destruction...Confusion...
Seemed forever present...

Where Black children would grow up
And have less than a chance
For survival in the World of Competition

Where the Community's good people...
Would be overshadowed by the evildoers...

Yes... We artists would go...
And not be afraid...
To express CONCERN and LOVE...
We would give our very best...Without selfishness

We learned that it would require more...
Than painting a Wall...
Yes... More would be required...
Then just painting a Wall...
Much more...

The late Elliot Hunter... Myrna Weaver...And
Lenore...Franklin...
Would often drive the Community youth...
To beaches...And parks...
To go swimming and picnicking...
Katherine Akin... would encourage teenagers...
To continue their education...

Darrell Cowherd…Bill Walker… Billy Abernathy…
Bobby Sengstacke…Roy Lewis…
Would encourage youth…
Who would express an interest in photography…

Norman Paris… Wadsworth Jarrell ….
Edward Christine… Carolyn Lawrence…
Barbara Jones….Florence Price…David Bradford…
Would always give their undivided attention
To the Community

Sylvia Abernathy…the Wall's designer…
Was always charming…
The Community truly loved her…

When the 43rd Street Langley young ladies
Set eyes on Jeff Donaldson…
One of the founders of OBA-Ci…
Well…
It was…Love…Love…Love…
Eda appeared on the scene…
Just prior to the completion of
The Wall of Respect…
He too…Would be unselfish…
With his time… and energy…
Eda painted lovely murals…
For the Community Organization's Office…
At his own expense…

At a much later date…
Will Hancock painted portraits of local heroes…
For the Wall of Respect…
Later…
Eddie Harris…Louis Boys…
Jim Malone…also a great artist… from Detroit…
Painted on the Wall of Truth…

Which was across the street…
From the Wall of Respect…

Yes…We…
The artists from OBA-Ci…
Went to 43rd and Langley Street…

We…
The OBA-Ci Artists…
The OBA-Ci Community Workshop…
The OBA-Ci Writers' Workshop…
We…Sponsored the WALL OF RESPECT…
WE paid a decorator to prime the surface of the Wall…
We purchased brushes…paint…
We rented scaffolds…

OBA-Ci Writers' Workshop provided the research…
OBA-Ci Community Workshop entertained the Community…
And read poetry…

Yes…
We went with the Spirit of Concern…
We went with the Spirit of Giving…
We went with Spirit of Respect…
We went with the Spirit of Love…

Yes…
We went where fools dare not tread…
To 43rd and Langley Street…
On the Southeast corner…
In the City of Chicago…
In the year of 1967…

There…where people…
Would come by the thousands…
To see the artists painting

The Wall of Respect...

People of different cultures...
The Rich... The Poor... The Famous...The Powerful...
Scholars... Writers...
Priests...Nuns...Ministers...
PEOPLE...

People from everywhere...
England...Germany...Africa...
Latin America... France...
Yes...PEOPLE...

People from the Media...
Channel 2...Channel 7...Channel 11...
Chicago Tribune... Chicago Daily News...
Chicago Sun Times... The Mohammed Speaks...
And the Chicago Defender...

Jim Tilmon used the Wall of Respect
As the Background for his TV show...Our People...
Snick used the Wall for rallies...
Esquire Magazine features the Wall as a centered Spread...

The Corner...
At 43rd and Langley Street...
Was no longer the place...
Where fools...or wise people...
Would dare not tread...

THE WALL OF RESPECT
Would be viewed...
By hundreds of thousands of people...

They came by night
They came by day…
They came in the wee hours of the morning…

Although many loved and admired the Wall…
Some disliked it…
Yes…
The Wall of Respect…
Generated mixed feelings within people…

The Community People
Expressed Joy…Respect…and Love
For OBA-Ci's Artists…Writers…Actors…and Actresses...

The feelings of Trust…Respect…and Love…
Was Mutual…
Between the Artists and Community…
The Atmosphere was filled with Jubilance…

During this time of Jubilee…
My thoughts turned to Brother Al Saladin
Brother Saladin… A Brilliant person…
Memories…Remembering that he was
The first person…
With whom I shared the idea of painting the Wall…
My question to Brother Saladin was
Would he be interested in collaborating with me…
He agreed…
By saying he would write poetry
On the Wall… memories…

Memories…Remembering that
I phoned Mitchell Carlton the following day…
Explaining the Wall idea to him…
He, too, expressed an interest…

A few days thereafter...
We visited the 43rd Street Langley Wall...
We also visited 43rd Street Evans Wall...
While there... I discussed Al Saladin with Caton...
Caton was agreeable with that idea...

After the neighborhood visit...
The foremost thought of my thoughts...
Was how to earn enough money...
To sponsor the Wall Project...
My time was to begin work
By May 1, '67...

Two weeks later...
I would search the neighborhood throughout...
Looking for Brother Al Saladin...
But he was to be found no place...

Memories continued...
Memories of the following day...
When I received a phone call
From a very great friend... Billy Abernathy...
Who spoke of a group of artist...
Who were having meaningful meetings...
He went on to explain that
Jeff Donaldson was one of the founders of the artist school...
The question from Billy was...
Would I be interested in attending the next meeting...
My reply was yes...
If my memory serves me correctly...
Abernathy invited Caton...
Mitchell was present at the meeting...

Caton would later explain
His lack of interest...He was not impressed...
I was deeply saddened...

I explained to Caton...
My idea of sharing the Wall Project with OBA-Ci...
That didn't impress him in the least...
After a few more meetings
With the OBA-Ci group...
I introduced the concept of an
Outdoor wall painting...
The OBA-Ci artists
Expressed respects for the thought...
I, in turn, said I would
Welcome their participation...
They agreed...

After the meeting that night...
We visited the community at 43rd and Langley Street...
At the Southeast corner...
It was in the middle of February...
11:20 p.m.
Tuesday ...1967...

During the planning stages...Mrs. Sylvia Abernathy
Created the most workable design
By separating the wall into seven spaces
For the artist to paint their compositions...
Mrs. Sylvia Abernathy presented a brilliant plan...
And we... the artists of OBA-Ci were very proud...

Memories continue to surround me... Memories...
Remembering people...places...
Remembering painting murals
For Black Churches on the Southside of Chicago...
Mt. Pisgah Missionary Baptist Church
True Life Missionary Baptist Church... Bethany ...
Yes... Painting wherever I could...

Painting for the Willie Smith…Hans Tigart…
Fika Imports…Goodman Dean and Scott…
Yes… raining…

Learning to paint
Was the foremost thought of my thoughts…
My concentration
Was never sidetracked from learning…
Lack of money didn't matter…
Even though people would laugh
And call me "Raggedy Ass"
It didn't matter…
Wearing paint splattered khaki pants
With tennis shoes…Year in…Year out…
No…It didn't matter…

(Extracted from a poem by one of its founders, William Walker)
(Courtesy of William Walker, Chicago Public Art Council and Jeff Huebner)

THE WALL OF RESPECT TO FESTAC "77"

Roy Lewis

The first artist was the Creator; His Blend of Time, Space and Distance will never be duplicated. Yet artists try, and since the first cave drawing to the electronic transmitting of images and sound through space, artists have been trying to outdo the Master Artist.

On May 28, 1967, at Lincoln Center in Chicago, we came together to create an organization that would be called Organization of Black American Culture (OBAC). Our purpose was to bring together community art, music, dance, drama, and writing to enhance the spirit and vigor in the Black community. The opening introduction was given by Gerald McWorter, one of the founding members. He danced with singer Terry Scott and we knew we were off on the right foot. David Moore or "Moose" read from his "Hip Generation" poem, Jeff Donaldson preached, and we had some music by the Fred Hampton Quartet. We left there fired up; we had filled out forms that categorized us as artists, musicians, and community workshop performers.

The visual artists group met two or three weeks later at Mirna Weaver's Studio on Stony Island. We discussed ideals, goals, and what we were going to do. Bill Walker proposed doing a mural drawing on 43rd and Langley, because he had been doing work in that neighborhood and felt we would be well-received. The idea was discussed back and forth, and we decided to go down and see the wall. It was decided that the wall would serve our needs and bring some art to the community. I photographed the wall for the rest of the group to study and use for their painting. Sylvia Abernathy's layout was selected to use as the blueprint on the wall area and selected artists decided what section they would work on. There were to be seven sections: (1) Rhythm and Blues, (2) Jazz, (3) Theater, (4) Statesmen, (5) Religion, (6) Literature, and (7) Sports. The community liked the idea and helped with the painting of the primer coat, and was always there to give moral support. It was truly art and the people as one.

As the WALL progressed, the word spread and people from all over the country would drive by and check out the WALL. As we came close to finishing, political action groups decided to hold a rally at the WALL. They decided that OBAC, as an organization, should not attend. That was a mistake, so we issued a statement about what OBAC was, our purpose and goals, listing the sections and thanking the community. The rally went on as planned and some of OBAC's visual artists attended and were introduced. Nobody was killed and there was no riot, just speakers and people being militant. So the wall was doing what it was supposed to do; that was to promote culture in the community and to create change.

Later some OBAC artists decided to change a section on the WALL without checking with the other artists. They painted the section Black, and painted it in a style that did not fit into the original style. After that, negative things began to happen like gang members being killed, as the purpose of the wall changed when it began to be used for other reasons. It was decided that the WALL needed a name; WALL OF RESPECT was chosen. That magical afternoon on August 27, 1967, just three months after the first meeting of OBAC; Gwendolyn Brooks read poetry, Phil Cohran gave a message in music, and Val Gray Ward gave the word. The WALL and community became one. When Columbia College organized a conference on Black Art with people coming from all over the U.S., local artists decided we would have to confront them. COBRA was created from OBAC artists. We confronted Columbia officials about how they could speak for Black artists without asking Black artists.

The WALL went through several stages, and what began as the mighty WALL OF RESPECT became the WALL of individuals. During 1971-72 the WALL was torn down with some of the panels going to Malcolm X College. On the positive side, Jeff Donaldson called a conference in 1970 at Northwestern called CONFABA. Artists, musicians, poets, and writers came together to discuss the direction art, music, and literature would go in the 70s and 80s. Next came the 2nd World Festival of African Art and Culture, which was held in Lagos, Nigeria at FESTAC '77 in 1977.

FESTAC '77 is regarded as one of the most important international gatherings of Black people in modern times. For a thirty-day period (Jan. 15 to Feb. 15, 1977), 16,000 Africans and African descendents from 70 nations gathered together for visual art exhibits, as well as musical, dance, theatrical and literary presentations. The first two weeks also included a colloquium where writers and scholars from the African diaspora exchanged ideas in an effort to improve the international standing of Black people. 482 African-Americans from the United States participated in this grand festival, with representatives from most major cities.

"GIVE THE DRUMMER SOME":
RHYTHM, REVOLUTION AND THE CHICAGO SUN DRUMMER

Amira Millicent Davis

During the height of the Black Arts/Black Power movement, seven men came together in Chicago to form a drum and percussion group, called the Sun Drummer. The group was committed to restoring drum culture for African America. In Africa, as in many other world civilizations, the drum was (and is) an instrument of healing and a central means of communication among humans and between humans and the spiritual realm. The African drum had traveled to the Americas with enslaved captives, but had been strictly regulated and eventually restricted through custom and law. Initially difficult to enforce, suppression of the drum intensified following the Stono Rebellion of 1739, in which a group of nearly 80 enslaved Africans killed over 20 whites.[1] The loss of the drum in African America represented a sociocultural, psychic, and spiritual rupture. The goal of the Sun Drummer, as reported by the man considered to be the group's founder, Harold Hampton "Atu" Murray,[2]

---

[1] The African drum had been part of North America's historical record as early as 1653. It was outlawed due to fears that it communicated coded messages only understood by other Africans as a call to revolt. Under the influences of the French, enslaved Africans in New Orleans were allowed to play drums and engage in traditional African spirituality in Congo Square every Sunday until 1815 when it underwent prohibition. Drums were viewed as un-Christian and potentially dangerous signaling devices. States crafted legislation forbidding the playing of drums...The South Carolina Slave Act of 1740... limited the privileges of slaves including forbidding slaves to drum, assemble, grow their own food, or earn their own money. Other colonies enacted similar laws. In the section of the Georgia legal code dealing with "Privileges and Disabilities of Slaves," paragraph 45 read:

> ...it is absolutely necessary to the safety of this province, that all due care be taken to restrain the wandering and meeting of Negroes and other slaves, at all times, and more especially on Saturday nights, Sundays, and other holydays, and their using and carrying mischievous and dangerous weapons, or using and keeping drums, horns, or other loud instruments, which may call together or give sign or notice to one another of their wicked designs and intensions; . . . and whatsoever master or owner or overseer shall

permit or suffer his or their slave or slaves at any time hereafter to beat drums, blow horns, or other loud instruments, . . . shall forfeit thirty shillings sterling for every such offence." (Prince)

[2] Harold Hampton was also known as Sir Harold and Black Harold. During a brief stay in Ghana from 1973-74, Atu married and received the name Ni (Chief) Kwaku (born on Wednesday) Atuquey (sir name – first born son) Ife Doyin Adebeyo (luck is like honey, the crown brings joy) chief of children.

was to return the drum to the village and use it as a medium to transform individual group members and Chicago's emerging Black (em)power(ed) community, awakening in both an African consciousness.

During the period between 1960 and 1975, conjuring men and women, artists, and intellectuals created a new Black identity. It was forged in the fires of African and Third World liberation struggles, the assassinations of Lumumba, Malcolm, and Cabral, as well as the numerous urban revolts that raged across the United States. This essay explores the Sun Drummer as a cultural artifact of that era. Hand drums and hand drummers—especially African-American hand drummers—have for the most part, been excluded from writings about Black musical culture in the United States. Their cultural work has been relegated to the arcane category of folk music as if, as Amilcar Cabral argues in *Return to the Source* (1972), the roots of revolution lie outside the people. This project is an attempt to rectify that omission and re-present the Sun Drummer as a vital part of Chicago's Black Arts/Black Power Movement. The Sun Drummer also provides a lens for reviewing the "revolutionary" versus "cultural" binary within the Black Nationalist tradition, demonstrating the power of the drum as being equal to or greater than that of the gun in bringing about cultural and political revolution; thus, revealing yet another meaning of "Black Power." This work is based on interviews with some of the original group members, and a review of relevant literature that reveals the Sun Drummer as an enduring institution in Chicago's Black Arts Movement that continues to inform the cultural work of artists around the country.[3]

The Making of a Sun Drummer

Atu was born August 10, 1940 in Birmingham, Alabama. He migrated to Chicago in 1944 with his mother, a concert pianist, and his brother. Atu taught himself how to play the flute, baritone sax, obo, ethnic wind instruments, hand drums (earth drum, air drums, stick drums), shekere, and African thumb piano. He was also a master carver, making works of art from tree trunks and branches. In 1960 he left Chicago to become a citizen of the world. His first stop was New York where he says he spent long hours in the library reading and copying books in order to learn "the relationship of all things to all things."[4] He also

[3] The author, along with other women, began playing drums in the mid-80s. We were taught by members of the Sun Drummer in Chicago and we incorporate their songs into our performances. I've used Sun Drummer songs and rhythms as a performer and arts-in-education provider in schools, communities, and cultural institutions throughout the Midwest for over 25 years. The songs are also known to be taught in Chicago's African-centered schools. The original members of the group continue to refer to themselves as Sun Drummer, as do drummers in cities like Detroit who claim an association with the Society.

[4] Phone interview with Atu October 31-November 1, 2005.

studied drumming and drum making with the pre-eminent African-American drummer, Chief James Hawthorne Bey. In 1964 he left New York to spend a year in St. Kitts, Virgin Island where he performed as Sir Harold in a duo with Sir Zambo. He returned to New York and continued studying, carving, and mastering the drum. It was during this time, when he was involved with the "African nationalists' pioneer movement," serving as a liaison between "all nationalists groups." He had the opportunity to meet and perform for Malcolm X and other nationalists, providing cultural entertainment as a musician and drummer for community events, as well as being a source of "spiritual information and affirmations." In 1967 Atu recorded an album called *Message to Our Ancestors* (1967, UNI Records) with the hand drummer, Big Black.

Harold "Atu Murray, aka Black Harold (1960)

Atu returned to Chicago in 1969. Tim "Eusi" Holly had heard this album and was impressed by the musicianship of the two performers. By chance, Eusi had taken his drum for repair to a well-known downtown Chicago drum shop, Drums Unlimited. There he met "Black Harold," the name by which Atu was known at that time. Eusi shared with Black Harold how he thought the drumming on the album was extraordinary and that the drummers were an inspiration to him. Atu invited Eusi to meet him at sunrise the next morning on Chicago's lakefront near 57th Street where he'd be playing for Jewel McLaren, a Chicago area dancer. Eusi said he'd gladly accepted the invitation and called off work to attend. Following that experience, the two men would frequently play together, eventually inviting others to join them.[5]

The first group of men who would become the Sun Drummer came together in the fall of 1970 in the basement of Atu's mother's home on the South Side of Chicago. In addition to Atu and Eusi, the original seven members of the organization were Louis "Kewu Saba" Goggins, Paul "Sura" DuPart (aka "Hazrus"), Gary "Selah" Allen, Larry "Enoch" Williamson, and Alfred "Oye Bisi" Nalls (now deceased). Later members included Clifford "Kahil El'Zabar" Blackburn, Andrew "Gafi-El" Taylor, Bart Thomas, Milton "Sanidi" Haynes, Alvin "Moseh" Milon, and Herbert "Babu Atiba" Walker. Others associated with the Sun

[5] Interview, Eusi Tim Holly, November 4, 2013

Drummer included Alvino Shinn, George "NeNe" Favors, Famoudou Don Moye, Calvin Stewart, "Dacha," Steve "Komoyaka" King, Maurice "Rockameem" Bell, and Musa Mosley, the Log Drummer. They came from the city's South and West Sides, from low-income and middle-class families. Some had college degrees, and some were married or single. They were all drummers, but Atu was recognized as the most knowledgeable in regards to musicianship, rhythmic techniques, drum making abilities, and metaphysical concepts. For most, he held the status of a drumming guru. An often repeated legend about Atu was that he walked around during Chicago's frigid winters wearing only sandals and a dashiki, claiming that his body's natural heat would protect him from illness. The men interpreted his actions as a sign of a profound level of spirituality.[6] Not every Black man who drummed was called to be Sun Drummer. Although Eusi made it clear there was no one leader of the group—they were all leaders at any time depending on the event—men who were uncomfortable with either Atu's ideas or the discipline he demanded, left the group.

Atu named the group the Sun Drummer in the singular to demonstrate unity: a philosophy reflected in Garvey's pronouncement of "one God, one aim, one destiny." The goal of the Sun Drummer was to impart to its members the values of personal excellence, self-discipline, and self-dedication. Under Atu's guidance, they studied the laws and principles of nature. He also stressed their responsibility to elevate the people in their roles as musicians, historians, athletes, and diplomats. However, the most vital skill of the Sun Drummer, according to Atu, was "in getting Black people to think and perform together in oneness," and to become agents of their own liberation. Atu reminded the men that the "one" in music was the foundation upon which all rhythm was based, and it also represented the sense of unity that was central to an African worldview. In addition to performing for community rituals and celebrations, they also served as cultural ambassadors, making cross-cultural connections across ethnic and ideological lines in the wide range of venues in which they performed, from colleges to strip clubs. Using homemade drums, bells, shakers, and songs, the Sun Drummer called into being an African National Consciousness (Richards, 1993).

Sura, Eusi, Kahil, Oye, Enoch, Atiba, Sun Drummer

The Sun Drummer did its first public performance in February of 1971 at Northeastern University. Eusi's wife, a student at the university, was part of a Black student group and

[6] During a fundraiser for Atu held in Atlanta, Georgia in October, 2013, Baba G said, "[w]hen I saw Atu walk across the lake in Washington Park wearing only sandals in sub-zero weather, it was at that time I knew that Jesus was bald and a Black man." Atu eventually developed tuberculosis and was hospitalized for several months after which time he took a more conservative approach to life in Chicago.

had been able to contract the Sun Drummer for a fashion show. For the next 3-4 years, following that performance, the Sun Drummer frequently performed throughout the city and at cultural venues around the Midwest. One such performance was at the American Indian Center for a fundraising event arranged by Dennis Banks, cofounder and long-time leader of the American Indian Movement. The Sun Drummer was called to perform with every dancer and group desirous of reclaiming traditional elements of rhythm and movement: e.g. Jewel McLaren, Julian Swain, Darlene Blackburn, The Earth Dancers (Eusi's wife's group), The Black Body Dancers, Hebrew Israelite dancers, Arnel Pugh, and Alyo Tolbert. The group performed at the lakefront wedding of Don L. and Carol Lee (Haki and Safisha Madhubuti). Eusi says the group had a long running gig every Friday night at the Safari Room on Chicago's West Side. Additionally, individuals performing under the Sun Drummer title played and recorded with groups like The Pharaohs, McCoy Tyner, Rahsan Roland Kirk, Nina Simone, and Von and Chico Freeman. In 1974 several group members performed on stage with Famoudou Konate and the Guinea Ballet at the Chicago Opera House. The Sun Drummer was regularly invited by Father George Clements of Holy Angels Church to play at various events organized at the church. However, at the other extreme the Sun Drummer also performed in venues at odds with the philosophy of the organization. Some of the men performed at night clubs behind strippers. One of the drummers recalled a memorable engagement with Kita Lolita, a stripper who performed with two bowls of fire and a white boa constrictor. The venue was on the north side, and it paid "good money."

Members of the Sun Drummer also had their own group projects. Mosheh says that he came to the Sun Drummer as a teenager who regularly worked with several groups. Famoudou Don Moye worked with the Art Ensemble of Chicago, playing trap set with a host of well-known musicians, when he had the opportunity to share his studio apartment in Chicago's Musicians' Building on 53rd and Drexel Avenue with Atu, following his return from Ghana in 1974. According to Moye, "we played, prayed and shared the pains and pleasures of drum making all day, every day 'cuz Atu didn't allow no slack."[7] It was in that period, as a result of the "intense energy," that Moye developed his own concept of Sun Percussion. Similarly, Kahil El'Zabar, known as being a consummate performer and business man, formed the Ethnic Heritage Ensemble. Oye Bisi Nalls is said to have recorded more music than other members, having played with the Pharaohs and other notable groups at the time.

The Sun Drummer came together for the purpose of creating an essentially African-

[7] Facebook comments from Famoudou Don Moye, March 20, 2013.

[8] According to Mosheh, Atu felt that each society had its own drum and relationship with the drum based on their location. As a city beside the lake, the Sun Drummer drew from its unique geographic and historical location.

American drum culture that didn't seek to replicate traditions found in Africa.[8] The men organized around the drum, songs, rhythm, and dance. In Atu's thinking, one was incomplete without the others and none could stand alone. Having studied with African-American, Native American, and Ghanaian drum makers, he opined that any cultural group had the responsibility for making and naming their own instruments for the performance of communal rituals and celebrations, such as: weddings, funerals, naming ceremonies, ritual and secular dances, and African martial arts. To that end, the drummers were required to learn how to make their own drums and other instruments. Atu had hoped that making and playing drums would lead the men to desire land ownership and become producers rather than consumers. He also sought to develop a synergistic connection to the earth through contact with the trees that the men would hollow for the drum shell and to the animals whose skin became the head. Sule Greg Wilson (1992) writes in *The Drummers Path*,

Sun Drummer American Indian Center c. 1974 Atu Murray, Atiba Storey, Eusi Tim Holly, Bibi Moore

> Yes; there is Spirit in the body of the drum carved out of the trunk of a tree; there is a Spirit in the skin of the drum itself. All this, plus the Spirit of the person playing the drum, becomes an irresistible force against any immovable object. (p. xii)

Mosheh says the men came to the group playing Mexican and Cuban congas, drums they purchased from pawn shops. "We started converting them to tack heads. We started riding around with sterno cans and hot plates to keep the skin tight. So you were always pulling and tacking. If it's a damp day, you'd pull out your sterno cans."[9] The men were making slat drums, as well as drums from tree trunks, traveling as far as Atlanta with Musa to get wood for drums. Other types of drums made included air drums, log drums, "council drums," and a large hollowed out tree trunk that requires four men to carry it on their shoulders, while two others walk alongside it, striking it with sticks. The Sun Drummer had played this massive log drum one year during the Bud Biliken Parade. Perhaps with the exception of that drum, it was Atu's custom to make drums in sets of seven, seven being a sacred spiritual number—the energy of the mystics.

---

[9] Interview with Mosheh Milon Sr. by phone May 15, 2013.

The Sun Drummer as a Masculinist Cultural Revolutionary Black Nationalist Organization

Ostensibly, the Sun Drummer as a whole, was a cultural nationalist group, adopting the names, the garb, the symbols, and ceremonies of Africa; reinventing a hybrid African-American culture. Many members, like so many at the time, traversed ideological identities to incorporate nationalistic activities that reflected territorial/separatist, revolutionary, cultural, and pluralist (nation within a nation) tendencies. The timeline of the Sun Drummer coincided with a conscious awakening of poor and working-class African-Americans that was perhaps unconsciously, linked to resistance movements waged by marginalized communities in the United States: e.g. Native Americans, Latino, women, gays, and antiwar activists, as well as those in Africa and so-called Third World countries waging anticolonial battles. At the time of the Sun Drummer's formation, Chicago was a fertile ground for Black revolutionary thought and activity. The tensions simmering from decades of race riots spilled over in April 1968 following the assassination of Martin Luther King, Jr. and again in August 1968 during the Chicago Democratic Party Convention. The assassinations of Fred Hampton and Mark Clark a year later in December 1969 exposed the wanton brutality of state repression. Their deaths, as well as the death of Malcolm X four years earlier, laid the foundation for uprising and rebellion among the city's young warriors. Malcolm had outlined a clear set of objectives for their activism in the charter of the Organization of African American Unity (OAAU) that he had been scheduled to deliver on the day of his death.

Like Atu in his work with Malcolm X and African Nationalists organizations in New York, many members of the Sun Drummer had previously been involved in Black Nationalist activities, ranging from the Black Panther Party to the Black Hebrew Israelites (BHI). Selah and Enoch had both been members of the Chicago chapter of the Black Panther Party. Enoch reports that it was through the Panthers and the revolutionary music of Jimi Hendrix and John Coltrane, that he got exposed to Blackness. Both men say they left the party after the deaths of Hampton and Clark. Selah said the chapter had awaited word to "make a move," but when they were ordered to stand down, he became disenchanted with the Party. "Fred was killed in December of 1969, and I turned in my resignation from the Party in January. For me there was nowhere left to go in the Party."[10] Eusi also cites the deaths of Clark and Hampton as a turning point in his movement activities. He was raised in an apostolic family in which his father, uncle, and grandfather were ministers, and his grandfather had also been involved with Marcus Garvey's Universal Negro Improvement

[10] Interview with Gary "Selah" Allen, Chicago, Illinois, September 17, 2005.

Association (UNIA). Although Eusi claims never to have been a "card carrying" member of any organization, he had extensive knowledge of the beginnings of the Chicago's BPP under Hampton's leadership. As a result of his organizing activities and connections with several campus organizations, Fred asked him to "check out people for him." "I provided intelligence,"[11] Eusi responded. Famoudou Don Moye didn't report an active involvement with the BPP, but he says he played for several Black Panther Party Benefits in Paris in 1969 and '70 with The Art Ensemble of Chicago, and other African-American musicians at that time. The Art Ensemble of Chicago's theme song, "Theme for Odwalla," written by Roscoe Mitchel, was first performed in early 1970 at one of the Black Panther Party Benefit Concerts at Theatre La Mutualité in Paris.[12]

Atiba recalls his consciousness being altered after reading Malcolm X's autobiography. It was while he was a student at Malcolm X College on Chicago's West Side, where he was studying criminal justice, when he met a group of Vietnam veterans who called themselves the Mau Mau. Atiba's involvement with the group was short-lived. He left the group after being unable to dissuade them from an ill-conceived plot that actually "went down" after his departure from the group.[13] The foiled attempt resulted in the arrest of six of the men for attempted murder.[14] It was at that point Atiba decided to follow another path to liberation. He would eventually become involved with the BHI community along with his brother, Sherman "Eli Hoe Nai" Walker, who was also a musician. The brothers had strong influences on Mosheh. It was under Atiba's direction when Mosheh joined the Sun Drummer. He had seen the men sitting at the courtyard bench of the Dearborn Public Housing units where they all lived, playing drums and doing "Black consciousness chants." Although Mosheh says he was never involved in any of the revolutionary nationalist groups, he identified with the Black consciousness movement. He joined the brothers in the BHI community, attracted to their search to find Africa in the Bible.

---

[11] Phone interview with Tim Eusi Holly, May 28, 2013.

[12] Facebook comments from Famoudou Don Moye, March 20, 2013.

[13] Interview with Atiba, September 17, 2005.

[14] An excerpt from Van DeBurg's New Day in Babylon details the results of their ill-conceived plot:

> [Chicago, 1972]. Six young blacks were arrested and accused of taking part in nine recent murders throughout Illinois. At their arraignment, the suspects appeared with the arms extended in the Black Power salute. Police told reporters that they were part of a nationwide league of embittered black combat veterans who had to "kill a whitey to get into the gang." Cook County officials claimed that the arrests thwarted the group's plan to begin a systematic cop-killing spree. Dashing any sense of relief this news may have encouraged, Tribune headlines screamed, "Murder Gang 3,000 Strong, De Mau Mau taking over for the Panthers" (p. 69)

For the revolutionary artist, the objective was to weaponize art to bring about a cultural and social revolution. Art was used to bring people together, transform their consciousness, and mobilize them to confront global white supremacy, industrial capitalism, and imperialism. With its own special "*ase*" (the ability to make things happen), the drum was both lethal and restorative. Wilson (1992) notes,

> Artists and musicians are manipulating power in the form of mood-altering sonics and information coded in iconic form—colors, patterns of line and movement, garments and images"....performing is much more than "having fun" or a "night's gig." "...there is a consciousness, a spiritual and social awareness that must be adhered to. (p. xiv)

Wilson goes further to say that "women and men have observed and studied for thousands of years to learn just what it takes to alter their own, or another's state of consciousness" (p. xv). Thus, the drum was reclaimed as an instrument of power. However, in the philosophy of the Sun Drummer, as set forth by Atu, men were the only ones who could evoke this transformation using the drum. Although women were objects for the restorative power of the drums, they were excluded from playing them.

According to Enoch, a secret male society formed to teach the principles of manhood, as was traditionally done through the rites of passage in Africa. Atu taught that the drum is a phallic symbol in which the trunk is the shaft of a man's penis and the skin represented the head. When the fresh skins (cow or goat) are placed on the drum casing, the excess skin—foreskin—is cut away like circumcision. Women of childbearing/menstruating years were not supposed to touch men's drums. Neither were they supposed to play drums with their hands, but rather with sticks, and then only in their own company or societies. Women were allowed to play bell with the men or dance to their rhythms, but even in those positions women were excluded from Sun Drummer membership.[15] Despite the reality of Black women as activists and revolutionaries, the Sun Drummer, like other Civil Rights/Black Power groups, reproduced an African interpretation of Abrahamic patriarchy; Black Power was as much about rescuing Black masculinity as liberating Black people from the throes of white supremacy. The group reflected the relationship between mass mobilization, political rhetoric, art/spirituality, and masculinity. Mosheh reaffirmed the Sun Drummer as a male dominated group.

> Atu liked ladies a lot, but he thought of women, in my view, as being sort of inferior. That was my impression. It was in evident in the songs Atu wrote, "a woman needs a man to be a man; a woman needs a man to understand....His thinking was totally macho and that ladies were an accompaniment to...the Sun Drummer.

[15] The prohibition of women drummers was ironic given the fact that Chief Bey often said his first drum teacher was a woman in South Carolina, Isame Andrews, in the 1920s.

Cheryl "Chaveevah" Banks was a dancer with Black Body, UHCC, and Muntu, whose husband Shlomo, briefly played with the Sun Drummer. She says that coming from a tradition where a woman left her father's house for her husband's, she didn't find Atu's position on women to be patriarchal or a statement of women's inferiority.[16] She admits she enjoyed the chauvinism and protective nature. Additionally, she said there was never a time that Atu didn't greet her in a way that recognized her beauty and womanhood. Atu's admiration of women was expressed in several of the songs he wrote for the Sun Drummer.

Conjuring an African National Consciousness: Songs of the Sun Drummer

Atu authored over eighty songs for the Sun Drummer. The songs were "transcendental," instructive, informative, provocative and compelling; urging the masses to think, act, and be different. In their simplicity, he says the songs could help anyone know how to resolve their differences. Atu was a linguist who understood and used spoken language the same way he used the language of the drum and all the other instruments he played. Instead of mimicking the sounds of an unknown African dialect, he wrote simple songs in vernacular English, which resonated with poor, working-class, African-American communities. In this regard Atu may have been influenced by musician and philosopher, Sun Ra, with whom he had worked.[17] In "To the Peoples of the Earth" Sun Ra wrote:

> Proper evaluation of words and letters
> In their phonetic and associated sense
> Can bring the peoples of earth
> Into the clear light of pure Cosmic Wisdom (Ongiri, 2000, p. 82)

Although not overtly promoting a political platform, the Sun Drummer understood a cultural revolution required broad-based support from the masses and an organic form of leadership that was responsive to them, an idea evident in the Sun Drummer chant, "A Body without a Head."

> A body without a head, ain't no good
> A tree without roots sure can't be wood
> Us, we, together we shine
> Doing your own thing ain't none of mine.

---

[16] Phone interview with Cheryl Chaveevah Banks-Ferguson, October 29, 2013.

[17] Atu would later be featured along with Pharoah Sanders on Sun Ra's 1976 release under the name of "Black Harold," Sun Ra and His Arkestra Featuring Pharoah Sanders /Featuring Black Harold, (Saturn Records, Chicago).

Evident in this song are the principles of unity (umoja) and collective work and responsibility (ujima) from the Seven Principles (Nguzo Saba) set forth by Maulana Ron Karenga: creator of Kwanzaa and noted theorist of the Black Arts/Black Power movement. Atu's songs also demonstrate a connection between Black artistic production and other kinds of functional African-American survival practices. For example, "Running in the Streets" is a cautionary tale for children as a deterrent for delinquency that simultaneously spoke to the disenfranchised element within the Black community.

> Running in the streets, made of concrete,
> No love will you find. Just hearts made of limestone.
> If we use our heads, we won't die in the land of the dead.

Atu drew inspiration for his songs from metaphysical precepts and principles. "Open my Eye" focused on the power of the third eye to apperceive transcendental truths.

> Open my eye to the light of understanding. Open my eye to the light of true commanding.
> Open my eye to the knowledge of the way. Oh, oh, oh on this day.
> We be the gifts, the gifts to the people. Behold my church, and look in my steeple.
> See me in my need, oh see me in my Father's seed.
> See me on my way to a new, new day.

Sun Drummer songs fulfilled the fundamental criteria of Black Arts production, speaking directly to the needs and aspirations of Black America. Additionally, as Karenga expressed in his manifesto "On Black Art," Sun Drummer songs were "functional, collective and committed." Again, Negritude offers a referent for themes and prescriptions covered in Sun Drummer songs. Their songs

> make possible…a return from exile, an abnegation of the alienation and loss through a symbolic return to authentic, natural African sources. Hence the themes: continuity, flow, timelessness, earth, nature, the rhythm of life, ritualizing the earth and life, the permanence of tribal masks, the power of the earthly black woman. (Newman, p. 56)

Atu may have been chauvinistic in his approach to women, an approach perceived as hypermasculine and misogynistic by some, but the following Sun Drummer chant expresses Atu's reverence for the African woman as the Mother of all humanity.

> Call: "It's only a woman who can be the mother of a man"
> Response: Respect your mother
> Call: "It's only a woman who can be the mother of a man"
> Response: Respect your woman

The Sun Drummer members, as true militant revolutionaries, weaponized their art knowing that Black art had to respond positively to the reality of revolution. These songs were not only used as a source of entertainment, but to transmit and reinforce positive cultural values necessary for the important task of post-revolution nation building. The Sun

Drummer used the power of the drum to connect to the physical, astral, and higher spiritual domains; using the vibratory effects of word sounds to bring about cultural awakening for their many audiences in and around the Chicagoland area. Perhaps Atu prophesied the enduring legacy of the Sun Drummer in the chant, "Indestructible Consciousness": "I-I-I-I-I will never die. Cuz I-I-I-I-I be indestructible consciousness."

The Sundown of the Sun Drummer

The Sun Drummer had been able to capitalize on the momentum of moving people, providing the rhythm to their freedom dance. The popularity of African-American drumming created opportunities for the Sun Drummer to work and travel. Unsurprisingly, the decline of the Sun Drummer coincided with the end of the Black Power/Black Arts Movement. As the enthusiasm that drove the combined movement began to dissipate into anti-Black government propaganda and violent repression of what was essentially a cultural revolution, so too did the number of well-paying gigs. Many of the Sun Drummer members were married during their years in the group. They began complaining that they couldn't continue playing every week for just $50. "We had families to take care of."

Money was just one of their problems. From the group's inception, men were coming and going for one reason or another. As a result, by 1974, the Sun Drummer had become the Chicago Sun Drummer Society. Although not the original intent of early members, naming the group a "Society" allowed the Sun Drummer to maintain its existence as a brotherhood.[18] Prior to 1974, Atu had left the group for a brief stay in Ghana where he married, studied drumming, and continued to perfect his craft as a carver. It was while he was in Ghana that Atiba assumed a quasi-leadership role, and it was under him when more drummers from the Black Hebrew Israelite (BHI) community joined the Society.[19] *Transitions East* was a South Side restaurant and community space belonging to the BHI, offering community dance classes taught by Alyo Tolbert, a student of Darlene Blackburn. Using the drums they had made, men from the Sun Drummer played for Tolbert's first African dance group, Unifying Humanity through Cultural Creativity (UHCC), under the auspices of

---

[18] Ashenafi Kebede writes in his work Roots of Black Music. The Vocal, Instrumental, and Dance Heritage of Africa and Black America (1972, African World Press) that most musicians belonged to a "guild, a religious brotherhood, or an association in order to protect or advance their mutual interests." Many times these guilds, brotherhoods or societies follow a lineage, producing generations of musicians to uphold and advance the traditions established by the group.

[19] Atiba became the Assistant Artistic Director of Muntu Dance Theater, a position he's held for nearly three decades.

the Hebrew Israelites. In 1972, Tolbert renamed the group *Muntu*, a Bantu word meaning "the essence of humanity." As Alyo continued to study West African dance and strove for a more authentic representation of drum and dance culture, (particularly from the Old Malian Empire), there was a need for drummers willing to learn, study, and play djembe. Mosheh said that when the Sun Drummer began making and playing air drums, "it didn't matter if you had $7,000 to buy a djembe, there were no djembes to be purchased. We made our own."

The air drum Atu had taught the men to make, was similar to the West African djembe; it was strapped to the body, held between the legs, and played while standing. Beginning in the early 1960s, drummers wanting to learn djembe were able to travel to New York to study with Malinke master drummer, Ladji Camara, who had immigrated to the United States. Later, in 1968, Katherine Dunham brought Senegalese drummer Mor Thiam to East St. Louis to work with her and members of the Black Artists' Group (BAG) at Southern Illinois University-Edwardsville. Thiam became a teacher for Chicago area drummers. The djembe was quickly gaining popularity, as was the demand for the drum, creating an international market. Some of the Sun Drummer men remained loyal to earth drums and congas, but those working with Muntu purchased and learned the djembe along with other West African drums, leading to the transformation of the Sun Drummer Society.

Atu, 73, currently lives and works in Atlanta, but is actively making plans to relocate to Ghana. For years Enoch and Mosheh played with Atiba in Muntu Dance Theater, later leaving for their own endeavors: Enoch in Chicago and Mosheh in California. Kahil El'Zabar continued to develop his own project, the Ethnic Heritage Ensemble. Famoudou Don Moye traveled with the Sun Percussion, as well as with other groups, while living in Morocco. Eusi resides in Atlanta with his family where he runs a security business, playing occasionally. Selah, Sura, and Kewu make infrequent appearances at Chicago's 63rd Street Beach Drum Circle. At least two, Oye Bisi and Gafi-El, made their transition to the next plane. Yet, despite its splintering, the Sun Drummer lives on.

Conclusion

The Sun Drummer saw the promotion of Black culture and the tradition of the drum as a necessary "revolutionary" act. The songs of the Sun Drummer were reflective of the new Black aesthetic announced during the Black Arts Movement, developed from the ideological framework of earlier Francophone writers from the African diaspora who articulated the concept of "Negritude." Negritude, like Black Cultural Nationalism, was often characterized as apolitical. However, taking part in a revolution of culture is a deeply political act, a Gramscian War of Position.

> Negritude is self-assertion, self-esteem, a retention of dignity, self-pride, cultural identity by affirming the beauty of blackness. Negritude is non-political nationalism, a way to assert independence, but within it is the notion that political independence is possible if cultural independence is assured. (Newman, 1987, p. 52)

Atu sought to reclaim the beauty of African culture, as reimagined in the Americas where it emerged as a hybrid, hyphenated, African-American culture. The Sun Drummer dedicated itself to preserving the knowledge of the drum and its spiritual connection to the earth, ancestors, and people. This reclamation involved intensive study and research in order to recapture the original value of the drum and return it to its place of distinction in the global African village. By engaging in the practice of recovery and restoration, the Sun Drummer waged a revolution as powerful as any armed struggle. They were able to mend the rupture created by the theft of Africans from their land and traditions, suturing the gaping wound of the Middle Passage (Ma'afa), and healing the people of the Holocaust of enslavement. In doing so, they were able to recreate a tradition of drumming that has been passed on through the many men, and even women, who were taught and inspired by the Sun Drummer. At a recent fundraiser held for Atu in Atlanta, Georgia, people came from various parts of the country to celebrate him. Each had a testimony of the impact his work had on their artistic development. He performed a ceremony in which he symbolically passed the torch to a young drummer, representing the forward flow of African-American culture. Sun Drummer songs are still being sung, and the name of the Sun Drummer resonates as strongly as the African heart in the breast of the people. For that we owe and express gratitude to Atu and the men of the Sun Drummer. Long live the Sun Drummer. So it is said. So let it be.

REFERENCES

Cabral, A. (1973). *Return to the source: Selected speeches of Amilcar Cabral.* New York: Monthly Review Press.

Epstein, D.J. (2003). *Sinful tunes and spirituals: Black folk music to the Civil War.* Urbana, IL: University of Illinois Press

Newman, R. (1987). *Black Power and Black religion: Essays and reviews.* Cornwall, CT: Locust Hill Press.

Ongiri, A. (2000). *Black arts for a Black People: The cultural politics of the Black Power Movement and the search for a Black aesthetic.* Ithaca, NY: Cornell University Press.

Prince, O.H. (1822). *A digest of the laws of the State of Georgia: Containing all statutes and the substance of all resolutions of a general and public nature, and now in force, which have been passed in this state, previous to the session of the General Assembly of December, 1820*. Grantland and Orme, 1822. Law (Google eBook, p. 454)

Richards, D.M. (1993). *The African aesthetic and national consciousness. In K. Welsh-Asante (Ed.). The African aesthetic: Keeper of the Traditions*, pp. 63-82. Westport, CT: Praeger.

Van Deburg, W.L. (1992). *New day in Babylon: The Black Power Movement and American culture, 1965-1975*. Chicago, IL: University of Chicago Press.

Wilson, S.G. (1992). *The drummer's path. Moving the spirit with ritual and traditional drumming*. Rochester, VT: Destiny Books.

A REVOLUTIONARY LIFE

Soyini Walton

The roots of my involvement in the Black Power movement run deep. My journey as a conscious and active participant in the Black Power movement began at the feet of my father, Mr. Russell Ricks. Daddy was a great intellect and an avid reader. His thirst for knowledge led him to greatly enhance the modest education he received at DuSable High School and Roosevelt University. His poor eyesight afforded him an early discharge from the United States Army, but it never prevented him from his voracious reading. His mother, Willa Ricks, was a domestic worker and found it necessary to put Daddy in Catholic boarding school in Milwaukee. That experience opened up a lot of questions for him about religion, spirituality and morality. Daddy remained an agnostic for the rest of his life. Removing the confines of one's own religious constraints allowed him to investigate and appreciate various political, cultural, economic and nationalist movements.

One thing that became crystal clear to my father as a result of his life experiences, as a black man living in America, and from his studies is that European white people are ruthless, power mongers. I learned very early from him about the way the world works.

My father's knowledge-base and understandings were further enhanced by his travels all over the world. He and my mother visited all of the continents and met people from many cultures and stations in life. Daddy perceived that the poverty and hunger of downtrodden people in third world countries was partly a result of religious missionary movements. It was through this lens that I was able to see that what I had learned in "his-story" books was just that: someone else's story. This set the stage for me to very easily embrace an African-centered world view.

My mother, Doris Ricks, imbued in me a love of music and from her I was exposed to the depth, variety and realm of Black music. My mother was a budding professional singer working the concert circuit before she settled into the life of being a fulltime mother and housewife. She had a beautiful contralto soprano voice. Our home was filled with the sounds of great black jazz and other genres of black music. I learned from my mother to celebrate and nurture myself no matter what the circumstance. She taught me that our home is a sacred place for family, and I learned from her how to make a home a wonderful place.

These were the beginnings of my "African self." The catalyst that really ignited my passion to be my African self was Don L. Lee. I met him on the evening of June 9, 1968 at Kennedy-King College. There was some type of Civil Rights event or gathering that we both attended. We got involved in a conversation about the movement and about the condition and status of Black people. He was well-versed, intriguing and tall, skinny and handsome. I gladly accepted his invitation to come by his apartment to continue the discussion.

I followed him to a basement apartment on 62nd and Ada. Once inside, I was surprised to find that it was a half-space, a half built out studio space in the front part of the basement of this two-flat building. However, the space was cozy, inviting, and yet cool on that warm June night. Books were everywhere. We sat and talked for hours, and I was enthralled by Don's passion and intensity concerning the challenges facing Black people. He was worldly and well read. He gave me copies of *Think Black* and *Black Pride*. These were his very first published books. They were books of poetry that he had managed to self-publish. He explained to me that in order to market the books, he would stand on street corners and sell the books to people passing by. I was very impressed with Don. I left his apartment that evening feeling very inspired.

The next morning, I got up and washed my hair, and with that action, I washed out my "press and curl." I felt new and beautiful and very authentic as I combed out my full "natural" or Afro. I have worn my hair in natural styles ever since that day.

Don and I grew to be good friends. Don had a vision and I wanted to be a part of it. Don had founded Third World Press in 1967. Being in Don's company gave me the opportunity to meet other notable people in the literary field and in the arts. Some of those people were Walter Bradford, Jewel Latimore, Carolyn Rodgers, David Llorens, Angela Jackson, and Sterling Plumpp. They would stop by "the apartment" to see Don and talk about the explosive new movement in literature and the arts in which Black people were raising their voices using various mediums.

Don was gaining some notoriety with his writings and speaking. He was invited to be an adjunct professor at Cornell University in Ithaca, New York. He vacated "the apartment" and left for Ithaca.

Third World Press had no operating space and no address. Don (now known as Haki Madhubuti) made an agreement with Curtis Ellis for the use of his bookstore space, allowing the Press to use the book store's address for sending and receiving mail. I delivered and picked up mail for TWP at that location and also shipped out orders of books for the fledgling press.

Haki wanted to have me start training in order to better help him with the Press, so he arranged for me to spend some time with Dudley Randall of Broadside Press in Detroit. That was a great opportunity to actually be a guest in the home of Dudley who, like Haki, was passionate about publishing for our people. Dudley had started Broadside Press some years earlier and had set up a good system for printing and distribution of the "broadsides." I learned a lot from this very warm and patient man.

I had the good fortune to be invited to a special gathering of writers. Haki and Gwendolyn Brooks, our Illinois Poet Laureate, had become very close. Even then, Haki described Ms. Brooks as his spiritual mother. Mama Gwen opened her home once a month on Sundays for writers to drop by. They came to sit at the feet of one of the greatest writers of all time. They came to share their work and to be encouraged by Mama Gwen and each other. Though Mama Gwen was highly revered by the group, she was also energized by the young writers, and she humbly felt that she was a student as well. They formed a new revolutionary choir of voices, each one singing his/her own part and yet communicating the profound message of the day: we are building a new consciousness word by word—and we don't have to follow your rules. This great camaraderie included some of the writers mentioned above.

In 1967, I discovered the Afro Arts Theater. Phil Cochran and his family and his band, the Pharaohs, had reopened the old Oakland theatre and were putting on shows there. Phil is a student of ancient cultures and the music and instruments of our African cultures, thus the name Pharaohs for the band. There was also a sisterhood among the wives of the band members. I got to know them and got involved with the sisters. I remember specifically Blondell Satterfield and Clara Handy. They were beautiful sisters who were studying and practicing the art of homemaking, caring for the body and natural healing, natural beauty methods for skin and hair, and sewing and crafts. I wanted this type of sisterhood. It was with the Afro Arts group that I first heard of Kwanzaa, and in 1967 I celebrated Kwanzaa with them.

The Kuumba workshop was also using the Afro Arts Theatre space for rehearsals and shows. It was during this time that I met Val Gray Ward and I became involved with Kuumba Theatre for a brief time. Kuumba was such a fascinating group. Val was and is very intense, and she is an extraordinary dramatist. Kuumba theatre brought the writings of the revolutionary poets and playwrights alive!

This era of our new African-centered consciousness and cultural consciousness was filled with the sights, sounds and smells of our new African-cultural selves. The sights, sounds and smells were intoxicating and memorable. We were angry, yet we were awed as we experienced the results of our art, music, African-inspired beauty, and ways of being.

We soothed our anger with the wonderful music of John Coltrane, Pharoah Sanders, Leon Thomas, Doug and Jean Carn, Grady Tate, Donny Hathaway and Lonnie Liston Smith, just to name a few. The newly formed Association for the Advancement of Creative Musicians (AACM) provided another musical voice that spoke of breaking barriers. We listened as we worked, relaxed, and planned. The music was a foundation for our ideas.

We inspired each other with our colorful, intricate African attire and vibrant "Afro" hairstyles. We were a sight to behold to each other. The artists gave us so much to ponder, and such a visual treat. I remember being so inspired by the expressions of Barbara Jones-Hogu (who actually shared tie dye techniques with me), and Murray DePillars and Omar Lama (artists whom I knew personally).

Many of us changed the way we ate during this time of awakening. We began to eat less processed foods, more whole grains, and we used herbs for a variety of purposes. The first time I experienced the fragrance and taste of peppermint tea, it was like ambrosia to me. The Sisters of the Afro Arts Theatre taught me how to bake whole wheat bread. Not only was the bread delicious and nutritious, but the fragrance of bread baking in the oven was just heavenly! This was truly a time of rebirth for me; it was intense, emotional and sensuous.

AFRICOBRA: AESTHETIC, VISION, AND IMPACT

Arlene Crawford

The artistic image is not intended to represent the thing itself, but rather, the reality of the force the thing contains.

—James Baldwin

As a child of the 1960s, I witnessed both the Civil Rights and Black Power Movements. I was also blessed to have mentors who modeled a dedication to art and emphasized the importance of African American cultural identity.

In college, I met and studied with Nelson Stevens. Nelson had been recruited to teach at Northern Illinois University (NIU) as a result of student demonstrations that, among other things, demanded more Black faculty and staff be hired. Like many of my peers, I desperately wanted to study with faculty who looked like me, came from the same cultural experience, and could point the way for dynamic engagement with art forms that could express the beauty of Black America and contain messages of empowerment.

Nelson taught studio drawing, painting, and the history of African American Art in NIU's Art department. During this time, he became a member of the African Commune of Bad Relevant Artists (AfriCOBRA). His teaching expanded and enriched my study, and I was excited to be mentored by him. He introduced me to AfriCOBRA members: Jeff Donaldson, Barbara Jones, and Napoleon Jones-Henderson. As an aspiring artist, I quickly embraced the ideas and images of (AfriCOBRA) as a way to empower African American people through visual art. I also joined the National Conference of Artists (NCA) as a student, where I was introduced to many more Black artists and educators from Chicago, as well as from across the country.

Nelson extended his commitment to the art and values of AfriCOBRA when he established a forum with Black students at NIU, which led to the formation of the Color Rappers, a student organization. Through it, Nelson helped Black students attend NCA conferences around the country and encouraged us to pursue networking and art-making.

All these activities resonated in my artistic soul, and for me, the Black Arts Movement became a REAL and PERSONAL movement, a lifestyle to which I became committed. My experiences at NIU became the foundation for my artistic vision and my work as an artist.

My vision was also shaped by scholar and writer Larry Neal who stated, "The main tenet of Black Power is the necessity for Black people to define the world in their own terms. The black artist has made the same point in the context of aesthetics." According to Neal, in a 1978 interview published in *DRUM* Magazine, the Black aesthetic would provide a theoretical point of view that would allow scholars to study black art forms such as blues, black rhythmic patterns, and elements that could be "the ingredients that constitute a way of proceeding creatively."1 In other words, Neal insisted that Black art be studied according to its own theoretical basis, rather than viewing all art as the same and understood with the same theories.

Neal insisted:

> A perception of things, like a way of playing the blues ... If you are trying to get to your cultural identity, the Black aesthetic mode forces you to look at Black culture in terms of specific uses of these items for art. There is a certain kind of aesthetic thrust a Black artist can use, call it a cultural construct.[2]

AfriCOBRA artists manifested their own meanings based on an African cultural continuum of thought and aesthetics:

> The Image, frontal/sublime; Expressive awesomeness: like Hip walk and Together talk"; Rhythm, rhythm, rhythm, free symmetry, repetition with change; Patterns in color, in form, and in design; Colors, Kool-Aid and bright, SHINE; infusion of Pan-African elements and symbols; Words, words, words; Words as pictures, Image text; Organic looking, feeling forms; Real and over real; the plus and the minus; the abstract and concrete meet; 'mimesis at midpoint'; these are their ingredients.[3]

In order to fully "check out" the images of AfriCOBRA and understand their cultural construct, it is necessary to "check out" the lushness of their aesthetic tenets such as shine, expressive awesomeness, and mimesis at midpoint. "Mimesis at midpoint is defined as: design that marks the spot where the real and the unreal, the objective and the nonobjective, the plus and the minus meet. A point exactly between absolute abstractions and absolute naturalism."[4]

The Black Arts Movement (BAM) has shaped my aesthetic influences. BAM is a continuum of the intellectual and cultural achievements of the Harlem Renaissance. That was a time when the creative "Talented Tenth" sought content and inspiration from African culture and history. For me, the Black Arts Movement was an extension or transliteration of that cultural imprint brought into the 60s. African culture is the stalk from which Black people spring; it holds a core foundation to our spiritual, psychology and social development. The experiences of slavery, reconstruction, civil rights and other altering events have had a profound effect on the art and consciousness of Black people. For me, artistic subject matter is inspired by our origins, our history and our declarations of self-determination. It is the Black artists who will determine what is beautiful, whole and authentic about Black people and their community. And a form of self-determination is identifying and validating their aesthetic principles.

As a Black artist, I found a specific purpose for my own work, creating art that is functional, collective, and committed, while also using forms and images which will define, identify, and direct. The following are some of the elements that I use within my work:

> Frontality of the form—representational images, which help the viewer identify the subject;
>
> Rhythm / syncopation / improvisation—principles key to African and Black American music (i.e. jazz or rather Black Classical music), R&B and the Blues;
>
> Color—Bright and vital, Kool-aide colors, like the visual energy that Black people use to adorn themselves.

The message conveyed its function is inherent in the visual statement. I choose words or symbols to communicate some of these themes: who we were, who we are, who we hope to become and our contributions to life and values. I prefaced this article with a quote from James Baldwin, which is taken from his book, *Nobody Knows my Name*. This statement speaks of the power of the artistic image to represent the reality of the force behind the image, which is at the core of my work as well.

For example with my work "Impression of a Drum" – My "mimesis at midpoint" is on the DRUM. The work is my tribute of Larry Neal: cultural critic and definer of the BAM. He is a DRUM; he is a communicator, telling the truth. Using the abstracted notion of the DRUM as a communicator, like its use in Africa, the DRUM kept us connected and informed. I'm just drawing from my memory of a conversation I once had with him. Larry's message, his drum speak, was the truth for our aesthetic. He was speaking to the power of the visual to de-colonize minds as a strategy for liberation. A new aesthetic, which is predicated on ethics, asks the question: "whose vision of the world is finally more meaningful, ours or the oppressors?"

AfriCOBRA reconstructed social definitions and created a language to discuss image-making that was relevant to the time. Expression was rooted in rhythm, patterns in color/form, and language as a visual emphasis within a work of art. AfriCOBRA sought to produce a celebratory art reflecting cultural balance and aesthetic hegemony. Jeff Donaldson's, founder of AfriCOBRA, intentions are clear:

> Our people are our standard for excellence. Striving for images that African people can relate to directly without formal art training and/or experience... images that appeal to the senses...it is our hope that intelligent definitions of the past and perceptive identifications in the present will project nation-full direction in the future.

Nelson Steven's "Jihad Nation" is a prime example. There are two commonly accepted meanings of jihad: an inner spiritual struggle and an outer physical struggle. The "greater jihad" is the inner struggle of a believer to fulfill his religious duties. This non-violent meaning is stressed by both Muslim and non-Muslim authors.

As we examine Nelson's "Jihad Nation," you see a brother—the front of his head—the seat of his mind and spirit confronted with the revolutionary Red/Black/Green—Africa—the Ankh or key to life from the Kemetic image language, and you contemplate his inner and outer quest for Nationhood.

The Black Arts Movement (BAM) was calling for artists to create art not for themselves, nor for the sake of art, but rather one should create for the liberation of the minds of all Black people. The art should address positivity and reflect values that will strengthen our people, committing them to nationhood and unity. The images, that the Black artist creates, are concerned with African heritage as much as with our contemporary reality, and those images should always be relevant to the era in which they exist. "BAM is radically opposed to any concept of the artist that alienates him from his community," similar to what Hip Hop was about when it first developed. The message was dedicated to community and liberation. It was then an outgrowth of BAM—but it has been corrupted, and with it our culture and community have been under fire.

The Black Arts Movement scholar, Margo Crawford says, and I'm paraphrasing here, "Images can be real and 'overreal' because they can produce the concrete reorientation of the black gaze that allows a person to see his or herself through their own eyes and also, the excessive dimensions of what one discovers with this new black gaze—the layers and layers of decolonizing, alternative worldviews. The messages delivered through art can be direct and intentionally political, without cancelling out the subjective responses that shape an aesthetic experience, like 'expressive awesomeness.'"[5]

"The WE in YOU is the Nation Calling, I AM because WE ARE." AfriCOBRA was, and continues to stand as, the aesthetic voice to the larger history of Chicago's cultural impact on the Black Arts Movement of America.

AfriCOBRA: Impact Now and onto Tomorrow

OBAC, AACM and AfriCOBRA all sprang from the same era in their institutional roots. The Association for the Advancement of Creative Musicians' (AACM) mantra is "Music, Ancient to the Future"; as I see it, AACM's goal and purpose is to create in that continuum. This makes me ponder AfriCOBRA's ongoing mission. Black Arts and Aesthetics have had the most effective intervention in the history of Black resistance here in America.

Clyde Taylor, emeritus professor of the Gallatin School at NYU, reflects that:

> Black Arts was a fresh modernism ...celebrating vernacular rural and urban values of survival and expression, revivifying the connection with Africa, honoring the African American history of resistance and struggle and its many heroes, revering new ways of interacting with mass media and their version of popular culture, vindicating black speech idiom, discovering anew the beauty of the black face and body and announcing bold new ways of confronting white racism. *After the Black Arts Movement*/ Nka, Fall 2011.[6]

Today's interest in the Black Arts Movement is being examined by some of this country's leading and progressive universities; here in Chicago, Northwestern University, the University of Chicago, Columbia College and DePaul University are all offering course curriculum content for their students on this subject matter. I think it further illustrates the impact this particular history is having on the consciousness of today's population, who elected America's first Black President. My daughter is subject to saying that, "there is no coincidence, life co-insides." As a child of the "60's", I understood that "Black was a complexion of the Mind". Daniel Widener echoes this same idea when observing that Benedict Anderson argues persuasively in his work, *Imagined Communities* (London, Verso, 1991), that the "nationalist sentiment was first and foremost a conscious intellectual act." Widener further explains that, "it is possible to see music, history, spirituality and even concepts like 'improvisation,' 'soul,' and 'blackness' as forming the outline of a creative, oppositional cultural set within the boundaries of a 'nation to be.'" "*Studios in the Street – Creative Community and Visual Arts*" (Nka Journal of Contemporary African Art, Fall 2011)[7]

I see this all as validating the continuation of the Black artist to further unite our community. AfriCOBRA's impact influenced other artists to practice the power of self-determination, defining/redefining aesthetics, and identifying our authentic and universal cultural values. AfriCOBRA's Kujichagulia, as it continues into this millennium, will seek to remain relevant to the community, or it will cease to be. For it is the goal of African people to survive and to believe "with all our heart in our people, our parents, our teachers, our leaders and the righteousness and victory of our struggle" (Nguzo Saba).[8]

Alain Locke states,

> ...in Africa things can be beautiful and objects of utility at the same time. Their art is never divorced from the vital context of everyday life, the art embodies and vindicates one of the soundest and most basic of aesthetic principles, beauty in use. (Locke, A. Negro Art, Past and Present, J.B. Lyon Press, NY)[9]

The rich history of all that has come before, coupled with the current works of AfriCOBRA, strive towards a common community goal—utilizing the beauty of history and struggle to create a constant and cohesive voice that not only sings, but creates a means and path to "Unite."

NOTES

[1] Lisa DiRocco, "Aesthetics and Culture: A View by Larry Neal," *Drum Magazine* IX (1978), 10.

[2] *Ibid.*

[3] Donaldson, J., "AfriCOBRA Manifesto" *Black World,* (Chicago, 1970.)

[4] Originally published in the exhibition catalogue Afri-Cobra III (Amherst: University of Massachusetts, 1973)

[5] Stephen Henderson "Understanding the New Black Poetry, Black Speech and Black Music as Poetic Reference" (New York, William Morrow & Company, Inc. 1973).

[6] "After the Black Arts Movement" *Nka Journal of Contemporary African Art* 29 (Fall 2011) 63-71.

[7] Benedict Anderson, Imagined Communities, quoted in Daniel Widener, "Studios in the Streets: Creative Community and Visual Arts" (Nka Journal of Contemporary African Art 29, Fall 2011) 40.

[8] Maulana Karenga, "*Kwanzaa: Origin, Concepts, Practice*" (Inglewood, CA Kwaidia Publication, 1977)

[9] Alain Locke, "*Negro Art, Past & Present*" (Washington, DC: Associates in Negro Folk Education, 1936) 97.

DRUM magazine was the student produced Black Literary and Art Publication of the University of Massachusetts at Amherst, of which Nelson Stevens was the faculty advisor. Brother Larry Neal had died suddenly in January of 1981; the spring issue of *DRUM* was dedicated to him, and on the cover was his picture—that picture was my original inspiration for the work. It was to be my portrait of him. I had met Larry Neal through Nelson. The man also loved the drum—I believe Art Blakely was his favorite drummer, but, I could be wrong.

A CONVERSATION WITH KELAN PHIL COHRAN

Useni Eugene Perkins

PERKINS: I understand you were born in Oxford, Mississippi, but spent most of your time in St. Louis when you were young.

COHRAN: Yes, I was born on May 8, 1927 in Oxford, Mississippi and when I was nine I left and came to Troy, Mississippi. I spent four years in Troy where I was introduced to the trumpet. I was also Valedictorian of my class and the principal recommended I be sent to a special school at Lincoln University Laboratory High School. At Lincoln University, I developed as a scholar and began to research the way of life. Although I was a high school student I also attended college where I majored in chemistry.

PERKINS: Why did you come to Chicago to live?

COHRAN: I came to Chicago because of Musicology.

PERKINS: Who were some of the people that impressed you when you first came to Chicago?

COHRAN: When I first came to Chicago, I played with Morris Ellis and Johnny Rivlin. Johnny was red hot and playing at the Corner Bar where they had nightly jam sessions. This was the hottest place in town. I came to Chicago in January of 1953 and lived on the west side until I could get situated. I got a job at Kuppenheimer & Co. clothing manufacturer where they made the lining for their suits.

PERKINS: What influence did Sun Ra have on your music and life?

COHRAN: I was already a composer and musicologist when I worked with Sun Ra between '53 and '61 because that's why I came to Chicago. Sun Ra helped to influence my life

because I was trying to make sense out of stupidity. He pointed out how ridiculous it was that we accept this way of life. I then began to develop my own concept of life and I tried to set an example for others. When I left Sun Ra, I developed a tremendous audience. I would like to write a book on him because he did a lot for me. But my development came when I was young. As a child I had an analytical and critical mind. I was always to myself and my mother used to tell me to go out and play with the other kids. It was not because I didn't like them, it's just that there were many other things I believed were more important.
.

PERKINS: What motivated you to become one of the founders of the Association for the Advancement of Creative Musicians (AACM)?

COHRAN: Well first of all we had undergone a drastic reduction in gigs for musicians and no one spoke up about it. The jobs just vanished. . First, we tried to deal with the problem but it was because of a pattern in City Hall that changed the tax laws for places with bands. The new tax laws made it difficult for club owners to make any money and, therefore, musicians were out of work.

PERKINS: So you got together with Richard Abrams and Steve McCall.

COHRAN: We had all come together because we were musicians. That was our life, we didn't care to do other type of work.. That meant that we had to be in a fertile environment and we come up and say "hey, how are you doing? Why don't we do something tonight? You know a lot of guys and I know a lot of guys, let's get all the guys we know together and do something." Well I said I was a photo technician with the police department for six years and he said okay and we sent out postcards to invite other musicians.. So I brought my group and they brought their group and about 40 guys showed up and these were some of the best musicians in the city. .

PERKINS: Was Lester Bowie there?

COHRAN: Lester wasn't there, He was in St. Louis at that time. Lester was a great musician and came to Chicago in the summer of 1966. But slit with because they went to University of Chicago to Mandell Hall and I did not want to be affiliated with that institution. I told them that was the end of my tenure with the group.. You know you all go your way and I'll go mine way but we would still be friends. So I went my own way and made a positive living with my music.

PERKINS: Some people believe that you did not get any recognition in terms of your contribution in helping develop the sound that Earth, Wind, and Fire had, is that true?

COHRAN: Well most of the members use to play with me. They all went to Crane High School and Crane Jr College. After they won a competition at Notre Dame University, they vowed to always stick together. Satterfield was working for Chess Records which was trying to get hooked into the Black community. I told them that Chess Records was already trying to take our culture and are now spitting in our face. You see I know what it is to oppose these people because they are military and don't know what art is. I have never seen an expression come out of them that I would fully except—maybe except for Judy Garland and Bing Crosby. I had developed a sound that was unique and others wanted to imitate it. Our music was different. Nobody had ever heard it before. When I was a lieutenant in the Nation of Islam in 1962, I would go fishing with Malcolm X. Once I asked him to give me the authority to form a national orchestra for the nation but never got a response from him. I left the nation after that.

PERKINS: Although you play many instruments, especially the trumpet, most people know you from playin the frankiephone. Can you comment on that?

COHRAN: Yes, I dedicated it to Sun Ra because he wanted us to get out of the box. He knew that our biggest problem was that we were thinking along organized lines formed by somebody else. He said we should be digging for our gold so we can enrich the world and it was the most powerful thing we can do. So I redefined my life as music and I redefined music as my life. The first thing I would discover by playing one note all day for a week as much as I could take and went as far as the mind could extend that note. Then I did other things I thought were spectacular. The mind alters so much because of the sound that when you get deep into it- you know we are a sound people. That's one of the doorways to our connection to everything.

PERKINS: How did you become involved in the On The Beach Program during the late sixties, which became the most outstanding cultural program in Chicago?

COHRAN: In the country, in the world. Betty Montgomey should be given all the credit for this program. She had the resources, she had the consciousness, and the generosity to come to people like me, and people like yourself, and ask us what she should do. I thought that was the stroke of the time and I will always give her credit for being the doorway to opening this concept. We had a concert every week and built a tremendous fan base. We had people like Oscar Brown Jr. to perform, Rev. Spencer Jackson and his Family and Darlene Blackburn and her dancers.

PERKINS: After the On The Beach Program what motivated you to start the Afro Arts Theater?

COHRAN: Well I have always been the managerial type and believed we should continue the On The Beach concept and extend it to include all cultural forms, It also provided opportunities for musicians to perform and provide cultural programs that raised the consciousness of our people.

PERKINS: What were some of the reasons the Afro Arts Theater closed?

COHRAN: There were many. First, we had people like Stokely Carmichael, Leroi Jones, Bobby Seale and Dennis Brutus, the South African poet, to speak at the theater, which did not go well with City Hall. Secondly, we began to get building code violations which we felt were bogus and put us in a difficult situation. And we had some internal problems that contributed to our closure.

PERKINS: What are some of the important things you feel came out of the sixties and seventies?

COHRAN: Black people finally began to accept that we are a separate people and have a separate destiny. I think that covers all of it because as long as we were following their program—we would never have our own. The minute we decided to have our own program, the squeakiest wheels got oiled.

PERKINS: So you feel the struggle for integration did not really help Black people.

COHRAN: Yes ultimately! Because in the end we would all have to come together. There was no way we can live with enemies. That's a stupid concept! We would have to find ways to compromise and that's what missing because the level of understanding never gets high enough for people to get to that point.

(Interview – May 16, 2015)

CRISIS IN BLACK THEATER

Useni Eugene Perkins

For many years now, the status of Black theater in Chicago has been unpredictable, fragile, and lacking in leadership and direction. Despite its rich tradition in the arts, Chicago's Black cultural community has been unable to build and sustain a viable theater movement. Although the streets in the Black community are saturated with talent, there exist little evidence today of a theater movement in Chicago, which is structured to absorb this talent into ongoing theater. While there are many Black theater groups in Chicago, there is an absence of a collective ideology to define their goals and purpose. Instead, most of these groups seem to be content in doing their own "thang," and while many give excellent productions, the meager audiences they often perform for leave much to be desired. At a time when Black culture is supposed to be flourishing, Black theater in Chicago continues to flounder as though it is lost in a maze. This is not to suggest that the theater has no roots in Chicago's Black community. On the contrary, we have always had a steady progression of theater groups since the federally sponsored art projects of the middle Thirties. Some groups like the Federal Theater, Abbott Theater, Chicago Negro Arts Theater, Negro Peoples Theater, Skyloft Players, Drama Inc., Center Aisle, Du Bois Theater Guild, Newer Still Productions, Tempo Players and the Penthouse Players have all played an important role in the development of Black theater in Chicago. Of course, some people may argue that many of these groups lacked a "Black Aesthetic" and; therefore, should not be categorized as Black theater. But the rationale for such an argument fails to take into account the social and political climate of the Thirties and Forties, which shaped these groups.

During this period, theater was seen as an amalgamating institution, and most Black participants were trying to prove themselves capable of mastering the craft of European theater rather than building a theater with nationalistic overtones. And we should not overlook the fact that these groups helped to influence the careers of Theodore Ward (Federal Theater and Skyloft Players), Lillian Thompkins (Drama Inc.), Margaret Burroughs (Chicago Negro Arts Theater), Micki Grant (Center Aisle), Richard Durham, Oscar Brown

Jr. and Vernon Jarrett (Du Bois Theater Guild), Walter Lott (Tempo Players), John Houston (Newer Still Productions), David Crowder and Frank London Brown (Penthouse Players) and a host of other people who are active in theater today.

Admittedly, productions such as *The Man Who Came To Dinner* (Tempo Players), *Three Men On A Horse* (Skyloft Players), and (can you imagine) *Jane Eyre* (Drama Inc.) did little to enhance or develop a Black theater ideology based on Black culture, but they did help to provide a training ground for the development of performers, stagehands and directors.

On the other side of the coin, one can get some consolation that a thread of "Black Consciousness" was able to weave itself through this cultural schizophrenia. Theodore Ward's controversial play, *Big White Fog,* had its world premier at the Great Northern Theater in 1938, under the auspices of the Federal Theater. Later, in 1951, the Skyloft Players performed Mr. Ward's *Throw Back* and *Whole Hog or Nothing.* Langston Hughes, who played a prominent role in starting one of Chicago's earliest Black theater groups, the Skyloft Players, had many of his plays performed in Chicago. The Skyloft Players presented his *Sun Do Move,* and the Negro Peoples Theater produced Mr. Hughes' *Even The Dead Arise* and *Don't You Want To Be Free* at the Lincoln Center. The Du Bois Theater Guild, whose founding members included Richard Durham, Vernon Jarrett, Oscar Brown Jr. and Janice Kingslow (who once performed the feature role in *Anna Lucasta,*) was one of the vanguard groups to stress "Black Awareness" in its theater philosophy. Although the groups did produce some plays by white playwrights, the most notable being Clifford Odets' *Waiting For Lefty*, is better remembered for its Destination Freedom series, which emphasized Black achievement and was presented on the radio and in live performances. During the late Fifties the Penthouse Players were presenting plays by David Crowder and Frank London Brown (*This Is Life and Short Ribs*), and did many performances of Conrad Kent Rivers' poetic collage, "To Make A Poet Black." In 1963 the Tempo Players presented "Psalms of Protest," a chronicle of the Black struggle in music and song, which was compiled by Joan (Abena) Brown and Harold Johnson, who later was to direct Channel 11's television series, *Bird Of The Iron Feather.*

For a brief period after "Psalms of Protest," there was a lull in Black theater, and even Chicago's turbulent autumn winds could not arouse any interest in it. This cessation was also due to the fact that many theater people went to Harlem and off-Broadway in hopes of improving their careers. I suppose such an exodus should be anticipated in view of the broader theater opportunities in New York. A rundown of theater people working in New York, and other cities, would, no doubt, reveal that a sizable number of them got their rudimentary training in Chicago.

Black theater received some adrenalin in 1965, when Oscar Brown Jr.'s tantalizing musical, *Summer In The City,* opened at the Harper Theater in Hyde Park. Although the motif of the production had an integrated background, the gut and beauty of it came entirely from Black life. Despite large crowds and excellent reviews, *Summer In The City* was not a financial success, and plans for its revival the following year were cancelled. Two years later Oscar Brown Jr. was to direct members of the Black P Stone Rangers in a musical called *Opportunity, Please Knock,* which enjoyed local success and eventually gained national acclaim when the group traveled to the West Coast and appeared on a national television show. When the group came back to Chicago, a controversy over alleged misuse of funds developed, and what had started out as an enterprising project quickly dissolved. After this abortive venture, Oscar Brown Jr. tried to open a theater for youth, but his plans never materialized. The role Oscar Brown Jr. played in trying to develop Black theater in Chicago deserves more attention than it receives. When one closely inspects the lineage of Black theater in Chicago, the name of Oscar Brown Jr. appears frequently and prominently.

The failure of early Black theater groups to develop an ideology that could serve as a framework for future groups, has been one reason Black theater in Chicago is in its present state of disorganization. New institutions are shaped by tradition and example. The legacy and models that these early groups left did not lend themselves to fostering an ongoing theater movement. Although individuals from some of the groups like Harold Johnson (Tempo Players), John Houston (Newer Still), Edward Copeland (Skyloft Players), Claudia McCormick and Clarence Taylor (Skyloft Players), are sharing their skills and training with young people today; Black theater in Chicago still suffers from the lack of a viable reference and collective organization.

In 1966 a marked change in Black theater began to take place in Chicago. No doubt this resurgence was influenced by the fervor of the Black Power movement, which had been ushered in during the freedom march on Jackson, Mississippi. As a result, the direction of Black theater in Chicago assumed a more militant posture, and some of its principal advocates were indoctrinated in Black nationalism. But because at first the concept of Black Power was not clearly defined, groups began to create their own definitions. And in their eagerness to assert their new-found Blackness, many groups spent more time bickering among themselves than developing structures and goals which could help clarify their confusion. Due to their inter-group squabbling, there was more rhetoric than programs, and more romance than realism.

However, as the mood of the Black community became more intense, the challenge to Black theater became greater. If Black theater was to become a relevant institution, it became apparent that it must relate to the political climate of the Black community. And in the wake of the Black rebellion that scorched the streets of Chicago; artists, writers, musicians and dramatists began to search for ways to politicize their art.

One of the first programs to mirror this new consciousness was called "On The Beach," a cultural project conceived by Mrs. Betty Montgomery House during the summer of 1967. Consisting of poetry, music, dance and drama, "On The Beach" attracted thousands of people who trekked to 63rd on the lake front to see such performers such as, Phil Cohran and the Artistic Heritage Ensemble, the Darlene Blackburn Dancers, Rev. Spencer Jackson Family, special guest artists, and original theater productions directed by Larry Kabaka.

"On The Beach" was financed by Metropolitan YMCA of Chicago which, undoubtedly, saw it as a buffer to pacify the tensions that were brewing in the Black community. Despite the success of the program, the funds for "On The Beach" were stopped after the second year, when the climate in the Black Community became more relaxed. The curtailment of funds by the YMCA was a clear notice to Black groups that they could not rely on benevolent tokenism to finance their programs on a continuing basis. On Chicago's West Side, the House of Umoja, a community operated cultural center, met a similar fate when its funds from the Wieboldt Foundation were not renewed.

The year 1967 also saw the Organization of Black American Culture (OBAC) come into being. The need for such a group was obvious; although interest in Black culture had increased considerably in Chicago, writers, artists and dramatists continued to lack direction and a clarification of the relationship of their art to the community. From its constituency, workshops in art, writing and drama were organized for the purpose of helping each group develop a philosophical frame of reference for its art which then could be functionalized to meet the cultural needs of the Black community. In 1967 Black Art still meant different things to different people. The task of the writer, artist and dramatist became one of synthesizing their agreements and modifying their differences so that they could develop a collective definition of their functions. To some extent the writers and artists were able to accomplish this task, but those who participated in the drama workshop were unable to resolve differences or put into operation any collective programs. Consequently, the artists and writers became the nerve of OBAC and began initiating community based projects. The OBAC artists helped to paint the Wall of Respect, a mural which depicted Black people who had made contributions to the Black community. The writers started holding weekly meetings at the Du Sable Museum of African-American History, until they moved to a converted storefront on 35th Street. Eventually, most of the artists departed (many joined a group called the Coalition of Black Revolutionary Artists—COBRA) and OBAC was left with a group of aspiring young writers. While the artists and writers had organized themselves around common goals and community projects, the people associated with theater continued to bicker between themselves and to grope for direction.

As these events were transpiring, Theodore Ward was formulating plans to open a theater that would "train Black youth and adults in theater craftsmanship as well as provide an outlet for Negro drama, which expresses some vital part of Negro life and spirit." The South Side Center of the Performing Arts (SSCPA) moved into the Louis Theater, a landmark cinema house on 35th Street, in the fall of 1967. On October 6, the SSCPA opened with Mr. Ward's own play, *Our Lan,* a historical drama of the Black man's struggle during Reconstruction. As significant as the occasion was, the SSCPA failed to generate sufficient publicity from the media. As one would expect, the white newspapers ignored it completely, but even the so-called Black newspapers were derelict in their reporting. It was nearly two months before *Our Lan* received one review by a Black critic. Nevertheless, *Our Lan* ran for 10 months (no doubt a record for a Black play in Chicago); and although it encountered many difficulties, the performances were usually excellent.

In an effort to attract a larger and more diversified audience, the SSCPA followed Our Lan with some of the contemporary Black plays which were being ballyhooed as relevant Black theater. Ronald Milner's, *Who's Got His Own* and *The Monster,* met with some success. Then came Ed Bullins' allegorical *Son Come Home* and Bill Harris'; *No Use Cryin',* a poignant drama about Black family life. But these plays failed to draw many people, and SSCPA was destined for oblivion.

Many reasons were given for its closing. Some felt that the SSCPA's location on 35th Street deterred many people from coming to the theater. It is true that the area along 35th Street, where the Louis Theater was located, did not resemble Main Street America. Mr. Ward even admitted that the Louis Theater's location became threatening to the white actors who performed there. Also, the Illinois Institute of Technology, which had played an important role in the beginning, withdrew its resources because of environmental phobia. But I feel that the major reasons were the lack of participation from the Black middle class and the small support of the Black media. Although many middle-class Blacks lived within walking distance of the Louis Theater, in the integrated South Commons, Prairie Shores and Lake Meadows apartments, they avoided the SSCPA as if it had the bubonic plague. And the performance of the Black media was inexcusable. Both the Johnson Publishing Company and the Chicago Defender were located close to the Louis Theater, but neither took time to feature an article about it.

The closing of the SSCPA was just another in a long line of catastrophes that have impeded the progress of Black theater in Chicago. However, when the Louis Theater did reopen, it housed an institution that the Black community always finds time to support, the Christian Church.

Two months after the arrival of the SSCPA, the Affro Arts Theater opened its doors on a bleak evening in December. The Affro Arts Theater had been an outgrowth of the "On

The Beach" program and was the brainchild of Phil Cohran. The opening of the Affro Arts Theater was met with great enthusiasm, and the theater quickly became the hub of Black Art in Chicago. Besides the weekly appearances of Phil Cohran and the Artistic Heritage Ensemble, performers such as Oscar Brown Jr., Ronald Kirk, Olatunji, the Ghana Dance Ensemble and Josephine Baker graced its stage. Although the Affro Arts Theater did not feature drama plays such as, Jimmy Garrett's *We Own The Night*, Marvin X's *Take Care Of Business* and the Rev. Spencer Jackson's *A New Day* were performed there.

For two years the Affro Arts Theater was the most active cultural center in the Black community, but in 1969, it became beset with a series of problems that it was unable to overcome. Community attendance began dropping. Internal disputes between those who operated it became immutable, and city officials began to harass the theater for alleged building code violations. Phil Cohran eventually departed, and the Pharaohs, who dropped the name Artistic Heritage Ensemble, took over the distraction of the theater. The result of all this culminated in the demise of the Affro Arts Theater, which still stands today at Oakwood Boulevard and Drexel Boulevard, as a tarnished memory of what Black theater used to be.

Because the SSCPA and the Affro Arts Theater closed down at approximately the same time, one might speculate that these undertakings were ill timed. While this might be true, each theater had its own profile and did not seem to be in direct competition with the other. Even though there did exist ideological differences between the two theaters, it would have been interesting to see what would have taken place if the skills and talents of both groups had complemented each other more.

While the Affro Arts Theater and the South Side Center of the Performing Arts were having their problems, another theater group located in the Parkway Community Center was also struggling to remain open. The original Parkway Community Center, located at 51st Street and Dr. M. L. King Drive, had been the home of the Skyloft Players; but after it relocated to 67th and Eberhart, it lacked facilities to continue theater. However, when it became affiliated with the Hull House Associates, a new theater was built and its drama program continued. But as an extension of the white-orientated Hull House Associates' Theater program, the Parkway Community Center found itself doing such plays as *Call Me By My Rightful Name, Sponomo, Slow Dance On The Killing Ground, The Laundromat,* and *Tiger Tiger Burning Bright,* all written by white playwrights. Finally, Hull House made some token concessions and Parkway did William Wellington Mackey's *Requiem For Brother X,* James Baldwin's *Amen Corner* and Imamu Amiri Baraka's *The Slave.*

Also, as an added token, Hull House opened an Underground Theater in the basement of one of the apartments in the Ikes-Dearborn Homes, a housing project of the Chicago Housing Authority. But neither the atmosphere nor the plays presented there were appealing enough to attract many people and the venture did not last too long. And when Hull House withdrew its support, it also took its electrical equipment, thereby making it impossible to keep the theater open.

Since the administration of Hull House had never fully involved Blacks in policy-making roles, the Parkway Community Center remained a white artifact that lacked understanding of the Black theater. And when many of its white patrons became insecure about coming to Parkway after the summer rebellions, attendance dropped sharply and finally the theater closed. Thereafter, various Black groups attempted to rejuvenate interest in theater at Parkway but failed due to the shortage of funds, disorganization, and, more acutely, the lack of an operating philosophy.

After a two year drought, theater had returned to Parkway. In 1972, the X (Experimental)-Bag reopened the theater in hopes of providing the Black community with relevant plays that would reflect a range of themes from the Black Experience. Under the capable guidance of veteran performers Clarence Taylor and Claudia McCormick, the X-Bag has already presented two excellent productions: Lonne Elder III's Ceremonies In *Dark Old Men* and Ronald Milner's *Who's Got His Own.* And in each production the X-Bag introduced new talent, which is always a good sign for a developing theater group. The future of X-Bag will not only depend upon the qualities of its productions and the dedication of its members, but also its ability to generate greater interest and support from the Black community, two things which Black theater in Chicago has not even come close to achieving.

Between 1969 and 1971, Black theater in Chicago was quite fragmented. John Houston and his Newer Still Productions did manage to perform Douglas Turner Ward's *Happy Ending* and Langston Hughes' *Simply Heavenly* on occasions, and one of the Chicago Park District's drama groups would do its annual re-run of Lorraine Hansberry's *Raisin In The Sun.* Oscar Brown Jr.'s production of *Big Time Buck White* drew mixed reactions, and an original musical/drama by folksinger Ira Rogers, "To Reach A Circle," met with some success during its short run. And for a brief period, Rodney Graham's New Era Theater produced some of the most stimulating drama to come out of Chicago's Black community in years. Its production of Ed Bullins', *In New England Winter,* was a fascinating theater experience. Also, the New Era Theater's weekly presentations at the Afram Gallery were beautiful vignettes of Black life. Another group, Destination Blacks Unlimited, was also able to provide the Black community with some refreshing drama during its brief existence.

But these were only isolated productions which focused on individual achievements, and they did not stress a collective theater consciousness that was sorely needed to stimulate greater interest in Black theater.

Then in 1969, the Kuumba Workshop was founded by Val Gray Ward, a dramatist who has been called by Gwendolyn Brooks "a little black stampede." For the past year Kuumba has been the only Black theater group to offer continuous weekly performances. In view of the status of Black theater in Chicago, this is, indeed, an achievement. During this period it has presented Ted Shine's *Contribution,* Joseph White's *The Leader,* Alice Childress' *Mojo, Wine In The Wilderness,* and *The Image Makers* (by this author), a satire on the current super heroes in Black movies.

After each performance, Kuumba presents a stunning ritual entitled "Destruction or Unity," which features music, poetry and dance. The rituals have had a great impact on audiences and, perhaps, come closer to expressing Black life than most plays. Kuumba, which means "creativity" in Swahili, takes great pride in being a "cleansing force" in the Black community, and has performed in: prisons, churches, community centers, schools, as well as given benefits for the Republic of North Africa, CORE, Afro American Patrolmen's League, Provident Hospital, Du Sable Museum of African American History, and many community organizations.

At present, Kuumba is performing at the South Side Community Art Center, one of the Black community's oldest cultural institutions, but is seeking a larger and more permanent facility which could be converted into a resident Black theater. But even if it is successful in accomplishing this goal, Kuumba will still be faced with the problem of generating greater public support of Black theater. For despite its being one of the most active Black theater groups in Chicago, Kuumba, like the others, still finds itself performing to small audiences.

Other groups who are trying to improve the image of Black theater in Chicago are Ebony Talent, Inc., TAIFA, Black Heritage Theatrical Players, and Unify Humanity Through Cultural Creativity. Ebony Talent's production of N. R. Davidson's *El Hajj Malik* was one of the highlights in Black theater during 1972. Directed by the talented Harold Johnson, this poetic drama of Malcolm X's life was presented at a number of colleges and high schools. At present, Ebony Talent has only a touring group but is making plans for establishing a resident theater group, drama workshops and a children's theater.

The TAIFA Builders (Swahili for Nation) was formed as the result of some of its members participating in the SSCPA and later the Independence Professional Artists groups. Consisting primarily of young people, the group is attempting to bring to the community the most contemporary forms of Black theater. An example of this was seen in its production of Joseph Walker's *Ododo*, a musical epic in two acts, at the Lincoln Center in February. Other plays which the group has performed include Sonia Sanchez's *Sister Sonji*, Ben Caldwell's *Militant Preacher* and Joseph White's *Ole Judge Moses.* TAIFA's director, Pemon Rami, is very critical of the Black theater scene in Chicago and feels that too many groups have resigned themselves to performing traditional plays and do not put enough energy into promotion and publicity. Unify Humanity Through Cultural Creativity (U.H.C.C.) is a newly formed group that has yet to build a firm base but hopes to focus on ritualistic drama that can blend the various forms of Black Art into a cohesive spiritual experience.

Rev. Spencer Jackson, founder and director of the Black Heritage Theatrical Players, has an impressive list of theater credits. Once the pastor of a church and a choir director, Rev. Jackson and his family, all talented performers, have used their religious background to bring a unique dimension to the Black theater. A prolific author, Rev. Jackson has written two plays, *New Day* and *Come Home,* which have been produced in Chicago.

The most crippling force impeding the development of a strong Black theater in Chicago is the lack of unity and coordination among theater groups. In 1970 there was an effort made to hold a Chicago Black Theater Conference, which, hopefully, would serve as a conduit for exchanging information and developing collective strategies. But after a series of unproductive meetings, the conference was discarded when some participants suggested that they apply for funds from the Department of Human Resources. Naturally the funds never were provided. Also, many of Chicago's theater personalities did not participate in these meetings. Actually, the conference needed few funds to achieve its goals, only the willingness of brothers and sisters to come together around a common problem.

An example of Umoja (unity) was exemplified at a Kwanza Theater Festival held last December. At this "Celebration of Black Life," over 20 groups participated in a two-day festival; including the North Chicago Cultural Workshop, which featured every aspect of Black theater. What dampened the beauty of this event was the few people who attended. The small attendance could be attributed to many factors, but the failure to properly promote and publicize the festival was, undoubtedly, the most flagrant cause. And because it was held on the West Side of Chicago, at Providence St. Mel High School, the "plantation mentality" of some brothers and sisters kept them from wholeheartedly supporting it. Nonetheless, the Kwanza Theater Festival did demonstrate that Black theater groups in Chicago could come together for a common purpose, something which has been missing in the past.

The Black community must also share the blame for the plight of Black theater in Chicago. None of Chicago's so-called civil-rights groups, social clubs, fraternities or business institutions have shown any real concern for Black theater. Yet some of these same groups will sponsor theater parties for downtown theaters and dinner playhouses. While Black theater should try to relate to the total Black community, it cannot do so without a financial base. And, for the most part, this base must be provided by those who are most capable of doing it, the Black middle class. When one takes into account that most Black theater groups in Chicago depend upon volunteers and few performers are ever paid, the Black community should at least, try to re-enforce this type of dedication and commitment.

Even the colleges in Chicago ignore the need to develop Black theater. Only one school, Malcolm X Community College, has attempted to develop an ongoing Black Theater program. Under the artistic guidance of Ulyssis Duke Jenkins, an associate professor in fine arts, Malcolm X has presented a number of Black plays. The other colleges continue to do traditional white plays, although many have larger Black student enrollments and are located in Black communities. An example of this overt toadying to the white aesthetic can be seen in the Kennedy-King College's Professional Drama Guild 1973 scheduled list of plays which includes *Allegro, She Stoops To Conquer, Come Back Little Sheba* and *Dracula.* This is an insult to the Black community despite the Guild's claim of being "America's FIRST TRULY INTEGRATED Professional Company…" We should all know by now that "integration" only means Black subordination.

The future of Black theater in Chicago remains grim. While some cities—New York, Detroit, Newark and Cleveland—are trying to support Black theater, the potential of Black theater in Chicago remains in a retarded state. When one gleans through the various Black Cultural magazines, Chicago's Black theater is seldom mentioned or rarely receives a footnote. Of course, there is Black theater talent in Chicago, and there are dedicated Black theater groups. But talent and groups are not the only elements that make theater. Black theater must be expressed in terms of some operational philosophy which gives it being and purpose. Just to prefix "Black" to something doesn't define its true substance. The Irish Theater did not come into being simply because it was Irish. It came into existence because it was a living extension of Irish culture, and was able to develop Irish playwrights, like Sean O'Casey and J. M. Synge, who reflected Irish culture in their plays. Yet Black theater in this country, to give a broader example, is so diffused that we find ourselves imitating white culture in such maligned productions as *Hello Dolly* and *Golden Boy*. And even many of our plays by Black playwrights leave much to be desired in that many tend to be only cracked mirrors of the so-called pathology in our communities.

What can be done to remedy this situation in Chicago? The task will not be simple, but I've attempted to list a few suggestions:

1. Form a theater consortium which would consist of representatives from all Black theater groups and interested brothers and sisters;
2. Publish a monthly bulletin about Black theater, listening plays, events, performers, etc.;
3. Develop better means for promoting and publishing plays;

4. Seek support of Black businesses, social clubs and community organizations;
5. Get local stores to serve as ticket centers and to distribute publicity;
6. Establish joint projects between the different theater groups;
7. Avoid repetition of plays and do more plays by community based playwrights;
8. Organize workshops for playwrights which can also perform readings of their plays;
9. Develop Black critics who are sensitive to Black theater; and
10. Create a collective theater philosophy.

The late Lorraine Hansberry's prize-winning play, *Raisin In The Sun,* used Chicago's Black community as its landscape. It is my hope that this same landscape will someday be cultivated to raise the status of Black theater so that it, too, can bask in the sun.

GWENDOLYN BROOKS: NOURISHED BY CHICAGO

Haki R. Madhubuti

There are races and there is the race, questionable calls and the call, commitments and the committed. Gwendolyn Brooks entered my young life at a time when I needed to see a Black artist, preferably a Black poet of stature, meaning, melody, music and muscle who, under any circumstances would not run from the initial and critical call to be one's self and to best represent that self and selfhood in her or his art. Brooks, Gwendolyn Brooks, provided for me that opening, that promise, that "yes" to what, we younger poets of that Black period needed—not a question mark, but the organic energy which served as a catalyst for the emerging Black Arts Movement. Her work was part of the initial impetus that aided cultural workers to create an unambiguous Black aesthetic, a Black journey, course, and signature, i.e. Black Arts.

It can be stated without contradiction, that Gwendolyn Brooks was one of a very few iconic American-born poets who lived to experience, enjoy and sometimes relax in a national, multicultural, multilayered community of non-poets, poets, people and institutions (schools, colleges, universities, museums, libraries, community centers, bookstores, houses of worship, and local, state and federal structures) who truly appreciated and loved her and her poetry.

As we celebrate her centennial year, her work lives on in the many genres of poetry, children's books, fiction, essays, and interviews of the first Black person to win the Pulitzer Prize (the nation's highest and most prestigious literary award). Today, we find ourselves still amazed at the quality and expansive output of this major American poet. In this centennial year, Ms. Brooks' work takes on new meaning and carries greater weight than all the oceans and mountains combined if they could also be read as literature. She can also be defined by her many honors other than the Pulitzer such as: Consultant to the Library of Congress (the last consultant before the honor was renamed Poet Laureate of the United States), the Poet laureate of the State of Illinois, NEH Jefferson Lectureship, over seventy honorary degrees, distinguished professorships at multiple colleges and universities with numerous schools, university centers and libraries named in her honor tracking her poetic journey across this vast land. Her history also includes multiple volumes of poetry, criticism, and biographies, detailing her place in African American and American letters. The most recent book to be published honoring the life of Ms. Brooks is the highly-recommended *Seasons: A Gwendolyn Brooks Experience*, edited by Nora Brooks Blakely and Cynthia Walls with illustrations by Jan Spivey Gilchrist.

One of Ms. Brooks' major contributions to American literature is her role as one of the few precursors and participants in the Black Arts Movement, that Black literary explosion that helped changed the national conversation and position on race and Black culture (1965-1976). Her poetry and many acts of personal kindness had already positioned her as a key resource and poet, like Langston Hughes, who understood what it meant to be a Black artist and not an artist who happens to be Black. She did not wear her race/color on her sleeve. She carried it in her heart, and wrote it on the page. Her poetry from *A Street in Bronzeville* (1945) to *In Montgomery* (2003) represents a Black linguistic exploration in a language that not only connects, but easily places her in a universe reserved for the very best of the nation's poets.

She was consistently and lovingly "nourished" on the South Side of Chicago. She embraced young people and especially, children of all cultures. She had always lived among her own people. Her respect for all artists and their art is unparalleled. She had stated that "art is refining and evocative translation of the materials of the world."

For all of her life, she and her family lived modestly with careful thought as to how she uses her resources. That she supported independent Black institutions, art institutions, libraries, and individual artists is well known. Much of this is in the furtherance of "Art." She writes in the poem of the same name:

> Art can survive
> the last bugle of the last bureaucrat, can survive
> the inarticulate choirs of makeiteers,
> the stolid in stately places,
> all flabby gallantries, all that will fall....
>
> We hail
> what heals and sponsors and restores.

She lived for her work and for us. She left Harper & Row in 1969 to publish with the upstart and revolutionary publishing house, Broadside Press of Detroit. This single act was viewed by many young Black poets as a gigantic statement and affirmation of support and commitment, which cemented her place in the history of independent Black institution-building in the nation. She would go on to publish with Third World Press, and briefly start her own companies, Brooks Press and one named after her father, The David Company.

We must never forget that it was Ms. Brooks' poetry that propelled her into never-to-be-forgotten land, placed her without her permission among the finest poets/writers of any generation anywhere. She was our loud and quiet language-maker.

We will always remember her somewhere between brilliant and genius in the neighborhood of great and unforgettable, as our unique word giver and kind heart. She lived among us in a time of unwellness and deep need, while refusing first-class passage and caviar. She remained attached to her language, her people, and all children. She was our kindness and there will be no final words.

Finally (I know that this is a fact) her poetry and her life actions over fifty-five years intimately touched more poets, people, children, and the non-poetry reading public than any other writer/poet of her generation. She was not trapped at any level by the multiple layers of accommodation, fame, or fortune. She emerged as our able witness and deep participant, and translated our many troubles into the language of *can-do*. Published here, is one of the two extended interviews I did with Gwendolyn Brooks; it was published in *Black Books Bulletin 2* in 1974.

BLACK BOOKS BULLETIN INTERVIEWS GWENDOLYN BROOKS

"There is indeed a new black today. He is different from any the world has known. He's a tall-walker. Almost firm. By many of his own brothers he is not understood. And he is understood by no white. Not the wise white; not the schooled white; not the kind white. Your least pre-requisite toward an understanding of the new black is an exceptional Doctorate which can be conferred only upon those with the proper properties of bitter birth and intrinsic sorrow. I know this is infuriating, especially to those professional Negro-understanders, some of them very kind, with special portfolio, special savvy. But I cannot say anything other, because nothing other is the truth." These words, this precise utterance is Gwendolyn Brooks today, is Gwendolyn Brooks post-1967, a quiet force cutting through the real dirt with new and energetic words of uncompromising richness that are to many people unexpected, but welcomed by millions.

Gwendolyn Brooks is an African poet living and writing in America whose work for the most part has been "conditioned" by her experiences in America. By acknowledging her Africanness, her blackness, she reverses the trend of being defined by the negative to her own definition in the positive. She, in effect, gives direction in her new definition which, if it does nothing else, forces her reader to question that definition.

To question is the beginning of empowerment. Why does Gwendolyn Brooks call herself an African? Almost for the same reason that Europeans call themselves Europeans, that Chinese call themselves Chinese, that Russians call themselves Russian, that Americans call themselves Americans—people find a sense of being, a sense of worth and substance with being associated with land. Associations with final root gives us not only a history (which did not start and will not end in this country), but proclaims us heirs to a future and it is best when we, while young, find ourselves talking, acting, living and reflecting in accordance with that future, which is best understood in the context of the past.

Characteristically she has said that

> My aim, in my next future, is to write poems that will somehow successfully "call" (see Imamu Baraka's "SOS") all, black people: black people in taverns, black people in alleys, black people in gutters, schools, offices, factories, prisons, the consulate; I wish to reach black people in pulpits, black people in mines, on farms,

> on thrones; Not always to "teach"—I shall wish often to entertain, to illumine. My newish voice will not be an imitation of the contemporary young black voice, which I so admire, but an extending adaptation of today's Gwendolyn Brook's voice.

Gwendolyn Brooks is the example for us all, a consistent monument in the real, unaware of the beauty and strength she has radiated. Above all, she is the continuing storm that walks with the English language as lions walk with Africa. Her pressure is above boiling, cooking new food for our children to grow on.

BBB: Gwen, we would like to start off by asking you a question that has probably been asked of you quite a bit, but we believe that it is fundamental in our understanding of you and your work. Why do you write?

BROOKS: That question has been asked many times before and I've sort of divided my writing life into three parts. I write in the first department which started at the age of seven, or so my mother tells me, and ends about the age of thirteen, to "express myself." I wrote about dandelions and clouds, love and enemies, friends, anything that seemed sort of nice around me and my environs. This department ended about when I was thirteen when I went to Hyde Park high school here in Chicago, which was then chiefly white, and that was my first study exposure to prejudice because of race. I then wrote a poem, a sonnet which I named "To the Hinderer", and this was the beginning of my integration stage. I began to sense that if we screamed loudly enough and showed how truly wonderful we were, that sooner or later they would open up their arms and embrace us and invite us to share the feast. I kept believing that until 1957. This was the third department of my writing activity. And then because of the new young influences, Don L. Lee chiefly among them, I began to understand that Black Afrikans should be concerned about Blackness. And I believe that with Don and other young writers, that Black poetry is written by Blacks, about Blacks, to Blacks. That is where I am now and expect to stay.

BBB: Do you see anything in the present situation of Afrikans here in this country and on the continent that would cause you to think that we are likely to endure the future?

BROOKS: That we are likely to endure the future?

BBB: That is in terms of Black people surviving. It seems that the greatest killer in the Black community is education and drugs. And of course the crime rates are very high. And we understand the reasons for this, but what strengths do you see within the context of our community, which will allow us to survive the last quarter of the century?

BROOKS: What strengths do I see within the community? I wouldn't want to be that specific, but I feel that Blacks are very strong, look what we have survived already. And I think that we ourselves collectively will develop answers for these threats, these oppressions. Perhaps we will have to be a little harder on ourselves then we have been. Perhaps from somewhere there will have to come a force that will really have to deal unmercifully with those elements.

BBB: Would you like to say a little bit about the workshop that you ran in the late sixties and early seventies. Especially the ones that you conducted with the Blackstone Rangers?

BROOKS: I had only one workshop which as soon as the older people joined it was no longer called a workshop. I started it because I was excited by Oscar Brown Jr.'s show *Opportunity Please Knock*, and I asked him were there some writers among those people, and if so, I would like to start a workshop for them. And a few of them came. That was a very interesting experience. They looked at me, I looked at them. I remember one who has kept up with me pretty much until the present; Peanuts, Richard Washington. He had a real interest in some of the younger Rangers and tried to be a good influence among them. But when the older people came, college students and community organizers, well, we became just a bunch of friends. We left the first Presbyterian Church and started meeting at my house where we are sitting now, this very day. And we had some very exciting times. They made it very plain that they did not want me to "teach" them anything about the sonnet form or such." Some of them feel a little different now and I don't know whether I should be happy about that or not. But, as I say, we were friends that talked about our poetry and read our poetry to each other. And also talked about what was going on in society. They taught me many things that I had not known before.

BBB: In keeping with that, what are some of the major changes in your life that have taken place over the last decade?

BROOKS: Over the last decade, yes. Well, this is 1974. Well, my real changes came in 1967 when I first met these young people who could really see what was happening all around them and were kind enough to let me know too. They recommended books to me, that I read. Such books as *Report From Iron Mountain,* of the possibility and the desirability of peace, and *The Rich and the Super Rich and The Choice,* which are books that I am always recommending to people now. Also the *Autobiography of Malcolm X* really influenced my changes.

BBB: One of the significant acts that we have noticed with you has been the consistent helping of Black institutions. We know that you are on the Board of Directors of the *Institute of Positive Education* and that you left *Harper and Row* for a Black publishing company in Detroit, *Broadside Press.* Would you comment on that?

BROOKS: Yes, I didn't leave Harper and Row because they were doing anything to me. Or I didn't know of anything that they were doing to me that was of an evil nature. But I had been telling young poets to support the Black presses. Whenever I went to colleges to visit or to read my poetry I would tell them that this was something that they should feel as a commitment. And it seemed strange for myself to continue with a white publishing company when I was giving this advice.

BBB: How have you found it working with Broadside Press? I know that one of the problems you had with Harper and Row was that your books were not widely distributed in the Black community. And we found also that in many cases they were not distributed outside of the continental U.S.A. In terms of distribution, quality of the books and production, do you see any qualitative difference between Harper and Row and Broadside Press?

BROOKS: Well, about distribution, who would know better than BBB. Of course Black publishers have an immense problem with distribution. I think that we will have to continue to work with it, but there doesn't seem to me to be the great, great worry that some of us have felt it to be. I think that what a lot of young people told me in the late sixties was true. They believed that we should stress brotherhood and a caring for each other. And I think that Black writers, for the time being at least, will have to give up the idea of becoming millionaires, and famous and profiting at any level. They may even have to let go of a few dollars that they have to aid these presses so that they can attract future writers.

BBB: So, essentially you are saying that Black writers should aid institutions, especially publishing institutions, and that they cannot hopefully, at this time, live off the returns that a book has made.

BROOKS: Indeed no! You are asking me how I have found working with Broadside Press and I can include Third World Press there too. It's been an ideal experience. It really has been a working together.

BBB: In reading *Report From Part One*, the first part of your autobiography, it seems that you constantly revealed that an important part of your life involved conflict between you, the writer, and the individual family member. Maybe conflict is the wrong term, but you found that preserving the sacredness of your family is very important. How do you reserve the conflict between the artist and the family, if there is one? Are those three separate entities or are they one.

BROOKS: We are talking about the family in the private sense, or the family in the extended sense?

BBB: We are talking about the family in the private sense.

BROOKS: Well, with many Blacks there are going to be problems, but I think that that is just part of our growth. And those of us who are committed to Blackness and to the future and the nourishment of Blackness will have to strive straight ahead in spite of problems here and there along the way. But we are all living in an interesting and dangerous time and we can expect problems, problems that are sometimes painful; sometimes deadly. The family, actually, is a major source of strength.

BBB: How do you propose to deal with the problems? For in many cases we talk about the "writer" or the "artist" being torn apart inside because of the individual or personal family problems. What would you suggest for the young writers in terms of dealing with his or her personal problems?

BROOKS: Write about the.

BBB: We know that your work has changed greatly. When I say greatly we are talking about in terms of style. In the sense that there seems to be more of the quicker, sharper poems. It seems that these shorter and quicker poems communicate more effectively than the longer works. Also, we would like to know could you possibly say now your work would have developed differently, if you had read something like Chancellor Williams' *The Destruction of Black Civilization* as a young girl?

BROOKS: I wish I might have had such an opportunity as a young girl, as a young woman even ten years ago. But about changes in my style, I have not yet achieved the changes that I want. I was fascinated about seven years ago, when we used to go out, Don and me and the others, to taverns and other places and read our poetry. And I've always felt that it was most important that these people who made taverns their home still were able to find Don's poetry relevant and to sit there among the drinks and enjoy it and learn from it. If I had read some of the sonnets that I had written, the intricate and embroidered sonnets, I'm sure that they would have thrown their drinks at me. And I want to develop a style that will appeal to these people, the people who make the street their customary habitat, people in prisons. And of course I have to be very careful about including prisoners, because some our best work is coming from prisons. Where people are at last having time to sit down and think over their lives and then to reflect, meditate and develop their thoughts in poetry and exciting fiction. This new style, I guess, should be rather short, because most people in this rushy time are not going to take the time to sit down and read an epic. One exception to that might be a long poem such as Okot p'Bitek's *Song of Lawino*, which is easy to get into and easy to stay into.

BBB: Speaking of writers, the Afrikan writer as an example, we found that out of the sixties, there was a wave of young writers producing, and in many cases functioning within the context of Black publishing houses. And we found that in some cases that these writers were able to attract a following, but we find also that you had already established a following in the context of the Black and white literary world now leaving a major house and coming to a small Black publishing house and we found at the same time other "Black" writers leaving Black houses going to the white publishing houses. What do you think about that?

BROOKS: I deplore it of course. I think that these people have decided that they want "success" in the American send of the word. They want to turn out pretty little books. Although our own books are beautiful, they expect to make money which is an illusion. I certainly never made money as a publishee of Harper and Row. And I began with them in 1945. I even published a novel there, *Maude Martha,* which I'm going to begin a brief sequel to this summer, Broadside Press will bring it out, but it's going to be very short. So, I'm very sorry that these people have wandered away and I hope that they will come back. Now I realize that Black publishers have some problems too. Some of these folks are saying that, well, we can't get published by Black publishers. I think that there is an answer to that and that is that we need more Black publishing companies. So instead of going to white companies I suggest that a few of them might get together and start yet another Black publishing company that is urgently needed.

BBB: You were in Africa a few years ago. Did your return home leave a mark on your future work: If so, how? And do you plan to return again soon?

BROOKS: This summer, I'm going to West Africa. I went to East Africa in 1971 and I'm sorry that the only literary product from that trip was the chapter, "African Fragment," in my autobiography. I do expect some day to write some poems and when I go to West Africa, I'm certainly going to keep a day by day diary from which poems and other things might come.

BBB: What countries do you plan to visit in West Africa?

BROOKS: Ghana. I think only Ghana.

BBB: What are your plans for future work, novels, novellas; you mentioned a small novel among others. What about biographical essays, what about political or literary essays? What ae you working on now?

BROOKS: I just finished a tiny book of poems called Beckoning, some of the poems in there are an attempt at the new style we were talking about before. No essays, I plan to concentrate on poetry and fiction.

BBB: Are you your own worst critic?

BROOKS: I think so.

BBB: In terms of your future work, do you plan on publishing any essay – collection of essays?

BROOKS: 'm really not brilliant enough to bring out a book of essays.

BBB: What about literary reviews?

BROOKS: I've stopped writing reviews many years ago for that very reason. I think that people that write reviews should know about everything, should have read just about everything. And neither is true about myself.

BBB: You are now the editor of an annual publication called the *Black Position.* How has it been doing and what do you see as the future for it? What is coming out in the next issue?

BROOKS: I don't think in terms of how it has been doing. I'm very happy about it. It has some excellent essays in it by the real Black thinkers of today, including Dudley Randall, Hoyt Fuller, Lerone Bennett, Don Lee, and this upcoming issue is going to feature a twenty-eight page interview with Chancellor Williams, by George Kent. George Kent is interviewing him and has written an essay on the book, *Destruction of Black Civilization.* And it also features a long essay that I think is most provocative, and it's going to get letters, by Saundra Towns, and it's called "The Black Woman as Whore: the Genesis of the Myth." I think lots of people will write letters.

BBB: When is that issue coming out?

BROOKS: In just a couple of weeks. We are waiting for page proofs. It also contains a chapter from Willie Keriopestile's autobiography.

BBB: Who of the young writers today are moving and functioning as you see it in a correct direction?

BROOKS: I'm sorry that you asked me that question because it's very difficult for me to say much on that score. Suffice it to say that if you are thinking about successors to Don L. Lee, these people who came up along at his time. I can't name any. Among others I like a lot of the work of Lucille Clifton. I think she is gathering more and more subscribers. I'm always meeting people who are asking if I've read her books. I admire and respect Audrey Ward. Her work many Black people find exceedingly difficult. And so a lot of our people are not going to buy her books. But she's an excellent poet

BBB: What about some of the writers that came out of the sixties in terms of their production? What about Etheridge Knight?

BROOKS: Etheridge Knight as you know has a new book, *Belly Song.* I admire it, I admire a good deal of it, but I prefer *Poems From Prison.*

BBB: What about Mari Evans?

BROOKS: Oh yes, she's one of our best poets. She writes in a way that people who wouldn't dream of paying ten dollars for a book of poetry can relate to and would buy the book. And, she too publishes with a Black publisher, Third World Press, I believe.

BBB: What about Sonia Sanchez?

BROOKS: Sonia is experimenting in feeling here and there, and I don't know just what she's going to come up with, but just now she is publishing simpler kinds of poems. She seems to be very much interested in love songs. She says that she wants to write an epic. She's good.

BBB: What about Imamu Baraka?

BROOKS: I don't think that anybody can speak for him, because he changes constantly and I understand that he isn't doing much writing now. So I don't know just what his present status is.

BBB: Nikki Giovanni?

BROOKS: She is young and I believe that she will have many changes in her life—I have in mine—she isn't nearly fifty-six, so we'll just have to wait and see what happens in the future.

BBB: Michael Harper?

BROOKS: Michael Harper is an excellent writer, and an excellent poet, one who really knows language and knows what to do with it. My favorite poem of his is, and this will tip you off I suppose to the kind of thing that I like, "The Algiers Motel Incident."

BBB: What about Ishmael Reed?

BROOKS: I really don't feel qualified to say a good deal bout Ishmael Reed because I haven't read much of his work. I have read some of his poetry and I consider it good. And he too, like Michael Harper, is an excellent manipulator of language. I think that these people will be doing exciting things in the future.

BBB: Much of the major writing that came out of the sixties in terms of Black people was published first in the *Liberator, Soul Book, Black World, Essence* and *Ebony*. What do you see in terms of the future of Black magazines and the media?

BROOKS: You left *Journal of Black Poetry* and *Black Scholar.* These, along with *Black World* and *Black Collegian.* Though I haven't read *Black Collegian* for quite some time, are my favorites. Of course, everybody reads *Ebony* and what others did you mention?

BBB: *Essence, Liberator* and *Soul Book.*

BROOKS: I think everybody buys or turns over the pages of *Essence* on the stand. It is said that when *Liberator* and *Soul Book* did live that they were very important. My interest in a Black magazine is that its focus be Black and for my magazine, *The Black Position*, I'm interested in stating and featuring the *Black position.*

BBB: What do you think that position is? What would you say to somebody who said what do you mean by Black?

BROOKS: Well, my stress is on Black unity so I favor those things that create and sustain Black unity.

BBB: When Maulana Karenga talks about Black unity, he talks about not only color but culture and consciousness. And we find today that in many cases Black people here are trying to regain their culture which gives them a sense of identity, purpose and direction. And on the other hand you find that some of the elders steadfastly stay with the old terminology. To the young, Afrikan and Black mean the same thing. And of course the older generation still uses negro. What do you say to a person who continues to use a term such as negro, which undoubtedly has been proven to many of the young to be not only disgusting but insulting and degrading, and of course is a term that defines us from somebody else's frame of reference.

BROOKS: I agree with that. I deplore the word negro, colored and all the rest of that stuff, but when you mention the elders, may I say that many of the younger are going back to where some of us were some years ago. And I find this most upsetting. And a lot of the young women who wore naturals for many years are now straightening their hair. And many of them are using the work negro themselves. And their emphasis is on "America" and all things "American." They are interested in money and fancy clothes. I shouldn't say fancy clothes, I should say American clothes, because many of them have turned their back on anything Black and Afrikan.

BBB: You have of course met and talked with and, at one level have been friends with the last generation of writers: John Killens, James Baldwin, Margaret Danner and Langston Hughes. For example, John O. Killens and Langston Hughes we know have helped many young writers. Could you comment on your association with Langston Hughes?

BROOKS: I met Langston Hughes when I was sixteen. When I went to Metropolitan Community Church to show him some him some of my poems at the behest of my mother who accompanied me and saw to it that I did this. He was most kind and read the poems right there after his reading and told me that I had talent and that I should keep writing. Later I met him again because he came to a poetry workshop that a reader on the staff of *Poetry Magazine* had started at the Southside Community Art Center. Her name was Inez Cunningham Stark. And he attended one of the meetings people who belonged to this group were, Bill Couch, Margaret Burroughs, Fern Gayden, Margaret Cunningham, who is now Margaret Danner, and Edward Bland. Langston Hughes was mostly excited about the work that we were reading and he predicted a beautiful future for all of us. Later on still, I gave a party for him when I lived at 623 sixty-third street and there were about seventy-five people or so crowded into our little two room kitchenette, and nobody had a better time than Langston Hughes who was real "folk." Never any airs or pomposities from him. And as you say, he has helped a great many young people. Showing interest in their work and encouraging them.

BBB: Many young writers see you as you saw Langston Hughes, in terms of giving direction and aiding in many ways, in terms of helping them get published and financially also. Do you think that this is the role of the elder writer in relationship to the younger writer?

BROOKS: I certainly do. I think that this should be their prime function other than their writing. I think that a writer as old as myself in spite of early difficulties has had time to achieve, if there is going to be any achievement. It's hard for youngsters coming along to gain exposure, sometimes just to eat.

BBB: But it was hard for you too. It wasn't an easy trail to where you are now. And it is still not easy.

BROOKS: Well as far as eating was concerned. I must give my husband credit who had a hard time supporting his family for over twenty years. I mean that was the only place that money was coming from. And it was very hard for him.

BBB: In that respect, what do you think about the women's liberation movement?

BROOKS: I've been on panels with a good many of the women's liberers and I'm very disturbed by the fact that so many of them seem to despise men, really seem to hate men. And for Black women to hate Black men is contradictory to what we are about. And I don't want to see our Black women going that route. I don't like this nose thumbing at Black men. I think that that's another divisionary tactic that we need to be very wary of. We should be about *Black liberation*—which includes women and men.

BBB: Why do you live in Chicago? Why not Miami or the West Coast? Why did you choose Chicago?

BROOKS: I didn't choose Chicago, but I've grown up here and just stayed in the neighborhood that is familiar. When I got to Dar Es Salaam, I got so excited about the beauty there, that I had the idea of being around layers and layers of Black people that I thought of getting a house there, but I don't know how practical that would be. I think that there is plenty of work for me to do right here because there are plenty of Black people here. Well, here I am today. Things may change tomorrow, but I am here today.

BBB Are you satisfied with your life as it stands now?

BROOKS: No, who could be satisfied with my production and the way we are treated in this country. But the last thing in the world I intend to do is to imitate other people's way of writing, but I would be much happier if I had written poems that so many black people found relevant. I'm not happy about the things that are going on in this world. But I do whatever I can to rectify what I see as rectifiable. All my energy and resources will be used for the benefit of my people.

BBB: Many people feel that your work is much more political now which I would argue with because I think that it has always been political because it positively dealt with Black people I think that everything is political but some people feel that your work is much more distinguishably "Black" and therefore makes it that much more political.

BROOKS: Well isn't that interesting that to be Black is to be political. That word doesn't bother me either. I don't sit down and say, well today I'm going to write a political poem and it will scare all the whites. I don't have that in my mind at all. I really believe what the young said that Black poetry is written by Blacks, about Blacks to Blacks and that is really all that I have in my mind.

BBB: I would leave the phrase that Chancellor Williams emphasized and that is Black unity. I think that that should be our flag. The unity of Black people is the only way I see of saving the Black race and the reason Chancellor Williams' book, T*he Destruction of Black Civilization* is not in the best sellers list because he points this out in very clear terms what Black people should be doing for our survival. Read the chapter "A View From the Bridge" in the revised edition.

BBB: Thank you Gwen.

BROOKS: It is I who should be thanking you.

(Gwen Brooks was interviewed by the Editor. June, 1974)

SECTION TWO

INSTITUTION BUILDING AND COMMUNITY ADVOCACY

"To build institutions is to physically construct thoughts and actions. You cannot institutionalize thoughts and actions at a mass level without institutions. To construct and build is not an end in itself, but one of the larger means toward the end that comes about because of work, study and creativity in schools, hospitals, community centers, co operative businesses, parks, places of worship, and so on. In building, we create concrete models in the community that black people can relate to, respect and support."

FROM PLAN TO PLANET LIFE STUDIES:
THE NEED FOR AFRICAN MINDS AND INSTITUTIONS
by Haki R. Madhubuti

THE ROLE OF THE LABOR MOVEMENT IN CHICAGO 1960-1975: FROM THE UPTURN TO THE BEGINNING OF THE DOWNTURN

Timuel D. Black

In the spring of 1960, at the annual meeting of the American Federation of Labor and Congress of Industrial Organizations (AFLCIO), the president of that national conglomerate of union leaders shouted out to Mr. A. Phillip Randolph, the national head of the brotherhood of Sleeping Car Porters, "Who the hell chose you to be the spokesman for the Negro people?" At that time, not only was Mr. Randolph the chief of the Brotherhood of Sleeping Car Porters, he was nationally and internationally known for his personal activities locally, nationally and internationally in civil rights and civil liberties affairs. He was an admirer and supporter of Mahatma Gandhi's pacifistic ideas and a promoter of Nelson Mandela and the South African Freedom Movement. In 1941 he threatened President Franklin D. Roosevelt with a labor march on Washington if the president didn't sign an executive order providing equal work opportunities in the war industries for all Americans. This was in the beginning of WWII. We were on the verge of entering the war but also were the major supplier to our allies. To avoid international embarrassment, the U.S. claimed that the war was being fought by ally nations against Nazi Germany and Italy for global equality and justice. President Roosevelt prepared and signed executive order number 8802, which was the first Fair Employment Practices Act (FEPCT) in the history of the United States. After the signing, A. Phillip Randolph asked the leader of an important labor union why capable black railroad workers could not get jobs in the drilling industry and in other areas besides porters and cooks. Then the president of the AFLCIO responded to Mr. Randolph in a vicious and disrespectful manner. Immediately after that insult and confrontation, many black workers from other unions and their white union and non-union friends came together in Detroit during the Fourth of July weekend of 1960 to form the Negro-American Labor Council (NALC) and unanimously elect Mr. Randolph as its first national president.

The council's initial purpose was to voice opposition to AFLCIO's president. The council's inaugural conference was held in 1960. There were many unions represented there: United

Auto Workers (UAW), The United Steel Workers (USW), The United Parking House Workers (UPHW), The Brotherhood of Sleeping Car Porters and Waiters, The International Building Trades (IBF) and many others. Every big city, industrial, commercial or agricultural area elected its local officers at the conference. Timuel D. Black of the Chicago Teachers Union (CTO) was nominated and elected to be president of the local chapter of NALC. My good friend Willoughby Abner, regional education director of the UAW and the former president of Chicago's NAACP, was elected as vice president. For me and many other black unions and their supporters, that convention was the highlight of 1960. We returned to Chicago immediately and began to broaden our base with unions like members of the Chicago Teachers Union (CTU), the Ladies Garment Workers, UF, CW, SCME, ATU, IBT, SELU, The Retail Clerks Union and others. We were South Siders, West Siders, North Siders, male and female, Catholics, Protestants, atheists and Jews, democrats, republicans, socialists, independents, etc. With that broad base of unionists and friends, we felt confident that we could not only bring about more equality and fairness in the Chicago job market, but we could have a positive impact on the political, social and economic life in Chicago as well. We met monthly in the United Parking House Worker center at 49th and Wabash, now called the Charles Hayes Family Investment Center. There we planned and targeted job areas, and developed strategies and tactics to accomplish our goals.

We first targeted the West Side, from east of Western, over to Halsted. We researched and targeted large and small businesses as to the race and gender of their employees. Also, we researched the employees' communities, wages, salaries and working environments. We used West Side labor leaders to take the leadership and responsibility for bringing the communities together for this adventure. We were quite successful. Churches, schools, community leaders and even local politicians worked together to bring more labor equality in that area. We next moved to the Lake Street Corridor to the north with the same east-west boundaries. These ideas, plans, types of strategies and tactics were necessary. We then continued into the Englewood community and focused on the vast Halsted Street shopping district, and met similar success. These activities by the members of the Negro American Labor Council (NALC) continued until 1966. In 1966, Dr. Martin Luther King, Jr. recruited Rev. Jesse Jackson to take over the leadership of a newly created arm of The Southern Christian Leader Conference (SCLC), which was named Operation Breadbasket. SCLC expanded and was renamed as Operation PUSH (People United to Save Humanity). Also, by this time NALC was suffering from internal friction over accusations that certain members in Chicago, New York, Cleveland and Detroit were members of the Communist party. Mr. Randolph, who was an active Democratic Socialist, publicly detested communism, and launched an investigation into those accusations. In protest to this investigation, many members began to leave NALC, which weakened its base. I stayed because of what I thought was the larger issue—jobs for our people.

Going back a bit, in 1961 at our second annual meeting in Yonkers, New York, Dr. Martin Luther King, Jr. was our featured speaker. The banquet hall was jam packed. Ed Nixon, who was a Montgomery member of the Brotherhood of Sleeping Car Porters, was an attendee. Nixon recruited Dr. King to lead the Montgomery, Alabama bus boycott in 1955. He and Rosa Parks had carefully planned and launched that boycott. When they approached religious leaders in Montgomery to take over the leadership of the proposed boycott, they were rejected until Mr. Nixon approached newly approved twenty-six-year-old Dr. Martin Luther King, Jr. Dr. King Jr. accepted the invitation and the boycotts and marches immediately followed. We in the North, particularly labor leaders in Chicago and other big cities, picketed and boycotted the bus company in Montgomery that segregated and insulted its Black passengers throughout the South. Thus, because Mr. Ed Nixon was an active member of the Brotherhood of Sleeping Car Porters, a lifelong relationship between labor and Civil Rights Movement began. Pacifist Bayard Rustin, an ardent advisor to Mr. Randolph, acted as the continuous link between the persons and groups. Also, it was at the second annual meeting of the NALC in Yonkers, New York in 1961, that we heard Dr. King express his opposition to the war in Vietnam and the military's racist treatment of Black and Hispanics who were being sent to the combat zones of Vietnam. Thus, we had two charismatic pacifists and good American leaders working together to bring peace, equality and justice to our nation and to the world. They continued to work together until their deaths.

Richard Daley, in collaboration with black ministers and the Chicago Urban League, a shattered NAACP, took control of the NALC and focused mainly on jobs and education. The defacto segregation of all Chicago Public Schools contributed to Washburn Trade School excluding Black students and making it extremely difficult for them to acquire trade union credentials. Because of this exclusion, Black students were denied jobs in the building trades such as brick masonry, plumbing, electricity, etc. Also, Black students were not being properly educated in language, writing, speaking and reading, to prepare them to go on to higher education some level of professionalism. On both of these levels, NALC led picket lines and testified before city, county and state levels, particularly elected politicians and appointed officials. Generally, there were attempts to ignore, discredit or reject our demands.

However, because of our experiences in life, pertaining to racial and class struggles, some progress was made. Washburn, which had been built and supported by public money, was taken from the control of bigoted unions and integrated into the city colleges of Chicago, which opened it to all people, regardless of race, ethnicity or gender. Through untiring efforts (and occasional arrests of people like labor activist Rosie Simpson and prominent comedian Dick Gregory) and a suit in federal court (in which this writer was a plaintiff), public schools became less rigidly segregated. However, with this official change, many white parents took their children out of public schools and sent them to private schools, or they moved to the suburbs in quest of "better schools." At this juncture, because of the declining interest in quality education by certain powerful politicians and the breakdown of parental and community participation, the quality of education (except in certain select schools) declined. This decline disheartened many black parents. Though the Chicago Teachers Union (CTU) and the newly formed Cook County College Teachers Union (CCCTU) became stronger during this period; their interest and participation in quality education declined. Negro American Council membership in these unions was relatively small and weak. However, NALC members who were also union teachers, carried the banner of NALC at all meetings, but could not speak officially for our unions.

Most teachers who had school aged children did not send them to public schools. But it was the intense political pressure of leadership members of NALC that caused a bill to pass in the city council that required all public school employees to live within city boundaries. That rule was rescinded in 2010, because both CTU and CCCTU hardly ever received broad public support as their unions weakened. Also, partly because of age, relatively few members of NALC had children in public schools from 1960-1975. However, during this same period, the NALC was politically active in the community. Several members, on both the South Side and West Side ran for public office, usually as independent democrats. In 1966, led by members of NALC, demonstrations were organized at the United Parking House Workers' Union Hall at 4854 S. Wabash to oppose the republican convention, which was held at the Convention Center of the Stockyards. Richard Nixon was their nominee. The marchers and protestors strongly supported U.S. Massachusetts Senator John F. Kennedy, who was the first Catholic president in U.S. history. Kennedy, along with his political activist brothers Robert and Ted, became strong supporters of Dr. King and the Civil Rights Movement. These political, social and job seeking activities continued on during this period in 1963.

After former U.S. congressman Augustus "Gus" Savage withdrew his name from consideration for candidate for 4th Ward alderman, I was asked by the independent voters of Illinois (IVI) to replace him as their candidate in the 1963 race against incumbent Ward Alderman Claude W. Holman. Holman had previously been selected by this organization of political independents as a running mate of independent 5th Ward Alderman Leon Despres on the promise that he would work with Despres to try to get city council support for open housing in all parts of Chicago. Such a local victory would have been in tune with the U.S. Supreme court decision in 1948 (*Shelley v. Kramer*), which ruled that restrictive covenants in housing were unenforceable anywhere in the U.S. This suit had been originally launched by Chicagoans Carl Hansberry, C. Francis Stratford (John Rogers' grandfather) and Atty. Earl B. Dickerson and supported by local and national NAACP's legal defense.

Thurgood Marshall, who later became a Supreme Court Justice, and Holman had agreed to cooperate with Despres in trying to make this a reality in Chicago. He was running against a white conservative republican. The Black and White labor, civil rights, and civil liberty forces in the 4th Ward came together to support him. Holman immediately became a captive and supporter of Richard J. Daley, who had become mayor of the city of Chicago, only because of the massive turnaround and support of Black voters urged on by Black machine politician Congressman William J. Dawson. Daley betrayed their trust and support by taking local government jobs from Dawson's control and centralizing them in his office. He then transferred the Black political control from Dawson's patronage to his political control. The political allegiance shifted so sharply that the six Black aldermen became sarcastically labeled "The Silent Six," because in such issues as fair and open housing and public school integration, they would either support Daley's restrictive controls or remain silent. Claude Holman would be the most open virulent supporter of Daley, and a vicious public attacker of Alderman Leon Despres: who was strongly supported by the Negro American Labor Council and other liberal political groups such as the Independent Voters of Illinois. By this time, the NALC's base had eroded because of the accusations of Mr. Randolph and others that the largest local branches, and particularly in the Chicago branch, were deeply infused and controlled by members of the Communist Party.

As the race for 4th Ward alderman started, we quickly began to organize for money and troops. Meanwhile, in order to capture the seat held by an independent, Leon Despres and Daley's organization launched a hard fifth campaign with a well-known Black lawyer, whose daughter was a student in one of my classes at Hyde Park High School. Because of Despres' long history as a supporter of Black causes and as legal counsel for organized labor, his office called Walter Reuther: president of the United Automobile Workers Union (UAW), to throw their physical and monetary support to Despres. They agreed, and therefore severely and immediately damaged our campaign. Though I had the visible support of such notables as writer and actor Oscar Brown Jr. and comedian Dick Gregory, access to important organizing centers and churches were made inaccessible to us and on Election Day; my supporters were denied access even to the local polling stations. Thus, understandably, we lost.

However, in this contest we learned many things. We laid the groundwork for many political changes for the future, including the 1983 election of Harold Washington as the first Black mayor in Chicago's history. During this campaign, we involved many young people eighteen and under, in organizing, presenting and articulating important issues, learning to be active and independent in their communities, and to help others beyond their families and communities. However, plantation politics began to take place and some of our Black politicians acquiesced to its divisive tactics. This form of political manipulation can be traced to the days of legalized slavery when some slaves were called "house n------" (those more favored by slave master) and "field n------" (those regulated to service in the cotton, tobacco or other subservient fields of slave labor). This momentum, supported by labor forces, carried the Civil Rights Movement into the glorious May Birmingham march for jobs, initiated by Birmingham, Alabama minister Rev. Fred Shuttlesworth, who made several trips for support in Chicago's labor and religious leadership.

By this time a new coalition of Civil Rights organizations in Chicago had emerged, which called themselves The Triple CO (Chicago Committee for Civil Rights Organizations). Some of us believed that it was formed to control or quell the growing street organizations and demonstrations such as SNCC (Student Nonviolent Coordinating Committee), CORE (Congress of Racial Equality), and the Negro American Labor Council. Led by the leadership of the NAACP and Chicago Urban League, we were urged by our national leaders to join the CCCO. We joined, but the conflict on issues such as housing, education, etc. between the radical and the more conservative leaders of each of the groups made it difficult to reach a group consensus. Finally, when Mr. Randolph announced in a national board meeting of the NALC in New York that we were going to call for a march on Washington "for jobs and freedom" as we had done before WWII, we were stunned. Those who were there wondered how such an appeal could be successful, given the nationwide breaches between our so-called well known civil leaders. Well, we did not take into consideration the strong ties that developed between Dr. King and Mr. Randolph and kept alive by Randolph's advocate and messenger Bayard Rustin. Labor leaders had played a big role in the Montgomery bus boycott and in organizing the Birmingham protests. The Birmingham clash between protestors and the police beatings of adults and children outside the Sixteenth Street Baptist Church was seen on t.v. screens worldwide. The magnificent "Letter from a Birmingham Jail" was distributed all over the world. Mr. Randolph immediately asked Dr. King to share the leadership with him in organizing the 1963 March on Washington for jobs and freedom. Because of the envy of Dr. King by the national leaders of the NAACP and the Urban League, there was a reluctance to publicly support him at first. Mr. Randolph and Dr. King asked Bayard Rustin to ask me and Lawrence Landry (now deceased), of the Congress of Racial Equality (CORE), to take over the leadership and organizing of Chicago contingent on the planned march on Washington.

Under the leadership of the late Charles Hayes and labor activist Addie Wyatt, we were given space in the headquarters union of stockyard workers. We were flooded with volunteers and demands for reservations to Chicagoans in the march. The local NAACP and Urban League eventually began to join us in the organizing of this historic event. Their resources were invaluable. The late Hyde Park labor activist Sam Ackermann took the leadership in organizing whites from various neighborhoods. Chicago members of the Brotherhood of Sleeping Car Porters arranged for adequate railroad transportation for us to and from Washington, D.C. for the 27th and the 28th of August. In the coaches alone, we carried more than two thousand people. Then there were those who drove in autos, busses, etc. We had celebrities such as singer and movie performer, Etta Motem-Barnett and writer and social activist, "Studs" Terkel, and many more well-known people, including my wife and two children. The march on Washington and Dr. King's march in Chicago in 1966 for fair housing helped set the stage for the 1983 election of Harold Washington. The struggles of the progressive activities of labor leaders paved the way for Chicagoan Carol Mosley-Braun to become the first African American woman to become a U.S. Senator from Illinois. Although today's labor unions and organizations may not be as strong as they were in the sixties; nonetheless, they played an important role in the election of Senator Barack Hussein Obama as America's first Black president. When Obama first announced he was going to run for president, he sought and won the support of the Coalition of Black Trade Unionists. Let's keep on laboring!

UNITED AFRIKANS FOR ONE MOTHERLAND, INTERNATIONAL (UFOMI)

Sarudzayi Sevanhu

In 1971 I began attending classes taught by a young man named Ruwa Chiri, whose influence has affected the rest of my life.

Maruwa Saunyama Chiri was born on February 17, 1943 in the town of Umtali, in Manyikaland province of then Southern Rhodesia; a territory of the British colonial federation of the Rhodesias and Nyasaland in southern Africa. His parents were involved with the Methodist Church Mission, so he attended the regular mission schools and followed the usual requirement to take a "Christian" or European name. Through his church contacts, Ernest Weighmor Chiri came to the United States to further his studies in July 1962. Initially placed with a white host family in Rochester, New York, Ruwa began to feel the contradictions of racial attitudes in the U.S. and eventually moved away.

Ruwa attended MacMurray College in Jacksonville, Illinois and Chicago's Roosevelt University. By the mid-sixties he was part of the Chicago community of artists, activists, and organizers. He worked with Wali Saddiq (Lou House) in the International Black Studies Program and later spent time with SNCC's Mississippi Project in Holmes County with Rap Brown's brother, Ed. In 1968 Ruwa married Mozella Duncan, an activist who had worked with Operation Breadbasket. He became a father to a son, Tiriwangani, in 1969 and became permanently separated from his family the next year.

The Black Nationalist movement had grown into many community organizations, artistic and literary associations, and educational units since the call for Black Power in 1966. Ruwa naturally involved himself in several of these endeavors. He worked in a training program with the Vice Lords youth gang on the West Side. He also taught classes at Ruth B. Lott School, located at 4521 S. Oakenwald Avenue. The Ruth B. Lott School (later called Ile Iwe Ominara) was an independent early childhood school operated by the Black Women's Committee, whose members included Dorothy Roberson, Betty Randall, Lois Ricks and others. He also taught at the African independent McKissick School in Milwaukee.

Ruwa held a class in contemporary African affairs on Saturday mornings at the Communiversity, which offered free community classes at Northeastern Illinois University Center for Inner City Studies facilities at 700 E. Oakwood Blvd. After Ruwa's class, several people congregated to ask him further questions about African news and affairs. Several of these attendees came together at the instigation of James Robinson, and formed a new organization that we called United Afrikans For One Motherland, International (UFOMI). We met in September 1971 and in subsequent meetings incorporated, wrote and adopted a constitution. We eventually lost most of the founding members.

We set up a rather elaborate structure for such a small group of people. There were four standing committees: international affairs, economic development, education/culture, and social affairs/public relations. Each of which had detailed, elaborate plans to be executed. James Robinson was elected director with Ruwa as his assistant; I was secretary; Kanzetta Howell was treasurer; and three other people were coordinators of publications.

By January 1972, with few of the original members, we decided to form the Arusha-Konakri Institute (AKI) as an institutional part of UFOMI, where we would hold political education classes. Arrangements were made with Willie Curtis at St. Agatha's Catholic Church on West Douglas Boulevard to use the facilities for classes on Saturdays.

I remember that first Saturday we went over to begin our classes. It was cold! We took a large coffee maker to provide herb tea for our participants and ended up warming our frozen hands on the urn. Of course, nobody showed up but our people. The following Saturday was more fruitful. We had twenty to twenty-five people attending, at least half of whom were young people who were also members of The Kadre.

The Pan-Afrikan Kadre youth had been meeting at the King Library on 35th Street for study sessions. Its founder, Arnold Gray, had asked four adults to be advisors—Ruwa, along with Linda White and Catherine Jackson, who were history teachers at Dunbar High School, and me. Through this association, the Pan-Afrikan Kadre members began to work with the Institute while they continued their own study group.

We held classes in African politics and Swahili taught by Brothers Wambui and Njoroge from Kenya. After a few weeks, the young people had developed a program for children which they called YAPAKI (Young Afrikans Program of the Arusha Konakri Institute). Some of these young people were Rujeko (Virginia Brunson), Haruna (Deborah Taylor), Nyasha (Diane Spencer), and my daughter Sheila. They recruited youngsters from the neighborhood, our children, and their brothers and sisters to participate in the classes. Classes were taught in geo-politics, African dance, and Swahili. The turnout was low. We didn't realize until much later and after much failure that the neighborhood parents were hesitant to send their small children into a place where older neighborhood teenagers habituated, whom they suspected of using or selling narcotics. The older teenagers were members of the Zulus, the youth program for high school drop-outs at St. Agatha's Church, run by Willie Curtis. Some of them did occasionally sit in on our classes.

Afrika Must Unite Magazine

Ruwa Chiri was a prolific writer. His writing included essays on political topics, newspaper articles, and poetry. One of the poems that gained some attention was a response to the well-received and timely poem by Eugene Perkins, *An Apology to My African Brother.* Further encouraging Pan-African unity, Ruwa wrote *An Acknowledgement of My Afro-American Brother.* He also wrote for *Communiviews* and other local newsletters.

One of the many things I found out in working with organizations is the far-reaching effect of propaganda—the ability to project an organization greater than its actual productivity and resources. Through Ruwa's efforts, UFOMI developed as its propaganda medium our magazine, *Afrika Must Unite (AMU)*, which we began publishing in November 1971 as "a bi-monthly journal of fact and commentary published by the International Affairs Committee of UFOMI." Our first issue was a four-page typewritten newsletter dated November 31 [sic], which was printed at the local instant printing establishment. The first five hundred copies went rapidly at twenty-five cents each. Our excellent sales force was The Kadre.

The second issue, published two weeks later, had grown to six pages. We could not continue to publish bi-monthly, so by February 1972, we issued *AMU* as a "monthly analysis of news and opinion;" published by the Arusha-Konakri Institute of UFOMI. By now we had a distinctive masthead that we used throughout the life of the magazine. The magazine had grown to twenty-eight pages with letters from the readers and several articles, including one from Africans in Australia who had attended the Congress of African People conference in Atlanta, 1970. We were able to publish fairly regularly during the first half of 1972. The June/July issue marked a new accomplishment—we were no longer typing our copy. It was typeset and printed by a company in central Illinois.

Ruwa did most of the writing for the magazine and all the editing. Although we occasionally included articles from other writers, one of the positive aspects of the magazine was its feature of young people's writing. We had begun an Afrikan Scholar's Program where the youth who worked with us did research on topics of their choice under Ruwa's supervision. The young people were students at Lindbloom, Kenwood, Dunbar, and Metro High Schools. We were able to publish some of their work in *AMU*—poetry and essays—works by fifteen- and sixteen-year-old students: Rujeko Tasika (Virginia Smith), Nyasha

Dzeshato (Diane Spencer), Rakina Lumumba, Chavunduka Sevanhu (Sheila Pearson), and Gerald Prestwood. One of our co-sponsors of The Kadre and Dunbar High School social studies teacher, Linda White (now Ifé Carruthers), also contributed to the magazine as writer and photographer.

Ruwa introduced the concept of spelling Afrika with a "k" as a reclamation of our culture. Amiri Baraka popularized the spelling and it was used throughout the seventies and beyond by many organizers and writers.

When we had to change printers, we began to do our own layout. The November 1972 issue was a good looking one, featuring a cover picture and interview with Mme. Jeanne Cisse, Guinea's ambassador to the United Nations, serving as the first woman president of the Security Council. It was also at this time that we became sophisticated and began to call the magazine "a journal of current Afrikan affairs." Our correspondents were located in New York, Washington, D.C., Guyana, Australia, Tanzania, Kenya and Canada.

Publishing and distributing the magazine became a major task. By the end of 1972 we no longer held classes at St. Agatha's; in fact, Cardinal Cody was closing the building. We used Ruwa's apartment at 7831 S. Ridgeland for many activities, but we stopped having classes. Ruwa edited the articles that he had chosen for an issue and I typed the edited copy, along with Nyasha: one of our young sisters who worked several evenings a week. We spent a lot of nights staying up trying to meet deadlines with the printers. We also spent lots of nights listening to Ruwa. There were several of us who went to the Institute every day, except Sundays and occasionally Saturdays. Most of the workers came at varying times set by Ruwa or when called upon. About a dozen young people came after school until about eight or nine o'clock. Kebba (Kenneth Wright), a student at Dunbar High School and Kadre member, became a mainstay in the distribution of the magazine and Arnold Gray of the Kadre, a student at Roosevelt University, was the bookkeeper for a time.

The adults who worked with us were not on a schedule, except Kanzetta Howell. Kanzetta was originally treasurer but had become librarian. She collected and archived magazines and other written material from various organizations around the U.S. and the world. Linda White provided photos of the various events for *Afrika Must Unite*. Over time we held different positions with the magazine. I moved from secretary to director of the Institute; Tommy Bordain was an editorial assistant at one time and another young student, Nhamo, worked on various aspects. It all depended on Ruwa's judgment.

Jerry Christmas, another public school teacher, and Linda (Tsitsi) Porter were our French translators, most often translating President Sekou Toure's speeches from the Guinean national newspaper, *Horoya,* which Stokely Carmichael had arranged for us to receive from Guinea. With the death of Kwame Nkrumah, we looked upon Sekou Toure as the leading live representative of pan-Afrikanism. Ruwa had led a contingent of demonstrators who closed down the Portuguese airline, TAP, when NATO-backed Portuguese forces invaded Guinea on November 22, 1970.[1]

Ruwa wanted so badly to head a functioning organization and particularly to publish a reputable journal; however, he had difficulty getting along with brothers in everyday working situations. Arnold Gray, who also wanted to lead a group, was in his early twenties and would not submit totally to Ruwa's direction. There was never a confrontation between them, but subtle disagreements were often present in their interactions. Finally, Arnold, who had changed his name to Mansong Kulubally, withdrew from UFOMI with his pan-Afrikan Kadre group (later known as Black Body). Rujeko and my daughter, Chavunduka, remained members of UFOMI and the Kadre. Gerald Prestwood, who was given the name Kofi Baako, took over Kenneth Wright's duties as circulation manager. I took over the bookkeeping duties with other administration activities. Fortunately, the key responsibilities were still managed, but we keenly felt the loss of the young people and their vitality. They did; however, still support our programs and continued to help sell the magazine.

A Change of Name

Changing one's "slave name" for an African one was very popular around this time. I had long wanted an African name—one given to me by an African born on the continent. Somehow I felt it would be more legitimate because they would better understand the cultural significance of the name. Ruwa gave names that had political significance, but he refused to give names to adults unless they had shown a commitment to work for the people. He had already given names to Rujeko, Haruna and Nyasha: the teenaged sisters who had worked with him the previous three years with the Pan African Students Organization in the Americas (PASOA).

When UFOMI celebrated Afrika Freedom Week in April 1972, Ruwa surprised me by including a naming ceremony for my family. I became Sarudzayi Chapupu Sevanhu, meaning, "Choose the whirlwind, revolt, as a people." My daughter, Sheila, became Chavunduka Ifungwa Sevanhu (It is our minds that have been stirred, as a people); and my son, John Marcellus, became Kanazvada Tichatora Nhaka Sevanhu, meaning, "We shall take back the land of our ancestors, as a people."

[1] SOBU Newsletter, December 12, 1970, p. 4

Afrikan Seaman's Program

Afrika Must Unite was the one program of which we were very proud, although we only published twelve issues from November 1971 to April 1974. We had agents in several cities in the U.S. as well as Toronto, London, Guyana, Liberia, and Dar es Salaam. We sold through our correspondents, bookstores, other organizations and directly at large meetings and conferences. In the summer of 1972, we found an unexpected outlet for *AMU*, though not an income-producing one.

Ruwa had talked about the Africans from the continent who used to meet Ghana's *Black Star Line* ships a few years earlier. We checked the newspapers for arrival time and went down to the Chicago Port at Navy Pier to meet the *Black Star Line* of Ghana, West Africa. There we first met the *Birim River* ship, but were unable to board because of restrictions from Port authorities. Lexie Spurlock, one of our supporters, later went to the ship and brought some of the crew to the Institute where we had food and a long discussion. Nana Aykin and his fellow-crew had planned to look up members of the Black Panther Party so they could set up a chapter in Ghana. Instead, we revived their memories of the days of the Young Pioneers and the Convention People's Party of Kwame Nkrumah. They took boxes of *Africa Must Unite* and distributed them in Ghana and up and down the coast of West Africa. They also set up a chapter of UFOMI in Tema, Ghana.

We continued to meet the ships—the *Nakwa River, Offin River, Subin River, Klorte Lagoon* and *Sukumo River*. We went on board the ships; prepared meals for the crew at the Institute and they for us on the ship; poured libations; took pictures; danced and had a good time as we talked politics. On the *Sukumo River* we even met an African captain.[2] After a couple of years, this connection was ended when the ships were re-routed to Thunder Bay, Ontario, Canada.

We received many letters from those who obtained copies of *Africa Must Unite*, even from Cameroon, where a brother requested that we publish in French. Little did he know that we could barely publish in English. Our resources were always so meager. We were never able to get any serious display advertising. Most of our revenue came from subscriptions, direct sales of the magazine, Ruwa's speaking honorariums, and donations. We usually had trouble collecting from many of our agents. But we were beginning to get a varied readership—all parts of the United States, Toronto, Jamaica, Guyana, Surinam, London, Hong Kong, India, and many parts of Africa. We had secured subscriptions from a few non-African libraries and institutions like Northwestern University, Southern Illinois

[2] "African Sea Captain," Muhammad Speaks, June 15, 1973, p. 14.

University, Hoover Institute, and General Motors, among others. But the outlet that gave us the most satisfaction was the seaman's program because it allowed us to liken ourselves to Marcus Garvey's UNIA, which also distributed information through African sailors.[3]

National and Other Local Organizing

UFOMI was very involved in the collective organizing of the period, sometimes initiating or co-sponsoring many of the activities. Most of the people and organizations coming out of the civil rights, then Black Power, movements were just beginning to recognize their connection to Africa. Unlike so many Africans who had come to America to go to school, Ruwa was fully integrated into life in the Black community, thus he was sought often as the "African representative."

Organized near the end of 1971, UFOMI quickly became involved in the upcoming national activities of the following year. Ruwa was asked to be on the steering committee for the National Black Political Convention, held in Gary, Indiana on March 10-12, 1972.[4] He wrote a paper that he presented to the Task Force on International Affairs, "Towards a Black Foreign Policy." It was an historical meeting where over four thousand delegates and an equal number of alternates and observers came from all areas of the U.S. and all sectors of the African community.[5] Ruwa and I were delegates from Illinois and took members of the Pan-Afrikan Kadre with us to Gary where they sold *Afrika Must Unite* and collected funds for our Refugee Program. Ruwa and I both served in the subsequent National Black Assembly and I was elected as one of the three delegates from Illinois to the National Black Political Council, along with Sanii Andika of Peoria and Charles Koen of Cairo.

Ruwa was also on the steering committee for African Liberation Day, 1972. UFOMI called together the various organizations in Chicago to plan for our participation in African Liberation Day, May 27, 1972.Three busloads of participants paid fifteen dollars each to go to Washington, D.C. for ALD. It was an exciting occasion. Up to thirty thousand people had come to Washington to support the liberation struggles in Africa, most of them under thirty years of age.

Always thinking ahead, Ruwa issued a paper called "Black Nationalism in the Sevenites: Toward Mass Politics (A Call to All Serious Nationalist Organizations and Individuals in the Chicago Area)." In it he emphasized the importance of united activities and a unified voice that would strengthen the nationalist movement, particularly in Chicago. Once again

---

[3] "Tony Martin Race First, (Westport, Conn.: Greenwood Press, 1976) p. 96

[4] "The Gary Convention and the Crisis of American Politics", Black World, October 1972, p. 21

[5] "ALD, International Success," Black World, June 10, 1972.

called together a meeting of the nationalist organizations on September 9, 1972 and UFOMI proposed the creation of a unified institutional structure of local nationalist organizations. The newly-named Confederation of Nationalist and Pan-African Organizations included: the Afrikan Information Center/Catalyst, African People's Union/ Shule Watoto, Communiversity, Pan-Afrika Kadre/Black Body, Black Music Workshop, Black Women's Committee/Baraza Wa Afrika, Institute of Positive Education, Kuumba Workshop, Republic of New Afrika, Topographical Research Center, UFOMI and U.H.C.C. (Unify Humanity Through Cultural Creativity).

Despite decreased personal involvement by Ruwa, UFOMI continued its presence through Kanzetta Howell and Kofi Baako. Among the Confederation's many activities, such as a citywide memorial to slain liberation leader, Amilcar Cabral of Guinea-Bissau; observance of the Sharpeville Massacre; and African Liberation Day 1973, one event that lasted in one form or another over many years was the establishment of a citywide Kwanzaa celebration. On the last day of the 1972 Kwanzaa, January 1, 1973, the Confederation sponsored the first citywide Karamu ya Imani at the (black-owned) Ridgeland Club, 7330 S. Ridgeland. Over five hundred people, wearing their African attire, attended a full evening of activities. From three to five p.m. they observed performances by the students of the four independent schools. From five to seven p.m., a repast of fruits and juices accompanied the music of Phil Cohran and the Black Music Workshop. From seven to nine p.m. they participated in the ritual, reviewed the past year's work and made a commitment to the struggle for the upcoming year. From nine to eleven p.m. they shared the feast of delicious food prepared by the organizations with Cecil Troy's (black-owned) Grove Fresh juices.

UFOMI on the Road

We were young and full of energy, ready to hit the road at any time. We put quite a few miles on airplanes, but mostly on rented cars in order to take the younger people along. Kebba (Kenneth Wright) was one of the few teenagers who could drive and drove very well. He helped me drive several young people to conferences including Youngstown, Ohio's Freedom, Inc. headed by Ron Daniels; and San Diego for the second conference of the Congress of Afrikan People in September 1972, where we got a chance to hear several heroes speak, like C.L.R. James, and to see and hear most of the leaders and artists in the nationalist movement.

November 23-25, 1972, we traveled to Durham, North Carolina where we held the Kwame Nkrumah Conference on Afrikan Students, Youth and Development sponsored by the Afrikan Youth Movement for Liberation and Unity (New York City), Arusha-Konarki Institute, Ghanaian Student Union in the Americas and Kwame Nkrumah Institute of London. About two hundred students from eighteen African and two Caribbean countries and the U.S. were in attendance. A secretariat was set up to further communications and to organize for a second conference in Ghana the next year. Unfortunately, as soon as we returned to our homes, students began to have immigration problems, lost visas, and experienced FBI visits to themselves and family members.

The Last Days with Ruwa

Soon Ruwa also began to experience increased pressure from the immigration service. In January 1974, the commissioner at the immigration office called Ruwa to his office where reportedly he had been told to find some country to accept him because he had to leave the U.S. before the end of the year. He was very depressed, but when we returned to the Institute, he began making plans for continuing UFOMI from Canada.

I had returned to Wendell Phillips High School after a year's sabbatical, so several days later when I went to the Institute after work and when I didn't see Ruwa, I checked his apartment below. I left a note on the door that I found untouched the next day. By then I was totally puzzled and worried about his whereabouts. Later that night Ruwa called from New York, using a pseudonym. He was staying with Elombe Brath of the African Nationalist Pioneer Movement in New York and planned to go down to Greensboro, North Carolina for the African Liberation Support Committee's meeting over the weekend. He called again that Sunday evening from Greensboro asking me to wire him airfare to the Guinean Embassy in New York. The next night, he said he would return to Chicago Tuesday afternoon.

Tuesday evening I went to the Institute after work, expecting Ruwa anytime. Only my eleven-year old son, Nhaka, and I were working at the Institute that evening when around four o'clock the telephone rang. The man on the other end asked for me and said he was calling from the coroner's office in New York City and that they had Ruwa's body at the morgue. When I composed myself, I got into my car and, in spite of bad brakes, drove the ice-covered streets to Lu Palmer's *Black X-Press* newspaper office on 35th.

Lu called New York to verify what I had been told. Lu Palmer, a veteran journalist and a former columnist for major Chicago newspapers, now published his own newspaper, Black Xpress, to which Ruwa contributed articles on African politics. The coroner's office explained that on Tuesday, February 4, 1974 at 4:23 a.m., a subway train had struck and killed him.

The next morning Ruwa's brother Itayi Chiri, Kofi Baako, Wale Amusa (a Nigerian brother who worked with us in Champaign, Illinois) and I, went to New York. Itayi and his cousin identified and claimed the body. The transport authorities told us the motorman saw a body lying across the tracks, seven hundred-fifty feet inside the tunnel, just past 110th and Lenox Avenue. The driver reportedly was unable to stop before six of the cars had run over the body.

Elombe Brath explained to us how Ruwa had gone to some of the embassies regarding his immigration and had been promised some help. They were leaving Elombe's house Monday night to go to where Ruwa would be spending the night. Elombe stopped to talk to someone and when he looked around, Ruwa had disappeared. Elombe called to Ruwa and since he did not see him, returned to his own house and was unaware of what happened until about six p.m. Tuesday, when the police called him.

His cousin, Rukudzo Murapa, and other brothers arranged for the African-American Institute (which had sponsored Ruwa's coming to the U.S.) to send his remains back to Zimbabwe. Kofi and I returned to Chicago to make arrangements for a memorial on Ruwa's birthday to be held simultaneously with one in New York City.

Wali Siddiq (formerly Lou House) arranged free use of the A. R. Leak Funeral Home's main chapel for the memorial service on February 17, when Ruwa would have been thirty-one years old. Many Africans turned out to pay tribute to his memory, for although he sometimes was a difficult person to get along with, his contributions to our struggle could not be denied. He was one of the few Africans born in Africa who spent all his time in this country working for African liberation. He was always insistent that we are all Africans, even when he sometimes felt excluded from some privileges because he hadn't come from the "hood." Mail poured in from around the country and Africa, expressing grief at the loss of the hard-working African who insisted on spelling Afrika with a "k."

REBEL WORKER ABOUT CHANGE: PERSON TO NATION

(Nyala) Joan Smith Cooper

These are my experiences from 1960 to 1975 as a very ordinary person taking part in an extraordinary movement; one that formed the new era of Civil Rights in Chicago.[1] Those years brought me into adulthood with a sense of self, taught me what it means to be intricately bound within the destiny of a people, and gave me a special family and the vehicle of my work to help me make a difference. It was, for me, taking part in a rebellion of a new sort that would open new avenues for those to come. During these times in Chicago, it was through struggle that Black professionals began to experience themselves as "change agents"[2] rather than an extension of management. The concept of change agent, as expressed by Charles V. Hamilton, was and is essential to Black unity because in the minds of so many, class (as defined by education) had overshadowed race and human dignity.

It is quite right to begin my narrative in 1960. I was eighteen years old and the 1960-61 academic year would be the first to let me walk by myself. That year would raise the level of my consciousness to what it means to be Black in America. It was my senior year at Providence High School, 119 S. Central Park on Chicago's West Side. You know it now as Providence-St. Mel. That year there were thirteen African Americans among the 1,100 girls enrolled. I lived on 15th and Lawndale in a neighborhood that had been abandoned by the Jewish people. All that remained of their stay was two buildings, the Jewish Peoples' Institute (JPI) that became an upper grade center and Herzle Junior College that soon housed grades one through six. Starting with Negro blue collar workers trying to escape the high rents of the South Side, Lawndale had quickly become synonymous with the poverty of the newest Black migrants who had left the fields of the South. In Lawndale the Vice Lords emerged as the dominant gang. The stretch of blocks between 15th and Central Park where I would board the bus to school and 119 S. Central Park was relatively short; I had even walked it. But, how different was the daily philosophy. There were lessons to be learned in both places that sometimes conflicted.

In Lawndale, an intricate part of the 43rd Ward, Chicago Democratic politics were legendary. My mother was an assistant precinct captain under Alderman Ben Lewis. My sister and I had lessons on how to pass out campaign literature, stuff mailboxes, and hold the silver dollars or bottles of perfume that were to be given as voters exited the polling places. It sparked my interest in meeting people. At school, all the other girls celebrated their heritage on St. Patrick's Day (Irish) or St. Joseph's Day (Italian); there were no Black Catholic Saints for me or the other twelve Black Provites to celebrate. Africa would have to be the way to be proud of being from Lawndale. I spent class time drawing African masks and shields. Fortunately, while attending a Crusade for Christ Mission Conference, I met Mary Jo Kasindi, a young woman from Tanzania who was attending St. Mary of Notre Dame College. Africa was starting to free itself of colonial rule. She felt isolated as one of the few Blacks on her campus. When the top ten percent of my class was invited to a mixer at Notre Dame University, I was eager to keep my word to visit Mary Jo and perhaps attend an Independence party for Tanzania. Approximately twenty Provites made the trip with two chaperones on the train ride to South Bend, Indiana. I had no idea of where I really was (that is, me in my charcoal gray kick-pleat skirt, powder pink polyester puff jacket [you know the kind that your mother buys you for Easter?], and nearly two-inch heels), when I stepped out from the Morris Inn onto the promanade to walk across the Notre Dame campus to find St. Mary's College. I, the girl from Lawndale in the glory of my first solo initiated venture, walked down the open campus midway, totally unaware. Guess I was just interested in the sound of my shoe heels clicking on the concrete. Pow! The first hit was sharp and stinging as something pierced the back of my leg. Oh, my head! Again, pow. Showers of rocks were pelting me! From where? I saw no one, only the gaping open dark windows of the Roman-like grand buildings with Greek letters. Fraternity houses, these must be fraternity houses. Sharp stones kept hitting my head, which had thinly pressed hair. Stunned, with a dawning awareness that I would have to run…run in the shoes that my inexperienced ankles could hardly keep my feet going in a straight line in? Stunned, that in this Catholic kingdom, something, someone, me, was not welcome. Run, run faster. Remember the signs of the South: "Run, Nigger, Run! If you can't read, run anyway!" You are Black and South Bend. Indiana is not just the home of Notre Dame; it is also the home of the Indiana Klu Klux Klan. I had to understand that I was a representative of Black people, my people.

The summers of my youth spent in Hopkinsville, Kentucky should have prepared me more for this. How could I have forgotten that my Aunt Evelyn would have to call the local Catholic Church to tell them that her nieces from Chicago would be coming to go to Mass at their whites—only church, in order to have their Mass-books signed? I knew about the 1955 killing of Emmett Till and didn't even think of sitting down at the soda fountain in their downtown restaurant when my cousin, Darlene, did and got us thrown out. Jim Crow also promptly directed us to the side door of the Princess Theater to take our seats in the "crow's nest" to see a movie. Yet that day at Notre Dame, I just wasn't prepared; I must have forgot. *How could a lone girl be treated as such a hated object because of the color of her skin?* I had also forgotten how us Black kids had been chased from the Chicago Park District playground that stretched from 26th to 29th and Wentworth. The police told us later that the Italians, to keep the Negroes who had moved into the newly built Dearborn Homes Chicago Housing Project on the other side of the tracks (28th to 30th and State), would grab young Black girls and rape them in public on top of the railroad tracks at the east boundary to the park. I had forgotten how this had touched our family. It caused our flight from the tiny South Side apartment, which our parents could not afford, landing us on the West Side. I should not have forgotten these lessons that said my life was intricately bound with the destiny of my people, Black people. That fall season of 1960 rocked my world, literally and figuratively!

Discrimination was everywhere you turned. But, us Negroes were expected to just keep shuffl'n and turning. My family was my strength. I am the second daughter of God-fearing Black parents, Glyen and Ophelia Smith, who wanted the best education for their children. My mother had a seventh grade education and my father never attended school. They were a very proud, hardworking couple. I have a younger brother who, along with my sister, would be part of emerging programs that represented change and a return to dignity. My sister, Glyendoleon, would be in the first class of health advocates who Dr. Haughton designed to assist the patients of Cook County Hospital. The program was unique because participants had to be from poor areas and the program included earning an Associate of Arts degree from Malcolm X College. My brother, Glyenn, would be the primary operator of Teen Town Restaurant along with Art & Soul, which were business enterprises on 16th Street undertaken by the Vice Lords through the W. Clement Stone Foundation and University of Illinois. With all the comings and goings, we were quite a family. And yet we would continue to work for substandard wages.

I had started to work towards the end of my first year in high school by pretending to be a year older in order to get a social security card and a work permit. Hospitals did employ teenagers for some jobs. For the most part, white kids were Candy Stripers; Black kids worked food service. My starting pay was seventy-five cents an hour; after one year, it went up to one dollar an hour. I worked four hours, four days a week after school and a full eight hours on Saturdays and Sundays at Mercy Hospital on 26th and Prairie. During the summer, I worked full time to give the regulars a chance for vacation. This went on for three and a half years. All of my other time was spent studying, except whenever I danced downstairs at Budland, 64th and Cottage Grove. I graduated from high school earning one dollar an hour.

Nevertheless, the fall of 1961 found me enrolled at St. Xavier College, 103rd and Central Park Ave. I would later tell those close to me that I chose my schools as a survival strategy; I wanted to know what white people knew so I could get their feet off my neck. I couldn't leave Chicago to go to Marquette University in Wisconsin to pursue journalism because my father was very ill. Besides, we were too poor for me to go away to a Black college; the United Negro College Fund just never seemed to get around to me. And I couldn't afford the clothes to pledge to a sorority, which I thought was a necessity in the historic Black colleges. From 1961 to 1964 there was only one other Negro student beside myself, Denise Carver, attending this small liberal arts college of some five hundred women who had "run" from 49th and Cottage Grove.[3] I worked at the main post office a minimum of sixteen hours a week as a short hour substitute clerk to pay the tuition. As a worker, I identified with my parents; as a student, I didn't have a family role model.

But in March 1965 one of my classmates, Maureen Ryan, and another classmate's sister "Pidgy" Brown came to campus after class to tell what is was like when they went with Reverend Dick Lawrence to Selma, Alabama. They talked about Dr. Martin Luther King, Jr. and the horrendous hatred and jeers that met them at the Edmund Pettus Bridge. I thought, "These girls are doing this for the rights of my people? I'm Black and I care; I should be out there!" The Lawndale in me was ready to fight!

Meanwhile, my political education was being informed from contacts at the main post office. The lessons were taught by masters in life and every school of thought that inflamed the spirit. For Black professionals who worked in glass ceiling jobs and lived in segregated neighborhoods that were "red-lined" to overcharge for goods and every service, their professional jobs did not pay enough to support their families. So they also moonlighted at the post office. My friend, Simone Collier, and I had started dialoging with a highly conscious young man, a detail clerk named Bernard, who invited us to the opening of Solidarity Bookshop on Armitage on the near North Side. My lessons would take on a new dimension. The owners (Franklin, Penelope, Tor, and Bernard) were young Wobblies, a new wave of the Industrial Workers of the World (IWW).[4] "One of the IWW's most important contributions to the labor movement was to give a broader push towards social justice. When it was founded it was the only American union to welcome all workers, including women, immigrants, and African Americans, into the same organization."[5] The older Wobblies like Fred Thompson and Carlos Cortez still kept the IWW office at 2422 N. Halsted Street. Young and old were alike in political perspectives; most were anarcho-syndicalists who rejected concepts of both private property and organized government in favor of voluntary association and cooperation. In May 1886, Chicago anarchists had spearheaded the movement for the eight-hour work day and tried to organize previously unorganized workers. The major confrontation was the Haymarket Riot[5] in which the Chicago Police, on horseback, descended upon protesting workers. The discussions at Solidarity followed the tradition of "social issues of the day," comraderie, and the best get-down music. Black people would be drawn from Hyde Park and Woodlawn like Ron Woodard and Seward Wrist on his motorcycle. Enigmatic Black poet, Joffrey Stewart, was a frequent visitor. Friends then and over the years who would come to the bookshop included John Stucky and Don Watanabe. Nevertheless, my time at Solidarity was relatively short, productive, and enjoyable. I read, studied, and even fell in love. I moved from Lawndale to Lincoln Park. Having taken journalism in high school and as the literary editor of our Twin Towers newsmagazine, I was glad to take part in the printing and assembling of the first issues of *The Rebel Worker,* a tabloid newspaper aimed at young people. We would then sell the paper on Wells Street. I learned the language of protest and mastered the media—leaflets, hand bills, picket signs. And I was not exactly nonviolent.

In June1965, having gone from Lawndale to selling newspapers on Wells Strret and lawlessly picketing at munitions plants, to my surprise, I graduated from college with majors in psychology and philosophy. That summer I worked at St. Bernard's Hospital's Project Early Bird (a pilot study that would become the national Head Start Program), completing psychological write-ups on preschool children. I was still not making enough money to quit the post office. By the fall of 1965 my Solidarity friends encouraged me to go to work at the Department of Public Aid because there was a new independent union trying to organize there. It would be called the Independent Union of Public Aid Employees (IUPAE).[6] It was different from other unions because it combined professional social workers with masters degrees in social work along with: certified social workers (BA degrees with additional required course in social work), case managers (BA degrees), and clerical staff into one bargaining unit. Social workers had previously been treated like hospital and other "essential" personnel. Social workers had formed professional associations, but never organized as a labor force before. Sure enough, I was hired in September and joined the IUPAE Union, but before I could complete the three-month probationary period, I was suspended for a one-hour picket outside before coming into work. That action gained us union recognition and the right to organize. While I had been unable to participate in the Civil Rights March on Washington, I managed to finish out 1965 by participating in the anti-war march to the Washington Monument lead by Dr. Benjamin Spock against the Vietnam War.[7]

July 1966 was my chance to put myself on the line in peaceful protest for the civil rights of Black people. Dr. Martin Luther King, Jr., to challenge the strict racial segregation in

Chicago's housing, had moved into an apartment on 15th and Hamlin, just two blocks from where I had lived with my family and where my mother still lived in Lawndale. Reverend Dick Lawrence called for volunteers to join Dr. King to march for the creation of open housing in Marquette Park.[8] This was profoundly meaningful for me because during my time at St. Xavier as a "day-hop," I had ridden four buses from 15th and Lawndale to 103rd and Central Park for three and a half years to get to class. I transferred to each bus, the racial antagonism from white high school students and many adults boarding the bus intensified with each leg of the journey. The 16th Street bus would be full of Black people; the Kedzie bus as it went from 16th Street to 67th Street would drop off the few Black and Latino students going to Farragut and Harrison High Schools quickly and by 31st Street would begin the hostile stream of whites. At 67th Street (Marquette Park), I would take a Kedzie Ave. extension bus to 103rd, then transfer to the 103rd Street bus to take me west to Central Park. The last hostile group would be white boys headed to Brother Rice High School. The hostility towards me was strong and included hateful stares, stepping on my toes, shoving against my knees, as well as taunts and curses. Now, to return to Marquette Park, to march for open housing in that neighborhood where I had witnessed and faced such degradation, meant that other Black people would have a chance to live in this area and bring change to the racial climate. The day of the march, the behavior of the antagonizing crowd was the worst that even Dr. King had ever experienced. I was blessed that one of the Black policemen, Sergeant Williams, who also had been a short hour sub at the P.O., saw me and asked, "Joanie, what are you doing here?" There was no time to answer because the bricks and bottles were raining down. I didn't need to ask myself that question. I was part of the movement. The old Notre Dame experience was nothing compared to this. White people, some who were probably relatives of my college classmates, threw rocks and bottles, spat in our faces, and released their dogs on us. Within the next week, I would also march with Dr. King in Belmont-Cragin on the northwest side of town, which was the neighborhood of some of my high school classmates. I was re-visiting and marching in nonviolent protest back into the places where I had been most denied my dignity as a person of the Black race. I was standing up for civil rights, representing my people, and making a difference. That year, the Union called a short strike and won "Dues Check-off."

The year 1967 would be a different story. The Union drafted a contract. The Cook County Board of Commissioners refused to come to the table to negotiate it. We went on strike in a cold Chicago winter, and the County Board of Commissioners left us out there. Striking public aid workers were ignored because no one seemed to care about public aid recipients; it was a popular notion that the recipients were Black unwed mothers, an unpopular constituency. There was considerable Black leadership active in the Union (I may not remember all the names and also mix up the office locations). Bruce Mims and Dan Knight were the union representatives from the Kenwood office, Tom Hopkins and Al Hogan from Woodlawn, and George Bruno from the general assistance office on Roosevelt Road. Also prominent were Dave Shirley, Larry Jones, Ed Robinson, George Forney, and Tom Young. Barbara Merrill and Amanda Marsh were representatives for clerical staff members. The Union Stewards, where I worked, the Oakland District Office at 608 S. Dearborn—the old Transportation Building—were my friends, Cecile Singer and Carol Travis. I was the alternate delegate; Bulah Barber and Letisha (Tish) Taylor were the lead for our clerical membership. It was clear that our only ally would be the people on welfare. The Oakland District office joined with the Kenwood Office to meet with the Kenwood Oakland Community Organization (KOCO), to develop a strategy to get the county to negotiate. A union representing county employees joined with a community organization that also represented public aid recipients who had not been heard of before.[9] The then very young Reverend Jessie Louis Jackson had come to Chicago and was serving an internship at KOCO. The meetings between the Union and KOCO were intense because of the historical adversary role that the system had cast social workers in—"Go out there and find a man in the house and cut that mother's check off." The Union's Ed Robinson and KOCO's Jessie Jackson, would continually lock horns debating how the two groups could be stronger together. Eventually, we had to agree not to let either one of them speak. The welfare rights movement emerged; Marian Staples in the Cabrini-Green area and Dovie Coleman and Ginger Mack were outstanding in organizing. Later, I would go to Toronto with Ginger, as the National Organization of Women (NOW) and Women Strike for Peace in Canada addressed the problems of women of color and the struggle with welfare systems. The Chicago Packing House, named for all the workers in the flourishing meat packing industry who would have languished without a labor union, was the site of our mass rallies during the strike. Among politicians who joined us in the struggle was State Representative Charlie Hayes. Eventually, it was decided that union members would have to engage in civil disobedience to bring attention to the strike and force county commissioners to the bargaining table. Myself (still the rebel worker) and twelve others were to arrive at George Dunn's office (he was President of the Cook County Board) and demand to be seen. This time when we were not given an appointment, we would refuse to leave. Everything was set; strategy, attorneys, and bail were all supposed to be in place. But when Marty Morgenstern, a union organizer from New York, saw us, he said, "Oh no! You gotta look like white colla' workers!" We were in clothes like people who had been on strike for six weeks—shabby. The next day we came well-dressed like professionals. At the end of the day we were arrested, handcuffed, and taken to a jail under the County Building. It was more than terrifying. After being booked, many began to panic, especially when we were forced to have mug shots and were transferred to the main lockup at 11th and State Street. The attorneys took a while to come. We were convicted. Arnold R. Weber was appointed as the federal arbitrator for the contract negotiations. The Commissioners came to the table and we went back to work in the spring, triumphant![10] Those arrested had been told that if we were convicted, the Union would appeal. We never won the appeal on the convictions and when I moved to California in 1984, I still had to explain my conviction on the psychology licensure application.

Many of us were union activists who would also go on to form The Concerned Black Public Aid Employees group that created and promoted Black awareness in the workplace. When I was looking to gain some strategic insight into how best to go about organizing Black people working in the Welfare Department, my first opportunity to contact Bobby E. Wright came. I had been told that he was this dynamic truant officer in the Public School System who had been very instrumental in working with Al Raby. They worked to get rid of the "Willis Wagons,"[11] atrocious temporary trailers that were put up on school grounds to keep Black children trapped within the boundaries of the Black ghetto. Al Raby and Dr. King had founded the Chicago Coordinating Committee of Community Organizations (CCCO) that gave birth to The Chicago Freedom Movement. I reached Bobby by phone. He was under tremendous pressure and surveillance because of his organizing activity. He was encouraging while stressing several points.

The Union bulletin boards began to display information about Black events, and soul food pot lucks started to appear in celebration of Black culture in district offices. Black people wore their hair in natural styles and began to wear African prints and dashikis to work. A Union member, George Forney, who was authentic in his carriage and apparel, seemed to attract the wrath of the administration. People were actually fired from their jobs for embracing their African heritage. Criticism also came from some in the Black community; they called those who began to identify with African culture in order to establish a positive identity, cultural nationalists. The inference was that our commitment to the liberation of Black people did not extend beyond the external trappings to action. I was *in action.*

Professor Charles V. Hamilton, a political scientist, taught at Roosevelt University from 1967 to 1969. With Stokely Carmicheal, he had co-authored the book *Black Power.*[11] I was fortunate to be in the first class that he had created for social workers, teachers, and policemen. Members of the IUPAE, The Black Patrolman Association under Renault Robinson, and the Federation of Black Teachers were solicited. It was a class to formalize the concept of change agent as an avenue for professionals to use themselves in a way that would advance human dignity and empowerment of constituent populations. Change agent was *the concept* for me; lessons well-taught and well-learned guided me in my work.

Following Dr. King's assassination in April 1968, riots swept through Chicago's Black community. I was still living in the Old Town area at 1717 N. Hudson and was one-seventh supportive owner of The Guild Bookstore on Halsted near Webster. Suddenly, everything changed in that liberal neighborhood. Now, everything was black and white. When the National Guard Federal troops rolled under my windows of the coach house that faced on Fern Court, they were looking for Black people from the Cabrini-Green Projects who had come across North Avenue (1600 North). Time to get back on the South Side! So, without ceremony, I headed south.

Public Welfare had also begun to change. William "Bill" Robinson, a Black man, became the Director of the Cook County Department of Public Aid; Charles McDowell, a Black man, became the District Office Supervisor for the Oakland office. The office had moved to the "Back of the Yards" neighborhood and occupied the old Drovers' Bank building. Cecile, Carole, and I requested to attend the 1968 National Conference on Social Welfare (NCSW) in San Francisco. Mr. McDowell gave us the challenge that in order to be approved to go, we would need to successfully rehouse nearly fifty residents of a nursing home who had just been shut down by Licensing. We drove to San Francisco. This would also be the year of the Farm Works strike against the California grape growers. Caesar Chavez and Rev. Jesse Jackson addressed the group to protest the social work needs of the Black community were not being addressed. Black social workers walked out, totally disrupting the conference. Bill Robinson also walked out with us and came to the re-assembled group of Black social workers. He seemed so genuine in throwing his arms up and saying something like, "I've tried to give hope to all the little Black children in public aid who are fatherless. I tell them: *I'm* your daddy!" He then went on to say to the group, "Free me from old social work traditions, so I can do a better job as director of this agency." I stood up, identifying myself as one of his case workers, and loudly replied. Other strategists of the re-assembled group outlined issues and ways that people could go back home and begin to do social work in a different way. I was most impressed with the articulate interpretation of issues outlined by Carole Adams, who I later found was from Chicago and a member of a group called The Catalyst. I found out that The Catalyst was a body of "Black people with skills dedicated to the liberation of the Black community by any means necessary." The group was meeting at the Parkway Community Center, where Leon Chestang was the director. I became a member of The Catalyst. This would become my extended family ever since. I knew some of the members from public aid like my old friends, Bruce Mims and Willeva Lindsey. Unlike other groups that elected officers, The Catalyst managed quite well with a fluid steering committee and Elders for consulting: Charlie Ross, Audrey Johnson, Joan Phillips Brown, Earl Doty, Eugene Perkins, Carole Adams, Chris Narcisse, Kermit Coleman, Levert King, Clyde French, Don Linder, Chuck Curry, James Stephenson, Rev. T.C. Vivian, William "Bill" Boline, Mattie Hopkins, Lloyd Sanders, Brother Hannibal Afrik, Timuel Black, Isabel Edwards, Cynthia Williams, Jerry Wilson, James I. Cage, Lerone Bennett, Jr., and Rev. James Mack to name just a few. As follow-up to the walk-out at the NCSW conference, Blacks in social work from all over the country met in Chicago and talked about whether to form an association and about the true nature of an association of Black social workers. I especially remember Ed Pitt from New York, who electrified his challenging comments. I witnessed a polarization of ideas between political activism, which would bring attention and action to issues affecting the Black community and, at the other end of the spectrum, a rather non-political organization. The Catalyst was clearly committed to action. It followed the inaugural first conference of the Association of Black Social Workers in Philadelphia. I attended for the first day, saw the movement of the group, and left before the end of the conference. I continued as a Catalyst member. We soon adopted a Pan-African focus and I chose the name *Nyala*, "swift and sweet messenger," to help teach my lessons to others.

In 1969 at public aid, Lenora Cartwright had begun to select individuals from the social work staff who could be counted on to respond to extraordinary situations. These positions would have a different title and high pay. I was considered, but not selected. However, when she left public aid to launch the Department of Urban Studies at the University of Illinois at Chicago Circle, she contacted me about another new program there. So, in August 1969, I left public aid to be part of the first program to bring minority students into the newly built University of Illinois at Chicago Circle campus. With Jake Jennings in the chancellor's office and James Griggs as director, the Educational Assistance Program (EAP) emerged. Key heads were Herb Scott, Murray DePillars and Chuck Anderson. To name some of the team, my co-counselors and instructors were: Sharon Jackson, Jessica (Tem) Yasui, Horace MacDougal, Paul Vega, Kathy Brown, Jim Pleasant, James Crawford, Beverly Fanniel, Joaquin Dias, and Ernie Berman. Outreach and recruitment staff included John Long, Dennis Daniels, and Theresa Powell. Marie Johnson was in the student counseling center and helped with the interface to that unit. The major contribution of this program was to bring the next generation of students of color—Black, Brown, Red—into an academic program that would help them to take educated leadership in their communities. One of the most renown of this first wave of students was Ellis Cose, award-winning journalist and author. These kinds of programs at open colleges and universities were open to urban youth without regard to income level. They began to spring up around the country. As an academic and counseling advisor, I was able to use my background in psychology and social work to help lift these students as they competed among Chicago's best for grades. Sometimes, in their classrooms they were met with more cynicism and racism because they had entered through the EAP.

During my first year at the University, it was necessary for me to take a leave of absence to help assist a close Chicago friend who had been put in prison in Rome. I could not reveal the real purpose of my leave to the Program. For over two months I wanted to visit Italy, Holland, Germany, France, Spain and North Africa before returning home. The trip would provide me with an international understanding of how Black people are viewed and treated outside the United States. When I returned I had more encouragement for my students in their aspirations. Jim Griggs also encouraged the EAP staff to continue their education. Having realized that we could not expect others to foster our growth as a People, it was clear that we needed more Black professors. So, in the fall of 1971, I officially entered the doctoral program in psychology at Circle, taking my rebel worker, change agent and Catalyst mentality right along.

As a graduate student in psychology, I was six years older than the other students who had come straight from undergraduate school. My year was the first that Black students enrolled in graduate psychology. It never occurred to me when I was working at the main P.O. and looking out the window along the Congress Expressway, seeing them build Circle campus, that I would be a university student there! I needed to seek Black mentors in my field. My classmate, Larry Byrd, who was from Atlanta and had attended Morehouse College, told me about the Black Student Psychological Association (BSPA) and the Association of Black Psychologists (ABPsi). Prentice Jackson was president of the BSPA. Bobby Wright emerged again. Since our last contact in the sixties, he had completed his Ph.D. in psychology at University of Chicago, along with the sister, Bobbie Hamilton, in record time. They welcomed me to the Chicago Area ABPsi, which had been strong until Black psychologists walked out of the American Psychological Association (September 1968) to form the Association of Black Psychologists. Larry Byrd and I would manage to convince U of I to give us a University car to drive to Detroit to attend my first national ABPsi conference in 1973. I found an able mentor in Dr. Joseph L. White. It was his article, "Towards a Black Psychology," in *Ebony* magazine that first used the term "Black psychology" in print, putting it into the lexicon.

By 1975 I had completed the MA research and was far enough along to start work for Dr. Bobby E. Wright at the Garfield Park Comprehensive Community Mental Health Center while completing the doctoral requirements. The Garfield Park CCMHC at Kedzie and Roosevelt Road was just a few blocks from the high school that I had attended and an old public aid office had been across the street. I had made it back to the West Side.

Now, I would have a chance to meet the mental health needs of the Black community that had been ruptured by poverty and the riots of the sixties. I would also help to foster the development of consciously committed Black mental health professionals. Within a short time, I was the first Black person to earn a Ph.D. in Psychology from the University of Illinois at Chicago Circle. After receiving my degree, I was bombarded with hysterical cheering, especially by every Black person there. It was as though I was a member of their family; And indeed I was and still am. I was thrilled to be seen as part of my people, to have gone from person to nation. Bobby would soon deliver his landmark work, "The Psychopathic White Racial Personality," and I would go on to work for him for that community for the next eight years, sharing the uplifting change agent and Catalyst philosophy.

NOTES:

[1] Please forgive my lapses of memory that may have caused me to leave out some names and mixed up some dates or events. Errors and omissions will be acknowledged if brought to my attention.

[2] Carmichael, S. & Hamilton, C.V. *Black Power: The Politics of Liberation in America.* New York, Vintage Books, 1967.

[3] Quoted from Sr. Paula, R.S.M. It seemed that almost every day in her Social Science class, she would give an opinionated history of the Sisters of Mercy that said they had to move their college and Motherhouse from the corner of 29th and Wabash, and then again from 49th and Cottage Grove, because of the Negro people moving into the neighborhood and being unable to afford the tuition. Then, she would call on me with some innocuous question that I would be unable to answer because I was choked with rage. When I complained to the president, I was transferred out of the class.

[4] Industrial Workers of the World, Internet Homepage: iww.org downloaded 1-30-08. Also Wikipedia: http://en.wikipedia.org/wiki/Industrial_Workers_of_the_World

[5] Deaths, Disturbances, Disasters, and Disorders in Chicago: a selected bibliography of materials in the municipal reference collection of the Chicago Public Library. Complied by O'Brien, E. & Benedict, L.

[6] *Labor Studies Journal,* 27.1, 25-43. The West Virginia University Press, 2002.

[7] King Encyclopedia, http://www.stanford.edu/group/King/about_king/encyclopedia/vietnam.htm Downloaded 1-30-08.

[8] Worten, H., Edwards, S. & Stokes, D (2002) An Activist AFSCME Local Confronts Welfare Reform, Labor Studies Journal 27.1 (2002), downloaded 1/30/08 from http://muse.jhu.edu/demo/labor_studies_journal/v027/27.1worthen.html

[9] Weber, A.R. "Paradise Lost; Or Whatever Happened to the Chicago Social Workers?" *Industrial and Labor Relations Review,* Vol. 22, No. 3 (Apr., 1969), pp. 323-338doi:10.2307/2522170.

[10] Carmichael, S. & Hamilton, C.V. *Black Power: The Politics of Liberation in America.* New York, Vintage Books, 1967.

[11] Just a closing note: Before retiring from the Los Angeles County Department of Health Services, King-Drew Medical Center in 2002, where I had also served as Interim Academic Chair of the Department of Psychiatry and Human Behavior (1993-1996), I had a chance, thanks to SEIU, to get on that picket line with that bullhorn one more time.

A VOYAGE OF DISCOVERY

Edward L. Palmer

I had been on the Chicago police force for about a year when Mayor Richard J. Daley issued his "shoot to kill" order after the Black uprisings and the looting on Chicago's West Side following Dr. Martin Luther King, Jr's assassination. I juxtaposed this kill order in my hometown with the cover picture on *Life* magazine of an eleven or twelve-year-old Black boy lying dead in the street. He had been shot by police in Newark, New Jersey, after he took a six pack of beer worth, at that time, ninety-nine cents.

Some of us Black policemen had a real fear that other Black leaders, who were unarmed, and Black people in general could also be killed by White reactionaries. I organized a small group of fellow Black Chicago policemen—Renault "Reggie" Robinson, Curtis Cowsen, Willie Ware, Wilbur Crooks, and Jack Dubonnet—to found the Afro-American Patrolmen's League with the intention of protecting the Black community and our leaders. Tom Mitchell, who was not on the force but later became our Information Officer, rounded out our original group. Howard Saffold joined later. We met initially in my apartment at 7639 South Luella, and then we chipped-in to rent office space on East 63rd Street.

We announced the launch of the League at our new headquarters. Explaining why we had formed the League, I asserted, "No longer will we be brutal pawns in a chess game against our own community. But rather, we still stand and protect our communities."

Black people all over the country were rising up demanding their rights as citizens, as human beings. From an initial group of about ten Black policemen, who had been regarded as Uncle Toms or in famed Black Panther leader Fred Hampton's words "Dashiki pigs," there emerged a group of Black policemen willing to affirm their commitment to people in the community where they lived. Fred would later tell me that I stood a good chance of being assassinated, ironically, because I was "more dangerous" than he was. A month later Fred Hampton and Mark Clark were killed by Chicago police.

I knew early on that no matter how strongly our band of Black policemen was committed, we needed more than our group to defend the Black community. So I came up with the idea of an umbrella of support, which meant getting endorsements for the League from almost all Black organizations in Chicago. This created an environment in which an attack on a few valiant Black policemen would be seen as an attack on the entire Black community.

I also suggested to Richard Durham, who was, though not a Muslim, the editor of *Muhammad Speaks* newspaper, that the Black community should also support us. Dick—who was one of the premier Black intellectuals, journalists and activists of our era, and also a compatriot of Oscar Brown, Jr., Studs Terkel, Harold Washington, Ishmael Flores, Louis Martin and Charlie Hayes—turned my ideas upside down. He stressed that the police, especially Black policemen, needed to support the Black community. This became the basis of the League's slogan: "We Support the Black Community."

Support came from Black people across the South and West Sides of the city. Frederick Douglass "Doug" Andrews, head of the Garfield Organization on the West Side of Chicago, was one of our staunchest advocates.

As well as knowing we needed broad support, I knew that we needed to have more than a policeman's sense of the Black community, and we needed to know how organizations worked. I asked Bill Berry, head of the Chicago Urban League, to help us. We got a grant from the Ford Foundation to hold seminars for Black policemen. About thirty Black policemen attended the seminars at the University of Chicago in 1968.

Among the people who addressed the seminars were Earl Durham, University of Chicago School of Social Work administration, and Richard Rubenstein, assistant director of the Adlai Stevenson Institute. More seminars were held at Dartmouth College in New Hampshire, organized by the Adlai Stevenson Institute. Participants included Professor Jonathan Mirksy, a professor at Dartmouth; the head of the National Security Council; the editor of the *Cleveland Plain Dealer* and Marshall Field. The conferences developed in us a greater awareness that we were not simply policemen, but we had become men. We had truly become protectors of our community, and we were now accepted as members of that community.

Dick Durham, who by this time had built *Muhammad Speaks* newspaper into the largest Black newspaper in history, became an advisor to me personally and to the League. As editor of the newspaper, which had extensive international news, Dick exerted great intellectual power. I was honored when he told me that he was going to model a PBS series, *Bird of the Iron Feather,* after my life and for which he paid me a consultant's fee.

The Afro-American Patrolman's League took seriously its responsibility to protect Black leaders. At Stokely Carmichael's request, the League escorted him when he was in Chicago to speak.

On one memorable occasion, Reverend Jesse Jackson was scheduled to testify before a U.S. Congressional hearing on Blacks and the construction trade. Rev. Jackson had asked for federal protection. Rev. Jackson and I, accompanied by other League members, met with then Assistant U.S. Attorney Tom Todd in a parking lot at 51st and State Street. But since Attorney Todd was accompanied by only two agents, I told Rev. Jackson that the League would provide protection.

We formed a phalanx of armed Black Chicago policemen and escorted Rev. Jackson to the Old Custom House on Canal Street and into the hearing room, to the outrage of some five to ten thousand angry white construction workers who surrounded the building to keep him from testifying. Mayor Richard J. Daley condemned this effort and threatened to remove League members from the police force.

In an unforgettable meeting after the event, Rev. Jackson and I caucused with Congressman Ralph Metcalfe at his home. The Congressman subsequently prevailed on the Mayor to rescind his threat.

The League also became embroiled in Cardinal Cody's refusal to appoint Father George Clements, a strong supporter of the League, as Pastor of St. Dorothy's Church because he was considered too militant. We organized pressure on Cardinal Cody, who did appoint Father Clements Pastor of Holy Angels.

During its early days, the League had a number of accomplishments that laid the groundwork for subsequent achievements:

1. The League broke the shibboleth that Black policemen were conspirators and complicit in the oppression of Black communities. The breakthrough may have been more symbolic, but it had huge ramifications then and later. For example, in Doris Kearn's book about Lyndon Johnson, she suggests that he thought the country was on the brink of anarchy in the 1960s. In response to one of Detroit's uprisings, LBJ called on the 82nd or 101st Airborne Division (my memory is shaky here) to quell the disturbances. Many of these soldiers were Black and from inner city areas, and they refused to go, saying if some formerly "Uncle Tom" Black Chicago policemen could stand up for their community so could they.
2. The League took a forceful stand on renaming Crane Junior College as Malcolm X College.
3. The League strenuously opposed Mayor Daley's "shoot to kill" edict and the placement of shotguns in police squad cars. The outcry against these practices eventually led to the discontinuation of the edict and the removal of the shotguns.

4. The League took a principled stand by refusing to agree with the official Chicago police position on Fred Hampton's death. By this time, some League members had become more cautious about taking what could be dangerous positions, and some did not want to take any position on Fred Hampton's death. The *Chicago Sun Times* newspaper initially buried the story in the back pages. Courageous journalists at the paper, including Michael Miner, threatened to resign if the paper did not put the story on the front pages, which it did shortly thereafter.

   I insisted that we all go see how Fred was killed. Reggie, Curtis, Saffold and I went to the house where Fred had died. It was clear from the trajectory of the bullets that they were only incoming, and the mattresses were soaked with blood. After seeing the scene of this slaughter, it was our consensus that the League had to speak out, which further consolidated the Black community's respect for us.
5. Because of the attention the League got in Chicago, other similar groups formed in Detroit (Frank Blunt), New York (Lennie Weir), and San Francisco (Richard Hungiston).

Around 1970 there was a coup in the League, and I was removed from leadership. Some members felt that my militant positions were injurious to the League. I had been on a leave of absence from the police force for about a year, during this time I was head of security at Malcolm X College. When I applied to return to the Chicago Police Department, I was informed that my leave had not been honored. I was formally removed from the police department's rolls. This turned out to be a blessing in disguise. I am now engaged in wider, more progressive, more encompassing international work and leadership.

LOOKING BACK AT THE BLACK STRUGGLE IN CHICAGO: 1960-1975

Hannibal Barcar Shabazz aka Robert C. Butler

This paper will specifically discuss the role(s) this writer played in the Black struggle in Chicago from 1967 through 1972 as related to: participating in marches, demonstrations with Chicago Public School teachers and students, and community organizing in the Cabrini-Green Projects on the near North Side of Chicago; the Lawndale community on the West Side of Chicago; DePaul University of Chicago; Malcolm X Community College's Nat Turner campus (formerly located in the Jewtown community at 12th Place and Newberry); and the University of Chicago. In addition, this paper will inform its readers how this writer used his base in Chicago to close the gap between Blacks in both the North and South who were struggling to bring about Black liberation as well as speaking at numerous white Northern college campuses in an attempt to recruit Black students and educate as many students as he could. Lastly, this writer will discuss how he went about building Black unity and relationships with others who were involved in the Black struggle in Chicago as well as across the country and the lessons learned from his involvement in these struggles.

Chicago Public School Kids and Teachers Demonstrating/ Marching on the Board of Education Downtown at 211 Wells Street

As a FTB (full time basis) substitute teacher with the Chicago Board of Education for grades kindergarten through eighth grade during the 1967-1968 school year, I was assigned to teach at inner city schools on both the South and West Side of Chicago. As an organizer for Black liberation, I had positioned myself quite well. Every day I went to schools like John Thomas Ferrin, Mary C. Terrell, DuSable Upper Grade Center, Hess Upper Grade Center and others, to educate and agitate fellow teachers, janitors, dining room workers and students of the need for Black Power, Black unity, Black pride, and Black excellence.

Some of the most productive work I was able to do was on the West Side of Chicago at Hess Upper Grade Center, which is located in the Lawndale community. This community had a population of approximately 265,000 inhabitants (mostly African American). Moreover, this community housed the 23rd Ward and the 11th police precinct. Deceased United States Congressperson George Collins and his wife Cardiss, who later replaced him in Congress after he died in an airplane crash, were just some of the people I worked with in the Lawndale Community. I mentioned the 11th police precinct because in the late 1960s my organization's focus, the All African Peoples Alliance, was on community control; we helped to expose various white police officers in the 11th precinct who were members of the Klu Klux Klan.

Although the Conservative Vice Lords, a street gang, controlled the streets of the Lawndale community, I dealt directly with members of another street gang, the Enchanted Lovers. Two of the leaders, Johnny and Frog, lived less than two minutes from our organizational headquarters located at 3316 West Roosevelt Road.

Hess Upper Grade Center is important because three very important people worked there: Principal Nola Joy, Sandra Pye, and Pat Jones (my AKA sister who I knew from my many organizing efforts at the University of Illinois in Champaign-Urbana). These three individuals had no problem whatsoever with Black Power, community control, or Black excellence for Black kids in the Chicago Public School System. Needless to say, I formed a very close bond with them.

Cabrini-Green Projects and the Near North Side

From July 1967 until March 1970, I lived in Old Town Gardens on the Near North Side at 1350 North Sedgewick Street, which was located two blocks from the Cabrini-Green Projects. Living in Old Town Gardens afforded me the opportunity to meet a lot of people who lived in Cabrini-Green and the surrounding area. Also, it made it possible for me to meet and work with now deceased United States House of Representative member, Sidney Yates. I wrote articles about the conditions in the Cook County Jail for his newsletter.

Going in and out of Cabrini-Green on an almost daily basis allowed me to meet Brothers Danny Underwood, James Edwards (who was later murdered), the Walla Walla Basics (African drummers who attended Waller High School on the Near North Side), various gang leaders, and community organizers in the area. It was through Brother James Edwards that I was introduced to Joyce Brown and Bob Brown, two members of Chicago SNCC (Student Nonviolent Coordinating Committee). At the time they were organizing resistance groups against the Vietnam War. I later met Jessie White and his tumblers, who practiced in a space owned by Old Town Gardens.

During the first year that I lived in Old Town Gardens, I made a lot of friends. I visited every night club in the area and had a very thorough knowledge of the key players in the Near North Side African American community and also the adjacent Old Town music area along the 1300/1400 blocks of Wells and LaSalle streets.

By the spring of 1968, Danny Underwood, a young militant nineteen-year-old Cabrini-Green resident, and I started a group called BAD (Black Active and Determined). Many of our initial members were students from Waller High School on the Near North Side of Chicago. One of our most talented members was a sister by the name of Linda. Not only was she a natural-born leader, she was also smart as a whip and as militant as Angela Davis and Kathleen Cleaver. Our city-wide organization of young, militant high school students from all over Chicago, along with militant full-time and part-time Chicago Public School teachers, organized a school boycott over the issues of better food in school cafeterias and the hiring of African American photographers to take the graduation pictures of African American high school students. I was also able to hook up with two of my former buddies from the University of Wisconsin-Madison, Jacqueline Jackson (from the West Side of Chicago) and Larry Woods (former state champion hurdler and wide receiver from Maywood Proviso East High School).

By May of 1968, BAD had organized enough African American students at Waller High School to force the school principal and the Board of Education to implement an African American history class. A good sister, who was a recent graduate at the time from the Chicago Art Institute, was very instrumental in helping us push for African American history to be taught at the school.

As the 1967-68 school year came to a close, I made a calculated decision to leave the Chicago Public School System as a substitute teacher and to take the job as director of Development of Neighborhood Resources (DNR) with Chicago Commons, a social service agency. My office was located in the middle of the Cabrini-Green Housing Projects. Initially, I operated out of the Olivet Community Center, which was eventually closed down, and later out of Olivet Catholic Church, which was located down the street. This new position provided me the opportunity to come into contact with every resident who lived in Cabrini-Green. I called my new job "organizer's heaven". I say this because I was my own boss. Also, I had Danny Underwood, a life long resident of Cabrini-Green and the co-founder of BAD. Later, Leroy Walker a.k.a Solomon Oyuko Kenyatta (a former pimp, gang banger and resident of Cabrini-Green) moved in with me due to homelessness; he helped me in my organizing efforts. Also Johnnie Dee Swain, a classmate of mine at Tennessee

State University in Nashville, Tennessee, came to live with me in Chicago after spending a year in law school at the University of Wisconsin-Madison. What Johnnie Swain lacked in community organizing skills, he made up for with his theoretician and tactical skills. We all had been thoroughly trained in the politics of Black Power, Black Nationalism, Pan Africanism, Negritude, and radicalism during our stay at Tennessee State University. The writings, tapes, and records of Malcolm X were our breakfast, and the writings of W.E.B. DuBois and Osageyfo Kwame Nkrumah were our lunch and dinner.

Being the director of the DNR program also afforded me the opportunity to meet people like: Al Raby, Tim Black, members from the West Side Organization (WSO), Professor Irvin Spergel at the University of Chicago, E. Duke McNeil from TWO (The Woodlawn Organization), Margaret Burroughs from the DuSable Museum, poet Haki Madhubuti (formerly Don Lee), Useni Eugene Perkins, Communist Brother Claude Lightfoot, the Honorable Elijah Muhammad, Jessie Jackson, gang leader Jeff Fort, Bob Lucas and Curtis Burrell and various other members from KOCO (Kenwood-Oakland Community Organization), Warner Sanders of BBF (Better Boys Foundation), Mayor Harold Washington, Brothers James Turner and John Bracey from Northwestern University, Faith Christmas from the Chicago Defender, and many others in the "hood" struggling for Black liberation and nation building "by any means necessary".

Although as director of the DNR program I was able to serve Black people, my hands were often kept tied by those over me. This resulted in me attending countless business meetings downtown, which I felt were not directly related to those whom I served in Cabrini-Green. Although my supervisor saw value in the organizing work I was doing, they did not approve of me leading the CTA bus boycotts. Consequently, I turned in my resignation in December 1968. I enrolled in the graduate school program of sociology at DePaul University for the winter quarter of 1969. Fortunately, I had the opportunity to study under Drs. James McKeown (former University of Chicago Fulbright Scholar) and Luvenia Raymond (a Brazilian anthropologist and scholar who studied under famous anthropologist Levi-Strauss at Indiana University).

Battling With the President and Other Racists at DePaul University

Little did I know that DePaul University, both its downtown and Lincoln Park campuses, were hot beds of racism. From January 1969, when I initially enrolled in the graduate program in sociology, until I graduated in June 1970, I spent the vast majority of the time I was on campus educating and agitating. I educated Black folk and agitated white folk.

Because I was a graduate student and a research assistant, it did not take long for both Black and white students to get to know me or hear about me. I preached Black Power and Black Nationalism day in and day out, both in and out of class. Due to me being a very good student, the only people that openly challenged my ideas were Dr. Luvenia Raymond (an anthropology professor), Richard Crowe and his Young Republican organization on campus, the University president and his henchmen, and a few conservative African American students marginally associated with the Black Student Union.

The in-class verbal exchanges I had with Dr. Raymond were over race versus culture. Of course, my position always centered on "race matters". She disagreed with me vehemently. Johnnie Dee Swain, also enrolled in the graduate program in sociology at DePaul, was always there to support my Black Nationalist/Black Power assertions. If it had not been for Captain Ed Scarborough, also an African American graduate student in sociology and head of DePaul's ROTC program, the university administration would have gotten rid of me the first day I enrolled. Not once did Captain Ed Scarborough fail to intercede on my behalf when I got into conflicting situations with the white folk at DePaul University.

During my second quarter at DePaul, I convinced Ervin Mayfield and several other key members of the Black Student Union, such as Lillian Jefferson and John Motely, that we should present a set of demands to the university that would make things better for African American students and Black/white relations at the university. After we threatened to take over the basketball court at half time when DePaul was scheduled to play Niagra University on nationwide television, the President of the university decided to meet with African American students at a "town meeting" at the Near North Side Campus. The game was also of national interest because Calvin Murphy, an all-American and the nation's leading scorer, played for Niagra University.

The condition under which President Cordieau agreed he would meet with Black students was that I would not be allowed to say anything during the meeting. Believe it or not, the majority of the Black Student Union members agreed with this condition. Of course, at the meeting, President Cordieau denied every one of our just demands. Consequently, we got in touch with Fred Hampton and other Black Panther Party members from the Chicago area and the Young Lords (a near North Side Puerto Rican street gang), who helped protest and let the university administration at DePaul know we meant business about our reasonable demands. Ultimately, we took over the campus center at the Near North Side campus where all of the classes were held. We chained and locked every door in the building. What we heard on the radio while we had the building under siege was entirely different than what really was going on. As usual, many in the administration blamed me for the takeover of the campus center building. Consequently, both the university administration and the sociology graduate program faculty recommended me for a teaching job at Malcolm X Community College in order to get me out of their hair. Moreover, white students and their parents booed me when I walked across the stage when I received my Master's Degree in sociology in June 1970. Not only was I booed when I crossed the stage displaying my Black Power fist, I also was momentarily placed under arrest on stage by DePaul security officers to let me know that white folks ran the show at DePaul, not me.

On The Battlefield at Malcolm X Community College and the University of Chicago

When I first started teaching at Malcolm X Community College in the Fall of 1969, there were two campuses—the Denmark Vessey and the Nat Turner campuses. The Vessey campus was located by the Cook County Hospital near Madison Street and Ashland Avenue, and the Turner campus was located at 12th Place and Newbury, in "Jewtown," near the University of Illinois at Chicago campus.

I enrolled in the doctoral program in sociology at the University of Chicago; at the same time, I accepted the position to teach full-time in the Social Science Department at Malcolm X Community College. Dr. James McKeown was chiefly responsible for developing my interest in applying to the Ph.D. program in sociology at the University of Chicago; after all, he had been a Fulbright Scholar there and one of UC's most distinguished graduates. Dr. McKeown used every skill and contact he had at his disposal to get me away from DePaul University, so I would not wreak any more havoc there. It was Dr. David Street, in the sociology department at the University of Chicago, that made it possible for me to receive a National Institute of Mental Health fellowship (NIMH); thus, sealing the deal for me to matriculate toward a doctorate degree at the University of Chicago.

Both institutions, the Nat Turner Campus at Malcolm X and the University of Chicago, provided fertile soil for me to continue my organizing activities as well as educate and agitate. It was at Malcolm X that I met Black Panthers Fred Hampton and Bobby Rush, and Dr. Bobby Wright, Dr. Charles G. Hurst (President of Malcolm X), Buzz Palmer, Phil Cohran, and countless other comrades fighting for black liberation. Also, I met and trained a large number of freedom fighters during my brief time teaching at the Nat Turner Campus. Among the best of them were: Terrance McClay (Mansa Musa), Diane Mabin, Erzella Woods, Debra Mahone, Victor Adams, Geri Ousley, Pharoh (Allan Jones) and Michael Singleton.

At the University of Chicago, I was afforded the opportunity to meet and associate with such brilliant African-Americans as Drs. John Hope Franklin, Allison Davis, Charles Long (the faculty advisor of my campus organization, the All African Peoples Alliance), Alphonso Pinkney (visiting Sociology professor from Hunter College in New York), and doctoral students Harold Rodgers, Anderson Thompson, Ather Hunt, James "Red" Moore, Roberta Gill, Shemilis Tellis from Ethiopia and other international graduate students, Marion Sleet, and undergraduate students Dorothy Foster, Maja Jackson, Stan Willis, and many others.

Rather than spend our time reading the Maroon, the student newspaper at the University of Chicago, my campus organization, The All African Peoples Alliance, published an eight-page tab newspaper titled *The Black Light*. Dorothy Foster, Maja Jackson and I were very instrumental in getting this paper published monthly.

As I began to gain momentum with my organizing, educating and agitating tactics at both Malcolm X Community College and the University of Chicago, I decided it was the right time to base our struggle and organizing efforts in the Black community. The critical question that others and I had to answer was, which Black community in the city of Chicago?

Lawndale Here We Come: The All African Peoples Alliance

By April 1970, I had thoroughly convinced the students, especially those from Malcolm X and the University of Chicago, that I had been organizing around the city and that the university was an extension of the community rather than the other way around. Because the community was the key element in our struggle to organize Black people toward nation building and Black liberation, it became paramount that we start there and work our way toward the college campuses. The students from the University of Chicago and Malcolm X Community College that joined me in the struggle in the Lawndale community, clearly understood that if our mission was to be accomplished, we must be community-oriented as well as see the need to build strong relationships in the Black Community. We began our work in the Lawndale community at 3316 West Roosevelt Road, in an extremely large storefront building we rented out from the people who lived upstairs. The name of our international organization was the All African Peoples Alliance. We painted the outside and the inside of our multi-purpose storefront building red, black, and green (red for the blood that Black people have shed in the liberation struggle, black for our people, and green for the land we are going to acquire in our struggle for Black liberation).

The programs we offered were many: free breakfast programs for school children, karate classes, after-school knowledge sharing (tutoring) programs for elementary and upper grade center students, firearm training, African drum and dance classes, Kiswahili classes, the monthly publication of the All African Peoples Alliance newspaper, political education classes, a church service every Sunday evening, community organizing (primarily pushing for community control of the schools in the Lawndale area), community control of the 11th precinct police station in the Lawndale community, roundtable discussions of important Black books, publishing my books, a Black speakers bureau, and communicating with people through our massive mailing list.

Because of my courage, leadership skills and strong revolutionary will, I was elected the permanent International Governor of our international organization. One of my current best friends in the Chicago area, Mansa Musa, aka AME Pastor Terrance McClay, was elected the permanent vice international governor as a result of his strong leadership skills, outstanding courage, and revolutionary fervor. In sum, we had a very strong organization chiefly composed of young college students, but we also attracted many community residents such as Sister Mary Hill (wife of dance show host Bill Hill); her two high school daughters, Warijia and Warijima; and many of her friends who worked at the Dr. Martin Luther King Health Center on Crenshaw in the Lawndale community. Also, we attracted gangbangers from the Enchanted Lovers, especially two of the leaders, Frog and Johnny.

Our one act street plays and African drummers, such as those from the Walla Walla Basics (Brother Calvin and his friends) and Akin Babatunde (a Chicago native who was attending the University of Illinois), proved to be very effective in drawing both younger and older people, high school students, dropouts, and the elderly into our facility. We even held the first Kwanzaa celebration in the city of Chicago from December 26, 1970 through January 1, 1971. Although it was the first Kwanzaa ever held in the city of Chicago, it was also the third ever held in the United States. The first Kwanzaa ever held in the United States was held in South Central Los Angeles, California, by the U.S. organization headed by Maulana Ron Karenga (slave name Ron Everett, who obtained his undergraduate degree from Howard University and his doctorate degree from UCLA in African Studies). The second Kwanzaa ever held in the United States was in Newark, New Jersey, by Imamu Amiri Baraka (formerly known as LeRoi Jones the poet, who also received his undergraduate degree from Howard University and his graduate degree from Columbia University in New York).

Everybody attended the first Kwanzaa our organization sponsored. Not only did we serve food, shell peanuts, and herb tea each day as we moved toward karamu day, but we also had nightly panel discussions facilitated by Ruwa Chiri, a brother from Zimbawi, and me. Brothers and sisters from the continent of Africa could dialogue with brothers and sisters in the Black Diaspora. Phil Cohran, dancers Arnell Pugh and Julian Swain, the Sun Drummers, the Darlene Blackburn Dance Troupe, the ABC Center Dancers, and poet Cleveland Webber, were also featured at this political and festive event.

After one year in operation, the All African Peoples Alliance had become very effective in helping to organize the Lawndale African American community on the West Side of Chicago. However, one of the biggest mistakes we made was when I went on Wali Saddik's WLS Sunday night radio show and bad mouthed Bob Haggerty of Sears and Roebuck. As a result of this public attack, the Chicago Building Codes' people declared our building as being unfit and in violation of various building codes. Consequently, we had to vacate the building. Within one week, we moved our organization to St. Agatha Catholic Church. Brother Willie, a Chicago Youth Organization worker, was chiefly responsible for organizing this move. Although we worked vigorously to organize the young people in and around St. Agatha Catholic Church, the multiple attacks, verbal and otherwise, we suffered from the Chicago Police Department in the surrounding area, resulted in the decision to relocate the government of the All African Peoples Alliance from Chicago to Champaign-Urbana, Illinois, and later to Knoxville, Tennessee.

Conclusion: Lessons Learned

Looking back at the struggle in Chicago during 1960-1975, I learned that spending time talking about the white man in the news media is not the answer to our problem as a people. We have got to realize that our struggle for Black liberation and nation building is not going to be achieved overnight. We must not only keep in mind that our struggle is protracted, but also we must prepare or develop successors to continue the struggle. I learned that we cannot get discouraged because other black folk do not see the need to get involved in the black liberation and nation building struggle. In reality, the only thing that matters is that we determine in our hearts that we are going to stay on the battlefield until we die! As Fredrick Douglass used to say, "Dare to struggle, dare to win!" I do not know what you came to do, but I came to struggle against any and every form of oppression: white, black, yellow, brown or red.

INTERVIEW WITH HENRY ENGLISH

Useni Eugene Perkins

This interview between Henry English and Useni Eugene Perkins took place on September 22, 2014 at the office of the Black United Fund.

USENI EUGENE PERKINS: What was the general climate of Chicago's West Side where you lived during the 1960's?

HENRY ENGLISH: Well, you know, coming back out of the military in 1966, I decided that when I got out of the Marine Corp that I would go back to school. The closest junior college to me was Crane College so I entered Crane, September of '66. After getting out of the Marine Corp, I took a job at Delcore Aluminum and I worked a 3 to 11 shift, which was the ideal shift for me to attend school. That particular period was calm, and people were still kind of buzzing around trying to figure out how to move forward. When I started at Crane Community College, I took 9 hours and later on I just happened to take a job at Crane. Also, at the time, many people were being laid off at Delcore. I had just been there over a year and it made me eligible for a 12-week vacation. So instead of being laid off, I took the vacation time, which allowed me to become more active with Crane.

PERKINS: What motivated you to join the Chicago Chapter of the Black Panther Party?

ENGLISH: Well, we have to go back because what motivated me was my involvement with student government. I also began working with the Yearbook staff which made me become more involved with student government. Stan Wills, also a veteran, headed the African American Club and we became close friends. Alonzo Evrich was president of student government and our student advisor was Ellie Evans, an English teacher at the University of Chicago. After Alonzo left Crane to attend Chicago Teacher's College, Stan and I decided to run for president and vice-president respectively. We both won and now were in the forefront of student government. At that time Rufus Walls was the leader of the African American

Club. Eventually, Stan became the president of the African American Club and we began a movement to name the school after Malcolm X.

PERKINS: How well did you know Fred Hampton, the chairman of The Chicago Chapter?

ENGLISH: I first met Fred Hampton on the West Side after Dr. King was assassinated in 1968 and the West Side began to erupt in rebellion. I remember I was over on the South Side visiting a friend that day and as I was returning to the west side I could see flames everywhere. As I was headed home, the National Guard was patrolling the streets with tanks and armor trucks. The following day, the student government decided to hold a memorial for Dr. King and invited Fred, who was from Maywood and an activist in the NAACP to speak. We also invited Don Lee (now Haki Madhubuti). Fred gave a fiery speech and I thought the (nigger) must be crazy. That was the first time I met Fred. The second time I met Fred was in the basement of a home on the South Side with Bobby Rush and Billy "Che" Brooks. That was the beginning of the formation of the Black Panther Party moving from the South Side to the West Side.

PERKINS: What were some of the other Political Activist groups that you were involved in on the West Side or even the South Side?

ENGLISH: We had Nancy Jefferson who headed the West Side Association. Nancy played a critical role in this whole process of renaming Crane Jr. College to Malcolm X College. She was a strong supporter of our student organization and whenever we had a problem she would have our back. We all were very appreciative of the West Side Association and it gave us more confidence to know that she was behind us. I could also name Lugman, who headed the Black Hand Society and Russ Meek. There were also other groups like Robert Butler (aka Brother Hannibal) who headed the All African's People Organization and Rev. Archie Hartgrave and his West Side Organization. Although these groups may have had different ideologies they shared a common protest against injustice. With the support of these diverse groups, we were in a better position to strengthen our movement to rename Crane Jr. College to Malcolm X College when we met with Shabat.

PERKINS: Who was Shabat?

ENGLISH: Oscar E. Shabat was Chancellor of Chicago City Junior Colleges. He decided to hire activity directors from each college to bring the leadership of City Colleges together.

We had a big meeting in Lake Geneva and that was really the defining moment when we were able to exert a lot of influence over the mission and administration of the city colleges. I became the founding President of the City College Student Government.

PERKINS: As one of the primary leaders of that movement, what are some of the obstacles you faced?

ENGLISH: There were a number of different obstacles, but none that we could not overcome. At this time there were two groups in the city colleges—the older ones and the new ones. Because members from the older group—like Stan, Robert Clay and myself had been in the service we didn't have much fear and believed we could accomplish what we set out to do. This attitude began to trickle down to the younger groups who looked to us for leadership. It is not that we felt invincible but we believed that we could shut down the whole system with just a phone call if we had to.

PERKINS: How could you do that?

ENGLISH: Because we could call all the Presidents and say we're shutting it down.

PERKINS: What was your relationship with Renault Robinson who I believe was one of the founders of African American Patrolmen's League?

ENGLISH: My relationship as a student was with Buzz Palmer who headed the security at Malcom X. Buzz worked for the Chicago Police Department and was a friend of Renault. Actually, it was Buzz who was the founder of the African American Police Association and he was sympathetic to our movement. My relationship with the African American Police dates back to its beginning. Also, it was around this time that we sent representatives from the party to secure an official charter from the National Chapter of the Black Panther Party in Oakland, California.

PERKINS: Did you meet Huey Newton at the time?

ENGLISH: I didn't go with our representatives because at the time I was in jail. However, I took the lead when the west side chapter was approved and as I stated earlier met with Fred, and Bobby on the south side to form our Central Committee which was located in an office on Madison Street.

PERKINS: Did you know "Fats" Crawford from the Deacons for Defense?

ENGLISH: Yeah I knew "Fats" I met him at the meeting I told you about in the basement of South Stewart Street.

PERKINS: Okay, while Malcolm X was being built, where were classes held and who were some of the instructors that taught at Malcolm X during that time?

ENGLISH: The list is too long for me to remember all of their names. But it did represent almost every activist and political group in Chicago. Some of the instructors were Lou Palmer, Kermit Coleman, Anderson Thompson, Russ Meek, Bobby Wright and Phil Cohran, who wrote the school song for Malcolm X College.

PERKINS: Where were classes held while Malcolm X College was being built?

ENGLISH: I believe it was located some where near the Market area. We were recruiting high school students to take our place and I was getting ready to transition out. I was ready to move out and ended up in New Hampshire with the Party. When I returned to Chicago it was difficult to tell the Party from the Student Government. I served on the Central Committee of the Party and also was President of the Student Government. This was a crucial period because there were some people who didn't want to name the school after Malcolm X.

PERKINS: Did that surprise you?

ENGLISH: Well yeah it surprised me. But what surprised me the most was that the City Colleges commissioned a survey to determine what the name should be and the one that received the most votes was Booker T. Washington. Nobody was going to buy that one so the case was closed. We start calling the new building Malcolm X College and began sending out literature with the name Malcolm X on it. We also had our basketball team wear red and Black uniforms and began to fly the Black Liberation flag.

PERKINS: I understand Dr. Nathan Hare was being considered for the Presidency of Malcolm X. Was he interested or give me some information.

ENGLISH: That's correct. But the student government wanted to hire Barbara King.

PERKINS: Who was she?

ENGLISH: At present she is a minister and has one of the largest congregations in the suburbs of Atlanta, Georgia. When she was at Crane, she was an Assistant Dean and had a strong bond with the students. At that time this was a major achievement to have a Black woman as Assistant Dean of a college. As President of Student Government I placed her name to be considered for the position of president. But while I was incarcerated her name was removed from the list of potential candidates.

PERKINS: Why were you incarcerated?

ENGLISH: As a result of us leaving the West Side to meet with some members of the Black P stone Nation. And we were fully armed. We had received a threatening letter from them and we wanted to let them know we were about helping Black people and not killing black people.

PERKINS: Was Jeff Fort at the meeting?

ENGLISH: No. When we got to the meeting we marched down the street with our guns on our shoulders and went to their headquarters. Jeff was not there and they said ya'll folks are crazy coming over here with your guns on your shoulders and your pistols on your waist. We knew they had more guns but we wanted them to know we were pro community and that our battle was not with them but the forces oppressing the Black community.

PERKINS: That was a bold move.

ENGLISH: We met up with Sengali, the spokesperson for the Stones, who set up the meeting for that night. On our way back to the west side, the driver made a bad turn and we were pulled over by the police and I was one of those individuals in the car.

PERKINS: What relationship did you have with Bobby Gore and the Vice Lords on the West Side?

ENGLISH: I didn't have that much of a relationship with him because my assignment as a student
organizer was mostly spent organizing student organizations at other City Colleges. When

we first began organizing we all were speaking at the various colleges whether if was the University of Chicago, University of Illinois or Northeastern University. We decided that one speaker would be better and Fred was chosen to be that speaker because he was very passionate and a charismatic speaker. He could recite passages from Malcolm's writings with ease and could be challenging with his oratorical skills. A lot of people don't understand why Fred became the point person for the Party. The reason he became the point person was we decided only one person was needed to articulate the Party's views. Fred was not over the organization, where people get confused, he was the spokesperson for the organization.

PERKINS: Do you think one reason the Chicago Chapter of the Black Panther Party was in conflict with the Vice Lords was because the police believed the Party would politicize the gangs to become more of a political threat to Mayor Daley and his machine?

ENGLISH: We tried to politicize everybody. Some of the gangs didn't realize if they changed their ways, they could become an asset to the struggle.

PERKINS: How did Dr. Charles Hurst become the first president of Malcolm X?

ENGLISH: I went to jail.

PERKINS: What do you mean by that?

ENGLISH: I was in jail when Hurst was interviewed for the position and he impressed everybody. Hurst had a PhD in communications and was an elegant speaker. After I got out of jail I met with Sabbath to discuss if someone else other than Hurst could be considered for the presidency. I suggested he also consider Barbara King for the position who had the support of the student body. He was not pleased with my suggestion and said we should have a revote among the students. I told him I didn't have that kind of authority and the decision would have to be made by the student government. If the revote came out in favor of Hurst then I would be obligated to follow what that vote dictated. So we had a revote and it ended up being Charlie Hurst. What we didn't know at the time was that he and Dr. Nathan Hare, who was also interviewed for the position, were not on friendly terms. In fact Hurst was largely responsible for Hare being released from Howard University where they both had taught. Dr. Hare was also a boxer who often moonlighted to pursue this activity without getting permission from the university. Hurst had informed the university about this which resulted in Hare losing his job as a member of the faculty.

PERKINS: So why did Malcolm X College become, I would say, the epic center for the struggle not only on the West Side, but the South Side?

ENGLISH: It began at that meeting in Geneva when we seized power over all the City Colleges. We had influence over all the student leadership and had a base for bringing the colleges together to address a particular issue. For example, when we were fighting to have the school named Malcolm X, students came downtown from every one of the colleges to give their support at a press conference to announce the naming of Malcolm X College. And when Hurst spoke in behalf of all the colleges, he made a rousing appeal that Malcolm X was the appropriate name for our new college. He was a hell of a speaker!
It should also be noted that doing our struggle to rename Crane College to Malcolm X College, we had the support of such leaders as Did Gregory, James Montgomery, Jesse Jackson, and Harold Washington who, as you know, became Chicago's first Black mayor.

PERKINS: Thank you Henry for your informative remarks.

BLACK MOVEMENT IN CHICAGO—1967-1975: FROM STUDENT ACTIVISM TO COMMUNITY BUILDING

Dorothy Odell Foster

My connection to the Black movement in Chicago evolved through three phases: an awakening into a new identity as a part of the Black student movement at the University of Chicago; moving into the grassroots Black community struggle on Chicago's West Side; and working alongside Black contractors and construction workers struggling for economic parity. For each phase I will look at the people who were struggling with me, how we defined our struggle, what we accomplished, and what we learned.

Coming of Age as a Black Student on a White Campus

When I arrived at the University of Chicago in September 1967, I joined thirty-four other incoming Black freshmen from all parts of the country. Out of about 730 freshmen, we were the largest group of Blacks ever admitted to the University at one time. We came as part of an effort to attract the best and brightest of Black students from North and South, East and West, urban and rural. Together there were almost more of us than all the current undergraduate Blacks on campus.

We were warmly embraced by a core of Black upperclassmen who had come together in a group called SPLIBS (a local slang for Blacks). They had already began thinking about agitating and rebelling and were buoyed by our boost in numbers.

The first hurdle to overcome was the sense of individualism and isolation. The notion that "I am here and I can do it on my own" began to fade for many of us because we realized that if we were going to "survive and succeed," we needed each other.

During the fall and winter quarters we mostly talked, but it was a purposeful ongoing conversation that had a radical nature all its own. For many of us it was the first time we felt free to talk about hostilities we felt from white students, teachers, and the administration.

We discovered that some administrators did not believe so many Black students could successfully matriculate at the University of Chicago. It was as if we had been brought in as an experiment that was destined to fail. As one of my academic advisors reminded me during my initial interview, "You know your SAT scores were not among the highest." Somewhere, I found the courage to argue that I knew "that they were not among the lowest either." Many of us had come from predominantly white high schools where lowered expectations were commonplace, but the difference was that now we had others with whom to compare our experiences. We also began to develop a worldview through which we could understand the individual acts of racism and discrimination that we had endured.

All this talking among Black students resulted in a shift in consciousness for me. I was born in the South during the vibrant emergence of the Civil Rights Movement. I was five-years-old when the U.S. Supreme Court ruled on *Brown vs. the Board of Education*, but in Tuscaloosa, Alabama, I attended segregated schools in my sophomore year of high school. In 1956, at the height of the Montgomery Bus Boycott, domestic workers in Tuscaloosa and other Blacks also refused to ride the buses. But, as a seven-year-old, I knew that while Blacks were being brave many were afraid of the reprisals from white bosses and whites "who wore white sheets and rode in the night". Just four years before coming to Chicago, I was fourteen and in Sunday school when four little girls were killed while attending 16th Street Baptist Church in Birmingham—only sixty miles away from my hometown. So the Civil Rights Movement was not a newsworthy abstraction for me—it was real and personal and I knew that struggle required courage. Consequences were real and in many instances deadly.

University students taking the time to talk about what it meant to be Black in American shifted the focus of my perceptions about what we, as Black people, were struggling for and against.

In the South the solution appeared to be integration or desegregation at the least. We thought if we could just go where whites went to eat, study, shop, live and work with them, then they would recognize our humanity and all the opportunities of the American Dream would open up to us. In fact, I had spent two years living with a white family in State College, Pennsylvania, along with three other Black southern students, with sponsorship of a group of American Friends or Quakers. We had integrated the almost all-white State College High.

Coming to Chicago and engaging in long discussions with young Blacks who had grown up in Woodlawn, Englewood, Chatham and Morgan Park, we learned that Chicago was not the Promised Land for Blacks.

Painfully, through personal testimony, we learned that Blacks could not live wherever they chose in Chicago. In fact, it was eye-opening to learn the history of how the communities close around the campus had become part of restrictive covenants designed to keep Blacks out of Hyde Park and the University community.

Opportunities for jobs, careers, and business ownership were also serious problems in the North. But what was emerging was not a call for integration, but cries for justice, equality, and freedom that took on a historic and international resonance.

True to our calling as scholars, we were encouraged to read and study. Reading and discussing our "Black book list" often kept us busy late into the night after classes and studying—and for some it became what we chose to do instead of the rigorous University curriculum.

The reading list included: *Souls of Black Folks* by W.E.B DuBois, *Black Skin, White Masks* and *Wretched of the Earth* by Dr. Frantz Fanon. The struggle began to take on a revolutionary, Third World context. We also had the benefit of graduate students like Harold Rogers, who had studied Egyptian culture and movements, and Don Robotham, who was prominent in Jamaican freedom movements.

In the South, Dr. Martin Luther King, Jr. and the Southern Christian Leadership Conference (SCLC) used strategies and tactics for change that were clearly nonviolent protests and peaceful civil disobedience. But Chicagoans who met with us on campus were already being influenced by a new generation of leaders, such as Stokely Carmichael and the Student Nonviolent Coordinating Committee (SNCC). As we sought alliances with other Black student organizations on campuses like Roosevelt University, Northwestern University, Lake Forest College and as far away as Valparaiso University in Indiana, different strategies and tactics took prominence.

In 1968 Fred Hampton organized the Chicago Chapter of the Black Panther Party. National leaders of those movements, such as Bob Brown and Bobby Rush, were frequently on the agenda at our Black student meetings whenever they were in town. Speeches from icons like Huey P. Newton, Aldridge Cleaver, H. Rap Brown and Stokely Carmichael were recorded, printed, excerpted, memorized and codified. Rather than nonviolence, a mantra of "by any means necessary" developed and took precedence.

Growing up in the South, Judeo-Christian values permeated the struggle and in fact we knew that "God was on our side" and "Jesus had your back" in the Civil Rights Movement. But within the Black student study circles, new and different religious beliefs emerged to capture our hearts and spirits. With Chicago being the home of Elijah Muhammad and the Black Muslim Movement, some students began to study Islam as a way of life. Some of them gave up finding a church home in Chicago and began to attend the local Nation of Islam mosque, which was very close to the campus.

As part of our cultural immersion into everything African, "natural" spirituality with an African beat seemed very attractive. Studying new ways to look at Black struggle became very organized. There were classes in off-campus Woodlawn apartments with teachers like Bob Rhodes, a much older graduate student who had developed a body of knowledge around Marxist-Leninist thought. We studied dialectical materialism, other aspects of radical thought, the struggles in Algeria, Africa, and Cuba and how it all could apply to the Black struggle in Chicago. The needs were clear and basic on the macro level—Black people needed jobs and decent homes and good schools for their children. On an emotional level there was a clear call for freedom, justice, and the right to be ourselves. And we had a new name for ourselves—we were Black.

Certain historic events help to determine the momentum and the dynamics of the Black student movement on the U of C campus. On April 4, 1968, in the spring quarter of my freshman year, Dr. Martin Luther King, Jr. was assassinated and riots broke out in Chicago, most notably on the West Side and in the South Side communities adjacent to the University. Most of us left campus out of fear and anger, but also because of a sense of frustration. We had a need to separate from the white establishment. On the other hand, there was a strong desire to close ranks with one another and with the larger Black community.

The problem was that we did not yet have established ties with the Black community outside of the campus, so we went to large Hyde Park apartments that were home to upperclassmen and graduate students. Contrary to a notion that became popular in rap culture later, "This revolution was televised." And we watched it unfold as Bob Rhodes, among the chief Marxist-Leninist scholars, pointed out the similarities and differences with revolutions around the world. He also used his knowledge of Marxist and Leninist thinking to predict what would happen next. To be honest, we also ate and drank all we could find. Some of us danced all night while others played Bid Whist into the wee hours. A few brave souls actually ventured into the West Side and unwittingly found themselves between rioting Blacks and armed Illinois National Guardsmen.

That summer, my involvement in the Black Chicago movement accelerated. I worked on the West Side teaching GED and basic literacy classes out of Crane Junior College and a community-based office at the Better Boys Foundation in the Lawndale community. I worked alongside community leaders like Sister Christine Johnson, who had been a Black Muslim for many years in Chicago. She was a grassroots Black historian steeped in mystery and mysticism.

I had a chance to see firsthand the devastation that the riots had left behind. There were burnt-out stores and blocks that would not be re-built for many years to come. I also got a chance to see how difficult it is to reverse the vestiges of a dysfunctional educational system and the lack of living-wage job opportunities in the lives of individual Black folks. It was hard work and often you did not feel that you could make a difference without real, systemic changes.

In the fall of 1968 after the campus rebellion at Columbia University in New York City, U of C Black students launched a loosely-organized takeover of the administration building on Ellis Avenue. It began around ten in the morning. We barricaded ourselves into some offices and made our presence known. I am not even sure if we had written demands as we went in or if we developed them as we went along. Rather timid revolutionaries, some of the younger students actually called home to tell parents what we were doing and asked for permission to participate. As predicted, after parents argued that such actions might get a student expelled or cause them to lose scholarship dollars, several reported that they would have to leave the takeover immediately. In fact, shortly after the demand for food and water was met, the makeshift sit-in ended before the regular closing business hours that day. We lost some credibility as true revolutionaries, but it did get the attention of the administration in a positive way.

During the fall of 1968 interactions between Black students and administrators shifted. Some things that we had loosely discussed began to happen. An even larger group of Black freshmen arrived on campus. We had more interactions with Black faculty, such as Dr. Charles Long of the Divinity School and noted scientist Dr. Charles Bowman. Walter Walker from the highly regard School of Social Work was given a vice presidency and some liaison responsibilities between the University and the Woodlawn community. Students were invited to sit in on discussions about the University's relationship with the Black community. We got to see alliances between University leaders, such as Julian Levy, brother of University president Edward Levi, and The Woodlawn Organization, represented by Leon Finney.

The University offered the Black student organization a Black Student Center. We debated for nearly a year whether we should take it and what we would do with it. In fact, we debated for so long that the administration reluctantly rescinded the offer.

Later in 1970 the University asked for our blessing for a new program that worked with famed Chicago coach, Larry Hawkins. Hawkins would run programs for Black Chicago youth—mentoring, tutoring and helping them to get into colleges and universities in the area. Black students refused to support it, but Hawkins thought it could help a lot of struggling Black students who would otherwise be lost within Chicago's failing education system. Despite our misgivings about the program, Hawkins nurtured a relationship with U of C that has helped thousands of students over the past several decades.

This scenario illustrates the primary deficiency of the Black student struggle at the University in the late 1960s and early 1970s. We were more emotionally driven to embrace Blackness as a style and had not yet developed any substantive strategies for how such a movement could improve the lives of the larger Black community or even our lives as students on a predominantly white campus. But given where most of us had come from—homes and communities that did not appreciate or recognize anything that related to Blackness or Africa as culturally valid—we achieved a great deal in our own consciousness. A foundation was laid that allowed us to build a platform for community action as we matured individually and affiliated with other aspects of the struggle of Black freedom in Chicago and beyond.

Looking back, it was significant for my development as a Black woman that I had the opportunity to meet young Black Chicagoans who had been nurtured in the history and politics of this city. People like Linda Murray, who taught us a new way to think about race and class and who challenged what we knew about history and the news of the day. The University had brought in several older students like Standish Willis, a Chicago bus driver who brought an uncanny sense of realism and clarity to the theory of the Black revolutionary struggle for many of us. And there was the late Adine Simmons, one of the first Black residence hall assistants on campus, who inspired us with a new sense of "Say it Loud, I'm Black and I'm Proud." She also planted a depth of caring for Black people that has shaped the passion and compassion for the people within our struggles for freedom.

From the Gargoyles and Quadrangles to A West Side Grassroots Storefront Movement

When I returned to the University in the summer of 1970 after a nine-month working sabbatical as a Robert Kennedy Fellow, I returned as a much more mature advocate for change. During the time away, I had worked within the Newark, New Jersey school system representing the concerns of welfare mothers of at-risk elementary school children for the Newark Area Planning Association.

Back on campus as a Black sister in good standing, I immediately took a job as a counselor to incoming Black freshmen arriving several weeks before classes started in September. The program was designed to provide them with a head start orientation for survival and success in an extremely competitive academic environment.

That same summer, I met Hannibal Barcar Shabazz, head of a fledgling group of West Side cultural nationalists called the All African Peoples Alliance. With our headquarters at Roosevelt and Kedzie, the Alliance recruited students, mostly females from college and university campuses such as Roosevelt, DePaul and U of C.

In organization and philosophy, the Alliance was a blend of the Black Panther Party and the cultural nationalists led by Maulana Ron Karenga. The group had a rigorous set of programs that attracted idealistic Black students: after-school tutoring, breakfast programs for hungry school children, and free bus programs, which took mostly poor Black women to work outside of their communities. We provided weekly karate self-defense classes for children and adults. There was also a rousing Sunday evening worship service that included a message by Shabazz and movement songs adapted from Negro spirituals, civil rights songs, and popular music. For instance, we took Sly and the Family Stone's "Thank You for Letting Me Be Myself," adding the names Ron Maulana Karenga, Imamu Amiri Baraka and other cultural nationalist leaders. We had a ten-point program and a chronology of struggle that included moving to the South and preparation for armed struggle. Core members of the group like me lived very austere and disciplined lives. We read for two hours a day and wrote reports on what we read related to the struggle.

We ate one meal a day, as suggested by the Honorable Elijah Muhammad. There were private target practice classes; although we did not directly espouse violence, we did believe in self-defense "by any means necessary."

We dressed in African garb, which resulted in our car being shot at by South Side gang members who confused us with a sect of the Black Peace Stone Nation, who also dressed in African attire.

We all took African-inspired names. Mine was Moombi Dido Shabazz. Moombi was the Mother Earth of Kenya people, likened to Eve in the Christian Bible. Dido was the mother of historical figure Hannibal. And, according to Elijah Muhammad, all Black people originated from the tribe of Shabazz.

In real terms we developed strong alliances with West Side leaders, such as the wife of popular local TV personality Big Bill Hill. Sister Hill was linked to the Martin Luther King Health Center and neighborhood churches and schools, all of which were valuable linkages to our community credibility as we sought to organize.

Our quest for cultural consciousness led to the first Kwanzaa celebration during December 1970. I had gotten from Amiri Baraka's organization in Newark a complete handbook of the tradition celebration developed by Karenga. This provided a detailed roadmap of the words, symbols, and activities for a new Black community event to replace or supplement the Christmas season.

That first celebration was very successful and we shared the information with several other groups who joined in the celebrations in the years to come. We featured musician, ethno-musicologist, and cultural icon, Phil Cohran, in our events. We also had a close alignment with Hannibal Afrik (Harold Charles), West Side teacher and organizer.

The two things that the All African Peoples Alliance excelled at was building tangible, solid, and consistent programs for the community and creating strong alliances with community based leadership and complementary organizations.

The challenge was that there was no funding, except the donations we raised on Sundays, because all the programs were free. Government, foundation, and corporate funding were not an option. So while a lot of thought had gone into planning activities, there was no strategic thinking about sustainability.

As many of the women began to have children, the issue of support became more critical.

From a social point of view, as we sought to replace Christian values, mores and family structures with African-centered concepts, the transitions were not smooth or comfortable for all of us. Many of the men, especially the leaders, wanted to adopt plural family lifestyles without fully understanding the underlying responsibilities of multiple "wives" and the children who came with them. The results often brought confusion and emotional turmoil. The group tried very hard to live by the creed "Putting principles over personalities" in all our work, but often personalities and personal dysfunction got in the way. Ultimately, these personal conflicts led to the demise of the group.

After my son, Samory Amilcar Shabazz, was born in June 1971, people like myself refocused on education and the ways to take the principles into a more traditional career and family life.

Moving on to Community Building with United Builders

After graduating from the University of Chicago in the winter of 1972, I had the opportunity to move into another phase of the Black struggle in Chicago as a result of my employment with the United Builders Association, an affiliate of CEDCO (Chicago Economic Development Corporation). UBA was headed by Paul King, Jr., who was also a pivotal mover in the National Association of Minority Contractors.

I started out as a research manager, which gave me an opportunity to learn about how the Chicago movement of Black contractors and construction workers had an integral part of the struggle for justice and equality across the nation. It was a perfect transition for me because it had a clear focus: jobs and business opportunities for Blacks in Chicago.

My previous work on the West Side had shown that these were core issues for the Black community. Alongside education, economic self-sufficiency was pivotal in attacking the evils of injustice and inequity suffered by the masses of Black people.

We worked alongside of developing young businessmen like Glenn Harston, who was making a name for himself in the structural steel arena where there were no Black companies getting the work.

On a daily basis I felt that UBA promoted and encouraged the totality of the Nguzo Saba principles of: collective work and responsibility, unity, self-determination, cooperative economics, purpose, faith and creativity without the cultural trappings of the Swahili words or African garb.

The other principle I learned while working closely with Paul King was that to actively engage in the Black struggle, you had to engage in politics—locally and nationally. You could not ignore it or run away from it. You had to find a way to make politics and politicians work for you. The goals were still radical because nothing challenged the establishment more than the notion that they would have to share the economic pie. But the strategies and tactics differed. By the time I joined United Builders most of the direct street action and civil disobedience had already been deployed successfully. By 1972, the threat of hundreds of Black people shutting down construction sites was a very effective strategy. But more often it involved negotiating around measurable and achievable goals for Black economic progress and preparing Blacks to walk in the doors that had been opened. During those two years, our local and national efforts shifted to ways of removing systemic and institutional obstacles. These obstacles included access to capital for Black business people and the management skills needed to support those businesses as they grew.

On a daily basis I had the opportunity to research opportunities for struggling Black businesses to uncover free and low-cost resources to help Black contractors with accounting and other management tools so that they could survive.

The process was much the same for me as it had been in the early University of Chicago days; I studied and read. But now instead of Fanon and Malcolm X, I was perusing the *Wall Street Journal* and *Crain's Business Magazine*. Instead of researching African culture, names and languages, I was in the library stacks hunting for everything I could find on affirmative action and minority set-asides. The priorities of my struggle had moved from style to substance, from theory to practice. So while I put away my African garb and nobody called me Sister Dido, there was clearly a history of struggle entwined in the history of Black contractors. Strategically working along Black men and women who were challenging the system to open up jobs and business opportunities was met with overt and covert resistance in Chicago more fiercely than almost any other city in America.

Much of the testimony and news articles that I worked on with Paul King clearly outlined that this struggle had a long history of achievement on the part of Blacks and resistance on the part of whites in America. More importantly, the quest for Black Power to be gained in this arena encompassed the power to transform the lives of Black families and Black communities in an authentic revolutionary movement.

In many ways I had come full circle in my own consciousness and my capacity to struggle. Much of what we learned in 1967 and 1968 on a white university campus, about how to work together as Blacks, served me well in my job alongside others in that small United Builders office on 31st and Wentworth.

All that I had learned about the plight of everyday Black folks, shackled and beaten down by institutional racism on Chicago's West Side, gave me purpose and focus for my work to empower Blacks in the construction industry. It all made sense and I had a framework within which to feel that our struggles would make a difference.

NOTES OF ANOTHER NATIVE SON: A PERSONAL JOURNEY THROUGH INTEGRATION IDEAS INTO AFRICAN-CENTEREDNESS

Donn F. Bailey

INTRODUCTION

I have been privileged over my thirty-six year career at the Center for Inner City Studies (CICS) of Northeastern Illinois University in Chicago to have worked with a number of great teachers and unique scholars. With a special note of gratitude, I acknowledge my collegial relationship with Jacob H. Carruthers, Anderson Thompson, Sonja H. Stone, Nancy L. Arnez, Elkin Sithole, Robert Starks and Donald H. Smith. I learned a great deal from them all.

This chapter is written to give some detail to my involvement in being up close and personal in the founding of CICS and its growth and development from the summer of 1965 to 1975. Many significant events and worthy contributions have occurred after 1975; but I have been asked to focus my attention on the period between 1960 through 1975.

I intend to honor my editor's instruction; however, I believe I must preface this fifteen year period with a brief analysis of who I am and how I grew from being a social and educational integrationist to an African-centered educator.

This transformation became apparent in my field of speech-language pathology and as a contributor to the original curriculum of the Master's program. In the summer of 1965, Dr. Donald H. Smith, the founding director of CICS from 1966-1968, began to design a Masters degree program in inner city studies for experienced teachers who taught in schools that had a majority of so-called "disadvantaged children". In the spring of 1966, CICS was awarded 350,000 dollars from the U.S. Department of Health Education and Welfare through a grant written by Dr. Smith. Some of his early collaborators in this endeavor were Nancy Arnez, Barbara Sizemore, Stanley Newman, Rose Brandzel, Dan

Kuzahara, Edward Barnes, Harry Woodward and me. The course of study was built on the educational model of "cultural disadvantagement."

With the hiring of new full-time faculty members at CICS during 1968 and 1970, namely Jake Carruthers, Andy Thompson, Sonja Stone, Elkin Sithole, Bob Starks, and Carol Adams, the original CICS graduate curriculum underwent a significant transformation.

Early Years (1930s, 1940s and 1950s):

I was born in February 1932 in New Castle, Indiana, a small town of sixteen thousand people northeast of Indianapolis. My childhood and teenage life were ordinary for a "colored boy" in the Midwest. Since the town was small, the children of the three hundred Black folk in New Castle went to school with white kids. However, in a deeper sense, New Castle was de facto segregated. Blacks were confined to certain residential areas. Clothing stores refused to allow us to try on clothes. We could not sit down in restaurants. We were not permitted to swim in the Baker's Field swimming pool. We were sent to the balcony in the Princess Theater, etc.

My hardworking parents, Walter and Thelma, taught my older brother Rex, my younger sister Kay and me to "go along to get along" and "don't make waves." The town was notorious in its acceptance of the KKK philosophy. I remember the Klan marches around the courthouse square at the July 4th celebrations. After the parade, the KKK would circle that courthouse for hours.

Our dad; however, told us to behave and be proud of the Bailey name. He also told Rex and me not to take "crap" from anyone and to protect our sister. He worked for thirty-nine years in the local Chrysler plant and had his run-ins with white coworkers. During this time, we were encouraged to compete aggressively in school and truly believe we were as good as anyone and in some cases, better. However, we were cautioned that we had to prove it in the classroom and in all of our school activities. Graduating with honors from New Castle High School in 1949, Indiana University with BS and MA degrees during the 1950s, and a doctorate from Pennsylvania State University in 1974, I felt real pride in "putting a lie" to one of my teacher's assessments in 1947. She advised me that going to college was not realistic and to prepare myself to work in the Chrysler factory. Mom and Dad said, "Forget Miss Ritter; you're going to IU and you better graduate!" I did graduate and so did my brother and sister (so much for effective high school counseling in the 1940s).

My training as a speech-language therapist at IU included several academic assumptions of the 1950s and 1960s. The field of speech pathology recognized Standard

American English as the premier language goal for everyone. The other assumption was that social and regional dialects were regarded as low-prestige, socio-cultural elements in American English that had to be replaced. I remember the fall semester of 1960 when my supervisor, Miss Kratovil, paid me a visit at Willard Elementary School to observe my teaching performance. Willard School was an inner city school with an enrollment of nearly thirteen hundred children, all Black. While there she asked to see my "waiting list". This was a list of children who had been tested and assessed as having speech disorders. After reviewing it, she wondered why I had only forty names listed. She indicated that nearly all of the fifty-five speech therapists in the Division of Speech Correction in Chicago Public Schools had more than a hundred children waiting to be taught (it is noted here that of the fifty-five speech therapists on staff at the Division in 1959-1960 only five were Black).

My response to her inquiry as to why I had only 40 children waiting to be taught was quite simple. I told Miss Kratovil that I recorded only those children who had speech disorders. Further, I informed her that most Black children may have southern dialects or ethnic speech differences; but they were not children with *defects* ("bafroom" for "bathroom", or "swimp" for "shrimp", and ethnic syntax like "I be busy" or "she done been gone" for "she has gone" are not *disorders*). They are speech *differences* that may be addressed by speech teachers later in the third, fourth or fifth grades if those differences persist or become problematic in reading proficiency. When or if those differences are formally addressed by a speech specialist, those differences would be approached with a methodology that encouraged the children to work toward *enhancing* their dialect range. I instructed Miss Kratovil that Black children's first-learned dialect must not be attacked by teachers as bad or inferior because they learned their speech habits from their parents, relatives and friends. As such, it would be a grave mistake to condemn their speech. A good, effective teacher should always find ways to teach an extended dialect. When a child's speech is attacked as inadequate, the teacher is essentially attacking that child's home and friends. In the child's mind that is a declaration of war on their "Momma".

Thereafter, Miss Kratovil viewed me as an opponent to her way of thinking. I became an "arrogant Negro" because my language ideas varied widely with the conventional approach of the American Speech-Language and Hearing Association in 1960.

The restrictive policy of speech differences of Blacks was challenged by a group of speech-language pathologists who were members of the Black Caucus of ASHA in Denver, CO, in 1967 when we "took over" its convention. The Black Caucus members of ASHA joined with specific linguists who supported our position on Black dialect. We developed language learning ideas that highlighted the linguistic truism that Black speech/Black dialect/Ebonics had to be regarded as a legitimate language system of a legitimate group of people. "Black speech is legitimate because the Black people who use it are legitimate." We further pushed for the acceptance of Black dialect and instituted educational activities that stimulated and extended Black children's language range. We fought within the profession to oppose rigorously those speech-language pathologists who advocated *replacing* the dialect with so-called Standard American English. Those of us who waged this battle for policy change defended the dialect as an important form of language that was learned in the home and community. We felt that it must be accepted and built upon as a foundation. We felt that Black children would be less likely to oppose language change if they truly believed that their first-learned language was all right. "It's OK to sound Black" was our theme; Jesse Jackson sounds Black; Malcolm X sounded Black; certainly Martin Luther King sounded Black. Sounding Black is crucial if you use that language to further the cause of Black liberation.

This fight continued through the early years of the 1970s. As a result of this struggle, a number of African American speech-language pathologists split from ASHA as a Black Caucus entity and established and developed a separate institution. The National Black Association for Speech-Language and Hearing (NBASLH) was conceptualized. This writer, along with Eugene Wiggins and Njeri Nuru, became the signatories of the NBASLH charter and its constitution. The charter was issued in Washington, D.C. in 1977.

The Curriculum Reconstruction at CICS:

With the movement in my profession and given the change in my personal development, I became more restless with speech pathology and began my search for a theory, function and structure of what had become identified as Black English or Ebonics. Lorenzo Turner, Ernie Smith, Orlando Taylor and others helped me begin to see similarities in so-called Black English here in America with languages in the African Caribbean Basin and some West African languages, like Wolof.

This research effort became imperative in 1968 with the hiring of Dr. Jacob H. Carruthers and Dr. Elkin Sithole, the elevation of Dr. Anderson Thompson to full-time status, the appointment of Dr. Sonja H. Stone as chairperson of the department of inner city studies education, and Dr. Nancy L. Arnez as the second director of CICS. This cadre of African thinkers encouraged me to listen, learn and read African analysis of pre-colonial Africa, western philosophy, western civilization, and the doctrine and practice of white supremacy. I became a "student of the struggle", or as Dr. Carruthers identified it: "How we got into this mess!"

I remember one incident that happened around this time. Many events were taking place in this country: the Detroit, Watts, and Newark uprisings along with protests against the war in Vietnam. Sonja Stone was my officemate; so we had many conversations about life. One day, Sonja stopped me in mid-sentence while I was talking about school desegregation efforts in the South and in Chicago. She remarked in mocked surprise, "You're an integrationist, aren't you?" My long-winded explanation about being involved in street demonstrations, housing marches and Dr. King's workshop activities compelled her to cut me off. She said, "OK, OK Donn, you're a militant integrationist!" We laughed and she gave me one of her "poor baby" looks and said, "That's all right Donn, you'll learn. I believe in you!" And learn, I did. I sat in on Jake's classes and Andy's classes. I read new material and discovered other African thinkers and writers who introduced me to deep African thought. I began to understand from my colleagues that racial integration, as depicted in America, will not help us to build a "nation within a nation." CICS faculty colloquia taught me to understand fully what Jacob Carruthers and Anderson Thompson were teaching our students:

- Many African warriors have fought the wrong battles because the true nature of the enemy has been disguised.
- Wanting and struggling to be treated as equals in the American/European world must stop.
- Stop analyzing the victim and begin to analyze the victimizer. "Study him and his institutions!"
- Stop defending Western civilization.
- There are twin pillars of the European worldview. Those pillars are Western civilization and white supremacy. One cannot separate those twins.

Those so-called "commandments" and others that I extracted from Jake and Andy's class lectures afforded me an opportunity to grow, develop and transform my thinking. This African-centered thought process forced me to rethink my position on school integration, Western philosophy, racism, white supremacy, and the concept of human speech.

While I was away from CICS and working toward my doctorate at Penn State (1969-1971), my colleagues in Chicago were busy transforming the CICS Master's curriculum and drafting an undergraduate curriculum that fit well into the reconstructed graduate degree at CICS/NEIU.

Below are course titles that reflect the rejection of the cultural deprivation or the cultural disadvantagement education models and the acceptance of an African-centered model.

The faculty at CICS has struggled mightily over the years to develop a discipline of study and research that is based upon the true, vital interests of Africans here in this country, Africans elsewhere on the continent, and in the Diaspora.

The original curriculum for the Masters degree included:

- Graduate Study of the Disadvantaged
- Language Behavior of the Disadvantaged
- Problems in Testing the Disadvantaged
- Literature of the Disadvantaged
- Teaching in Disadvantaged Schools
- Pathology of the Ghetto, etc.
- Racism in Theory and Fact

The reconstructed Masters degree program includes eighteen hours required, twelve hours elective in a thirty-hour program:

- Graduate Study in the Inner City
- The Inner City Community: its Politics, Economics and Structure
- Theory and Methodology of Ethnic Group Research
- Business Welfare and Labor Systems in America
- Problems in Testing Inner City Children
- Literature of Ethnic Groups
- Behavior Patterns in the Inner City
- Idioms of African Communities
- History and Philosophy of Black Education
- Curriculum Development in the Inner City
- Cultures of the Inner City
- Methods of Teaching in the Inner City
- Research Methods in Inner City Studies
- Research Writing
- Research and Thesis

Below are some of the course offerings in the undergraduate program (general education courses omitted):

- Introduction to Inner City Studies
- Development of Inner City Children

- The Paraprofessional in the Inner City
- Introduction to Ethno-Musicology
- Colonial Systems
- Revolutionary Movements
- Urban Art Forms
- Introduction to African Civilizations

Establishing a discipline of study which challenged the conventional wisdom of "researching the victim" was a large undertaking. However, in the words of Jacob Carruthers, it was not only necessary that faculty members at CICS do this in their field of competence, but that they *must* do it because "The inner city must study, simply because it has been studied about so much." Members of the CICS faculty must represent the interests of inner city residents. We must "research not only the research; but also the researchers and their interests." Carruthers also pointed out in his work that in 1900, Blacks were a country or rural problem because most of us lived in the country. In 1970, America faced an urban problem because most of us lived in cities. And in 2050, Carruthers points out that Black people may be a suburban problem because by then most of us will have, willingly or not, gone to the suburbs. This tragic drive to "get out of the ghetto" has tremendous dimensions that are suicidal for us as a people, and cannot be pursued in this chapter. Suffice to say, this issue has always been a problem area for America. The truth is, wherever the Black race has been located/confined/contained, America has a problem with that area.

THE 1960S: DON'T CALL THEM BAGGAGE

Atty. Thomas N. Todd

I was born in Alabama in 1938. But I was reborn in Louisiana and Chicago in the 1960s. Alabama played one more key role at the beginning of the decade.

The latter part of the 1950s were difficult for me. In 1958 my mother died, and in 1959 I was "washed out" of the Reserve Officer Training Course (R.O.T.C.). Both of these events were needless to say very, very unsettling to a twenty-year-old graduating college senior.

After graduating from Southern University in Baton Rouge, Louisiana, in August of 1959, I had lost my Army commission and was unemployed. I returned to Mobile, Alabama, without belaboring the point. It was during this period that I "grew up," matured and made decisions that would affect my life forever. The first one of these was to go back to Southern University's Law School in Baton Rouge, Louisiana. But before returning to Baton Rouge and having turned twenty-one in September 1959, I started my rebirth by working as a volunteer with the local chapter of the NAACP in Prichard, Alabama. First, I taught literacy in preparation for a voter registration drive, and prepared to take the literacy test myself to qualify to vote.

In January of 1960 I took the two and one-half hour literacy test. My problem was with the interpretation of the Due Process clause of the 14th Amendment of the U.S. Constitution. For the sake of brevity, let's just say I qualified to vote and received my voter registration card for 3 dollars (the poll tax for two years).

In September 1960 I enrolled at Southern University's Law School in Baton Rouge, Louisiana. As a reminder of the climate during the time, there were freedom riders, lunch counter sit-ins, protest marches, and organized efforts to get Blacks registered to vote, just to mention a few. Students from Southern were marching against Jim Crow every day in Baton Rouge. You could smell the scent of tear gas and see the tattered clothes of students who had been attacked by dogs.

Because I left Southern University as an undergraduate, developed a reputation as a speaker, and headed several student organizations; a delegation from the marchers visited me at the law school to ask me to join their protest.

At twenty-one years of age I had to make one of the biggest decisions of my entire life. Should I join the protests? If so, this will surely lead to an arrest and perhaps conviction; thus, effectively ending my chances of ever becoming a lawyer in Louisiana by never being able to take the bar exam. Or should I stay in school, finish, pass the bar, become licensed, and then spend the rest of my life trying to use my law degree and license to help Blacks and oppressed people?

After much agonizing I chose the latter. It was not easy, but I reasoned that the marchers had enough Black students protesting. However, they did not have enough Black lawyers. Having made the decision, I made a contract with myself to spend portions of the rest of my life trying to help. I finished law school in June of 1963, passed the two and a half hour written bar examination in July, and was sworn into the Louisiana Supreme Court on August 28, 1963, the same day of the March on Washington.

In September 1963 I went to Washington, D.C., to take a job on the solicitor's staff of the U.S. Department of Labor. It was not long before my personal civil rights problem reared its head. I found out "accidentally" that my office mate, who was a white Yale Law School graduate, was awaiting the results of the bar examination. Consequently, he was not a licensed attorney, but rather a law clerk. Notwithstanding the fact that I had graduated from law school with honors, passed the bar examination and had been licensed to practice law, he was hired at two pay grades above mine. Note that this was 1963, the president was John F. Kennedy and this occurred in what was called the "New Frontier."

Well, I filed a civil rights complaint and won. Their defense was, "We have never had a graduate from your law school work here before, so we didn't apply the same rules." My law school (like my college, high school, junior high school, and elementary school) was all Black and segregated.

1964-1967

I was commissioned in the Judge Advocate General's (JAG) Corps of the U.S. Army (legal branch) in 1964. After training, which included legal courses at the University of Virginia's Law School in Charlottesville, Virginia, I was assigned to Fort Sheridan just north of Chicago in Highwood, Illinois. It was my first time ever in the Chicago area. In fact, many of us living in Alabama had relatives and friends who had returned home to visit and said, "Blacks were free in Chicago." They were wrong.

I was the only Black in the JAG Office as a 1st Lieutenant and one of few Black officers on the base. It did not take long before full truth manifested itself. Not only was there racism on the Army base, but it was also rampant in the surrounding areas. Soon after I got to Fort Sheridan, Major Dee Bennett, the Civil Rights Officer, contacted me about the post problems; Major Bennett was a Black Chicagoan. We used testers—one white, one Black—to expose housing discrimination in the North Shore. The Black tester was told "no vacancies." The white tester was shown the property and given an application. We broke up the practice.

Black women came to us saying that the large cosmetic companies would not makeup Black women's faces at the Post-Exchange. We broke up the practice. Then the Black women enlisted in the Women Army Corps (WACS) came to us, stating they received non-judicial company punishment more than white WACS for basically the same offenses. We broke it up. Word got around that there were people on the base who would fight for civil rights.

In November of 1965, I was volunteered for duty in the Dominican Republic. I negotiated to come back to Chicago once the temporary assignment was over. While in the Dominican Republic, I had to defend some Black soldiers accused of various crimes. My duties included paying Dominicans for damage and sometimes death caused by American Soldiers.

I returned to Chicago in April of 1966 and my last big criminal/civil rights case involved two Black soldiers accused of kidnapping a white woman in Indiana. The offense carried with it a sentence up to life in prison. White state troopers stopped my client and another soldier; the question was asked, "What are you doing with the white woman, Nigger?" One of the soldiers got six months; the other one, my client, got a year and a half. He was the driver and more involved. It is fair to say that no matter where I was in the Army involvement with racial matters was frequent.

1967-1970

After getting out of the military in September of 1967, I was hired as an Assistant U.S. Attorney by Edward V. Harahan, the U.S. Attorney. Because of my trial experience in the military, I was assigned mostly criminal cases early on. But, remembering my personal contract and constitutional law, I knew this office had jurisdiction over civil rights matters. It had never really used that authority. This is what I wanted to do. My chance came when a new U.S. Attorney was appointed. He showed an interest in Civil Rights. Later, I was contacted by a community group regarding the practice of selling Black property on contract (no mortgage) at tremendously inflated prices, and then taking the property back after one payment was missed. The organization which contacted me was the Contract Buyers League.

At a state hearing into this matter, without authority, permission, and hesitation, I stated that the U.S. Attorney's Office would investigate. The statement made headlines, complete with pictures. Although mildly admonished by the U.S. Attorney, we did indeed investigate and ended up filing an Amicus Brief on behalf of the homeowners.

Interestingly, while working in this office, I met Lu Palmer, Renault Robinson, Reverend Jesse L. Jackson Sr., Arthur Fletcher, Senator Richard Newhouse, Nancy Jefferson, Attorney Robert L. Tucker, Attorney E. Duke McNeil, Warren Bacon, Dr. Manford Byrd and many other persons who were involved in the Chicago Black community at that time.

Based upon the needs discovered in Chicago, I went on to establish the first Civil Rights Office in the nation in a local U.S. Attorney's office. The office consisted of a secretary and me.

During my stay in the office there were other major events. Among them were the National Democratic Convention in 1968, the days of rage, and the assassination of Fred Hampton and Mark Clark, members of the Black Panther Party. I also developed the first case for civil rights deprivation against the Chicago Police Department, which ended in an acquittal handled by white lawyers from the office. The second indictment came from a complaint that white police officers were beating Black students from Tilden High School on the South Side of Chicago, filed by Jeff Fort of the Black P. Stone Nation.

This time I took the complaint; I investigated the matter, presented it to the Federal Grand Jury, and tried the case with a representative of the U.S. Justice Department in Washington, D.C. The jury at the trial hung 11-1 for a conviction, allowing us to retry the police, but the U.S. Attorney's office refused. I dissented with the best language I could muster in expressing my disagreement. One other noteworthy case came from working with the U.S. Department of Justice in Washington when we filed the first racial housing discrimination case in the nation under the *1968 Federal Housing Act*.

From what I experienced early in the 1960s, in the Deep South and later in "Up South" Chicago, one principle loomed large. Those of us who were blessed to get an education and put into positions to make a difference developed a feeling that what we received came from the collective efforts of many people from our community. Although we may have possessed some skills and talents, credit must go to those who "plowed up the fields" in the words of Frederick Douglass, without whom we could not have gotten where we were. We owed the sit-in demonstrations, the Freedom Riders, and the boycotts, to those who personally sacrificed careers, money and sometimes their lives to press the issue of fairness and equality for Blacks. We felt greatly indebted to Black educators especially; they would not allow obstacles to prevent us from excelling, counseling that we had to sometimes work four times as hard as whites.

Because of this history there was always, with me at least, a feeling that we had an obligation to give back, reach out, and in the words of the early Black Womens' Clubs, "Lift as we Climb."

From 1970 to 1971, all of my earlier living experiences—segregation in the Deep

South, segregated education from elementary school to law school, my military and judicial experiences in Washington, D.C.—converged. They formed the backdrop for what was to be my greatest challenge and opportunity.

In 1970 I joined the law faculty at Northwestern Law School to teach. Here I would teach, among other things, Constitutional Law, Advanced Problems in Constitutional Law, and Law and Racism, a course I designed. And for the first time in my professional career, I could engage in private practice. I could litigate in the area of voter rights, reapportionment and other civil rights areas designed to help empower Black people.

Then, in 1971, one of the greatest opportunities presented itself. The Reverend Jesse Jackson, Sr. extended an invitation to join him in Bread Basket and the local chapter of the Southern Christian Leadership Conference (SCLC). Now after all of these years, after the law school promise, I could join the front ranks of what was perhaps the most viable Civil Rights organization at the time—Operation Bread Basket, organized by Dr. Martin Luther King, Jr. and refined by Reverend Jackson, his staff, and an army of volunteers.

An integral part of Bread Basket was the Saturday morning forum, which was broadcasted live on the radio. I was again given an opportunity to teach. I joined some of the most notable people in our community, or any other, at one of the most powerful platforms Blacks ever received. I used my experience, my knowledge, and what talents I had to try to teach our community about contemporary legal, civil rights, and human rights problems facing us. I have always believed that education is still the key.

This forum used educational, economic, and political principles combined with entertainment and sports, wrapped in the Black religious experience. No platform before or since has ever rivaled the Saturday morning forum. I don't want to dwell too much on my personal involvement. It's not about that. What it is about are the people from all walks of life—mostly black, but also white, Hispanic, Asian, Native Americans and others; mostly Christian, but also Jewish, Islamic, nonbelievers, and many, many others using their talents and resources to help others, not just themselves. The forum was continued under the banner of Operation PUSH (People United to Save Humanities).

Another activity, for lack of a better word, was the phenomenal Black Expo (later renamed PUSH Expo). Once a year, business people, educators, religious people, news people, sports people, entertainers and others in the thousands made a pilgrimage to Chicago for what was called Harambee. There have been few experiences in my life where the kind of feeling of kinship, coupled with a feeling of growing power combined to create what only can be called electric. The elderly, school children, and people from all walks of life came.

Between the Saturday morning forum and the Black Expo, many careers were enhanced and many political careers launched. In fact, some are benefiting from these and other activities now; these people are clueless as to what happened then and how some of these things are helping them even today. "Those who do not know their history will not recognize it when they see it again."

Many of our "newly arrived" Negroes feel no obligations to the sixties, nor do they even acknowledge the significance of the era. In fact, some have criticized us for being "stuck in the sixties", and they have accepted the characterization of the sixties as creating "baggage." Needless to say, they are directly and indirectly benefiting from the sixties' fruits, especially the 1964 Civil Rights Act, the 1965 Voters Rights Act, and the 1968 Fair Housing Act. I have never seen so many people benefit from history and legacy while renouncing both as being insignificant today. Because of the blatant contradiction in their position, I call them "history hustlers" and "legacy pimps."

I am a creature of the 1960s, plus a beneficiary of the 1960s. And I am proud to be both. Consequently, to call the sixties baggage, simply put, is "fighting words." Don't call it baggage. Furthermore, don't call the killing of the four little girls in the 16th Street Baptist Church in Birmingham, Alabama, baggage; or, the civil rights workers and the assassinations of Medger Evers, Malcolm X, and Dr. Martin Luther King, Jr. For many of us, the sixties are sacred. Don't call it baggage.

Because of this attitude, the period of 1960-1975, for me, was one of the most active and productive periods for Blacks in my lifetime. People were working to make a difference, to give back and to help improve the lives of others, not just for themselves.

Herein for me lies one of the significant differences between those of us who came of age in the 1960s and many of those who, even today, are benefiting from the sixties struggle—we felt, and still feel, an obligation to that struggle and a kinship to that period, never forgotten.

Blacks viewed themselves as representatives of the Black community to the white establishment. Today, many view their roles as representatives from the white establishment to the Black community. They knew that they didn't get to where they are by themselves. They knew that they were standing on somebody else's shoulders, reaping the harvest of seeds planted by someone else—that somebody marched to get them where they are, that somebody cried to get them where they are and somebody died to get them where they are. They didn't do it by themselves. This was a kind of collective self-determination.

But now with all of the educated new Negroes graduating from what they call elite (white) schools, with all of their credentials—they are functioning close to the old plantation models of slavery where Blacks had no education. In the words of the Dred Scott Decision, "No right which a white man is bound to respect."

We have lost grounds while being told that tremendous progress is being made. It is the evolution of a circle.

IN THE BLACK

Damali Carol Adams

I arrived in Chicago on September 1, 1966, fleeing Boston like a runaway slave. Having just obtained my master's degree from Boston University, I was anxious to escape New England's peculiar brand of racism. I was a child of the South, born and educated in Louisville, Kentucky and then moved to Nashville, Tennessee to attend the famed Fisk University. I had grown up in the most segregated of circumstances and became a civil rights activist in my teen years, but no one had ever put "Nigger Go Home" signs on my threshold until I went to Boston.

Going back to Louisville never crossed my mind. I had seen too many educated Black people working as janitors or in the post office. My cousins and big sister had all moved to places where the climate seemed more suitable for upward mobility. In retrospect, I regret that none of us understood the value of sacrifice and groundwork laid by the previous generation of Adamses, and thus did not take up their mantle at home.

I had relatives in Detroit, East St. Louis, New York, and Cleveland—so why Chicago? My scholarly interests and personal preferences had whittled down my choices to Atlanta or Chicago. I knew I wanted to continue my graduate studies. I was concerned about job prospects and the social and cultural environment. Chicago quickly became the frontrunner. I had read Silberman's *Crisis in Black and White* and could envision myself organizing in Woodlawn. I was preparing to be a sociologist and knew that its American home was at the University of Chicago, but one final fact made Chicago my destination of choice. I read that there were 1,000,000 Black people in that city, and soon I was humming "Going to Chicago. Sorry, but I can't take you!"

Unlike the thousands of Black people that had migrated to Chicago in the wake of their pioneering relatives, I did not have family rolling out the welcome mat in the Windy City. So I did what my mother had done when she struck out on her own in Louisville and what young women had done for years; I went down to the YWCA. Located in an imposing mansion on Dearborn and Oak, it would be my home for a month while I situated myself in Chicago.

Jobs were plentiful and my background suited me for the work of the day. I was, however, quickly eliminated from consideration by the city of Chicago when my civil rights background came to light. The Irish bureaucrat that interviewed me for the Joint Commission on Youth Welfare (or some such title) said one couldn't work for the city and picket the mayor, and I was the type that might do just that. I wrote scores of letters, interviewed in a variety of places, but it was ultimately the Fisk network that led me to my first job. One of my sister's classmates, Annie Blair, worked at the Welfare Council of Metropolitan Chicago and she referred me to a position in their research department. At about the same time, I was offered a spot at the Jewish Foundation, but the Welfare Council paid slightly more and I'd have a friend there. That singular decision played a major role in helping me find place and purpose in Chicago, and I never looked back.

Soon I would meet another colleague at the Welfare Council, Charles Ross, and he invited me to the meeting that changed my life.

Feeling that African American social workers were being required to represent the oppressor, rather than the oppressed, three bold Chicagoans called a meeting of that group to discuss how we could use our positions in the interest of our people. The conveners of that meeting were Al Raby, Joan Phillips Brown (now known as Abena Joan Brown), and Warner Saunders. The meeting was held at Brown's home, and a revolution was seeded in that place.

Stunned at the brilliance and boldness of those gathered that night, I was uncharacteristically silent. I didn't know anyone there but Charlie and felt like such a novice in the midst of this new breed of professionals. There wasn't a handkerchief head in the bunch! A new army was being formed and I was ready to enlist!

Soon this group was to expand beyond social workers to include artists, lawyers, teachers, and a few folk in the corporate world. Those activists were to become change agents, not just for Chicago but for the entire Black world.

To discuss its mission with a larger audience, the group organized a meeting called The Confab at Crerar Presbyterian Church on Chicago's south side. Advertising pioneer Vince Cullers was a member of Crerar and he not only secured the church for us, but designed the striking conference materials as well, something he and Larry Shaw would do repeatedly.

As our numbers grew, we could no longer continue to meet in private homes. Through Bill Duncan we established our first regular meeting place in the theater at Parkway Community House. We met on Saturday afternoons, after Breadbasket and before Lu Palmer's Bookshelf. Believe it or not, folks were so dedicated at that time that some people managed to go to all three and squeeze the Communiversity in as well. We were ravenous about reading and discussing what we read well into the evening, where we often ended up at the Queen of the Sea restaurant on Stony Island dissecting Harold Cruse's seminal work, *Crisis of the Negro* Intellectual.

It was at one of those Saturday meetings that we decided a name for our group. I suggested The Catalyst, because I felt we were surely going to ignite change. Others agreed and we stayed together under that name for many years, even as the group focus metamorphosed over time (but more on that later). We didn't want a president (being anti-charismatic leadership and all), but we did name someone "convener." We determined that our conveners would be male, because we were aware of the anti-male bias the dominant culture had about Black men and wanted to force them to have to deal with that which they feared most, not because of sexism or subordination. Anyone who knew The Catalyst knew the women were warriors in their own right!

We had been meeting and honing our philosophy and strategies for some time when a cataclysmic chain of events urged our militancy into full bloom—the assassination of Dr. Martin Luther King, Jr. and the subsequent uprising in black communities throughout the nation, including the west side of Chicago. Many of our members worked on the west side at agencies such as the Better Boys Foundation, the Better Boys Republic, Marillac House, and the Marcy Newberry Center. Stores and houses burned down and people in distress received very little emergency assistance from the establishment agencies. The Red Cross stated that they did not feel compelled to respond because it was "not a natural disaster," and many Catalyst members were disturbed by the non-response of their employers as well. Angry and fed up, we decided it was time to stage our coming-out party and put these agencies on point!

We decided to summon the heads of the city's social welfare agencies to what we dubbed "The Confrontation in Black and White," an apt name since all the agency executive directors and the boards of directors were all white. We sent telegrams to these guys (yes, they were all males, too) indicating that they were to show up at the Afro Arts Theater at 39th and Drexel Boulevard to discuss the racism rampant in organizations that purported to be about uplifting the human condition. The telegrams were signed "The Catalyst" and, just as we thought, they were all set to ignore this anonymous invitation. However, at exactly eleven A.M. the day the telegrams were delivered, Catalyst members who worked at these agencies presented themselves at the offices of the directors. They identified themselves as members of The Catalyst, and suggested it would be in their best interest to show up.

This was to be the first of many public events designed to make our presence felt and to dramatize the fact that our zeal to work for the people was far stronger than our desire to keep our jobs. The Afro Arts Theater was the perfect venue for the launch of our Afrocentric Code of Ethics, aptly called "This Is Our Bag," and the issuance of a list of demands to the social services establishment.

The scathing preamble to our declarations of independence read thusly:

We MUST recognize that the traditional role of the highly trained among us had been to act as a buffer between a hostile and unsympathetic community and our people. As Black people, we must determine that this is a condition that we cannot and will not tolerate any longer.

Our Saturday meetings grew even larger and we soon organized committees, among them Direct Action and Skills Bank. The former planned our strategic demonstrations and the latter was a way we could list our skills, so that we could tap into our own talent when we needed expertise. It was through the Skills Bank that I became a close friend and mentee to Jacob Jennings, who worked as a community affairs liaison for the University of Illinois Chicago Circle and later for the Illinois Department of Higher Education. I had registered in the Skills Bank as a researcher and when they needed some research done at the University, he retained me. From that point on, I was his discovery, a sister who could research and write.

People brought their problems to The Catalyst Saturday meetings—everything from being told they couldn't wear natural hairdos or African garb at work, to being denied professional advancement because of race. We had a committee that would go to the complainant's job and represent their case. Most of the time we won!

Disgusted by the lack of African American representation on the boards of the city's flagship social agencies, we decided to once again engage in public direct action. The United Way's annual dinner was a huge function and all major social service agencies bought tables and one or two of us "tokens" were usually seated. We plotted to take over the microphone at this event and demand that Blacks be placed on the boards of these agencies and that we have a say at where United Way dollars were going, otherwise we would stop contributing. That evening, after dinner had been served, a cadre of Black men representing The Catalyst took over the stage. They read our demands, while the members in the audience stood at attention (Chuck Curry, Don Linder, Earl Doty, and Levert King were part of that contingent). It made the newspapers the next day and change in the months to come, but not before we made good on our threat to withdraw our contributions from the United Way!

As the saying goes, "When we fight, we win," and The Catalyst had a long series of victories as a result of our actions. We count among them the seating of Blacks on the board of the United Way and changes in the way grants were distributed that resulted in more equity. Eventually, Jerome Stevenson, an early member, became the executive director of the United Way.

We also confronted WTTW about not having any Black programming on their station. Harold Johnson, a director and Catalyst member, and Oscar Brown, Jr. had an idea for a Black soap opera they wanted to produce. In typical Catalyst fashion, a group of us went to call on them and soon *Bird of the Iron Feather* could be seen on public television.

The Catalyst also got involved in Chicago's blood-sport—politics. Our first campaign was the election of Fred Hubbard as alderman of the second ward. This was a significant campaign in that we were trying to dismantle the Negro political hacks who always seemed to represent old Daley, rather than the interests of Black people. The legendary Machine "Boss" William Dawson was running Lawrence Woods, his administrative assistant, who we felt would continue the old-style plantation politics. We saw Fred as an excellent candidate; he was a social worker and founder of Independent People's Organization, and he promised independence and empowerment. We strategized, raised funds and knocked on doors, helping to build a successful team for Fred. He trounced Woods, two to one. It was our first political victory, but it had a strange ending. Fred, who was reputed to have a gambling addiction, literally disappeared in May of 1971 (the *Chicago Defender* ran a headline saying "Ald. Fred Hubbard: Call Your Office") with 100,000 dollars in federal funds. The money was allegedly embezzled from The Chicago Plan for Equal Opportunity, a project designed to get minorities into the construction industry. Fred was subsequently found and convicted, never to be heard from again.

Catalyst founder Charles O. Ross convinced us to become a part of history in the bid to elect Richard Gordon Hatcher, mayor of the city of Gary, Indiana. We held his first Chicago fundraiser and were an integral part of his victory on November 7, 1967. Hatcher became one of the first Black mayors of a northern city and held the post for twenty years.

Bolstered by these two successful elections, we set our sights even higher. Declaring that it was time for a Black mayor in Chicago, The Catalyst produced buttons that proclaimed "Chicago—Black Mayor '71." Twelve years later, when we worked to elect Harold Washington, I often wore that button alongside that ubiquitous blue Washington for Mayor button people prized so much.

While all of this was going on, things were buzzing on the cultural scene as well. Catalyst members were also in the epicenter of this movement. Joan Brown and Harold Johnson started Ebony Talent Associates as an agency to represent Black artists. Eugene Perkins was not just doing his thing as a social worker (with Warner Saunders at the Better Boys Foundation), but writing and publishing as well. The Catalyst published a cultural arts directory, listing outlets for Black cultural expression. Black is truly beautiful, and we intended to represent.

The Vince Cullers agency was poised to take advantage of this movement. A gifted artist and owner of the nation's first ad agency, Catalyst member Vince Cullers, produced the first print advertisements that reflected the spirit of the times. Larry Shaw, a man of similar talents, joined the agency. While they turned out beautiful printed materials for all of our events, they revolutionized the way Black people were shown. Their work was so beautiful, people framed them and I created my own Wall of Respect by making a collage that featured their work.

We knew we were fine, but now we wanted to be beautiful! Blackness was celebrated everywhere and The Catalyst decided to have our first major fundraiser around that theme. Called "A Night of Blackness," it was held at the High Chaparral on Stony Island. We raised enough money that night to operate for a year. We all decked out in our finest African-inspired attire and my Catalyst sister, Willeva Lindsey, and I headed to Lou Byrd's barbershop on 71st Street to get one of those Afros for which he was famous (Lou was responsible for most of the Afro hairdos in the ad campaigns discussed earlier).

Historians, scholars, and authors were also part of The Catalyst. Among them: Anderson Thompson, Charles Hamilton (who authored *Black Power* with Stokeley Carmichael), and Lerone Bennett. Students were beginning to clamor for Black studies classes and some of us answered that call as well. Charles Hamilton was already making his mark at Roosevelt University. Jim Craigen went to DePaul University. I taught the first African American studies class at Crane Junior College. Joan Brown taught at Mundelein. Anderson Thompson left Forrestville High School to go to Northeastern Illinois University's new Center for Inner City Studies, located in the Abraham Lincoln Center on Oakwood Boulevard. Harold Pates went to Loop College. We did some team teaching too, Willeva Lindsey and me, at Valperaiso University in Indiana and Loyola University's Lake Shore campus. I also taught African American history at Central YMCA Community College with Anderson Thompson, Larry Shaw, and Harold Pates; it later evolved into a consulting firm, which we called the African American History.

The academy provided the perfect platform from which to raise the consciousness of our students, conduct research and codify new social constructs, and continue our own studies with scholars from around the country.

Black History Week had emerged as a time in which we tried to cram so many activities that we were conflicting with each other. A number of organizations decided to get together to produce a joint calendar and held a meeting at the Black People's Topographical Research Center (called "The Top" for short) on 75th Street. There was no way a week could contain our collective creativity, so I came up with a novel idea—let's expand to a month. We all agreed and decided to call it Black Liberation Month. We did that for a number of years. Other cities joined in, but most used the more timid Black History Month designation. Eventually, everyone used that title, but it all started in Chicago (a little known Black history fact!). Since The Top met its demise years ago, Anderson Thompson is probably the only person who has this documentation.

The Catalyst's contribution to Black Liberation Month was a day-long event held at the Harris YWCA, called Black FolkUs. Workshops, lectures, storytelling, an African marketplace, swimming (old Y guys like Lloyd Saunders and Levert King would lifeguard), and fabulous cuisine were all a part of this family event. Each year there would be a theme that was integral to our movement—organizing, education, economic development, etc. Our announcements were graphically outstanding, designed by outstanding artists like Calvin Jones and Emmit McBain. We would utilize the entire Y, which was easy since the organization seemed to be run by Catalsyt women—Arney Jonson, the director of Harris; Joan Brown; Doris Wilson, who went on to become the director of the YWCA; Willeva Lindsey later became the director of the YW at Ida B. Wells; and I eventually became a board member of the Chicago Y. Hundreds of people came to Black FolkUs and our children grew up looking forward to this event. It truly was a time for us to spend the day focusing on issues of importance to our liberation. Joan Brown and Doris Wilson revolutionized the YWCA. How do you think that venerable women's organization came to make their mission the elimination of racism?

Our movement into Pan-Africanism has been central to our evolution. That will be another chapter, for another book. Hopefully, a book I will write. What we do and how we do it bears telling. It will be a cook book, a philosophy tome, a tell-all (well, maybe not all), a love story, an epic historical account of a body of work accomplished by people dedicated to their race and to the absolute belief and confidence that we could accomplish our purpose.

Much came out of The Catalyst movement and there are many stories to be told. We are institution builders, organizers, theorists and practitioners. We made house and field one. We've built schools and theaters. But most of all, we have kept the faith. There is no separation in us, only work, and we still put our work in every day. You don't have to look for us in the whirlwind; we ARE the whirlwind, and WE DON'T STOP. WE WON'T STOP!

THE ORIGINAL RAINBOW COALITION OF CHICAGO AND THE POLITICS OF SOLIDARITY

Antonio R. Lopez

"A lot of people are running around talking about fighting fire with fire. They say theyre going to fight racism with racism. But we claim that you fight fire best with water. We say you fight racism with solidarity. We say you dont fight capitalism with black capitalism. You fight capitalism with socialism."

Fred Hampton

The calculated assassination of Fred Hampton by a tactical police force on December 4, 1969 stands out in the violent racial history of Chicago as the clearest example of state-sanctioned terrorism and institutional racism. While we will never forget or forgive what occurred in the early morning hours at 2337 W. Monroe, we should also remember why the FBI, the Cook County State's Attorney and Chicago police were compelled to eliminate the leader of the Illinois Black Panther Party and kill and injure his comrades.[7] Part of this memory should include the Black Panthers' commitment to build a Rainbow Coalition with the Young Lords Organization, the Young Patriots, the American Indian Movement, Rising Up Angry, and others. In this chapter, I examine the politics of solidarity in Chicago during the

[7] During the raid Defense Captain Mark Clark from Peoria was killed by police. Seven Panthers survived the raid conducted by a police force under the direction of States Attorney Edward Hanrahan. On the events of the raid see, Jeffrey Haas, *The Assassination of Fred Hampton: How the FBI and the Chicago Police Murdered a Black Panther,* (Lawrence Hill Books: Chicago, 2010), and Ward Churchill and Jim Vander Wall, *Agents of Repression: The FBI's Secret War Against the Black Panthers and the American Indian Movement* (South End Press: Cambridge, 2002).

late 1960s to explain why the original Rainbow Coalition threatened those in power.[8]

The Rainbow Coalition formed in Chicago sometime in late 1968 or early 1969. When asked about the origins of the alliance in a May 25, 1969 *Chicago Sun Times* interview, Chairman Fred Hampton explained,

> This coalition took place around five months ago. We had a section chief who was working out on the North Side, and he ran into these people. He worked with them. We gave them books to read, and things like that, and they started, you know, to come along those lines. We talked about common interests, and common enemies, and when we found we had these things in common we decided to form a coalition. The coalition was also to show that we believe in solidarity in practice.[9]

Hampton's use of the pronoun "we" during this discussion of the origins of the original Rainbow Coalition deserves attention. At first, "we" refers to the Illinois Black Panther Party, a chapter of the revolutionary organization founded in Oakland, California in 1966.[10] Then, it subtly changes to signify the Rainbow Coalition (previously "these people"), before returning to refer to the Chicago Panthers once again. I contend this fluid use of "we" by Hampton reflected a dynamic politics of solidarity that developed among Rainbow Coalition activists. Aside from the revolutionary ideology, the charismatic leadership, the courage to confront common enemies, and the moving dreams of liberation, this transformative understanding of solidarity in practice undermined the politics of race upheld by the Daley regime during the late 1960s.

In the face of growing protest during the late 1960s, Mayor Richard J. Daley reinforced a political culture that maintained power relations in Chicago. During his inauguration speech on April 20, 1967, for example: Daley related his plans for Chicago, his role as mayor, and his view of activists that opposed his plans. Using his standard bravado Daley proclaimed,

> Today, the people are looking to us to carry out the objectives enunciated in the Comprehensive Plan for Chicago. Published last December, the Plan has the major objective of improving the quality of life. Its focus is directed to three related human concerns: the expansion of human opportunities; the improvement of the environment in which we live; the strengthening of the economy which sustains every man, woman and child in this city...[11]

---

[8] The Rainbow Coalition under analysis in this chapter pre-dates the National Rainbow Coalition formed by Reverend Jesse Jackson during his presidential campaign in 1984.

[9] *Chicago Sun Times,* May 25, 1969, p78.

[10] The origins of the Black Panther Party are also traced to the foundation of the Lowndes County Freedom Organization in Alabama in 1966 by SNCC.

[11] "Inaugural Address of Mayor Richard J. Daley, April 20, 1967," http://www.chipublib.org/cplbooksmovies/cplarchive/mayors/rj_daley_inaug04.php

The problems they present will not be solved by demonstrations in the streets, but by demonstrations of understanding and compassion. In fact, the greatest peril to the success of these endeavors is the threat to the rights of others that lies in violence and intimidation. The greatest protection of the rights of all is the preservation of law and order—and as long as I am Mayor, law and order will prevail. The truth is that only a tiny minority of our citizens—a relative handful—are engaged in creating violence and dissension with calculated appeals to hatred and emotion. Unfortunately theirs are the loudest voices, theirs are the most vociferous and irresponsible claims and charges.

Following a landslide election victory in the aftermath of Dr. Martin Luther King's desegregation campaigns in the city, Daley defined the people of Chicago as lawful citizens united by their respect for the rights of others and a rational desire for capitalist development. His abstract description of the people of Chicago; however, disguised a racialized politics of solidarity that casted those who protested racism, exploitation, and the benevolence of urban planning as irrational threats to social stability. By framing acts of dissention as violent enemies of the people, Daley projected this politics of race and representation as the non-violent, protector of stability, quality of life, and freedom.

The mayor's racialized vision of the people of Chicago and war on behalf of stability were contradictory as they both required the threat of instability in order to exist. His fiery politics of solidarity, in other words, thrived upon the actions of "radicals," as they fulfilled the notion that non-radical, rational, law-abiding citizens, required protection. Reflecting upon Daley's political culture and whether the Chicago Panthers desired to radicalize the people, Fred Hampton explained, "Well, we believe in heightening contradictions. But I don't see where any confrontation has to be forced—in the city of Chicago or anywhere else. I think that Mayor Daley's a walking contradiction himself."[12] The insidiousness of this Manichean field of politics was that intensifying efforts by people of color for economic justice, rights, and self-determination could be used to consolidate Daley's political culture that dismissed those very demands as sources of instability. During the late 1960s Chicago was a site of profound urban upheavals and social movements that called for radical social change and racial solidarity. As much as these movements cultivated racial pride and fertilized the soil of resistance in communities of color, they equally reinforced the racialized politics of solidarity that the Daley Machine thrived upon.[13]

---

[12] *Chicago Sun Times,* May 25, 1969, p78

[13] On the neighborhood level this political culture justified the saturated policing of communities of color as sites of potential instability. On the individual level it excused police brutality as skin color remained a marker of potential violence.

As in other northern cities where institutional racism and urban despair persisted, Chicago was rocked by urban uprisings on the West Side on August 1965 in the Division Street riots of June 1966 and again in Lawndale in April of 1968. In these uprisings, hundreds of Blacks and Puerto Ricans responded to acts of police brutality and racial violence by protesting in the streets, destroying exploitative businesses, and confronting the police.[14] These conflicts were ignited by particular acts of racial violence, but were fueled by years of frustration towards economic exploitation, the invisibility of poor people of color, and police violence. For example, in "Los Motines de Chicago," a song produced in the days following the Division Street uprising in Humboldt Park, rage and feelings about ethnic identity that permeated the Puerto Rican barrio are communicated. After recounting the events that resulted in the unjust shooting of a Puerto Rican youth by the police, the decíma asserts,

El jibaro esta despierto.
Ya ha nacido un nueva dia
El Boricua no tenia
Derechos en este estado
Y por eso se rebelaron
Contra de la policía[15]

In the same spirit, the poet Don L. Lee expressed an oppositional rage and racial consciousness felt by many during the late 1960s given the persistence of anti-black racism and cultural mis-education. In his introduction to *Think Black* (1966), Lee exclaimed,

> We must destroy Faulkner, Dick, Jane, and other perpetuators of evil. It's time for Du Bois, Nat Turner and Kwame Nkrumah. As Frantz Fanon points out: destroy the culture and you destroy the people. This must not happen. Black artists are culture stabilizers, bringing back old values and introducing new ones. Black art will talk to the people and with the will of the people stop the impending "protective custody."[16]

As powerful expressions of urban defiance and identity, Lee's call for Black art and "Los Motines de Chicago" are examples of the fire of intra-racial solidarity that burned in the minds of many oppressed people of color during the late 1960s in Chicago. Whereas

---

[14] The August 1965 uprising was triggered by the death of a woman killed by a fire truck responding to an open fire hydrant opened by children of the community. The April 1968 uprising was in the aftermath of Dr. MLK's assassination in Memphis and resulted in Daley's infamous "shoot to kill" order.

[15] Simón Gomez, "Los Motines de Chicago," *Dialogo,* no. 2, (1997), p 28.

[16] The introduction to *Think Black* (1966) is quoted from Haki R. Madhubuti, Liberation Narratives: New and Collected Poems, 1966-2009, (Third World Press, Chicago, 2009) p 29.

Daley's politics of solidarity waged war upon racialized threats to an abstract people of Chicago, movements that cultivated a politics of anti-racism waged war on a hostile society through racial pride. It was this dichotomous power struggle involving the politics of race and solidarity, this fire versus fire, that the Illinois Black Panther Party, the Young Lords Organization, the Young Patriots, Rising Up Angry, and others intervened in when they formed the original Rainbow Coalition.

The Rainbow Coalition linked ongoing struggles for economic justice, dignity, and self-determination in Lawndale, Uptown, and Lincoln Park. Formed in the summer of 1968, the Illinois chapter of the Black Panther Party became the most vocal advocate of Black power, community control, and self-defense in Lawndale.[17] Through its ten-point platform, survival programs, and the charismatic leadership of Chairman Fred Hampton, the Chicago Panthers galvanized the Black freedom struggle in Chicago. Influenced by their example, the Young Lords street gang transformed into the Young Lords Organization to mobilize poor residents in Lincoln Park against gentrification and urban removal.[18] Likewise, the Young Patriots, and Rising Up Angry organized among poor white migrants living in the Uptown area of the city. As a location where large numbers of Native Americans were relocated, Uptown was also a place where the American Indian Movement was active. By forming the Rainbow Coalition, activists were able to demonstrate the ways ethnic experiences of oppression in Chicago were connected.

Throughout 1969, the organizations involved in the original Rainbow Coalition worked tirelessly to address the problems of poor people and to educate their communities about the inter-related nature of oppression in Chicago. In Uptown, Lawndale, and Lincoln Park the groups that coalesced into the Rainbow Coalition: published newspapers, opened health clinics, served children through breakfast programs, occupied institutions hostile to community needs, and staged protests and rallies that promoted solidarity. In a recent interview Omar López, the Minister of Information of the Young Lords Organization, explained the decision to form an alliance and described the level of solidarity that existed in Chicago. He recalled,

---

[17] Jon F. Rice, "Black Radicalism on Chicago's West Side: A History of the Illinois Black Panther Party." (PhD dissertation., University of Northern Illinois, 1998).

[18] On the Young Lords see, Felix M. Padilla, *Puerto Rican Chicago,* (Notre Dame: University of Notre Dame Press, 1987), Johanna Fernandez, "Between Social Services Reform and Revolutionary Politics: Late Sixties Radicalism, and Community Organizing in New York City," in *Freedom North: Black Freedom Struggles outside the South,* 1940-1980. Ed. by Jeanne Theoharis and Komozi Woodard. (New York: Pal-grave, 2003), Judson Jeffries, "From Gangbangers to Urban Revolutionaries: The Young Lords of Chicago," *Journal of the Illinois State Historical Society,* v. 96 (Autumn, 2003): 299-304. Lilia Fernández, "Latina/o Migration and Community Formation in Postwar Chicago: Mexicans, Puerto Ricans, Gender, and Politics, 1945-1975," (PhD dissertation, University of California San Diego, 2005).

> The concept of the Rainbow Coalition is something that evolves....There was all of this interaction and interactivity, so all of that contributed to the concept. There came a point where we said, if we come together as a coalition, we'll have more power city-wide. And the fact is we all have the same problems, we all have to deal with the same authorities, so we need to come together as a coalition. And nothing is stronger than having a multi-national coalition, a multi-racial coalition. I don't know exactly who came up with the name the Rainbow Coalition, but it came out of all of that work that was going on already. It was a question of just structuring it and naming it.[19]

From all of this meaningful work emerged an insurgent politics of solidarity in practice that undermined the racialized political culture upheld by the Daley regime. In the months prior to his assassination, Chairman Fred Hampton was the leading voice that articulated this politics of the people and the need for continued solidarity in practice.

In his speeches, interviews, and actions, Fred Hampton moved activists of all ethnic backgrounds to serve the needs of the people. In August of 1969, in one of his most famous speeches delivered at the Peoples Church on the West Side, Hampton began his speech by saying,

> Power to the people! White Power to white people, Brown Power to brown people, Yellow Power to yellow people, Black Power to black people, X power to those we left out, and Panther Power to the Vanguard Party!

After an animated speech that urged audience members to be revolutionaries, he finished by saying:

> I believe that I'm going to die as a revolutionary in the international proletariat struggle. And I hope that each of you will be able to die in the international revolutionary proletarian struggle or you'll be able to live in it. And I think that struggle's going to come. Why don't you live for the people? Why don't you struggle for the people? Why don't you die for the people?[20]

I suggest that his opening statements and final prophetic words charted a transformative understanding of political solidarity that reveals the significance of the original Rainbow Coalition. In his introduction, Hampton saluted all power movements as equally important demands for self-determination. His closing remarks, on the other hand, related his sincere commitment to the international class struggle, and called on those present to commit their lives to the people. Though the struggle between these two political perspectives seems irreparable, Hampton reconciled them in these two proclamations. A politics of interna-

---

[19] Omar López, Interview with the author, January 10, 2010.[15] Simón Gomez, "Los Motines de Chicago," *Dialogo,* no. 2, (1997), p 28.

[20] Quoted in Haas, *The Assassination of Fred Hampton* p. 4.

tional class struggle, waged through serving the poor people of every race in Chicago, required an anti-racist politics of solidarity that involved active unity between poor people and activists. As an alliance that practiced this politics of solidarity, the Rainbow Coalition cultivated a dynamic political culture that could expose the inter-related racial and class interests protected by Daley's regime.

In an article entitled "To My People, The Poor, The Youth, The Oppressed," José Cha Cha Jiménez, the leader of the Young Lord Organization, reflected on the struggle and wrote:

> I just wonder how long it will take us to wake up. How long will it take us to see. Will we forget our martyrs and let them die and suffer in vain… We are going to have to learn to be like the elephant who never forgets because they do not owe us money. They owe us something more precious, our human rights, our human freedom. They are going to have to stop calling us niggers, spics, hillbillies and chinks. But that is not all. No, that's not all. They are going to have to start sharing the wealth that they have collected off the sweat of our backs. And giving a few of us homes, educations, employment, etc. is not going to stop us from our struggle. They have to give the pie to all of us to share equally because poor people have had enough.[21]

Given that Daley's regime depended upon the threat of "radicals," the words of Jiménez give us a clue as to why the Rainbow Coalition's politics of solidarity was a real threat that had to be broken apart. Whereas Daley's racialized political culture thrived upon social movements that advocated a politics of intra-racial solidarity, the Rainbow Coalition's politics of solidarity in practice disallowed racialized groups (all those called niggers, spics, hillbillies and chinks) from seeing each other as threats to seemingly separate racial agendas for "homes, education, employment etc." Perhaps this is what Bob Lee, a Black Panther Field Marshal who organized in Uptown, meant when he recalled in an interview, "The FBI were always watching us. But the Rainbow Coalition was their worst nightmare. It was Daley's worst nightmare too."[22] Considering that Daley squared off with Dr. Martin Luther King, Jr. and thousands of anti-war protestors during the late 1960s, it is hard to believe that a coalition of dedicated grassroots activists could scare Daley. Yet by allowing poor people of every ethnicity to see their common interests and common enemies, the original Rainbow Coalition had the invincible Daley spooked.

---

[21] José Cha Cha Jiménez, "To My People, The Poor, The Youth, The Oppressed," *Young Lords Organization March* 25, 1969, vol.1 no.2, p 8.

[22] Quoted in James Tracy, *The (Original) Rainbow Coalition,* http://www.areachicago.org/p/issues/solidarities/original-rainbow coalition/.

Conclusion

The original Rainbow Coalition is an extraordinary example that oppressed groups in Chicago have overcome the hyper-segregation of the city to struggle for freedom together. To be sure, the original Rainbow Coalition was not some romantic model of inter-racial harmony. As an alliance formed during a time of intense cultural nationalism and anti-racist outrage, the move towards an inclusive sense of community was contentious and was embraced to different degrees amongst activists. Yet in its refusal to fight with fire and its commitment to solidarity in practice, the original Rainbow Coalition exposed the racial and class interests of the Daley regime and the ways it benefited from divided movements. In a recent interview Nwaji Nefahito, a survivor of the December 4, 1969 police raid, summarized the Daley strategy. She explained, "If you play all of the different parts against each other, they can never come together and the people in power don't have anything to worry about."[23] I believe that as someone who called for people to embrace a politics of solidarity in practice, Chairman Fred Hampton would agree with Nefahito's assessment. We should always remember the day when he was assassinated and who was responsible. We should also remember the politics of solidarity he stood for and the people he referred to when he said "we."

I am that clear thought before you lift the safety
Tellin you to break chains like Haiti
I am Black, Brown, Grey and Hazy...
We are the products of rundowns and street sweeps
The rhythm that the beat keeps
The movement that Fred speaks...

I am...We are

[23] Nwaji Nefajito, Interview with the author, January 13, 2010.

AD HOC ACTIVISM AND CHICAGO'S WEST SIDE

Brenetta Howell Barrett

Ever since I can remember, my mother would tell me and anyone else who would listen that I taught myself to read from local newspapers at about three or four years of age. While I wasn't offended by the plaudits or incredible "oohs" and "wows," I pressed my mother for most of her life to tell me which adult friend or relative had helped me learn to read. She insisted that I did so on my own and encouraged my interest in reading, nonetheless. The hunger developed for reading, books, topical publications, and language propelled me into the 1960s and beyond.

Armed with a hard-won high school diploma, I took an ad hoc approach to continuing education and training. My commitment to self-teaching became the bedrock for future community, professional, political, administrative, and executive positions I would hold between 1960 and 1975 in the public, private, and third sectors of endeavor.

Thanks to a prior year of work with the Lawndale/Westside Booster newspapers, by 1960, I had become immersed in journalistic pursuits as a reporter, columnist, and associate editor. These newspapers were published by Augustus "Gus" Savage, outspoken activist and writer, who was ably assisted by his wife, Eunice. Others who played key roles in the continuing crusading, advocacy, and publication of these important information bearers included Herman Cromwell "Gil" Gilbert, Albert "Al" Janney, and Bennett J. Johnson.

Not only was I provided the opportunity to identify, develop, and use skills which were dormant for years, I was able to experience and contribute to the Boosters' community appeal through the involvement of its staff in social and political community events. I began my work at the Booster office in North Lawndale as a volunteer.

The year 1960 and the balance of the decade and a half that followed catapulted me onto a variety of activist, community organizing, political, journalistic, economic/business development, and leadership platforms.

The Chicago struggle for justice, parity, and expression of progressive thought, was nowhere more daring, adventuresome, educational, or historic than on Chicago's West Side. The years 1960 through 1975 were punctuated very sharply for me by their quantitative and qualitative events. There were numerous notable happenings, and a cast of many characters was centrally- or peripherally-associated with them.

Recalling the 1960s brings forth images of some people and events bubbling in the cauldron of perfidy, need, exploitation, dependence, independence, achievement, resistance, and Black pride that was the West Side. My personal involvement with battles against, and commitment to, these elements was woven throughout a series of activities, affiliations, occupations, and alliances which were integral parts of the West Side persona. These include various categories of employment, volunteer work, civic/community leadership, as hoc education, and fellowship.

The Black Press/Journalism

I was referred by my husband to Gus Savage, a customer of the lounge and function hall we owned at Roosevelt and Kedzie (The Club Pyramid). I met with Gus and Gil, managing editor/columnist. After writing and submitting an article to them on the spot, I immediately became a member of the editorial team. I wrote for the Booster newspapers and shared political leanings with Gus, Gil, Al, and Bennett long after the newspapers ceased being published in 1961. My association with these comrades never wavered and never ended. Gus Savage recommended me to Charles "Chuck" Stone, then editor-in-chief of the *Chicago Defender* newspaper, as a potential West Side editor and writer for the Defender who could manage its office in what was called the Henry Fort Building, after its African American owner. It was located at 2400 West Madison, and was also a Defender circulation center. I got the job and stayed in the position until the office was closed (The Chicago Urban League had an office there, briefly). Although I was transferred to the main office at 2400 South Michigan and became a member of the editorial pool, I continued to write from a West Side perspective. I was a reporter, columnist, and editor, who also wrote feature stories on the Civil Rights Movement. Often, I helped create the stories on my own time through my personal activism. David Llorens, from *JET* magazine, and I frequently discussed the irony in this situation as we covered various protest marches and demonstrations (as a teenager, I had a Chicago Defender newspaper route for several years).

The *Chicago Courier* newspaper was another place where I could write, advance progressive ideas and activities, and work with experienced, reputable journalists like Lutrell "Lu" Palmer and Burleigh Hines. I helped Clarence Lane effect West Side circulation of the *Courier*. I served as managing editor for another publication, the *Chicago News Star*, which was based in North Lawndale, distributed also in East and West Garfield Park, and in the Near West Side community. Clarence Lane was its publisher. A number of other short-lived print media emerged on the West Side. Volunteering when asked, I stayed with them until they folded, for various reasons, during the '60s.

The Westside Journal, published by Donald McIlvaine and his wife, Heruanita, in 1972 allowed me to write a regular column, editorials, and to become an associate editor. Sometimes, my columns were antithetical to positions taken by high-profile politicians and other Westside Journal supporters or advertisers. Don wore other hats as an artist, youth mentor, and co-founder with Bernard Clay of the Westside Arts Council. Youths were encouraged, taught, and had their works displayed and sold in North Lawndale and elsewhere. The young artists earned money from the sales and improved their skills under Don's tutelage.

Bernard Clay founded and served as executive director of Introspect Youth Services in 1975. IYS began to assist thousands of Westside youths and adults to enter and graduate from colleges and universities around the country.

Chicago's Westside Black Press was represented primarily by the *Lawndale Booster* (which expanded and was subsequently renamed the *Westside Booster*) and, later, the *Westside Journal*. They captured and projected many key producers, players, and wannabes onto the broader community stage.

The *Booster* has associates and staff with backgrounds in the political, business, communications, educational, civic, entertainment, journalistic, and civil rights arenas. Some were local community activists and leaders who shared the progressive leanings of the newspaper and its publisher, Gus Savage. Gus was a North Lawndale resident. He was known for his "take no prisoners" attitude regarding those, he felt, who abused or threatened harm to the best interests of the Black community.

Don McIlvaine drew some criticism as *Westside Journal* publisher because he relied heavily on advertising revenues from area taverns, bars, lounges, and clubs. They, in turn, relied heavily on the sales of alcohol and tobacco products. Nonetheless, his work with youths drew praise from many sources. This newspaper, like the *Booster*, was popular with nightlifers and daytimers alike.

Both newspapers, along with several others that had very short lives, filled vital roles in educating, informing, training, and unifying residents. These tasks were accomplished via their editorials, columns, news coverage, and creative promotions such as the Booster's "Mayor of Lawndale" contest, and the "Annual Awards Banquet."

McIlvaine and Savage recognized that patrons of local taverns and lounges were citizens, voters, workers, leaders, entrepreneurs, activists, churchgoers, and lawmakers, as well as aspirants to those positions. These "watering holes" were not only reliable meet and greet social centers, but served as incubators and classrooms for the development of community thought, mobilization, and action. They were great sites for newspaper distribution, leafleting, and petition campaigns, as were barbershops and beauty shops. They were all noteworthy informal discussion centers. The newspapers left in these businesses, where they could often be read leisurely, aided the political growth of their customers and staff by publishing the profiles, positions, and records of elected officials and/or candidates for office.

Perspectives on the period 1960-1975 regarding politics and political activism on Chicago's West Side are mainly seen through the prism of some of my own experiences, associations, and connections with a broad array of individuals and organizations. Off times, events, personalities, and information didn't make it to the West Side. This resulted in the West Side being taken to them.

The *Lawndale Drum* was a North Lawndale-based newspaper whose resonant beat was heard and felt by Blacks throughout the West Side communities. Its publisher was Sigmonde Wimberli, a poet, journalist, and activist member of the Lawndale Peoples Planning and Action Committee, which fought for employment, housing, and political equity.

Because the Greater West Side was frequently overlooked, or was included in community and citywide events as an afterthought, I wound up being called upon to represent this part of town on numerous occasions. In other instances, when I was tapped as a resource for a worthy cause, I was often able to refer or suggest other people to meet the need.

Embracing the Crucible

Some organizations, individuals, and events which changed the political landscape of the West Side, while affecting every other aspect of its community fabric included, in the 1960s:

- The West Side Organization (WSO) led by Chester Robinson, as a community-based organization on the Near West Side, served the ABLA Homes public housing development.
- The Westside Christian Parish, headed by the Reverend Dr. Archie Hargraves, a storefront church and ministry source for activists on the Near West Side.
- The Garfield Organization (GO), led by Frederick Douglass "Doug" Andrews; he acquired several Burger King franchises and provided jobs for numerous westsiders.

- The Deacons for Defense and Justice, organized and led by Edward "Fats" Crawford to ensure self-defense at the individual and community levels the Deacons felt were needed. The organization originated in Louisiana.
- Lawndale Peoples Planning and Action Conference, led by Attorney Cecil Butler and Michael W. Scott, for housing development and training of residents in this field. Numerous residents became housing managers.
- Westside UNIT of NAACP, fought with the National NAACP office in New York, and was finally allowed to become the Westside NAACP BRANCH (fight led by Carter Jones, Bennett Johnson, Faith Rich, Brenetta M. Howell (who was an officer and was later installed as vice president, along with other officers by Circuit Court Judge Mark Jones)).
- The Black Panther Party, established in 1968, with office and service facilities on Chicago's West Side, provided food for hungry bodies and hungry minds. It was led by young Chairman Fred Hampton, born in Maywood, Illinois (a Chicago western suburb). The charismatic leader was assassinated while he slept in the West Side apartment where he lived on December 4, 1969, along with Mark Clark. Ronald "Doc" Satchel, who organized and ran the BPP Health Clinic, was critically wounded.
- The Chicago Economic Development Corporation's West Side branch office, at Kedzie Avenue and Roosevelt Road, became the number one producer of Small Business Administration-approved loans for Black-owned businesses in Chicago (68% of all loans granted through four CEDCO branch offices around the city, including two on the South Side). I was the branch manager. This success led to permission for me to do more organizing of small, local Black firms in the name of CEDCO. This followed my convening and development of the Westside Business Advising Council and Women's Business Development Program as CEDCO projects.

Key West Side branch business counselors included Melvin Eiland, who progressed to becoming a shopping mall developer, completing two such projects (one each in North Lawndale and on the Near West Side). Another was Jesse Madison, whom I recruited from a major downtown corporation. He advanced to the position of CEDCO Associate Director for Administration. Later, he was elected a state representative to the Illinois State Legislature.

CEDCO's West Side branch office was the springboard for another significant economic justice victory by helping to create the Chicago Business Opportunity Fair. The branch staff established a contractual relationship between the North Lawndale-based Western Electric Company and Fred Miller, a westside entrepreneur who manufactured wooden pallets consistently purchased by the majority firm.

CBOF, a spin-off of this venture, was the area's premier event for bringing together minority vendors/suppliers and large corporate purchasers. The first event was coordinated by the branch manager, and George Johnsen, and Henry Wilson of Western Electric. It was held at the International Amphitheatre.

In September 1969, the first ever CBOF award was presented to Brenetta M. Howell "In Appreciation for Opening Squeaky Doors." The award, a wooden plaque embellished with an attached bronze oil can and hinges, was the precursor to the coveted Gold Oil Can Award presented by CEDCO for many years thereafter to minority and majority businesses for exceptional partnering performances.

In the spring and summer of 1967, I was repeatedly struck by the number of vehicles belonging to construction general contracting and subcontracting firms with European names, suburban addresses, and no visible Black personnel on the West Side. I lived and worked in these neighborhoods.

When I took my concerns, as West Side CEDCO branch manager, to Garland Guice, executive director, he listened carefully. I told him I wanted to organize Black construction-related business owners in the area and conduct a "full court press" to achieve meaningful general contracting and subcontracting opportunities. He informed me that a similar effort on the South Side had failed, and he gave me the go-ahead.

Shortly thereafter, I convened a meeting of a group who, in September 1967, allowed me to name their burgeoning alliance The West Side Builders Association. This became its permanent name. We met for a few more months in 1967 on the fourth floor of the building that housed the Lawndale Urban Progress Center, a satellite of the Chicago Committee on Urban Opportunity, at 3140 West Roosevelt Road. The first meeting was attended by local contractors C. C. Turner, Alonzo Travis, Roosevelt Betts, and Loise Turner. Since the elevator in the building was frequently out of order and the only available space was on that top floor, we began meeting at the Pulaski Road barbershop of Loise Turner.

As word spread of our efforts, we were joined by other contractors such as Bob Andres, Luster Jackson, and Ernie Taylor. We were able to assist Taylor Electric in attaining a subcontract for most of a total of $250,000 in subcontracts for WSBA members. Journalist Francis Ward covered our efforts and wrote an article for the Chicago American about this victory.

By this time, we were also gaining attention from city, state, and county agency personnel who began to attend WSBA meetings at Turner's Barbershop. New attendees also increasingly included small contractors from the south and north sides of town. CEDCO board members who were bankers, corporate executives, and nonprofit organization leaders from entities such as the Chicago Urban League, Chicago South Side and West Side Chicago NAACP became involved. CEDCO was able to get a nearly half-million dollar federal grant to staff and expand this effort.

I was promoted to Associate Director for Community and Public Relations (with personnel-related duties re: training, manual development and production, and recruitment orientation) and transferred to CEDCO's downtown office. The grant permitted Garland Gaice and me to develop job descriptions and prospective staff profiles, working with C.C. Turner who was then WSBA president. We hired Paul King, Consuelo Miller and staff for WSBA.

Our initial efforts with WSBA became more successful and soon I was getting calls and letters of inquiry and invitations to come and assist with such projects in places like Milwaukee, Wisconsin; Columbus, Ohio; and Springfield, Illinois.

This group of small business persons were invited to attend business conferences, trainings, and bid briefings which they had not experienced previously. They also gained political wisdom and grew in understanding the potential power they held. An unsuccessful attempt to elect Robert Biggs 29th Ward alderman in 1963 as part of a Black independent fight against the Richard J. Daley Democratic Party machine led to the creation of Protest at the Polls. A dedicated group of political activists from throughout the city, led by Blacks and including sympathizers of various racial and ethnic backgrounds, held an organizing meeting at Metropolitan Community Church with such well-known leaders as Gus Savage, Bennett Johnson, Rosie Simpson, Clory Bryant, and others. I was elected secretary. In 1964, PATP sponsored the congressional candidacies of three of its members. They were Ahmed (A.A. "Sammy") Rayner, 1st Congressional District (South Side); Brenetta M. Howell, 6th Congressional District (West Side); and Clory Bryant, 9th Congressional District (North Side).

None of these candidates won. However, the body of knowledge and experience that was developed was extremely valuable and contributed to the development of PATP's early members and supporters, as well as latecomers. PATP-affiliated candidates were soon to be found in city, state, county, and federal campaigns all over Chicago.

Lessons Learned (partial listing)

- Communicate with oneself (orally, in writing, visually, etc.)
- Always remind oneself to:
  - ✓ Define and recognize oppression
  - ✓ Be clear about NEEDED change as well as expected change
  - ✓ Commit to working for empowerment of the powerless
  - ✓ Accept multigenerational leadership and structural unity in the quest for justice
  - ✓ Seek truth beyond the headlines and the headliners
  - ✓ Bring lessons learned and respect for tactical differences to contemporary movements and activism
  - ✓ Vow to become or remain involved in community betterment efforts local, worldwide, etc.)
  - ✓ Don't dismiss the potential in the POWER OF ONE to get a ball rolling for Justice (educational, economic, political, social, etc.)
  - ✓ Seek and ask for help to identify resources and move towards positive change
  - ✓ Expertise is not always needed to tackle a persistent problem
- Ensure that FREEDOM is more than just a slogan tossed around and about casually
- Instill fresh meaning into each letter of this powerful work by reviewing and pledging to fight for FREEDOM with:
  - ✓ F: fidelity
  - ✓ R: Research
  - ✓ E: Enthusiasm
  - ✓ E: Empathy
  - ✓ D: Documentation
  - ✓ O: Opportunity
  - ✓ M: Mindfulness
- Be PRESENT: LISTEN/SPEAK UP/ACT
- Continue to believe that WE CAN ALL DO SOMETHING!!

WASHINGTON SPEAKS: NO MERCY PERCY?

Harold Washington

The recent and unfortunate drug raids on the homes of two innocent white families in Collinsville, Illinois, could eventually lead to a re-examination of all the repressive criminal measures that have been passed during the five-year Nixon presidency.

Such laws as No Knock, Stop-Frisk, Preventive Detention, Excessive bail proposals, permissive wire-tapping and forced sobriety tests have served during the past five years to lay siege upon Black, Puerto Rican and poor communities through this country.

These laws have given racist law enforcement officers and law and order nuts a field day. Black people generally were aware that these laws were not directed toward the elimination of street crime (which every right thinking individual wants to control because our fathers, mothers, women and daughters must walk the streets), but rather were directed toward the repression of legitimate voices of dissent.

Black people, and particularly Black Legislators who fought such laws, were labeled as coddlers of criminal elements.

Many of us; however, got trapped by the propaganda, which cried for an excessive amount of power in the hands of law enforcement officers in order to prevent encroaching crime. Those that did are now beginning to see their mistake.

The white media, which one would expect to be just as diligent in the protection of the rights of individuals as they are in the protection of the freedom of the press, were in the forefront of those who condoned many of these repressive measures.

It was only when Nixon's Supreme Court condoned throwing newspaper reporters into jail that the news media began to exercise any concern about the steady encroachment upon the freedom of people who walk the streets or merely sit in their homes and become victims of excessive police control.

Their attitudes are similar to those of the white community, generally in the area of marijuana and hard dope. As long as marijuana and hard dope were considered a Black problem, the white community did not concern itself.

When they discovered that marijuana and addictive drugs were being used in abundance by suburban white kids, the attitude toward strong punishment for the use of such illegal contraband began to soften.

And so it is with the federal use of No-Knock laws, innocent people have had their doors broken down by brutal, insensitive federal agents.

Now the white community is up in arms, and our good Senator Charles Percy, whose voice has been singularly quiet regarding Stop-Frisk and other abuses of Black people, is mouthing statements daily to the effect that no-knock laws should be repealed.

I agree that the federal No-Knock law should not only be repealed but should never have been made law. I would think much more of men like Senator Percy, if they used the examples and lessons of Watergate and the excessive No-Knock laws to assist Black Legislators, such as myself, in rolling back and repealing the numerous repressive measures.

I would like to hear the good senior Senator from the State of Illinois come out strongly against Stop-Frisk, preventative detention, inordinate Army, FBI and CIA surveillance of ordinary citizens, known and repeated instances of police brutality, arrogance and disdain perpetrated against innocent Black citizens.

If I direct my remarks against Senator Charles Percy, it is only because he has been singularly quiet while the iron heel of repression has come down on the necks of Black people and threatened such fine individuals as Renault Robinson of the Afro-American Patrolmen's League.

I did not hear the good Senator even raise a query when Judge Sydney Jones was mistreated by Chicago's finest. Percy stood mute while Congressman Ralph H. Metcalfe organized his Concerned Citizens for Black Police Reform.

I did not see Senator Percy joining other black citizens or me in attempting to repeal the Illinois Stop-Frisk Law.

It was only when white folks in southern Illinois became innocent victims of No-Knock that the good Senator began to express his concern about that narrow, repressive law alongside the many others that you and I have suffered under for far too long.

I say this to all the Senator Percys who care to read:

> If you wish to catapult your political ambitions toward the presidency of these United States, it is about time that you concern yourselves with the fact that Black people demand adequate, professional police protection and will never have it unless repressive criminal laws are repealed. Also, people like the good Senator need to make it clear that they will not tolerate police arrogance and brutality.

What do you think?

(Reprinted from The Black Express *Law and Prisons from the Vivian Harsh Collection—August 18, 1973 written by +then-State Representative Harold Washington.)*

THE CONSERVATIVE VICE LORDS: "A COMMUNITY ORGANIZATION"

Benneth Lee

"The Rise of a Nation Begins in the home of its people"

African Proverb

The sixties were a time of the Civil Rights and the Black Power Movements. In Chicago, Blacks were faced with conditions that resulted in most young people becoming involved in petty crime, drug usage and street gangs to cope with their desperate circumstances. Living in slum conditions with limited resources shaped the value system of the young people who were merely trying to survive.

As a youth in the sixties, on the west side of Chicago, I was exposed to hustling, petty crime and gang life at an early age. The Conservative Vice Lords, an older group of brothers, sought out to provide more positive alternatives and opportunities for us younger brothers. They became a chartered community organization and set up social, educational, cultural and economical opportunities to help us cope with the adverse conditions in our communities.

Being young and responsive to racial tension and a lack of positive alternatives, I developed a world-view from an adolescent and cultural shame perspective. Today, as an adult looking at the conditions young people are faced with (street-crime, drug trafficking, violence and street gangs) I am inspired to look at the conditions and the movement of the sixties from a mature and cultural context. I want to look at the efforts the Vice Lords made to bring about a better opportunity for us younger brothers at that time and what caused their failures in their desperate attempt to do so.

The Vice Lords had twenty-six sets that made up the Vice Lord Nation. It was the older Vice Lords that became "Conservative" Vice Lords Inc., a legitimate charted community organization designed to provide positive alternatives for inner-city west side youth. They received funds from private charitable organizations and companies in the community to fund their efforts in providing education, economical and cultural opportunities for these youth.

The Cicero Vice Lords were the older brothers from the Austin community, the set I came from. They became a Vice Lord branch in the year 1966. They consisted of older brothers in their late teens and early twenties. They had connections with the Conservative Vice Lords who had introduced them to the movement of becoming a grass roots organization to advocate and provide alternatives for the youth. Slim, the leader of the Cicero Vice Lords, had moved from Sixteenth Street and started the first branch of Vice Lords in the Austin area. His mission of duplicating what the conservative Vice Lords had accomplished in North Lawndale was difficult due to the opposition he was confronted with, especially the whites who were the majority in the Austin community. Their plight was different from the Conservative Vice Lords because of the geographic characteristics of over-crowding other Black families who fought over the limited resources available to them. The Conservative Vice Lords lived in a predominantly Black community; the Cicero Vice Lords lived in a predominantly white community. Because of the need to defend ourselves against our white adversaries, it was important that we supported each other. We, the young brothers, looked at this as racial solidarity, a means of survival and what being a Vice Lord was all about.

The majority of the Vice Lord sets were involved in street crime, drugs and Black on Black crime. Because we were all Vice Lords, the Conservative Vice Lords received negative press coverage for what other sets were doing. It wasn't until I was in Statesville Maximum security prison (1978) that I met some of the founders of the Conservative Vice Lords, and I learned about their goals and what Vice Lords were supposed to stand for. The Conservative Vice Lords' whole concept was to teach each set how to tap into the resources within their perspective area and create positive alternatives for the youth.

The Vice Lords Becoming the "Conservative" Vice Lord Inc.

It is clear that the media has an influence on how one group of people perceive another. When stories are told about the clash between blacks and whites, the whites are looked upon as victims of black criminal behavior. The fact that black youth defend themselves from white racist attacks is often overlooked and never reported from the black youths' perspective. It was during the early 1950s when blacks on the west side of Chicago were fighting whites for housing, jobs and use of public facilities. The media would portray whites as being attacked by violent black groups invading their communities. These groups were identified as "Black Street Gangs." Because of this image given to Black youth and their supporters, opportunities for obtaining funds for community programs became a challenge.

The oldest and second largest street gang in Chicago was the Vice Lords. They were predominately Black and were formed in the late 50s as a club in the Illinois State Training School for Boys at St. Charles, Illinois. As several members were released in 1958, they relocated to the Lawndale area of Chicago's west side; they then grew into many factions that had distinctive names and leaders. The Factions included: Unknown Vice Lords, 4 Corner Hustlers, Traveling Vice Lords, Cicero Mafia Insane Vice Lords, Undertaker Vice Lords, Imperial Insane Vice Lords, Renegade Vice Lords, Central Insane Vice Lords, and Conservative Vice Lords.

In 1966 Dr. Martin Luther King, Jr. started his northern freedom campaign in Chicago. He met with the Vice Lords and other Black gang members when he moved into the Lawndale community. He appealed to them to practice nonviolence and to join in his movement to fight for tenant rights. Several of the gangs joined Dr. King and served as marshals when he marched through the white hostile community of Marquette Park. Fred Hampton, who led the Illinois chapter of the Black Panther Party, met regularly with the leadership of the three largest gangs at that time: the Vice Lords, Blackstone Rangers and the Disciples. Some of these meetings were held at the Better Boys Foundation, headed by Warner Saunders.

It was then that the Vice Lords, Blackstone Rangers, and Disciples formed the first city-wide coalition of its kind to fight for jobs and civil rights. Jesse Jackson and other civil rights leaders worked with the gangs in their campaigns for jobs in the construction industry.

New Image Building Period

In 1968 the Vice Lords declared that they were no longer a street gang. In a story covered by the *Chicago Daily Defender* (May 28), members of the Vice Lords assert "We're no Gang," declaring their intention to "...take the bottom of our bag, turn it upside down and shock people all over the world with some of the positive changes we can and are making. We no longer want to be classified as a 'gang'." Bobby Gore, one of the leaders of the Conservative Vice Lords, wrote a letter to the Chicago Defender that criticized it for continuing to call the Vice Lords a gang. He contended that "We are a corporation charted in the state of Illinois. Our goals are constructive. We have our own little bag called 'ghetto sophistication'." Bobby went on to ask a pertinent question, and then answered it himself. "Who came up with the idea that we have people to waste? We've been labeled the worst kind of people… gangs. I mean we can't find a single person in our group who can't be used for something. And society has proved to us that the only helping hand we'll find is at the end of our own arm."

On March 19, 1969, the Vice Lords took a leadership role in boycotting businesses in the Black community that did not hire or address the needs of the Black people. Seventy members of the Conservative Vice Lords joined a coalition of about sixty community groups that launched a boycott against Red Rooster stores. Richard Kay, vice president of the supermarkets, also attended the meeting with his wife and participated in the evening activities enthusiastically. One of the main speakers at the rally was Jessie Jackson, national head of Operation Breadbasket, who charged black people to stand up with dignity and demand respect.

Some of the organizations on the west side of Chicago that participated in the boycotts were PPAC (People Planning Action Committee), Deacons of Defense and the Westside Association for Community Action.

Another organization that played a major role in addressing the mistreatment of Blacks on the west side was The Black Hand Society; it was made up of many grassroots organizations and street gangs that had joined together in peace. Its members would have secret meetings to strategize on how to address issues such as police brutality, poor schools, and the unjust arrest of Blacks on the west side; they also would organize around political issues and promote a particular political candidate. Chicago's west side was predominately democratic and controlled by the Daley machine. Because of the power of this Democratic machine, the Black Hand Society was underground, making power moves to get desired results for Blacks on the west side, avoiding public confrontation and coercion from the machine. The leaders of the street organizations were becoming politicized and moving with the agenda of the Black Nationalists; because of this, the young people were receiving guidance to move into the science of Black Power. With this shift of Black Power consciousness within street organizations, they became a threat to the Democratic machine.

Because there existed a hostile relationship between the Black community and the police on the west side, Renault Robinson and Edward "Buzz" Palmer, both Black police officers, organized the Afro American Policeman League. They began their first meeting at the Better Boys Foundation and developed programs to provide a new image of Black police officers assigned to the Black Community.

The Conservative Vice Lords were moving as a vanguard for the Black community on the west side. They organized with the belief that Black politicians and clergyman were not doing enough to address the issues that led to Black-on-Black Crime and violence because it was a position in opposition to the Democratic machine. The Conservative Vice Lords were wise enough to see that the slum lords, poor schools and racist business owners in the Black community suppressed it, and that suppression resulted in Black-on-Black crime and violence. Leonard "Goat" Parks, first president of CVL INC., said:

> The conditions in which Blacks are forced to live under [Poor schools, high unemployment] are the root cause of the crime and violence among Blacks. CVL is an organization that is designed to fight for better conditions and the future of our youth. We will show other Vice Lord sets how to organize and develop opportunities for themselves. They don't have to wait on us, but learn to do it for themselves by shutting down any business that do not hire Black people and voting and elected official out of office that do not work on the behalf of Black people. (*Lord Thang, CVL and David Dawley production 1968*)

The Conservative Vice Lords, in their efforts to shut down construction sites that did not hire Blacks in the community, discovered that their issues were shared by youth groups on the south side. This common concern gave birth to LSD (Lords Stones and Disciples). The LSD challenged the Building Association of Chicago and city planners on the issue of Blacks being discriminated against in securing construction jobs within their own community. LSD joined efforts with the Coalition for United Community Action, a group of community-based organizations, to become a stronger force to challenge the unions and contractors that kept Blacks out of construction work.

Chicago Today covered a story on the United Community Action meeting with the construction industry (August 22, 1969). "Leaders of the Coalition for United Community Action appeared jubilant after conferring with representatives of the construction industry about more jobs for Blacks in the building trades."

Eleven Blacks met with eleven white representatives from the Building Associations of Chicago and the Chicago Building Trades Council. David Reed, spokesman for the Blacks, commented "There was a very high level of understanding by both sides of the problems." He felt that future meetings would be fruitful. The conference was the result of the picketing of Blacks which halted 80 million dollars-worth of construction on 20 south side sites since July 22 of this year.

The Suppression of a Black Community Organization "The Democratic Machine"

The Chicago political machine has an Imperialistic legacy of suppressing Blacks from forming programs to advance themselves from the oppressive conditions that are a challenge in the inner city Black communities. Because of the Black Power movement during 1963-1968, the white power structure (Daley's political machine) within the city of Chicago demonstrated its power in discriminating against Black organizations that were formed to address the needs of the Blacks in their various communities. Street gangs were influenced by some of the leaders of that time and joined the Black Power Movement. Due to this new relationship between the street gangs and community leaders, the politics of the Black community began to be controlled by the Blacks within the community. Dr. Martin Luther King, Jr. moved his civil rights' movement to the north and eventually to Chicago's west side. There he met with leaders of the various gangs and appealed to them for their help in his fight for better housing and labor equality for Black people.

Although organizations in Chicago's Black communities, such as the NAACP and the Chicago Urban League, were fighting for civil rights and equality, Fred Hampton of the Black Panthers called a meeting with the heads of the three street gangs. They agreed to move as one group on the issue of jobs and improving the social services needed in the black community. The Black Panther Party for Self Defense collaborated with the three major street organizations in the Black community. What I think was happening was that the new coalition had the potential of bringing the street organizations into a leading role within the Black movement. Their suppression was the destruction of democracy in Chicago and the victory of a neo-colonial ruling strategy through Black preachers and politicians.

Dr. Martin Luther King's movement on open housing and summits on civil rights was evidence that a Civil Rights Movement was not the way to go in the north. They met opposition from Mayor Richard Daley's political machine. The LSD coalition joined the Black Power Movement and gained influence with Chicago Black politics. Mayor Daley noticed that his favored politicians in the Black community were being outvoted by the LSD coalition's candidates, and he began a war against gangs. His method was clear: he planned to frame the new coalition as gangs and discredit them as grass roots organizations. Dailey and, at that time, state's attorney Edward Hanrahan, issued a report that marked a significant change in public policy towards street gangs. Their objective was to influence the public by showing gangs as wayward youth, causing them to be seen as threats to their communities. From that point on, the law enforcers were going to treat gang members as criminals. This new approach opened the doors for the FBI to investigate the activities of street gangs (like they did with Martin Luther King, Jr., the Black Panthers and the Nation of Islam) with its COINTELPRO (counter intelligence) program.

The philosophy of that time was that infusing massive amounts of money could help solve the problems of America's inner cities. Community organizers and social welfare agencies began to lobby for monies to trickle down to the black communities, to open programs and to meet the need of the black Community. The Vice lords applied and got their article of corporation and became "Conservative Vice Lords Inc.". David Dawley, author of A Nation of Lords, was very instrumental in developing programs for the Vice Lords. He wrote to Washington, DC, on the behalf of the Vice Lords stating, "Through the Vice Lords we have an opportunity to develop the most exciting social action project in America, the possibility of organizing a large section of one of the major cities in the United States and of building a new model of social and economic development."

The Vice Lords have demonstrated good faith by meeting throughout the summer with police, businessmen and bureaucrats. While other cities have had riots, the Vice Lords, Roman Saints and Cobras have assisted the city-wide campaign to 'keep a cool summer.' But without money, without a vote of confidence, and at least a test of intentions, the Vice Lords will remain cut off from society as a hoodlum group.

Conclusion

The sixties was a period when Black People were fighting for their right to vote, to live in decent neighborhoods and to go to schools to receive a quality education. Because of the atmosphere of fighting for civil rights and Black power in the Black community, street gangs saw a way to support the efforts of Black people by joining the fight for the rights and opportunities of Black youth. The legacy the media left, about the street leaders in the sixties, was to "never trust young Black leadership."

MY PERSONAL STRUGGLE IN THE CIVIL RIGHTS MOVEMENT

Afi Samella B. Abdullah

Little did I know in 1963, one year prior to my faculty appointment at Northwestern Medical School, Black medical doctors had been discriminated against and denied hospital privileges in most private hospitals prior to the Civil Rights Movement. Board certifications were rather restrictive in admitting Blacks, and the availability of these specialties were in socially exclusive institutions. Even the Physicians' Honor Society allowed no chapters at Meharry or Howard, where approximately ninety percent of Black health care professionals were educated. On June 12, 1963, a multiethnic group of physicians picketed the American Medical Association's convention "to speak out immediately and unequivocally against racial segregation and discrimination...wherever [they] exist in medicine and health services" (Clayton & Byrd, 2003, V.II, p.271).

Black physicians became increasingly militant and participated in marches and demonstrations. Also, they began providing medical care to civil rights groups and local communities. This group of racially mixed physicians were supported by the NAACP, American Jewish Conference, CORE, SCLC, SNCC and the National Catholic Conference for Interracial Justice. These efforts later advanced to protection and care of civil rights workers, providing health education, developing rural and mobile health centers, surveying medical needs, and documenting discriminatory patterns in health services in the North and South. Had I known all of this at that time, I might not have chosen to apply for an academic and clinical position in a medical school and its clinic.

It was my faith in God, my belief in my grandmother's struggles, and my reflection on my sorority's litany to live "life with vision, meeting challenges, through commitment, dedication, fellowship/sense of community, personal endurance, and perseverance" that inspired me to take the position and manage the challenge. The white medical staff and administrators at Northwestern University's Chicago-based medical complex soon learned the value of a so-called Negro turned Black, and a Black social worker turning militant. Stereotypes were decidedly offset and confronted as professionalism was practiced. As

I gained acceptance, I modified my personal image and began wearing a short Afro hairstyle. When the director inquired if I cut my hair due to any scalp disease, I proudly informed her that I would no longer wear my hair straightened. I would wear it in its natural kinky condition as a testament to my being African. With the support of the director of social work and the initial employment interviewer, staff meetings on inequalities and injustices were conducted, and community leaders and organizers were invited to speak on a regular basis. I am pleased that my grandmother, the daughter of a formerly enslaved African woman, lived long enough to see me become a "race woman" like herself.

The white professionals at Northwestern verbalized fears of Black Power, Power to the People, and Burn Baby Burn slogans with little understanding of the slogans' origins. They attributed these fearful slogans to the Black Muslims and not to the political leaders. White professionals went so far as to question their household help in efforts to contradict my assertiveness. They seemed to feel some relief from their household servants about their guilty feelings regarding oppression and domination. That consoled them only momentarily, for it was soon clear that the house servants failed to express their concerns or feelings about the socio-economic plight of the masses of Blacks in Chicago. Ultimately, some of the faculty and staff had to denounce the complacency of their household help in the view of the uprisings and insurrections (which they called riots) that broke out in Northern cities during the mid-sixties. The television news consistently exposed the brutality and violence imposed on the peaceful, nonviolent civil rights workers in the South. The questions came to me. "What do they want?" "Why are they burning and destroying their own communities?" I was pleased to respond to these questions that these communities did not belong to the people who lived there. These communities were ghetto colonies owned by white people, who exploited the people rendering insufficient services for overpriced products (rentals, groceries, cars, retail items). I orchestrated in-service training on the Civil Rights Movement. "What We Want" was the theme and invited nationalists, militants and civil rights workers to speak.

Northerners watched the television reports of Freedom Riders, college student sit-in movements, brutality of Southern police, hangings, murders, and fires while denying the brutality in the North. Lynchings by members of the White Citizens Council in their attempts to maintain segregation, economic/social inequality, and injustices toward Black people were prevalent and expected—because that was the South. The monumental Southern Christian Leadership Conference's (SCLC) March on Washington with the passive theme of "We Shall Overcome" seemed acceptable to Northerners who were still in denial about their racial discrimination and oppression. Since the Northerners pointed the finger at Southerners as racist, they were helped to view their political positions more realistically.

The discrimination against Black physicians was discussed within the context of the Urban League's 1956 report that "Black physicians were victims of discrimination in Chicago and other cities," and "only 7.1 percent served at predominantly white hospitals" (Clayton & Byrd, 2003 V II, p. 254).

Dr. King came to Chicago and took up residence on the West Side, where several uprisings had occurred. The evening television news displayed him suffering attacks from police dogs and fire hoses, in a manner similar to the violence he experienced in the South. He was jailed. I left work to hear Dr. King speak in Grant Park. I spent many evenings listening to Stokely Carmichael, director of SNCC, speak to the Black community. I was introduced to Black culture, Black art, and Black politics in a Black arts theater. I watched Malcolm X being interviewed by a white journalist on television. I was immediately impressed with his candor, knowledge, and assertive outspokenness. I stopped wearing the usual attire of the stiff and rigid social worker. I wore ethnic clothes that helped shape my identity and complemented my short Afro haircut.

Many so-called Chicago Negroes who recognized the degrees of oppression began dressing accordingly, wearing their kinky hair in natural short or long styles. This style of wear was being emulated by professional Negroes in the fields of social work, psychology, medicine, law, psychiatry, academia, journalism, and nursing. Elected officials, being responsible to the community, were accepted into the group and held accountable. This association was for liberation of self, family, profession, and community. This multi-disciplinary organization was named the Association of Black Catalysts. The mission was "unity for survival." The agenda was Black identity, Black unification, Black linkages and Black facilitation. The question was, "Can you afford not to be Black?" This question was pertinent and relevant because each Negro professional had endured miseducation (lies about geography and history) and dis-education (distortions of truths) during the course of their matriculations at colleges and universities which upheld and practiced white supremacy domination theories. We became further aware that the more higher education received, the more indoctrinated a Black person became in white supremacy and Black inferiority theories.

It became evident that Black people in America required some soul cleansing and cognitive revitalization to rid themselves of the systemic and institutional indoctrinations that led to internalization of white supremacy racism. We understood the need to develop positive identifications with our African heritage and to build institutions (culture, politics, social systems, structures and organizations).

The Association of Black Catalysts was created in recognition of the need to formalize a value system for framing, collaborating and uniting our thoughts and goals. We also developed a code of ethics for modulating our behaviors in the interests of the total Black community. The Black Catalysts consisted of multi-disciplined Black professional "movers and shakers," who aggressively practiced unity, self-determination, cooperative economics, faith, and creativity. Community-determined leadership prevailed as the group operated within a code of ethics for Black people (see appendix 2—this is Our Bag!). Each member utilized his/her professional skills and research abilities to research the public and private institutions servicing the Black communities. We utilized published annual reports and census data, in addition to conducting surveys of each institution's advertised demographic data and on-site personnel. Discrimination policies and practices, including hiring and retention, were documented. We subsequently formed small teams of members who made strategic visits to these institutions, shared our knowledge of their unconstitutional practices, with specific strategies for removal of their institutional racist policies and programs. We had learned from our places of employment that institutional racism was so embedded in the fabric of our society that white people really needed to hear from Black professionals how their specific institutions were racist. These confrontational visits were a successful means of communicating that educated Black people who were just as "sick and tired of being sick and tired" as Rosa Parks and Dr. Martin Luther King, Jr.

Members of the Black Catalysts also recognized that each member needed to maintain their memberships in their respective national professional associations, and confront them with demands for recognizing and prioritizing the needs of the Black professionals and the Black communities served.

The confrontations on the American Medical Association by the National Medical Association began in 1963 (Clayton & Bryd, V. II, 2003, p. 273). The Black nursing profession began its struggle following World War II in 1945, with a campaign against racial discrimination with the War Department. 1

The Black social workers organized nationally at the 1968 Conference on Social Welfare when they collectively walked out of the Convention and formed a steering committee that returned with a signed position statement of the new National Association of Black Social Workers. This statement addressed ten racist positions and demanded acknowledgment of institutional racism reflected in ethnic composition and representation of the board and committees; theories-based misinterpretations; failure to support social welfare that maintains unequal participation; failure to support the national welfare rights; and awarding the secretary of health, education and welfare, who denied practicing white racism. I was one of the twelve Steering Committee members who helped write, sign and deliver the position statement on the platform of the Hilton Hotel in San Francisco, California (Jaggers, G. 2003).

Black psychologists organized nationally at the American Psychological Association's 1968 convention when they collectively walked out of the convention, under the leadership of Robert Williams and Joseph White, pledging themselves to be Black people first and psychologists second. They did so with a mandate to support each other and to prioritize and address their psychological needs and concerns, including: the recruitment, retention and graduation of psychology students and to improve the training of psychologists who seek to work with Black people (Guthrie, 1998). I am a past president (1998-1999) and a member of the Council of Elders in the International Association of Black psychologists.

Potential lessons to be learned:

1. One's socioeconomic status of childhood should be no hindrance to one's adult status for some forms of deprivation can inspire one to want more and move toward self-improvement, knowledge and social and political skills.
2. One should do more than read a book and pass an exam. One should value the merits of an education for:
    a. The advancement of acquiring knowledge.
    b. The enhancement of abilities to do for self and community.
3. Learn to conduct research and enhance one's ability to perform as a critical thinker (The Black Catalyst members used our skills to confront racism. The Black professionals used knowledge of self, ancestral history, ancient African principles, and faith in our Creator to be self-determined). We must:
    a. Recognize that a problem exists, gather data, evaluate and analyze data.
    b. Summarize data, test reliability and validity. If needed, redo re search.
    c. Make presentation on data and list/demand recommendations for changes.

REFERENCES

Abdullah, S. (2007). Memoirs about the sixties Struggle as related to offsprings.

Clayton & Byrd (2003). *An American Health Dilemma* V. II. Routledge: NY.

Guthrie, Robert (1998). *Even the Rat was White*. Allyn & Bacon: Boston, Mass.
Http: www.abpsi.org/about_abpsi.htm.
Jagger, G. (2003). *That Rare Moment in History* V. I. Jagger: Detroit, MI
http:www.nabsw.org/mserver/mission.

Washington, H. (2006). *Medical Apartheid*. Doubleday: USA.

MY INVOLVEMENT IN THE BLACK STRUGGLE 1960-1975

Conrad Worrill

I was born in Pasadena, California in 1941. My early training for the activities of the movement began while I was a very young child in Pasadena. My mentors and teachers at the time were my mother and father. I classify the role of my own family's work in Pasadena as "race people." My mother was the first Black person to sing in the Pasadena Civic Chorus. When I was a young boy my father was very active in fighting for racial equality in his leadership roles as the Youth Program Director of the Pasadena YMCA and in the Pasadena NAACP. He often spoke of his involvement in desegregating the public swimming pools, as well as fighting for Blacks to have the opportunity to join the police force, to become civil service postal workers, and to eat downtown in the so-called fine restaurants in Pasadena. During NAACP membership meetings I often heard the discussions about tactics and strategies to demolish racial discrimination in all sectors of life in Pasadena. Many events that impacted my consciousness were occurrences in family gatherings and various community organizations like school, church, and other enclaves of the Black community.

Socio-historical occurrences during the fifties began to shape my consciousness. For example, the murder of Emmett Till in August 1955, at the age of fifteen, impacted me on a deep psychological level as I was the same age at the time of his death. Also, the organizing around support for Mamie Till Mobley, his mother, was taking place on the block on which I lived—56th and Maryland—in Mr. Al Benson's house, the noted Black disc jockey. So, I was conscious of this moment in history where a young Black man had gone to Mississippi for the summer and allegedly whistled at a white woman to later be found brutally assassinated. This event in history captured the attention of Black people and American society across the country. In fact, Jet magazine put a picture of Emmett Till's defaced body on its cover. Seeing him in his casket, which his mother demanded to be open in order for the world to see the brutality of racism, had a deep impact on my soul like it did on other Blacks in this country.

I was additionally affected by hearing about Thurgood Marshall and the NAACP's involvement in *Brown v. Board of Education.* Also, in 1955 Black people in Montgomery, Alabama were refusing to ride public transportation in an effort to break down the barriers of racial segregation. The success of this movement, a bus boycott that lasted from December 1, 1955 until December 20, 1956, forced the power structure in Montgomery to end racial segregation in public transportation, and declared laws requiring segregated buses as unconstitutional. During this time, because of Martin Luther King's involvement in the Montgomery boycott, I began to hear about the leadership of Dr. Martin Luther King, Jr. Dr. King organized around issues such as Blacks' right to vote, labor rights, and desegregation. Dr. King's involvement in the Civil Rights Movement really resonated with me when in 1956, Dr. King was invited to Chicago to speak to the Democratic National Convention's committee concerning desegregation of schools. Other examples of events during that period were the establishment of the Southern Christian Leadership Conference by Dr. King, Dr. Abernathy, Charles Steele, and Fred Shuttlesworth; the "Little Rock Nine," the involvement of college students in the Woolworth lunch counter sit-in; and the formation of the Student Nonviolent Coordination Committee. These moments in history impacted me deeply, personally, intellectually, and spiritually.

1960 was a critical period in my life. I moved back to Pasadena to attend Pasadena City College, attempting to complete my first year of undergraduate school. This endeavor was a total failure; by the spring of 1960 I had been dismissed from the college for a variety of reasons. My expulsion from school propelled me back to Chicago to face the wrath of my father and family for failing at my first attempt at college. The experience of this failure was devastating to my psyche. By 1960 I was eighteen years old and disoriented, not knowing what direction my life should take after being thrown out of college. So I returned to Chicago and attended local junior colleges. I played basketball and ran with my partners, who were all athletes. Escaping the challenges and responsibilities of moving my life forward, I played a lot of basketball. For this brief moment basketball courts all over Chicago bore the weight of my failure from college.

On the other hand, I had clearly begun to be captivated by the speaking and writing of Malcolm X. One Sunday in 1961 I witnessed, with my father, Malcolm being interviewed on NBC in a program called *Open Mind.* In this interview, Malcolm was a master at articulating and conceptualizing ideas that inspired me immensely. He articulated ideas of self-determination and Black Nationalism for our political, economic, social and cultural advancement as a people. When he finished, I said to my father that Malcolm was the smartest Black man I had ever seen and heard thus far in my life. My father's response was, if this brother kept talking like this, they would kill him. Little did I know that years later Malcolm's ideas would influence me greatly. Because the Honorable Elijah Muhammad and the Nation of Islam's headquarters were on the south side of Chicago, I now had an opportunity to interact with many of the brothers and sisters who were part of the Nation as well as brothers and sisters, such as the Deacons for Defense, Fats Crawford and Russ Meeks of the West Side and others who were a part of the Black Nationalist Wing of the Black Movement.

This eventually led me to an early marriage and, because of my inactivity, unemployment, and failure to register, being drafted to the United States Army on May 4, 1962. This, of course, was something I had not planned for. However, before I knew it, I was on my way to Fort Knox, Kentucky. Being drafted into the military began to challenge my spirit since I still had not come to grips with what I wanted to do with my life. At the conclusion of eight weeks of basic training in August of 1962, I was assigned my military occupational specialty, and then informed that I would be assigned duty overseas to Okinawa. I was outdone. Okinawa is seventy miles long and seventeen miles wide, bordered on one side by the East China Sea and on the other by the Pacific Ocean, the last place I wanted to be. The island was made up of indigenous Asian people called the Okinawans, who had been occupied in World War II by the invasion of the United States military. Thus, in my consciousness, I began to understand the United States' occupation in the lands of other people.

On April 6, 1964 I was discharged from the military. I came back to Chicago to reconnect with my friends and family. I was eager to seek out what was going on with Black people organizing in Chicago. I had heard about various organizations that were active in Chicago. While on my tour of duty I learned about the assassination of Medger Evers and the bombing at Sixteenth Street Baptist Church in Birmingham, Alabama, which killed four little girls: Addie Mae Collins, Denise McNair, Carole Robertson and Cynthia Wesley. I had also heard about the school boycott that took place in Chicago on October 21, 1963. 220,000 students stayed home from school and boycotted around the issues of Willis Wagons, double shifts, and to generally protest the poor conditions of Chicago's inner city schools. I wanted to meet some of the players who organized this movement, since the issue of education was still critical in this city.

I had heard there was a coalition of organizations in Chicago called the Coordinating Council of Community Organizations (CCCO), which was made up of a number of block clubs and community organizations throughout the city. I found out where they were meeting and started volunteering to help with their numerous community organizing projects. These meetings included participation from Congress of Racial Equality, the National Association for the Advancement of Colored People, the Friends of Student Nonviolent Coordinating Committee (SNCC), Chatham Community Organization Block Clubs, Lawndale Community Block Clubs, a variety of church groups, personalities such as Al Raby and Larry Landry, and other young organizers.

After being discharged and returning home, I began attending George Williams College and working odd jobs; however, I spent most of my spare time trying to be connected to the organizing around issues like fair housing that was taking place in Chicago. By 1965, Jesse Jackson had come to Chicago to study at the Chicago Theological Seminary where Rev. Archie Hargrave was a professor. Jesse began to work with KOCO—the Kenwood Oakland Community Organization, an organization where I was also a volunteer. The culmination of these organizations represented a young network of emerging activists developing across Chicago. These activists were dedicated to issues such as open and fair housing, fighting restrictive covenants, voting rights, education, and challenging the racism and police brutality of the Chicago Police Department. Chicago was a hotbed of activism sparking my inner soul.

In the aftermath of the assassination of Malcolm in 1965, I was on fire to be at the center of whatever would propel our people to bring down the walls of racial injustice and white supremacy. Although I loved the oratory of Dr. King, somehow in my soul the ideas of Malcolm seemed more rational to me in terms of Black people's fight for self-determination, self-definition, community control, and controlling our own destiny. Therefore, I listened to all of Malcolm's speeches and read all of his writings while concurrently reading and listening to the speeches of Hon. Elijah Muhammad, who was on radio every Sunday.

I became fully immersed into the nucleus of the activism in Chicago's Black Movement by doing what organizers called "grunt work." Along with many other young men and women, we were the core group that passed out thousands and thousands of flyers for every event or activity that was going on in the city. I would suffice to say, my first contributory involvement in the Black Movement of Chicago was on the streets, interacting with people and disseminating information through flyers and leaflets about upcoming events. I was learning to become skillful in the arts, geography, and strategies of literature dissemination to get information clandestinely and efficiently distributed to the people I loved by passing out flyers on the street.

"Grunt work" was an important strategy because at that time, other than mainstream radio and television, the main way to reach people was to put written information into their hands or to send out letters in the mail. As a matter of fact, this is how I met Jorja English, Lu Palmer's wife, who ran off hundreds and hundreds of flyers in the offices of CCCO on a mimeograph machine. I had the pleasure of having lots of ink get all over my clothes from her mimeograph machine. Little did I know, I was being trained in some of the major areas of community organization in terms of what it takes to mobilize people, to encourage people, and to get information out to people through street activities and street mobilization. What I was being trained in at the time of my involvement was the art and skill of mass propaganda: how to design a flyer, how to manufacture a flyer, what to include, and how to make the flyer attractive so people could read it quickly and get the information. Jorja English, who I had the honor of being mentored by, was a master at the art form of producing flyers. Thus, I began to have a profound appreciation for the creation of propaganda materials for mass dissemination.

In 1965 I was heavily involved in the movement and a full-fledged student at George Williams College. It had historically been located in the West Hyde Park community, but has since then moved to Downers Grove, Illinois. I went to George Williams College because I could attend with free tuition. My father was a YMCA professional and I still had this yearning to obtain a bachelor's degree to make him, my mother, and rest of my family happy. Between juggling activities in the movement, working, and going to school, I was becoming a full-fledged activist in Chicago. I was learning the art of reading the newspaper, listening to the radio carefully, and keeping up with national trends and international events. I was constantly engaged in political dialogue with activists such as Rev. John Porter, Earl Durham, Useni Eugene Perkins, Warner Saunders, Fred Hampton, Leon Harris and Obaseki Hodari about the movement and its impact on people of African descent. I developed a routine of getting up in the morning and listening to the radio while getting all of the newspapers that I could read before starting my day and arming myself for political discussion on the streets.

Dr. King's visits to Chicago in Winter 1966 and Summer 1966 during his campaign to end discrimination in employment, education and housing, sparked a great debate in the city. I began to understand more and more the role of electoral politics in decision making and public policy; up to this point, I had limited understanding of the connection. However, when Black preachers and politicians, such as Rev. J. H. Jackson, Congressman William Dawson, Alderman Claude Homan and Alderman Kenneth Campbell called a press conference with Mayor Daley denouncing Dr. King's presence or the need for him to come to Chicago, many young men and women and the larger Black communities were outraged. When Dr. King finally did come to Chicago on August 31, 1966, he spoke at Liberty Baptist Church located at 49th and South Park. I was in attendance for that speech. Dr. King announced his open housing initiative along with his campaign for economic justice in the north. I was there at all the meetings, which fired me up and prepared me to assist the campaign and fight against racial injustice.

My main role; however, was still to be a participant and helper for whatever project emerged. Occasionally, I would have an assignment to convene a meeting, to chair a meeting, or to implement an agenda for a meeting. Still, mostly I was a trooper who was on the ground taking direction from the broad leadership—Al Raby, Larry Landry, Rosie Simpson, Bob Lucas, Tim Black and Dick Gregory—and putting these ideas out in the street. We saw the fruits of our contributions to the community. Mobilizing a mass meeting, a community forum, or a large public gathering allowed for the Black Movement in Chicago to continue and grow. We knew then that our strategies worked because of the large masses of African descent people that showed up to community rallies and meetings concerning issues relevant to a better quality of life for us in Chicago. Not only were we learning the creative and essential strategy of formulating flyers, we were learning how to rouse unity, collaboration and participation in the community, as well as to disseminate this information throughout the entire city of Chicago. Because of the terrain, I began to learn very carefully the various neighborhoods, wards, precincts, and diverse populations of the city. Now information dissemination became a much more tactical task, beyond just the creation of the flyer, but also knowing where to place them and how to create a logistical methodology for dissemination of thousands upon thousands of leaflets became critical. I was impassioned to learn how to effectively do this. When I reflect on this particular period, I was in training for what ultimately became a part of my life's work.

I was thrust into student leadership due to my previous training and experiences in Chicago. While driving to George Williams College in Downers Grove every day, I would pick up and have political conversations with Black students who did not have transportation. I did not know then that the Black Student Movement on college campuses throughout the United States would now become something that we were a part of on our little campus in the western suburb of Downers Grove, Illinois. Students were organizing around the demands that were emerging from Black Student Movements, which were impacting higher education around increased Black admissions to the hiring of more Black professors in predominately white colleges and universities throughout the United States. In fact, these demands escalated as young college students took hold of the notion of Black Power, which was the slogan made popular in 1966 through the utterances and public speeches of Stokely Carmichael, aka Kwame Ture. This slogan was infused in our souls shortly after Brother Kwame made the call for Black Power on June 16, 1966 in Lowndes County, Alabama at a voter registration rally. Shortly after, he came to Chicago and spoke at the Afro-Arts Theatre that was headed by Phil Cohran. I had an opportunity to be at that meeting and to sit and talk with him, to feel his energy and spirit as he spoke on the south side calling for the need of Black people to struggle for Black Power and self-determination. I supported and worked with the Friends of SNCC, where I met one of our greatest movement organizers, Bob Brown. Over the years, I learned a great deal from Brother Bob about community organizing.

It's important to know that my political consciousness was clearly being shaped to conceptualize the struggle for the liberation of Black People. My consciousness around our ability to control our own destinies without outside interference was not only about Black people in this country, but African descent people throughout the Diaspora. It does not mean that one does not have assistance from others, but it does mean one is not dominated by others. It was in that spirit that I began to politically identify myself as a Black Nationalist, because Black Nationalism now became the way I saw our ancestors struggling around two basic sets of ideas that I was beginning to read and study: the struggle for civil rights and integration and the struggle for Pan-African Nationalism with the right to self-determination. I was able to read about some of the great nationalist heroes who had been sort of left out of our history—Martin R. Delaney, Bishop Henry McNeal Turner, Edward Wilmot Blyden—and of course, I began to read extensively on the contributions of the Honorable Marcus Mosiah Garvey and the Universal Negro Improvement Association.

By 1966 and 1967, through my own volition, I had done a lot of reading about the history of our people, the repatriation movement, and the desire of our people prior to the Civil War to be repatriated back to Africa. I also read about the struggles of Black people in what was called the westward movement and the Black Town Movement, the efforts of Black people flee the plantations and settle in Kansas and Oklahoma, establishing free Black communities. Their struggles became ideas I saw that related to what Black people should really be struggling for, to control our own politics, to control our own economics, to control our own education, and to build our own institutions. We were steeped in our history in this country where Black people had built our own institutions, had created our own educational and religious institutions, and that the idea of integration was not the goal that I personally was pursuing. I learned that there is a difference between integration and desegregation.

These were lessons that were emerging at this particular time and it became quite clear to me—I had to make a choice as to who I was going to become—the goals and objectives that I was going to be a part of in terms of the history of Black people in this country. I consciously choose to become a Pan-African Nationalist, a person who believes that people of African descent throughout the world share the same racial, cultural, social and economic conditions as a result of their African ancestry. Not only did I now choose the path of Black Nationalism and Pan-Africanism, I began to hear about the struggles on the continent of Africa through interactions with other movement activists and other nationalists from around the country. Across the nation, we began to hear of Mulana Karenga, Amiri Baraka, Rap Brown, Mack Stanford, Jitu Wausi, Dr. John Henrik Clarke, and Yosef Ben-Jochannan. We began to hear whispers of these scholar activists in our interactions with this nationalist wing of the movement, which I now began to identify.

It was out of this rising consciousness, which was sprouting everywhere, that we were able to challenge the administrators at George Williams College: a small Christian YMCA training school where I was still trying to complete all of my requirements for my undergraduate degree. I became a student leader at George Williams College. Other committed students and I took the spirit of the Black Student Movement that was impacting universities across America. University students across the country utilized tactics, such as shutting down and taking over administration buildings, while demanding that these colleges and universities be more attentive to the needs of Black students in order to increase their opportunities in higher education. This became a full-blown movement and we, in our efforts at George Williams, demanded the same. Black students of George Williams College made demands for equity in higher education to the administration, President Hamlin, and all the administrators associated with that college.

We infused the kind of consciousness and spirit that declared it was all right to be Black with the emergence of Black consciousness, while slowly shifting away from referring to ourselves as a Negro people. By 1968, as I had finally finished my degree requirements, James Brown had written the song that inspired us all, "Say It Loud, I'm Black and I'm Proud," and Nina Simone had created the song titled "Young, Gifted and Black." As well recognizable manifestations of popular culture, these two songs singularly, by 1968, fired up Black people from one end of the country to the other. It was so hot internally in the Black community because the Black student movement was on fire and young Black people, students, and non-students across the United States were laying to rest the idea that we were Negro people. This led to discussions in churches, schools, and seminars on how we even got to be classified, identified, and accepting of being a Negro. We realized how this was totally out of order, totally inappropriate, and why we should shift our nomenclature to see ourselves as a proud, Black people, as people of African ancestry. So the Black Power movement transitioned into this Black consciousness movement and many Black people moved away from identifying themselves as Negroes. It was a movement we participated in and one by which I was an inspired advocate. At George Williams College, we stopped all the Black people and challenged them to never say that we were Negroes ever again; we would not allow white people to identify or refer to us as Negroes either.

In 1967 Harold Cruse's book, *The Crisis of the Negro Intellectual,* was released. We were also into the writings of Frantz Fanon and his book, *The Wretched of the Earth,* and we were introduced to the writings of Carter G. Woodson, particularly his book *The Mis-Education of the Negro*. By the time I was recruited to attend the University of Chicago Graduate School in Social Service Administration, I had had several years' preparation in community organizing. As a student activist, with several years of volunteer participation in the movement, the synergy and spirit of my own personal involvement had now trained me to become part of the Black student leadership movement in the United States.

Upon official completion of my undergraduate degree, I was employed on the west side at the Sears YMCA in the Lawndale community as Program Director. Because of my employment at the YMCA, Lawndale became a community in which I began to utilize my early training as a community organizer and activist. During my years at the Sears YMCA, I wanted to have deep involvement in the youth after-school programming and its importance in helping young people with their homework. I attempted to create programs at the Y that would help young people understand the importance of becoming steeped in their own history and culture. I was able to organize trips for our young people to visit other young people throughout the city, to have youth forums and exchanges, and I was able to invite young people from other cities to come and participate as well. In addition, my interest and background in athletics also helped me organize basketball tournaments, swimming programs, and other athletic or recreational activities that were used as organizing tools to mobilize our people to participate in YMCA programs.

In my capacity as program director of the YMCA, I interfaced frequently with Lawndale social service agencies. Consequently, it was in Lawndale's social service agencies that I met key activist and organizers of West Side Chicago: Useni Eugene Perkins, Warner Saunders, Cecil Butler, Leaders of the Vice Lords, leaders of the Roman Saints, Chester Robinson of the West Side Organization, Doug Andrews of the Garfield Organization, Danny Davis, Ed Smith, Nancy Jefferson, and many others. The YMCA became my employment entity that I used to connect to the larger community of Lawndale and to the Black Movement at large. But on April 4, 1968, as I was driving in my Volkswagen on the Eisenhower Expressway with a few people in my car, I heard on the car's radio that Dr. Martin Luther King, Jr. had been assassinated. I abruptly got over in the right lane in time to exit at Homan Avenue, 3400 West, and drove directly to my office at the Sears Y. Within an hour, we began hearing reports that the west side was up in smoke. The impacts of Dr. King's assassination and of Malcolm X's assassination affect me personally even to this day. But Dr. King's assassination propelled Black people to angrily react throughout the United States as cities across the country went up in smoke. This led the Black movement to raise questions as to which direction to take now. The debate over violence and non-violence became an acute discussion within our communities.

I began hearing of an organization that had been established in Detroit, Michigan called the Republic of New Africa. The Republic of New Africa was taking the position that we should create, within the five states of the South, our own nation and we should secede from the United States, fighting by whatever means necessary to take these five states. The philosophies of the Republic of New Africa helped me to further understand through a programmatic thrust that Malcolm X's idea of self-determination and self-reliance was possible. At the same time, various forms of Black Nationalism were beginning to come into fruition and further shape my consciousness as a Black Nationalist. The Black Panther Party that originated in Oakland, California also began to take shape in Illinois. During this time

I interned with Fred Hampton in Maywood, Illinois as an advisor in a graduate internship at George Williams in Maywood NAACP Youth Council. I helped organize some of their youth activities (i.e., field trips, athletics, recreational activities and Black History programs). Fred Hampton eventually became the Chairman of the Illinois Chapter of the Black Panther Party, on the West Side at 2400 W. Madison. Through my YMCA programming, I was able to help the Panthers by organizing their free breakfast programs, Black history programs, and the young people with whom the Panthers were working with on the near West Side.

In 1969 a lady contacted me by the name of Abena Joan Brown. I had known of Abena because of her leadership in the YWCA Movement and the arts. She had recently been the leader of forming a group called Catalyst, which was made up of Black social workers and social service practitioners. Abena said to me that I should go back to school because she had finished from the University of Chicago herself and there were some scholarship opportunities available. Abena Joan Brown was so passionate about this opportunity to attend the University of Chicago that to appease her, I showed up on campus and started taking classes. Before I knew it, I had finished one semester at the University of Chicago's so-called renowned School of Social Work and Social Service Administration in the fall of 1969.

It was at the University of Chicago where I received a great boost of confidence-building as I sat in the classes witnessing how white supremacy percolated through the curriculum at the highest level. I understood that this credentialing process was not connected to the real conditions of African descent people. The social work program offered a pathological model of training to social work practitioners. This further instilled in me the need for self-determination of African descent people. Being in the University of Chicago's graduate program did, however, give me an avenue to student activism. Mile Simms, who is now the owner of Au Natural food store, and I began to organize Black students on the University of Chicago. We created and participated in cultural programs, community networking and dissemination of information concerning broader Black issues and had social gatherings.

It was during my second year at the School of Social Service Administration that one of my professors, Charles Ross from Gary, Indiana, was running for Congress. Charles Ross had been Richard Gordon Hatcher's campaign manager in his victorious win as mayor in 1967. I completed my field work assignment during the Congressional campaign of Professor Ross as his assistant campaign manager. This placed me deeply in the nuts and bolts of how to organize a political campaign at the precinct level and ward level. I also learned how to raise money, how to create press releases, and how to write speeches for candidates. I learned how to conceptualize issues in the area of this particular Congressional race. Along with some of the other students, such as Cheryl Simms, Melailai Nuru, Harold Singer, Harry Singletary, and Lacy Day, we assisted Professor Ross in his second unsuccessful bid to unseat this white Congressional candidate who had been a Congressman representing Gary, Indiana for more than twenty-eight years.

Even though Professor Ross was unsuccessful in his Congressional bid, we forced Ray J. Madden for the first time in many years to act. We forced him to actually come back to Gary and campaign for his seat, because in years previous to that, he did not campaign. Black people just voted for this white man and he was reelected by a majority of the vote, so we had a close election. We forced Ray J. Madden to have to campaign. My experiences of working with Charles Ross (aka Mawanzaa) was one of my most rewarding organizing projects. It helped me understand voter registration rules and regulations, how to get a candidate on the ballot, building a candidate, raising money for a candidate, and generally how to organize a campaign. Being assistant campaign manager for Professor Ross immersed me in the nuts and bolts of electoral politics that became a major strategy in my future organizing activities, especially as it culminated in my involvement in Harold Washington's successful bid to run for mayor in 1982 and 1983.

During this period when I attended the University of Chicago's School of Social Service Administration, I always kept connections with three of my friends from my athletic days—Leon Cedric Harris, Jack DeBonis, and Obaseki Hodari. These relationships led to my introduction to the Communiversity, housed inside the Center for Inner City Studies, in 1969. Leon Harris was pursuing his master's degree in the newly developed graduate program in inner city studies education. Obaseki Hodari was participating with Leon Harris in the independent development of the Communiversity. The Communiversity was kind of like a think tank where we met, read literature specific to African people, had study groups, and were introduced to critical ideologies of discourse throughout the African Diaspora. We would stay up all night discussing the great works of Cheikh Anta Diop, and we became familiar with the writings of Martin R. Delaney, Bishop Henry McNeal Turner, Edward Wilmot Blyden and other Pan-African and nationalist thinkers of the nineteenth century. These writings grounded me into the tradition of Pan-Africanism and Black Nationalist thought.

While participating in the activities in the Communiversity (1969-1970), I was introduced to the brilliance of Dr. Anderson Thompson and Dr. Jacob Carruthers. My introduction to the Communiversity and meeting these incredible scholars was one of the most eye opening intellectual experiences that I had encountered thus far in my development. As a result, my world was turned upside down. In fact, I found myself in a total emersion of their re-conceptualization of my mis-eduation. I had no idea that years later I would actually be employed at the Center for Inner City Studies and that this initial introduction to Dr. Thompson and Dr. Carruthers would turn out to be a lifelong relationship of intellectual growth and development that enhanced my continued activism in the community. In my activist work I attempted to always put into practice what Dr. Anderson Thompson called the concept of African principle. The African principle, as Dr. Thompson described, was a principle that addressed the issue of "Whatever we do, it should be done around the greatest good for the greatest number of African people." The African principle in its most practical manifestation was center to my organizing practices. In applying that idea to my organizing work, it was always deeply rooted in my consciousness, whatever strategy, whatever project, whatever tactic I came up with.

Chicago was the seat of Johnson Publishing Company, Johnson Products, Seaway National Bank, and Independence Bank. But during the late sixties and seventies, there was a trend where other people were moving in, primarily Arabs and Koreans, and beginning to occupy businesses that Black people owned under another era. When this trend began to emerge, we took an aggressive campaign to challenge our people to once again take up this issue of creating small businesses. During this time I created an ad hoc group to address the emerging trend of Arab businesses in the Black community. To demonstrate the power of entrepreneurship, we would get up early in the morning to take young people down to South Water Market Street to see the Italians, Polish and Irish unload these trucks and farm these food items out to community stores.

Leon Harris and I also organized food co-ops that lasted for many, many years where we organized significant numbers of Black families connected with the Communiversity and our nationalistic organizations and institutes in Chicago to buy their food collectively. We also alerted Black people to the potential land value. We urged Black families that owned potentially valuable property to not sell it to outside people. We were successful to some extent in encouraging Black families who had traditionally owned property in Black neighborhoods to maintain these properties and pass it onto other family members. We weren't totally successful, but this area today has valuable land and many of the Black homeowners have held onto this valuable property.

After graduating from the University of Chicago in 1971, I was recruited by Dr. Ken Stoudent to receive a Doctoral fellowship at the University of Wisconsin. I commuted to Madison, Wisconsin, to begin my first semester at the University of Wisconsin as I completed my master's degree at the University of Chicago, while still participating at the Communiversity on Saturdays. The idea of working on a Ph.D. had not settled in. At the time, I formed a relationship with two other African American doctoral students, Ken Dowden and Eugene Robertson. We studied together and I began to become educated on what was required to complete a Ph.D. program in curriculum instruction and secondary social studies. For the next two years I was somewhat on sabbatical from the Chicago movement.

My periodic commute back and forth to Chicago kept me abreast of the movement that was going on in Chicago, the United States and the world. During this period I began to hear about the emergence of African Liberation Day activities to support the armed struggled in Mozambique, Angola and Guinea Bissau. The first African Liberation Day March Rally and Parade was held in Washington, D.C., May 27, 1972. Fifty thousand people of African descent from around the country participated in this major support rally and March. The emergence of the liberation movements in Mozambique, Angola and Guinea Bissau to overthrow the Portuguese rule in Africa began to lift up the questions of independence and eradication of apartheid in South Africa. Also, while in Madison, I drove to Gary, Indiana to participate in the historic National Black Political Convention. The convention attracted over ten thousand Black people from around the United States for the development of a Black political agenda that was emerging around the 1972 presidential election between George McGovern and Richard Nixon.

I completed my dissertation in the summer of 1973. Faced with the daunting task of finding employment, I visited the University of Wisconsin Placement Office for Doctoral Students and sent my résumé all over the country. I did not get one response for a job. Calvin Lockridge had been an activist and organizer in Chicago. He was running an educational program in southeast Washington, D.C., aimed at helping parents participate in the community control of schools. Brother Calvin heard that I had completed my Ph.D. and offered me a position as the lead organizer in Anacostia in southeast Washington, D.C. While I was considering this employment, one of the professors of George Williams College offered me a position as an assistant professor. I was appointed in September of 1973 as the assistant professor of urban studies at George Williams College in the western suburbs, the undergraduate school where I had completed my bachelor's degree.

In regards to my activism during 1973, my work was really around the question of power inside the Board of Education. The majority of school population by mid-1970s had become predominantly African American, so we were fighting for increased numbers of representation on the Chicago School Board to reflect the population of Black people. We were also fighting for increased administrative positions downtown. In fact, we were suggesting early on that Black people should have the superintendent's position of the Chicago School Board. So our fight in education had a lot to do not only with academic programs, intrusion, and infusion of African and African American content in the school curriculum, but also the politics, leadership and economics of the Chicago Public Schools, which is a major economic enterprise. We wanted to encourage Black people to have the opportunity to be vendors in the variety of goods and services necessary to run the Chicago Public School system.

It was during this period of moving back to Chicago, when I participated in Communiversity activities at the Center for Inner City Studies and was mentored by Dr. Thompson and Dr. Carruthers, that I began to look deeply at the impact of European thought and its social, systematic and institutional impact on African people. I assisted Dr. Thompson in developing his Association of African Historians, where we began to host conferences with other Pan-African and African-centered scholars such as John Henrik Clarke, Yusef Ben Jochannan, and Asa Hilliard. It was also during this period that a position became available at the Center for Inner City Studies. Dr. Carruthers' wife, Iva Carruthers, served as an advocate on my behalf and encouraged me to apply for this vacant tenured track possession in 1975. In 1975, I was interviewed by the staff, students, administration and faculty at the Center for Inner City Studies and I was selected to be on the staff at the Center for Inner City Studies of Northeastern Illinois University.

This was the blessing of my intellectual activist and organizing life. It put me in the presence of such scholars as Jacob Carruthers and Anderson Thomson, and they nurtured my intellectual and spiritual growth and development. Being at the Center for Inner City Studies put me in a position to have tentacles with the worldwide African community and from 1975 up to the present, I've been employed as a professor and am now director of the Carruthers Center of Northeastern Illinois University.

The lessons in my judgment for the youth of this generation, having clearly had a life propelled as a movement child of the 1960s, is that self-determination, self-definition, understanding who we are, where we came from, and how it manifests itself into our present condition and future for our race, is critical to any organizing, intellectual activity or career choices that we engage in. In addition, it is imperative that we create independent institution and economic strategies to finance our liberation. We can't achieve independence and self reliance until we have generated the will and commitment to go deep in our own pockets.

EXPLOSION OF STREET GANGS DURING CHICAGO'S BLACK STRUGGLE 1960-1975

Useni Eugene Perkins

The political potential of Black street gangs first became evident during Chicago's Freedom Movement in 1964. Gang members were encouraged to participate in rallies, act as marshals during demonstrations and take part in civil rights discussions. Leaders of the movement felt that this involvement would help it show greater strength and give gang members an opportunity to improve their civic image. But this move was not without criticism. Some people felt that gangs were only using the movement to put them in a negotiable position with community organizations to secure jobs for members. Conversely, community organizations that used gangs were accused of exploiting gang members only as a tool to further their own bases of power. Both accusations were probably correct, but vested interests always have a priority when goals depend upon reciprocal relationships.

At one time the Black Panther Party made efforts to politicize street gangs to get them involved in constructive community activities. However, this was during the period when the Black Panther Party was engaged in constant confrontations with the police and its own image was challenged as a subversive and violent organization. Also, many street gangs resisted these efforts because they felt that the Black Panther Party was infringing on their territories and would divert members from their groups. When the climate for an allegiance between street gangs and the Black Panther Party became favorable, the police had clamped down so hard on these groups that a coalition was not possible. Some people felt that the police had realized the potential of such a coalition and made every effort to abort its formation. It has also been speculated that the police executions of Fred Hampton, chairman of the Chicago Black Panther Party, and Mark Clark, chairman of the Illinois Black Panther Party, were linked with this crackdown. Before his death Chairman Hampton had been making some progress in mobilizing gang leaders around political issues.

Social service agencies were stymied in their efforts to redirect gang members. The traditional programs they administered failed to meet the needs of troubled youth. As a result, some social service agencies initiated non-traditional programs to service gang members. The strategy they used was to employ street workers or outreach workers to work directly with gang members in the streets. This strategy was first used in New York in its Mobilization for Youth programs and had achieved some mild success. To some degree this strategy was also successful in Chicago, but the resources available were minimal in comparison to the magnitude of the street gang problem.

By the early sixties Chicago's Black street gangs had grown to such proportions that they not only posed a threat to themselves but to the Black community as well. The fuse was now burning at a pace so rapid that it was only a matter of time for it to detonate an explosion, which would leave the Black community in a state of utter confusion and turmoil. No longer were gang members perceived as misguided youth who were merely going through the pains of adolescence. Now they were being perceived as predators who preyed on whomever they felt infringed on their lust for power. These predatory gangs were not content to emulate their predecessors. Instead, they turned to more criminal activities, and the control of turf became their number one priority. By controlling turf gangs were able to exercise their muscles to extort money from businesses and intimidate the Black community. Later, as these gangs became more powerful, many began to engage in the trafficking of drugs.

The recruitment of new members became the means by which gangs could expand their base power. Whereas membership in Black street gangs had once been mostly voluntary, it was now being forced upon non-gang members. The more powerful a gang was, the more difficult it became for non-gang members to resist recruitment. Those who did try to resist were placed in confrontational situations, which usually resulted in them being subjected to intimidation, threats or bodily harm. Many youth had no alternative but to join a gang lest they be victimized by it. In fact, in some communities it got to a point where being a gang member was the safest thing to do.

As gangs became stronger and more common, they began to appeal to non-gang members to join of their own volition. Being a gang member had become a status symbol, and for many alienated Black youths this was extremely important. It provided for the first time a sense of belonging, self-esteem and identity. When these needs are juxtaposed with the political climate of the sixties, one can begin to understand their importance. The sixties were a period when most youth, regardless of their racial or economic background, were striving to be recognized on their own terms. Youth movements were common across the nation, and it became apparent that young people no longer held the status quo as being an infallible norm for regulating their lives. Youth of the sixties wanted to become more involved in the political process and were willing to challenge traditional institutions in their newly discovered independence. Because of their unconventional lifestyles, these groups were viewed by the larger society as deviant minorities. Among these groups were the hippies, yippies, Black Panthers, US and SNCC. Although their goals were often different, the quest for social change was common to all. Despite their lack of political awareness, Black street gangs were expressing their own disenchantment in the only way they knew.

Contributing to the expansion of black street gangs in the sixties was the massive breakdown in major institutions. This collapse was so severe that institutions mandated to serve youth were conspicuously ineffective. For example, the Chicago public schools were more successful in literally pushing more Black youth out into the streets than they were in preparing them to achieve fundamental and essential academic skills. The crisis in public schools began in the fifties when there were sharp increases in Black student enrollment; concomitant to this escalation was the dramatic decline in white student enrollment. Everything indicated the quality of education in public schools was directly influenced by these transformations. School drop-out rates in some Black communities were as high as 40 percent, leaving many Black youth with nothing to do but waste their idle time in the streets. Then, too, even those Black students who remained in school were subjected to an apathetic educational environment. As a result, the public schools became a primary source for gang recruitment and turf identification. Schools in the sixties became incubators for the breeding of street gangs even if they were not directly responsible for these developments.

Other major institutions, such as the Department of Children and Family Services and the juvenile court, were equally negligent in serving the needs of Black youth. Both of these institutions were given cases involving Black youth, and both did very little to help Blacks make the types of social adjustments needed to successfully cope with the inequities in their environment. Thus, it should not have been a surprise that many Black youth felt alienated and found street gangs, they believed were sensitive to their needs. Although their perception may have been incorrect, street gangs were there to accept them as they were. And accept them they did! For those Black youth who had been turned out of school, exposed to the juvenile justice system and seemed to have no one to help them, the gangs were there to boost their lagging self-esteem. Now, for the first time, many of these alienated youth could feel wanted and important. Street gangs gave them a sense of identity and belonging they never had before. It didn't matter if they were subjected to strict regimentation and had to engage in criminal acts to prove their loyalty. They were willing to take the risk because gangs accepted them as they were.

The first blast of the Black street gang explosion had occurred. For ten years, approximately from 1965 to 1975, Black street gangs were to inflict a wound on the Black community that has yet to heal. A pattern of gang behavior had developed that was diametrically in conflict with traditional mores in the Black community. Standards which had previously been honored by Black youth were being completely discarded by Black street gang members who began to establish their own rules of conduct.

On the South Side, the Blackstone Rangers were now the Mighty P. Stone Nation, the Devil Disciples changed to the Black Disciples, and the Vice Lords now prefixed their name with Conservative. But the Egyptian Cobras, once the Vice Lords' archrival, had lost much of their power and disintegrated into a number of splinter groups. These groups controlled the vast majority of Black gang members in Chicago, and they were determined to maintain their lofty position, regardless of whom they exploited or victimized.

Of these gangs, however, the Mighty P. Stone Nation achieved the greatest notoriety. In fact, the Mighty P. Stone Nation was probably the largest street gang in the nation, and its reputation received celebrity status. At one time, some of its members toured the country in a production called "Opportunity Knocks" that was conceived and directed by Oscar Brown, Jr.; and Sammy Davis, Jr. had performed a fundraiser on their behalf. Also, Jeff Fort, the "chief" of the Mighty P. Stone Nation, and Mickey Cogwell were invited by the White House to attend the inauguration of President Richard Nixon in 1968. It has been alleged that the invitation was made to reciprocate the Mighty P. Stone Nation's role in trying to persuade Blacks to vote for Nixon. Although this allegation was never formally substantiated, the Mighty P. Stone Nation was wooed by many special interest groups. Many of these groups consisted of white liberals who saw the Mighty P. Stone Nation as a means to propagate their own beliefs. These white liberals were awed by the potential political power of the Mighty P. Stone Nation, and they attempted to translate this power into constructive activities. While this in itself was noteworthy, the romantic image many had of this street gang made it difficult for them to realize the magnitude and complexity of the problem. As a result, the support they gave was often self-serving, contradictory and short-lived. Rarely did they consult with Blacks who had been working with Black street gangs.

While Chicago claimed some of the most notorious Black street gangs, other cities such as Los Angeles, Philadelphia, Newark, Detroit and New York were being besieged by similar gang problems. Many of these gangs interacted with each other, and in 1967 a meeting was held that consisted of major gang leaders. The meeting took place in Resurrection City in Washington, D.C., a site erected as a gathering place for civil rights groups. The outcome of this meeting was not made public, but shortly afterward a national coalition of street gangs was organized and supported with government funds. Leaders from Chicago's Black gangs played a prominent role in this development.

The sixties continued to be a turbulent period for Black street gangs in Chicago. They continued to increase in size as well as in violence. Nothing seemed to suppress their growth or contain their violence—not well-intentioned community organizations, social service agencies, white liberals or even the police.

Later, a massive street worker program called STREETS emerged when three other agencies, the Chicago Boys Club, Chicago Youth Centers and Hull House Association, saw the need to coordinate their efforts. In 1967 this program was centralized under one agency called Youth Action, which was able to expand its services with the acquisition of federal funds. Still, the problem of gangs persisted and gang activity accelerated. Whereas gang involvement had formerly been seen as an inescapable stage in the lives of most ghetto colony youth, gangs now achieved greater sophistication, and it became advantageous for young adults to remain in their ranks.

Although many street workers performed their duties with great enthusiasm and dedication, their efforts were thwarted by the lack of cooperation from big businesses and other formal institutions. The business and political barons of Chicago were simply concerned with pacifying the activities of street gangs and not with providing their members with opportunities that would enable them to escape their world of oppression, and the street worker became the buffer agent by which this could be accomplished. Despite the large amount of funds allocated to street work programs, the Black street gang problem grew to even greater proportions.

As Black street gangs grew larger and more violent, it became increasingly difficult for street workers to maintain their limited influence over gang members. Then, too, there were accounts of some street workers over-identifying with the gangs, thereby neutralizing their ability to rationally assist gang members in changing their ways. Also, the political climate in Chicago was far from conducive to rehabilitating gang members. Cooperation between social agencies and law enforcement agencies left much to be desired, and both agencies accused each other of being responsible for the cleavage. On the one hand, social service agencies were accused of being overly paternalistic; while on the other hand, law enforcement agencies were accused of being too punitive. Gang members were the victims of their dilemma because neither agency was able to help them adjust to the realities of being oppressed and Black in a racist society. Consequently, gang members had little trust in either agency and established their own standards for coping with an environment that appeared to them to be either apathetic or hostile to their needs.

In 1968 a last-ditch effort was made to rehabilitate Black street gangs. Funds from private foundations and government agencies began to trickle into the hands of a few street gang organizations. Previously these funds had been given to community organizations who, in turn, were supposed to turn them into viable programs to help street gangs secure jobs for their members. But when this arrangement failed to achieve its goal, gang members were then asked to participate along with these organizations to develop more productive programs. One of these programs was Operation Bootstrap, which was designed to create economic opportunities for street gangs. The history of Operation Bootstrap was a short and unsuccessful one. The reasons for its failure were many. During its brief existence charges of mismanagement of funds, unfulfilled promises, political patronage and plain fraud were echoed by both the street gangs and participating agencies. As one gang member put it, "They gave us a strap, but not a boot for it to go on."

In North Lawndale, the Cobras received some assistance in setting up a gasoline station and car wash service. But this undertaking was short-lived. Due to inadequate facilities, insufficient funds, and the lack of proper management, the business lasted less than six months. Later, the Cobras managed a paper factory, which was far more successful. But this venture ended in disaster when the building burned down as the result of a fire, which some people believe was the work of an arsonist.

What really happened to the small business ventures of the few street gangs that had begun to achieve some economic stability? First, I suspect that they lacked sufficient on-going funds to have any long-term success. Second, they lacked sincere professional guidance, which could have helped to ensure better management. And third, the internal struggle for power between gang members, coupled with the gang mentality, undermined the few chances these groups had to achieve even a small degree of economic security.

As the financial resources of Black street gangs dwindled, so did their influence. Older gang members realized they needed funds to maintain their operations and to provide jobs for members. Also, many were becoming tired of constantly fighting each other and were receptive to gaining meaningful and legitimate jobs. The opportunity did come for some in the form of the Chicago Plan, a program designed to obtain jobs for minorities in building and trade unions. But these unions, true to their traditions, were not supportive of the Plan and resisted its implementation. Under the leadership of the Coalition for United Community Action (CUCA), Black street gangs were mobilized to stop work at construction sites to dramatize the racist policies of the building and trade unions. After a series of fiasco, violent demonstrations and political sabotage, the Chicago Plan faltered.

It is noteworthy that during these CUCA demonstrations, particularly the one that tried to shut down the construction site at the University of Illinois Chicago campus, several gang leaders were arrested; these arrests were followed by many more. By the early seventies, almost all of the major leaders of Black street gangs were incarcerated. The indictments that led to their incarceration ranged from weapons charges and racketeering to murder. Gang leaders claimed they were being convicted on trumped up charges and accused Black organizations of not coming to their defense. Furthermore, they claimed that some Black organizations had abandoned them when they no longer served their vested interests. There was some truth to these allegations because many Black organizations did sever their ties with Black street gangs after the abortive Chicago Plan. Previously, these organizations had been ambivalent about their involvement with Black street gangs. On one hand, they tried to redirect Black street gangs to engage in positive activities; on the other hand, many felt they were losing in their efforts to rehabilitate Black street gangs and thought it would be best to abolish them.

Following is a brief description of Chicago's Black Street Gangs during the sixties.

Period of Increased Expansion and Turbulence 1960-1970

1. Intense Gang Activity
2. Large Group Membership-Nations and Group Mergers
3. Very High Frequency of Delinquency
4. Very High Frequency of Criminal Activity
5. Highly Organized
6. Increased Expansion and Mobility
7. Age Range 8-35
8. Interested Inter-Group Conflict
9. Intense Recruitment
10. Turf Domination & Economic Expansion

(Excerpt from Explosion of Chicago's Black Street Gangs 1900 to Present *by Useni Eugene Perkins, Third World Press 1987)*

CHICAGO'S BLACK LIBERATION MOVEMENT 1960-1975

Rev. Curtis Burrell

What brought me back to Chicago in the summer of 1965? A kind of scary and unbelievable thing when you look back on it; physically, spiritually, and metaphysically, the things that caused me to go back were all wrapped into one energy: the only answer to this question is God.

I came back to the city of Chicago on a conscious, divine mission. As I say many times, this is a saga of an evolution of a man from victim to victor, from defeat to triumph over death and destruction, unto life and the proliferation of hope that comes from within.

The journey started in St. Louis, Missouri in 1932, the year of my birth. I was born and raised in the area that was referred to as downtown, which was the northeast area of the city, during the days of the Great Depression and segregation. If I was to use a geographical and pictorial image as a metaphor, I would start at the point of decline into a valley. I'd reached its floor for a short jog, and then with diving intervention and inner-compliance I'd ascend to the top of the hill—thank God! On that valley floor, the right sense of direction with the working method was invisible. I stepped into and was carried in the traps that laid within and without; for years I remained delinquent in major characteristics of a responsible citizen and a human being. As a willing victim and prodigal son form intelligence, the consequences of this past end on the valley floor was predictable: crying, drug addiction and prison was the culmination.

In 1956, while alone one afternoon in a small eight by eight prison cell in the Missouri State Penitentiary in Jefferson City, I had this epiphany, a spiritual big bang in consciousness and an infusion of a divine image that opened a path to a new paradigm. There was no Bible, no preacher, no religious literature; there was no audible voice nor human form. But there was this indelible and deep impression from a higher place, which if I had given it a song, it would have said, "Come, ask no silly questions even if you are called to jump into the unknown, unto death...Come." Further interpretation of the epiphany said, "Now, sail your ship back into the infinite ocean." And thus we have the metaphor of what was meant when the Bible spoke of the man who "waited diligently on the Lord, who heard his cry and brought me up also out of a horrible pit and out of the miry clay and set my feet upon a rock and established my goings." I took the leap of faith and became a new man in Christ, which awakened my soul consciousness; this is sometimes referred to as "being born again." It is said that when this happens old things pass away and all things become new. The first old thing to pass away from me was educational ignorance. Having been a high school dropout, I immediately gathered and read all of my prison books aloud and assigned myself to a program and regimen of study. This enabled me to pass the GED test later, which I needed to enter college.

America had a big bang epiphany moment of its own in 1956 when a really fragile Black lady riding a Montgomery segregated city bus decided to discontinue her participation in the criminality of an unjust legal system by refusing to get up and give her seat to a demanding white male passenger. Mother Rosa Parks launched into orbit a satellite of consciousness that reverberated around the Earth and created the mantras "Freedoms Now" and "We Shall Overcome." Her resistance to evil conjured up for the betterment of humanity the work of Rev. Dr. Martin Luther King, Jr. After the diving initiation in the cell, I returned to my righteous mind. My upgraded behavior changed and earned me trustee status in prison; I was moved to one of the prison farms.

Soon to be released and having no place to live, I was introduced to the Midianite Ministries and Rev. Hubert Swartzentruber, pastor from the mission in my St. Louis neighborhood where I was returning, and another minister, Rev. Muntu Gingrich. He was from the mission in a little town called Cherry Box, Missouri. Hubert and I made an arrangement that in exchange for room and board I would do the maintenance on the building and help teach the various programs of the church. This saved me from being homeless.

In the winter of 1959 Hubert got me enrolled in the Midianite Bible Institute where he had attended in Kitchnawaterloo, Ontario, Canada. In 1960 I enrolled at the Heston Midianite College in Heston, Kansas from a scholarship arranged by Allen White, a local Midianite inventor at the Heston Manufacturing Company. He was a member of the Whitewater Midianite Church in Whitewater, Kansas. I completed the program at the junior college in two years, but I stayed another year to help counsel some students from home at the Poor Idle housing projects. I encouraged the college to extend scholarships to youth from my neighborhood; we enrolled five or six students that year. I was twenty-seven years old, and had found my calling. In the summer of 1962 I, along with other Midianite tenants, volunteered for a peace project that was constructed by the Midianite Central Committee. They secured a building in Atlanta called the Midianite House. Its address was 540 Houston Northeast. Dr. Vincent Harding was the director. We shared the same square block and alleyway with Dr. Martin Luther King. Dr. Harding spent time counseling and strategizing with him. That's how Dr. King and the SCLC launched their Albany campaign in southwest Georgia. Everyone in the Midianite House joined the SCLC in Albany. There we met well-known civil rights fighters, the first being Dr. King, Rev. Abernathy, Rev. Y.T. Walker, Rev. C.T. Vivian, and Bernice Regan Johnson. That summer I also taught summer vacation Bible school at the churches of Dr. King, Rev. Abernathy and Rev. William Holmes Waters. I graduated from Goshen Midianite College in 1963 with a B.A. and finished in 1966 at the adjacent Midianite Biblical Seminaries at Goshen, Elkhart, Indiana. But after the final year of seminary in the summer of 1965, the congregation at the Woodlawn Midianite Church located at 46th and Woodlawn, sent me an invitation to serve that summer at their church. That appeal was based on a need to face the growing neighborhood challenges of deterioration, gang threats, gentrification, and the combined community ills of lack of health care, high death rates, unemployment, poor education, and welfare reform. The church also wanted to observe me to see if I was qualified to assist the Rev. Delta France. Dr. Harding had been a member of this congregation when he was at the nearby University of Chicago in the sixties earning his Ph.D. Rev. Ed Riddick of Operation Breadbasket, who continued his membership up until the time of the church arson in the summer of 1970, was also a member there.

Many social dynamics changed the consciousness of America during the sixties. There was the Vietnam war and the divisive dynamics that surrounded it: the "drop out and turn on" hippie movement, the rise of the Black Panthers, protests and demonstrations from coast to coast and border to border, the Cold War, the fear of Russia and the threat of communism. Centered in Chicago, influenced significantly by the city was the revelation of the government's Counter Intelligence Program (COINTELPRO), the Black struggle for liberation and racial equality, Black people's self-redefinition and history. Of course, the Nation of Islam, with its headquarters on the South Side close to the residency of the Honorable Elijah Muhammad, were only a few blocks from my church at 49th and Woodlawn. We were highlighted for raising Black consciousness by Malcolm X and Muhammad Ali, who also lived in the neighborhood in the 4900 block on Woodlawn. And then there was Stokley Carmichael raising the declaration of Black Power.

Chicago's prominence in the Black struggle became apparent with Dr. King bringing his Southern movement of integration "up south" and claiming his residence on the West Side. His push for open housing in what he called "the most segregated city in America" added to this becoming the number one civil rights confrontation in the country at that time. During the summer of 1965, prior to King's arrival in the West Side, a group of community pastors and ministers in the North Kenwood-Oakland area donated one of our churches at least once a week to discuss social issues of the community and try to come up with some solutions. We concluded that we needed a permanent organization, an organized body of residents who would commit to social problems; they'd make demands of the responsible city bodies and their services to direct their attention to the legitimate concerns of overcrowding and the social pathos we faced. The pastors and churches who galvanized this group were as follows: my own Woodlawn Midianite Church with Revs. Delta France and Curtis E. Burrell, Jr., St. James United Methodist Church at 46th and Ellis with Rev. Henry Harding presiding, priest Paul Robemyer at the St. Ambrose Roman Catholic Church located at 47th and Ellis, Kenwood United Church of Christ with Rev. Herbert Eaton at 46th and Woodlawn, their assistant Marion Phillips, a young brother from the Chicago Theological Seminary, and Christ the King Lutheran Church with the Rev. William Griffin located at 37th and Lake Park. We were serious about what we had to do, but had little funds to do it. However, we were committed and continually worked at our task, our calling.

In the winter of 1965 the group named itself the Kenwood-Oakland Community Organization, KOCO for short. I had returned to finish my last year in seminary. Dr. King had set up Operation Breadbasket. Its office was located in the 300 block east of 47th Street. During the winter of 1965 Rev. Jesse Jackson became the first KOCO director for a few short months. At the end of the summer of 1967, I made the trip to Heston, Kansas where I married a young Midianite-Amish girl. We met while I was helping to conduct a youth evangelism gathering and that relationship later developed at my church in St. Louis, Missouri where she had come to finish her nursing degree. We married and moved to Chicago for my last year of study.

In the summer of 1966 after graduating in June, I moved back to Chicago to reengage in the work that I had helped start last summer. The Woodlawn Midianite Church sent me a definite invitation to come and assist with the church's ministry as associate pastor with Delta France. We now continued to help grow the KOCO movement in the neighborhood. The only finances came from contributions from the churches, the pastors involved and voluntary office work. The funds were minimal. The brother who asked to be the next director was James McGowan. Those of us who supported it contributed as best we could to supplement the money needed for Mr. McGowan and his family. Other contributions were made by the United Church of Christ and the Chicago Theological Seminary. They turned over a building they owned next to the Kenwood United Church at 46th and Greenwood. They had another facility at 4500 S. Greenwood, which they allowed a local group of community activists, the Protector Rights, to use. They allowed them to occupy this house until the Blackstone Rangers took it from them. The other group that gave aid as it could was the Jewish Council on Urban Affairs (JCUA). They contributed a small, yearly stipend and added to our professional staff by giving us Bob Gordon, who was a professional photographer and architect. Bob produced our first publication, a brochure in black and white, which laid out pictorial views of our vision, the upgrading of the Kenwood-Oakland areas. A major section of this publication was dedicated to offering an alternative for the debated location of the much-needed new high school which would replace Old Forrestville High School that would ease some of its problems. The location that we chose for the property was different from the one the Chicago Board of Education was looking at. Our location was the square block bound by Drexel Blvd., Ellis Ave., 45th and 44th Streets. On the Drexel side of that block, the old Walgreen mansion stood. I personally surveyed this area.

African American residents were frightened by the deteriorating factors in the community and had resigned themselves to move to a "better area." Thus, Black removal and gentrification was in full effect. Our Black foundations had been frightened away by the increased deterioration of the fabric that keeps a community healthy and growing in its own best interest. Another promotion that KOCO in those early days helped produce was one offered by NBC and noted by Scott Craig. It was a video production called "A People's Thing."

Having had personal contact with and participation in the Albany campaign with Dr. King and SCLC during his visit to Chicago, I had my church and KOCO invite him to hold a rally in our neighborhood focusing our main concerns. He came along with Al Raby and Dick Gregory, the convener of the Coordinating Council of Community Organizations. The St. James Methodist Church allowed the rally to be held in its parking lot, which is still there at 46th and Ellis. The rally was poorly attended. My church then hosted Dr. King with a dinner in the parlor at 46th and Woodlawn.

During the summer of 1966, there was a giant citywide rally at Soldiers Field. Dr. King was to be the central speaker. This gathering was very well attended. Breaking unexpectedly onto the stage was a long, unending line of Black youth, mostly males. They began to slowly proceed with a huge banner showing a 50 caliber machine gun. The awe and silence of the crowed was deafening. Dick Gregory brought calm by calling for "peace and unity and making a place for our neglected youth." They attended and won a place at the table, by force, a place which still remains undefined. KOCO would later become one of the places that would give a definition. Jeff Fort and his Black P. Stone Nation had introduced themselves. Their message was loud and clear: "Cut us in or cut it out." All leaders and social activists in the Black liberation movement, including the SCLC, now gave recognition to this new face. This uninvited guest who had just crashed the party, beating its chest and growling like an untamed animal, gave its messages. Oscar Brown, Jr. applied his theatrical talents and creative genius to developing a play using the Black youth of the Woodlawn community to sing and dance. The play was titled *Opportunity Please Knock* and was performed at the church of Rev. John Fry at 64th and Kimbark.

KOCO, whose motto was "Black people serious about one another," continued its serious work of organizing and confronting the issues. One major program we initiated was around the issue of healthcare. We invited medical personnel from Howard University in Washington, D.C. to come and help stage a campaign to pressure the city to establish a community health clinic. There were many changes and battles we had to go through, but this was eventually accomplished and became Homan Clinic, which at that time was housed in a new building at 43rd and Vincennes. Later it moved to another new structure at 43rd and Berkeley. As Chicago policies would have it, the clinic was named after the person who had vigorously opposed its creation—the infamous alderman of the 4th ward, Claude B. Homan, one of the mayor's silent Negroes on the city council. Both of these people had declared that there was no segregation in Chicago. The clinic still bears his name.

The tension from improving and organizing the Black community was citywide in the mid-sixties. Dr. Archie Hargrave, a teacher at the Chicago Theological Seminary on the campus of the University of Chicago, and Rev. C.T. Vivian of the SCLC formed a citywide group called the Coalition for United Community Action. It was made up of thirty organizations, activists and twenty churches, including the street nations, Lords, Stones and Disciples. Once a week we would meet at the Presbyterian Church, one of the historical churches of the Underground Railroad. This church was located at Warren and Ashland. Some of the people in the organizations composing this body were Meredith Gilbert of the Lawndale Peoples Planning and Action Council (LPPAC), the West Side Organization, the well-known Dr. Conrad Worrill, the Honorable Anos M. Lukeman, "Fats" Crawford, Doug Andrews, Paul King, David Reed, Carl Lattimer, Sally Johnson, Nancy Jefferson, Marion Stamps, Rev. Thurston, Rev. A.I. Dunlap, Rev. John Porter, Rev. Curtis Burrell, Paul Jones, Calvin Lockridge, Rev. Mingle of the Morning Start Church, and Rev. James Mack of the Grace Presbyterian Church to name a few. Our group took on overarching issues. One which still stands and is still being fought is Black participation in the building trades and the unions' contractors. We took on this confrontation, which was brought on as a result of the coalition's involvement in what was then to become the model cities program. We had gotten word from a close friend, Al Mellons, of plans being constructed by the office of Housing and Urban Development under Arthur Fletcher at that time, who would soon be making this package available to Mayor Daley. Mellons told us that we should be present at a gathering to be held on the far North Shore at Illinois Beach State Park. I was chairman of the coalition's model cities program. We showed up and made quite an impression. Not long afterwards, Irvin France, the mayor's urban project director, called me into his office and presented the coalition with an offer to be included in the Kenwood-Oakland area section of the model cities program.

However, at our following meeting Meredith Gilbert observed a major flaw. As things stood in the building and trade industry, the unions and the contracts, Black people would not be getting a fair share of the work to be done. The coalition, therefore, called and engineered a boycott, shutting down construction being done in the Black communities of Chicago. Within thirty days, over one hundred million dollars' worth of work was halted. This was started by stopping the construction on the annex of the First National Bank at Dearborn and Jackson while simultaneously shutting down the office of the trades unions on North Wells and the rail line work that was being done on the South Side. Our work stoppage spilled over into other neighborhoods. Regular negotiating sessions were convened with Mayor Daley as their chair, including the presence of the coalition and building contractors, major ones and unions. The street protests and demonstrations that we conducted each morning were brought to a halt when Rev. Jesse Jackson intervened at a major confrontation that was being held on buildings that were underway on the campus of the University of Illinois at Chicago (UIC) at Halsted and Roosevelt. This struggle for Black people trying to get into the building industry, which was closed to Black participation, continued until today, as highlighted by the unions' closing down of the Washburn Trade School several years earlier and moving out of the city.

Another major development coming out of the involvement in the coalition was information that the Community Renewal Society (CRS), an arm of the United Church of Christ, had designed a program similar to the stated intent of the model cities, the difference being that the control would be placed into the hands of the independent community organizations. This program was called Toward Responsible Freedom (TRF). Rev. Donald Benedict was its director and Rev. Ruben Shears was the liaison between TRF and the community. We could see that independence had not yet arrived. This program would have a five-year lifecycle and resources.

The value of the program would be approximately 3.5 million dollars, which would include office space, staff, clerical and community organizers, seed money, and professional help in the areas of economic development, social welfare, legal, housing and health. However, all the elements of the community would have to be involved and take part. A meeting was established to call all known community people to do so. Upon hearing of this program, I took this information back to the KOCO board of directors. We began courting Rev. Benedict and Rev. Shears. We needed this program, as it would provide sufficient monetary and moral support that KOCO needed to manifest its comprehensive vision. Our prayers were being answered, we perceived. But the final bolt left to be tightened was whether KOCO and the Stones could work together in the TRF program under the direction of KOCO, with Rev. Burrell as its chairman. Therefore, CRS arranged a meeting with KOCO and Jeff Forte and his group one Sunday afternoon at the Chicago Theological Seminary. Jeff Forte and some of his people came to the meeting and met with the KOCO board and myself where we agreed to cooperate together under the direction of KOCO. Forte declared that his desire was to work with the youth. He was hired as the position of youth director later on. However, there was so much bad press that Forte soon resigned that position. The KOCO board members present besides myself were James McGowan, Thomas "Blood" Mickles, Ginger Mack, James Payne, Ruby Mora and Leota Johnson. Together we agreed to this precarious matrimony between KOCO and the Blackstone Rangers. This was in 1967. James McGowan was prophetic and insightful when he stated to me in private that he was leaving to return to Detroit and would not take the chance of working with Jeff Forte. So Brother McGowan jumped ship. The rest of the crew continued the journey. With the new funding and the addition of the Blackstone participation, KOCO swelled up like a person on steroids. Daddy-O Daley, who then had a program on WVON, called me "the gangster preacher" while interviewing me on his show.

As we continued our efforts to work together in the community, the percentage of office staff and organizing staff that was with the Stone Nation increased. The spokesman for Jeff and the P. Stone Nation became the chief organizer. Several girlfriends became secretaries and office helpers. The quality of teamwork disintegrated. My frustration began to grow. KOCO had made an arrangement in our economic development program with the A.I. Zollinger plastics industry of Downers Grove to train our people from the neighborhood in the growing plastics industry. We had three eight-hour crews transported by our private VW micro bus, which we stored in one of the garages in the alley behind Gills Liquor Store on 47th and Kimbark. One afternoon when I entered the office there was a museum-type silence with strange figures standing around. A gunshot rang out from the basement and soon Chester Evans, one of the Stone enforcers, appeared. This had sent off a shock wave in the office. He came upstairs and told me that Chief was on the way and wanted to talk to you, Blood and several other staff members. Soon Forte came in and said, "Hi, Rev. I want the three of you to ride with us to the Forest Preserve out in Palos Heights and have a talk." They had commanded the vehicle used to transport the work crew to Downers Grove, and thus were hampering our economics program. I refused to go. Some of my professional staff ran away. The economic developer, Mr. Tony Statinger, said that he was going to Washington to work with the Nixon poverty program.

I felt threatened and intimidated in my small office space. Then I began to hear of extracurricular activities of extortion and intimidation that the Blackstones were conducting outside the KOCO parameters. There was an effort to extort money from people like Daddy-O Daley and his partner, Jacoby Dickens, at their 87th and Cottage Grove bowling alley. Mr. Dickens was later shot. I think he recovered. Also, there was a forceful back-off with a confrontation between the Blackstone Rangers and the Black Panther Party over territory. The Stones did not want the Panthers there. Then the South Mall Hotel at 67th and Stony Island was taken over by the Stones. At another meeting, the one that they called Crazy Paul Morton led in a group of enforcers and introduced a plan to go to the churches and take a special collection for the P. Stone Nation. Another egregious activity that they conducted outside the KOCO program was their "don't vote campaign." They graffitied support for President Nixon on the walls in the neighborhood. The Republican Party showed its gratitude by giving an all-expenses paid trip to the Nixon inauguration to a Blackstone Rangers representative, so Mr. Mickey Caldwell, the leader of the Cobra Stones, went to the White House representing Black P. Stone in 1969.

From that time, a deep transformation began to evolve in my consciousness that would climax on June 17, 1970. I complained to Jeff Forte about the growing discord and lack of cooperation between myself and the staff. He and I then had a private meeting in the KOCO office on 47th Street and another at my house, along with some of his "mains." Here he told the group that he and I were one. That he was Zorro and I was Don Diego, the same person. It really sounded dramatic and interesting. However, it was meaningless. The deterioration continued. I was deeply conflicted. I was back at the crossroads. My being was challenged. The deeper question raised by Shakespeare arose in me—to be or not to be. To be real or not to be real. I began to realize that I had to separate myself from this situation, which threatened to cast aside my new and transformed life and pitch me into a downward spiral. To continue in being or unite with non-being. Since material gain and social status was never a desire to any degree on my part, sacrificing material and social elevation was not a problem for me. My exodus and ascent from the valley floor and this other imprisonment started.

I paid a ministerial visit to Rev. Jesse Jackson, who was convalescing in the St. Joseph Hospital on the North Shore. When I visited he was telling me of the threats that he and his family were getting from the Stones. In his words, "Leaning on me for eighty thousand dollars." I told him that I, too, was under threats and if I had him as backup, I would engage in confrontation. He then said that he knew of some brothers serious about Black liberation and if I ever needed help, let him know and he would call them. With this in mind, I began to secretly put together my plan. I kept it quiet from everyone; only the spirit of God knew. I took a solo retreat for three days at a friend's Michigan cabin; it was located on a small lake. There I meditated and prayed for a length of time. I was brought to the same conclusion as a famous biblical character. Her better-known name is Esther, but her Hebrew name is Hadassha. She, along with the Hebrew people in southern Judah, was transferred to Persia under King Nebuchadnezzar. This was the time of the Media-Persia Empire. They were threatened with extermination and genocide by a hater named Haman. Her uncle, who posed as her father, was named Mordecai. Esther became queen because the king found disfavor in his earlier queen, but found delight in her. But as the laws of Media-Persia said in those days, you did not enter the king's chamber unless he called you; to do otherwise meant death. She told this to her uncle and he let her know that she had come to the king for a reason. Then she made up her mind, prayed, and meditated. She declared to herself that she would go in and see the king unannounced—I will do this thing and if I perish, I perish. And so I concluded, I will go back and I will do this thing and if I perish, I perish. I returned to my Chicago office with the following plan and script in mind. I wrote these words on the office blackboard: "Attention all KOCO staff—as of Friday noon, you may pick up your checks because this office will be temporarily closed for the purpose of inventory and re-evaluation. Signed, Chairman Rev. Curtis E. Burrell, Jr." I then went to the Chicago Defender and let it be known that I had fired the staff and all of the Stones. I also appeared at Operation Breadbasket at the Capital Theater and 79th and Halsted. Having posted this on the blackboard, this declaration for which I had intentionally not sought advice nor approval from the board of directors, immediately a thug representative of the Stones who had been on the staff came into my office. This was one of the close associates of Minister Leonard Sengali, one of his right-hand men. "All right, Burrell, I want you to sign my vacation check and I don't care about this so-and-so job." I refused and stated, "Brother, you stay on vacation, you only come twice a month, on the first and fifteenth to pick up your check." He began to call me names and curse me, showing total disrespect and blocking my doorway to my small office with his body. I was prepared for this, and eventually I opened my Samsonite briefcase where I had a loaded .9 mm Browning automatic gun. I pulled it out and, looking him in his eyes, I told him, "Move, let me past." When he refused and kept on pulling up his pants, I looked him right in his eyes and pointed the gun down at the floor. I had been taking target practice at Blue Island. My gun was registered. I fired three shots—these became the shots that were heard around the world, especially around Chicago—setting many people free, even up on the North Side. The first person to hear about these shots was Rev. Jackson. I had parked across the street illegally in front of a bus stop. The KOCO office was across from what is now Bally's at 47th and Kenwood. I had my new 1970 black Monte Carlo illegally parked in front of this bus stop with another weapon in the trunk. There were some Stones standing in the office when I came out. They were surprised by the gunfire, but offered no opposition. I got into my car and calmly took off toward Lake Shore Drive and headed north to St. Joseph Hospital to see Rev. Jackson. When I told him what had happened, he chuckled in approval and a little surprise. He got on the phone and dialed. "Hey, W.L." This was W.L. Lillard of the Lillard Security Agency on the West Side, the same brother who had backed up security guards a few years earlier down in Cairo, Illinois when they were conflicting with the Ku Klux Klan. "Hey, W.L. I've got Rev. Burrell here. He just fired at Stones and shot his way out of his office. He needs your services." I contacted Reuben Shears and Don Benedict and they agreed to hire Lillard immediately, who immediately whisked me off to 26th and California to the office of the infamous Edward Hanrahan. They had, a year earlier, assassinated Fred Hampton and Mark

Clark in 1969. This was June 17, 1970. W.L., being a law man himself, had to let Hanrahan know that a conflict had ignited and was brewing between myself and the Stones, and that some violence had actually occurred. As we returned to 47th Street, the drama began to unfold citywide. That Saturday at Rev. Jackson's instruction to director Rev. Calvin Morris at Operation Breadbasket, I was allowed to make an announcement from the stage (I had threatened to do so out on the curb if they had not). The Chicago news media—TV, radio, magazines, *JET* magazine—let this drama dominate the news for the whole summer of 1970, and there was an immediate violent response. The KOCO office had a bomb thrown in its office door. Someone fired about thirteen bullets through the front window of my home. I got my family out of town to a place of safety. My response was to announce an invitation to walk with me in the well-publicized Walk Against Fear. We led a small group of supporters down Lake Park Avenue, starting at 47th and Lake Park, down to 37th and Lake Park. This included some ministers, some news reporters like Charles Armstrong and Lu Palmer, my bodyguards and a few faithful and brave souls. Rev. Reuben Shears was there, as was Rev. Marion Phillips. Across the street on the east side of Lake Park was Jeff Forte and his group. On July 30, 1970 Tommy Picou of the *Chicago Defender* wrote a very touching and supportive editorial in my support. There was a great response from all over the city at all levels, including the Black legislators in Springfield, who had invented the term Walk Against Fear. The brothers from the Topographical Center, located on Cottage Grove and 65th or 66th, came—and there were unknown persons who came into the city with out-of-town plates on their cars into Blackstone territory, causing consternation and confusion and bewilderment.

There was much fear and trembling on the part of many "movement people" because my dismissal of the Stones presented a backlash that affected their funding, thus causing collateral damage to their programs. So they sought immediate funds on which to survive. A meeting was convened at the Urban League at 45th and Michigan. I was denounced by two well-known reverends and civil rights community organizing activists. These leaders said that I should have been murdered like Martin Luther King, Jr. and Christ for the good of mankind. Such crazy fear had locked up, tilted, and twisted reasoning on the part of these so-called leaders. There were even several letters from the Ku Klux Klan threatening me stating that "the hairs were on my neck." Later, Fort and his main twenty-one called a midday meeting in the gymnasium of Rev. Fry's church on 64th and Kimbark. They wanted me to state to them publicly what I was doing and what I was calling for. Accompanying me were my bodyguards and about two hundred grassroots community Black men. The Stones didn't display any armed hostility nor verbal threats. They wanted to listen and hear me. I called for change, repentance, and a trial to be held for those who were guilty of harming communities and individuals. I called for them to cease this terrorism. This caused

Lamar Bell, also called BOP, to ask me how they could trust me. I said in response to that question, it was not about how much they could trust me, but about them doing the right thing. My appeal was not received nor welcomed, as shown by the next acts of violence taken against me.

The Rev. John Barber had been a staff member with Operation Breadbasket and Rev. Jackson's close associate. He was writing a biography of Rev. Jackson. He needed a place to stay and a salaried position because Breadbasket could no longer afford to keep him there. I gave him both the room off of my third floor study and a job with KOCO. I spoke with Rev. Shears and the KOCO board of directors about offering Rev. Barber the opened position as director of education, the position that had been left by Sis. Willeva Lindsey. Reuben, John, myself and about three bodyguards were holding negotiations with John Barber about the duties and the salaries of this new position. Another guard had camouflaged himself in a nearby parked car. The windows of the church parlor where we were meeting were at street level. This was the same parlor where we had hosted Dr. Martin Luther King, Jr. a year or so earlier. Suddenly, shots were fired through the window. The church had been surrounded by a body of about twenty youth. One of the guards cracked the heavy oak door leading to the streets, caught sight of the direction of the gunfire, and dashed out in a counter-attack, shooting, but not fatally, at one of the attackers; this made headlines. At a press conference Rev. Barber, who was not a man to be made afraid or threatened, caused fear in the Stones. His words and demeanor were like fire and thunder out of Bible prophets and Revelations. He declared war on Black boys who tried to frighten and assassinate righteous Black men. This drama happened near my birthday, July 27, 1970. The church building was destroyed by arson early on the morning of July 30.

Out of this conflict Rev. Barber produced what was to be called Black Men Moving. Rev. Jackson then offered to come to the church to hold a press conference in my place, saying that I must be too shocked and broken to do so. I turned down his offer, stating that this was my church and that I was pastor in charge of it all. Then Rev. C.T. Vivian came by the freshly burned out church and accused me of being at fault, saying that I had it coming. I should have known better, he said. I had to stop one of the guards from manhandling him. Rev. Vivian had been threatened by collateral damage. Rev. Barber and I called on Senator Charles Percy to help by launching an investigation of street gangs and their influence in Chicago. We were sent plane tickets and other expenses to come before the Senate subcommittee and the crimes investigation sub-committee to give testimony. We went and testified before the U.S. Senate in the fall of 1970. Following this, Rev. Barber and I went to Englewood, Colorado to talk with Charles Kettering, whose foundation was funding the Rangers. We appealed to him to shift some of those funds to rebuild the church since his money had helped support the forces responsible for the crime. He refused, saying that he funded education and not construction. In a freak accident later on he was killed by an automobile while crossing the street near his Colorado home.

On August 5, 1970 Rev. Ralph Abernathy and the president of the SCLC's Atlanta office announced that they would send a team to look into the conflicts between Rev. Barber, Rev. Curtis and the Blackstone Rangers. The SCLC had a meeting place in the Holiday Inn Loop hotel, which was on the border of Dan Ryan and Halsted. No solution was reached because the so-called leadership was found to be only a façade. These leaders were afraid of calling out and facing the disorder and irresponsibility in our communities, which made unification an impossibility. The leadership did not see or understand that repairs begin internally with the act of the will, without which one remains a victim by his own inactions and complaints.

Following the church arson, Rev. Barber introduced me to Rev. James Bevel. He had just arrived from Baltimore with a rather large group of people promoting their newly founded organization, which was called Making a Nation (MAN), based upon the acquisition of land, community living, and being honest with one another. They needed housing and I offered them temporary shelter in my home. I also took on Herman Neal of the MAN group as one of my community organizers.

Another interesting individual was Robert "Bob" Lucas, who had been hired by KOCO at my invitation to become the director of our newly formed leadership training program. His organization, Community Organization for Racial Equality (CORE), could no longer employ him and he needed a job. We hired him. Lucas was there when I fired the Blackstones. He was never comfortable with my arbitrary act and remained my critic. He then led a conspiracy to take me to court and gain a court injunction to keep me out of the office with the threat of jail. I was accused and charged with violating the KOCO constitution for acting undemocratic when I fired the Stones. I never set foot again in the KOCO office.

Today, there is a group called KOCO, who has the same emblem that we had. Their office is located at 1006 E. 43rd Street. I have never met anyone there, although I went in personally to introduce myself and offer any help that I could if they ever wanted to call on me. I have not heard anything as of yet.

I would like to name the personalities who either participated directly with KOCO by coming into our office or in various programs that coordinated our efforts on: familiar persons such as Brother Richard Barnett, Hannibal Afrik, the late Ralph Abernathy, Doris Lomax, Connie Howard, Willeva Lindsey, Carole Adams, the Great Muhammad Ali, Sister Christine Johnson, George O'Hare, Dick Gregory, Sue Duncan, Al Raby, Timuel Black, Rev. Dr. King, Rev. James Bevel, Jeff Fort, Cecil Butler, Danny Davis, Gus Savage, Fred Hampton, Rev. Jesse Jackson, Andrew Heard, Bill Wallace, Sen. Richard Newhouse, Charles Armstrong, Anna Langford, Anderson Thomas, Lu Palmer, Georgia English, Patty Williams,

Finest Henderson, Paul Hall, Phil Koran, Kermit Coleman, Don Mobley, and Judge Eugene Pincham. I'm sure I have missed a few, but these are some of the great souls that we have had the honor and privilege of touching the hem of the garment thereof.

Community Action Activities Consciousness has not been dormant for one moment since the courts conspiratorial from the KOCO operation ejected me. Herbert Passion was the judge who ruled against me and threatened me with jail. The Passions are a family that operated the Passion Construction Company, which was one of the companies that contractors on the Dan Ryan had closed down during our boycotts. Therefore, I was a marked man. The activities had not been dormant.

There are three watersheds that I would like to point out, which continues the flow of self-determination, self-direction, self-definition and self-evaluation. One is called New Wineskins, which is my own self-developed nickel and nail economic base providing sustainable income since 1972 for myself and others. It is based on the principle of letting down your bucket where you are without complaining that there are no resources, proving that outside funding is not a must to continue a sustainable economic development for a people. Many people have been helped by my programs. To learn about Wineskins, I would suggest that the reader go to my webpage, www.thewineskins.net, to be updated on our activities. Many have moved on from my school and are able even now to go out because my children were raised during the period from this transformation and this drama. I presently make my living from the products that we have created at New Wineskins. We did not start off creating leather products as we do now. We are looking to create our ideas into marketable items. New Wineskins is one of those things that we have continued out of our consciousness and community responsibility, along with a New Age Troupe. To get more insight on the New Age Troupe, we invite you to go to www.nat.org, and they would more than happily fill you in on details about the troupe and its founder. The second group showing an active community consciousness has no name. These are people who have the authentic dedication to community improvement and self-determination that our earlier group had brought into the original KOCO. That group was organized by one Mary Borderline of the long-established honorable Borderline family of North Kenwood.

It was after the KOCO office ejection by Judge Passion that I continued the idea of independent economic development. Having no resources except a little bit of insurance money from the burned-out church, a small group of people and I continued to put forth efforts to let down our buckets where we were. While developing an economic program from 1972 onward, I met the most unforgettable character that I would ever meet in my life. It would have been enriching if many Black leaders had met this Black man from Mississippi, Dr. David Berry, who introduced us to a level of consciousness which we are void of still. We run into too much confusion and failure because his message and his example remain unknown. He called his message the New Age Truth. One of the problems with leaders in the movement is that we allowed them to ascend when they were false or pseudo-prophets, wolves in sheep's clothing, Trojan horses, camouflaged within the house; they were willing to sacrifice unity and righteous vision for self-aggrandizement. There was no light to shine to show who was who and what was what, what was genuine and what was fake. In meeting with Dr. Berry and the New Age Truth, one of the treasures given to us was the knowledge of the two cells and their continual contest for dominion of our minds—man's universal mind, particularly the minds of Black people. The Black liberation struggle since the sixties up until now has not accessed this insight and ancient wisdom. Thus, we have invited into the house disabling havoc and defeat, even in the face of sure victories.

Looking back over the years and the history and struggle in this community, I can see that the early days were full of attempted redemption based upon sympathy and compassion but it was like trying to construct a building with a weak foundation upon the sand. We had a partial vision, because we left out the force of a single-minded union. A single destination had not come into focus; there was blindness on the part of would-be leaders. The core problem had not yet been seen. It took all of this drama to see the illness. Funding and social programs blurred clear-sightedness and bypassed the real and true thing, which was doing for self as righteous, loving people such as the Hon. Marcus Garvey, the Hon. Booker T. Washington, the Hon. George Washington Carver, and the Hon. Elijah Muhammad.

We did not get a vision and commitment to self-knowledge based on faith; rather, we were welfare-minded, making excuses that we could not lift ourselves up by our bootstraps rather than making the boot and the straps. Let down your nets where you are. Use your magic, create something out of nothing, and sit down with like-minded people. The promised land is here. We are only a thought and a will away from it. In the words of Denzel Washington in *The Great Debaters,* "There is no enemy who defeat me nor us." Coming through the sixties and seventies has been the fiery furnace which has brought out the pure gold of the present consciousness.

CHICAGO FREEDOM MOVEMENT RECOLLECTIONS FROM A DR. KING FOOT SOLDIER

Rev. Al Sampson

I was a young field organizer barely out of Massachusetts when Dr. Martin Luther King, Jr., president of the Southern Christian Leadership Conference (SCLC), moved to Chicago and launched what would be known as the Chicago Freedom Movement. Having worked side by side with Dr. King throughout the South as an SCLC staff member, I was both thrilled and honored to be asked by him to join him in Chicago for what would become his only campaign to bring economic and racial justice to African Americans living in the North.

Ordained by Dr. King in 1966, I felt I had been adequately trained for this unique assignment. However, nothing could prepare any of us for the level of betrayal and hostility among Northern Blacks against our efforts to end economic apartheid in America. In the South, Blacks reluctantly worked with southern white racists to thwart our efforts, while in Chicago, many prominent Black politicians, preachers and business leaders openly worked hand in hand with the Richard J. Daley administration and others to stop our campaign. Today many of them remain on the wrong side of history, having worked tirelessly to slow the tide of racial progress in America.

Much has been written about Dr. King's Chicago crusade. In my view, there are three themes that should be explored when recalling what the Chicago Freedom Movement became, two of which remain overlooked or purposely misunderstood by the recorders of history. The first theme centers on so-called cultural nationalists who publicly misinterpreted our human rights struggle as integrationist. The second examines the marriage between the Black church and the community at-large. The third gives central focus to the economic exploitation of the poor through the housing industry.

It should also be noted that the White Liberal Element (WLE) within the Chicago Freedom Movement eventually double-crossed its African American partners. Forty years later this broken, progressive alliance, born in the sixties, has heralded the demise of

African American political and cultural institutions in Chicago.

The Black Power ethos of the time embodied a radicalized discourse based on cultural symbolism and activity designed to translate a newfound sense of self into social and political power. Cultural nationalists throughout the sixties and seventies took pride in redefining our human and civil rights struggles through a false prism of accommodation. Nothing could be more insane. It is even more troubling when one realizes that many of these critics never participated in the Chicago Freedom Movement at all. These are the same cultural nationalists who have never even developed a dashiki clothing factory to clothe themselves. And today, they have turned over their own holiday—Kwanzaa—to corporate interests.

Many were armchair theorists who never engaged in any real sociopolitical campaign to rid poor people of the long arm of American apartheid. While thousands marched in the South and ultimately joined the launch of the Chicago Freedom Movement in the mid-1960s, the cultural nationalists worked to compartmentalize our efforts as something less than revolutionary.

Building a movement out of the African liberation motif required a cultural and spiritual expression that gave the people a language of liberation from Alabama to Illinois. The thirteen-year southern movement—which began with the lynching of Emmett Till in August of 1955 and peaked four months later when Rosa Parks refused to submit to transit segregation laws—involved numerous legal fights, international lobbying, political organizing, fundraising, and the consistent and direct confrontation of racist whites determined to uphold the legacy of slavery and institutional racism.

Dr. King's idyllic actions were more radical than many of those who identified themselves as nationalists at the time, those who demanded Black Power but had no real means to achieve it beyond racial rhetoric designed for the psychological benefit of Black people. However, the northern Chicago Freedom Movement was the close cousin to our southern Civil Rights Movement, and both were designed to break down the artificial barriers of racial segregation and economic exploitation. It should also be noted that the only institution that Blacks controlled independently of white power structures was the church, and therefore it was fitting and natural that the Civil Rights Movement and the campaigns it sparked throughout the North were also born on this base.

My definition of a nationalist is an individual or institution that recognizes the history and culture of an African people in America. The notion of integration is problematic because it makes an assumption that one can become a part of that which he has ownership of. Just because a person is invited into a house does not make that person a member of the family. Supreme Court Justice Thurgood Marshall once remarked that America couldn't talk about a melting pot society when we are not in the pot. Andrew Young said it another way—U.S. society's relationship to Blacks is not like a bowl of chicken soup where all of the ingredients meld to make one concoction. Instead it is more like beef stew, where each ingredient maintains its identity and unique place in the mix. Therefore, it goes without saying that our spiritual and cultural genius have never been lost during the search for our "Americaness." In recognizing the "twoness," as identified by Dr. W.E.B. Dubois, Black people did not have to reject one in order to embrace the other. Though society has tried, our spiritual and cultural identity remains intact and cannot be broken. Therefore those of us who came out of the southern struggle for civil rights did not need the rhetoric of Stokely Carmichael, who cried "Black Power," or the lyrics of James Brown who sang, "Say It Loud I'm Black and I'm Proud," to encourage us in self-awareness and self-determination. We saw our non-violent direct action as a continuation of the ongoing freedom struggle initiated by our people when they were thrown in the bowels of slave ships in 1619. Our freedom struggle is not an integrationist struggle, it is a liberationist struggle.

When SCLC embarked on Chicago in the summer of 1966, it was natural for us to identify our base with a Black church. Stroy Freeman, pastor of New Friendship Baptist Church, provided us the necessary base of operation. Rev. Freeman and liberation pastors such as Liberty Baptist Church's A.P. Jackson and Friendship Baptist Church's Shelvin Hall, understood that the suffering of the people could never be alleviated by teaching a watered down Christianity devoid of liberation and direct action. Therefore, when he opened the doors of his church and exposed it to firebombing and other vandalism, we recognized these acts were anti-integrationalist attacks. These were race-based attacks against the church as an institution of liberation by racist, Nazi, Eastern European demagogues. The Black church was not firebombed, nor were Civil Rights workers gravely injured or killed because of integration; they were victims of racists who saw our efforts as a movement to end American apartheid and bring economic, political and social justice to the disenfranchised.

Simultaneously we experienced the patterns of apartheid in Montgomery or on Greyhound buses or at southern lunch counters, while experiencing the imaginary boundaries of apartheid in Chicago with segregated housing and police brutality. Both involved the economic exploitation of the people through institutional racism. We learned in the South that you could have a Ph.D., D.D. or no D and in the North you could wear a Dashiki or Brooks Brothers suit, be a Baptist or Catholic and your Blackness relegated you to an apartheid arrangement that you agreed to with silent consent. Therefore when SCLC came to Chicago, it was a natural progression of the movement to end American apartheid. For us it was simply moving from "Down South" to "Up South."

The Chicago Freedom Movement was a multicultural consortium of churches, community groups and individuals across religion, culture and class. Dr. King said for this movement to work we needed "operational unity." He used this concept as the rallying cry to build a northern campaign that would withstand fragmentation once pressure was applied. For more than a decade SCLC had trained freedom workers on the theory of nonviolent liberation within the context of Christianity and by using Jesus as the ultimate model for liberation and social justice. Given the large number of African Americans in Chicago and the unique political landscape which saw the rise of many Blacks politicians and wealthy business people, SCLC believed the City of Big Shoulders would make the best model for future northern campaigns. Yet, our efforts were met with resistance by many churches who feared repercussions from the political and economic power structure. Preachers closed their doors to SCLC and Dr. King because their religion made them comfortable with political subdivision of power. For them, it was perfectly fine to live within an apartheid relationship because at least they were able to manage the pain among those who suffered the most from its effects.

Dr. King called this putting a ceiling on the mental skies of the children. Therefore, we had not only the burden of organizing externally, but we had to fight our own base of support internally. Some Black leaders, ministers and businessmen, at the behest of Mayor Richard J. Daley, began to attack Dr. King as an outside agitator and worked with white politicians to thwart the Chicago Freedom Movement. Many publicly asked him to leave the city and to take his nonviolent activism with him.

So Chicago became a battleground to remove the mental ceilings and destroy the stronghold of institutional racism that relegated Blacks and the poor to bad housing, impoverished neighborhoods, reoccurring poverty and social despair. Dr. King's very presence disturbed the pathological arrangement that the "slaves" had with their "masters." Because of his and Ralph Abernathy's escalated campaigns in the north, police, FBI, CIA and other intelligence gathering agencies began to step up their espionage in order to stop the burgeoning northern movement.

The housing crisis (residential segregation) in Chicago can be summed up simply by noting that this crisis created yet another artificial barrier designed to keep Blacks from enjoying consistent upward mobility.

Rev. James Bevel, Andy Young, Larry Patterson, and I were assigned to organize the street organizations into nonviolent troops for social change. I was one of the staff members invited to live with Dr. King at 1550 S. Hamlin, a dilapidated apartment he shared with his wife Coretta, for the duration of his stay in Chicago. The field staff began meeting with leaders of the Black Stone Rangers, Disciples, Cobras, Latin Kings and others to talk about the principles of nonviolence, the need for operational unity, and to outline concrete and achievable goals. After considerable dialogue, we gathered them all in a convention of sorts where they were addressed by Dr. King and other leaders of the movement. We explained they could be important to the community as developers, rather than destroyers. This sort of organizing was critical to us because it made no sense to Dr. King to have access to the parents in the pulpits on Sunday, but no access to the children who were in the streets on Friday. It was not unusual to see us in the pool halls talking with young men and women, including King, who was pretty good with a pool stick. We needed their numbers and their discipline for the many marches we had planned, particularly the one in Marquette Park on Chicago's Southwest Side.

Dr. King didn't want any ignorant warriors. Therefore, it was important to teach seven steps of non-violent activity: information, education, purification, negotiation, confrontation, reconciliation and recreation (recreating what was destroyed).

It should also be noted that SCLC's move to organize the street organizations (gangs) into a disciplined unit for nonviolent confrontation frightened the intelligence community. The United States was watching a wave of political liberation sweeping through Africa and the Caribbean. King had been invited to Ghana personally by Kwame Nkrumah to witness his inauguration as the first black prime minister of that nation. The liberation movements of Africa sought to free our brothers and sisters from the control of the British, French, Belgian and other colonists. In the United States we fought a similar battle against immigrant whites and others committed to keeping Blacks in a state of servitude and second-class citizenship. The Balfour Agreement that chopped Black Africa into fifty-four different nations was no different to us than the residential covenants that sought to chop up the political and cultural base of northern Blacks. We later learned a Blackstone Ranger who had attended our organizing meetings would later testify against Jeff Fort as a spy for one of the law enforcement agencies. Had SCLC advocated violence, many of us, including me, would have been indicted and possibly imprisoned indefinitely—as so many Black freedom fighters are today.

During the Marquette Park march, when Dr. King was hit in the head, the street leaders nearly lost it. Later, they demanded blood. They wanted to go back to Marquette Park and give the whites a taste of "Black Power." Dr. King was a powerful listener. As the young men expressed anger and outrage, he suddenly asked them a question. "If a house is burning would you put more fire on the fire?" The street leaders became indignant and accused Dr. King of insulting their intelligence. "Man everybody knows you fight fire with water," they yelled. "Exactly," King said, "that is what nonviolence is." This powerful orator then went on to explain that it was futile to strike back at the whites with violence because Blacks could never match the violence of whites because we had neither the firepower, nor the law on our side. To do so, King argued, would cause untold atrocities against innocent Blacks who would suffer the wrath of the white power structure. This would also give cover to the violent white cowards who were attempting to provoke violent confrontation. Further, if we had allowed the younger Blacks to disrupt the movement with violence, we would have lost the White Liberal Element within the growing movement. Reason prevailed.

Aside from marches, the Chicago Freedom Movement convened an emergency housing summit. Dr. King trusted White Liberal Element leaders, such as Jack McDermott and Dale Williams of the American Friends Service Committee, Don Benedict of the Community Renewal Society, as well as Black establishment leaders like Bill Berry of the Chicago Urban League and Al Raby, a leader of the Chicago's Coordinating Committee of Community Organizations. The white liberal wing of the movement has never been properly studied nor have we fully examined their close relationships with real estate and banking industries. Many of them lacked the moral judgment to serve the community any good. Whites who sought to join our freedom struggle wanted political manipulation rather than liberation and would have rather conceded true justice for the right to simply manage the economic sanctions against Blacks. They wanted to measure what type of freedom would be granted and they trusted the political system to implement the reforms without any input from the community whatsoever.

We had been engaging in field tests where we would send a white couple and a black couple into a real estate office to determine if the firm engaged in red-lining and block busting. Chicago's economic apartheid and affront to open housing was spearheaded by real estate, insurance, mortgage companies and banks.

Out of that conference developed a ten-point covenant. By being one of the signatures to that agreement, Dr. King trusted white liberals to live up to their end of the bargain. When Dr. King left Chicago, the WLE and their black allies were not prepared to sustain the movement. When you cannot sustain something, you work to contain it—and here lies the double-cross. The metropolitan Open Housing Movement launched a goal of dropping Black folk into single family housing in the suburbs. There was also the Oak Park Area Association, which worked to steer Blacks across Madison Avenue. The Neighborhood Housing Institute steered Blacks in another direction in South Shore. The Beverly Area Planning Association (BAPA) also developed a quota "steering" system that led to panic legislation being developed at the state level in order to protect white homeowners from the influx of African Americans into "their" communities. The White Liberal Establishment also helped to create the surge in African American poverty in public housing and was in the forefront of fighting for Section 8 certificates that allowed people to move from their slum community to any other community in the country (therefore leading to gentrification at the expense of the Section 8 certificate).

Between 1954 and 1967, the Chicago Housing Authority constructed more than 10,300 public housing units, of which only sixty-three were built outside poor, racially segregated areas. The Gautreaux Decision was the first desegregation lawsuit of its kind. However, it wound up creating so-called "scattered site" housing over a period of twenty years, further leading to the destruction of the African American economic political base, all under the guise of deconcentration.

Chicago's public housing was designed to perpetrate a pattern of economic exploitation of the poor in general, and African-Americans in particular. For example, southern Blacks moving north were used to living in open spaces, being able to cultivate land and grow their own food. They were not accustomed to Chicago's high-rise housing, as designed by city planners, nor were they used to living in cramped spaces without privacy and protection. When people received their public housing unit, the first indication of their upcoming exploitation was the size of the kitchen. With little shelf space and a very small refrigerator, residents realized they would not be able to hold adequate quantities of food to sustain their families for the month. Therefore, they would have to walk down several flights of stairs (due to broken elevators) several times a week, only to be exploited by local merchants. The attack on the social, physical and mental health of poor blacks can be traced through the attack on "soul food," which consists mostly of fresh vegetables. But people living in public housing were unable to obtain them due to "food deserts," the lack of quality produce and grocery stores near their communities. Public housing changed the way southern people lived into an urban reality on how northern people died.

Jesus had an agrarian relationship with scripture because he often talked of seeds, harvest and planting. The Black church understood the seeds of survival were captured in soul food vegetables (this is why my church is the only church in America that has a department of agriculture in its ministry). None of us ever died from eating soul food—though many succumb to the things they put in it—because the genetic code of sweet potatoes, yams, green beans, Crowder peas, collard and mustard greens, and watermelon remains pure and unbreakable. Dr. George Washington Carver showed Albert Einstein that the theory of our relativity was not E = mc2, but it was three hundred goodies in a sweet potato and peanut, which was relative to us in feeding ourselves as a nation within a nation.

It is sad that in the wake of such findings, our community has never developed a wholesale or retail distribution network from Chicago to Wilcox County, Alabama; or from Florida to the West Side of Chicago; or from Louisiana to St. Louis. The Black farmers have no way of distributing healthy food products to the very people who need them the most. Therefore, we are stuck with the Jolly Green Giant and the Bird's Eye man rather than the food grown on granddaddy's farm. There is no economic reciprocity amongst us other than through our only independent institution of the Black church.

The Black church was the catalyst for the change during the Chicago Freedom Movement because it was the only institution that was independent and accountable to the people. It was very painful for Dr. King to see the many levels that our people were exploited in Chicago—a city rich in Black culture and political activism. Ironically, it was J.H. Jackson, president of the national Baptist Convention, and his band of establishment churches that hurt Dr. King's Chicago campaign the most.

When Dr. King challenged the church, he wound up forcing the people to identify if their religious leaders were working for or against them. In fact, because of our work, four types of churches emerged in the black community:

A. Entertainment Church: People get the Holy Ghost on Sunday and have to deal with Casper the Ghost on Monday. Theses churches focus on gospel music, expressive praise and worship, and dramatic preaching as a form of spiritual recreation and escape. These churches can be likened to neon signs advertising "Fig Tree," but once a person gets close, he or she notices there are no figs on the tree at all. There is no socio-economic agenda beyond tithes and offerings.

B. Containment Church: The talented Tenth are shut behind its doors. The congregation consists mostly of middle class and upper middle class Blacks who are comfortable on the plantation and are content with having first-class credentials but being relegated to second-class citizenship. Its members may work with the poor and the oppressed but will never do any meaningful works that will help move those groups into a higher clad. A social worker may have a client for twenty years and the only person whose condition has improved will be the social worker's.

C. Prosperity and Pain Churches: Though these churches prosper financially, they do not invest economically in the community from which it draws its wealth—thus creating a double sort of pain among the poor and oppressed. These members ride by the problems of drugs, crime, exploitation and racism on the way to church and see no correlation to their behavior to that of the community. Pastors of these churches keep their members focused on individual wealth rather than community wealth.

D. The Martin Luther King, Jr. Church—Liberation Church: Dr. King took the church out of the church and put it in the community where it belonged. When he was assassinated in 1968, the church went back indoors and this is where it has remained ever since. The Liberation Church gets its job description from Isaiah 61. It believes that struggle is from the streets up and that the oppressed have no choice but to withdraw from elicit relationships. This church made Jesus into a liberator of the oppressed who engaged in nonviolent direct action.

The 1960s was a time of transformation for many of us, and the Chicago Freedom Movement was a part of that growth. While cultural nationalists debated how to best preserve and define the racial history of Black America, and the White Liberal Element debated on how best to contain any such movement, the Liberation Church of Dr. Martin Luther King, Jr. fought to expand economic opportunity and political power among the poor and the oppressed, regardless of race.

In retrospect, the Chicago Freedom Movement was a noble gesture born out of history's unbroken continuity of Black struggle. It opened up the pathology of institutional racism and legally codified forms of white supremacy, changing the way people lived in Chicago and Cook County. In its wake, operational unity was sacrificed for greed, political access and personal upward mobility, while the masses continue to struggle for economic parity and racial justice.

CONGRESS OF RACIAL EQUALITY (CORE): IMPACT AND ACTIONS

Robert Lucas with Douglas Gill

In 1968, I was chair of Chicago CORE (Congress for Racial Equality); and I was chair of the North Central Regional CORE (inclusive of Wisconsin, Michigan, Indiana, Ohio, Missouri and Illinois). My task as regional chairman was to organize the CORE National Convention to be held in Columbus, Ohio in 1968. I had to go on the road in the months and weeks leading to the conference, including Columbus. In the buildup to the convention, I was talking about mobilizing; they heard revolution.

It seemed people came out "armed for bear hunting." The CORE National Convention got hijacked by the militant wing of the black liberation movement. Guns were conspicuous, everywhere. Nearly everyone had a strange satchel or bag, or a midriff bulge about the trunk of their bodies.

Everybody was talking about revolution. CORE never got to any convention business. Why? Because the National Action Council (the NAC), CORE's board of directors, had to go into emergency session every day to consider another aspect of the black revolution's prospects.

We did not take care of any business. Our elections and agenda of action were ambushed. Therefore, we decided to have a mini-convention in St. Louis to elect the slate of national officers. Floyd McKissick was tied up with the Soul City initiative outside of Hendersonville, North Carolina. He was, essentially, distracted and bought off by big foundation funding. Money was pouring into the enterprise. McKissick had a golden goose. He became a prophet of "black capitalism."

CORE was ripe for a takeover or a power play. Roy Innis, in that period, had endorsed Richard Nixon for President and came out with the "Black capitalism" agenda. Innis was the Assistant National Director. By default, he became national director when McKissick set up his enterprise in Soul City. Black capitalism was a failed strategy and was dead on arrival inside CORE.[24]

Earlier, in 1966, Chicago CORE had called for continued preparations for a march on Cicero, Illinois, just west of Chicago. This was in the wake of Martin Luther King's housing action campaign in Chicago.[25] The strategic thrust to end the slums appeared a failure; yet the launching of a more militant freedom movement was an outcome of that failure to end the slums. That seems ironic but that was the effect of the movement, which we had built.

When King withdrew, Chicago CORE agreed to sponsor the Cicero March. The CORE chapters had broad discretion to act, locally, on an independent agenda or issue, even if at variance with the national organization. Some leaders did not support Chicago CORE's call to march on Cicero even though it did not violate the letter or the spirit of the CORE Constitution.

We had got ready to March on Cicero. The mainstream leadership both black and white was in opposition. Some wanted to stop King by stopping the Cicero March. Some wanted to stop me by stopping the CORE national sponsorship of the March. The CORE leadership could not prevent us from going to Cicero, as local CORE representatives.

In St. Louis, Roy Innis wanted to take away local chapter autonomy and get elected National Director. We could not stop him if we voted these agenda items out on the floor. But there was another strategy in the hopper. We did not have enough votes to stop him on the convention floor. I was scheduled to speak on some matter of platitudes. I could not think of a coherent plan to stop the Innis train from leaving the station. So, what could be done?

At the end of my speech, I left the stage and kept walking. I walked down the aisle, into the lobby and nearly half of the delegates walked out. Over fifty delegates followed me out, disrupting quorum. These were more delegates than we had counted on. A few Innis supporters got caught up in the moment and walked out with us. Some others were just going to the restrooms. We went off to some hotel, near the Convention, in downtown St. Louis; and we decided to meet in Columbus, Ohio, in October to form a new organization.

---

[24] See Allen 1970, Ofari 1970

[25] Here is the prevalent view on the history of the Cicero March: "*Cicero was taken up and abandoned several times as site for a civil rights march in the mid-1960s. The American Friends Service Committee, the Rev. Martin Luther King, and many affiliated organizations, including churches, were conducting marches against housing and school de facto segregation and inequality in Chicago and several suburbs, but the leaders feared too violent a response in Chicago Lawn and Cicero. Eventually, a substantial march (met by catcalls, flying bottles and bricks) was conducted in Chicago Lawn, but only a splinter group marched in Cicero. Chicago CORE –led by Lucas, was that splinter group.*

My activism began while I was at the Chicago Post Office. I was hired at the Post Office in late 1954. I stayed with the Post Office from 1954 until October 1967. Beginning in 1959, I was as active in CORE as much as I was on my job with the Post Office. I was with the Post Office until Henry McGee fired me in 1967.

Thereafter, I started going in and out of Detroit with James Boggs. Everyone had code names, or they were close to it. About eight of us in Chicago had joined the revolutionary circle. We had a truly revolutionary group around 1970-72. Institutional and policy change was too limited to address the challenges facing the country in this period.

CORE had placed me in KOCO (Kenwood Oakland Community Organization) in 1967. Subsequently, I had become the coordinator of the Leadership Training Program, via a Ford Foundation grant, provided to KOCO in 1969. Then I became the working Chairman of KOCO in 1972. Due to a lot of legal confusion, it was not until six months later that I actually took over at KOCO.

I was in Boggs's organization from 1971 to 1973 along with a handful of other Chicago black activists, including Edwin "Buzz" Palmer. Buzz was in the Chicago Police Department and got fired because of some allegations. But he was to remain among the principals in the Afro American Patrolmen's League. Earlier, Buzz had met with Boggs and brought the idea of forging unity with him back to the group. We joined. This transition turned out to be a short stint—marked by trying to apply a theory of social change in a community-based rather than a factory-based urban setting.

We had first encountered the reality and the real possibilities of informants operating inside movement organizations in the mid-1960s. This presence and our security became much more critical over the next few years. When informants were first identified, the impulse was to ostracize them and to boot them out. This was fruitless because now we did not know who among out midst were the police. We eventually found a more strategic use for them. Rather than turning them out, we decide to hold them dear to us. We figured that the next spy might not be so easily identifiable.

We treated them like unwanted wives. That is, we treated them like it was "cheaper to keep her." We knew who they were, but we might not find out who the next ones to come might be. There was one guy in our ranks who we found out was a spy. We sent him to get us lunch, to mop the floor, and other menial tasks. I had him drive me to my speaking engagements. One was to St. Joseph College in Rensselaer, Indiana. We never told him anything of substance, except what we wanted the police to know.

By the early 1970s, the black middle-class, pretty much, stopped participating in locally controlled municipal and state elections. They were inclined to lean on national Democratic Party candidates, hoping to revitalize the Roosevelt-Truman tradition in liberal social policies. To them, Chicago politics were nearly hopeless. Nevertheless, some of us did not give up the fight.

The Civil Rights Movement in Chicago was a qualified success; yet it failed. It failed not because of the actors and participants, but because of the intractable positions of white power elites that were linked to ethnic bases and were unwilling to go forward on a progressive agenda. They wanted to take back gains made during the War years and the 1950s. They wound up losing much more ground, due to the irrepressibility of the movement for social change.

When I joined CORE in 1959, it seemed that some sharecroppers in Tennessee, near Memphis, had tried to register to vote, the owners put the tenants off the farmlands near there. They were put up in tents. This was the first "tent city;" it was in Tennessee, than in Washington DC., with Dr. King and Robert Abernathy.

In those days there were not many socially aware Blacks. In the wake of this development, the "plantation politicians" did not like it. The William Dawson's, the Claude Holman's, and the Metcalfe's loathed this development because it challenged their position of political mis-leadership and cowardice before "Machine" power in Chicago.[26]

When I first met Bennett Johnson, the civil rights and social justice activist, it was around this struggle. Bennett, along with Brenetta Howell Barrett, Herman Gilbert, and Gus Savage, started the Negro Voter's League, on the west side of Chicago. These people were my heroes, back in the day. They ran a black legalist for City Clerk's office and they shocked everyone, when the candidate garnered 60,000 voters. This was a shock to the patronage system. It motivated other, would be, black politicians.

One of the so-called "silent six," (they were the silent six because they never said anything in City Council) Claude Holman was Alderman of the Chicago, 4th Ward. When

[25] William "Bill" Dawson (1886-1970), US Congressman from the 1st Congressional District of Illinois from 1946-1970. Dawson reputedly controlled the South side policy racket for a long time and was a principal in the establishment of currency exchanges, affectionately called "ghetto banks" in Chicago. Dawson was a long time Ward Committeeman and head of the black sub-machine, a subdivision of the Chicago patronage system. Claude Holman was a Chicago machine political hack who, as 4th Ward Alderman, was branded one of the "silent six," who never said anything publicly. During the R. J. Daley era his ward was one of the "automatic five" that the machine could count on to deliver a regular party vote in just the amount to suppress voter returns, thereby saving the bosses having to pay the voters. They could also be counted on to deliver massive votes in Gubernatorial, Senatorial and Presidential elections. Ralph Metcalfe Sr. was former 3rd Ward Alderman and Congressman who succeeded Dawson in Congress. Metcalfe Sr., the former Olympic sprinter and longtime protégé of William Dawson, succeeded Dawson in 1971 in Congress. Dawson was on of the silent six and the automatic Five in the Dawson sub-machine,. See J. Q. WIlson op. cIt.

Holman died in 1973 and they needed a replacement for him. Tim Evans was, nominated; that meant, "appointed." He was appointed by the Mayor to succeed Holman. Mayor Daley (I) told the 4th Ward, precinct captains that: "I want Tim." They thought themselves obliged to grant Daley his wish. They voted in Tim as Alderman.

Herman (Gilbert) and Bennett (Johnson) were in the same class as Brenetta (Barrett). They were militants. Bennett's militancy cost him his job. He had taught English in the Chicago Public Schools (CPS). Of the four of them, Gus (Savage) was the driving force. He was strategic in his thinking. They put out a booster newspaper. It was a voice of the independent radicalism, emerging in Chicago and was outside the "Machine."

(This brief paper is taken from the yet to be published memoir of the late Robert Lucas. It is co-written with Dr. Douglas Gill and included in this book because of the important role Robert Lucas played in Chicago's Black Struggle during the 60's.)

AFRIKAN LIBERATION DAY CELEBRATION

Photos courtesy of Kofi Moyo

Don L. Lee (Haki Madhubuti), Lerone Bennett, Jr., unidentified person and nephew of President Sekou Toure of Guinea

Dick Gregory

Afrikan Liberation Day Parade on State Street enroute to Washington Park

Dr. Anderson Thompson
Scholar/Historian
(Courtesy of Conrad Worrill)

(From left to right) Dr. Conrad Worrill, Dr. Jacob Carruthers, Ife Carruthers and Chester Spears
(Courtesy of Conrad Worrill)

Kelan Phi Cohran, Musician, Teacher, Composer
(Courtesy of Kofi Moyo)

Vernon Jarrett, Sterling Brown, Useni Eugene Perkins and Russell Patrice Perkins
(Courtesy of Useni Eugene Perkins)

Gwendolyn Brooks, Illinois Poet Laureate

John Lewis, founding member of the African American History Roundtable (Courtesy of Betty Lewis)

Ruwa Chiri, Pan-Afrikan Freedom Fighter from Zimbabwe (Courtesy of Sarudzayi Sevanhu)

(From left to right) Clarence Taylor, Okoro Harold Johnson and Abena Joan Brown (Courtesy of Useni Eugene Perkins)

Lerone Bennett, Jr., Historian/Scholar (Courtesy of Kofi Moyo)

Norman Brazelton, Barber with Bill "Skip" Davis (Courtesy of Norman Brazelton)

Dr. Margaret Goss Burroughs, Dr. Haki R. Madhubuti and Charlie Burroughs at Third World Press Anniversary
(Courtesy of Haki R. Madhubuti)

Afrikan community at grave of Dr. Bobby E. Wright at Oakwood Cemetary
(Courtesy of Conrad Worrill)

The Catalyst Family
(Courtesy of Useni Eugene Perkins)

(From left to right) Larry Crowe, Woodie King, Jr., Jackie Taylor, Haki R. Madhubuti, Ron Milner and Useni Eugene Perkins
(Courtesy of Useni Eugene Perkins)

(From left to right) Bob Crawford, Muhal Richard Abrams, Barbara Jones, Dr. Jeff Donaldson and Douglas Williams
(Courtesy of Roy Lewis)

(From left to right) Dr. Jacob Carruthers, Hannibal Tirus Afri, Dr. Conrad Worrill and Pat Hill
(Courtesy of Conrad Worrill)

(From left to right) Dr. George Kent, Val Gray Ward, Hoyt Fuller and Pemon Rami (Courtesy of Useni Eugene Perkins)

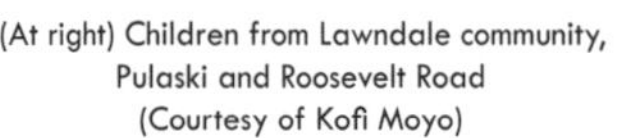

(At right) Children from Lawndale community, Pulaski and Roosevelt Road
(Courtesy of Kofi Moyo)

TELLING THE STORY OF THE CHICAGO AREA FRIENDS OF THE STUDENT NONVIOLENT COORDINATING COMMITTEE (CAFSNCC): PRESERVING THE PAST, INFORMING THE FUTURE

Fannie Rushing

In the early 1960s the Student Nonviolent Coordinating Committee (SNCC) was formed to coordinate the student sit-in movement for civil rights in the South.[31] As the movement grew and spread across the nation, support groups were formed in the major cities of the North. One of those northern groups was the Chicago Area Friends of SNCC (CAFSNCC). Its original purpose was to raise money and support the Southern movement. The oppressive and horrendous conditions that thousands of African Americans were experiencing in Chicago soon made it impossible for CAFSNCC to be a viable organization without becoming involved in local struggles. Between 1962 and 1965, CAFSNCC was catapulted into the leadership of the local movement in Chicago. This is a brief look at this little-known history, a review of some of the key moments within these struggles, the lessons learned and their ramifications for today and the future.

In the early sixties, SNCC was one of the least known of the major civil rights groups. It was distinguished from other organizations in ways that had implications for CAFSNCC and the early movement in Chicago. SNCC was organized by African American young people (at first primarily students); however, it soon became (and this was one of its strengths) an

[31] Specifically, the organization was formed at a conference held over Easter weekend (April 15-17, 1960) at one of the Historically Black Colleges and Universities (HBCU) Shaw University, the alma mater of the Fundi/Teacher, mentor and friend of SNCC, Ms. Ella Baker.

inter-generational organization that could seek counsel with Ella Baker, Fannie Lou Hamer, Mildred Forman Page and many others.

The organization was a secular, ecumenical one that drew on various traditions and respected diversity. SNCC was committed to participatory democracy and group consensus rather than to a leadership hierarchy that made decisions for everyone. Perhaps most importantly, it believed in understanding local struggles, listening to local people, and working with local organizations to realize their aspirations and goals as opposed to imposing an agenda from outside.

The involvement of CAFSNCC in local struggles did divert funds and attention away from its primary purpose of being a support organization for the Southern movement. This soon brought about a conflict within the organization in relationship to structure and purpose. However, given SNCC's commitment to listening to local people and local organizing, it was ethically difficult to say that CAFSNCC could not involve itself in these issues. In addition, James Forman, the executive secretary of SNCC, was from Chicago and had lived the Black experience in the city. It was he, along with his former teaching colleague Sylvia Fischer, who had been instrumental in founding CAFSNCC. Also, many of the Southern SNCC field staff, Jimmy Travis, Curtis Muhammad (Hayes), Charles (Chuck) McDew, and many others had been in Chicago for relatively long periods of time for fundraising, health care or the collecting of resources and were very familiar with the particular conditions in Chicago. The long debate sparked by this contradiction was instrumental in shaping and refining SNCC and CAFSNCC's understanding of the fundamental nature of racism and the struggle against it whether in the South or in the North.

CAFSNCC began to be pushed further beyond fundraising for the South when the CAFSNCC office and CAFSNCC were chosen by the other civil rights organizations in the city to coordinate the Chicago component of the 1963 March on Washington. The March allowed African Americans from all over the country to make a national statement about the ongoing nature of their oppression throughout the United States. Given that CAFSNCC did such a successful job in mobilizing and coordinating the Chicago contingent of the march, it is not surprising that other organizations in the city began to see the potential of CAFSNCC for organizing. The March on Washington highlighted the conditions of African Americans throughout the United States, and Chicago was no exception.

The Chicago Public School system was designed to facilitate the integration of the European immigrant population into the United States of the 19th and early 20th centuries. Having accomplished that goal by the mid-20th century, one of the primary goals of the public school system was the continued viability of the schools for the descendants of those earlier immigrants. Although the European immigrant population was diverse, a patchwork of self-contained, ethnically specific neighborhoods developed. Using a "neighborhood plan" tied the school system to residency. Extreme racial discrimination in housing meant that African Americans would be relegated to only certain areas on the South and West Sides designated for "coloreds/Negroes/Blacks" and that their children could only go to schools in those areas.[32]

Although the battle against the legal segregation of the public schools of Chicago had been fought and won by the African American community in the late 19th century, the public schools of twentieth century Chicago had become as segregated de facto as any schools in the South where there was legal segregation. In Chicago, de facto segregation was maintained by an all-white school board handpicked by the late mayor, Richard J. Daley. He and an avowedly racist superintendent of schools, Benjamin Willis, committed to the neighborhood school policy.[33]

By mid-century, as the white population of the city began its migration to the suburbs, the African American population of the city reached the largest numbers to date. It was a population with a large youth component. Schools in white areas drained by the suburban march had empty classrooms; whereas, schools in Black areas had bulging classrooms of fifty to fifty-five students often attending in double shifts. The logical solution outside of a segregationist construct would have been to abandon the neighborhood school policy and use empty classrooms to relieve overcrowding. Instead, in 1961, to prevent integration of the schools, Superintendent Willis came up with the idea and convinced the school board to approve the purchase of trailers to be used in the Black areas.[34]

In Chicago racism, segregation and discrimination were woven through the very fabric of the city, interconnecting and encompassing schools, housing, jobs and politics. A challenge to one part of the system challenged all the component parts. Although at various times, CAFSNCC challenged all the parts, it was the school system that was the most glaring

---

32 There were no signs indicating where those areas were, but who could and could not enter the "white only" areas was as established a policy as if there had been posted signs saying "white only" as in the South or Bantustan in apartheid South Africa. Not to know this would result in the Chicago Race Riot of 1918, when a fourteen-year-old boy swimming on an inner tube in Lake Michigan accidently drifted into the "white only" area and was stoned to death by a crowd of angry whites. Not satisfied by the death of the boy, gangs of whites stormed through the Black community, beating, burning, looting and killing until the National Guard finally restored "unequal" order—a story repeated on a much smaller scale whenever some hapless individual wandered into one of these areas.

33 Richard J. Daley (Boss) served as mayor of Chicago from 1955 until his death in 1976. Benjamin Willis had been selected to be superintendent of schools in 1953, a capacity he served in until driven from office by the citywide civil rights movement in 1966.

34 Long before the Federal Emergency Management Agency (FEMA) was hustling African Americans affected by Katrina into substandard trailers, Willis was hustling African American children into trailers and using them for classrooms.

for CAFSNCC and most of the major civil rights groups: Chicago Urban League, National Association for the Advancement of Colored People (NAACP), community organizations within the African American communities, The Woodlawn Organization (TWO) and liberal Euro American groups such as the Catholic Interracial Council (CIC) and Teachers for Integrated Schools (TIS). To mount a successful attack on de facto segregation required a citywide consensus and strategy.

The Coordinating Council of Community Organizations (CCCO) had been formed to mobilize for the March on Washington. The success of the march suggested that this was a forum where a campaign against de facto segregation could be launched. By the fall of 1963, the CCCO consisted of all the major civil rights groups, community organizations in the African American communities and some liberal Euro American groups. It was a tenuous coalition with many differing tendencies, principles and agendas. Coming up with common principles and agendas proved to be very difficult, but were ultimately determined by the overall severity of the problem. There were organizations such as the Chicago Urban League, that for years had been compiling statistics on the problem, those such as TWO that had been fighting against the Willis Wagons from the beginning, and CORE and CAFSNCC ready to adopt direct action tactics and strategies as extreme as the problem.

Precisely how the idea came about to call for a student boycott of the schools is determined by which of the members of the CCCO or participants you ask; it is shaded in the memories of all. The reasoning for calling the boycott is much clearer. The Board of Education received a per diem for each student enrolled in school per day. If students were not in school, it decreased the amount received. If the majority of the enrolled students boycotted the schools for one day, there would be a drastic reduction in the dollar amounts received by the school system.

In the organizing that led up to the first school boycott, the objectives and demands of the CCCO were made very clear: the end to overcrowding, double shifts and the Willis Wagons and the development of a long-range plan for ending segregation in the public schools. The CCCO issued a call for the first school boycott for October 22, 1963. Although the call came from the coalition, much of the organizing was carried out by CAFSNCC. This happened for several reasons: the reputation gained by CAFSNCC for organizing the Chicago contingent of the March on Washington; a commitment to organizing from the base; the ability to engage young people in the cause through the youth arm of CAFSNCC, High School SNCC; and the rhetoric and militancy of the fiery young co-chair of CAFSNCC, Lawrence Landry.

The Daley political machine, while allied with Willis and the school board, tried everything to prevent the boycott from taking place. However, they categorically refused to do the thing that could have prevented the boycott: getting rid of Willis and his wagons. The first school boycott virtually closed the Chicago Public Schools. More than 250,000 students boycotted the public schools and, instead, attended Freedom Schools throughout the city run by churches and community groups.

At the close of the school day, as was planned, students, parents, community activists, ministers and organizers staged an orderly, disciplined march in the downtown business district from the school board offices to City Hall. In spite of critics who had predicted chaos, the crowd of more than 300,000 marched, sang and protested without a single incident. The massive police presence assembled by the city to protect property was completely unnecessary, as movement picket captains and parade marshals saw to it that demonstrators obeyed every rule, and assembled and disassembled with precision.

Freedom Day I, October 22, 1963, sent a clear message to the Daley Machine, the school board and Willis. Determined to preserve inequality, segregation and discrimination, they became defensive and even more intransigent. A defiant and imperious Willis touted his credentials as an educator, claiming to know more about what was best for the school system than students, parents or the community. The mayor and the school board made it equally clear that Willis had their full support. At the same time conditions within the schools were deteriorating, making it evident that the struggle had just begun.

Inside the CCCO plans were being made to continue the fight. The tensions and contradictions within the fragile coalition began to heighten. What was happening within CCCO was not any different from what was happening in the United States in general as the Civil Rights Movement began spreading, deepening in intensity and moving in more militant directions. The struggle was making the diversity within the African American community more apparent.

By the beginning of 1964 the convener of the CCCO was Al Raby, an African American school teacher and head of the primarily white organization, Teachers for Integrated Schools. The media and the machine had begun to identify what they called the "moderate" forces within the coalition and those termed the "militants." The moderates—The Urban League, the NAACP, white liberal groups and some of the community groups—coalesced around Raby. The militants—CORE, CAFSNCC and some of the community groups—found their voice in the University of Chicago graduate social worker turned activist and co-chair of CAFSNCC, Lawrence Landry. The media and the machine tried to siphon off the moderates, raising Raby up in the press and speaking first to him while vilifying both SNCC in the South and CAFSNCC in Chicago.

The differences within the CCCO erupted over which strategy would accomplish the groups' common goal of getting rid of Willis and his wagons and improving education for African American students. The first boycott got the attention of the media, the mayor, Willis and the school board. The question was whether there should be another boycott or some other tactic such as negotiations. The answer was that the success of another boycott would solidify the position and allow negotiations from a position of strength. This hard-won debate by the militants, however, was about to split the organization in half. The second school boycott was called for February of 1964.

Knowing what the movement was capable of achieving, the Daley Machine used every device to prevent the boycott. Given the pressure brought to bear on CAFSNCC, it is amazing that a second boycott did take place. Church doors and others that had been open for the first boycott were now closed to the movement by order of Mayor Richard J. Daley. Perhaps the numbers were not as large as the first boycott, but they were large enough to establish that if not all the Black community was angry about the issue of schools, at least a significant portion was, and they were prepared to fight the battle "by any means necessary." And more importantly, the Daley Machine was not able to prevent them from struggling for change. The demonstrations and boycotts really signaled the beginning of the end of Benjamin Willis. By 1966 he was gone and a new era was starting in Chicago.

The involvement in, and success of the boycotts, made CAFSNCC begin to focus even more on Chicago problems. CAFSNCC made a decision to open a storefront community center (Freedom Center on 43rd and Cottage Grove.) It was to be in a separate location from the CAFSNCC office, funded separately, with its own agenda and staff. Monroe Sharp and Nate Jackson, two local people who had started working with CAFSNCC during the boycott, were to run the center and begin organizing around local issues. The community identified two issues as priorities: schools and housing. The Freedom Center was open and staff were working on the organizing of rent strikes by the spring of 1965. The center did not last for very long because forces unknown to us were already systematically planning its demise. Later, we would all come to know these forces as the Red Squad and the Counter Intelligence Program (COINTELPRO).[35] We now know that this program had been in existence at least since 1956 and that it allegedly ended in 1971.

What originally drew CAFSNCC into the CCCO and the movement around schools, were the Willis Wagons, overcrowding and segregation. However, in the course of struggle it became apparent that those things were only a part of the problem. What did it matter

[35] The Red Squad, a then secret division within the Chicago Police Department charged with spying on social activist organizations and people. It paled in comparison to the more sinister, sophisticated and comprehensive program of the FBI, COINTELPRO. J. Edgar Hoover, as the director of the FBI, was allowed large sums of money and license to subvert and destroy people and organizations involved in civil rights and social justice. COINTELPRO's activities went far beyond spying to actively destroying people and organizations through character assassination, torture, murder, creating fake organizations, disrupting meetings or anything to keep organizations from functioning.

if the wagons left AND the classrooms were less crowded and desegregated if students continued to learn the same curriculum, one that prepared them to uncritically reproduce the same relationships of domination and subordination. The real objectives should be those of the SNCC Freedom Schools of the South: teaching people to think critically, to analyze and evaluate their own issues in relationship to those of the larger society, and to change society to meet the needs of their own communities. In keeping with these ideas, CAFSNCC began organizing to create a Residential Freedom School for the summer of 1965.

The Residential Freedom School was to bring together students from schools in the North and schools in the South, so they could examine their common problems and develop a better understanding of the national system of racism, segregation and discrimination. It was to last for eight weeks, four of them in Chicago and four in Cordell, Georgia, where SNCC had a field project. Ambitiously, there were to be forty students, twenty from the South and twenty from the North. There were four full-time SNCC staff people: Judy Richardson, Sharon Jackson, John Love and Fannie Rushing, and various organizers scheduled to move in and out as guests. Although it was agreed that there would be Black history, the rest of the curriculum, following the Freedom School model, was to be open-ended. Rather than being committed to cover certain material within a given time frame, teachers were encouraged to be flexible and let the students' questions dictate the curriculum. Additionally, field trips had been arranged to places where students could raise questions about the similarities and differences between the North and the South, such as trips to the housing projects, Cook County Hospital and City Hall.

The Residential Freedom School proved to be a real organizing vehicle in the community since, as usual, CAFSNCC did not have any money. The school was completely supported by the community. Reverend Tynes at Monumental Baptist Church allowed the church to be used for the school. Women in the church helped with preparing food. The students were housed in the community. People donated all the food that was used.

With respect to the goals of the project, extraordinary experiences were had by all involved students as well as teachers. The Southern students could see that in the North there were neither signs nor legal impediments to equality, yet the Black condition was as much one of subordination as what they experienced in the South. For example, although Blacks could vote in Chicago, the only choice that they had was to vote for their continued subordination to the Daley Machine, his Black-face henchmen Congressman William Dawson and the Silent Six in the city council.[36] The Northern students came to realize that their

[36] As congressman of the First Congressional District, William Dawson was the most powerful African American politician in the city. However, he was the representative of Daley to the African American community, not the congressman for the African American community. Dawson was called the "Man," meaning Daley's man. Similarly, the growth of the size of the African American community resulted in six aldermanic seats in the city council. These

lives were just as threatened from gang violence in the North, as Southern students were from white terrorist gangs such as the KKK in the South. As teachers, we were amazed at the courage and bravery of the Southern students and their determination to make change even in the face of death. The northern students, in spite of the poor formal education they were receiving in school, had an extraordinary ability to evaluate their social reality critically and to look for solutions to problems.

The Freedom School, like the Freedom Center, had a shorter life in Chicago than planned and for many of the same reasons. They were in a neighborhood of great poverty and one that was seeing a growth in the development of larger and larger street gangs. The Southern Civil Rights Movement had not yet addressed these issues. The civil rights movement was drawing to a close and the Black Liberation Movement was just beginning. New strategies and tactics for change were being created. Finally, the Red Squad and COINTELPRO were perfecting their techniques for destabilizing organizations. For all these reasons, by the fall of 1965 the office and Freedom Center were closed and the organization of CAFSNCC came to an end.

These brief remarks could not possibly tell the entire or only story of CAFSNCC and the many people who were part of it, nor is it a comprehensive presentation of all the events of the period. The CAFSNCC story is an important story of the moment when the many strands within the African American community of Chicago came together to make their contribution to the freedom struggle. It was a moment when the African American people combined their strengths, demanded control of their communities and were able to change the existing reality to one that served their needs.

Three years ago some of the remaining members of CAFSNCC realized that many key people of the Civil Rights era were dying. They came together to initiate the Chicago SNCC History Project, 1960-1965. It is an oral history and archival project designed to recover and preserve the stories of the hundreds of people involved in whatever way with the organization and a creation of those important moments of Black history in Chicago in the early 1960s. The project began with a conference at Roosevelt University. It brought together people from across the nation who had been involved with SNCC and CAFSNCC, including in particular the SNCC Freedom Singers who told the story of the movement through music; a special memorial service to remember the then recently deceased James Forman, the executive secretary of SNCC; and the many freedom fighters who had

[36] Black aldermen were known as the "Silent Six" because they were silent on all the issues unless Daley told them to speak. CAFSNCC had participated in various campaigns to get rid of Dawson and the Silent Six, to no avail. However, the civil rights movement was gaining so much momentum that soon a serious fissure within the Daley Machine occurred when one of the six, Ralph Metcalfe, was forced to break with Daley in order to continue the support of his constituents.

departed this life.

After the conference it was decided to place all the materials and oral histories collected in an archive at the Carter G. Woodson Public Library, which houses the Vivian C. Harsh collection of African American history and is one of the most utilized public libraries in the city. Then the process of collecting oral histories began. In the fall of 2007 the Chicago SNCC History Project began working with students in three public high schools: Hyde Park, DuSable and Phillips. A group of approximately twenty students were identified by the service learning teachers as students who would be interested in the oral history project. After an intense six-week training program on the history of the movement, these students were taught how to do oral histories. They were then sent out into the community to find relatives or friends who had been involved in the Civil Rights Movement of the early sixties. Ultimately, these students will train others how to do so. The oral history tapes that they create will be stored at Carter G. Woodson. The Chicago SNCC History Project, 1960-1965, was created to preserve the past and in so doing pass on the history of Black empowerment as a legacy to a new generation so that they might use it to make their history their own.

THE PEOPLE'S BARBER: INTERVIEW WITH NORMAN BRAZELTON

Useni Eugene Perkins

PERKINS: Norman could you provide me a brief statement about your background and why did you decide to come to Chicago in the sixties?

BRAZELTON: I am the second eldest born to Mr. and Mrs. Curtis & Josephine Brazelton. I was raised with my siblings Norris Gene and Evelyn in South Haven, Michigan. I attended High School at Central and graduated in 1957.

I moved to Chicago to pursue an education degree at Woodrow Wilson Jr. College, as a Physical Education teacher. I stayed with my Uncle Frank who lived on the south side. Shortly after I moved I started working at Gills Grocery Land on 69th and Wentworth.

One Saturday night I was invited out by some friends to see the singing group The Pastels in Altgeld Gardens. The show was great but after the program a fight broke out on our way home. I told my Uncle Frank about the fight and he called my father who quickly picked me up and took me back to South Haven. I was confused and didn't know what I was going to do or what I wanted to do. I took the next year visiting family in California and trying to find myself.

In 1959 I came back to Chicago and started working at Speigel's for the Christmas rush and I got laid off. Then, I got a job at Evans Fur Company and I got laid off. Every time I got a job I could never keep it. In between jobs I was always asked by someone if I could cut their hair. I talked to my mother and told her of my troubles keeping a job and how I had been cutting hair on the side. She reminded me of how I always like cutting hair, and said "maybe that is your calling." She said she thought it was my gift, my God given talent.

I needed money so I found a job at Republic Steel and worked there for 3 months until I was fired. I drew my unemployment and that's when I decided I was going to Euroline Barber College. A couple of months into the program a gentleman named Arthur Hearn came to the college looking for a barber to work in his shop. He asked me how many hours I had, I told him I had only been enrolled for 2 months. He watched me cut hair and told me to take his card and said "you can cut hair good" and that I was good enough to work in his shop. I went to visit his shop on a day he was short a barber and very busy. He asked me did I bring my tools, "I said, no sir." He pointed to a chair and station where a barber used to work and told a young boy to get in the chair and I have been cutting hair ever since. I transferred to McCoy Barber College and got my license and never looked back. I continued to work for Arthur for the next eight years.

PERKINS: I understand that Arthur played an important role in your early career.

BRAZELTON: Yes Arthur was very instrumental in my career and personal life. He introduced me to the Muslim religion and the Nation of Islam. I became interested listening to a lot of Arthur's clients who were Muslims and members of the Nation of Islam. They came to the shop weekly to get their hair cut. They talked about empowering black men to own their own business and what our black community needed. I was so interested, I joined and served under the honorable Elijah Muhammad and Wallace D. Muhammad. I was a member for 10 years and I don't regret it.

PERKINS: When did the Afro or natural become popular in your barber shop?

BRAZELTON: During the '60s and '70s the "Natural" had been the popular hairstyle to cut. Toward the late '60s the trends of barbering and hair styles were changing. An adult haircut was $2.25 and $1.50 for children. The hairstyle that stands out the most to me was the Afro. The afro was created by Willie Morrow. It became popular not only for its precise round shape, but also because it required more than the normal barbering tools of clippers and shears. You had to have a pick and hair spray. The "clinched fist" pick became an iconic symbol for black pride and identity during the 60's and 70's Black Pride Movement. Its long metal teeth were perfect for picking coiled hair and shaping the Afro. I won many afro styling competitions.

PERKINS: Who were some of the noted people who you served?

BRAZELTON: In 1960 I was able to open my own barber shop, Lake Village at 1218 E. 47th Street. My clientele was growing fast. I began doing more locally known dignitaries such as; Reverend Clarence Cobb, Alderman Tim Evans, Singer Jerry Butler, Chicago Bulls athletes Clem Haskins and Walt Bellamy. I also had as customers such national celebrities as Meadowlark Lemon of the Globetrotters and the greatest heavyweight boxer of all time Muhammad Ali. All these men inspired me because they were doing something to help the Black community..

PERKINS: Could you comment on your struggle with the Barber's Union and how it affected your business?

BRAZELTON: I was a member of the Local 939 all black union for twenty years. I became a member like most barbers who wanted to join a Black owned organization. I had been a member of AFLCIO, who offered health benefits and retirement plans. When I moved my shop to Hyde Park at 1604 E 53rd Street, the shop was the largest barber and beauty Black owned shop in the city. I had 13 chairs, 7 barbers on one side and 6 beauticians adjoining on the other side. The union wanted me to sign up all of my beauticians, some of which were already in the union and make them pay dues. They began picketing, harassing and threatening me. They tried to intimidate and force my stylist to join and pay into their barber union. It was not affecting my business or clientele until one night I received a call that the shop had burned. The shop was gone.

PERKINS: I understand that you knew some members of the Blackstone Rangers and Rev. Curtis Burrell.

BRAZELTON: Yes the Blackstone Rangers was a very popular Chicago gang. I first met the Rangers through Curtis Burrell who was the Chairman of KOCO. He worked with the Blackstone Rangers and rival gangs. KOCO was dedicated to the community residents, but I mostly remember it helped inner city kids find jobs and enroll in trade schools. The program had many Blackstone Rangers as participants. I became most of their barbers. I cut Curtis Burrell hair but I never cut Jeff Fort's hair. The Blackstone Rangers had taken over some businesses in the area but not mine. They watched out for me and protected me.

PERKINS: How did you become involved in teaching barber classes at Pontiac Prison in the sixties?

BRAZELTON: I was at the State of Illinois Barber Competition when I was approached by a white lady named Mrs. Ruck. She complimented me on a haircut and styling of a young man and asked could she introduce me to her husband. He asked my name and said I got a problem. I am a Caucasian barber and I have a class of all black barbers at the Pontiac Correctional Prison, can you help me. I said yes, I got three barbers from the shop and once a month we went to the Pontiac Correctional Prison to teach barbering and the newest hairstyles. Jr. Chamber of Commerce sponsored the grant that paid us. I reached out to local Black hair product companies requesting donations of shampoo, sprays and we would take those with us.

PERKINS: What are some other highlights which you remembered during the sixties?

.

BRAZELTON: I was a member of Operation Push. It was an organization that helped the community and represented its residents. Rev. Barrow also helped me several times and was an advocate for my shop when it was being picketed by the union and supported me when the shop was burned down. As I look back at those days, a lot of things were going on and I was fortunate to have known many of the Black activists who were fighting to make things better for all people. Incidentally, I also cut and styled Rev. Jesse Jackson Sr., and his sons Usef, Jonathan and Jesse Jr.,. Thank you Brother Useni for allowing me to contribute to your book.

SECTION THREE

POLITICAL AWARENESS

"The Negro entered the struggle for political power in Chicago with many disadvantages. As one student has observed, individual success in politics depends on access to large campaign funds, on the support of the daily newspapers, on a certain measure of social prestige, and on political experience and insight. The Negro had none of these advantages."

Black Metropolis by
St. Claire Drake and Horace H. Cayton

REFLECTIONS FROM DANNY DAVIS

Congressman Danny Davis

I was born on September 6, 1941 and came north in 1961 during the last big wave of black migration from the South. The pattern was that as children grew up and became adults (in some cases after going to college), they left home. In some instances whole families would leave, but my family left Arkansas one by one. There was usually somebody from my hometown who had already moved to Chicago, had housing and a job, and had a place for us to live in the city until such time as we could find our own housing.

I came to Chicago soon after receiving my B.A. degree, although I stayed home for a couple months to help my father harvest his crops because we were sharecroppers. Once we finished with the harvest in July 1961, I left Arkansas and traveled north to Chicago where I had two sisters living in the North Lawndale community. By that time North Lawndale was considered a big "problem area" in the city. It was 5 ½ square miles wide with a population of 125,000 squeezed into a very small area, so it was too many people living in too little space. There was no place to move in the city since to the west of us Cicero was forbidden territory to African Americans. Instead, we went further north of our neighborhood, but even that was limited in terms of available housing for African Americans.

My first job in Chicago was at the post office, and soon after I became a teacher at Magellan School at 3600 W. Ogden. The student body was all African American, and the school was for over-aged, underachieving kids who were between 15 and 17 years old with a reading score of 4.0. Our kids had been to correctional schools like Logan or Montefiore or they came straight from co-ed facilities at St. Charles or Geneva. A few of them were girls who had become pregnant the year before. So, Magellan School was a repository for kids with troubled pasts. When we opened the kids were given the opportunity to name the school. They suggested the name Magellan both in honor of Ferdinand Magellan, the famous explorer, and to recognize that our school was a new experiment and exploration by the Chicago Public School system. Magellan worked quite well because it had small class sizes and dedicated teachers.

We were all new, young teachers in those years, full of hope and belief in the Civil Rights Movement, how we could be a part of it, and a desire to make certain the kids learned. I liked it there so much that I used to arrive at school every morning before 8:00 am. The janitor and I became the best of friends because I would be waiting there for him to open the door. I taught for six years in the Chicago Public Schools system and when I left I was so dedicated to my job that I had only taken two days off: one day to be examined for the Army and another day because I was dating a young lady who wanted to go to the zoo.

I decided to go to Chicago State for my master's degree because it was accessible and I could attend in the evenings after teaching. A bunch of us did the same thing, and by going a couple evenings a week we were able to get six credits a semester and do it without any real disruption.

I actually had two jobs while I went to graduate school: teaching at Magellan and my part-time job at the post office. Then I added a third job by working at Sears, Roebuck.

I became involved in the Civil Rights Movement and we just considered it a normal thing to do because we had started joining the protests when I was in college in Arkansas. Dr. Martin Luther King, Jr. had come to speak to us and we had demonstrations and protests against discrimination. The atmosphere of change was so great at that time, as well as the possibility of things being different. It led to programs resulting from the Civil Rights Movement, and my involvement in the Movement contributed to my active participation in politics.

In addition to my regular teaching I was also instructing GED students at night at a community agency called the Lawndale Urban Progress Center. I taught an elderly lady how to read and she was so overjoyed that she said to me, "You've got to meet my goddaughter because both of you like to do things for people." So, I met Rose Marie Love, a precinct captain who was working at the Urban Progress Center. Rose was a real advocate for the neighborhood and the people, so we would talk every night after my class because she was the assistant director and responsible for closing up the Center at night. She was also on the board of the Greater Lawndale Conservation Commission, and then Chairman of the Commission's personnel committee. The executive director had just been fired and Rose convinced me to apply for the job. I said, "Okay, it sounds like some interesting stuff" and took the job in 1969. Also, I was involved in the Lawndale community, going to meetings, and getting my "feet wet."

The Greater Lawndale Conservation Commission was the main neighborhood organization in North Lawndale at the time, although the Lawndale People's Planning and Action Conference was emerging. These two groups had a big split, as they became involved in a community organization dispute. Warner Saunders was a key player in the other group. The people who remained were more closely aligned with City Hall. The split between the two Lawndale organizations was based on opposing views about how to redevelop the neighborhood as well as their relationship with City Hall. One group figured that it was better to do whatever City Hall said while the other group had some younger and more action-oriented people who opposed that approach.

Even though I was with the Greater Lawndale Conservation Commission when the split came, I was more philosophically aligned with the other group and didn't view them as the enemy. I didn't last too long with the Conservation Commission and quit to become part of a new community health center known as the Martin Luther King, Jr. Health Center. I had the position of director of training, and that's how I developed my interest in health care. Then I decided to get a Ph.D, with a focus on health, and became involved nationally in the National Association of Community Health Centers and locally in the West Side Association for Community Action in the late 60s.

In the sixties, my congressman was white and even after the area changed the last congressman elected was a white man. When Brennetta Howe Barrett ran for Congress, her white opponent had died the Friday before the election. The dead congressman still got elected and that became an incentive for us to change the political environment in the neighborhood. As I became involved in politics, I learned that practically everybody was part of the Democratic "Machine." You would be dealing with somebody and think that because the person was a civic leader or had a political job that they were free to do what they wanted to do. Then, you would discover that the arms of the "machine" were long and wide. Although you may not have had to deal with City Hall on all of these issues, people felt like they were required to do it. City Hall was perceived to be all-encompassing and all-empowering by a vast majority of the people.

Toward the end of the 1960s, one of the most important issues was to expose the great disparities that existed between African Americans and whites. That was the big revolution in the minds of black people and when poor blacks arrived in search of the "promised land," they discovered that they had moved North just to live in another kind of slavery on Chicago's West and South Sides. That "slavery" meant living in overcrowded, rat and roach infested tenements. Many of these people had never seen rats and roaches because they lived out in the country where they had plenty of space. Although they had lived in shacks and shanties in the South, those structures could be kept clean. Even though some African Americans thought about moving back South, they knew that the only jobs were sharecropping and picking cotton for $.30 an hour. The only real option for African Americans in Chicago was to improve their own living conditions. Of course, African Americans loved going back South for visits, especially if they had a car to show off in their hometowns and appear to have newfound wealth. In truth, they had just enough money to buy gas to get back to Chicago.

By the mid-60s, Dr. Martin Luther King, Jr. had become such an icon for African Americans that those of us caught up in the notion of change worshipped him and the positions he took on the issues. You could walk down the streets of Chicago's West Side and listen to his speeches playing on music store public address systems. We all tried to emulate King's speech, and you could listen to him and feel chills and shudders running through your body. When he was assassinated, of course there was no way we could contain our reactions to his death. Some thought that there may be a way to curtail some of the violence and, initially, we were out on the streets trying to protect our children and help control the situation. However, we immediately discovered that it was impossible.

Sadly, the resulting rioting and looting led to great destruction in the West Side. During the weekend following his assassination, I was in a car with a friend of mine who was very middle class. As a matter of fact, his school and hometown were named after his father, so it was not like he didn't have certain values. We were in the car when all of a sudden he began to drive crazily. I said to him, "Man, you're running the lights. Why are you doing that?"

His response was, "Everybody's running the lights."

I said, "But, just because everybody's running the lights doesn't mean we have to do the same thing since the police could arrest you."

He said, "Today, we are the police!" He drove his car right through the glass window of a supermarket and just jumped out and began gathering up cartons of cigarettes and whiskey and putting them into the car.

My reaction was to get out of his car. I was a young school teacher and I didn't want to be arrested. He said, "Aw, c'mon man, what are you waiting on? Everybody's doing it." But I ignored his comments and just got out of the car. In my mind it didn't change him or make him a bad person. Like so many other people, he was simply caught up in the emotions of the moment and expressing uncontrollable rage about what had happened to Dr. King. People in the neighborhood who were breaking the law by looting saw all of this simply as acts of civil disobedience. But I had grown up in an environment of order and respect for the law. My mother used to tell us to do what is right, and that "wrong is wrong" and "right is right." So, all of those events after the assassination were different experiences for me.

Although some wealthier African Americans did move to suburban communities, they got out of the city because they didn't feel that they should subject their children to life in the ghetto. While I have always stayed, I could understand why some of the people decided they had to go. It is unfortunate that we have not done enough to help people from our community with their upward mobility, but the 60s got us to start thinking about how to make that happen. When you think of the impact that John F. Kennedy and Martin Luther King, Jr. had on us, the federal and local governments, and the Civil Rights and anti-war movements, they were an important way to get people involved in their communities. As a result, I would maintain that the 1960s was one of the most important decades in contemporary American life.

[Reprinted from Chicago in the Sixties: Remembering a Time of Change, *edited by Neal Samors]*

THE GREATEST BLACK GENERATION

Rev. Kwame John R. Porter

I am grateful to Useni E. Perkins for suggesting that I join others in reflecting and writing about my experiences in the Chicago Freedom struggles from 1960 until 1975. I have chosen to write on this topic for two reasons. First, I tend to think and write in generational terms. Second, I read award winning journalist, Tom Brokow's multi-volume book, *The Greatest Generation*. Brokow chose the post-depression World War II generation (1929-50) as the greatest American generation. While Brokow chronicles the many achievements of that generation, he gave only scant recognition to the many sacrifices and achievements of African-Americans.

It is difficult singling out any one generation as greater than another. I believe that we can cite examples of sacrifices and achievements in each Black generation since 1619. However, in a short essay, I can only summarize their contributions. My assigned task is to spend most of this essay on "The Greatest Generation between 1960 and 1975." Each Black generation continued the Freedom struggle passed onto it from the generation that came before them. A generation is believed to be about 25 to 30 years. The first generation was from the West Coast of Africa. They did not volunteer to come to America. These captive Africans were brought to Jamestown, Virginia in 1619 and to Plymouth, Massachusetts in 1620.

The first generation (i.e. a strong core of them on every plantation) passed on at least four things to the next generation from 1619 until 1800: a sense of undying hope for freedom, resistance, surviving and ways of escaping (running away from the plantation) slavery. From these experiences those in the South formed the first African Baptist churches. Those in the North founded the African Methodist Episcopal (AME) and the African Methodist Episcopal Zion churches (AMEZ). Slave revolts shook up the slave system and laid the foundation for Dr. Martin R. Delaney's 1852 Back to Africa Movement. The U.S. government passed the Fugitive Slave Act in 1851 as a means of helping the South hunt down Africans who escaped from slavery. The Abolitionist Movement started during this period. The following generational events helped to shape the freedom struggle for this era: the Civil War, the Reconstruction Era, the Post Reconstruction Era, the birth of the Ku Klux Klan (KKK), the birth of Jim Crow and legal segregation in 1876, the first great Northern Migration, the Plessey vs. Ferguson decision, the Hayes vs. Tilden Compromise and the founding of the historic Black Colleges and Universities (1860-1900), the 13th, 14th, and 15th Amendments to the U.S. Constitution.

Some of the key 19th century leaders were Frederick Douglass, Henry Highland Garnett, Henry McNeil Turner, Sojourner Truth, Edward Blyden, Harriett Tubman, Booker T. Washington, Ida B. Wells, Martin R. Delaney, Nat Turner, the 22 Blacks elected to the U.S. Congress, etc. During this era the 13th Amendment, abolishing slavery, the 14th Amendment, the equal protection clause, and the 15th Amendment, the right to vote were passed. The institutional development of the Black struggle was carried on into the early 20th century with the founding of the Niagara Movement (Forerunner of the NAACP), the National Urban League, the National Council of Colored Women, the rapid growth of Black Methodist, Baptist, and Pentecostal denominations. During the 1920s, New York's Harlem Renaissance became the cultural, literary and entertainment capital of Black America.

Marcus Garvey founded the Universal Negro Improvement Association (UNIA), which had a membership of 2 million based in New York and in cities across the country. Jack Johnson reigned as the first great Black heavy weight boxing champion (1900-1915). During U.S. President Franklin Delano Roosevelt's tenure (1932-45), a Black cabinet of leaders emerged as advisor to the President on colored issues. Included in this generation of leaders were Dr. Mary McLeod Bethune, Dr. Jane Nabrit, Attorney Charles Houston, Dr. Adam Clayton Powell, Sr., Walter White and Ralph Bunche. Dr. Bethune influenced national policy by working with Eleanor Roosevelt, the President's wife.

Joe Louis was our second great heavy weight champion (1937-50). Jesse Owens was our first Olympic track great (1936), the Black Tuskegee Airmen distinguished themselves during WWII, and George Washington Carver literally saved white Southern agriculture during the early part of the 20th century. The white medical establishment (U.S. Public Health Establishment) experimented on 399 Black men with syphilis from 1932-1972 in the poorest counties in Alabama. Most of these poor, illiterate sharecroppers consented to the experiment even though penicillin as a cure had been invented. Over half of these men died because they did not receive penicillin. Black journalists continue to tell and write our story through Black newspapers and print materials. Paul Robeson and Roland Hayes became international literary stage and screen stars. Lena Horne received national fame through the 1947 movie, Stormy Weather. President Harry S. Truman desegregated the U.S. Armed forces in 1945. (He also dropped the atomic bombs on the Japanese cities of

Hiroshima and Nagasaki, killing thousands of Japanese people in 1945.) John H. Johnson, President of Johnson Publishing Company, founded Ebony and Jet Magazine in 1942. Restrictive Housing covenants were passed in 1948 to prevent Blacks, Asians, Latinos, and other non-whites from renting, buying, and owning housing and businesses in white areas. The largest Black churches in Chicago during the 1940s were Pilgrim Baptist, Progressive Baptist, Tabernacle Baptist, Quinn Chapel AME, First Baptist on the West Side, St. Paul C.O.G.I.C., Liberty Baptist, St. Mark Methodist, etc.

During the late 1940s into the 1950s, Blacks began dominating such music as jazz, blues, rhythm and blues, Gospel music, and crossover balance. Singers Nat King Cole, Sam Cooke, Sarah Vaughn, Ella Fitzgerald, Dinah Washington, Billy Eckstein, Joe Williams, Mahalia Jackson, Shirley Ceasar, Roberta Martin, The Five Blind Boys, and the Soul Stirrers emerged as the top Black singers of that era. Jackie Robinson integrated Major League baseball (MLB) in 1945-1947. The National Football League (NFL) and the National Basketball Association (NBA) began integrating its teams in 1947. The Harlem Globetrotters were the most popular basketball team in the world during this period. Paul Robeson was under attack for accepting an international Peace prize from Russia. The Rev. George Lee was killed by the KKK for attempting to register Black people to vote in Belzoni, Mississippi in 1951. The U.S. Supreme Court outlawed racial segregation in public schools on May 17, 1954. On August 28, 1955 14-year-old Emmett Till from Chicago's South Side was brutally murdered by the KKK in Money, Mississippi. In December 5, 1955, Rosa Parks refused to give up her seat to a white man. Black people boycotted the busses in Montgomery, Alabama for 385 days. Dr. King and a group of Southern Ministers founded the Southern Christian Leadership Conference (SCLC) in 1957. Ghana became the first independent African nation in 1957. In 1957 Mrs. Daisy Bates, a NAACP leader, led nine brave Black high school students into the all-white central High School of Little Rock, Arkansas. President Dwight Eisenhower had to call up the National Guard to protect these Black students from thousands of racist whites who tried to prevent them from entering.

In Chicago the democratic machine formed the Chicago Housing Authority (CHA), which built over fifty 28-story high-rise buildings to contain the growing Black population (Cabrini Green - 1942; Stateway Gardens - 1955; Robert Taylor Homes - 1962). The Chicago political machine also took over the Chicago NAACP Chapter—the strongest NAACP chapter in the country. As a result, they registered over 2000 people who voted out the militant NAACP leadership. In 1955 Mayor Richard J. Daley emerged to become the most powerful machine based mayor in Chicago's history.

Chicago as an industrial center had declined by the mid-1950s. Gone were over 500,000 jobs in the meat packing companies, steel and auto industries, railroad industries, long shore man industries, light and heavy manufacturing, etc. The growth and expansion of the retail industry declined in Chicago's Black communities (this opened the door for Asians, Arabs, and others to take over the retail industry in Black communities). Blacks continued to be locked out of the building and trade unions and their control over training. The only areas where Blacks experienced some growth were in politics, sports, entertainment, beauty/barber shops, the funeral business, and the church.

This intergenerational greatness from 1619-1960 became the foundation for the late 20th century Freedom (Civil Rights) Movement.

1960-1965

During the 1960s, Muhammad Ali emerged as our new national boxing hero. Malcolm X and the Honorable Elijah Muhammad became household names alongside Dr. Martin Luther King, Jr., Stokely Carmichael, and the Black Panthers, renewing interest in Africa. *Ebony* and *Jet* Magazine continued to inspire Black people with images of local and global progress for Africans and African Americans. On February 1, 1960 the sit-in movement began when four Black students from North Carolina A&T refused to move to the "Colored section" of a local Woolworth (5 and 10 cents) restaurant section of the store. In 1961 the Freedom Riders were born in Nashville, Tennessee when white and Black students integrated interstate bus stations. Also in 1961 Margaret Burroughs founded the DuSable Museum of African American History and named it after Chicago's founder Jean Baptiste Pointe DuSable, a Haitian trader who was the first permanent settler.

There were people like myself who became involved in the freedom struggle from its beginnings in 1960. I promised Dr. Martin Luther King, Jr. in 1958-1959 that he could count on me during and after seminary. I was part of the leadership group that created a C.O.R.E. (Congress of Racial Equality) chapter in Evanston, Illinois in February 1960. I became a student assistant at the Normal Park Methodist Church in Chicago's Englewood community in 1960-1962 (the late Rev. Harry Conner was the pastor of Normal Park Methodist Church). In April 1962, I was appointed Pastor of the Christ United Methodist Church in the Englewood community.

In July 1962 I received a telegram from Dr. Martin Luther King, Jr. inviting me to join him at SCLC's 1st mass nonviolent demonstration in Albany, Georgia. After praying with my wife, I decided to join Dr. King and others in this demonstration. After six days in an Albany jail, I came back to Englewood to begin organizing in three ways:

1. I began appealing to Dr. King and the SCLC to start a chapter in Chicago.
2. I began organizing a local Englewood civic group (The Englewood Civic Organization).
3. A group of us joined the newly organized CCCO (Coordinating Council of Community Organizations). From 1961-66 the CCCO was comprised of sixty citywide organizations that were formed to challenge the almost absolute control that the Mayor of Chicago had over the city (Richard J. Daley, 1955-76). We organized two massive school boycotts, which forced the mayor to shut down the Chicago Public School (CPS) system.

The Freedom Movement Leaders during this period in Chicago included: Bill Berry, President of the Chicago Urban League; Albert Raby, Public School Teacher and Co-Convener of CCCO; Attorney James Montgomery and Attorney Anna R. Langford; Rev. Arthur Brazier, President of The Woodlawn Organization (T.W.O.); Bob Squires, T.W.O. Executive Director; Jorja English, Secretary CCCO; Larry Landry, Organizer of the first mass Chicago school boycott; Chester Robinson, Executive Director, Westside Organization; Nancy Jefferson, Westside Leader; Brenetta Barrett Howell, Executive Director of Illinois Black United Fund; Robert Lucas, Chairman of Chicago's C.O.R.E.; Frederick Douglas Andrews, Westside Leader; Bill Hogan, Catholic Interracial Council; John Egan, Catholic Interracial Council; John McDermott, Catholic Interracial Council; Attorney E. Duke McNeil, T.W.O. Leader; Squire Lance, T.W.O. Organizer; Joseph Gardner, T.W.O. Organizer; Bennett Johnson, Past Press; Attorney Kermit Coleman; Attorney Bill Cousins; Rose Simpson, Englewood Leader; Attorney Larry Kenon; Dr. Timuel Black, Historian; Dr. Anderson Thompson, Historian; Dr. Harold Pates, retired Chicago City College President; Rev. Earl Sardin, Community Activist from the 1930s and 40s; Dr. Conrad Worrill, Director of the Jacob H. Carruthers center for Inner-city Studies; Dr. Earl Durham, Social Work Administrator; Dr. James Mack, Pastor of the South Congregational Church, Secretary, CCCO; Dr. Barbara Sizemore, Author and Educator; William L. Dawson, Major Democratic Power Broker between 1940-80; Don Rose, Political Strategist, Alderman Leon DesPres, Rev. Ed Riddick and Rev. Bill Griffin, Lutheran Church of Chicago.

The writings of Lerone Bennett, *Before the Mayflower* (1962); James Baldwin, *The Fire Next Time* (1963); Alex Haley, *Autobiography of Malcolm X* (1965); Dr. Martin Luther King, Jr., *Stride Toward Freedom* (1957); the Nation of Islam's Newspaper, *Mohammed Speaks;* Brother Curtis Ellis's first Black bookstore located on 64th & Cottage Grove called **Ellis's Bookstore** gave our movement updated intellectual credibility in the eyes of the world and made the Chicago Freedom movement one of the most important in our struggle.

We in Chicago, adopted some of the freedom songs from the Southern movement: "We Shall Overcome," "Ain't Gonna Let Nobody Turn Me Around," "Oh Freedom," "This Little Light of Mine," "If You Miss Me at the Back of the Bus," "God on Their Side," "The Day They Killed Medgar Evers," "Where Have All the Young Men Gone," "We Shall Not Be Moved," "Michael Row Your Boat Ashore," "If I Had A Hammer," "Blowing in the Wind," etc.

1965-1975

During this phase of our struggle, several new leaders and organizations emerged. While a few individual pastors were included during the 1960-65 phase, Black Pastors and churches (in fact, Black, white and mixed churches) were involved: Rev. Clay Evans - Pastor, Fellowship Baptist Church; Father George Clements - Pastor, Holy Angels Catholic Church, Rev. Jesse L. Jackson - National Director, Operation Bread Basket; Rev. Willie T. Barrow - Vice President, Operation Bread Basket; Dr. Calvin Morris - Assistant Director, Operation Bread Basket; Dr. Arthur Griffith - Pastor, First Congregation Baptist Church; Dr. Shelvin Hall - Pastor, Friendship Baptist Church; Dr. Maceo Pembroke - Pastor, St. Mark United Methodist Church; Warren Avenue Congregational Church; Bishop Louis H. Ford, late President of the Church Of God In Christ; Dr. Hycel Taylor - Pastor, Second Baptist Church of Evanston, Illinois and Professor/Director of The Church and the Black Experience at Garrett Evangelical Theological Seminary; the founding of Black Methodist for Church Renewal. On the national scene President Johnson appointed Thurgood Marshall to the U.S. Supreme Court. The Rev. Clarence Hilliard and Dr. William H. Bentley were - Leaders of the National Black Evangelical Association; Dr. A.P. Jackson - Pastor, Liberty Baptist Church; Rev. Henry O. Hardy- Pastor, Cosmopolitan Community Church; Rev. T.L. Barrett - Pastor, Life center Church; and Rev. John R. Porter, Chicago Center for Black Religious Studies and Pastor of Christ United Methodist Church. A secret group found the Black People's Topographical Center on E 75th street.

The phenomenal growth of Chicago's Black Youth Gangs is to be noted: Bobby Gore, President of the Vice Lords; Jeff Fort, President of the Blackstone Rangers/El Rukens; David Barksdale and Larry Hoover, Co-Presidents of the Black Gangster Disciples; Mickey Cogwell, Founder of the Mickey Cobras (Cobra Stones). The underground drug economy fueled territorial rivalries leading to a growth in homicides. The Illinois Black Panther Party, led by Chairman Fred Hampton, Mark Clark, and Bobby Rush came into being in 1967 to defend the Black community against Police violence and other forms of corruptions. Useni Eugene Perkins became the first major writer to address this problem when he wrote, *Home is a Dirty Street: The Social Oppression of Black Children* (1975).

The Chicago Black arts movement came into being and began creating outdoor and indoor murals all over Chicago, raising up a new generation of Black poets and writers and producing several new forms of Black music. Phil Cohran, Oscar Brown, Jr., Richard Abrams, Co Co Taylor, bobby Guy, Albertina Walker, the Barrett Sisters, the Staples singers, Curtis Mayfield, Jerry Butler, The Dells, Gene Chandler, The Impressions, Aretha Franklin, The Temptations, The Jackson Five, The Supremes, Chuck Jackson, Isaac Hayes, James Brown, Ray Charles, and others were leaders in creating a new African and freedom music. Also during this time in Chicago, Val Gray Ward created the Kuumba Theater on the South Side, Abena Joan Brown created ETA theatre on the South Side and Jackie Taylor founded the Black Ensemble on the North Side. Haki Madhubuti emerged as a renowned Chicago poet and publisher at Third World Press during this period.

Chicago became the cultural center for Kwanzaa celebrations. Kwanzaa is an Africanized non-heroic cultural holiday founded by Dr. Maulana Ron Karenga in 1967. In Chicago Malcolm X College, Kennedy King College, Olive Harvey College and the South Shore Cultural Center served as the primary centers where annual celebrations are held.

Dr. Martin Luther King, Jr. and the Southern Christian Leadership Conference (SCLC) staff were invited to Chicago by CCCO, SCLC and other Chicago groups in 1966, creating the Chicago Freedom Movement. Dr. King and Al Raby served as Co-Conveners of the Chicago Freedom Movement. The Chicago Freedom Movement successfully broke racially segregated housing through a series of mass demonstration in all white communities. This movement opened up the restricted housing market for thousands of Blacks, Hispanics, Asians, and Arabs throughout the city. These communities include Belmont-Cragan, South Deering, Gage Park, Marquette Park, etc.

The assassination of Dr. Martin Luther King, Jr. on April 4, 1968 was a defining moment for America. Dr. King was the moral and prophetic epicenter for black people and America. His death created a vacuum, which no one has been able to fill and which represented the end of the Civil Rights era. Mayor Daley issued a "shoot to kill" order in the late summer of 1968 during the turbulent Democratic National Convention, which was held in Chicago during this time. A Black leader issued a counter statement which said, "All white people must be out of the Black community by 6:00pm daily." For a brief time Chicagoans, Black as well as white, were petrified with fear. Chicagoans continued the freedom struggle and the Rev. Jesse Louis Jackson, Sr. and Operation Bread Basket emerged with a portion of the King dream.

The U.S. Government apparently decided to destroy the Black Panther Party nationally. In Chicago, on December 4, 1969, the Illinois Black Panther Chairmen, Fred Hampton and

Mark Clark were assassinated on the Westside of Chicago by Chicago Police. No one was ever brought to justice for their murders.

The Black Political base expanded from the "silent" six Negro aldermen (1960-65) to twice that number by 1975. The Black Chicago population had grown from 500,000 in 1965 to over 1 million in 1975. Blacks began to flex their voting muscle and saw that within a few years they could control more than one U.S. Congressional District. Black representation in the U.S. Congress increased from 5 Congressman to 20 Congressman by 1975. The Public School system continues to deny full and equal access to a quality education for all Black children. Whites sought to gerrymander school districts so that white children would attend white public and private schools. The late Dr. Barbara Sizemore and other serious Black educators attacked these attempts at limiting the quality of educational opportunities for Black children. Dr. Donald Smith founded the Center for Inner City Studies at Northeastern Illinois University in 1967-69. Thousands of jobs continued to leave the urban sectors of America. Black Public School children continued to drop out in record numbers, perform poorly on test, and fill up jails and juvenile detention centers. This continues to be our greatest challenge, creating a public school system which will guarantee each child a quality education and equal protection under the U.S. Constitution. And another is opening up the building trades and career studies which lead to permanent employment and good paying jobs for Black men and women.

In this limited version of the struggle, we stand on the shoulders of living and deceased generations of Africans who make it possible for us to continue this great emancipation struggle today. This generation must continue to struggle for freedom and fulfill the unfinished agenda of those who went before them.

REFERENCES AND NOTES

Baldwin, James (1963). *The Fire Next Time.* Dial Press.

Bennett, Jr., Lerone (1966) *Before the Mayflower A History of the Black Negro in America 1619-1966 The Classic Account of the Struggles and Triumphs of Black Americans.* Chicago Johnson Publishing.

Brooks, Gwendolyn, *Bronzeville Boys and Girls* (1945). Harper Collins.

Cayton, Horace, *Black Metropolis: A Study of Negro Life. Life in a Northern City* (1945). University of Chicago Press.

Drake, St. Claire, Black Metropolis: A Study of Negro Life. Life in a Northern City (1945). University of Chicago Press.

DuBois, W.E.B. (1903) The Souls of Black Folks: Essays and Sketches. Chicago –A.C. McClurg & Co.

Franklin, John Hope. (1947) *From Slavery to Freedom: A History of African Americans.* McGraw-Hill Education.

Frost, Robert. (1874-1963) Poet.

Gates, John Henry. (2000) *Africana: The encyclopedia of the African and African American Experience.* Perseus

Haley, Alex. (1965) *The Autobiography of Malcolm X*

King, Jr., Martin Luther. (1957) *Stride Toward Freedom*

Perkins, Useni. (1975) *Home is a Dirty Street: The Social Oppression of Black Children.* Third World Press.

Perkins, Useni. (1986) *The Explosion of Chicago's Black Street Gangs: 1900-2000.* Third World Press.

Ralph, James, *Chicago Freedom Movement.*

Royko, Mike. (1972) *Boss: Richard J. Daley of Chicago.* Dutton.

Travis, Dempsey. (1981) *An Autobiography of Black Chicago.* Urban Research Institute.

Woodson, Carter G. (1933) *The Miseducation of the Negro.* Africa World Press

ONE MAN'S VIEW OF THE STRUGGLE

Charles Davis

When the civil rights activities of the 1960s and 1970s are discussed in my presence, I am reminded of the response of Madame Patel (at the time the African National Congress Party Whip in the Parliament of the Republic of South Africa), when she was asked by a friend, "When did you join the Movement?"

"If you were educated, you were always part of the Movement," Mme. Patel answered my friend, and this, I am sure caused him to think of the broader implications of his question. Her answer is also instructive to anyone who wishes to understand the activities and changes that took place during one of the most exciting and encouraging periods in the human rights struggle in America. Mme. Patel, it should be noted, is Black and the granddaughter of the late Prof. Z. K. Matthews. She spent part of her life in exile in England. After returning to South Africa at the end of the Apartheid era, she joined the leadership of her party and was elected to the legislature.

She is a part of the continuum of the human rights struggle that is worldwide. Her grandfather was the principal of the Fort Hare School, a college for Blacks in South Africa. The school trained many like Mme. Patel and her parents, who were forced to leave the country for their activism; and others like Nelson Mandela, who stayed at home and were jailed. Prof. Matthews visited the U.S. in 1948 and warned that the National Party that was coming into power would initiate more drastic repression of Blacks than what already existed in segregated South Africa. The brutal repression he warned of provoked domestic violence and international condemnation, and after twenty years the National Party was forced to relinquish power.

This anecdotal reference to three generations of activism in one family is unfamiliar to most Americans. This reality hints at the disconnection between activists in the sixties and seventies, and their elders who, educated or not, were "...always part of the Movement."

I was an observer of, and sometimes a participant, in the changes leading up to the sixties and seventies. My work, and later my business gave me these opportunities. Beginning in 1946, I worked for the *Chicago Defender* as a reporter, editor, and member of management. This enabled me to learn of just about every reported incident in the struggle around the country and to cover many locally on a daily basis for years leading up to the 1960s. This included lynchings and other murders, riots, job discrimination, police brutality, mob violence, destruction of property, miscarriages of justice and exclusion from the polls. I was also able to learn of protests that were beginning to develop here and there.

This privileged position—and it was a privilege to sit within that flow of information—also enabled me to see the victories for human rights that were being won around the world and the country, as well as those here in Chicago. I saw the decline of lynching, the end of poll taxes, "White Only" primary elections, and the end of segregation in interstate travel and public accommodations as tactical victories in a war that definitely was being won. I saw the rise of Blacks in organized sports and commercial entertainment, the opening of previously restricted residential areas, the dramatic increases in Black elected officeholders and the growth of a new class of entrepreneurs and business people as fruits of those victories. For my own part, I joined the NAACP and served as its secretary for twenty-five years.

I left the *Defender* in 1959 and started my own business. I briefly served the Chicago Commission on Human Relations and counseled several corporations on employment practices and public policy regarding the Black community. I also served two national organizations of Blacks, which enabled me to observe the changing picture of race relations in major, and some smaller, ones around the country. I was encouraged that change was taking place, and that more gains were imminently possible.

I remained optimistic that the civil rights struggle was being won, even as local school issues approached the boiling point.

It was in this frame of mind that I entered the 1960s. I was convinced that the national momentum of change, and the new economic and political strength of Blacks in Chicago, provided the leverage necessary to settle grievances and negotiate solutions to lingering problems of race relations here.

I approached the late Edwin C. "Bill" Berry about organizing a council of community organizations that could bring issues to a forum and reach concerns on major issues in cooperation with Black aldermen and Mayor Richard J. Daley, whom I believed to be a political realist. We envisioned a rotating chair so that all interests would be represented.

I miscalculated on more than one level. After months of "noodling" we formed the organization and labeled it the Coordinating Council of Community Organizations, but the Black aldermen declined to join. The idea of a rotating chair was quickly swept aside by skilled community organizers who gained control of the organization and called for direct action, rather than negotiation as its main tactic. The community-based flavor of the CCCO soon disappeared and a charismatic late bloomer, Albert Raby, was installed as the spokesman and public face. Two bright, angry young men, Lawrence Landry and Nahaz Rogers, joined the ranks as did Rev. Lynwood Stevenson and Rev. (now Bishop) Arthur Brazier, State Sen. Richard Newhouse, and others who were attracted by the goals of open occupancy, and reforms by School Superintendent Benjamin Willis.

CCCO invited Dr. Martin Luther King to Chicago, which "Bill" Berry had earlier called the most segregated city in the North. Dr. King accepted, and CCCO installed him in a Westside apartment. They also persuaded him to lead a march for open occupancy into the racially hostile Marquette Park community. The resistance to that march is well known. Dr. King, who opposed violence, moved back to Atlanta to pursue other priorities. However, Blacks did move into Marquette Park.

Through direct action, CCCO succeeded in bringing the drive to resolve school issues, housing discrimination and other grievances, to a level of public attention that demanded action. However, to some extent, it was involved in the wrecking of a stretch of West Madison St. as a retail center. Lawrence Landry and Nahaz Rogers organized a street meeting to protest the fatal injury to a young woman by a city fire truck. The meeting was taken over from them by others, who stirred the crowd into a fury and went on to loot stores and destroy property. The destruction was nearly completed a few years later by the rioting after Dr. King was killed. Most of the scars remain.

CCCO went into decline after a short life and disappeared for want of support. In preempting the community organizations that formed its original base, the leaders shut off its source of funding, and replacement sources were not found. CCCO undoubtedly contributed to the Movement that continues today using less confrontational tactics. This one man wonders if more could have been achieved in the sixties if united Black community organizations had taken their goals and grievances to the center of power with negotiation as their first resort.

DIVIDE AND CONQUER: A PROFILE OF THE SIXTIES

Atty. Eric E. Graham

The system of privilege in the United States is established by custom, the Constitution, state legislation, judicial decisions, and business decisions by the managers of capitalist enterprises. Voting has made possible greater participation of the formerly excluded members of the United States society and produced a type of parliamentary democracy. Labor unions have been able, in some cases, to force the owners of industry to humanize their distribution of profits to some extent. Welfare legislation has allowed some relief from the problems of starvation and homelessness. But privilege and the control of resources continues to be, to a large degree, in a relatively few hands.

African Americans, first as slaves, and later as slaves who were granted emancipation from slavery, have had a special set of problems in becoming accommodated by the system of politics and economics that exists in the United States.

Violent revolution tried by slaves was met by violent means that smashed the revolts. In later years, different strategies have been employed to try to reach an accommodation with the laws and customs of the United States.

One of the customs was the separation of citizens of the United States into communities, which, if white, would attempt to keep black people out. Agreements were written into contracts for the sale of property and into deeds of conveyance, which provided for penalties if the owner attempted to sell to an African American. It followed that African American politicians would make this an issue in their political campaigns. Like the people in the New Testament who wanted to please Caesar at all costs, African American politicians in Chicago sided with the white mayor of the city. They did not vote in favor of a law that would allow for open occupancy; that would make it unlawful by contract or real estate deed or conduct to keep people from being able to live anywhere in Chicago regardless of their race.

The conduct of the six Black aldermen, who were labeled the Silent Six because they did not speak out against the segregationist position, was a form of accommodation to political life in Chicago. What does a politician have to do to be able to get a piece of the pie for himself, his close political associates, and hopefully his constituents? How can he do this without offending the arbiters of privilege?

In the biblical example, Jesus was sacrificed so Caesar would not be offended. In Chicago, open occupancy, a right dear to all African Americans, was sacrificed to avoid offending the white European who ran the city of Chicago through his control of patronage or privilege in the city.

One of the Jews who agreed that Jesus should be crucified said that it would be better for Jesus to die rather than to have the Romans kill thousands if they believed Jesus would lead a revolt. Similar reasoning was used to explain the conduct of the Silent Six. Patronage jobs and favors would be on a wholesale basis denied if blacks appeared to want to stage a political revolt.

Opposing the powers that are in the United States means standing up to the national government, which has shown its ability to devastate its enemies in peace and war. It means on the local level challenging a system that leads to job offerings for the faithful and vengeance against opponents.

What we frequently ask of African American leaders is that they make a suicidal effort to confront a problem. Knowing of the violence and hostility of the sheriffs in the South in states like Alabama, from a practical point of view the sit-ins were to a great extent a suicidal challenge. However, the sit-ins were not intended to be practical or suicidal. They were intended to challenge the spirit that existed in the American conscience, placed there by a God who knows about the hateful nature of humans, but also reserves for himself the power to have the hater overwhelmed by a nonviolent spiritually motivated challenge. The redemptive power of unmerited suffering was brought into play by nonviolent sit-ins and demonstrations.

Many of us who did not have the hope that haters would have a change of heart in our lifetimes, but then saw them moved by men of faith, now believed the gospel of love would prevail. The judicial process by which evil wrongs were restrained and civil rights respected was an interesting transition. Conservatives today point to the mindset of the founding fathers when opposing most of the views that are considered progressive. The Bill of Rights was added in after the Constitution was written and accepted. We live in fear that the conservative views of the present set of justices will set us back to the views of the founding fathers. We must remember that some of the founding fathers were slaveholders. They were trying to reach an accommodation with urban business people who had no interest in the preservation of slavery as an institution or many other things that were dear to the heart of the Southern agriculturist.

The Supreme Court on the question of the privilege of equal educational opportunity said at first that if separate facilities were provided in a segregated system, the Constitutional right of African American citizens would have been respected. It later concluded that separate but equal was not right and that all citizens should have an equal opportunity to share the privilege.

In 1965 the Friends of the Student Nonviolent Coordinating Committee was led in Chicago by Lawrence Landry. He became the leader of a movement for ending an unequal system of educational opportunity that existed in Chicago. Students were being sent to neighborhood schools that were overcrowded, understaffed, and without traditional classrooms. The Superintendent of Schools approved and furnished buses as substitute classrooms. These were called Willis Wagons.

In the 1960s office space in the Loop area of Chicago was generally not available to black lawyers. McCoy Ming and Leighton, Euclid Taylor, Claude Holman, Rogers, Strayhorn and Harth, and a few others had space.

In 1958 Raymond Ewell, Maurice Dixon and I secured space at 166 W. Washington and shared the space with several other lawyers who served the Civil Rights Movement. Leo Holt and James Montgomery had Al Raby as a client. James Walton led a revolt against the Neinstein machine on the West Side. I represented Lawrence Landry and Renault Robinson, and Douglas Andrews. All of us joined in assisting Dr. Martin Luther King when he came to Chicago. Dick Newhouse was also part of this group but his input was more political than legal.

I remember vividly the day that Dr. King went to Marquette Park. King and his civil rights entourage came to our office and met with the lawyers, then left for Marquette Park with Newhouse and some of the lawyers in his entourage. The NAACP had contributed money for bail bonds, which some of the lawyers in the office administered. We had to keep track of the arrests so that bonds could be posted and refunds collected after trial.

The players in the political and civil life of Chicago in the period from 1960 to 1975 appear to have been motivated by idealism, anger, pragmatism and cynicism. Sometimes they were dominated by one form of motivation and other times by another or a combination of two or more motivations. My observations were made from the point of view of "the man next to the man" and a member of the multitude. My advice was sought as an attorney on legal matters and as a person who had an idea about several things.

In 1960 I got married and had settled down to the task of being a husband and father. However, the brutal treatment of the students beaten and abused by Bull Conner, a sheriff in Alabama, converted my wife and me to the cause of activism.

Lawrence Landry, the head of Friends of the Student Nonviolent Coordinating Committee in Chicago, had been a friend since the early fifties when I lived on the same block with his family during my attendance at the University of Chicago Law School. Larry had graduated from the University of Chicago as a sociologist and was in the process of garnering a national reputation as an expert on juvenile delinquency. He was employed by the City of Chicago. Mayor Richard Daley had described him as the leading expert in these matters and he was in the good graces of the Chicago Machine.

The head of the Chicago Public School system, Benjamin Willis, in an attempt to maintain the segregated system of enrollment in the schools of Chicago, tried various ways of redrawing attendance lines so that black students would remain in their areas. When the number of students in the Woodlawn area became too great and relief was not possible by way of these attendance lines, trailers called "Willis Wagons" were purchased and used as classrooms. This of course was inappropriate and led to the formation of a coalition of activists led by Landry, who were committed to dealing with the immediate problem of Willis Wagons and the ultimate elimination of the segregated system of attendance lines and quality of facilities. Led by a spirit of idealism and responding to the anger of the mistreated, Landry, Al Raby and other leaders began a series of actions culminating in a successful boycott of the public schools in Chicago.

The Machine did not take kindly to Landry's role in this matter and he was relieved of his employment by Daley. Unemployed, Landry became a full-time freedom fighter. He joined with an activated community to engage in a series of marches and sit-ins which disrupted and called attention to the serious nature of the unequal distribution of educational and other resources.

Landry was joined in his activist movement by Douglas Andrews, a charismatic leader who had an association with and the ability to bring into activist action large numbers of people. Doug became a friend, student and follower of Landry and his methods. He became involved with ACT, a national group headed by Landry, which included leaders of the movement for black liberation from racism all over the country. Dick Gregory and Nahaz Rogers were local leaders, as well as Stanley Branche from Philadelphia, Jesse Gray from New York, and others. A young Marion Berry, who later became the mayor of Washington, D.C., was also a member.

The protest movement in Chicago, as elsewhere, was always met by confrontation with the police, arrests, swift convictions, and brutality. Several forms of resistance and replies to the conditions were made by the activists, including sit-ins, boycotts and protest marches. Dr. Martin Luther King and Al Raby also led protests in Chicago. Doug and six other West Side activists were accused of conspiracy to commit arson after a fire had been lit on the West Side. A search of their meeting place disclosed information about making Molotov cocktails—a device for starting fires. I represented the group in court and, to our delight and surprise, an all white suburban jury found them all not guilty.

Malcolm X College was built and began operations under a new resident, Dr. Charles Hurst, as president. I was surprised to receive a call from Dr. Hurst requesting my help. He said that the Panthers had declared their revolutionary right to declare a holiday in the Malcolm X community. He feared there would be problems with the financing of the students who, out of fear or respect, stayed away from school on the Panther-declared holiday. Someone told him that Doug and his street gang friends could scare the Panthers off and restore order. He did not want to call the police because of general community fear and distrust of the police. I called Doug and he responded, and order was restored at Malcolm X College. This began a relationship between Doug and Dr. Hurst that lead to a variety of events. Doug and his troops became members of the security team at Malcolm X. This duo eventually became supporters of the Nixon administration. Doug started the Garfield Organization, an umbrella group of West Side organizations, and undertook a variety of community-based initiatives. Some which required government grants. Doug and Dr. Hurst secured funding from the Nixon administration for many of them. When questioned by his friends, who were supporters of the Democratic Party, as to why he could support Nixon: Dr. Hurst responded that it was necessary for the Democrats to know they did not have a lock on all black votes. Secondly, Nixon was too vicious to be allowed to be making decisions about blacks with no blacks in attendance.

Unable to find work in Chicago, Lawrence Landry moved to Washington, D.C. Daley blocked his employment at Brandies University and from Democratic dominated entities everywhere. Unable to deal with the Democrats, Landry sought contracts for his management consulting company with the Republican Administration. Nahaz Rogers joined Landry's Consulting Group and together they were successful.

Dick Newhouse, a graduate of Boston College and the University of Chicago Law School with no political background, got together with a few of his friends and decided to run for the position of State Senator for the Illinois Legislature. Most of the knowledgeable members of his organizing committee decided that this would not work and quit coming to meetings. I assumed the management of the campaign. He won and gained a reputation as an independent Democrat, which meant that he would normally vote with the Democrats but reserved the right to get out of lock step when the party was out of line with his principles.

In the exercise of his political independence, Newhouse challenged the Democratic party to name a Black as the head of the Senate. He threatened to vote with Republicans and cast the deciding vote for a Republican if the Democrats did not select a Black president. Cecil Partee became the first Black president of the Illinois Legislature based on this threat. Ultimately, Dick became lionized and hated by his fellow Democrats, including some of the Black ones. Another example of Newhouse's use of his independence was his endorsement of Richard Ogilvie to be governor of Illinois. Hurst and Newhouse were main supporters of Oglivie and enjoyed several political favors after Ogilvie's victory.

During the Newhouse campaign for his first term, a young gang leader, Jeff Fort, would sometimes come into the campaign office between gang banging activities accompanied by Watusi, the gang enforcer. They were in their early teens and taking money from young students was their crime. Newhouse pledged that if they would try to do the right thing, he would help them. Newhouse joined my law office after his election. As a result of the promise of help from Newhouse, Jeff appeared in the office and asked to be represented. Since Dick had never represented a criminal defendant, he asked me to go to court. Jeff received a slap on the wrist after his mother assured the court that if Jeff Fort were dealt with leniently, he would never again be any trouble to the community. This statement turned out to be incorrect.

Dick received many requests for legal help, which our office attended to. One of these was the request to execute the documentation for the Afro-American Patrolman's League to become a not-for-profit corporation of the State of Illinois. Again, it became my job to do the legal work. In addition, I counseled the cofounders of the League, Renault Robinson and Edward Buzz Palmer, in conducting organizational meetings and procedures. Included in this task was creating a statement of purpose that would be strong, legal and satisfactory to an aggressive group of protest-oriented young black policemen. Father George Clemens was influential in setting the course for the league and contributed to the statement of purpose.

An interesting set of events led to the formation of the Garfield Organization, led by Doug Andrews in activist, political and business matters. The son of the president of Midas Muffler had taken over the company. I was able to convince him that the energies of Doug and his cohorts could be used to create business enterprises as a source of employment and reduction of youthful antisocial activities. A franchise was created and delivered to the Garfield Organization. It operated successfully until a theft by an officer of the franchise funds forced it into insolvency.

Dick Newhouse, Renault Robinson, and the Afro-American Patrolman League collaborated in a series of meetings and legislative hearings on questions of police brutality and other matters of the administration of criminal justice. The question of health care, admission of blacks to medical school, and retention of hospitals in the Black community became an issue. Buzz Palmer on the South Side, and Danny Davis on the West Side, were directors of arms of the Comprehensive Health Planning Agency. Comprand, Buzz Palmer's organization, continued operations after the closing of the Comprehensive Health Planning Agency. The University of Illinois was dropped by Buzz and Danny to become a provider of black medical professionals. Danny Davis has employed his background in health care provision to assist his constituents now that he is in Congress. The University of Illinois has responded to Buzz and Comprand in a variety of ways beneficial to black citizens of Chicago.

Dick Newhouse initiated the Black Legislative Clearinghouse, starting with his original supporters as incorporators and saw it develop into a national teacher of legislative action to black politicians. The Newhouse way was employed to a large degree by the campaigns of Hatcher in Gary and Harold Ford in Memphis. Newhouse ran for mayor in Chicago in 1974 and received about fifty thousand votes—the first time that a Black candidate for mayor received votes in all precincts, foretelling the possibility that ended in the Washington victory. I was allowed to write the editorial for the *Sun Times* on one occasion as a compromise because of the unfairness of the coverage during the campaign.

Dr. King's visit to Chicago involved Newhouse, who marched with King in Marquette Park and Doug Andrews and Company on the West Side, when Curlie and Goat, part of the Andrews entourage, were his protectors. Dr. King also had the assistance of Al Raby, a schoolteacher, who became a protest leader. During Dr. King's stay in Chicago he nailed on the door of City Hall a document outlining criticisms and demands addressed to Mayor Daley regarding injustices in housing and other matters. A popular television commentator had a program in which his criticism of civic and political leaders was common. Regarding the King posting on City Hall, he said that he had talked to Cecil Partee and other prominent, sensible blacks, and that they all thought it was a foolish act. He gave a deadline for the replies. As the deadline approached, Cerillo McSween, national treasurer of the SCLC, and Dick Newhouse recognized that someone had to reply. I was selected, and appeared and explained that everything that King said was justified by the statistics and the reality of life in Chicago.

When Jesse Jackson came to Chicago he was introduced to the business community by Cerilo McSween. The earliest meetings with other members of the community were very small. My attempt to talk with the Cook County Bar Association was met by hostility. Claude Holman and other lawyers, who were prominent members of the association, resented Jackson and threatened anyone who would challenge Daley and Daley's programs.

Jackson quickly became a hero on the South Side and it became customary to stand and applaud when he entered a room. Operation Breadbasket became instrumental in using the threat of boycott and economic actions to assist the success of Black business. It was less successful initially in dealing with the problems of the poor and homeless. I was the first volunteer legal counsel for Jesse and Breadbasket.

Dissatisfaction with Breadbasket led to the formation of a chapter of SCLC loyal to King's emphasis on the poor and homeless. Cirilo McSween managed to be treasurer of SCLC nationally as well as a leader of Operation Breadbasket, particularly the businessmen's group, and mediated what could have been a destructive battle between the groups.

In 1966, as a volunteer attorney for the Cardinal's Committee for Spanish speaking, I represented hundreds of Puerto Ricans after a series of riots following the first Puerto Rican Day in Chicago. Mr. Samuel Betrances describes the riots and the turn of events as follows:

"In 1966 Puerto Ricans of Chicago took a tragedy and transformed it into a series of organized efforts to help our people gain a voice in the many forums in which decisions are made. In the ensuing decades, events would be discussed as happening either before or after the riot. The riot and our response to it would define our generation. Just as everyone today remembers where they were on the day that the planes flew into the Twin Towers of New York, Puerto Ricans of my generation remember where they were when the riot broke out on Division and Damen. It was that significant!"

Elijah Muhammad had a profound presence during the years involved. Aware of the fact that many of the well-educated black people, usually Christians, did not feel respectful of his black Muslims and did not associate very much with its leadership—he would invite non-Muslims to his home for dinner and conversation from time to time. Richard Durham, editor of Muhammad Speaks and a non-Muslim, would invite the guests. I was selected and met with Elijah Muhammad on two occasions under this program. In addition, I met with him on other occasions after writing a list of suggestions for the Nation of Islam with Lawrence Landry. Muhammad appeared to be very wise though not deep in his theology. One of my visits was shortly after the death of Malcolm X. Elijah's explanation was that Malcolm, though a genius as a lieutenant, had no talent for organizing the kind of institution he was trying to build, so he had united with bad people who were responsible for his death. In life he had maintained a posture of no intervention in political matters, but he still profoundly influenced black thinking about socialization of our community and political empowerment.

Between 1960 and 1975 the political climate was under a cloud represented by the Federal Government, which kept tabs on the language of the leaders of Blacks who engaged in revolutionary talk; ready to pounce on them if they exceeded norms and restrictions set by Washington. Telephones were tapped and the FBI monitored and physically followed leaders of the Civil Rights Movement. My telephone became inoperable because of the taps and had to be repaired. The crude technology during the time of Renault Robinson's inquisition allowed the tapper to almost participate in conversation and on one occasion, he interrupted the conversation completely when Renault made an insulting remark about the Police Superintendent.

I frequently played the role of suggesting changes in the choice of language for an angry Afrocentric leader who phrased his rhetoric in language that a prosecutor might consider to be felonious. The rhetoric of the Civil Rights Movement has been loaded with demands for freedom and threats of retaliation for present and past actions. The processors of political power and wealth and the poor—the enslaved and the unlettered have hoped for a means of closing the gap. This has been a capitalist country and freedom for the capitalist is the right to maximize profits without restraint. Workers have been indentured servants, kidnapped slaves, poor immigrants, sharecroppers, factory and office workers, and tradesman. The basic political, judicial and economic statement of rights, privileges, and limitations of rights and privileges has been the Constitution. In its early stages it did not have a Bill of Rights. African Americans became people and citizens by virtue of the amendments to the Bill of Rights.

Political independents were a special breed. While the majority of politicians seeking public office would join the Regular Democratic Organization, people like Sammy Rayner, Charles Chew, Dick Newhouse and Bill Cousins would declare themselves to be independent of the Machine and managed to be elected. An independent was frequently a lecturer, an elocutionist who made noble statements about ideas and ideals. He also gave voice to resentments that would not be expressed in regular organization sessions, but had to be answered. Harold Washington was able to be in both the independent and regular worlds. Dick Newhouse was usually an independent, but sometimes a Democrat. Charlie Chew angrily claimed Independence and then gave it up as he received favors from the Machine.

"What do you want?" was a question everyone was asked by the Machine. Much of what appears as progress in judicial and political progress appears to be promises kept. Blacks identified with the Machine have become Supreme Court justices, federal judges, mayors, presidents of the Illinois Senate, chief judges of the Circuit Court and president of Cook County.

Progress has been made. Things politically and legally are better. Praises are due to all the players whose roles have been complementary to each other.

1. Humans have demonstrated since the biblical narrative about creation that humans will lie, kill and conspire against each other individually and collectively. Exclusive possession of resources and privilege has been at the root of human activity both individually and collectively since the beginning.

2. Throughout history the planet Earth has been dominated by racial and ethnic people. Early on it appears that Ancient Egypt and other parts of the world were dominated by the resident populations of that area, which was not European. They employed a variety of means—some humane and some not so humane—to acquire and retain resources and privilege. Pharoh, an African, had to be begged to "let my people go."

3. From 1960 to 1975 the population of Chicago has been led by people who have changed roles and uniforms in a variety of ways to create a judicial and political climate that appears to have moved forward in many respects through fairness yet equality of opportunity has not been achieved.

4. The names of the judges and politicians have changed considerably. These are now Hispanics and African Americans playing many of the roles that had been reserved for Irish and Polish judges and political office holders.

LAW ENFORCEMENT AND THE FREEDOM MOVEMENT

Judge Mitchell Ware

Everyone with a television set had seen *The Untouchables* where Elliott Ness fought the Mafia. What most watchers did not know was that his boss was Malachai Harney. In 1960 Malachai Harney had retired from the federal government and was heading the fight against illegal drug traffic in Illinois. The Illinois Narcotics Division would not only be the regulatory agency for legitimate businesses, which dealt with narcotics and dangerous drugs, but it would also investigate and break up the illegal narcotics operations which appeared to be experiencing a major increase.

I had just become a state trooper when I was asked by Malachai Harney to become an agent. He did not have to elaborate about the growth of problems directly related to narcotics, which were clearly affecting the community in which I lived. I accepted the position and became an agent. I would be going after drug dealers. Chicago was the hub of illicit drug sales, and most of the work already was concentrated there.

I was not naïve. As a youth I had seen friends using illegal drugs. When our group of athletes went to play baseball, football or basketball, there was usually a separate group following us, smoking pot and talking about taking a "trip to the moon." I thought the drugs were affecting their minds and never liked to see them use drugs. It was disheartening to see the addicts going into the bushes near the baseball diamond and using a needle to inject dope. When some died of drug overdoses it validated my belief that drugs were horrible and reaffirmed my commitment to never use any.

Illegal drug sales on the streets of African American communities were outrageous. Drugs were all over. It was not unusual to learn about the misdeeds of junkies. After seeing the horror that junkies caused to ordinary hard-working citizens by their thefts, robberies, and murders, it was not difficult to persuade me to try to help stem the problems. As an agent first, then later as superintendent of the Illinois Division of Narcotic Control in 1969, it was my job to enforce drug trafficking laws. In 1972, as deputy superintendent of the Chicago Police Department in charge of the Bureau of Inspectional Services, there were fourteen hundred officers in the five divisions. The Vice Control Division embraced narcotics, gambling, prostitution, vice detection, and licensing units. The Intelligence Division contained organized crime, subversives and an analytical unit. The Internal Affairs Division had corrupt practices and excessive force units. Inspections were the quality control unit. They had a records unit and a follow-up unit. Gang Intelligence kept tabs on gang activity. Later, a special unit called C-5 was created in the Bureau to use unusual tactics, such as sting operations, to ferret out corruption in the police ranks.

Superintendent of the Illinois Narcotics Division

In 1969 I was appointed by Governor Richard Ogilvie to be the superintendent of the Illinois Division of Narcotic Control. After Illinois senator Fred Smith made the official nomination and the Senate approved, I became the first and only African American in the United States to head a statewide law enforcement agency.

During my first year in 1969, instead of meeting the past performance with the same number of agents working under my command, (with new and different standards and rules,) year-end statistics showed the agents had increased their arrests four hundred percent and their seizures of illicit drugs by a remarkable three thousand percent. The crime rate in Illinois and the use of narcotic drugs had gone down. It was almost prophetic; when illegal drug use increases, so does the crime rate. There is a definite correlation. When the Illinois crime rate went down the president recognized these awesome statistics and appointed Dr. Jerry Jaffe, a doctor from the University of Chicago who worked with our Methadone program, to be the "Drug Czar" to head a new federal program they wanted to use nationally. Unfortunately, it did not achieve the same success that was experienced in Illinois.

On January 1, 1970 the Illinois Bureau of Investigation was created and I was appointed superintendent. The existing Narcotics Division was joined by an Organized Crime Division and a General Crimes Division. I was in charge of what was soon to be recognized as possibly the best investigative agency in the country. This was an opportunity to show real leadership. The agents working with me had been selected from thousands of applicants and were far above average in ability and education. But most importantly they were hard workers with integrity, dedicated to the task of getting the job done. In its first year, 1970, IBI set a record that probably will never be duplicated. It achieved a ninety-seven percent conviction rate. An attack was launched on organized crime mobsters, resulting in the arrests and convictions of dozens of the top outfit mobsters, more than all the other law enforcement agencies in Illinois combined. Major complicated crimes were investigated and solved, including many which warranted the front page headlines of major newspapers. Millions of dollars of illegal drugs were confiscated and hundreds of drug peddlers were arrested and convicted.

In 1970, after testifying about drug abuse in the United States before the House Committee, I was appointed by the president as a commissioner on the National Commission on Marijuana and Drug Abuse. The task was to look at the drug situation throughout the world and report back to Congress on the true dangers of the various illicit drugs, with emphasis on marijuana and heroin and their effects on the United States population. At the conclusion of our study, we had prepared the most extensive and thorough report ever done on the extent of the drug problems throughout the world.

President Richard Nixon could not quarrel with the findings, but he was not entirely pleased with the recommendations. The majority of the commissioners, especially the doctors, recommended decriminalization of marijuana. Congressman Paul Rogers and I wrote a dissent. While we agreed that criminal penalties should be removed for simple users, we recommended that fines be kept in place to create a deterrent to help discourage the use of any intoxicating dangerous drug.

In the seventies many people in Chicago, especially in the minority communities, were growing cynical about police officers. The crime rate was increasing. Police officers were being accused of extortion and corruption. Many law-abiding citizens did not trust the Chicago police officers. Those in minority communities frequently viewed uniformed police officers as corrupt or violent. This same fear did not seem to be present in white areas of the city.

There was a much-used phrase when people in the black communities saw a police car headed their way, they said, “Here comes trouble.” In white communities when a police car was seen coming, it meant, “Here comes help.” The citizens were not only being short-changed by the police, but they were also being intimidated, robbed and terrorized by criminals.

When I had headed both the Illinois Narcotic Control Division and the Illinois Bureau of Investigation, they were both top notch, highly effective, widely respected, scandal-free law enforcement agencies. Because of this background, I was asked to come into the Chicago Police Department as deputy superintendent to help clean up the problems.

Acceptance of the position would pose a real personal challenge. It would require an enormous amount of work. I also knew that nothing was harder than internal investigations of corruption and brutality and that nothing could be more harmful to the community, the city, and the police department than the betrayal of trust by corrupt officers who have sworn to uphold the law. I knew there were some officers who rightfully deserved that reputation, but there were thousands who do not deserve anything but praise for the job they were doing.

News stories at the time fueled the flames to expedite efforts to clean up the problems of the department. Headlines almost daily told of police misconduct, including some indicating that the FBI was initiating a major investigation into police corruption. One of those stories was about a prominent black South Side dentist who had been beaten by the police. Dr. Herbert Odum was a close personal friend of U.S. Congressman and former Olympic track star, Ralph Metcalfe.

The investigation of the Odum matter appeared to be slow and inefficient when it appeared to be obvious that a motorist being stopped for a traffic violation should not end up beaten and hospitalized because of a verbal dispute with the police. When Congressman Metcalfe tried to help expedite the Odum investigation, the department seemed to ignore the congressman. This caused a major breach in the relationship between Congressman Metcalfe and Mayor Richard J. Daley, and the congressman led the fight for change in the department's internal affairs investigations.

Another headline followed a rare FBI news conference where Roy Moore, the special agent in charge of the Chicago office of the FBI had, in a very unusual act, announced to the press that the FBI was on the verge of arresting a Chicago police officer and cracking a police "hit squad," which was responsible for the murders of three black businessmen southeast of the Dan Ryan expressway. With knowledge of the obstacles, I accepted the challenge. On August 3, 1972, I became the youngest deputy superintendent and third in command of the Chicago Police Department.

After the appointment, a large file about three inches thick was given to me. It was titled "Hit Squad." It was the homicide investigation which supposedly was being worked jointly with the FBI task force investigating mob hits. It involved the murders of the three black businessmen, who appeared to also have been involved in the business of selling drugs. The news media were implying there was nothing being done to try to apprehend the murderer, because it appeared the shooter was a Chicago Police Officer. The three-inch thick confidential file contained written statements, photographs, ballistics, forensics, lab and coroners' reports, as well as the investigative reports from Homicide and Internal Affairs. The forensics report showed that bullets found in the deceased victims were of the same caliber as weapons frequently used by members of the department. The top suspect tentatively identified by the FBI in the file was Renault Robinson, who incidentally was believed by the FBI to be the head of the Afro-American Police League. Police officers Renault Robinson and Howard Saffold actually were principals in the Afro-American Police League.

They and other members of the League, including Officer Curtis Cowsen, had publicly and frequently stated they had tried, as their primary duty, to eliminate what they saw as police abuse of African American citizens in their communities. When either one of them observed arrest situations involving black arrestees, they became involved. Robinson, Saffold and Cowsen were consistently being accused of interfering with police investigations.

I felt right away that this murder allegation was preposterous and the look on my face must have said just that. I did realize that a lot of people resented Renault Robinson and that he had caused a lot of internal turmoil in the department. However, I had met Renault Robinson before and he just did not fit the murderer's role. Besides, Renault Robinson also was the plaintiff in a lawsuit filed and pending, against the police department alleging racial discrimination. On a vast number of occasions the outspoken officer Renault Robinson had publicly expressed that he was aware that he was constantly under police scrutiny and whenever I saw him, Renault Robinson acted as though he felt he was under surveillance.

When I asked, "Why would the head of the Afro-American Police League want to murder a dope peddler? It just does not add up," Mike Spiotto was quick to advise me that he felt the FBI had jumped the gun and was probably wrong about the murderer being Renault Robinson, but he did feel they were correct in their assessment of some type of police involvement.

I was told that Renault Robinson was currently assigned to patrol the "alley detail" behind police headquarters. I quickly triaged the file and asked Spiotto if he knew the reason that Renault Robinson had been given the alley detail. Spiotto said he had nothing to do with the assignment and felt that it might have been made in order to keep Robinson away from sensitive assignments where Robinson could do no harm to the department. When the briefing was completed I added ten additional investigators on this case and wanted a daily briefing. I would monitor the case until it was solved and an arrest was made.

Nearly seven months and thousands of investigative hours later, it was solved. The real suspect in the murders was a police sergeant named Stanley Robinson and a police detective named William Tolliver. But the most disgusting revelation was that an FBI informant named William O'Neal was in the police car with the police officers when the murders occurred and the FBI knew who the suspects were the day after the shootings; yet, they held the press conference and failed to tell us until our separate investigation discovered the identity of the suspects.

After the informant was identified, it turned out to be the same William O'Neal who set up the raid on the apartment of the Black Panthers where Mark Clark and Fred Hampton were killed.

Stanley Robinson and William Tolliver were both convicted and sentenced to the penitentiary. A few months later William O'Neal was found murdered.

Bussing—Willis Wagons

Bussing was being started by the Chicago Board of Education where black children were taken by bus to previously all-white schools in white neighborhoods. The day after it began, all five of the deputy superintendents sat down around the big conference table in the room adjoining the office of the recently appointed superintendent, James Rochford.

The first question asked by me was what plans were made to control the unruly mob of demonstrators opposing the bussing of first and second grade black students to the all-white grammar schools?

White hooligans were picketing the busses and taunting the black children as they went from the busses to the school. The police officers had formed protective lines and the children passed through without incident, but there were no black police officers. When I asked about the lack of an integrated force, the answer was to prevent violence. My response was that there will be some today. I directed certain commanders to send minority officers to the schools to arrest any of the demonstrators who threatened them or the children.

The same day, uniformed patrolmen at the scene showed up with an integrated force. The mixed forces of plainclothes detectives from my bureau were also there mingled with the crowd, the same way they blend in when demonstrations are held by any other disruptive crowd.

The mob jeering came to a halt. The crowd stopped yelling and threatening and stopped calling the children names. The demonstrations stopped with only two arrests. The school went about its business of teaching, with no further need for additional police officers.

Specific Incidents Involving Race

In 1969, while heading the Illinois Narcotics Division, I was asked by C. Bernard Carey to begin an investigation of the Honorable Elijah Muhammad and his Muslim religion. I refused.

First I asked, what crime is he or his followers suspected of committing? When there was no immediate logical answer, I brought the suggestion to an end by merely saying, "if ordered to begin an investigation of the Muslims, we also should begin an investigation of the Catholics and the Episcopalians and the Baptists and Methodists because more arrestees belong to those religions than Muslims." The pressure disappeared. There was no investigation.

Board of Education—Al Boutte

In 1969 Alvin Boutte was the president of the Chicago Board of Education and the first black to head the Board. Boutte also owned two drug stores in the black community. One of the tasks of my Narcotics Division was to check on the sales of controlled drugs by drug stores. The pharmacists were to use a triplicate prescription whenever controlled drugs were sold and they were not to sell more than a prescribed amount of exempt narcotic preparations within a twenty-four-hour period to the same customer. One of the pharmacists in an Alvin Boutte-owned drug store had violated that section of the law by selling too much of an exempt preparation. C. Bernard Carey wanted me to arrest Boutte.

When I declined to do so he went to the governor. I received a call from Governor Ogilvie asking me why I refused to arrest Boutte. The governor was told that even though the law allowed for a criminal charge to be placed against the CEO of a corporation when the drugs are sold, it had never been done before where there was no complicity by the CEO or owner.

Al Boutte at no time was seen in the drug store when any of the unlawful acts occurred, and there was no evidence that he had any knowledge of the unlawful sales of drugs by his pharmacist. When there appeared to be a question of protectionism, I ended it rapidly by saying that we also had been buying the same exempt narcotic preparations from Walgreen's and from Osco Drugs. I added that if we obtained a warrant to arrest Al Boutte, it was only fair that we also obtain arrest warrants for Charles Walgreen, the CEO of the Walgreen's chain, and for Richard Cline, the CEO of the Osco chain. That ended the conversation. Needless to say, Alvin Boutte was not arrested.

I had no involvement in the raid of the West Side apartment of the Black Panthers. When asked to look into irregularities in the actions taken by the Black Panther grand jury following the raid where Fred Hampton and Mark Clark were killed, I accepted the assignment with the clear understanding that I would report the true facts. A short time later when the grand jury returned its secret indictment and there was reluctance to open it, Chief Judge Joseph Power was told that the indictment had been properly returned and it had to be opened even though it would result in the indictments of Cook County states attorney Edward Hanrahan, a few of his assistants and a number of police officers. Even though the action was not welcomed, the law and facts were clear, and it would have been unjust not to do so.

When Buzz Palmer, Renault Robinson, Howard Saffold and Curtis Cowsen started the Afro-American Patrolmen's League, it caused considerable consternation in the Chicago Police Department. It was not a union in the acceptable sense of the word, but an association.

The stated purpose of the Afro-American Patrolmen's League was to help improve the relationship between police officers and the black communities they served. At times these black officers would go to the scene of arrests and observe the actions of the arresting officers. Othertimes, they actually intervened in the arrests. Even though their actions were sometimes controversial, they took bold actions that they felt were necessary to protect the black citizenry, which infuriated many police officers.

Even though their tactics were sometimes wrong, every black member of the department recognized that the majority of the actions were taken with a good purpose in mind. The intentions were good and most non-whites in high positions, including me, knew that it was necessary to help implement the goals through the appropriate channels.

NOBLE

In 1972 a band of high-ranking, brave black police officials, who had obtained leadership positions in law enforcement agencies throughout the United States, bound together to form an organization called NOBLE, an acronym for National Organization of Black Law Enforcement Executives.

The main thrust of the nationwide group was to increase minority representation in departments throughout the nation, use our best efforts to help get more high-ranking black officers in every department, and to train and sensitize white police officers in their dealings with minority communities. At that time, there were only three top black superintendents or chiefs in the nation. Last year, there were more than a thousand.

REFLECTIONS FROM WARNER SAUNDERS

Warner Saunders

I was born in 1935 in Chicago and lived at 432 E. 47th Street on the city's South Side. In 1953, after going to grammar and high school in Chicago, I decided to attend Xavier College in New Orleans. I received several athletic scholarship offers to white colleges, but I turned them all down. Xavier was a wonderful college. I made many friendships and we had the chance to explore New Orleans. I was a physical education major and after graduation I came back and began teaching at Hess Upper Grade School on Chicago's West Side at Douglas and St. Louis. The school was located in the old Jewish Peoples' Institute (JPI), but by that time North Lawndale was 99.9% black.

Once back in Chicago I joined the northern portion of the Civil Rights Movement. I also went south for a number of events, including voter registration, and continued my avocation of civil rights through involvement in several organizations. I was drafted into the Army in 1957 and served in the military for almost a year. In the late '50s you could get out of the Service after one year if you were a teacher in what was considered a "culturally deprived" area in need of teachers. I applied for it and went back to teaching school as Hess. After that I became very involved with street kids who included gang members belonging to the Vice Lords and the Cobras. I knew all those kids because I had taught them.

It felt good to be back in Chicago after spending my college days in legally segregated New Orleans and my year in the Army as a cryptographer at Ft. Benning in the Ku Klux Klan-infested state of Georgia. The de facto segregation of Chicago was not as constricting as the "in-your-face, 24-hours-a-day assault" I had known in the South. After all, Chicago was my home and I reasoned that the "devil I knew" was better than the "devil I didn't know." However, I was still a second-class citizen, albeit Northern-style. I started doing unofficial street work in 1963 and left teaching to become the Executive Director of the Better Boys Organization. That was where I really began much of my militant activity, including close interactions with the Black Panthers, such as Fred Hampton and Bobby Rush, who had become good friends. The Black Panthers had breakfast programs for the community, and I found myself in the middle of the Civil Rights ferment and it gave a lot of focus to my anger.

One of our targets in the 60s was Dr. Benjamin Willis, the superintendent of Chicago Public Schools and a staunch supporter of racially-segregated schools. In those days all-white Chicago schools were led by white principals, as were most if not all black schools. Dr. Willis created what became known as "Willis Wagons," temporary buildings constructed in the playgrounds of overcrowded black schools. Often, those schools were located on one side of a street, with underused white schools on the other side. Willis decided to build those temporary structures rather than send the black kids to the white schools. By 1965 Dr. Willis had become a symbol of Northern school segregation and the target of Chicago Civil Rights activists and protest marches.

In 1965 the West Side was beginning to show some positive signs of change, but there was an event at a West Side fire station that affected the African American community. Apparently, somebody pulled a false alarm and a hook and ladder fire truck pulled out of the station without somebody on the ladder section of the truck. The ladder swung around and hit a woman standing at the corner and killed her. The fire commissioner at that time was Commissioner Quinn and he appeared to respond in a cavalier manner at the woman's death. That was the start of probably the first riot in Chicago on the West Side and, because of it, the city and the state brought in the Illinois National Guard.

During the mid-1960s we had a burgeoning black community. Lawndale had quickly changed its racial makeup during the 1950s and 1960s when thousands of African Americans moved to Chicago from the South, primarily for economic reasons. Jobs were becoming very scarce in the South because new and modern machinery was replacing the picking of cotton by hand. There was also an enormous amount of competition between poor, Southern, rural blacks and poor, Southern, rural whites. That was perfect fodder for the Ku Klux Klan and during the 60s there was an upsurge in the beating and lynching of African Americans in the South, which contributed to the expansion of the Civil Rights Movement. As a result, Southern blacks were moving to Northern cities in great numbers seeking jobs and housing. It meant that there was a rapidly growing black community on the South Side of Chicago with few places to live and work.

Blacks began moving to the West Side while Jewish families and business moved out and started selling two-flat and three-flat apartment buildings to middle-class blacks who were moving away from poor urban blacks. That had always been the pattern in urban areas when the middle-class of any ethnic or racial group separates itself from its lower economic class. It was not a new pattern of change and by the early 60s, the communities that surrounded the South Side had border skirmishes with working-class whites who felt that they had no place to move.

Since I was an African American living on the black South Side of Chicago, it would have been difficult if not impossible to move to white neighborhoods without serious and often violent repercussions. We were also very aware that although there were no "for-whites-only" signs at Near North Side bars and clubs along Rush and Division Streets, those places were clearly hostile to black revelers. Black males, especially, were turned away from the doors by burly and determined bouncers. Few black businesses and professional people could rent Loop office space, and local beaches were segregated so that on hot summer days, the cooling waters of Lake Michigan flowed only toward 31st and 63rd Street beaches for blacks.

During those years, the Black Muslims led by Elijah Muhammad and Malcolm X grew into a very strong influence in the black community. Elijah was unquestionably "the man," and I remember being at a Black Muslim meeting at McCormick Place where Malcolm was speaking. In the middle of the speech Elijah Muhammad walked on stage and it was clear that "the man" was there. He was not as articulate as Malcolm, but Elijah Muhammad had a power that was so incredible that it stirred your vitals. He was a charismatic man with a very simple and appealing message that rejected the concept of integration with whites.

The message was, "Okay, you don't want to integrate. Then we will separate." I use that all the time to make a distinction between segregation and separation. You hear the two terms used interchangeably, but you can't use those two concepts in the same way. Segregation is when a greater power decides where a lesser power will live, work, and operate. Separation is when two equals decide they don't want to associate with one other. What was beginning to happen in the black community was the promotion of the concept of separation led by the Black Muslims. "You don't want us! Well, let me tell you something, buddy. We don't want you! Not only are you not superior to us, you are the devil!" That view had an amazing appeal for a very frustrated black community that had for all those years during the King movement, attempted to say that we were going to send you the best and brightest that we have, but were was rejected.

In 1966 Dr. Martin Luther King brought the Civil Rights Movement to Chicago. After an open-housing march through the white Southwest Side of Chicago, Dr. King said that he had never seen so much hate displayed—not even in the heart of Mississippi.

With the King Movement, I had found a place to channel my frustrations and energy, and had become a community activist. I participated in numerous marches and protests against the war in Vietnam and in favor of civil rights for African Americans in Chicago. It was an exhilarating time and I felt that I was an active part of it.

The war in Vietnam and the reaction to it was a major component in the changes of the 1960s, both in Chicago and across the nation. When Dr. King took a stand against the war, he brought the issue home to blacks despite the fact that many African Americans had wanted Dr. King to concentrate only on being a Civil Rights leader, rather than focusing his attention on the war. Black Civil Rights leaders were concerned with King's change of focus, and it is important to understand that in the North Dr. King was not immediately accepted with open arms by the black community. There was a feeling that he was too radical, and when he first arrived in Chicago, a majority of black ministers (the group that he got the strength from in SCLC) turned their backs on Dr. King. I believe that it was not to their economic advantage to support him because they appeared to be strongly influenced by the Democratic organization. Jobs had been meted out to them; they had their own little fiefdoms and Mayor Daley had "taken care" of them through their black aldermen and Congressmen. So they weren't about to deal with this "trouble maker."

When Dr. King moved to the West Side, we were very hard pressed to find many ministers who would visit him and support what he wanted to accomplish in Chicago. He marched in Cicero in 1965 and later in Marquette Park. To this day I am grateful to Reverend Clay Evans and Reverend Shelvin Hall because they ignored other ministers, which was not easy to do, and invited Dr. King to speak from their pulpits. There was a strong negative reaction at that time because Dr. King was considered to be an outside agitator in the eyes of the Democratic organization ("Machine").

His opponents felt he had come to Chicago to put new and dangerous ideas in the heads of the "happy black people." In those years it was a "happy" black community because it was bursting at the seams and in need of new housing. That led to the border skirmishes and the resistance between blacks and whites. The politicians did not want anyone to stir up anything and all they wanted was peace and quiet.

I have always lived on the South Side and in those years I was at an apartment in Prairie Shores. Then on April 4, 1968, Dr. King was assassinated in Memphis and that violent act altered the course of the non-violent movement in America and changed the direction of my life. His assassination split the city and led to riots and looting in many black neighborhoods. As the West Side of Chicago burned in the wake of Dr. King's murder, I was asked by the respected black disk jockey, Holmes "Daddy-O" Daylie, to accompany him to the local ABC television station to talk about "what could be done to stop the Negros from rioting." As a result of that appearance, a weekly public affairs half-hour show, aptly named "For Blacks Only," was created with "Daddy-O" and me as co-hosts.

During the 1968 Democratic National Convention, I was a marcher with Dick Gregory. My job was to recruit high school kids from the West Side to march against the war in Vietnam and in favor the Civil Rights Movement. I didn't want to be arrested, so I made certain that I wasn't in Grant Park when most of the protestors fought the police. Instead, I remained south of the Conrad Hilton that August night and was excited and exhilarated by what was happening in Chicago. The combination of Vietnam, the Civil Rights Movement, and the fact that the black community was beginning to show signs of standing up on its own two feet were so important that it didn't occur to me that anybody was going to get killed or that it was a riot since I just considered it a logical protest.

[Reprinted from Chicago in the Sixties: Remembering a Time of Change, *edited by Neal Samors]*

MY STRUGGLES IN THE 1960S AND THE EARLY 1970S

Robert Starks

While preparing to write this essay I was reminded of the extent to which the world has changed and how much it has remained the same since 1960. In the fifty years since 1960, America has gone through dramatic changes both good and disastrous, and the city of Chicago has been at the epicenter of many of those changes. America and the world saw profound changes in attitudes and approaches to civil rights, human rights, and democracy. In reality the struggles of African Americans in this country have given impetus and encouragement to peoples of struggle around the world. Thus, it is not surprising that the theme song of most mass demonstrations and struggles from Poland and East Germany to China and Tibet, as well as Africa and Latin America, is "We Shall Overcome," the theme song of the American civil rights movement of the 1960s. "We Shall Overcome" has been translated into more than fifty languages and is now sung enthusiastically by both the young and old throughout the world.

While it is clear that the struggles of African Americans did not begin in 1960, we witnessed the culmination of the post-World War II movement for desegregation and civil rights. No city in America had more glaring contradictions within its image as the "promised land" for African Americans than Chicago, which epitomizes machine politics built on a carefully constructed foundation of balkanized ethnicity and race. In reality it is one of the most segregated big cities in the nation. Chicago was well into industrial decline, with manufacturing job losses due to the flight of whites to the suburbs and the Sunbelt. This was a time of absolute decline in economic opportunity for Blacks.

At the same time the intense, struggle to bring down the barriers of segregation and inequality in the American South was pushed onto the political and social agenda of Chicago and the nation by the heroic, nonviolent movement led by Dr. Martin Luther King, Jr. Additionally, the promise of the newly installed John F. Kennedy administration would bring about meaningful change in the federal government's attitude toward race relations, which gave hope to Black Americans in both the South and the North.

At the beginning of the 1960s, America was a place of hope and fear for Blacks: the hope of a better world and the fear of the increasing anti-Black violence and white resentment that accompanied the push for equality. The veil of inequality haunted us wherever we were in America. We realized in the most profound manner that we were all victims of white supremacy and that resistance to change was not regional, it was universal. Thus, we understood that to change Birmingham, we had to change Boston, Chattanooga, and Chicago. The fight then, as now, had to be a fight to change America! We understood that we had to change the social, political, and economic order of the country if we were going to begin the assault on white supremacy.

After fifty years of struggle, resulting in some significant wins and some profound losses, we are now able to express our hopes and fears more precisely. While we knew then that we suffered from more than the simple reality of segregated communities, we also understood that we had to take on one enemy at a time. Further, those of us who were young and impatient wanted to bring on revolution immediately; we quickly came to realize that we had to start with our community where it was at the time, with the hope to take it where we wanted to go. We had to learn one of the bitter lessons of social change, i.e., there is nothing more powerful than an idea whose time has come. In the early 1960s Black Americans understood that their status in this country was one that encompassed every phase of American society and we had to change the entire white supremacist system. Most Black people in the movement recognized that the first step in eradicating white supremacy was bringing down the barriers of segregation. At ages fifteen and sixteen, I began trying to understand connections and make sense of a segregated world in which some Blacks thought it was okay to submit to white supremacy, while others were determined to defy it and seek change.

Engaging the Jesuits and Loyola University

In Mississippi my grandmother and I maintained an avid interest in current events and news. We read newspapers, magazines, and watched television eagerly to follow the unfolding of the Civil Rights Movement and Dr. Martin Luther King, Jr. At the same time, my grandmother cautiously guided me through the racism and constant threat of violence in the heart of KKK country. In fact, most of the adults in that community reminded all of the young men and boys that we lived in the immediate shadow of the time and place of the murder of Emmitt Till, in August of 1955. His body was thrown in the Tallahatchie River in Money, Mississippi, which was less than forty miles from my grandmother's house.

While in high school I followed the protests of the lunch counter sit-ins, the Freedom Bus Rides through the south, and the founding of the Student Nonviolent Coordinating Committee (SNCC). I was immediately attracted to the bold and brave young men and women who were putting their lives on the line for the cause of civil rights. One of my greatest wishes upon graduation was to join SNCC.

After graduating in 1961 from high school in Grenada, Mississippi, I came to Chicago to live with my mother and stepfather. I considered Mississippi my real home because it was where I was born, spent most of my formative years, and attended school—even though I spent most of my summers in Chicago with my mother.

I was on my way to DePaul University when some Jesuit priests, with whom I played basketball at St. Ignatius High School, persuaded me to switch to Loyola. In the fall of 1961, I began studying at Loyola at night while working at the Regal Theater on 47th and South Park Avenue. I got my first chance to join a demonstration with SNCC and CORE young people during the July 1-6, 1963 NAACP convention held in Chicago. I joined the march from downtown to Grant Park where Mayor Richard J. Daley and Rev. Joseph H. Jackson of Olivet Baptist Church were booed when each came to the stage to speak. Apparently the older people in the crowd, including Professor Timuel Black, were unaware of the prearranged plan to confront the mayor, just as I was. However, as a young idealist with radical political views, when the confrontation began I was glad to join in. Thus, on cue from a demonstrative and eager group led by John Bracey, who was then a student at Roosevelt University and now a history professor at the University of Massachusetts; all of the young people, both Black and white, began chanting "End slums!" and "Mayor Daley, end slums in Chicago!" The chanting drowned out the mayor's attempt to speak. He struggled to say to the crowd that there were no slums in his Chicago, and eventually he left the stage in a huff.

This was my introduction to Civil Rights protests. I was hooked and empowered by the experience. I was able to meet people who were the leaders of the Chicago Area Friends of SNCC and CORE, like Tim Black, Bob Lucas, Al Raby, Anna Langford, and many others at that demonstration and after that summer into fall of 1963.

1963 was a turbulent and exciting year in Chicago for the Civil Rights Movement. The Honorable Elijah Muhammad, leader of the Nation of Islam headquarters in Chicago's South Side, was at the height of his power and influence in Chicago and throughout the nation. Minister Malcolm X had already emerged as the national spokesman for Mr. Muhammad and he had attracted an audience of primarily young Black people far beyond the membership of the Nation. Dr. Martin Luther King, Jr. had become a regular visitor to Chicago and had several strong allies in the city by 1963, including Rev. Clay Evans, pastor of the Fellowship Baptist Church, and Rev. A.P. Jackson, pastor of Liberty Baptist Church, who were active in supporting the Civil Rights Movement.

The brutal murder of fourteen-year-old Black Chicagoan Emmitt Till in Money, Mississippi in August of 1955 and the December 1955 arrest of Mrs. Rosa Parks after she refused to move to the back of the bus in protest of Alabama's state mandated segregation of public transportation, were the events that gained attention around the world. Both of these incidents gave impetus to the Civil Rights Movement in the city and the election of Harold Washington the first Black mayor of the city, twenty years later in 1983. From 1959, with the candidacy of Lemuel Bentley, the first Black to run citywide for the office of city clerk, until 1983, brave men and women demanded and fought for Black political empowerment. This group included crusading newspaper owner Gus Savage, who was later elected congressman from the second congressional district; attorney James D. Montgomery, who later served as corporation counselor for Mayor Harold Washington; union leader Charles Hayes, who was later elected congressman of the first congressional district; Dempsey J. Travis, author, real estate mogul, NAACP officer, and civil rights activist; Tim Black, professor and civil rights activist; Al Raby, teacher and civil rights leader; A.A. (Sammy) Rayner, funeral director, civil rights activist and alderman; Bob Lucas, U.S. postal worker and leader of the Chicago CORE; attorney Anna Langford, first Black woman elected to the Chicago City Council; Rosie Simpson, civil rights activist; attorney R. Eugene Pincham, later elected as judge of the Illinois Appellate Court; Bennett Johnson, political consultant and civil rights activist; Jorga English (Palmer), writer, community organizer and civil rights activist; Lu Palmer, journalist and civil rights leader; Vernon Jarrett, journalist; Charles Davis, Sr., publicist and NAACP officer; Edwin (Bill) Berry, executive director of the Chicago Urban League; Dick Gregory, comedian and civil rights activist; attorney Lawrence Kennon, civil rights attorney; Brenetta Howell Barrett, civil rights activist and political consultant; Addie Wyatt, union leader and civil rights activist; Rev. Claude Wyatt, minister and civil rights leader; Ishmael Flory, communist party leader; and Richard Durham, writer and organizer. From 1963 to 1968, I met most of them in the course of my civil rights activity.

Between studying at Loyola, working at both the Regal Theater and Montgomery Ward, and spending a lot of my spare time working in civil rights, 1963 was a very busy year for me. This was the year that Governor George Wallace stood in the door at the University of Alabama to prevent Black students from integrating the school; Black Mississippi NAACP leader Medgar Evers was assassinated; the March on Washington occurred in August; in September the KKK bombed the Sixteenth Street Baptist Church in Birmingham, Alabama, killing four Black girls who were attending Sunday school; and in November, President Kennedy was assassinated in Dallas, Texas.

In addition to working with the Freedom School organizers from SNCC and the Coordinating Council of Community Organizations (CCCO) on the massive school boycott, I raised money for the March on Washington, going from door to door in my neighborhood.

It was in these two activities that I first met Lawrence Landry, Rosie Simpson, and James Foreman. The excitement and electricity of this activity at the Packinghouse Workers Union Hall at 48th and Wabash was a beacon to all of us young college students who were eager to join the fight at whatever level possible. Thus, 1963 was a year of triumph and tragedy. We saw some civil rights triumphs and many tragedies at the hands of the KKK and continued resistance from Chicago's "Boss Daley" and his "silent six" Black aldermen who consistently supported his policies.

1964

After SNCC announced its 1964 Mississippi Summer Project, led by people that I admired like Bob Moses, Marian Wright Edelman, Lorne Cress Love, Lawrence Landry and Monroe Sharp, I wanted to go but decided not to after realizing the need to work that summer in order to have money to go back to school in the fall. This was the summer that Chaney, Goodman and Schwerner were murdered by the KKK near Philadelphia, Mississippi; and Fannie Lou Hamer and the Mississippi Freedom Democratic Party upset the proceedings at the Democratic National Convention in Atlantic City, New Jersey. That fall, Dr. Martin Luther King, Jr. received the Nobel Peace Prize and Malcolm X made a pilgrimage to Mecca. Upon his return, he formed the Organization of Afro-American Unity (OAAU). Lastly, the Twenty-fourth Amendment to the Constitution was ratified, which eliminated poll taxes in federal elections. In the fall of 1964 I was able to return to Loyola as a full-time student where I met several fellow students who became solid friends. My close-knit group of friends included Leon Smith (deceased), Joseph Gardner (deceased), insurance executive Al Smith, attorney Gerald Peterson, attorney Weldon Rougeau, attorney Willie Brown, attorney Paula Lingo, and computer company executive Peter Kelly.

By the end of 1964 I was again exhausted from trying to keep up with all the extracurricular activities, maintaining my studies at Loyola, and keeping a job. Luckily, I worked at Montgomery Ward, which was only about eight blocks west of Loyola's Lewis Towers campus. I was able to go to work and leave at 5:00 p.m. to attend classes, which usually began around 6:30 p.m.

1965

I joined the Historical Society, the young Democrats, and the human relations club at Loyola. In these organizations I began to see how connections, family, race, and ethnicity gave some people unearned advantages and left most of us at a real disadvantage. This became crystal clear after sitting in classes with the Italian and Irish scions of Chicago politicians like Richard Daley and John D'Arco (John Daley and John D'Arco, Jr.), who had little or nothing to worry about when it came to grades, while most of us struggled, worked hard, and still got lower grades.

More than any other year of my life as a university student, in 1965 I was experiencing depression and disappointment with the government and the course of the Civil Rights Movement. I had abandoned a belief in the orthodoxy of nonviolence, and I had become a fervent admirer of Malcolm X and his notion of "liberation by any means necessary." Thus, when I watched the reports of Malcolm's assassination on that sad day in February, I was saddened, angry, and in mourning along with my fellow classmates for days. We were convinced that we had lost our "shining Prince." We were convinced that the revolution was just around the corner. Little did we know that the last five years of the 1960s would be even more violent and devastating to our communities.

Because of increasing involvement in SNCC, Black and white friends of mine and I organized the Loyola Friends of SNCC, which I chaired, and we began organizing on campus. One of our first efforts was supporting the Selma, Alabama campaign and the Lowndes County, Alabama movement to register voters, which was being spearheaded by SNCC and its charismatic leader, Stokely Carmichael, aka Kwame Toure, Cleve Sellers and Rap Brown. In the heat of this support effort, following that "Bloody Sunday", we solicited funds from our fellow students at the Loyola Lewis Towers campus student union. As I moved from table to table collecting money, I encountered a smart-mouthed redneck student who said in a loud voice, "I did not know that Selma was sick." At that point we began to tussle and engage in fisticuffs, ending in a mini riot. University officials called off the solicitation and forbade us from further solicitations on the grounds that we had not gotten official permission to collect donations.

Our Loyola SNCC group never allowed the occasional taunts and slurs from the white students at the university to divert us from our goal of supporting the civil rights movement and SNCC in particular. While we were quickly moving further to the left in our opposition to the war in Vietnam and our growing appeals to radicalism, we fully supported Dr. King's Selma to Montgomery march. We were horrified by the continued violence in the South, which resulted in the death of civil rights workers. We sent letters of support and money to the Selma workers. We followed closely the Watts riot in Los Angeles and correctly predicted further riots around the country.

One of the few bits of good news in that entire year was the signing of the Voting Rights Act. We were emboldened by the news that Dr. King was making plans to bring his SCLC movement to Chicago. Our SNCC group immediately made contact with the Chicago leadership and was eventually assigned to Rev. James Bevel as our contact. We then began attending meetings and rallies in support of Dr. King under Rev. Bevel's direction. I was already in regular contact with the Chicago Friends of SNCC office, led by James Foreman, Fannie Rushing, Bob Brown, Monroe Sharp, and Sylvia Fisher and her husband. I eagerly attended every speaking engagement and rally sponsored by SNCC that featured Stokely Carmichael.

1966

When Rap Brown and Stokely Carmichael announced that they wanted to encourage whites in SNCC to go back to their communities to organize and fight racism in their own backyards, we were told that this was the end of the organization. However, what these critics did not take into account was the fact that the Chicago Friends of SNCC's partnership with SCLC in the northern freedom movement energized SNCC and attracted more young people to its ranks. It was our group that rallied to the call of Bob Lucas to march into Gage Park and Cicero. It was our group that marched with Dr. King in his campaign for open housing.

The summer of 1966 was a very busy one for me. I was employed as a junior claims examiner at Prudential Life Insurance Company on North Michigan Avenue, where I worked from nine to five. After leaving Prudential I walked to City Hall and joined the marches to the Board of Education and sit-ins that protested the segregated schools. After demonstrating, I proceeded to the Federal Reserve Building where I worked as a check sorter until ten p.m. At the same time I was following the march through Mississippi, the shooting of James Meredith, SNCC's Willie Ricks' declaration of Black Power in the town square of Grenada, Mississippi, the racial disturbances in Chicago and the founding of the Black Panther Party.

1967

The winter, spring and summer of 1967 was an especially lively one for me and my fellow activists at Loyola. We were pleased with the appointment of Thurgood Marshall to the Supreme Court and the election of Carl Stokes as the first Black mayor of Cleveland, Ohio. However, our prediction of more riots and rebellions in major cities was more than fulfilled. We saw cities like Newark and Detroit go up in flames.

This was the year that I completed my BA at Loyola, and after years of student activism connecting me with college students from around the city, state, and the Midwest, it was clear that we needed to convene a meeting of some kind to discuss the next step in the student movement. My fellow Loyola activist Earl Jones, who was from Newark, and I contacted Stan Willis, who was at that time a student at Crane Junior College (soon to be renamed Malcolm X College). We decided to take up the challenge issued by the leadership of the Nation Black Power Conference held in Newark, New Jersey for Black students in three cities (Los Angeles, Chicago, and Baltimore) to hold a student conference during the Thanksgiving break. Stan Willis, Earl Jones, Ernestine Jackson and I met at Loyola and at my home in South Shore for more than a month to plan the conference.

We were fully aware of the rebellions being carried out by Black students in high schools and colleges demanding curriculum changes that reflected Black people, books by and written about Black people, and more Black teachers. The student movement was in sync with the national Black Power movement. Thus, we stated our goals and objectives as follows: (1) to establish a national Black communication system (2) to create awareness and provoke activity amongst students in the Midwest (3) to establish operational unity between Black students and the inner city community (4) to present meaningful alternatives to oppression (5) to establish a strong bond between Black students and the Black community and maintain the skills necessary for our liberation.

The first Midwestern Regional Conference of the Black Students' Alliance was held at Dr. John Porter's church, Christ Methodist, at 6401 S. Sangamon on November 23-25, 1967. Earl Jones and I were from Loyola, Stan Willis and Robert Clay represented Crane Junior College, James Harvey and James Crooks represented Wilson Junior College, Shedrick Sanders and Camille Landry represented the University of Illinois, Michael Orr represented Central YMCA College, James Moore represented Roosevelt University, and Linda Hughes represented the University of Pittsburgh.

Invited speakers included: Dick Gregory, Charles V. Hamilton, Lawrence Landry, Lerone Bennett, Ruwa Chiri, Odis Hyde, Nahaz Rogers, Bob Carter, Roscoe Mitchell, Muhammad Ali, Robert Brown, Alderman Sammy Rayner, Diane Nash Bevel, David Llorens, Elliott Evans, Russ Meeks, Dr. Hollis Lynch, Margaret Burroughs, Don L. Lee, Jewel Lattimore, Richard Abrams, Conrad Kent Rivers, Anthony Braxton, Bob Lucas, Rev. John Porter, and Lou House.

Workshops were allocated as follows: (1) Politics—Stan Willis and Robert Starks (2) Economics—Camille Landry (3) Education—Ernestine Jackson (4) Communications—Earl Jones and Jim Moore (5) Culture—Clifton Haywood (6) The role of Black men and Black women—James Crooks (brothers) and Linda Hughes (sisters). At the insistence of Bob Rhodes we added a workshop on political economy that he and Louis Randall conducted.

This conference was extremely successful and resulted in the development of the Communiversity, founded by Drs. Anderson Thompson and Harold Pates, which convened at the Center for Inner City Studies from 1968 to 1975. This conference and other regional Black student conferences also laid the foundation for the emergence of the Black Studies programs on college campuses. We helped further activate Black student organizing in high schools, and we gave momentum to the African American Student Association that was in its infancy.

Additionally, we raised the issue of Pan-Africanism, and Ruwa Chiri and Hollis Lynch led discussions on African liberation during the conference. We talked about South African apartheid. I had been put on the anti-apartheid mailing list by fellow student activist Weldon Rougeau and eagerly participated in this discussion. Perhaps the most dramatic presentations came from Rev. James Bevel and Dick Gregory, who revealed to us for the first time the plans for the protests of Black athletes at the 1968 Olympic Games in Mexico City, Mexico. Rev. James Bevel defended interracial mating as a means of increasing the number of Black soldiers in the "Black army of liberation." Russ Meeks urged us to get guns and fight to defend our communities. Perhaps the most important thing that came out of the 1967 conference was that it helped to prepare my generation of activists to begin organizing and working for the electoral progress that we were able to make in the seventies, eighties and nineties.

The overall events of 1967 presaged Black America's reaction to the tragedies of 1968. Black America, especially the youth, was fed up with the blatant racism and began a more comprehensive examination of it, concluding that we were facing a worldwide phenomenon called white supremacy and that the liberation of Africa was one of the major components of a victory over white supremacy. We emerged from this examination thoroughly committed to the philosophy of Pan-Africanism and Black Power.

1968

Of all the years in the 1960s, 1968 was the most earth-shattering. The events, tragedies and victories of 1968 forced all of those sitting on the fence to choose sides. It finally unleashed the enormous political, social and economic energy of Black people in this country and African peoples across the world and intensified their determination to fight. It demonstrated the real limits of a people who are uninvolved and uninformed. The push for Black studies was intensified, the number of Black elected officials began to multiply, affirmative action became a matter of public policy, Black opposition to the war in Vietnam became a national issue, and activity for Pan-Africanism was finally realized.

We should have known that 1968 would be a different kind of year with the February massacre of students at Orangeburg, South Carolina where many Black students were killed and wounded. We continued in the courts and on the streets unanimous in our criticism of the Nation Advisory Commission on Civil Disorders (the Kerner Commission Report) that was issued in February 1968. Our criticism was based upon our objection to the conclusion that the solution to the "urban problem," which was largely characterized as a "Black problem," was due to the concentration of Blacks in urban enclaves in the nation's largest cities. The report advocated a massive "de-concentration policy", in which Blacks would be given incentives to move to surrounding suburban communities. We immediately saw this as a move to lessen Black political power and influence by dispersing Black people throughout the metropolitan areas where their political power and influence would be minimal.

In the meantime we applauded Dr. King's stand against the war in Vietnam as we participated in demonstrations and rallies against the war. In 1967 I entered Loyola's graduate program in urban studies after earning my BA degree. I was given a recommendation for a job at the newly created Urban Education Center, which was in a building on the site of the future Malcolm X College. It was at the Urban Education Center where I worked with the directors, Dr. Myra Adams and Dr. Ross Adams, while continuing my studies. One of my students in this alternative high school program was Sam Jordan, aka Toure, who would later become a fireman and is now director of the local chapter of Ameri-I-Can, a Black youth violence prevention program. This was my first venture into the field of teaching. I had promised myself that I would not become a teacher; I had always wanted to go to law school and join a big law firm. However, I found teaching to be intriguing and quite satisfying.

It was during this teaching stint that on the tragic day of April 4, while entering my car after a day of working and an evening class at Loyola, I turned on my radio and heard the sad news that Dr. King had been assassinated. The tragedy of that day and that news will haunt me for the rest of my life! The next day, I went immediately to Loyola and gathered the Black student members of the LUASA (which I had organized a year earlier) in a meeting, as did my fellow students at Northwestern, U of I, and all of the Black colleges and universities in the country. We demanded full official recognition of LUASA, scholarships for Black students, aggressive recruitment of Black students from the inner city, and an official university memorial program to honor Dr. King.

At home I watched Rev. Jess Jackson and Mrs. Jackson (who lived across the street from me on Ridgeland Avenue) mourn the loss of Dr. King upon his return from Memphis. The staff and faculty at the Urban Education Center organized a memorial program for Dr. King and invited Russ Meeks as one of our guest speakers. Our students were genuinely saddened and outraged. Some of them later participated in the rebellion that occurred on the West Side of Chicago. My activist friends and I spent the following week in discussions with our intellectual leaders like Bob Rhodes, Gerald McWorter, and Nahaz Rogers, seeking guidance because we were convinced that the revolution was around the corner. We wanted to be ready for whatever developed. We explored every option, including mass exodus from America. We had many disagreements over the next steps to be taken. However, we all agreed that we had to go to the West Side and take money, food, and clothing to those who had been burned out by the rebellion following the King assassination. Further, we all agreed that we should support the newly formed Black Panther Party and join forces with West Sider "Fats" Crawford and Russ Meeks in their efforts to form a National Black Rifle Association.

We were pleased when President Johnson signed the Civil Rights Act of 1968, which banned discrimination in the sale and rental of housing. However, we were disappointed with the news of the assassination of Robert Kennedy in June 1968. We were in contact with fellow activists in Cleveland when rioting erupted there in late June. In August of that year Chicago became the epicenter of radicalism in the country. The Civil Rights forces, the anti-war forces and the poor people's movement/welfare rights groups converged in the city. This was one of the first times that radical Black, white, and Hispanic activists joined forces to protest. The protests were aimed at the Democratic Party and Hubert H. Humphrey, the Democratic Party presidential nominee who refused to denounce the war in Vietnam. After months of violence, threats of violence, and radical speech, seemingly the entire movement had assembled in downtown Chicago to confront the leadership of the Democratic Party.

Rioting lasted throughout the August 26-30 Democratic Convention along Michigan Avenue, in front of the hotels where the leadership was staying. Given the close relationships between the faculty of Loyola University and the Daley administration, whenever I participated in demonstrations in downtown Chicago I often encountered part-time Loyola University faculty members who were also City Corporation Counsel employees. During one night of the convention while a police riot was in progress, I passed myself off as a member of the press; I was able to go behind police lines where I came face to face with one of my grad school teachers who jokingly said, "Since you are a member of the press you may move forward!" I then stood on top of a police wagon and took photos and notes. The irony of this incident was that I knew many of the people like Bill Ayers and Marilyn Katz. If they had known that I was posing as a reporter to observe police violence, they would have denounced me as a traitor. Frankly, for a brief moment, I chuckled at the reality of seeing white demonstrators getting billy club beatings and tear gas after witnessing police violence being perpetrated on Black people for so long. The chuckle soon went silent after observing the brutality of the police and the fact that Black dissidents, including Bobby Seale, were being brutalized. This turbulent year ended with one of the biggest letdowns of all, the election of Richard Nixon as president.

The political fallout of the events of 1968 brought about government programs that were designed to quell the urban rebellions that were consuming the cities. One of these programs was the Concentrated Employment Program (CEP). CEP was a federal program that was supposed to help locate and develop jobs for inner city residents. The management consulting firm, Booz-Allen and Hamilton, was contacted to set up CEP programs in the Midwest. Ross Adams, a fellow teacher at the Urban Education Center, was a management consultant for this firm. He recommended me to the firm and I was hired as a management consultant. I became one of the three or four Blacks who were hired by the company. We were needed to help them gain entry into Black communities that whites were not welcomed in at that time. I set up the CEP office in East St. Louis, Illinois and worked in Minneapolis, Minnesota and New York City. By mid-1969 most of the CEP offices had been put in place and I was transferred to Booz-Allen Applied Research (BAHR, Inc.) where I worked until I was hired in mid-1969 into the research department of the Chicago Urban League.

1969

The Black Manifesto and James Foreman, Nixon's affirmative action program and the so-called "Black capitalism", were all themes that captured the imagination of young Black people in 1969. We all took sides in the great debate—should Black people join the Black capitalism bandwagon and sanction the economic system that enslaved our forefathers, or chart out a strident Black Nationalist/Black socialist course? We spent endless hours debating these ideas while reading and analyzing Karl Marx, Frederick Engels and the Black Nationalist writers like Harold Cruse. Psychologist Dr. Bobby Wright, who discussed the analysis of political economist, Bob Rhodes, Tony Montero, Harold Pates, Anderson Thompson, and Lorenzo Martin led loud and sometimes raucous opposition to some of these presentations at the Communiversity, Bob Rhodes' house, or at one of our campus hangouts at the University of Chicago.

All of this debate and discussion served as fuel for me in my MA program at Loyola. The Urban Studies program was an interdisciplinary program that employed the disciplines of economics, political science and sociology. Since I had received my BA in Political Science and had taken several economics and philosophy courses, I found these discussions exactly what I needed as validation for the arguments that I often found myself in during these classes. Later, it became clear to me that it was futile for me to argue with Loyola's mainstream instructors, who were convinced that the world was fine just the way it was and only needed a little tweaking here and there. I persevered and received my MA in Urban Studies in 1970.

Meanwhile, my experience at the Chicago Urban League was profoundly instructive. In the research department I was assigned the job of fact-finding and report writing, as well as working on a team that produced major annual research reports. My experience at Booz-Allen and Hamilton had prepared me for much of what was expected of me at the Urban League.

While at the League, I was reunited with civil rights activist Rosie Simpson, whom I had met while she was a stalwart fighter for the education of Black inner city children. She was working in the advocacy department with Connie Seals and Marian Henley. Edwin C. "Bill" Berry was the executive director of the Urban League and James Compton was a middle level administrator working under the tutelage of Mr. Berry in training as his successor.

It was also in 1969 when Bill Berry was one of the major principle actors in the planning of the Black Strategy Center, which was the white elites' concession to the Black community after the turbulence of the 1960s. Hampton McKinney, an assistant to Bill Berry, was appointed by Bill Berry to negotiate with the white civic elites who were members of the State Street Council and the men who were donating the money for the Center. McKinney chose me to accompany him to the meetings and take notes. My experience at Booz-Allen and Hamilton prepared me for the task as an assistant to McKinney. This was my first face-to-face contact with the movers and shakers of Chicago. I came away from these meetings realizing that these men were offering money and a commitment to a Black Strategy Center only because their backs were against the wall and they saw this as a liberal approach to appease the Black leadership.

John Higginson, a coworker in the research department and now a history professor at the University of Massachusetts, and I were summoned to the office of Mr. Berry when Rev. C.T. Vivian read the press statement that urged white people to leave the Black community by sundown for their own protection. We were ordered to help shape a response to the statement, which we later found out, was written by Jorja English (Palmer) and read by Rev. Vivian without careful review. Mr. Berry performed the role of apologist for the Black community in situations like this and he faced the news media with an apology we helped craft.

As newer radicals, Higginson and I took the initiative to demonstrate to Bill Berry the relevance of the Black Panther Party's Ten Point Program, after the assassination of Fred Hampton and Mark Clark. Again, upon being summoned to Berry's office to provide background material for his response to the assassinations, we urged him to have the Urban League adopt the Ten Point Program of the Black Panther Party. After our passionate and reasoned plea Berry looked up at us with tears in his eyes and said that we had "not learned a damn thing" that he had tried to teach us! He made it crystal clear to us that he was not about to embrace anything advocated by the Black Panther Party. He did, however, make it clear that he would go to the mat to uncover the truth behind the murders.

1970

1970 was a breakthrough year for me. In addition to my duties as a research specialist, I was regularly sent out to public forums and groups to represent the Urban League. I participated with the Chicago founders in the first celebration of Earth Day on April 22 of 1970. I was invited to represent the Chicago Urban League at Northern Illinois University in DeKalb, Illinois. It was after that speech when I was approached by a student leader, Jerald Durley (now Rev. Durley, pasturing a church in Atlanta with Rev. C.T. Vivian), Franklin Walker, and Parker Jenkins, who were staff members of the CHANCE program, a Black student recruiting program. They asked me if I would be interested in coming to NIU to put together a new Black Studies program. After a month of negotiations I agreed. I moved to DeKalb in September of 1970.

The move to DeKalb changed my plans and direction. I had completed my MA in Urban Studies and was on my way to law school at the University of Chicago when I realized that if I was going to be a professor in the university, I had to get a Ph.D. I immediately switched plans and entered the Ph.D. program in Political Science at the University of Chicago.

1971

In 1971 I was working at NIU and commuting to Chicago to take classes at U of C. That same year I was engaged to Judith Minor and we got married in August of that year. At Northern I was reunited with John Higginson, who was my coworker at the Urban League, and John Bracey, whom I had crossed paths with in my student activist days. In addition to professors Higginson and Bracey, the Black faculty also included Dr. Christopher Reed (now professor emeritus at Roosevelt University), all of whom were teaching in the History Department. Other Black faculty included the Rev. Dr. Eddie Williams, Jr. in Mathematics, Nelson Stevens from the Art Department and a member of the group AFRI-COBRA, and Dale Spann, also in the Art Department. Together, we created the most aggressive Black Studies program in the Midwest. After several meetings with Black students, and surveying their skills and interests, we formed the Black Drama Group, the Black Band Ensemble, the Black Dance Ensemble, and the Black History Club. We put these groups together under the Black studies umbrella and combined our efforts with the already existing Black Gospel Choir.

Most of the Black students were from inner city high schools in Chicago, and came to the university through the CHANCE program at the height of the Civil Rights Movement and the student protest movement. They were all very bright and extremely resourceful. Day after day I was called upon to get them out of some dispute or problem they had gotten themselves into with the university authorities, or some of the local merchants or police in DeKalb. We were given a little white house on the south edge of campus that the students dubbed the "Black House." We officially named it the Center for Black Studies. It was at the Center where we put together one of the most ambitious African Arts Festival programs in the country. At each program we featured a lecturer who would speak on a contemporary subject followed by top entertainment. For example, on one occasion we featured a lecture by John Woodford, then editor of Muhammad Speaks, followed by a Nina Simone concert. In 1971 and 1972 we featured concerts with artists like the Impressions, Dick Gregory, Leon Thomas, and Pharaoh Saunders, Osibisa, Leroi Jones and many others. All of these cultural events were supplemented by student trips to Washington, D.C., Black Expo, Operation PUSH, and other universities for performances. Meanwhile, the Black Studies faculty worked with me to construct a solid Black Studies minor curriculum including courses from the Art, Music, and Dance departments. Students were immersed in a solid, Pan-African cultural and academic experience. All have gone on to successful professional careers.

In the course of my travel back and forth to the University of Chicago I maintained contact with Dr. Carol Adams and Anderson Thompson, who were on the faculty at the Center for Inner City Studies (CICS) of Northeastern Illinois University. After getting married and expecting our first child, it was clear that the commute to Chicago was becoming more and more of a problem. I therefore eagerly accepted the offer from Drs. Carol Adams, Jacob Carruthers, and Nancy Arnaz (the director of CICS) to join the faculty. Thus, I was able to continue my study and reconnect with the movement community. The Center also provided me with fertile intellectual soil to continue to grow and develop as a Pan-Africanist. In addition to Carol Adams we had Dr. Joseph Pentecoste in Statistics, Dr. Donn Bailey in Linguistics, Dr. William Smith in Psychology, Dr. Elkin Sithole in Ethnomusicology, and several other adjunct instructors that included Lorenzo Martin (*Suburban Standard* newspaper), Harold Pates, and Professor Armstead Allen.

My first year at the Center was a year of learning for me. The university teaching experience that I brought with me from NIU was geared towards students who were young, recent high school graduates. The first students in my classes at NEIU were women teacher aides in a program that was designed to allow them to complete their BA degrees. Most of them were mature women who had been out of school for some time. They immediately informed me that my University of Chicago approach was not acceptable and I had to go back to the drawing board and come in with a more sensitive teaching approach. My first classes in September of 1972 did more than anything, before or since, to help me hone my teaching style and communications skills in the classroom.

1973-1975

The years between 1973 and 1975 brought me a fast pace of work and study, along with the birth of my first child in late 1972 and my wife Judith's employment in the Cultural Linguistic Approach Follow Through program at NEIU along with Bernetta Bush, now a retired judge, and Dr. Donald R. Linder.

At this time, the Center was the epicenter of Pan-African activism. We worked on the National Black Political Assembly and held endless meetings to help organize efforts for the advancement of local Black political empowerment. Upon coming to the Center I renewed my relationships with the political leaders and elected officials who I had worked with prior to going to DeKalb. I began by inviting Samuel Patch, a political ally of Harold Washington then in the Illinois State General Assembly; Senator Richard Newhouse, Cook County Board commissioner; John Stroger, State Comptroller/Attorney General; Roland Burris, and political operatives like Lu and Jorja Palmer to forums to speak to our students. These forums, combined with the continuity of the Communiversity and Pan-African organizing by my fellow faculty members Anderson Thompson and Lorenzo Martin and our activist students, put the Center on the front line of every major event and/or crisis that faced the Black community in Chicago and the rest of the nation.

By the end of 1975 we were already in touch with the national and international Pan-African intellectuals like: Cheik Anta Diop, John H. Clarke, Chancellor Williams, Harold Cruse, Chenwezu Bento and many others. We were also in contact with liberation fighters in Africa through Dr. Elkin Sithole, who was a South African Ethnomusicologist who maintained contact with the ANC leadership. Anderson Thompson had established contacts with the liberation fighters in other parts of Africa because of our work in the Communiversity, which in 1975 had gained international recognition. We worked with the organizers of the first African Liberation Day March and the declaration of Washington Park as Malcolm X Park. We worked with the group that organized N'COBRA. We worked very closely with Lu Palmer and his launching of the *Black X-Press* newspaper.

By 1975 I knew that I had found my place in academia, the Center for Inner Studies of Northeastern Illinois University. While I had interviewed at Roosevelt University and had been contacted by other universities and a research institution, I decided that Northeastern was the place for me unless I was offered an opportunity that was many times better. The clear advantage of working at CICS was the proximity of my home to the center, which was about five minutes away by car. I lived within walking distance of the University of Chicago where I was attending graduate school. Living in Hyde Park, I was close to my mother and mother-in-law, which allowed us access to reliable child care after the birth of my first child, Kenya. My wife Judith was hired by the Cultural Linguistic Approach Follow Through program, a research and development program that focused on Afro-centric teaching methods for children in the primary grades. This program was developed at CICS under the leadership of Dr. Nancy Arnez, the Center's director. I was able to expand my teacher education methods while serving along with Joseph Pentecoste, as a consultant to the Follow Through program. Program staff included Bernetta Bush, now a retired Cook County judge; Dr. Donald Linder, a Chicago Public Schools administrator; and Naomi Millender, a retired educational consultant.

Fellow faculty members at CICS were Dr. Jacob Carruthers, a political scientist who was a specialist in political philosophy; Dr. Anderson Thompson, a historian specializing in American and African history; Dr. William Smith, a psychologist specializing in human behavior; Dr. Carol Adams, a sociologist specializing in urban sociology; Dr. Joseph Pentecoste, a statistician and psychologist; Dr. Donn Bailey, a speech and linguistics specialist; Dr. Elkin Sithole, a South African ethnomusicologist; and Dr. Sherman Beverly, a historian specializing in urban history. We were all uniquely suited for an inner city studies curriculum.

We were in the process of defining and solidifying inner city studies as a new discipline when we became intellectually united in this process. First, we were faced with transforming a curriculum that was designed to train teachers in a master's degree program to encompass an incoming undergraduate program in Inner City Studies. Secondly, we had to establish the philosophical basis for this newly emerging discipline, which was by definition interdisciplinary. The interdisciplinary aspect of the curriculum, i.e. Political Science, Sociology, Economics, and History, placed it in a group similar to Urban Studies. My MA was in Urban Studies, with an emphasis in urban politics, which made me keenly aware of the fact that we had to steer a clear course that would make Inner City Studies distinctively different from Urban Studies. Our entire faculty was well aware of these realities and understood the need to make Inner City Studies a distinct discipline that was focused on the inner city, its African American residents, and the problems that they encounter in a white supremacist society.

However, it was Jacob Carruthers and Anderson Thompson who reminded us that we were African people who were members of the African family and as such we could not construct a comprehensive discipline if we confined it to the American shores and a European centered perspective. At the same time, we could not limit our examination of African American history and the history of African Americans in inner cities to the twentieth century. We had to construct a discipline that would encompass the whole history of the African experience from the beginning of human history to the building of the pyramids along the Nile to the Great Zimbabwe and all of the great civilizations of Africa that included all of the cities of ancient Africa. It was important to understand the relationship that African people have had to cities and civilizations prior to the invasion of the Arab slavers and the Europeans in the fifteenth century. It was clear to us that there was no other way we could fully understand the travails of African people from the beginning of human history to the present. We had to adopt an African-centered approach.

Most approaches to the study of the inner city and its African American residents begins at the dawn of the Great Migration of 1914-1918 and some so-called progressive approaches will begin the study at the end of the Civil War. We were determined to construct a curriculum and a discipline that would link the ancient African civilization, the traditional African family and community to African culture and spirituality, all of which have been passed on from generation to generation and remains within African American culture—African American existence in a society that brought them to these shores in chains, enslaved them, and created institutional racism as a virulent form of white supremacy that bred segregated inner cities and structural inequality.

All of my experiences in the movement, my formal study and training, as well as my observations of the transforming events of the 1960s, helped to prepare me for participation in the making of the first African-centered Inner City Studies discipline and curriculum. I am eternally grateful to my mother for her insistence that I network with as many people of different backgrounds as possible. Networking and working to become a good listener were two qualities that my mother and grandmother demanded of me as a child. Frankly, being able to listen to others and take seriously what it is that they are saying have been qualities that I have worked hard at sharpening all of my life. As a result of my struggle to be a good and keen listener, I have become a better teacher. While I come to my classroom presentations with more knowledge and understanding of the subjects than my students, I am constantly amazed at the questions that are raised as a result of lecture and discussions. Students are often unaware of the fact that in many cases their lively classroom exchanges result in my discovering more of the nuances of a given topic than I would have otherwise. This systematic, intellectual sharing of ideas, clarification of meaning, and conceptual calibrating sharpens my understanding of the subject. After rigorous discussions I am able to formulate the most appropriate manner in which that topic should be presented for maximum understanding.

It was after my first encounters with middle-aged teachers' aides, who had come back to CICS to complete their BA degrees, when I began to develop this pedagogic approach. These women in my first classes at CICS endured what I thought were gems of intellectual wisdom for about two weeks when they demanded that I abandon that approach and engage them in intellectual exchange that would allow them to better understand the concepts. The reality was that I was not listening. I was simply lecturing to a class that was eager to understand, but was better able to understand in a sharing environment. As part of my participation in the development of the African-centered approach to inner city studies, I began to understand that a sharing environment of exchange between teacher and students is in the tradition of the African griot and fully in the African educational tradition.

Lastly, we referred to ourselves as a family, the CICS family. This family included everyone in the building from the engineers and janitors to the students and faculty, as well as the members of our associated groups like the Communiversity, the African Historians Association, the Kemetic Institute, and later, the Task Force for Black Political Empowerment. It was this African-centered family atmosphere that was intellectually nurturing for members who had mutual respect for each other and their views. This environment has allowed me to grow and develop as a teacher and as a person.

My continued development from the 1970s to the present has been supported by the people that I have been able to meet and network with. We continued to grow as long as we live and our potential is only limited by the scope of our dreams. We are the products of the dreams of our ancestors and ourselves. Dreams are born out of our spirit. The African spirit is the only aspect of our being that has sustained us throughout our travails in this country. "African Spirituality," in the fabled words of the Black spiritual song, "It was good enough for my father and mother and it is good enough for me!" In the African oral tradition it is said that "the body of a man is very small compared with the spirit that inhabits it." In the tradition of the Eurocentric society of America we constantly stress to our children the importance of nurturing and developing our physical, psychological, and social aspects, while often neglecting our spiritual aspect. In order to grow and develop in a positive manner, we must give proper attention to the development of our spiritual growth. I hope to be able to continue to grow, to develop, and serve my community.

THE CHICAGO URBAN LEAGUE 1973 ANNUAL LUNCHEON SPEECH

James Compton

It is no news to anyone who so much as reads a daily paper, or follows the news offhandedly on television, that this city is in an acute social crisis. The crisis is both urban and radical, and the time available to us to make necessary adjustments is short. It is also clear that there is no institution of substance which is not involved, nor one which does not have a responsibility to discharge and a role to play in arriving at necessary social adjustments while there is still time.

It should not surprise you that I shall dwell now upon the racial aspects of the crisis, for it is born out of the open neglect of the troubles of tens of millions of Americans and the frightening divisiveness which this neglect has produced. What's more, this divisiveness is growing and the tensions it builds are becoming more dangerous.

The only practical answer to such a situation, quite obviously, is for all of us to come together in facing up to the facts and finding practical alternatives to the growing chaos.

And that is exactly why the Urban League is in business. Bringing people together is the method we've been using for many years and it is still our method. We believe that the real answers come when interracial cooperation is the rule, rather than the exception.

In this difficult year of 1973, we'll be driving harder than ever in the pursuit of our goals. But our way will still be to marshal the best strengths of the Black community and the white community to work together.

But events around us are changing so fast that the strategies we undertook in the past are not adequate to cover the growing list of problems that face us in 1973. The first thing this means is that we have to put more emphasis than ever on researching the problems, and on educating the total Chicago community. Facts are our number one weapon. The more we find them, and use them to educate and motivate the entire community, the more we all can move ahead. So you can count on me to push in this direction, toward mutual understanding, to the limit of our resources.

In all this we shall, of course, adhere to the Urban League rule of accountability and responsibility. We don't seek sensationalism, but we will reveal and report the good as well as the bad. And we will criticize wrong-doers, whatever their rank, whatever their color.

All this, I must remind you, is for the good of all of Chicago and while our obvious responsibility is to the minority American, we live up to our responsibility when we help the whole community; for no city can be healthy when so many are handicapped. No city can long remain great unless it eliminates the cancer which strikes at its heart.

That is why it is so extremely important for the ultimate survival of Chicago that the Chicago Urban League survives as a strong, healthy, and viable organization.

At the Urban League we have had unusual experience in analyzing the disastrous effects of the evil doctrines we have lived under for so many years. We have learned, through those years of experience, that interracial cooperation towards a common goal is the only effective and practical way to achieve a lasting solution to the main problems that threaten our lives and our city.

In order to ease the tensions and fears that exist between Blacks and whites in Chicago, the rational and racially balanced approach that the League personifies is a most essential approach.

The current situation in Gage Park offers an example of the kind of tension I'm talking about. Contrary to what the white parents in that community have stated, the issue here is not, and never has been, one of school overcrowding. But rather, it is the same old story of a neighborhood in transition that we have seen many, many times before. Only this time, the resident white people have gone to unusual lengths to try to enforce their racism.

The real issue before us is whether or not Black people and white people can live peacefully together in a truly integrated community. Whether the pattern that we have seen so many times before must continue to repeat itself with whites moving out. The quality and maintenance of the schools going down. The apartment buildings being neglected by their absentee owners, and the neighborhood gradually becoming ghetto. This is why the Chicago Urban League has involved itself in this critical situation. This is why we have investigated it, publicized our findings, and this is why we have gone to work to try to bring the two sides together in an atmosphere of mutual respect and cooperation.

For we know that if Gage Park goes the way of similar neighborhoods, then it will signal the continuation of a trend that has gone unchecked far too long.

Now, to get back to the broader question of what the Chicago Urban League plans to do about all this. What I have to say here may well be the most important thing that I could say to an audience such as this.

It is not a happy thing. In fact, I am saddened by the need to tell it. But the facts have to be presented.

Instead of dwelling on the very substantial good the League has done, I am going to give this frank appraisal.

First, although our contribution has been great, it is not enough to do the total job which must be done.

Second, although we have led and encouraged many others to do more and do better, the scale of that cooperation has been, and still is, far out of proportion to the real need.

It would be all too very easy for me to glorify here the results the Chicago Urban League has been able to produce. In proportion to the resources we've had to work with, the results have been superlative. But, it is high time now for all of us to realize that the problems facing Black and other minority residents in Chicago are deeply ingrained in the lifestyle and institutions of the city. The resources of the Urban League alone are far from adequate to deal with them all.

We have developed a program that we feel will generate better life chances, and chances for life, for many victimized people. But we are in no position to make the fundamental changes in the systems and institutions that govern our lives that are necessary to eliminate or even significantly alleviate the many problems that face our city's Black and poor people.

The truth of the matter is that we need a lot more help. We need the help of concerned people of all races and from all walks of life.

If there is to be any real change in the dismal future that is projected for poor people in this city, then it can only occur if a higher, more responsible type of leadership arises from both the Black and the white communities—the type of leadership that takes into account the morality and interests of all people. A leadership that is totally committed to the goal of equalizing the life chances and economic possibilities of all Chicagoans, regardless of race or origin of birth.

Now, let me take just a few moments to give you a picture of some of the problems that I'm talking about.

Three years ago, Bill Berry addressed a similar gathering. He said that the decade of the sixties was a decade of recognition in the field of race relations—a decade wherein Blacks and whites came closer together in an effort to understand the meaning of true citizenship equality more than ever before. He expressed expectations that the seventies would be a decade of execution during which the increased understanding generated during the sixties would begin to bear fruit in concrete improvements in the gross inequities that characterize American society. But I am sorry to report that instead of heightened interracial cooperation and understanding; the seventies have brought increased polarization. Far more of the economic and policy making sectors and the political leaders of the population have generally seen fit to turn their backs on the problems of the poor and the oppressed.

As University of Chicago sociologist and Chicago Urban League board member Dr. Philip M. Hauser recently stated: "If this nation continues to ignore its minority group problems, the future of Chicago and other metropolitan areas may well be the same as that which we read about every day in Northern Ireland."

Let's take a look at these specifics: Over the past few years, we have seen a great upsurge in the development and prosperity of this city. We have witnessed a large increase in construction in the Loop and adjacent areas, and we've seen thousands of workers pouring into newly completed buildings. We also see on the north side of the city many new luxury condominiums. But nowhere in this massive resurgence of city life do we see anything having more than a minimal effect on the housing of Black and poor people. In addition, during the year 1972, ninety percent of the people who came to the Urban League offices seeking jobs were unemployed. Sixty-six percent of these had been out of work for over fifteen weeks, and the majority had earned less than five thousand dollars per year on their previous jobs. During this period of unrivaled prosperity in our nation, unemployment among Blacks has risen from six point seven percent in 1968 to a reported present ten point two percent. And that ten percent doesn't include a vast number who aren't even reported as in the job market. Nor does that ten percent reflect the frightening higher percentage among our youth between the ages of sixteen and twenty-five. Compound these facts with the veteran returning home from Vietnam, trained for an occupation for which society has no demand—unable to find work or job training—thereby being left to erupt as a volcano in the streets of our cities.

During the period between 1955 and 1970, an excess of 150,000 jobs left the inner city for the suburbs—mostly beyond the range of inner city dwellers. This trend can be expected to continue, resulting in even greater unemployment for semi-skilled and unskilled Black workers.

During the past few years, between 20,000-30,000 jobs have developed in the city, but the majority of these are clerical and paraprofessional positions. These jobs haven't even been enough to provide places for the increased number of new white job seekers, much less provide employment for those whose jobs left the city. In addition, our current mass transportation system—which is being threatened with less service, increased fares, and fewer jobs—is totally inadequate to take inner city residents to the job markets that are opening up in suburban communities. To compound the evil, suburban housing is too expensive for most Black and other minority residents, and very little is being done to create new low and moderate income housing in suburban areas where it is so desperately needed.

And, as we look for a minute at the professional and managerial categories, where it is true that minorities have made 130 percent advancement in professional positions and sixty-seven percent advancement in managerial positions, it also should be remembered that the ten year base was very close to zero. As we further analyze this situation, it is very evident that the vast majority of these jobs are concentrated at the bottom of the corporate structure. The number of Black and other minority professionals who function within their corporations on anything close to a decision-making level is less than three percent.

Partially because of what I have just described, census bureau figures show us that the relative position of Black families as against that of whites is getting worse instead of better. In 1960, white families earned on an average of 2,900 dollars per year more than Black families. In 1970, the figures showed that white families earned 4,500 dollars per year more! And so, we are going backward rather than forward—retrogressing rather than progressing.

As we look at education, we find a system that is miserably failing to educate all of its children. Recently published reading scores showed students in the Chicago Public School system reading at below average levels. The rate of achievement in many of our schools in Black and minority areas is so poor, that if the human waste caused by poor education were the result of an act of God, rather than an act of man, these areas would be declared disaster areas.

By the failure of this state to adequately finance our public schools, we must realize that quality education is impossible. Therefore, our children are doomed to a life of failure. This means that far too many of them will become alcoholics, drug addicts, prisoners and a burden on society.

The money that we fail to spend today will have to be spent tomorrow in increased welfare costs, an expanded police department, and for the construction of reform schools and prisons.

Couple these facts with unjust courts, penal institutions which fail to reform or rehabilitate, and a police structure which disrespects and demeans minority citizens. Is it any wonder that our city isn't plagued with more crime than it is?

Each day, the Urban League's twenty-four hour Survival Line rings with calls from citizens reporting brutality and other forms of abuse suffered at the hands of police officers. In fact, we have found this situation so bad that we have joined with the Concerned Citizens for Police Reforms and the Afro-American Patrolmen's League in a suit against the Chicago Police Department. This is an effort to get policemen in our communities who can perform their duties with fairness and respect, and who, in turn, can be respected by the people they are paid to serve and protect.

Our current system of public assistance provides only the scantiest of livelihood to unfortunate human beings who simply have no other way to stay alive in this present-day society. If welfare costs are too high, it is because the relief rolls have to carry so many people who would much rather work but can't—either because there are no jobs for them, or because our educational system or our social structure have made it too difficult for them to qualify for jobs in a technological society. And I might say to those who preach the work ethic and condemn the jobless ones, that there are a lot of people in America who receive government checks in addition to those on welfare rolls.

We all, of course, are hopeful that the president has been successful in bringing peace abroad. We now must all work toward this end at home.

The twentieth century won't return to the period of lynching trees and legally sanctioned separation. But the forces of society that wish to keep Black people down have at their disposal much more subtle and sophisticated methods.

So long as our political, social, and economic powers continue to be directed at ends other than the assurance of full equality, the ghettos of this city will become festering, running sores of bitterness and resentment. The gap between the races will become greater, and polarization will increase. And the gathering storm of outrage and tensions will burst upon our city. It has been said that experience holds a dear school, and fools learn from no other.

In these crucial days of what sometimes appears to be a new post-reconstruction period, the Chicago Urban League has a vitally important role.

The Chicago Urban League is an effective instrument for the advancement of Black people. Our programs in education, community organization, leadership development, on-the-job training, comprehensive health care, and apprenticeship training have had their impact on the Black community, whose needs are growing and whose cause is just.

In addition to providing these services, the Chicago Urban League is, and will continue to be: a forceful advocate for the cause of Black people and other minorities, a bridge between the races seeking unity and harmony in a city torn by strife and division, and a staunch believer in an open, integrated, pluralistic society.

In October of last year, the Chicago Urban League launched a new effort to realize its ideal of justice, a new effort to change the way institutions have worked to discriminate and exclude.

As most of you already know, the Chicago Urban League has been chosen to administer the New Chicago Plan, a program sponsored by the Department of Labor, which is designed to provide approximately ten thousand jobs in the construction industry for minority Chicagoans over the next four years. Working along with the League in recruiting and monitoring the program are the Coalition for United Community Action and the Latin American Task Force. I must note, on this matter, that Chicago was fortunate to have the Urban League available for this particular task. It is doubtful that the necessary agreement by the unions, the employers and the government, could have been secured without having the League here to do the job. In addition to presenting an invaluable opportunity to many workers who have previously been excluded from the building trades, this program presents an invaluable opportunity to you who are present here today.

I commend those of you who have already devoted time and energy to making the plan a reality; but the real work still lies ahead, and it's going to take the full cooperation of many of you in this room, as well as many others who are not here today, to make it a success.

The New Chicago Plan presents an opportunity for government, business, and labor to show that they can work together with minority workers in a sincere and concerted effort to help them develop skills and training that will give all qualified minority craftsmen an opportunity to compete in this society.

It will take all of us working together to insure the success of this program, and I expect to be able to report to you next year on the great progress that your efforts have generated.

And, as I close today, I would like to offer you a challenge, and that is the challenge of getting off the sidelines and taking a real, personal part in doing what must be done to promote a better way of life and a better understanding among all Chicagoans.

In order to successfully answer the needs of Black and poor people in this city, the Chicago Urban League needs money; but money alone is not enough to accomplish our mission. And; therefore, I offer you another challenge, the challenge offered by Frederick Douglass way back in 1894 when he wrote: "Put away your prejudices. Banish the idea that one class must rule over another. Recognize the fact that the humblest citizens are as worthy of protection as are those of the highest and your problem will be solved...Based upon the eternal principles of truth, justice and humanity, with no class having cause for complaint or grievance, your republic will stand and flourish forever."

Thank you very much.

KENNON'S PERSPECTIVE ON THE 1960'S CIVIL RIGHTS MOVEMENT

Atty. Lawrence E. Kennon

The white Mainstream Sociologists characterize the 1960s and 1970s as a period of hedonistic, destructive and lawless behavior, filled with narcotics and sex. For African Americans it was an era of the Black Liberation Movement. We were engaged in destroying the American Apartheid segregation system, the period known as Jim Crow. The legally racist laws of enforced segregation of the South institutionally permeated the defacto activity of whites throughout the nation.

The 1954 *Brown v. Board of Education of Topeka Kansas* U.S. Supreme Court decision had been declared, calling for an end to segregation with all deliberate speed. By 1960, after six years, the "deliberate speed" requirement for the enforcement of the Decision had not compelled the retrenchment of the institutional engrossment of racism in our society, in the South nor the North. The North was never a mere spectator of the Southern brand of discrimination or claim of white supremacy. African Americans remained subordinated to white privilege in Chicago and throughout the North, except for individual signage. In Chicago, the ubiquitous existence of racism was unspoken but was manifested through the collective operations and machinations of everyday social and legal encounters.

I was born in 1929 in Chicago of Mississippi parents who shared with me and my siblings the culture and atrocities of the South. I graduated from DePaul University Law School and was drafted immediately into the U.S. Army in 1953. I returned to our West Side home in 1955, where my sister was the secretary of the West Side Unit of the NAACP. At the Main Branch General meetings, I met and was impressed by Timuel Black and Ishmael Flory, both of whom were conscientious and articulate. "Ish" was a communist and eagerly shared his Marxist theories to my sympathetic ears.

I was appointed as an assistant States Attorney in 1957. I shortly, along with my friend, William Henry (not the politician) organized the West Side Unit of the NAACP Youth Council, which in 1959 conducted a "Wade In," invading the segregated Rainbow Beach at 77th Street and the lake, which had theretofore been shut off from Black participation. It was a successful tactic, which was repeated for two years with full police and community support, until it was finally integrated.

There were two major crises in the 60s and 70s in Chicago. They were Housing and School Segregation. The continuing influx of African Americans from the South after the end of World War II caused the effect of extreme overcrowding in the African American Community. That community was confined within certain restricted geographical parameters within which they were corralled. Such a condition caused overcrowding within the school system. To accommodate the burgeoning incoming youths it was necessary to initiate double shifts within the same school buildings. Some districts even required triple shifts.

The overcrowding of housing and schooling was rampant. The growth of the African community was literally block to block. The first families to venture beyond the glass boundary lines were met with hostile resistance by whites through violent reactions in the form of physical confrontations, destruction of property or mob riots.

The community parents began efforts to enroll their children into schools outside the ghetto walls, and to extend those walls. These efforts were rebuffed by the white school system. The superintendent of schools was a prejudiced man named Dr. Benjamin Willis. The equally prejudiced school board consisted of only one Negro, in the person of Mrs. Wendell E. Green, the misguided wife of Judge Wendell E. Green. She is best described as an instrument of the oppressor, who voted 100 percent of the time with the white members of the board on every issue against the interests of the African American community.

Supt. Willis was unalterably opposed to allowing the African American children to be enrolled outside the Black boundaries. He contracted to have portable trailer type rooms installed on the grounds of the existent schools to accommodate the overflow of African American students, rather than to permit the enrollment extension beyond the Black borders. These "edifices" immediately became known as "Willis Wagons."

These conditions collectively created a shared feeling of frustration and outrage in the community and were ripe for unified protests. From the beginning of the 60s until the early 70s the growing discontent was manifested in a consistent series of protest rallies, boycotts, marches, sit-ins and so called riots. During this period there was a network of neighborhood block clubs and community organizations through which there was established a familiarity and a relationship with the community. Additionally there was the existence of the Daley machine under the auspices of the Democratic Party, operating through a system of Precinct Captains. Mayor Richard J. Daley was opposed and antagonistic to the Movement, resulting in the sometimes recalcitrant positions of the Captains. The *Chicago Defender* was both a recorder and a messenger, keeping us aware of the events and occurrences in the community.

In the 60s, the combined exercises of those of us engaged in the effort to overcome the nationwide oppression of African Americans as expressed in racist exclusion from the fruits of democracy, against the overt, aggressive, and in fact, criminal discriminatory actions of the government became popularly known as "the Movement." As such, the Movement was particularly contesting our exclusion from voting, housing and education. We undertook the struggle against unlawful harassment, brutality and arrests of African Americans and progressive whites, for exerting our constitutional rights. It was the unified movement toward justice. In Chicago the several independent organizations and community groups joined together in an effort to reject the "Willis Wagons" and to demand open enrollment to white schools beyond their neighborhood school districts. These groups were joined by the school teachers who also resented the overcrowded classrooms.

The Movement encompassed the entire organized African American community, including the National Association of Colored People (NAACP), The Urban League, and CORE. The Friends of SNCC, the Catholic Interracial Council and others.

There were marches on the West Side with picketing in front of real estate offices for open occupancy, and on the South Side, extending all the way to Gage Park seeking housing. However the major thrust was toward school expansion. The individual efforts were unsuccessful in responses from the school board or the superintendent.

After reviewing the independent efforts for open school enrollment, the leaders met, recognizing the confluence of groups with the same goals and formed an umbrella organization of the multiple protesting groups and teachers, under the banner of "The Coordinating Council of Community Organizations" (CCCO). This was an integrated organization seeking the integration of the Chicago schools. Thereafter the struggle engaged larger forces against the recalcitrant school administration.

My participation had begun in the early 60s. After our youth group opened Rainbow Beach the concentration was on open housing, open school enrollment and the rejection of the 'Willis Wagons." The repeated attempts of CCCO to have meetings with the school board or the Superintendent by Al Raby the Chairman of CCCO were unsuccessful. The Superintendent ignored or rejected his requests, and continued to add further wagons—reaching more than 600 wagons. The Mayor was targeted to overturn the Superintendent but he announced his backing of the wagons.

In response to the recalcitrance of the School Board, the CCCO and others held demonstrations before the school Board offices at 228 North LaSalle, and before the Mayor's office at the City Hall. Before the demonstrations the protesters met to rendezvous at the Soldiers Field, and later at the Buckingham Fountain to gather for the marches to the School Board or to City Hall. CCCO vowed to continue to demand removal of the Wagons and open enrollment until they were removed. The protesters were joined by Dick Gregory, who became one of the leaders, along with Bob Lucas and Larry Landry.

As the protests escalated Mayor Daley (the 1st) became more hostile, through the police force, and the police became more aggressive in their harassment and in the use of excessive force (brutality) against the marchers and the demonstrators.

Recognizing that the Board and Superintendent, backed by the mayor was refusing to surrender to their demands, Larry Landry organized a massive 5 day Boycott of the Schools over the strenuous objections of the Mayor and Superintendent. The Boycott was approximately 95 percent effective. During the Boycott many of the students and parents joined a march to the School Board offices and around to City Hall in protest.

For a period, the meetings, marches and demonstrations became almost daily events. There were nearly daily arrests of the protesters and demonstrators. They were held in lock-ups at the 11th Street lock-ups, and as the numbers increased, to 26th Street. Dr. Martin Luther King Jr. had introduced the notion of *Civil Disobedience* to unjust laws and restrictions, and the marchers expected the arrests.

A significant factor in the Movement was the "Movement Lawyers." These were an ad hoc group of attorneys who were dedicated to preserving the rights of protest, free of unlawful restrictions and abridgement of free speech and assembly by the government. The role of the pro bono movement lawyers was never to participate in the actual march, but to remain on the sidelines as observers to avoid arrest, to curtail some of the excessive actions of the Police officers and to record the almost daily arrests. We were then to represent the arrestees for bail hearings and later at trial. To understand our role, a description of the activities of the time will be helpful. Meetings were called by the leaders on the night or two before a march or demonstration at local churches or other venues. They would describe the issues, tactics and procedures for the next scheduled event. They would outline the behavior of the expected participants, the possibilities of arrest and bail; also the time and length of the demonstration, the spokes persons and the attorneys and would have discussions from the assembled parties.

The next day the group would meet at the prescribed rendezvous area and march to the protest site, i.e., CPS, Mayor's Office, school site, etc. When there was a marching permit (which the City labeled as a Parade permit) and agreement with the police would determine a proscribed route. Any deviation from the route would be declared illegal (which caused occasional confrontations and arrests). These restrictions were in fact unconstitutional infringements upon the 1st Amendment rights to express their grievances—in pre 9-11 era. We felt these marchers were members of the "Movement" all of whom were dedicated to the goal of equal education and the right to protest. This was the era of non-violent protest to which the demonstrators were committed, and should have been left in peace.

The Chicago Police were assigned in great numbers to the protest area, with back-up areas of squadrons and horses with potential to intimidate the marchers and to quell any possible outbreak at the scene. The police were dressed in combat uniforms, developed today as para-military dress. At the marches the police ordered, sometimes arbitrarily, the marchers to stay on the sidewalk, or in two's or when at a rally scene to "move on." When marchers refused to swiftly obey the commands the squadrons moved in and the masses were arrested. Initially the protestors remained over night until the next morning's bail hearings.

The volunteer lawyers would file appearances for all the detainees and represent them on bail hearings. The detainees were charged with disorderly conduct, failure to disperse, resisting arrest or assault on a police officer (a felony). The lawyers would then follow up for the trial dates. I first became involved in protest (civil rights) organizations when the education issues were originally addressed. When I observed protests on the West Side, before the original arrests, I recognized the need for lawyers whenever there is a protest. Later when I observed the initial arrests I would go to the scene or to the lock up to lend assistance. Soon a core group of lawyers would appear to represent the marchers.

I was the chairman of the civil rights committee of the Cook County Bar Association (CCBA). We would supply volunteer lawyers from our group. The National Lawyers Guild supplied a significant number of lawyers providing pro bono time. There became confusion in assigning the detainees to the regular court calls. The CCBA lawyers, with its president went to Judge Boyle, presiding judge and demanded that a night Mass Arrest Court be set up specifically to handle the many prisoners detained from the marches. The Judge agreed.

Thereafter, a night Court was established with a regularly assigned judge to hear Movement cases for setting bonds (This Court later evolved into the night Narcotics Court). The call would from time to time continue until the midnight hours. The pro bono lawyers would leave the midnight Court and have to return early the next morning to represent their paying clients.

Upon trial dates the same City Assistant Corporation Counsel represented the City in all of the cases. The police officers had sometimes arrested hundreds of so called "offenders" by the time their cases came up for trial. At times the officers had attacked the protesters with clubs or fists, injuring the individuals. To cover themselves they then charged the victim with assaulting an officer. Interestingly, in order to remember and to defend against charges of brutality, the officer would describe as his injury the very injury that he had inflicted against the now defendant. Many officers fabricated the facts of the arrest. They all denied the use of excessive force, but that they were victims of attack from the protesters. However, it should be remembered that the protesters were committed to non-violence and were not attacking officers.

As time progressed, among our celebrity clients were Dick Gregory and Al Raby. Our core group of lawyers was Leo Holt, who represented Al Raby, and Jean Williams, who represented Dick Gregory. I represented among the mass representative defendants. Another constant lawyer was Ira Silbar of the NLG. Cornelius Toole was a further member of the core group. (Leo Holt and Cornelius Toole later became Circuit Court Judges. Jean Williams became a Judge in the state of Arizona.)

Ultimately, the U.S. Supreme Court ruled to permit open occupancy and bussing and the Chicago children were permitted to cross school districting lines. The Willis Wagons were subsequently utilized as additional classroom space for the benefit of our children.

Today there is a surface ironic reverse parallel to the 60's school fiasco and the 2013 school controversy in that the 60's Board for its inadequate facilities added Willis Wagons, and today our brick and mortar school buildings are surplus, in a reversal of our past overcrowded condition, and this school Board subtracts or disposes of existing facilities.

Meanwhile, in late 1963 after the Birmingham church bombing, the death of President Kennedy and the tensions of continued Civil Rights activities, a Chicago fire engine from a Westside firehouse backed over a small black child. The community reacted with anger and erupted into a riot, burning stores and businesses owned by white businessmen. A series of looting and destruction venting the frustrations of the community ensued. Mass arrests took place throughout the community, of those involved and none involved alike.

Once again I, and other "movement" type lawyers responded to the call for the defense against mass arrest. This took place during a week when I had taken Attorney Kermit Coleman, a new lawyer at the time, to Jackson, Mississippi, from which we were assigned to Ruleville, to further defend and represent SNCC and local persons who were registering the locals to vote.

In 1964, SNCC had called for a Freedom Summer. They set up headquarters in Greenwood, Mississippi for their operations throughout the state to register the locals to vote, operating a Freedom School and teaching politics and government to people who were still living in a hostile Jim Crow environment, where voting by Blacks was considered illegal. SNCC issued a call for lawyers throughout the country to represent the arrested persons who dared to attempt to register to vote. Trumped up charges were made against Registrars and their clients. Local racists were attacking and harassing the workers as well as bombing and burning the local housing of those who register.

I went down to Jackson, Mississippi the same week that Goodman, Schwerner and Chaney came up missing. The lawyers at their own expense were rotating a week or more at a time. I went under the auspices of the National Lawyers Guild (NLG), who established a yearlong office in Jackson, operated by George W. Crockett of Detroit, Michigan. The Lawyers Committee for Civil Rights under Law also had established a Jackson office. On my tour was Nelson Brown and Henry McGee along with several white lawyers from the NLG. I had wished to be represented by the CCBA, but was discouraged by some elders in the Association because they maintained that such an action was political and that our Bar Association did not wish to alienate Mayor Daley. I was assigned to Greenwood, Mississippi, where several residents had been arrested for picketing a local white grocery store. At the end of our stay we were requested to return the following year to try some of the cases and to further represent the SNCC workers. One person was shot in Greenwood while I was there and there were several bombings in Ruleville, including the home of Fanny Lou Hamer.

In 1965, I returned with Coleman and was assigned to Ruleville, where we met Fanny Lou Hamer. All was quiet during the first part of the week. We heard on the news of rioting in Chicago. We advised Mrs. Hamer that our services were more urgently needed back in Chicago. We cut our stay short and returned to Chicago in the midst of the riot and severe Police confrontation.

The night courts had been set up and many of the same movement lawyers returned to represent those arrested during the riots. Although the goals were different, these defendants were expressing their outrage against an unfair oppressive system in the only outlet that they knew.

Although I did not agree with some of their tactics, I understood their frustrations and anger and knew that they deserved representation. Those cases were handled in the same manner as the Movement cases, except that the charges were greater. Even though many of the younger rioters were unaware and unable to articulate it, the frustrations arose from the same oppression.

In 1968, the assassination of Dr. Martin Luther King was more than the African American community could bear, precipitating a nationwide rebellion, called a riot by the media. It erupted causing massive destruction, burning, confusion pain and sorrow. Primarily on the West Side, buildings and businesses not previously destroyed were subjected to the outrage. Looting and pillage escalated. The natural response of African Americans was to ascend from protest to righteous rebellion. The king of non-violence had been violently destroyed.

Once again the core lawyers were called upon to represent the protest against the political assassination of the African American leader and all that that entailed. Again, hundreds were arrested by police in military riot gear. The police violently provoked confrontations and caused injury to persons being arrested in sweeps corralling the innocent along with the guilty. Complaints were raised about the sometimes brutal law enforcement, notwithstanding the merit of some of the arrests. The media and mainstream public denied any culpability of the police.

As lawyers, we engaged in an intense period of negotiations, arranging bonds, motions, and counseling families, etc. Again we operated in the night mass arrest courts after our daily court calls. Some of the cases extended throughout the year. The arrested persons had no money for attorney's fees, but were thankful for our services.

These cases were personally a bit perplexing to me. I could understand and empathize with the anger and frustrations experienced by the young and old who may have destroyed property or looted a store. These cases were similar to the riot cases I defended in 1965, but had more merit. They were more equivalent to the Movement cases. These persons were fighting back against the oppressor with their hands and feet as their only weapons. There was obvious political significance to the attack upon our entire community in Dr. King's death. Yet the self-destruction resulting in the acts of our own community destruction was fundamentally detrimental to our community. The actions perpetrated by the looters or burners were in fact criminal to the injury of other innocent people. Were the social contradictions outweighed by the complexity of the motivations of the perpetrators? As a lawyer, again, I recognized the right of all accused to legal representation. Was I to consider in this instance whether these defendants were heroes or villains? I had represented criminals who have no justification for their sometimes nefarious actions. The actions of those persons against the unjust system during the Movement years are not to be judged by the same barometer as other infractions.

The marches of the 60s and early 70s were essentially an effort by the Black community to gain equal rights under the authority of the 14th Amendment to the US constitution. The Movement effort was an integrated thrust to gain those equal rights, and whites were accepted readily into leadership positions pressing for the same goals. However, in approximately 1965, Stokely Carmichael (Kwame Toure) raised his right fist and demanded that Blacks should have Black Power. It was an astounding declaration for the time. He claimed that for Blacks to become free, we must ourselves be the thrust toward freedom. Thereafter the move shifted from equal rights demands to a thrust toward Black liberation. The Blacks took over the leadership of our efforts and the whites were slowly removed for violations or left the movement. There was a dynamic shift of the paradigm by the whites from the Civil Rights Movement to the Peace Movement in the white community. The Viet Nam war had loomed on the horizon and those parties who had been our Movement shifted to the Peace Movement, utilizing virtually every tactic of the Civil Rights Movement into the Peace Movement. The Peace Movement embraced also the Hippie community and the university intellectuals into their protests against the war.

Prior to 1968, the Black community activists declared that the Chicago Police were attacking our peaceful marchers and demonstrators. Those attacks increased against those arrested in the Martin Luther King rebellion where the Police would come with their clubs to beat us. The mainstream disregarded our claims and refused to believe that the Black demonstrators were beaten and were not the attackers.

In the 1968 Democratic Convention in Chicago where the demonstrations by the white Peace Movement occurred, the world had an opportunity to observe through television the Chicago police attacking the peaceful demonstrators, causing grave conflicts. For the first time the mainstream recognized the true conduct of the police against a peaceful demonstration, convincing the nation of the police tactics and vindicating our protests.

In the Black Movement, as we made our marches and demonstrations for equal and human rights, there was a marked absence of any of the Latinos, except in very small instances. The Asians were nowhere to be seen, and the Arabs were unknown and definitely not a part of those seeking equal rights for the African American community. As the years went by and the rights of the Black community progressed so that there became a recognition of the equality question, there was a switch from the Civil Rights under the 14th Amendment where we were seeking equality for the Blacks, to the 1st Amendment violations of freedom of speech for all, equals or non-equals. The present day, Movement for immigration seeks the input from all persons to help what has been illustrated as the Latinos being integrated into America. There is no apparent mention of the Haitians, Africans, Caribbean or other persons of color from the African Diaspora.

Further, the demands of the Arabs who are seeking equality and who claim discrimination are seeking the nationwide cooperation for their cause where they had never joined in the forces for Black equality, or efforts against racial discrimination of the African Americans. The Gay and Lesbian Movement today seeks the same considerations for equality as were demanded by the Blacks in the 60s and early 70s. They seek to compare their movement to the Black Movement, as do the Arabs. That is what can be called a *false equivalence* with respect to the Gay and Lesbian Movement and the Arab demands relative to the Civil Rights Movement in that the movements are patently unequal. The viciousness and hatred imposed in the oppression of African Americans is incomparable. The Gays and Lesbian were not noticeable as a group during the quest for equality and against discrimination of African Americans. Significantly among the Gays are a number of persons who reject Black equality in our country, and who exhibit some of the same racial tendencies as do the so called "straight."

We are left with a society that has become confused with respect to the media coverage of the African American experience because the media would have you believe that the African Americans have already achieved equal justice and equality, considering its omission in the news, guiding public discourse. The plight of the African Americans need never be addressed, it seems, but has been subsumed under the plights of the Latinas, the Arabs and the Gay and Lesbians. A person newly coming to America would be led to believe from the media that the fight for justice and equality has been won by the African Americans, leaving it only to Gays, Lesbians, Arabs and Latinas to gain full citizenship rights. Those groups are presently engaged in a latter day Civil Rights Movement, echoing all of the tactics of the Black Movement of the 60s and 70s, except that they do not have to contend with a hostile media. Sadly, it would appear that our long, hard fight of the 60s and 70s has left a legacy for everyone but us.

Our Movement has not ended. I am happy to have had the opportunity to contribute to the cause. However, in the spirit of continuing the quest for our well warranted, overdue yet unattained rightful position in our society, our young generation has the obligation to revisit the strategy of our past movement, as have other contemporary groups, utilize their momentum and utilize its positives for new measures for consummating the charge begun by even my elders, so long ago.

THREE EDITORIALS FROM *BLACK X-PRESS*

Lu Palmer

"City Cops Out on DuSable Monument"

June 23, 1973

On March 25, 1969 Mayor Richard J. Daley announced that a committee had been formed to "plan for establishment of a permanent memorial for Jean Baptiste Pointe DuSable, the first permanent resident of Chicago."

Some four years later, the Committee of Blacks and whites met in the First National Bank building and decided that the permanent memorial would be the DuSable Museum of African American History, which will soon move into its new home at 57th and Cottage Grove in Washington Park.

At first glance, this would seem like a satisfactory conclusion of a long, long battle to get the city to properly recognize DuSable as the father of this city. But for those who know something about the politics of the matter, it turns out that this decision was nothing more than a cop-out.

It's a cop-out because the city has neatly maneuvered to hide the "permanent memorial" for DuSable in the Black community and to continue its conspiracy of silence to keep white citizens from knowing that the Father of the Chicago was a Black man.

For years, many persons and groups have been battling to force Mayor Daley, and others in the power elite, to give DuSable the kind of recognition due him as founder of the city. There is nothing in the Loop—in the nerve center of the city—which proclaims DuSable as the city's founder.

We do not believe there ever has been any intention on the part of Daley and his cohorts to recognize the Black Father of Chicago. We have long contended that there is a conspiracy of silence so far as DuSable is concerned.

Aside from a high school and an alley on the South side, there is no honor given to this great pioneer. What is disturbing about the latest action by Daley's committee is that it places Mrs. Margaret Burroughs and her DuSable Museum in an awkward position. Blacks are supportive of the museum and are anxious for it to survive and grow now that it has a new location.

But Washington Park is in the Black community and whites are not going to journey into the ghetto—even though it is near the University of Chicago.

The point is not that we are so anxious for whites to visit the museum. The point is it is time that white folks recognize DuSable for what he was—and is—and give proper homage to him.

Jean Baptiste Pointe DuSable should be memorialized downtown on or near the spot where he established his trading post and that is pure and simple. If he had been a white man, there would be all kinds of statues or plazas or expressways named for him. But DuSable was Black and the White ruling elite doesn't want to advertise that fact.

It is unfortunate that Black Congressman Ralph Metcalfe was co-chairman of the committee which adopted the DuSable Museum as the permanent memorial for our Founding Father.

It is unfortunate that Leo Ellis, a Black man, introduced the motion which carried the action.

It is insulting that time after time decisions having profound effect on Black people are made in the First National Bank building where this action was taken.

This is indicative of the manner in which we as Blacks continue to succumb to the trappings, the machinations, and the mentality of white power.

Let it be understood that we have no quarrel with the DuSable Museum. Indeed, we applaud Margaret and Charles Burroughs for their noble efforts to keep alive Black culture and to provide honor to DuSable by renaming the museum in his honor.

There will be a fundraising affair—an auction—at the new museum building Sunday from noon to 6 p.m. 1.5 million dollars must be raised to renovate and maintain the 57th and Cottage headquarters.

Nothing definite came out of the First National Bank building meeting to indicate what kind of financial support the city will give to the Museum now that Chicago has adopted it as the "permanent memorial for DuSable."

So far as we are concerned, this matter is far from closed. We intend to continue fighting for Daley and the official administration to give DuSable his proper recognition. We do not feel that this was done by the action taken in connection with the DuSable Museum.

The conspiracy of silence continues. We will continue our campaign to force the city to erect a monument where it belongs, on or near the site where a Black man—DuSable—first settled, built a trading post, and became the Father of the City of Chicago.

"We Shall Overcome"

September 1, 1973

It's been a long time since I crossed arms, linked hands with the persons who were flanking me, and sang "We Shall Overcome."

But I did just that Sunday night in the Lake Meadows Restaurant at the close of the Martin Luther King, Jr. Movement's Poor People's Dinner.

I have to admit I felt kind of funny singing that song after all of these years because it seems that all we do is promise ourselves that "We Shall Overcome" when we ain't overcoming at all. And I also wondered as we sang "We Shall Overcome" in the first verse, then "I am not afraid" in the second verse and "God is one our side" in the third verse.

What I wondered is whether or not we were going to sing the fourth verse: "Black and white together."

But instead of the fourth verse—"Black and white together"—the song leader told us to hum on out to the end...

I was relieved that we didn't stand in the Lake Meadows Restaurant and sing "Black and white together." I'm not sure that I could have sung it. It was hard enough to sing "We Shall Overcome" because the singing, promising-ourselves-days were over.

The cold fact is that we are just not going to win a war for liberation locking arms and singing "We Shall Overcome." But I sang it Sunday night in that restaurant (patronized by Black folks and owned by white folks) because of a deep respect I have for the memory of Dr. Martin Luther King, Jr.

There is no question about Dr. King's leadership in the '60s. There is no question about his challenging the social consciousness of this nation. Nor is there any question about Dr. King's immeasurable impact upon the world.

But reality forces me to say that non-violence as a revolutionary tactic failed and always will. Reality also forces me to say that Dr. King's reach for an integrated society—his famous dream—was an unrealistic one for his time. And it is just as unrealistic now.

Before we tried so desperately last Sunday night to conjure up the magic of the King era by locking hands and singing "We Shall Overcome." I had listened to saxophonist Ben Branch recall his days with Dr. King and castigate those who do not recognize him as "the only Black hero."

I had heard the Rev. C.H. Turner, head of the Dr. Martin Luther King, Jr. Movement, talk about shutting down Commonwealth Edison construction sites at which Blacks from the neighborhood were not working, taking to the streets as in the days of King.

But it was the Rev. Al Sampson, who was also closely associated with Dr. King, who put the whole evening in perspective. And it is tragic that the program was so full of preliminaries that by the time Rev. Sampson spoke, most of the audience had drifted away.

Al Sampson gave an absolutely brilliant rendition of the meaning of Dr. King and a profound rendering of the tragedy of the years that have followed Dr. King's assassination.

I will not attempt to reconstruct Al Sampson's message because my tape recorder failed and I was too engrossed in what this young minster-activist was saying to take notes.

Suffice to say, Al Sampson made it clear that Blacks closely associated with Dr. King during his triumphant years were now "gambling for Martin's robe." He said these "leaders" think they can become another Martin Luther King, Jr. if by some means one of them could be anointed to take his place and wrap himself in "Martin's robe."

But the Rev. Al Sampson had harsh words for those who "wallow in Martin's blood" and bask in his shadow. He reminded his listeners that the spirit of a King would never seep into their hearts by the wearing of a Martin Luther King, Jr. button, or by framing his picture on a living room wall, or by celebrating a holiday in his memory.

"The real meaning of Dr. King must be internal. It cannot be external. He must live within you or he does not live at all," Rev. Sampson said.

The real strength of Dr. King, I think, is that he believed so deeply in what he preached. And even if what he preached is not realistic today, most of us in the '60s did believe in what we thought was "integration." Most of us did, indeed, believe that our salvation rested in becoming so absorbed by the system that we would finally some day be "accepted" by white people in America.

Black and white together…

I have a dream that someday…

Deep in my heart, I do believe, we shall overcome some day…

The papers have been full of long, analytical pieces trying to place America in focus 10 years after the March on Washington for Jobs and Freedom. It was August 28, 1963 when Dr. Martin Luther King, Jr. stood before a sea of Black and white faces around the Lincoln Memorial in Washington and chanted his memorable "I Have a Dream" speech.

"I have a dream…I have a dream that one day this nation will rise up and live by the true meaning of its creed: 'We hold these truths to be self evident that all men are created equal…'"

They say a quarter of a million people were there…people from all across the country. I don't know what white folks felt when they left this historic assemblage. I do know that they went back to their white world where they burrowed in deeper and refused to show their white faces when Black folks shifted the chant to "Black Power."

I suspect that most Black people left the Lincoln Memorial with their spirits lifted and their naïve souls really believing that the dreams would come true.

But, as the papers have reminded us, ten years have passed since the March on Washington and the white writers tried hard to make it appear that we have made some real progress over those ten years.

But there we were Sunday night in a restaurant (owned by white folks) in the Black southside—at a poor people's dinner with our hands locked singing "We Shall Overcome" just like 10 years ago.

And what was the dinner's sponsor—the Martin Luther King, Jr. Movement—asking for?

Men—Black men—to meet at 7 o'clock the next morning to protest because the white folks were digging ditches in a Black ghetto to lay pipes for Commonwealth Edison and the white construction bosses wouldn't hire Black people who lived right across the street.

In cement cages reaching into the sky.

"One Year After I Quit The Daily News"

January 12, 1974

On January 15th, a full year will have passed since I resigned my position as reporter-columnist for the *Chicago Daily News.* In my resignation letter, I wrote:

"I am a Black man first and a journalist second...My allegiances are first to the Black community and my loyalties to the objectives of my employer are secondary. I can no longer function effectively as an employee of the *Chicago Daily News.*"

A series of racist incidents had occurred to lead up to that resignation, a series of events which forced me to conclude that "the white Establishment press and the honest views of a Black journalist are totally incompatible. I am also convinced that the white Establishment is—and will continue to be—an arm of The System, and the concerns of Black people have no priority in that System nor in any of the satellite systems of which the institution of mass communications is one."

Following that resignation I was asked by many people, Black and white, if I was sorry that I had left what they considered to be a very prestigious job. Immediately after I quit the *Daily News* I said I was not in the least sorry. A year from now my answer will remain the same.

Indeed, I am happy, happy, happy that I left.

The reason I am happy can be articulated in terms of a reply to a quote from the celebrated *Chicago Daily News* columnist Mike Royko. Shortly after I split from the Daily News, the *Chicago Journalism Review* quoted Royko as saying:

"He gave up a very good job—I don't mean the money—he reached an awful lot of people. Not only through the *Daily News,* but over the wires. That's who he should be talking to—the whites. The Blacks don't need somebody to tell them what the social problems are. It's the white middle class people in the suburbs that he needed to reach.

"So whose thinking is Lu going to change now?"

On the first anniversary of my departure from the *Chicago Daily News,* it is appropriate to answer Mike Royko's question.

Royko is naïve if he thinks I was changing the minds of white, middle class suburbanites while I was writing for the *Daily News.* There is no question about the fact that I was reaching thousands of readers of the *Chicago Daily News* and thousands of others who were reading my column in other newspapers across the nation. And I was naïve enough—when I first went to the white press—to think that I could change some white folk's minds about the basic issues of racism, oppression, and repression.

But by the time I had gone through the white press' meat grinder for seven years, I was convinced that I wasn't even making a dent on the minds of the lofty white editors who messed over my columns, much less the readers. When it comes to racism, white folks close their ears to the truth.

I wasn't changing any white folks' minds writing for the *Chicago Daily News* and I finally had the good sense to realize it. As I said in a speech—"A Report to the Black Community"—on why I resigned from the white press:

"I'm glad that somebody said tonight that the issue is not Lu Palmer. Lu Palmer is symbolic of something. And what Lu Palmer is symbolic of is growth. After living for more than 50 years and spending 22 of those years in journalism, I finally recognized that you can't really fight the enemy with the enemy's own instrument."

In simpler words: if the white press is the enemy of Black people—which I think it is—then I cannot do battle against white racism and white oppression by communication through white folks' media.

So, Royko asks, whose thinking is Lu going to change now?

Black folks, that's who.

Royko's right when he says, "Blacks don't need somebody to tell them what the social problems are." But Black folks do need somebody to keep explaining why those social problems exist—really why. And that became this writer's mission on January 15, 1973: a total dedication to communicating to Black people without the intervention of white oppressive systems.

This mission moves on three fronts:

1. Lu's Notebook, daily commentary on four Black oriented radio stations, sponsored by Illinois Bell Telephone Company, with total control over the content of these broadcasts in the hands of this writer.
2. Lu's Bookshelf, a monthly analysis of books of vital interest to Blacks, which attracts from 500 to 700 Blacks each month. This program is underwritten by Urban Communications, a Black public relations firm.
3. The Black X-Press, an info-paper founded on May 19, 1973, to transmit to Black people new concepts and new truths, totally edited by Blacks.

There are more excited long range plans for the eventual development of an alternative Black communications system. But these plans must await the financial grounding of the struggling *Black X-Press,* which is held together by the sheer guts and determination of a handful of people and a larger group of Blacks who have enough confidence in what we are doing to subscribe, and whenever possible make financial contributions.

One year later, I repeat, I am happy that I left the *Daily News.* I am grateful to all who have given support to my mission. And I solicit greater financial support for the *Black X-Press* which at this writing, is alive, because a very few dedicated people are determined that it will not die.

(These articles are reprinted from the Black X-Press *collection of the Vivian Harsh Archives at The Carter G. Woodson Library.)*

FIRES OF LIBERATION BURN IN BLACK PEOPLE'S HEARTS

Nahaz Rogers

An open letter to The Reverends Ralph Abernathy, Andrew Young, and Jesse Jackson

Gentlemen:

As you ascend to the position of leadership, destiny is bound to thrust upon you and there are a few points I would ask you to consider. Putting aside the issue of violence or non-violence for the moment, let us deal with some areas of economics which should be looked at very closely if we, the black people of America, are to come into our own and not merely become a higher type of slave.

First, the idea that black America can find freedom and security by working hard and saving their money has no basis in fact. This country and no other country ever, arrived at a point of affluence by the hard work and frugality of its people. Europeans in Europe and those in America arrived at today's peak of affluence at the expense of the free or underpaid labor of the so-called underdeveloped countries of the world. In every case, articulate and well-trained natives of these underdeveloped countries helped the European exploiters rob and brutalize their own people.

Second, almost every candidate for the job of convincing the downtrodden and abused black masses to furnish cheap labor and permit outsiders to take control of the institutions of power was in their best interest, were Christians. This group of black lackeys could always be counted on to apologize for all the evils that white people heaped upon black people. But when black people made any move to throw off the yoke of oppression, they also could be counted on to attack the moves of the masses as acts of wanton violence.

Does it not seem strange to you that before they could get brown Vietnamese to "Tom" for whitey in South Vietnam, whitey had to convert the leadership class from Buddhism to Christianity?

The Indians who allowed the British to rape India were Christianized Indians. In the Islamic countries of Africa, it is the cadre of black Christians that permit, condone, and assist in the economic subjugation of that wealthy continent. Please don't react to this emotionally, but examine what is being said here with a kind heart and brotherly devotion.

In every country in Africa, with the exception of Egypt, black Christian Africans have joined into so-called business partnerships with Europeans, which includes American white; and in each of these countries the white have wound up with economic control. This is the newest form of colonialism.

The only area left in the United States for exploitation is the black ghetto. The black masses have served notice on the white power structure that it will no longer tolerate white enterprises extracting the life blood out of black neighborhoods.

This is what the fires are really about. Black people are saying the resources and labor that they expend must be used to build a meaningful community. A community where the institutions—social, economic, political, and religious—are owned, operated, and administrated in the best interest of black people.

This can only happen when black leadership confesses to one of two possible truths: Either black people are naturally inferior and must forever be dependent upon white people to survive, or face up once and for all to what the real truth has to be.

Any people who would really be free must take charge of their own destiny. If we fail in this, we not only will never be free, but only fools would think they were entitled to be free.

When Marie Antoinette said about the Parisians, "Let them eat cake"—the Parisians cut off her head and set fire to the town. The fires were called fires of liberation. Every Frenchman, no matter where he may be found in the world, celebrates Bastille Day each year.

The Boston Tea Party was no prayer meeting. History will have to evaluate the events surrounding our comrade's death. However, we must be mindful that the historians make evaluations based on personal points of view and national interest.

English historians saw the American Revolution quite differently from their counterparts in America. A wise people depend on their own scribes to interpret their positions in human affairs. For it is true that where there is no vision the people perish.

If after all the burning, as tragic as it may have been, our leadership group joins with the white power structure in reimposing itself on the blacks of the black masses, Martin Luther King, Jr. will indeed have died in vain. Prayers and tears are not enough—the price has been too great: over thirty people dead, by their count, thousands wounded, and tens of thousands jailed. There is no road back. Leadership must not permit the same old financial combines, with a Negro or two added for color, to reestablish themselves in the black ghetto.

The national income of black people in the United States is greater than the gross national product of the population of Canada. The number of blacks in America with college educations far exceeds the number of Canadians with college degrees.

These being the facts, there could be no valid reason why the enterprises and institutions in the black ghettos are not all black. For blacks to build stores and other buildings in the ghetto is nice, for blacks to be allowed to operate concerns in the ghetto may have value, but complete ownership and control must be the goal.

The eyes of the non-white world are upon the American blacks as they never have been before. To say that God is on our side is pure unadulterated nonsense. The other side wrote the Book and they say He is on their side. Every session of Congress, every session of the State Legislature, every session of the City Council, and don't forget the Klu Klux Klan and the White Citizen's Council, open their programs with prayer.

The point being that we can no longer expose ourselves to the World as a group of nitwits who want to take our troubles to the Lord and leave them there. King's death ought to convince us once and for all that there just ain't no Santa Claus, no Good Fairy, and no "pie-in-the-sky." If you want something for yourself, you have to get it for yourself. This is in no way an indictment of any religious view; it is simply an attempt to point out that a people cannot substitute religious dogma for economic, social, and political reasons.

As we ponder the impact of Reverend Martin Luther King, Jr.'s death and the outpourings of rage that followed, much harm can come from people who rush forth to excuse, justify, or lament these times. Sound judgment would insist that time be allowed to dictate our rationale in these matters.

Yet there are some things that must be attended to now. Those who choose to pick up the mantle must also deal with the challenge. Martin Luther King, Jr.'s brutal murder by this racist sick society is a milestone, a point in history from which we will reckon our future.

It indeed should make each of us reappraise our positions, reevaluate our determination, rededicate our persons, and resemble our forces for the journey ahead. From now on it will be a new ball game. The same old approach just will not suffice.

Reverend King served a great purpose in his too short lifetime and now he is with us no more. For anyone, no matter how bright, articulate, or committed they are, must realize Martin Luther King, Jr. was an institution unto himself. And neither single man nor group of men can give substance to his dream for dreams as by definition unreal.

New approaches must be found that use the best of what was in the King philosophy, coupling those with any others that prove sound and workable. The very difficult task of hammering out some meaningful working arrangement with blacks in this country and in other parts of the World, which are not Christian, must be attended to.

The instant Negro leader is coming off of the white mass media T.V., radio, newspaper, and magazine production lines in such numbers that it is hard to be sure who or what they are.

The white racist system is recalling, reviving, and renewing every old and young uncle Tom who ever served their needs in the past. Never before in the history of the World have so many lackeys been called leaders who represent so few, if any, people.

Negroes who the black masses know as tools of the system; Negroes whose only role has been to tell the black masses to slow down, take it easy, cool it, don't march in Memphis, don't boycott in Atlanta, don't picket in Chicago, don't boycott the Olympics.

This type of leadership could only have resulted in black people returning voluntarily to bondage. In the past few days we have been told that we were being led by Negroes whose only claim to fame, other than "Tomming," was that they could run fast, play baseball, and sell nuts, tap dance, kick footballs, shine shoes, clown around, marry white women, do the slow shuffle, "have white teeth and will grin."

In their desperation to ship blacks back into docile, dependable, responsible law abiding citizens, the government, T.V., newspaper, and radio people dug up Negroes who even they had long ago discarded as too out-of-date to be effective, Negroes who had gone back into the woodwork from which they came.

If anyone ever puts together all those tapes and articles that were used immediately after the vicious assassination of Martin Luther King, Jr., they will make the greatest comedy of all times. When desperation walks in the door, reason flees out the window.

Instant Negro leaders are like instant coffee, instant gelatin, or instant anything else. At best it is only a substitute for the real thing. People will only accept it if the genuine article is not available. Blacks have seen how costly it has been to follow leaders who were only fragments of this white racist society's imagination.

They now know that leaders made by NBC, CBS, ABC, *The New York Times, The Lost Angeles Sentinel, Time, Look,* and *Newsweek* can be influenced, manipulated, or unmade by this same group. The black masses will not, must not forget what happened to W.E.B. DuBois, Paul Robenson, Marcus Garvey, Brother Malcolm, and yes even Martin Luther King, Jr. The T.V., press, and radio had begun to attack King. He was no longer their fair-haired boy.

He had begun to deal in areas that white people felt black people had no business thinking about. They were well on the way to cutting off his flow of white funds and elite favors, and yet he was moving ahead, moving on up to higher ground.

This bright young Negro who had served white interests so well had, without their knowledge and as no part of their plan, emerged and evolved into Martin Luther King, Jr, the beautiful black man. In fact, he was beginning to become a thorn in their side, a pain in the neck.

The young Negro boy who had been such a comfort to white people, who had been so responsible in the past, was doing bold, imaginative, new things. White people didn't like this, and so he is dead. The T.V., press, and radio said Martin Luther King, Jr. is a menace to this society and we might be better off without him, and he is no more. Whom the Gods would destroy, they must first discredit.

Before any black person again jumps in front of the T.V. camera or the radio microphones, let him first do his homework lest all over again sharp interviewers and panelists make us look like idiots in this World of instant international communications.

Let us not make again the unpardonable mistake of claiming to speak for all the black people in America until we have spoken to all black people in America, but more importantly let those who do speak be sure that they know what the black masses in America are now saying.

(Reprinted from April 12-26, 1968 edition of The West Side Touch, *published by the West Side Organization.)*

DISPATCH FROM YESTERYEAR: MONROE ANDERSON REPORTS ON BEING IN THE FIRST WAVE OF BLACK JOURNALISTS GOING INTO THE WHITE MEDIA

Monroe Anderson

In the winter of 1968 I was on deadline, writing a movie review of *The Good, the Bad and the Ugly,* when my photography professor happened to pass through the newsroom of the *Indiana Daily Student*. He told me that a former student of his, Marv Kupfer, was a Midwest correspondent for *Newsweek* magazine, and that the Chicago bureau was looking for a black journalist because, "They're expecting a long hot summer."

That term, "a long hot summer," was code for what news reports called race riots and what I thought of as urban uprisings. The frustration with what was and what should have been had reached a boiling point in America's black communities from one coast to the other. The promise of the Civil Rights Movement was struggling while the prospect of Black Power was soaring in word, if not in deed.

In 1967, there were 125 urban uprisings in America with Newark, Detroit and Milwaukee experiencing that year's worst. National and local, Whites Only media, were discovering that when an economically depressed black neighborhood erupted, their reporters stood out like cold sores or age spots, making them handy targets for the ever-present brick throwers and the occasional sniper. The editors of all white media realized they needed, at least, a token black reporter who could blend in to witness and report the seething that was.

I came to appreciate that being in the right place at the right time armed with the right training and with the right connections has its advantages. I promptly followed up on my professor's tip, firing off an inquiry letter to *Newsweek's* Chicago bureau just days later. Shortly afterwards, I got a call. I was asked to come by the bureau when I came home for spring break.

I dropped off my portable typewriter and my luggage in Gary before driving on to Chicago. It was the day before my 21st birthday and the day after Dr. Martin Luther King Jr.'s assassination. Chicago's West Side was in flames.

It was the easiest job interview I have ever had. I left feeling that they wanted me to start right then.

I had come a long way from that day my seventh-grade English teacher at Gary Roosevelt, Mr. Guster, spotted my potential. After reading a composition paper I'd written for his class, he called me aside. "Good paper. Very good paper," he said. "You're a writer."

"Oh. Really?"

I'd had teachers tell me that I was talented. I'd had a fifth-grade teacher tell my mother that I was a genius. But Mr. Guster was the first to assign a specific facility to me. I was a writer. A Writer. From that day forward I stopped conscientiously studying my algebra and began thinking of myself as the next James Baldwin or Richard Wright.

When I grew up, I would write the Great American Negro novel. In the meantime, I introduced myself to journalism. I became editor of the eighth-grade page of the *Roosevelt News*. Three years later, as editor of the high school newspaper, I changed the name to the *Panther Post* as a nod to our school mascot and because, from early on, I've always found alliteration alluring.

In 1964, Les Brownlee, the first black reporter at the *Chicago Daily News,* visited Roosevelt to talk to the handful of students who were on the high school journalism staff. He told our small racially-segregated group from our racially-segregated school in our predominantly racially-segregated city that there was no better time than now for us to go into journalism; the color line was perforating. Since Brownlee was the only black reporter I'd ever met, it was easy to take his word as gospel. As soon as I got home, I announced to my mother that I was going to be a journalist. "There are no Negro journalists," my mother said, "Be a school teacher."

Brownlee's heads up was reinforced when I went to see Gretchen Kemp, my journalism counselor at Indiana University, following freshman orientation in 1965. After telling me that "Monroe Anderson" would make a great byline and chastising me for not having a pen on me because "a journalist is never caught without a pen," she told me that because I was a Negro, "If you graduate from Indiana University with a degree in journalism, you can write your own meal ticket."

I had nothing against writing my own meal ticket. But during my first two years of college I found my journalism classes less than fulfilling. One taught us the history of The Fourth Estate. Another taught us editing and layout. None threatened to defer my dream of becoming the next Baldwin. I'd already decided that I'd get a job as a journalist for a year, two tops, get paid while honing my writing skills, before moving on to penning that Great Negro American Novel.

The urban uprisings, with every episode dominating the front pages in the mornings and the lead story at night, were what made white editors come to the conclusion that they could use a black or two on their staffs.

The Report of the National Advisory Commission on Civil Disorders or the *Kerner Report*, pointed out these two obvious factors; one they had to know, the other was hiding in plain sight. The first was that the civil disorders resulted from black frustration at the lack of economic opportunity. "Our Nation Is Moving Toward Two Societies, One Black, One White—Separate and Unequal," the *Kerner Report* concluded.

The second factor hadn't been given a second thought by the whites running the news industry. "The press has too long basked in a white world looking out of it, if at all, with white men's eyes and white perspective."

The Commission's affirmation of the obvious would be a personal observation I would sorely make time after time during my three-decades-plus as a professional in America's media. And even now. The more things have changed, the more they have remained stuck in the status quo.

But things were promising when I started my internship at *Newsweek* in 1968. The magazine's Chicago bureau had hired a black intern and a black correspondent, Don Johnson. He came to Newsweek from the *Boston Globe*. He pretty much knew what to do and they pretty much knew what to do with him. Internships were still a novel concept. I was more or less in a grand experiment. My first assignment was to go hang out at bars on the South Side to see if I could overhear the reaction to the The Woodlawn Organization (TWO) scandal and what was being said about Jeff Fort and the Black Stone Rangers' involvement.

I was not really a Chicagoan. I was born and raised in Gary, Indiana, a southeast Chicago suburb. It's close. The western furthermost city limits of Gary is less than 10 miles from the eastern furthermost city limits of Chicago. But it's not the Black Metropolis. On the other hand, I grew up on Chicago media, reading the *Chicago Daily News*, watching WGN and the three network owned-and-operated TV stations, listening to WVON and WLS radio. I watched reports in 1963-64 about the boycotts and protests in reaction to Chicago setting up the Willis Wagons. I followed daily the events around Dr. King's stay and protests in Chicago during the summer of 1966 when I was back in Gary for the summer break, working in a steel mill to earn money to help pay for my sophomore year at IU. After reading and watching the news about the Wall of Respect and the Organization of Black American Culture, I'd made several trips to Chicago to attend OBAC meetings at the DuSable Museum when it was at 3806 S. Michigan Avenue.

But when *Newsweek* asked me to go to the South Side on a fishing expedition, I was at a lost. Other than what was in the newspapers, I knew nothing about TWO. I knew one thing about the Black Stone Rangers: They could be deadly. On assignment, I drove to the first bar I spotted and ordered a glass of Mateus. Since it was early in the afternoon, I could count the number of customers on one hand. Neither Jeff Fort nor The Woodlawn Organization was mentioned once. Two Mateuses, four cigarettes and an hour and a half later, I decided to call it a day and returned to Newsweek's North Michigan Avenue office to report that there was nothing to report.

I thought about that first experience a couple of years later while talking with one of my mentors, Sam Yette, *Newsweek's* first black Washington correspondent, who wrote the book, *The Choice: The Issue of Black Survival in America,* when he advised, "Don't let them make you into a spy."

That was the only time during my summer internship when I felt like I was supposed to be the black .007. Weeks after the TWO assignment, I was asked to report on "How the White Press Attempts to Reach the Black Community." One surefire strategy towards that end was to hire more black reporters. In reporting the story, I interviewed the four executive editors of the *Chicago Daily News*, the *Chicago Sun-Times*, the *Chicago Daily Tribune* and Chicago's American. In all four instances, as I finished the interview, each editor asked if I'd be interested in working at his newspaper.

The 1968 Democratic National Convention was the pivotal point in my trajectory. Four years after Brownlee encouraged me to become a journalist, I discovered first hand that he was not the only one. I met Robert Maynard, who at that time was a *Washington Post* reporter, but would later become the publisher and owner of the *Oakland Tribune*. I met Johnathan Rodgers, who was a *Newsweek* staff writer, but would later become the first and only black general manager, to date, of WBBM-TV before becoming the first and only black president, to date, of the CBS network. I met Sylvester Monroe, who had grown up in public housing and was then a St. George's prep school student. He was being groomed by *Newsweek* at the time to become a future journalist. Nineteen years later Monroe and I would work together at *Newsweek* on a cover story about him and 10 other black men who grew up in the Robert Taylor Homes. A year later, the *Newsweek* magazine report was expanded into the book, *Brothers: Black and Poor—A True Story of Courage and Survival.*

Newsweek was just one white media shop integrating its staff. Sometimes integration was accomplished by any means necessary. In 1967, the *Tribune* hired Joseph Boyce, a Chicago policeman, as its first black reporter and WMAQ hired Russ Ewing, a Chicago firefighter and piano salesman, as its first black TV reporter.

Newsweek's expectation of a long hot summer in Chicago was met but not entirely as expected. There was a riot in Chicago in the summer of '68 but it did not break out in the black community and the participants were not the usual suspects. "Unlike other recent big city riots, the events did not consist of looting and burning," reported *Rights in Conflict,* a study to the National Commission on the Causes and Prevention of Violence. "To a shocking extent, they consisted of crowd-police battles. The shock was intensified by the presence in the crowd of large numbers of innocent...citizens."

What came to be described as a police riot began on the Sunday night before the convention officially started. I was paired with John Culhane, who was one of *Newsweek's* four Midwest correspondents. We had just been dropped off at the corner of Clark Street and LaSalle Drive. We were both dressed in suits and ties. CPD-issued press credentials hung around our necks. We wore riot helmets that were supposed to go to the Detroit police but had somehow been commandeered by *Newsweek* for those of us on its street team.

From a block away, Culhane and I could see the rag-tag gathering of protesters in Lincoln Park. Most were hippies and other counter-culture youth. They had come to Chicago to protest the Vietnam Conflict because it was a war of oppression; because President Johnson had expanded it and his vice-president, Hubert Humphrey, who was going to be the Democrat's presidential standard-bearer, had made no promises to end it; and because most of them were of draft age.

In a press conference just before the DNC convention got underway, Abbie Hoffman and Jerry Rubin, co-founders of the Youth International Party introduced a 145 pound black and white boar, "Pigasus the Immortal," as the Yippies' candidate for president. In one of his characteristic radical street theater performances, Hoffman announced that he and his fellow Yippies were going to dump the hallucinogenic drug, LSD, into the Chicago water supply. Anyone who knew anything about the counter culture knew it was a put-on. Even if it were physically possible, which it wasn't, no one would have wasted that much valuable acid on the good citizens of Chicago. But Mayor Richard J. Daley, who was from a different time and mindset, took the threat seriously. No dirty hippies, Yippies or commie sympathizers were going to crash his party's party. The Boss's orders called for more cops in Lincoln Park than there were protesters.

The park was also swarming with reporters, photographers and cameramen. There were so many TV news crews covering the protesters that their camera lights turned the August 25 night into day. I was close enough to the action to see an object fly out of the crowd of about 1,000 protesters into the crowd of more than 5,000 Chicago cops on law and order duty. We didn't know it then but following an investigation, we'd later learn that an agent provocateur planted among the protesters threw a bottle at the cops.

It was routine for Chicago police to rough up blacks but this was different. A stream of bloodied protesters and spectators, virtually all white, streamed south on Clark Street. Culhane and I ran against the crowd so that we could see what was happening. We didn't get very far before we saw. It wasn't good. Baton swinging Chicago cops were willy-nilly striking anyone and everyone not dressed in uniform blues. We ran into the fenced-in front yard of Hermon Baptist Church, a house of worship established by black domestic workers in 1887. In American folklore, the church is supposed to be a sanctuary. It wasn't for us. Culhane yelled, "Press, press," while holding up his credentials as if they were a shield. They weren't. Two Chicago policemen ordered us to, "Come out of there motherfuckers" as they waited by the church's fence gate.

We followed their command and they, in turn, launched my career big time by giving me the dubious distinction of being one of the first journalists beaten by the Chicago Police at the DNC. The two cops stuck us on our heads before realizing we were wearing the same protective gear that they were wearing. They lowered their aim, hitting us on the back, the kidneys and legs. Although I had grown up in a blue-collar neighborhood, a block and a half away from Gary's Delaney public housing project, that was the first and only time I felt the sharp pain from the blow of a cop's nightstick.

The police had formed a gauntlet on the west side of Clark Street. They were systematically beating men and women, young and old, from one cop to the next. For Culhane and me it was a long quarter block as we were beaten and battered by the baton-happy cops.

We immediately called *Newsweek's* makeshift headquarters—their magazine had 55 reporters and editors covering the convention—to report what we had witnessed and endured. A Newsweek rental car picked us up and took us back to headquarters. Assuming that we had somehow provoked the police, Culhane and I were taken off the street team and forced to stay in the office manning the phone lines that Monday night. The CPD's intentional assault on the press continued on the city's streets. By Tuesday night, Culhane and I were back on the streets, chasing cops, as they were chasing protesters while being careful not to end up on the wrong end of their lead-cored wooden nightsticks again. There was tear gas in the air. There was a pitched battle with cops clubbing and protesters throwing anything they could get their hands on at the police. It was the most exciting thing I'd experienced. Before it was over, I realized that in practice journalism was far more exhilarating and engaging than it was in theory. As a journalist I got to witness history in the making, then got to write the first draft for the historians.

I was supposed to be a famous black novelist but then journalism got in the way. My *Newsweek* internship dramatically re-scripted the career storyline I'd been composing in my mind. Within that four-day span, the Writer became the Journalist. My great work of fiction would have to wait.

The day after the convention ended, we were picked up in a limousine and driven to the FBI's Chicago offices and interviewed. J. Edgar Hoover's men wanted to know if we could ID any of the cops. Of course, we could not. The police assigned to corral the demonstrators were a faceless mob. None wore nameplates on their uniforms. They hid behind the plastic face shields on their helmets. They had all removed their police badges under the guise that protesters might rip them off and use the pins on the back of them as weapons against the officers.

Being beaten by the Chicago police made me *Newsweek's* star trainee. I was photographed with *Newsweek's* four correspondents and one photographer who had also had a rendezvous with police behaving badly. Our picture ran at the front of the magazine on *Newsweek's* "Top of the Week" page and was distributed nationally via the Associated Press. I was flown to New York, put up at the Waldorf, interviewed WLIB-AM and introduced at a luncheon in Manhattan. When the luncheon ended, a well-heeled man who identified himself as a Yale-educated lawyer approached me, "Would you be interested in attending Yale Law School. I'm sure we can see that you're accepted."

No acceptance was necessary. I was going to be a journalist.

Many, many years later, I did write that novel, *Sweetspeare's Sirens: A Tell-All Memoir* by Pierce Trotter. When it's published, its readers will decide if it's the great one or not. Meanwhile I remain an independent journalist.

Looking back over the decades I've spent in American media—with apologies to another journalist who wrote the Great British Novel more than once—I can only report that, "It was the best of times, it was the worst of times."

SECTION FOUR

EDUCATIONAL ADVOCACY AND REFORM

"The education of African Americans has been profoundly shaped throughout history by two problems. One is access to educational opportunities and the other is the quality of accessible schooling. Unfortunately, the struggle for access diverted the energies of African Americans from the task of designing and providing quality schooling. In addition, the content of the schooling that African Americans did receive was designed to meet the needs of politically empowered European Americans and not the particular needs of African Americans."

The Search for Access and Content in the Education of African-Americans
by Joan Davis Ratterway

TOO MUCH SCHOOLING TOO LITTLE EDUCATION
edited by Mwalimu J. Shujaa

EDUCATION FOR LIBERATION: THE CHICAGO SELF-DETERMINATION MOVEMENT FOR COMMUNITY CONTROL OF SCHOOLS, 1960-1975

Hannibal Tirus Afrik aka Harold Charles

"In a racist and oppressive society, education for liberation becomes a subversive activity."
Anonymous

I came to Chicago's South Side in 1937 after returning from U.S. Army active duty in Germany. My plans were to enroll in graduate studies in medical technology and raise my family. Consequently, I was employed as a research biochemistry technologist in the Department of Biochemistry at the University of Illinois Medical Center and Research & Educational Hospital.

In the early 60s, Civil Rights organizing was being coordinated by several neighborhood groups, churches and residents within the South Side Woodlawn area. I became involved as a block captain and later as a delegate in my Hyde Park neighborhood, which gave me an opportunity to learn more about the lack of political power Black residents actually possessed. Through the tenacity and diligence of these community organizers, the new organization, T.W.O., was formed initially as a temporary formation and later ratified at a mass community forum to become the Woodlawn Organization.

At the August 1963, March on Washington, I was a delegate representing T.W.O. and focused with thousands of sisters and brothers in this historic event. One of the major impressions Dr. Martin L. King, Jr. articulated to the participants was a mandate to return home and continue to organize around the basic human needs of our people.

I accepted the challenge and in September 1963 I applied for a teaching assignment in the Chicago Public School System at a lower salary. In 1961 I received my master's in the Teaching of Science from Chicago Teachers College. Despite the efforts of the teacher personnel office to send me to a predominantly white school, because of my research and graduate studies background I persevered and came to Farragut High School, 2345 S. Christiana Avenue in the West Side's North Lawndale community.

Needless to say, I was somewhat naïve about Chicago's political system of controlling Black taxpayers even though there were several Black aldermen and other elected officials. There had been several Civil Rights marches and demonstrations against Superintendent Benjamin Willis' regime that placed Black elementary students on half-day school shifts and used portable classrooms (Willis Wagons) to handle the overcrowded student population, instead of building new schools. Eventually, the protests became successful and Willis was forced to resign.

However, the insidious institutionalized racism that prevailed within the Chicago Public School System was endemic and challenging. Farragut High School was a microcosm of the depths of white supremacy affecting the school administration, faculty, engineers, discipline, counseling departments and public safety.

Due to the stereotype of underachieving Black schools, particularly Farragut, there was no viable curriculum alternatives and relevant teaching methodology being instituted in West Side schools. The predominant theme of academic inferiority of Black students began with the school board, general superintendent, and department heads down to district level administrators, local principals and staff.

For me it was quite obvious that there needed to be basic changes at Farragut and when I was elevated to chair the Science Department in 1966, I had already formulated various school reform initiatives.

During the period of 1967-71 the parents and community of IS-201 and Ocean-Hill Brownsville District demonstrated against the New York Board of Education, demanding involvement and decision-making power in their neighborhood schools. The historic abuse of Black children and their parents became exposed and for a short time the parents achieved a victory when the School Board designated these schools to become a pilot project in community control.

When the Chicago Urban League sponsored a Town Forum on the Community Control of Schools Movement in 1969, several of the Harlem organizers presented workshops. After studying their strategies, I became convinced that Chicago schools could benefit from the community struggle and Farragut High School would be my primary target.

Historiography: Civil Rights Struggle For Desegregation

In the 1960s, Superintendent Benjamin Willis became the symbol of white supremacy with his arrogant, defiant and blatant neglect of Black students, parents and community leadership. Consequently, the Coordinating Council of Community Organizations (CCCO) became the umbrella group of seventeen Civil Rights organizations through a series of demonstrations, boycott strategies and court cases to demand the desegregation of Chicago Public Schools. Despite the national spotlight on de facto segregation, highlighted with complaints to the U.S. Office of Education, Mayor Richard Daley still maintained a stranglehold on upholding the status quo.

Ultimately, supporters of Willis prevailed to force the School Board to meet and vote to rehire Willis on October 14, 1963. Willis was re-instated as General Superintendent. This would not deter the community oppositions that led to a series of school boycotts, termed Freedom Days, beginning October 22, 1963 led by CCCO. The stated purpose was to protest the inferior education given to all children. Lawrence Landry became the chair of the boycott movement. The effects of the boycott resulted in 224,770 students reported absent from schools citywide.

In order to achieve their original thirteen demands, CCCO called for a second boycott February 25, 1964, but tensions were rising between Lawrence Landry, boycott committee chairman, and Al Raby, CCCO chairman, along with internal disagreements among some civil rights organizational members. Despite the split in allegiance by the Black community, 172,350 students were reported absent on February 25, 1964.

Through legal efforts to publicize the Chicago educational problems, CCCO submitted a complaint on July 4 and 27, 1965 charging that the actions of the school board and general superintendent were in violation of Title VI, Section 601 and that federal funds should be withheld. However, through strong political pressure by influential Chicago Daley supporters, the funds were released on October 5, 1965 under what has been described as the Whiston-Cohen Agreement. This was a definite victory for Mayor Daley because he refused to allow Civil Rights leaders to deny Chicago of any federal funds or to bring the national spotlight on negative social problems in the city.

Black Power: The Turbulent Era of Confrontational Strategies Civil Rights & School Struggle

The national Black Power Movement of the sixties and seventies was an evolutionary branch of the Civil Rights Movement. It was a decisive action of self-determination focusing on community control of cultural institutions, economics, and hopefully, political resources.

Throughout the Black community, 1968 was a pivotal period of activism for real community control. Student leaders emerged on the West Side and South Side high schools with protests demanding issues such as:

- Inclusion of community input in the decision-making process through recognition of concerned parents and residents.
- Approval of hiring Black administrators, administrative assistants and counselors.
- Requirement that Afro-American history be a one-year course for all students, inclusion of Black contributions to every subject and the invitation of Black professionals as lecturers.
- Elimination of the tracing system to develop students to their maximum educational potential.

On the West Side, several student protest organizations were formed, such as the New Breed, with dynamic leadership by Victor Adams and Sharron Mathews in the Harrison High School community that included Hispanic supporters.

As tensions increased following the April 4, 1968 assassination of Dr. King, a variety of social and educational confrontations emerged in South Side and West Side schools. At Farragut, High School students mobilized to vent their frustrations both within the school and in their neglected ghetto neighborhoods.

Student Mobilization

It has been documented that Farragut students left school early on April 5, 1968 and marched to Harrison, Crane, Marshall, Austin and other West Side schools to demonstrate and demand justice for Dr. King's murder. Somehow, the youths decided to go into the downtown Loop business section with their protest. Chicago policemen were equally determined to prevent any social confrontations in the Loop and forced these students to retreat to Madison Street back to the West Side. Along the way more frustrations were felt and by nightfall, the 1968 Chicago rebellion became so explosive that the Illinois National Guard was federalized for ten days and given orders by Mayor Daley to quell the disturbances at all costs: to "shoot to kill" protesters in order to regain law and order.

By mid-October 1968 student organizations came together and formed the Black Students for Defense as an umbrella organization consisting of thirteen public high schools and three private schools. On Sunday, October 13, students passed out flyers calling for "No School Monday Solidarity Day for Liberation." The boycott stated that unless their demands were met by Supt. Redmond by October 16, each Monday would be designated as the day for student boycotts.

On Monday, October 14, between 27,000 and 35,000 students participated in the boycott with about 3,000 students converging at a Rally at the South Side Afro-Arts Theater. After the rally, James Harvey, director of Afro-American Solidarity Organization, spoke in Washington Park and declared a new demand: the lifting of suspension for students of the boycott.

The second boycott occurred Monday, October 21, 1968 with Operation Breadbasket Teacher Division's 500-700 teachers in support. They also attended a rally at Fellowship Baptist Church, where Rev. Clay Evans was the pastor. The final student boycott occurred Monday, October 28, 1968 with only 8,000-9,000 participants.

On Wednesday, October 30, the Board of Education invited students and teachers to a special meeting to discuss students' demands. Among the teachers speaking were Harold Charles, Farragut Black Teacher Association; Roy Stell, Operation Breadbasket Teacher Division; and Bobby Wright, Black Teacher Caucus. The emphasis was on total community control and miseducation of Black students. The meeting ended abruptly after James Harvey, boycott organizer, challenged the integrity of the Board of Education and Supt. Redmond.

In a reversal of tactics there would be a boycott on Monday, November 4, but a call for sit-ins was publicized for Monday or Wednesday. Unfortunately, the sit-in failed as some principals ended school earlier in the day and police reinforcements were placed on duty in several schools. The Farragut Black Student Alliance (BSA) held out the longest and was the last school to end their sit-in before nightfall.

Some of the achievements of the student movement were:

- Afro-American studies became an institution in the school curriculum.
- Black administrators were increased.
- Community gained some voice in school decision through decentralization policies.
- Recognition by community that indeed students were interested in education.

At Farragut, the BSA was instrumental in organizing other West Side students to become cultural nationalists. From 1969-71, the BSA conducted after-school or Saturday academy sessions for elementary students at Marcy Center, Better Boys Foundation and Hess Upper Grade Center.

In 1970 the BSA created a Black Studies Workshop curriculum that enabled Farragut students to improve their standardized reading scores. This was intended to overcome the academic barriers of the public school tracking system, which stereotyped Black students as underachievers and functional illiterates. This curriculum was successful in increasing student scores by at least one grade level proficiency average in only one school semester. Consequently, their Black Studies Workshop became the first and only student-sponsored Chicago public school reading curriculum, and it emerged as the hallmark for student activism from 1970-1976.

The West Side Movement for Black Power

Upon the assassination of Dr. Martin Luther King Jr. on April 4, 1968, to many of us it became clear that the Civil Rights quest for economic and social justice from the oppressive white supremacist leadership across the country was in need of critical re-assessment.

The Lawndale community and the West Side in general had been active in community organizing for educational reform, particularly in 1968. Prior to this, Dr. King came to Chicago in January 1966 to begin the Chicago Freedom Movement and lived in an apartment on 1557 S. Hamlin Street. Unfortunately, at that time Chicago's Black leadership had a greater allegiance to Mayor Daley than to their constituents, in order to maintain their personal status quo of minimal power. Essentially, they were not willing to give up their minimal power for the civil rights and freedom of Blacks in the ghettos across the city.

Nevertheless, by 1968 an emphasis was shifting from civil rights to human rights and several grassroots and concerned parents emerged. The mood had turned to Black Power and there was little doubt about the ideological allegiance of warriors in the struggle. According to Stokely Carmichael and Charles Hamilton, Black Power is "a call for Black people in this country to unite, recognize their heritage and to build a sense of community. It is a call for Black people to define their own goals, lead their own organizations and support those organizations."

Among the grassroots organizations in this phase of the Liberation Struggle were:

- West Side Organization (Chester Robinson)
- Garfield Organization (Doug Andrews)
- Congress of Racial Equality-Westside Branch (James Cage)
- Student Non-Violent Coordinating Committee
- Black Impeachment Committee (Russ Meek)
- Lawndale Peoples' Planning and Action Conference
- Concerned People of the West Side

Several parent groups were involved through the Concerned Parents and People of the West Side, (Ted Bevy) and United Concerned Parents (Ida Mae Fletcher) and many local schools had a concerned parent unit.

Black Teachers On The Battlefield: 1968-1975

Throughout the Chicago Public School system, Black educators risked their jobs for the belief of equality for all children. Beginning with demands to the Board of Education directly, the racist Chicago Teachers Union and white supremacy climate of Mayor Daley's political Machine, courageous teachers challenged the status quo doctrine of educational "genocide" by any means necessary!

There were several prominent teacher organizations including:

- Teachers for Integrated Schools (Co-founded by Al Raby and Meyer Weinberg, 1961)
- Teachers Committee for Quality education (Timeul Black, Spokesman)
- Concerned Full-Time Basis Substitutes (James McQuirter)
- Operation Breadbasket Teacher Division (Harold Charles, Roy Stell, Mattie

Hopkins, David Harrison, Lillie Peoples and Sarah Cogins)

- Black Teachers Caucus (Bobby Wright, Grady Jordan, Al Cheatam)
- Farragut Black Teacher Association (Harold Charles)

Of all the teacher-oriented community organizations, the Operation Breadbasket Teacher Division was most effective in city-wide organizing. During their optimum years of productivity, 1969-1972, members attended the Wednesday meetings at the Colonial House on 79th Street. There were over one thousand members registered and weekly attendance averaged five hundred. During the week their Executive Committee met to develop strategies pertinent to our primary objective: community control of schools.

As part of a comprehensive plan to create our own demonstration alternative school, members participated in the 1970 summer-long Educators to Africa program sponsored by the African American Education Institute and Howard University. Teacher division members were on a mission to critically examine the Africanization process of West African school districts. Research was conducted during field trips and lectures in Ghana (Univ. Ghana-Legon, Univ. Science & Technology-Kumasi, and the Univ. Cape Coast). In addition, workshops were conducted at the Univ. Dahomey and Univ. of Togo, culminating in Nigeria at Univ. Ife, Univ. Lagos and Univ. Ibadan.

The Faragut Black Teacher Manifesto

Dr. King's murder on April 4, 1968 had become a symbol of rebellion throughout Chicago's West Side and across the country. An atmosphere had been created to shift civil rights to Black Power and community control of schools.

In a series of meetings during the summer of 1968, Harold Charles organized Farragut High School Black teachers in order to create a Black manifesto outlining thirteen non-negotiable demands for educational improvement on behalf of the students and parents. On the opening day of school, September 1968, the Black manifesto was then presented to Principal Joseph Carroll and the struggle for self-determination was launched. There were specific demands, recommendations and a timeline for implementation.

This was the first time that black teachers had organized their faculty and presented their educational program to the local and district school administration. The ultimate unification of the black community in support of their teachers signified the peak of Black Power and was destined to achieve positive educational improvement in our neighborhood schools.

On September 30, 1968 the Board of Education capitulated to the first demand for the assignment of a Black assistant principal. Arleen Hunter, a member of the Action Committee, was appointed to that position and, ironically, four other similar positions were opened city-wide to reflect the impression that the Black manifesto had achieved its goals.

However, over the next seventeen months, September 1968-February 1970, Principal Carroll either stonewalled or rejected full implementation of the remaining twelve demands. It then became necessary to mobilize for the removal of Principal Carroll "by any means necessary."

Sister Ida Mae Fletcher, chair of the Concerned Parents of the West Side, feared that further teacher confrontations would result in mass firings or re-assignments. On February 19, 1970 an in-service meeting was approved by District Ten superintendent Joseph Rosen to discuss the future of Farragut. After much discussion faculty members voted 150-20 to terminate Carroll's principalship. Joseph Rosen then notified the Board of Education of the faculty and concerned parents' decision, and Carroll was relieved of his duties and reassigned to administrative duties at the district office.

Another member of the Action Committee, Lawrence Flournoy, a popular counselor, was named interim principal and assumed his duties immediately. A new chapter in our concept of participatory education was developed by the formation of our School Policy Committee consisting of staff, students, teachers, parents, and community activists. During the weekly meetings after school, policies were discussed and enacted, which allowed all parties of educational reform to have decision-making power.

The resultant changes in the Farragut educational climate became historic with its all-school, self-improvement model to combat problems in: school/class attendance, tardiness, reduction in disciplinary incidents, increased academic achievement in local and district-mandated standardized test scores, decreases in school drop-outs, higher graduation rates and the resultant positive image compared to other high schools.

However, the Chicago Principals Association threatened the Board of Education with a lawsuit in 1970 for withholding a principal position and alleging that Lawrence Flournoy was ineligible as a candidate by Board standards. In order to maintain our movement for empowerment, the School Policy Committee agreed to interview prospective principal candidates and select a new principal. In 1971, after countless meetings, Elisha Walker was appointed Farragut's educational leader with the support of the School Policy Committee. This ended nearly three years of struggle and one and a half years of community control of Farragut. Our movement had been acclaimed as the first and only successful community control model in a Chicago public school. The process of interviewing and selecting future principals continued into the next decade.

In retrospect, Farragut teachers, students and parents came together, made demands and tirelessly organized demonstrations until those demands were met. Because of unity for Black Power, there were no teacher firings, student expulsion or parent reprisal and this model became an example for other schools.

Development of Independent Black Educational Institutions

POSTULATE:

> "Only when we are clear about the kind of society we wish to build, can we build an educational system to fit that society."
>
> **—Mwalumu Julius Nyerere**

One of the greatest tasks undertaken by the black community is to envision a new society for future generations. For those of us in the Chicago movement for community control of schools, we realized that in order to control public schools, educators and parents needed an active model to examine the critical areas of administration, staffing, curriculum, physical facility, economic resources, and community involvement among many other issues.

Chicago's Board of Education represented the basic premise of white supremacy as stated by Frederick Douglass: "Power concedes nothing without a demand; it never has and never will." After the Board of Education created the Woodlawn Experimental School Project (WESP) in the seventies, under the leadership of Barbara Sizemore, (former principal at Forestville Elementary School), it soon became apparent that the Board of Education had no real commitment to local control of schools. Despite great publicity at the onset, once educational issues became a power struggle between the University of Chicago and Woodlawn residents, the board rescinded the community contract and removed Sizemore for administrative reasons.

After the results of the futile Woodlawn Experimental School Project, concerned parents, educators and students became more politically astute to the realities of "benevolent racism." Whether liberal or conservative, white policy-makers were united in suppressing and co-opting Black activist leadership throughout the city.

It might be difficult for many blacks to understand, but in a system of white supremacy, oftentimes the oppressed buy into their own oppression if they believe they have a semblance of power within that system. For Cultural Nationalists there was no greater task than the education of our children for national liberation.

Since 1968, concerned educators, parents and students had struggled to gain community control, but in the final analysis the only tangible result was quasi-educational decentralization, which merely made local advisory groups symbols of partnership in school policy decision-making.

At Farragut, with a history of limited successful mobilizing for community control, it became necessary to re-access our objectives and forge a new agenda of Black empowerment. After extensive research and visitations to student-operated Freedom Schools in Milwaukee, Newark, NJ and Washington, D.C., the Farragut Black Student Alliance decided to organize a new model of African-centered education by adopting the Pan-African postulate of Tanzania's "Education for Self-reliance."

On February 5, 1972 three BSA junior and senior students, with the involvement of Harold Charles, Founding Elder, opened the Shule Ya Watoto (School for Children) in a storefront building on Roosevelt Road in North Lawndale; operated by the Lawndale Peoples' Planning and Action Conference. Beginning with five enrolled students, age five to nine, the Saturday Academy offered Rites of Passage socialization programs, such as science: math, communications, social studies, self-defense, Kiswahili, Black manhood/ womanhood, arts and crafts and cultural field trips.

After two years of the Saturday Academy, parents insisted that a pre-school full-time educational program be instituted. In September 1974 the Ashanti branch for children two to six years old was created and the Fulani branch on Saturday continued for elementary students seven to fourteen years old. Despite relocating the Shule to seven different locations on the West Side, the Shule Ya Watoto emerged as a model African-centered warrior institution for thirty-one years.

During the seventies several independent institutions were formed on the South Side:

- ILE IFE OMINARE School (Black Women's Committee)
- New Concept Development Center (Institute of Positive Education)
- Ujima Learning Center (Association of Black Sociologists)
- Blyden-Delany Academy (concerned parents and teachers)

In addition, several institutions were members of the Council of Independent Black Institutions (CIBI), a national umbrella organization, and locally with the Pan-African Nationalist Federation in Chicago as its education Committee. In 1973 the Education Committee spearheaded the observance of Kwanzaa KARAMU YA IMANI (feast of Faith) on January 1 and continued that role for over a decade.

Conclusion

The Black Nationalist ideology of the sixties and seventies created an understanding as to why community control of schools became a priority for Black people. One of our relevant statements was: "In a racially oppressive society, Education for Liberation becomes a subversive activity."

Additionally, a people seeking liberation cannot continue to be educated by those whom they seek liberation from! Black Nationalist ideology, combined with the failure of school desegregation efforts, created the realization for Black students, teachers, parents and community activists that the demands were reasonable and their tactics were necessary to achieve equality and empowerment.

PAMOJA TUTASHINDE (Together, we will win)

REFERENCES

Danns, Dionne. *Something Better For Our Children: Black Organizing in Chicago Public Schools,* 1963-71. (New York, Routeledge, 2003)

Perkins, Useni Eugene. *Home is a Dirty Street: The Social Oppression of Black Children.* (Chicago, Third World Press, 1975)

Madhubuti, *Haki From Plan To Planet-Life Studies: The Need for Afrikan Minds and Institutions.* (Chicago, Third World Press, 1973)

Anders, Elizabeth. *Everybody Runs Farragut.* (Chicago, Evergreen Magazine, 1971)

Afrik, Hannibal Tirus. *Operational Philosophy of the SHULE YA WATOTO.* (Chicago, Black Spear Press, 1980)

PATH TO A RELEVANT EDUCATION FOR BLACK STUDENTS

Barbara A. Sizemore

Anton Dvorak, My First Principalship

Mr. Minor encouraged me to take and pass the Chicago Public School's principal examination in 1961, and in January 1963, I was assigned to the principalship of the new Anton Dvorak Elementary School at 3615 West Sixteenth Street on Chicago's notorious west side. This part of Chicago was then called the port of entry for Mississippi migrants. This is also the section in which Martin Luther King, Jr. chose to locate his residence during his sojourn in the city. Sixteenth Street was called the "Street of Dreams" by local residents because of the volume of heroin sold on it in the 1960s. Most integrationists saw my new racially isolated school as a disaster about to happen and told me that my children didn't have a snowball's chance in hell for success.

The school opened on April 8, 1963. It was a Kindergarten to sixth, all Black, which is what we were calling ourselves then, non-graded elementary school of 1,263 students, approximately 60 percent of whom were born in Mississippi. These children had been attending school on double shift from September of 1962 to April of 1963. Some came to school at 8:00 A.M. and left at noon; others came at noon and left at 4:00 P.M. They shared books, materials, seats, supplies and sometimes teachers. The new school was structured to relieve overcrowding.

There were forty-two teachers: 65 percent were first-year assignments, 66 percent Black, 30 percent Jewish and 4 percent other whites. Georgia R. Williams; my double cousin Jo, the counselor; Mary J. Faust, the nurse; Gladys Berry, the librarian; and Clara K. Holton, the assistant principal were all Black. Clara K. Holton profoundly changed the direction of my professional life. She introduced me to the non-graded school.

The non-graded school concept operated from the premise that grouping children as learners by ages and grades, and then passing them in lockstep fashion from grade to grade because of age, was dysfunctional, since such grouping and promotion neither accounted for nor accommodated human incommensurability.

CPS called it Continuous Development. Students aged six and up were placed in teaching groups according to a constellation of ten factors. Teaching groups were called lanes and were lettered instead of numbered. There were actually three grades: kindergarten, primary and intermediate. There were two divisions, which were all male, each taught by a male teacher. Students were placed, by achievement in reading, in four lanes: A, B, C, D. This placement was determined by stanines. In a normal curve of distribution, such as reading test scores, there are nine stanines, with stanines one, two and three representing low achievement levels; four, five and six, representing average achievement levels; and seven, eight and nine, representing high achievement levels. Students at or beyond stanine level seven were placed in Lane A; stanines five and six in Lane B, and so on. Their ages ranged from six to eleven in the intermediate block/grade.

The reading and mathematics curriculum consisted of skills sequentially ordered in a hierarchy from simple to complex. Students progressed according to maturation and readiness and were exposed to knowledge through activities, tested to ascertain mastery, and given a new group of exercises when warranted. Students weren't penalized for not learning, but were given another chance to learn with a new set of experiences.

Of the schools in District Ten of the Chicago Public Schools, Dvorak ranked at the twentieth percentile in reading achievement in 1963. By 1964, it had risen. There were 184 students enrolled in kindergarten in October 1963. Of the 184 students, only forty-two (23 percent) were ready to read. Of the 205 students enrolled in kindergarten one year later, ninety-seven students (47 percent) were ready to read according to the Metropolitan Readiness Test administered in 1964. The students' skill mastery needs were diagnosed and taught by direct instruction. Phonics was an important part of reading instruction in both the kindergarten and the primary grades. Staff development was continuous. The faculty even provided in-service for other schools. We ran a tight ship and produced great students.

I tried to have a meeting with Martin Luther King, Jr. to discuss the students' achievement at Dvorak, but I never was able to do this. I did speak with Jesse Jackson. But, by that time, (1963–1965), the Civil Rights movement wanted enforcement of the Supreme Court's Decision in *Brown v. Board of Education,* which was ten years old. Chicago's schools were more segregated than ever. But the leaders of the Civil Rights Movement were sold on mixing up the races in the classrooms and Benjamin C. Willis, the superintendent of the Chicago Public Schools, was opposed to this and he became their target.

Consequently, I could not get anyone to take me seriously when I argued that Black students could excel, even in a segregated setting, if the teachers and the principal believed that they could and taught them to do so. I even argued about this issue with Ron Edmonds during those years. At that time, he agreed with the Movement. But the failure of integration to occur with all deliberate speed convinced him otherwise. The major problem with *Brown v. Board of Education* was the necessary assumption that anything all Black is no good. This was a reinforcement of Black inferiority and white supremacy. Many Chicagoans called me a traitor because of this, and accused me of defending Superintendent Willis and referred to me as Aunt JeBarbara.

Forrestville High, My Second Principalship

When the principalship for the Forrestville High School was advertised, friends advised me not to apply. The school was located in the center and converging boundaries of four warring gangs: The Blackstone Rangers, the youngest group, the East Side Disciples, the War Lords and the aging Four Treys. Drexel Avenue was the war zone line between the Blackstone Rangers and the East Side Disciples. Students could not come across Drexel Avenue to attend Forrestville without a fight. Sometimes guns were used and people were shot.

Forrestville started with a freshman class and was a grow-a-year high school. When I was assigned there as principal in September 1965, there were 1,159 students in ninth and tenth grades. The assistant principal who had been running the high school then was Anderson Thompson. He proved to be the next important person in my professional life. It was he who taught me how to be a high school principal in a time of turmoil and tension. Many teachers were full-time basis substitutes. Most people did not want to come into the area to teach. Several teachers were vocal dissidents opposed to racially isolated Black schools.

The Forrestville faculty was approximately 70 percent Black and 30 percent white. The administration, however, was entirely Black: Anderson Thompson, Frank Allen, William Hunter, Beverly Daniels and myself. Teachers immediately, upon my appointment, divided into two ideological camps: (1) those who believed that Blacks could be educated in a segregated setting and who wanted the new high school to be located in the Black community; and (2) those who wanted the new high school built in an area conducive to integration, and who believed that it was impossible to have an excellent education in a segregated high school. I took a position with the first category. It was war from the start.

The protest teachers considered me an Aunt Jemima, encouraged students to challenge the administration and, knowingly, incited the gang leaders to war. In the spring of 1966 the Council of Coordinating Community Organizations (CCCO), under the leadership of Al Raby, picketed the high school and recruited teachers as members.

In spite of these troubles, Anderson Thompson gave me some strong points on high school organization. Although he is a historian by training, his intuition for social dynamics of organizations is enormous. I told him that I entered the girls washroom one day and found some students smoking. When I told them to stop, they reminded me that my washroom was in my office. When I complained about this lack of respect he told me, "The biggest weapon teenagers have is anonymity." In five days I learned 900 names. After that, Mr. Thompson urged me to identify the leaders of all the organizations in and out of school. Whenever there was trouble we called these student leaders in to talk. Most of our students had trouble. At one time, over 60 percent of our male students were either on probation or had been incarcerated. Thompson's process was to identify students' needs, to win them over to his side by meeting those needs, to take a strong stand with the students when it met their needs, to defend his position and never to act as though he was afraid.

In two weeks, I knew the Forrestville student leaders. Interestingly, we found that certain gangs dominated the teams. Thompson suggested we meet with these leaders. From this meeting we learned that a gang war was imminent, involving a majority of our male students. Two days after the meeting, two gangs declared war and members of one of them shot into the school from a passing car. Luckily, no one was hurt. Students who lived at Forty-second and Oakenwald in a huge twenty-seven-story public housing project with large apartments of four bedrooms, could not come to school at all. Crossing Drexel meant death. We appealed for two uniformed juvenile officers to be assigned to the school. CCCO teachers criticized this recommendation, calling for the school to be closed. Grievances were sent to the Chicago Teachers Union in October of 1966. During that time James Redmond became the superintendent of schools. After a great deal of negotiation, begging and pleading, we were assigned two officers.

The first step enacted was disarmament. Weapons were taken from students and removed from school premises. The second step was an improvement in self-esteem. In the midst of this turmoil, self-image building assemblies called the "Men of Forrestville" were held each month for all male students and faculty, and "Women of Forrestville" for all female students and faculty. These programs produced the Magnificent Seven, a group of young male student orators who represented Fredrick Douglass; Martin Luther King, Jr.; W. E. B. Du Bois; Booker T. Washington; Malcolm X; Marcus Garvey; and Adam Clayton Powell. These students performed throughout the city, state, and nation. Social science and history teachers were given an African American centered curriculum to teach, starting with the Forrestville community and extending into the universe. And the division periods, sometimes called homerooms, were lengthened to establish a school family for our students. The third step was tackling the low achievement of many students. For example, those who were four years behind in reading were placed in English classes for reading.

In response, English teachers grieved to the union, protesting that they were not reading teachers. In November, teachers refused to do lunchroom duty, declaring the area unsafe for teachers. All administrators were assigned duty. There were four lunch periods from 10:20 A.M. to 1:00 P.M. I supervised the last lunch. For the rest of the term, CCCO teachers resisted any administrative attempts to improve the quality of education at Forrestville. Finally, unsatisfactory ratings were sent for twelve teachers charging them with insubordination and failure to exercise assigned duties. Since ten of them were substitutes, these were transferred out. New teachers were assigned to Forrestville the next term.

When I left Forrestville in 1967, it was on the brink of improving student achievement. I learned the hard way that Black academic achievement can occur only when there is an orderly climate conducive to learning, and where there is a principal convinced that Black students can learn, and where there is a consensus about the priority of achievement among the faculty. Forrestville produced the only Black National Merit Scholar in 1968 in the Chicago area, Carolyn Haynes, who went on to graduate from the University of Chicago.

The Center for Inner-City Studies, Northeastern Illinois University

In 1965, Dr. Donald H. Smith, then assistant professor of speech at Chicago Teachers College-North (CTC-N) and later assistant professor at Northeastern Illinois University, together with urban anthropologist Stanley Newman, submitted a proposal to the U.S. Office of Education under the Experienced Teacher Fellowship Program, which resulted in the Center for Inner City Studies (CICS). According to Gerald Butler (A Case Study in Urban Teacher Education: The Center for Inner City Studies: 1966-1971)2 CICS was one of the first institutions in the United States to dedicate itself to the preparation of teachers for service in the inner city ghetto areas. The program trained experienced teachers from all over America to be more effective with inner city youth. I became an adjunct faculty member of this program, as did Anderson Thompson, under the urging of Dr. Smith.

CICS had its legitimate base in the traditional academic center, but it was a radical departure from the general academic framework. In Northeastern Illinois University's "Center for Inner City Studies Report 1972–1973" it states that the primary concern of this organization was the "human condition in the inner city." It further explains that "the accepted categories of academic speculation are generally considered too limited and remote from the total life experience to produce the insights and ideas that would promote the relevant changes in human relations as they are determined by the real needs of inner city communities."

Gerald Butler commented that CICS's impetus was a letter from U.S. Congressman William L. Dawson, First District of Illinois (1943-1970), to Dr. Jerome Sachs, academic dean at Chicago Teachers College - North (CTC-N), outlining a preschool educational and activity program for four and five-year- old children who lived in the poorer precincts of the city. Faculty and administrators at Chicago Teachers College–South (CTC-S), however, felt that this was an infringement on their territory. The inhabitants of this predominantly Black neighborhood resented CTC-S for being a school that was predominantly White. Although Dr. Sachs responded favorably to it, Dawson's proposal was set aside.

In his book, *Climbin' Up the Mountain Children: The Journey of an African American Educator,*[3] Donald H. Smith notes: "I believed it was important to locate the program in the heart of the Black community, rather than at the college which was located in an all-white neighborhood. After a lot of exploration I came up on an ideal site." That ideal site was the Abraham Lincoln Center, a place with which Smith was familiar. He had attended its library as a little boy while living in the Ida B. Wells Housing Project. After a meeting with Mayor Richard J. Daley, Sr., Smith was able to get the building leased to the college.

During the spring of 1965, William Itkin, professor of psychology at CTC- N, submitted a proposal to the United States Office of Education (USOE) for funding of a National Defense Education Act (NDEA) institute for teachers of the disadvantaged. At that time, he was director of the college's Master's Degree Program for Teachers of the Culturally Disadvantaged. Itkin and Smith engaged a number of education people, of whom I was one, to present at this institute. Although the federal government did not fund it, Itkin and Smith managed to secure funding from acting dean, Robert Goldberg. Itkin was unable to devote sufficient time to the endeavor and most of the work fell on Smith, who became the college's catalyst for these ideas. Eventually, Smith and Newman secured funding for CICS and it opened on September 8, 1966.

Butler and other informants described Smith as highly regarded and dedicated to the advancement of Black people and other minorities. He had little difficulty assembling a group of six people of like mind. I was a member of this group, but without a doubt, Donald H. Smith was the brilliant visionary in this operation. Smith was so committed that he forfeited his position as assistant professor of speech when his faculty demanded that he give all of his professional energies to his duties on the main campus or resign. He resigned.

Between 1969 and 1970, five long-range programs were developed at CICS. The ExTFP, a program in which experienced teachers who wanted preparation for teaching in the inner city were recruited for a master's degree in education, was funded for three years. According to Butler, the program was structured around four principles: improvement of communication between teachers and students through mutual respect for language patterns; respect for ethnic minorities through knowledge and appreciation of their histories and cultures; empathy toward students through an awareness of, and respect for divergent lifestyles; and awareness of the individual worth of each student, combating the self-fulfilling prophesy syndrome. Confrontation of racism was a technique frequently used to carry out these principles. Students wrote to the USOE regarding their negative perception of this practice, complaining about the perceived lack of traditional course work usually given in graduate programs; emphasis by faculty on students attitudinal change; and a lack of rapport between faculty and fellows. The students asked that Smith be removed. Smith offers some insight into this in his book:

> In the midst of a tumultuous civil rights movement students and faculty were being obliged to examine their racist tendencies and ethnic stereotypes. The information we helped students to gather that first year proved so traumatic for some that a delegation of students met secretly with the college president and asked for my removal as director. (Smith, 2002)

He remained for another cycle and left at the end of the 1967–1968 school year when the faculty turned him down for promotion to full professor, but not until CICS had been evaluated and recognized by the faculty Senate as a permanent academic department. This testifies to the kind of leader Don was. He later said of this experience, "It was with pain that I left my beloved Center and my beloved Chicago." Sonja Stone was named acting director and chair of the Department of Inner City Studies and Dr. Arnez was selected to be director of ExTFP.

The Prospective Teachers Fellowship Program (PTFP) was funded in April 1967, before Dr. Smith's departure from CICS, for a period of five years. The unique feature of the PTFP was its emphasis on language development. Its recruits were college graduates who aspired to be teachers, and it offered a master's degree in education in inner city studies. Elise Tucker and Dr. Nancy L. Arnez co-directed this program. Arnez, Smith and Tucker created the Alternative Teacher Training Program long before those who now claim precedence.

Several programs were initiated through CICS under the dynamic leadership of Dr. Arnez. The Extended Day Program offered course work leading to a Master's Degree in Education for students who worked during the day. To accommodate these students' work schedules, classes were held late in the afternoon and early in the evening. The Career Opportunities Program (COP) and the Cultural Linguistic Follow-Through Model were both developed and implemented under Arnez's tenure. COP was designed to provide an opportunity for low-income people to enter the teaching profession and was sponsored by USOE. Teacher's aides enrolled in the courses at CICS while they still served in local schools. The first class began on July 1, 1970, with 116 participants. CICS also produced a national model for Follow-Through with its Cultural Linguistic Follow-Through Program developed by Dr. Arnez, Martha Bass, Renee Edmonds, Clara K. Holton and Edythe Stanford Williams and implemented in Chicago, Illinois; Akron, Ohio; Compton, California; and Topeka, Kansas during the 1969–1971 school years. The model was designed to improve the education of children in kindergarten through third grade. This model included the Ethno-Linguistic Oral

Language Technique, which was a framework for inclusion of the language of the child's culture in the content of the curriculum. The technique provided a means of utilizing, as a bridge to academic tasks, the rich background of stimulating experiences from community resources familiar to the child.

An outgrowth of CICS, initiated by Sonja Stone, was the Communiversity, which was a forum of Black intellectuals seeking and creating knowledge. It was the Communiversity that expanded my intellectual horizons. There were many courses and workshops on capitalism, enslavement, and Jim Crow, as well as African history, life and culture. There I was introduced to the works of men and women I had not known: John Henrik Clarke, Josef ben Jochannon, George Padmore, Zora Neale Hurston, Toni Cade Bambara, Sonia Sanchez, Haki Madhubuti and Mari Evans. The Communiversity was an important part of CICS and its legacy. I entertained many of these visiting lecturers at my home on Chicago's south side. So the Communiversity was not only an important part of CICS and its legacy, but it also impacted my personal life as well.

Donald H. Smith brought many faculty people together who later influenced my thinking about African and African American education: Nancy L. Arnez, who also wrote a book about my superintendency, and Sonja Stone, who introduced me to creative strategies for teaching. Moreover, Smith introduced me to consulting, which I have done for all of these nearly forty years. I also met Ruth Jones Farmer, now Swinson, from USOE and Arthur Thomas from Model Cities in Dayton, Ohio. Thomas later became the highly regarded president of Central State University in Xenia, Ohio. At CICS I also met Charles Smith of the Rockefeller Foundation, who later saved my professional life after I was fired from the D.C. superintendency.

Dr. Arnez was a very impressive intellectual leader with a vision for African American education and a mission to which she was devoted. She was also an accomplished poet. CICS grew under Dr. Arnez, adding many programs, including cultural events, such as "Rapsodi in Black" by Sonja Stone, a West Side youth school, the Career Opportunities Project with the Woodlawn Experimental School District and adult activities. After Smith's departure, the faculty adopted a sexist view regarding the participation of female faculty. I was very much opposed to this direction, as was Dr. Arnez, but the female faculty failed to articulate any effective protest. By 1972 I had separated myself from CICS.

I was gone from Chicago for twenty years (1972–1992). When I returned, searching for partners to work in the Chicago Public Schools, I found that CICS was somewhat indifferent. They were still training teachers, but, their emphasis was now on Africa and African culture under the leadership of Jacob Carruthers and Donn Bailey. I did some work with Anderson Thompson in several Chicago Public Schools for them, but I was never able to engage CICS in any of our school reform activities. In 1969, Donald H. Smith and Nancy

Levi Arnez wrote in the *Journal of Teacher Education*:[4]

> The central thesis of this article is that the key to improved instruction for educationally deprived children is improved training for their teachers. Ideally, this should commence during the undergraduate years, but even then, there will still remain a tremendous job of retraining teachers already in service. (Smith and Arnez, 1969)

They outlined their philosophy of educating African American and minority children who were poor in public schools. In a 2002 article titled, "High Performance in High Poverty Schools: 90/90/90 and Beyond," Douglas B. Reeves[5], president of the Center for Performance Assessment and on the faculty of several programs sponsored by the Harvard Graduate School of Education, reiterates the same observation. He noted: "The 90/90/90 research and the other evidence offered in this article falls far short of perfection. It does, however, contribute to the larger body of evidence, which, in its totality, suggests useful strategies for high poverty schools." Smith and Arnez saw the way to solve the achievement gap in 1969, and the permanence of CICS serves as Donald H. Smith's legacy to Chicago, his hometown.

In 1999, Carol Adams, then Director of CICS, submitted proposals to the CEO of Chicago Public Schools for a principals training institute. And in 2003, Conrad Worrill, then Acting Director of CICS, hired Grace Dawson as a faculty member to train principals. Dr. Grace Dawson had been the principal of Beethoven Elementary School located at Twenty-five West Forty-Seventh Street and in the center of the Robert R. Taylor Homes. The Taylor Homes are a public housing project stretching for miles down Chicago's State Street. When she failed her eighth graders, Arnez, Smith and I protested by writing a letter against her nomination for the 1989 Ida B. Wells Risk Takers Award. This award was given annually by the National Alliance of Black School Educators (NABSE). But in spite of our protest, she received the award.

After my return to Chicago, I realized that she had done so to dramatize the terrible inequities present in the distribution of resources among the Chicago public schools. Vallas later adopted her policy of retention, although I do not think retention, social promotion or referral to special education eliminates the causes of school failure. Those causes all stem from the regular education program.

Dawson went on to lay the foundation for Beethoven to be an effective school where a larger percentage of students there reached or exceeded the national norm in reading and mathematics on the Iowa Test of Basic Skills than students in similar schools. She also organized a Saturday school in her church for tutoring these children and providing experiences that would elevate and accelerate achievement. By 2002, under a succession of highly competent principals (former teachers under Dawson—among who were Lula Ford and Frances Oden), 45.9 percent of Beethoven's students reached or exceeded the national norm in reading on the Basic Skills test, and 54.9 percent reached or exceeded the national norm in mathematics. Dawson also served as Instructional Supervisor and Coordinator for the School Achievement Structure at DePaul University, mentoring principals of low achieving schools upon her retirement from CPS. She has contributed much to Chicago Public Schools and strengthened CICS's connection with school reform.

Director of Woodlawn Experimental School Project

Hedged in by the Black community, the University of Chicago was always in some kind of discussion about moving out of Chicago or containing the Black community. I entered the doctoral program there in 1962, but was never serious about completing it. At the time, the school of education at the University of Chicago had some distinguished professors: Roald Campbell, Luvern Cunningham, Franklin Seaberry Chase, Allison Davis and Donald Erickson. Later, Edgar Epps and Diane Slaughter-Defoe would join the faculty. Chase, Cunningham, Davis, Epps, Erickson, Paul E. Peterson, and Diane Slaughter-Defoe played important roles in my intellectual development from 1965 to 1970.

Bernard Charles Watson 'Bernie'6 was an intellectual giant from little Gary, Indiana. He completed the doctoral program at U of C in two years, while I took fifteen. In his book, *Negro Colored Black: Chasing the American Dream,* he said of U of C: "I entered the program in 1965; I intended to be out of there with my degree in 1967. Of course, everybody thought I was deranged when I said this—nobody finished a doctorate from U of C in that time—so I didn't mention it again." Later, Bernie would serve as deputy superintendent of schools in Philadelphia, vice president for academic administration at Temple University and president of the William Penn Foundation.

By 1969, Black Power was in vogue. Community control was the implementation of this ideology. Community control was a form of decentralization. Throughout the struggle for equal educational opportunity there have been cycles of desegregation and decentralization but never an effective assault on white supremacy and its consort, Black inferiority. Negro was out and Black was in, even though there was a growing preference for African culture, as illustrated by afros and such terms as "Africentered." Of course, this last term had to wait another ten years to pass into popular use.

I was studying at the University of Chicago for my doctorate (1967-1969) when I was chosen to be the director of the Woodlawn Experimental Schools Project (WESP) District, a

Title Three Elementary and Secondary Education Act (ESEA) government–funded program under Public Law 89–10. WESP was established by the University of Chicago in collaboration with the Chicago Board of Education and The Woodlawn Organization (TWO) to improve the quality of education in three Black schools: Wadsworth Elementary, Wadsworth Upper Grade Center and Hyde Park High School in East Woodlawn, the home of the Blackstone Rangers in District Fourteen of the CPS. At the time, East Woodlawn was the home of the Blackstone Rangers and was otherwise known as District fourteen of the CPS.

By this time, Black people in Chicago had given up on integration. While few noted the problem, most were still confusing segregation with racism or the belief in Black inferiority and white superiority. A new site in the community had been selected for Martin Luther King, Jr. Senior High School to replace the old Forrestville, assuring its racial isolation. The new high school had been planned by the faculty and administration of Forrestville and the specification sheets lay on my living room floor for six months.

Martin Luther King Jr. Senior High School was planned to be the premier performing arts high school of Chicago. The school was built around its two theaters, following Shakespeare's notion that the world is a stage and all of us are its actors. Every single occupation related to performing arts was represented in the curriculum, from using graphic arts to designing the playbills to constructing the sets and making the costumes. There was a ballet studio, an Olympic–sized gym, a television studio and a radio station. After serving as its director for three years, I left Chicago in 1972, and somehow the school was allowed to disintegrate. CPS built another performing arts high school outside of the community.

Although Superintendent Willis had been deposed, Chicago's schools were very much segregated; and those that were predominately Black were low achieving, except for a few bright spots where students were mostly middle class. WESP developed from a proposal for a Research and Development Center in Urban Education planned by the Committee on Urban Education (COUE) of the University of Chicago in 1965 and 1966.

WESP was governed by the Woodlawn Community Board (WCB), which originally consisted of seven members from each of the collaborating organizations: TWO, the University of Chicago, and the CPS. Later the university relinquished three seats to TWO. WESP consisted of three components: (1) the in-school, or the instructional, component controlled by the CPS; (2) the research component controlled by the University of Chicago; and (3) the community component controlled by TWO. The project had a director and a deputy director, Julius B. DeNye.

The in-school component consisted of an associate director in charge of that component, Clara K. Holton, two program officers in charge of each school, and consultants. The associate director in charge of in-school and the associate director in charge of the community supervised the forty-five community teachers. Theoretically, the principals and faculty of the three schools were part of the in-school component that provided in-service, curriculum supervision and new programs to the schools. The community component consisted of an associate director, Anthony Gibbs, two community organizers, twenty-five community agents and forty-five community teachers.

TWO was a strong and militant community organization that had been created by the vision of four Woodlawn pastors and through the efforts of the Industrial Areas Foundation directed by Saul Alinsky in the early 1960s. It was an organization of civic, religious, business and other community groups that had pledged themselves in a cooperative venture to work together for the improvement and the enrichment of life in modern urban society. Its basic aim was to take the initiative in developing adequate standards and values for community living by generating and maintaining community power.

Voting membership in TWO was by organization, each of which selected five delegates and two alternates to represent it at the delegates meeting, which was held at least once a month. However, in his testimony at the U.S. Senate's hearing investigating the Youth Demonstration Project in 1968, TWO president, Reverend Arthur Brazier, said that the basic unit of membership and participation in TWO was the Block Club. At that time, TWO had approximately ninety block clubs and neighborhood associations and eight standing committees, of which the schools committee was one. The thirty community agent slots and sixty community teacher positions provided by WESP considerably strengthened TWO. Although these positions dwindled as funding failed to keep up with fiscal needs, these people organized more than twenty-five parent councils and managed to send 100 to 200 people to the Woodlawn Community Board's monthly meetings.

Woodlawn is the community contiguous to the University of Chicago to the South. The Woodlawn Community Board (WCB) emanated from a letter written by the Reverend Arthur Brazier to Dr. Roald Campbell, chairman of the COUE. Reverend Brazier criticized the planning procedures and indicated that TWO did not support the use of Woodlawn as a research laboratory by the University of Chicago. Brazier deplored the university's failure to involve TWO in planning the research and development center it wanted to establish in Woodlawn. The Woodlawn Community Council was designed to resolve this conflict. When CPS joined the council, the name was changed to Woodlawn Community Board to avoid confusion with the District fourteen Council of the CPS.

The WCB was to set policy for WESP, but this policy was subject to veto by the CPS Board of Education. The problems around teachers' evaluations provide an example. For me, teacher and principal evaluation formed the crux of the Black student achievement. At both Dvorak and Forrestville, I had learned that many teachers will not teach Black students unless taught how to do so and then made to do it. Consequently, it seemed imperative to me that the WCB have control over principal and teacher evaluation. Friction between Anna Kolheim, the Black principal of Hyde Park High School, and her teachers started early in 1969. Grievances were lodged against the efficiency marks given by the principal, who was a "new" principal in the sense that she was giving marks to that faculty for the first time.

According to CPS Board rules, a new principal "shall give an efficiency grade to those teachers who are on their probationary period. He shall not grade other regularly certificated teachers whose work is satisfactory or better until he has served in that school at least five months." Additionally, the new principal was not bound by marks given by the previous administrator. In her reply to two of the teachers' grievances, the high school principal indicated that she had not visited the teachers' classrooms, nor held conferences. And in her statement before the union representative, the principal said she "assumed" that the classroom teaching was satisfactory.

Teachers were assigned to summer schools if they had excellent marks and qualifications, and promotions demanded superior or excellent ratings. The principal had been asked by the WCB to make her criteria known to the teachers; but I really wanted to change the procedures for teacher evaluation to fit the CAPTS (Community, Administrators, Parents, Teachers and Students) decision–making model, which had been designed by both the in-school and community components and around which a consensus had been developed in WESP.

CAPTS demanded that each group form and meet regularly to report to the WCB on its findings and deliberations. The vehicles for the operational functioning of CAPTS were: (1) the parent councils; (2) the Wadsworth Senate; and (3) the Hyde Park High School Senate. The community agents mobilized parents to form councils. The two Senates were to be established by the two principals in WESP. Neither ever materialized.

During the 1969–1970 school year, the high school principal described her criteria for the next teachers' evaluation (May 15, 1970). To be satisfactory, a teacher must do everything a teacher should do, such as prepare lessons, execute plans, arrive on time, meet classes on time, obey school rules and regulations. To be excellent, in addition to meeting the criteria for a satisfactory mark, a teacher must sponsor a club, contribute something to the community through outside efforts, and go beyond the call of duty. To be superior, in addition to meeting the criteria for satisfactory and excellent marks, a teacher must make a contribution to the literature of, or contribute something of worth to, the discipline and the profession.

Some teachers felt that the actual teaching job itself had diminished in value in the face of the new criteria, and they protested to the WCB. To provide teachers with the time to design their own criteria and evaluation process, WCB ordered the principal to give all teachers a superior mark for that term, to be changed, if necessary, according to criteria approved by the teachers and agreed upon by the principal in the CAPTS process. The high school principal complied with the WCB order but refused to sign her name, arguing that she was caught in a bind and forced to obey CPS rules when and if they differed from WCB's.

Edna C. Hickey, director of personnel at CPS, sent a copy of the following letter to me as director of WESP and to the WCB:

> Dear Mrs. Kolheim:
>
> The principal's signature must appear on the rating form. Please return your Efficiency Report (T.Per.104, Revised 1970) with the individual rating of each teacher indicated and signed by you. One copy is to be sent to Dr. Donald Blyth, District Superintendent, and one copy is to be retained by you.
>
> Sincerely,
> Edna C. Hickey
> Director
> Bureau of Teacher Personnel

On March 31, 1970, I held conferences with the teachers who had lodged grievances against the lowering of their efficiency marks by Anna Kolheim in May of 1969. Two of the teachers reported activities such as club sponsorships and involvement in community and related projects conducted during the 1968-1969 school year. These activities seemed to meet the criteria outlined by the high school principal for excellent teaching marks for that school year, and the lowering of the teachers' grades did appear to be arbitrary and capricious. Attempts to get an explanation from the high school principal proved fruitless and teacher morale began to disintegrate. "The problem facing the WESP staff was that it did not have the clear authority to implement a strategy of intervention, which could test this hypothesis: If you want to increase academic achievement, you have first to change the system so that those most immediately affected by the educational process have power to influence that process," noted John Hall Fish,7 a member of TWO, in *Black Power/White Control*.

Hiring Anna Kolheim, to fill the position of high school principal in WESP had been my idea. I cannot blame anyone else for it. When Reverend Brazier consulted me about the person for the job, she was my first choice. In fact, both officers in TWO and the area superintendent brought their perceptions of her stubbornness and willfulness to my attention. The area superintendent told Reverend Brazier that because of her past attitudes she was not only low on the list, but was unacceptable. Reverend Brazier supported my preference and she was appointed. So in this case I chose my own nemesis.

But I truly saw these characteristics as positive. Several friends who knew people working with her said that she was a person willing to fight the system, a person with courage, stamina, intelligence, industry and commitment. I knew a principal had to have plenty of heart, stamina, and guts. What I did not know was that Anna Kolheim's commitment was to herself, and that, in effect, when I became her superior I was the system she would fight. This, too, was a valuable lesson which I had to experience. A lesson that I experienced again, later in my career in the District of Columbia, before I learned it.

The WESP in-school component, after much involvement in Hyde Park, supported the teachers' efforts to solve this problem. What I learned from this struggle was that the WCB had no power to change CPS Board rules. The principal did indeed have the ability to thwart anything WCB wanted to do and could disregard the project director's orders. John Hall Fish noted in Black Power/White Control that the authority relationship between WESP and school personnel was at best ambiguous. During the last years of the project, the high school principal did not attend the WESP meetings, nor those of the final evaluation committee. It was at this point, one year before the project ended, that I knew the road ahead would be rocky and unproductive.

Conditions at Hyde Park High School went from bad to worse. WESP staff meetings were consumed in arbitrating difficulties between the community component and the principal on one side and the Hyde Park program officer, Joseph Montgomery, and me on the other. In June, 1970, teachers demanded better security in the school and criticized the administration for not taking sufficient action in the face of escalating conflict between the two major gangs, the Blackstone Rangers and the East Side Disciples. In his book *Black Power/White Control,* John Hall Fish wrote:

> In 1966, the Rangers, a small neighborhood gang since the late 1950s, were locked in combat with a rival gang, the East Side Disciples, which shared the Woodlawn turf. Attack, retaliation and escalation continued throughout the winter and spring of 1966. Partly for protection and survival and partly out of zeal, the Rangers entered into intense organizational activity, recruiting youth not only in Woodlawn but in neighboring communities and even distant parts of the city. The core leadership began talking about the Ranger Nation, a confederation of Ranger units. (Fish, 1973)

By 1970, the Ranger Nation was called the Blackstone Nation and could summon over 1000 members at short notice. John Hall Fish also commented that the Nation posed a threat to Woodlawn and to TWO since these youth were "products of the school system, welfare system, unemployment situation, police strategies and poverty" and that "what TWO had done and what TWO meant had not touched them."

A group of teachers mobilized by the WESP high school program officer sat in the deputy superintendent's office seeking help, since they had decided that WESP and WCB were incapable of any action. TWO and the associate director in charge of the community component had never trusted the teachers at the high school and resented this implication of impotence. This action moved TWO into the principal's camp.

In October 1970, students protested a rule governing student conduct, and the necessity for implementing the senate became paramount. In March 1971, students angry about the unimplemented senate decisions around Black History Month, protested against the administration's disapproval of a Black Student Union cultural assembly. Teachers boycotted the senate meeting that was called because they felt the administration had blocked senate actions concerned with security matters. The administration stated that some motions previously adopted were in violation of CPS Board rules. Students claimed that these arguments should have been presented by the administration up front.

On April 5, students were joined by several teachers in a boycott of boycotted classes at Hyde Park High School. The area superintendent placed the principal on a five–week sick leave. The faculty and students began to develop a collaborative relationship with the new acting principal, Spurgeon Gaskins. But on May 20, the WCB voted to return the principal to the school. There was actually nothing else they could do. CPS had no place to put her. WESP was running out of money, and there was no possibility that it could be refunded, especially with the controversies so widely publicized. Students and teachers were so outraged by her return that they went on strike. The high school was removed from my jurisdiction, and students and faculty were arrested. Five teachers were transferred, and WESP joined Ocean-Hill Brownsville as a tragic failure.

The student unrest was too much for CPS, in the face of the many activities of the Blackstone Nation. However, Anthony Gibbs had many contacts with the Nation, and several of their war counselors were alleged to have been community agents. In the spring of 1971, near the close of the program, community agent Frances Cain was distraught because the Nation was attempting to recruit her son, Vincent, who was determined not to join. Vincent was thirteen years old, very stubborn and proud. He claimed that he wasn't going to let anybody bully him. During this time executions were ordinary and the police seemed not to care. At the same time, someone produced a forged advertisement from the Ku Klux Klan offering to sell guns to the Blackstone Nation in support of the good work they were doing killing "ni**ers." Frances asked me to take Vincent to live with me for a while. So in June 1971, Vincent Cain came to live with me and my family. Vincent attended

Howalton Day School with Furman for seventh and eighth grade, Metro High School in Chicago and Woodrow Wilson Senior High School in D.C. He graduated from Wilson in June, 1975, and attended Morgan State University in Baltimore, Maryland for two years.

Three factors impeded progress in WESP: (1) the WCB did not have the power to enforce its policies or to hire and fire school personnel; (2) the WESP staff did not have the authority to assign, transfer or evaluate school personnel; and (3) as a consequence of this impotence, the project was used as a patronage program. It soon became obvious to me that there was no future for me in the CPS. The fracas over Hyde Park High School and WESP, and my role in advising the high school leaders of the boycott, had strengthened my reputation as a radical troublemaker among the CPS leadership. WESP taught me the impotence of poor people's chronic need to use schools to fulfill patronage and personal agendas.

The community component became a patronage organization. Because the WCB did not have the power to evaluate the CPS personnel, the in-school component was emasculated and stripped of any power, making the community component the power base. Unable to affect instruction or student achievement, it operated in the only realm possible, job creation and employment. TWO had no choice but to use its community component to organize community power against the CPS. It could not, through WCB, make the CPS recognize its decisions. While Local School Councils created in 1988 by the state legislature can hire, evaluate and fire the principal, they had no control whatsoever over the evaluation of teachers, nor their hiring or firing, nor could they in any way maintain a high quality of instruction in their schools.

Even though the high school dominated the WCB's agenda, it was not the sole problem in WESP. The performance of the deputy director was unsatisfactory. He would not do his work, and he was often late for appointments. More aggravating, he would approve expenditures of money without the project director's knowledge. As participants began to understand the futility of the operation, it was almost impossible to get serious work done. When the high school principal made it clear that she could stop anything from happening, other personnel decided to get the most they could get for as little effort as it took. Personnel started looking for jobs. Work in WESP remained undone. Ultimately, student achievement suffered.

Student achievement, the real target of the expenditure of the federal dollars, was almost forgotten in the conflict between the community, the teachers and the high school principal. Student achievement proved to be mixed. As expected, gains occurred in the area where there was the most teacher consensus: Wadsworth Elementary School.

In 1966, only 29.3 percent of first grade students were ready to read according to the Metropolitan Readiness Test. In 1969, the first year of WESP, 39.1 percent were ready; in 1970, 61.9 percent were ready, and in 1971, 66 percent were ready, due largely to the leadership provided by Clara K. Holton, Renee Edmonds and Ethyl Holmes. For the third grade, the mean score in reading before WESP was 2.920. After WESP, it was 3.108, where the result of the "T" test was significant. The "T" test is a statistical test that determines whether or not two populations are sufficiently dissimilar enough that one could say that one does not belong to the same population. In the case of Woodlawn Experimental Schools Project, students engaged in WESP from 1968—1971 were compared to those who were not.

The evaluation of student achievement was executed by psychologist James Savage and nuclear engineer Warren Miller, both from Northwestern University and hired to conduct the outside evaluation in determining the extent to which WESP accomplished its stated objectives regarding the academic performance of the students in the district, through the completion date of the project in June of 1971. The questions which the evaluators tried to answer were: (1) Is there a significant increase in mean scores of each subtest of the Metropolitan Achievement Test and the Davis Reading Test under WESP? (2) Do students' scores vary as a function of quartile rank? (3) Do students in the lower grades show greater relative improvement than students in the upper grades?

As expected, the younger the student, the better the performance. On average, post-WESP first graders achieved higher reading scores than pre- WESP first graders. Statistical analyses were conducted to determine whether the observed differences could have occurred by chance. WESP experiences appeared to be the most important variable. In terms of the mean subtest scores by quartiles for the reading test, the first graders in the lowest quartile showed the greatest percentage gain of the post-WESP first graders when compared to the pre-WESP first graders in the same quartile. The students in the third quartile showed the next highest percentage gain. Thus, there appeared to be a strong tendency for the students in the bottom half of the distribution of students to show the most beneficial effects from their WESP experiences, as they are mirrored in reading test scores. However, post-WESP students in the first and second quartiles showed non-significant percentage decreases when compared to their pre-WESP counterparts.

In June 1971, to bring me in line, I was assigned to Government Funded Programs under the supervision of James Moffatt, with whom I was never able to work out a satisfactory relationship. We first fought over the pictures hanging in my office space of Malcolm X, Angela Davis and Martin Luther King, Jr. I was ordered to remove them from my walls. I refused on the grounds of discrimination. Immediately, Richard Tygielski, my straw boss, began hounding me for their removal, although my white coworkers had pictures of their ethnic heroes and heroines on their walls, and many Catholics had crosses hanging over their desks with other religious artifacts. However, on February 29, 1972, Richard Tygielski sent a bulletin to everyone in the unit saying:

> I would appreciate your taking whatever steps are necessary with members of your staff to assure that the physical surroundings of the Department of Government Funded Programs are businesslike in nature. I am sure you will agree with me that personal pictures, check lists, calendars, etc., taped or stapled to the outer walls of the office do not create a businesslike tone for the general public. I appreciate your assistance in this matter.

This order hardly made me popular in my unit.

Although Mr. Moffatt reminded me daily that he was the only person who had been willing to hire me after the WESP fiasco, I seemed to be at odds with him on almost everything. We rarely agreed on procedures, processes or routines. The explosion came when he tried to involve me in his attempt to eliminate William Jones, then director of the Bureau of Dropout Prevention.

On July 14, 1972, I wrote my second letter to Mr. Manford Byrd, Deputy Superintendent of Schools for CPS, regarding the discrimination against Black directors in the Government Funded Programs unit. Mr. Moffatt had invited me to a meeting where his intent was to reprimand Mr. Jones and use me as a witness. I refused to be so used, and Mr. Moffatt indicated his intent to cite me for insubordination. I stormed out of the office and wrote my letter. I never received a response from Mr. Byrd; and Mr. Jones, with whom I have a common nephew, kept his position. In fact, his wife, Nina Flemister Jones, was promoted to director of personnel after Edna C. Hickey retired.

By this time I was in deep, deep trouble. I requested to be placed back in the field in a principalship, if possible. Isaac and Jessie Huey, whose son had been clubbed to death in Cicero in 1968, while searching for employment, mobilized a parent and community group to draft me as district superintendent, but Mr. Byrd would not be moved. So, I left CPS in December of 1972.

(Excerpted from Walking in Circles: The Black Struggle for School Reform, *Third World Press)*

MY EXPERIENCES TEACHING IN NORTH LAWNDALE IN THE 1960S

Theodis R. Leonard, Sr.

My preparation to become an educator began at an early age when my parents read to me and taught me speeches and my sister taught me my alphabet. While my parents did not finish elementary school, they always taught me the importance of getting an education. They pointed me to other relatives who were college graduates. They sent me to school and encouraged me to participate in extracurricular activities. I served as class president, local (Mileston Vocational High School) and state New Farmers of America (NFA) President, and delegate to a national convention. I did not play on any sports teams, but I managed high school baseball and basketball teams. This taught me leadership, organizational and teamwork skills.

I went into the Air Force after high school to earn money for college. I was honorably discharged in 1957, after having attained the rank of Staff Sergeant. I relocated to the West Side of Chicago and attended Chicago Teachers College (currently known as Chicago State University), where I continued to develop my speaking and leadership skills. I participated in Shakespearean dramas through the Little Theater. I improved my human relations skills by taking a course in urban studies and cultural relationships. I visited community centers as part of class projects and observed how students were taught divergent thinking skills (divergent thinking is dealing with open-ended questions, as opposed to closed-ended questions, or convergent thinking). The class also visited police headquarters to get a sense of what could happen if we did not teach the child about himself as a whole, within the context of his environment.

I found the courses in philosophy of education and methods of teaching to be an essential foundation for my career. The Chicago Teachers College approach focused very heavily upon the curriculum guides of the Chicago Public Schools. I learned to group students according to individual differences and participated in enrichment activities to correspond with each lesson. My preparation at Chicago Teachers College helped me to develop effective lesson plans and smoothly transition from college to teaching in Chicago Public Schools.

While I developed excellent theory and practice in Teachers College, I still needed more practical seasoning in my early days as an educator. I did pre-practice teaching and practice teaching at John Milton Gregory Elementary School in the North Lawndale community, on Chicago's West Side. Little did I know, when I started my student teaching in 1964 that I would spend the better part of my thirty-six-year career at the school.

At the time Gregory School served pre-school (Head Start) to sixth grade. The lead teacher was Bernard Niedjelski, who saw to it that I received all of the experiences that I needed to become a better teacher. This included teaching during the regular school day and after school, with a specialty in reading. Mr. Niedjelski served as a coach as I developed lesson plans and structured field trips.

It would be impossible to describe my tenure at Gregory School without first providing some context regarding the social, economic and political environment at the time. I started teaching eleven years after *Brown v. the Board of Education,* the landmark Supreme Court decision outlawing the practice of providing "separate but equal" educational facilities for black and white children. There was significant pressure to desegregate schools and provide equal opportunities for black children. President Lyndon Johnson had been elected in a landslide in 1964 and he felt the political conditions were right to push for Congressional action on an agenda of social reform, called The Great Society. A central program in that agenda was the Elementary and Secondary Education Act (ESEA) of 1965.[1]

ESEA was championed by Congressman Adam Clayton Powell from New York and administered by Francis Keppel, the Secretary of Education. The Act was intended to provide comprehensive assistance for impoverished students to improve their performance in school. Funds were provided to teach reading, mathematics, guidance and counseling, and camping. The program provided educational materials, books and equipment. It also provided staff development in the form of in-services, college courses, and consultants. ESEA was the pre-cursor for the No Child Left Behind Act of 2001.

There were several crucial educational issues during the sixties. They included: student population, new teachers, teacher salaries and benefits, quality education, segregation, and community involvement.

In many neighborhoods, schools changed from white to black, seemingly overnight. As more black students entered these schools, experienced and tenured teachers left and were replaced by new, inexperienced and untenured teachers—many of whom were draft-age and were subject to being called to military service. Not only were they teaching students of a different culture, some of the students had records of gang involvement and behavior problems.

---

[1] "Elementary and Secondary Education Act of 1965 (ESEA)", Association for Educational Communications and Technology, 2001.

To correct cultural and behavior problems, some officials of Chicago Public Schools went South and recruited black teachers from southern schools, colleges and universities who grew up and taught in cultures similar to the ones in which our students lived. While many of these teachers were not certified, they turned out to be among the most effective teachers at our school. They taught with care, concern and empathy for the students. Most of their students were well-disciplined and demonstrated academic progress. Our school consistently ranked among the top schools on the West Side of Chicago.

It should be noted that the black migration from the South was in full swing in the 1950s, and North Lawndale was a major destination. By the 1960s the North Lawndale population had reached its peak of over 120,000 people, many of whom had recently moved from the South. Gregory School had over 1,300 students, and overcrowding was a major issue. Some classes had as many as forty-eight students. This situation was not unique to Gregory School.

Benjamin Willis, the superintendent of Chicago Public Schools at the time, instituted the use of temporary mobile units to ease the overcrowding in black neighborhoods, rather than build new schools. The units, which resembled trailer homes, came to be known as "Willis Wagons." Gregory School had three such mobile units.

The overcrowding and influx of new teachers created an environment that was ripe for strengthening the labor movement within the Chicago Public Schools. Teachers' certification, salaries and benefits became issues around which to organize. Teachers became more active in the Chicago Teachers Union (CTU) and demanded higher salaries and benefits. Many of their demands were met, including higher salaries, better teacher pensions, and smaller class sizes.

The Chicago Public Schools began using the National Teacher's Examination to certify teachers, making it easier for people educated outside of Chicago to become certified. Teachers who were not certified by taking either the Chicago Teachers' Examination or the National Teachers' Examination advocated for automatic certification after having a certain number of years of successful teaching. This became a reality in the 1970s.

School issues were intertwined with community issues. Parents demanded quality education for their children and wanted the schools desegregated. This brought about significant pressure upon the schools. As a result, more paraprofessionals were added to the payrolls, parent involvement programs were added, and new schools were built throughout the community. Students from the community were allowed to attend schools in predominantly white neighborhoods through bussing, permissive transfers and admission to special schools outside of the neighborhoods. This advocacy set the stage for the creation of magnet schools like Whitney Young Magnet High School in 1975, which was built to address issues of school segregation. Local elementary schools, such as Howland (now closed) and Crown, also developed magnet programs to attract students from across the city.

Another feature of schools in the sixties was early childhood programs, including Head Start and all-day kindergarten. The federal Head Start program was launched in the summer of 1965 as part of President Johnson's "War on Poverty." The eight-week summer program was designed to provide low-income preschoolers a "head start" on school and life. From the beginning, it has been a comprehensive program that includes early childhood education, health and nutrition, social services and parent education, and empowers parents to participate fully as decision-makers and effective advocates for their children and their communities.[2] The Head Start program is rooted in the Civil Rights Movement. Students who participated in the program got a strong foundation for kindergarten, and their early results carried over to success in the regular school.

It is against this backdrop that I began teaching at Gregory School. ESEA provided the funding through which I taught after school, summer school and pull-out reading during the regular school day. I taught individualized reading skill-by skill to each student. I taught students how to locate answers, follow directions, use context clues, draw conclusions, and find the main idea in paragraphs and stories. I also taught them how to classify ideas, and assigned additional reading and book reports to supplement classroom exercises.

Prior to the enactment of ESEA, I observed that my class gained about one half year achievement for one year's work. After we received increased funding and resources from ESEA, I observed the same cohort to achieve at least one year's progress for one year's instruction. I also noticed that we had better results in our attempts to remediate basic skills in summer school.

The regular school hours were spent providing classroom instruction geared to move the entire class forward, while addressing individual students' needs. I divided my regular classes into as many as four groups, which were based upon the skill level and interests of the students. I took into account their facility with word recognition, vocabulary, reading comprehension and oral reading. I taught students a range of tactics, such as unlocking words and how to get meaning from context. I continuously used student lessons to diagnose reading skills, develop word games and quizzes. I also provided individual lessons from reading laboratories and book reports. I gave pre and post tests in reading and mathematics to measure and monitor student progress. I encouraged student learning by giving students awards for book reports and achievement on standardized tests. Students who were having difficulty were referred to after school programs to shore up their weaknesses.

---

[2] http://www.sccoe.k12.ca.us/depts/headstart/proghistory.asp Head Start of Santa Clara and San Benito Counties website.

Our curriculum included the scientific method, and I taught students how to carry out experiments based on class discussions. I also taught them to develop and test hypotheses and record their results and conclusions. The school held an annual science fair, which gave students an opportunity to share what they learned and to compete for awards.

I used the outdoors as an extension of the classroom to teach earth science, biology and mathematics. I took students on trips to Camp Duncan in Ingleside, Illinois. The students studied the weather, temperature and wind direction from a nature station. Students learned how to identify animals by the tracks in the snow, to identify trees by their leaves, and estimate the ages of trees by counting the number of rings in the trunk. I taught them how to collect cultures from pond water and to approximate the heights of trees by using protractors and the lengths of the trees' shadows (triangulation). Recreational activities like tobogganing and ice skating on the frozen pond counted towards the requirements for physical education.

I also used field trips to reinforce classroom learning. I took my students to places like the Museum of Science and Industry, the Adler Planetarium, the Shedd Aquarium, and the Chicago Historical Society. I also took them on tours of Chicago's City Hall, Springfield, Illinois, and to Washington, D.C. so that they could observe our government in action. We visited such historical sites as the Gettysburg Civil War Battlefield in Pennsylvania; President Washington's home in Mount Vernon, Virginia; and New Salem, Illinois, the village where President Lincoln grew up. As preparation for these field trips, a group of other teachers, parent chaperones and I taught students proper behavior on a bus, how to take notes, and good table manners in restaurants. We documented our trip through photographs and home movies. Our students made reports and took tests on what they learned from the field trips.

Gregory School's curriculum included career development for all of our sixth grade students. We helped them to get in touch with their feelings, develop study skills, test-taking skills, job applications, career clusters and how to deal with peer pressure. This program helped our students to become better students academically as well as socially. We were very proud to learn that our students were among some of the top performers at Manley Upper Grade Center (now Manley High School) and Webster Elementary School.

I found the school assembly programs to be an excellent outlet through which students could develop social skills and self confidence. As a rule, every class in the building would appear in an assembly program at least once per year and sing one or two songs. My first class performed in a play about Christopher Columbus and the discovery of America. I observed that students' participation in the play provided a number of benefits. They learned something about American history while developing their speaking skills. The students who had an interest in arts and crafts were able to showcase their talents by helping to design and build stage props.

One of the key ingredients to our success in the 1960s was the level of community engagement in our students' learning. The parents were active participants in the PTA and volunteer activities in the classroom and school office. Local churches, such as Carey Tercentenary African Methodist Episcopal Church, sponsored Boy Scout and Girl Scout councils. Students who participated in Scouting activities developed leadership and teamwork skills that seemed to help them more readily adapt to classroom and other settings. Sears, located across the street from the school, proved to be a great corporate neighbor. They sponsored our chapter of Junior Achievement, made their parking lot available for our recess, sponsored local Boy Scouts, and sponsored an annual community arts festival. The Archie Moore Gym (Better Boys Foundation) provided after school boxing and tutoring activities, and a Sharper Mind Program, which enhanced critical thinking skills. Indeed, the adage of "it takes a village to raise a child" was actually practiced and not used as lightly as it is today.

While we had our challenges with achievement gaps, discipline and behavioral problems, there seemed to have been a greater level of support and interventions in the 1960s. School guidance counselors helped teachers to implement programs for our students that included study skills, test taking skills and life skills.

We had classes dedicated to special education as opposed to mainstreaming special needs students, as is the practice today. The special education classes were taught by teachers who had a certificate in special education, as opposed to being taught by generalists or teachers who may have had a specialty in another area like reading, math or science. Special education students were placed in small groups and provided with special materials. Grouping students with similar skill levels allowed the teacher to tailor lessons geared toward individual students' needs. Under the current policies that provide for mainstreaming special needs children, teachers run the risk of teaching "over the heads" of students with special needs, while holding back students who typically perform at grade level. The disadvantage to providing special education classes was the fact that children were sometimes labeled as slow. I also observed that in some cases, students who were more aggressive, or active, were inappropriately placed in the special education track.

Some students who required more attention but did not have severe learning disabilities were placed in special schools, such as Roentgen, which was designed to help them catch up with mainstream students. Students were given remedial reading and mathematics, guidance and counseling, and test-taking skills in small classes.

The truant officer was a very important person in the lives of the students and in the operation of the school. He monitored student attendance and student progress in special schools. He also assisted in getting parents to school. Our truant officer also assisted in getting clothes and school supplies for needy students.

Students who were consistently disruptive in class, but were not delinquent, were often referred to schools such as Montifiore until their behavior improved. Teachers at Montifiore were skilled in discipline and correction techniques. Students who went afoul of the law were placed in a juvenile detention center at the Audy Home. They were taught the regular curriculum and required to serve a certain amount of time before they were allowed to return to school.

Parental School, located on the North Side of Chicago, addressed family and social issues. As the title suggests, this school worked to improve student learning by working with parents. Parents and teachers became partners in delivering educational experiences to students, and were quite effective. Unfortunately, this school no longer exists.

Some programs did not work as well as others. Among these were Closed Campus and Distar. Classes usually began at 9:00 A.M. and ended at 2:30 P.M. for closed campus schools. These schools did not provide outdoor recess, effectively reducing valuable time for physical education. Closed campus also affected the quality of teaching and learning. A shortened school day meant that up to one hour of teaching time was lost, and some classes were not taught as well as they should have been. To put this in perspective, schools that were not on closed campus held classes from 9:00 a.m. to 3:15 p.m. and had twenty-five minutes for recess, and forty minutes for lunch. Teachers were more refreshed after lunch, and the students were more attentive after having a combined recess and lunch break.

Distar, a reading program that focused heavily upon phonics, worked mainly with very young and severely retarded children. The rote learning process was very time consuming, and cut into time that could have been spent teaching other skills, such as comprehension and critical thinking. The strengths of the program included the fact that students were able to sound out words.

Recommendations

- To avoid undue political influence, Chicago Board of Education should be composed of different ethnic groups and people from all geographic locations throughout the city of Chicago.
- The Board of Education should be elected within geographic districts rather than appointed by the mayor.
- Board members should be required to participate in training programs to help them perform their jobs better.

- The Board of Education should have a search committee that will seek out nationally known educators with doctorate degrees in education and lifelong records of success in administration and education.
- Chicago Public Schools should build new schools like Renaissance 2010 schools and charter schools only after research says they are improvements over existing schools. Renaissance 2010 is an ambitious plan set forth by Mayor Daley in 2004 to build 125 new schools by 2010. The controversial plan entails closing low performing schools and reopening them as charter schools. The data suggest that these new schools don't perform significantly differently than their traditional counterparts.
- Adopt-a-School programs should be given back to CPS and not to the mayor.
- CPS should set up new parental schools like the ones they had in the 1960s. These schools could be residential for parents, teachers and students. They should have intensive parent training programs with career education programs. This is especially important in our current environment, with very young parents.
- CPS should reestablish the truant officer program to increase student attendance. There is a direct relationship between student attendance and school performance.
- Hire more paraprofessionals and train them as teachers and allow their work as paraprofessionals to serve as the first three years on the career ladder.
- Re-instate Project CANAL. Project CANAL provided teacher retraining on site, and proved that by retraining teachers and administrators and parents you can change the culture of your school and make it more successful.
- Do not hire community activists to work in programs in which they participated for at least five years after they last participated. This would minimize the chances for conflicts of interest.
- Eliminate undue political influences from the school system. Politicians often make decisions based upon what helps them personally and politically, as opposed to working in the best interest of the schools and the students.

A CONVERSATION WITH HAKI R. MADHUBUTI AND SAFISHA MADHUBUTI

Transcribed by Gwendolyn A. Mitchell

Haki R. Madhubuti began the interview with an opening statement that responded to the question: "What were historical and internal forces, decisions and developments that led to the inception of Third World Press, the Institute of Positive Education, and the School(s)?"

HAKI: I came out of the Black Empowerment, Civil Rights, and Black Arts Movements of the 1960s. In 1962, I found myself at the Du Sable Museum, which at that time was located in the home of Dr. Margaret Burroughs and Charlie Burroughs. I was able to observe, firsthand, two people, as well as their brother and sisters, in the arts putting all their energy into building a museum. The Du Sable was the first African American museum in the country. They had converted the first floor and basement of their home into the museum. During my first meeting, I was warmly greeted by Eugene Feldman, a Jewish man, who introduced me to them. I remember that Margaret Burroughs, who is a first–class artist, was in the kitchen working on a piece of linoleum that she was cutting into a unique piece of art.

From that point on I began to take careful mental notes on how this dedicated man and woman were building an institution, basically without the resources of people outside of their community. They had a desire and a mission in their hearts to make it work. That was the beginning, or the germination, of the idea inside of me that something could happen.

In 1966, I published my first book of poems, *Think Black*, at the encouragement of Margaret Burroughs. Shortly after that I was introduced to Dudley Randall, who was the founder and editor of Broadside Press, which was becoming the most important Black independent book publisher in the country. He and Margaret were co–editing a book on Malcolm X called *For Malcolm*, and I was asked to contribute a poem to this collection—in the interim I had been working on a second collection of poems, *Black Pride*, and I asked Dudley Randall to write the introduction. He did more than that; he offered to publish this new volume. He asked me to come to Detroit to finalize the poems for *Black Pride*. I was excited about that, because I was going to see another independent Black institution in its early days.

I was surprised, but not overly so, when I found that Broadside Press was in a room in the home of Vivian and Dudley Randall. As I walked into the one–room press, I was again encouraged to think (as I was by the Burroughs) that with a little dedication I, too, could make something similar happen.

During this same time I was involved in the Congress of Racial Equality (CORE) and the Student Non–violent Coordinating Committee (SNCC). I was also involved with the early formation of the Organization of Black American Culture (OBAC) Writers Workshop, and many of the poets and other writers gave readings in Chicago and elsewhere. So when I left Detroit, going back to Chicago, I was trying to think what I could do to help get the word out about Black writers.

The answer came a few months later. I had a poetry reading somewhere, was paid $400, and decided to use those funds to start a press. I was going to a community college at that time and met a writer named Jewel Latimore (Johari Amini); I had already met Carolyn Rodgers at a poetry reading. So I asked them to join me in this effort, and they both agreed. Third World Press's first publications were their books: *Songs of a Black Bird* by Carolyn and *Images in Black* by Johari. Carolyn Rodgers stayed with the press for six months. Johari Amini stayed dedicated to the press off and on for about ten years. She is now a chiropractor in Atlanta. So we continued to struggle with others to build the press.

At the same time, though, because of the influence of Margaret and Charlie Burroughs and Dudley Randall, I had been developing a philosophical side, in terms of the literature that I was reading, ranging from Franz Fanon to Malcolm X, both of whom also had a strong intellectual influence on me. I then met Hoyt W. Fuller, who was the managing editor of *Negro Digest*, which became *Black World Magazine*, the major journal of Black progressive ideas in the country at that time. Hoyt was the sponsor and guiding light of [the] OBAC Writers Workshop. During that same period, I met Barbara A. Sizemore, who was a very strong educator. She influenced me a great deal, especially my own views of women's liberation. Later in 1967, I met Gwendolyn Brooks. She became a pivotal figure in my life, not just because she was a poet, but primarily because she had a gigantic heart and saw something in me and some of the other writers whom I had worked with at that time. She started her own workshop, The Gwendolyn Brooks Workshop. And, of course, I became a member.

I had given a number of poetry readings around the country, and in 1969, was asked to read at the John Oliver Killens' Writers Conference at Fisk University. The reading was well received. I had started to develop a good reputation as a poet and public speaker and had published two books by that time. As a result of that reading, I was offered two jobs: one at Talladega College and one at Cornell University. I initially decided that I wanted to teach at Talladega, an all–Black college, and went through the regular job application process. The students wanted me to come, but the administrators said absolutely not. So I ended up going to Cornell.

Cornell was really a lightning bolt. I moved to Ithaca, New York and was a Black poet–in–residence at an Ivy League institution. I was able to view and experience racism and White supremacy at an intellectual and emotional level at a very elite institution. Prior to my appointment, the Black students had demonstrated to get someone in to teach Black courses, and that is why I was recruited. But before I could acquire the position, I was interviewed by five of the English professors (all White men).

Each began to question me about Black literature, since I was brought there to teach those courses. After the first round of questioning, I realized that the only thing that they (three or four of them) had read was maybe Richard Wright's *Black Boy* and Ralph Ellison's *Invisible Man.* I knew that if I was going to get this job, I had to go on the offense. And so for the second round of questions, I would turn around and ask them a question in a little more detailed way about the same text, or I would move to other texts, which I knew that they had not read. That went around one time, and I got the job. It was very clear that they did not want to be put in a position where they had to answer questions about Black literature, life and writing that they could not answer.

I was a visiting professor (my official title was Poet–in–Residence), the first Black in the history of Cornell University, and I was basically one of the few Black professors on campus. I interacted with most, if not all, of the Black students that were active and involved there. Later that year (1968–1969), the students (many of them were mine) took over the administration building. The university asked me to join their team to negotiate with the students, and I refused. However, one professor who did agree was Harry Edwards, a sociologist. Following that ordeal, the university appointed James Turner as the chair of the African American Studies Department. He asked me to stay, but there was no way I was going to stay up in that cold place, so I came back to Chicago. And I think that the spring of the following year, I met Safisha (formerly Carol Easton). She was teaching in an after–school program at that time, and was completing her Masters work in English at the University of Chicago. She was writing her thesis on the Black Arts Movement, and had contacted me for an interview and to give a poetry reading to her class. But in our conversations together, we often talked about the Chicago public school system, of which we were both products. Safisha made a statement, something like "we really need our own school." Having started TWP, being a poet in the Black Arts Movement and being pretty bold, I just said, "Yes, let's start a school."

SAFISHA: The Institute of Positive Education (IPE) was formed as a precursor to the school. The school started in 1972. We are talking about history.

HAKI: Yes, that is how we started, because we thought that TWP was very important in terms of publishing, but it was not an "activist" organization. We wanted a name that would not scare people away, and would not be too revolutionary either. We felt that people could not argue about the name "Institute of Positive Education." It became an umbrella organization that functioned in areas of education, communications and community activism. But the core programming to come out of IPE was the New Concept Development Center (NCDC), where Safisha became the primary administrator. At that time she was teaching at Kennedy King College.

Question: How have the cultural institutions that you have built been affected by your commitment to their independence?

HAKI: Well, let me just say this: when I was at Cornell, I wrote most of the poems for my third book. I shared the poems with Gwendolyn Brooks, and she was very excited about them. And I asked her if she would consider writing an introduction to the book. She said, yes.

Prior to my going to Cornell, I was reading at a jazz club on the Southside of Chicago. I read a poem that affected a young writer by the name of David Llorens, who wrote for *Ebony* and *Negro Digest*. The title of the poem was "In the Interest of Black Salvation," and he literally fell off his seat laughing at the poem. He was a Catholic, and the line from the poem was "Jesus saves, Jesus saves, Jesus saves S & H Green Stamps." We became friends. He convinced John H. Johnson to do a story on me at Cornell University. He included many of the poems from my upcoming collection of *Don't Cry Scream* in the article. The story came out in March of 1969, and *Don't Cry Scream* was published that same month and just took off. It sold literally fifty thousand copies the first year; and over the years—it is still in print—has sold over a hundred thousand copies. The article in *Ebony* magazine was one of the first articles that had been done on a "revolutionary" Black poet of the 1960s. It gave me national exposure. I put about ninety percent of the money that I received from the sales of *Don't Cry Scream* back into Third World Press and the Institute of Positive Education.

As a result of the success of *Don't Cry Scream* and the article in *Ebony*, I received a call from Andrew Billingsley, a sociologist, who at that time was the Provost and Vice President of Academic Affairs at Howard University. He asked me if I would come and teach there. The interesting thing about this is that I had always wanted to go to Howard. When I was younger I sold magazine subscriptions door–to–door in order to stay alive, and one of the sales lines I would say was "I was working my way through Howard University." They were starting an institute for the arts and humanities, and had already brought John Oliver Killens from Fisk University to be the fiction writer–in–residence. Jeff Donaldson, a fine visual artist, served on the faculty. The university had also recruited the great cultural critic, Dr. Stephen Henderson, as the director. They asked if I would come and be poet–in–residence.

So, I agreed to consider the position only if I could commute between Chicago and D.C. I just could not justify moving across the country again. At that time Safisha and I began to see each other, and we were building IPE and the Press, and I could not leave the city. There was too much at stake. Surprisingly, I talked Dr. Billingsley into allowing me to commute (which was unheard of at that time) from Chicago to D.C. every week. We negotiated a three–year contract. That contract turned into an eight–year commitment. That's how we were able to stay alive. I was able to continue scheduled readings and travel in order to bring money into the Press and the Institute.

In the meantime, Safisha and others were planning on starting a full–time school. We first started a day care program and an evening school for children in the community. We then expanded to a Saturday school. It became very popular. We had requests from inside and outside of our community to go full time. But the only way we could go full time was to have a full–time director. Safisha, along with others who were affiliated with the IPE at that time, and I talked this through. By that time she had received her Masters; but decided to leave a tenure–track position at Kennedy King College and come on full time as the director of the school.

Now her mother thought she had lost her mind. She said she had to be certified crazy to be following this poet. Well, in any case what happened was that she took the job as director. So she and others began working to build a school. We worked collectively to provide the philosophical direction for the institution. *Plan to Planet* (1973), my first book of political and cultural essays, came out of this struggle. We utilized ideas in that book to run the school. *Plan to Planet* was one of the few books that looked at building African–centered institutions in our communities.

SAFISHA: I want to further respond to the question concerning building cultural institutions and our commitment to their independence. Part of what happened during the period of the 1970s is that the whole spirit of activism was very much in the air. This is different from right now. We all felt that we were a part of something bigger than ourselves and bigger than the institution that we were trying to build. Over the years we developed a number of ways of trying to sustain the institution and maintain our independence. Everybody had to be committed to making very little money. As a way to grow and have a common vision of what we were trying to do, we, as an organization, were always involved in collective study. We would eat collectively at the Institute, which was at that point located at 78th and Ellis Avenue on the Southside of Chicago, actually across the street from the building where we are now located. Many of us made our own clothing. Haki had moved into a building on the next block, and it turned out several people moved out of the building, and we were able to negotiate a deal with the owner, where many of us were able to move into that building and live together. We called that building IPE Towers.

These were all ways in which we could sustain ourselves individually. It was also a period before many of us were married and had kids. There was this tension in terms of the ability to sustain an organization independently, once we made a decision that we were going to be independent. That fundamentally meant, at least at that time, that we just had more limited resources, and we had to be able to make every dollar stretch, and we also had to be very committed to doing this work without a lot of financial resources. That meant that we had to be inspired. We had to be frugal. I think the intuitional setting of doing things collectively—we ran together to maintain our health; ate together, which saved on food; collectively lived together, which saved on rent—influenced our decision to maintain an independent institution that we had to be able to sustain financially.

HAKI: One of the interesting things about that was we were all young and full of spirit about what the future could be. We involved ourselves totally, not just rhetorically. This was also evident in the books that Third World Press published and the programs sponsored by the Institute of Positive Education. At IPE, we started a pamphlet series, Black Pages, and a speakers' forum. In the early days we also started a food co–op. Safisha talked about our exercises, and one of the interesting things we did was run down to Grand Crossing Park, which is right across from here on 78th street. We would often discuss among ourselves what we could actually do if we had the facilities that we ran past every day—a Catholic Parish and school. And of course, twenty years later, we own the property.

So I'm saying, at one point, this vision of what can be—of what is possible—started with an idea. We stayed on Ellis in two storefronts until 1974, when we purchased property on South Cottage Grove Avenue. We were able to have a full–time school through the Institute of Positive Education, the New Concept Development Center; a bookstore, the African American Book Center; and the publishing company, Third World Press. We also made space and time for a magazine, the *Black Books Bulletin*, and the food co–op. At that time we had also become a part of Congress of African People, a national organization under the leadership of Amiri Baraka. We were just very involved.

SAFISHA: But before you go into that part, I think we should discuss some practical things that we were forced to do in order to maintain our stance of financial independence. First, virtually all of us worked across all three institutions. It wasn't until many years later that people began to specialize in working in the school or working in the press, but, in those early days, you would work in the press, you would work in the school, and you would work in the Institute.

When we moved to 75th and Cottage Grove, that building had to be totally revamped in order to pass the city codes to house the school. We were able to attract, and had even in our membership, some people who had technical skills. We have old pictures where you can see scaffolds as we built the second floor and the side of the building that was going to house Third World Press and the book store. That ability to continuously attract people who were willing to bring their skills to help us in the work has always been absolutely crucial to our ability to maintain our independence.

HAKI: That's very true, and we cannot minimize, at any level, the number of people who came through into the IPE, TWP and other institutions. It is very important to realize that these institutions were built as a result of very dedicated men and women (some are still with us today) who were committed to getting the work done. Safisha is absolutely correct about the work we put into doing everything.

But during that period from the 1970s on up, we continued to work nationally with two major organizations: the Congress of African People and the African Liberation Support Committee. By this time I had made my first trip to Africa in 1969. And so we were trying to hook up with African liberation movements. I think the key point of all of this is all of our members were keenly aware of international struggles, and we all were and still are very political. The politics, theory, and the practical—trying to mesh all of it—go together. We did not see ourselves as an appendage of the African liberation struggle; we saw ourselves as totally involved. We felt that our struggle here with apartheid in America was just as important as the struggle against apartheid in South Africa.

We felt that one of the answers was to begin to teach our own children. Some of these ideas are spelled out in Plan to Planet. Most specifically there was an answer to the question: how can you continue to move toward liberation if you allow the children to be taught by people who don't love them, who don't care for them, and who most certainly don't have their development or best interest in the center of their own hearts? This was the reason we felt that education was critical. We were involved in international structures, and education became very important in terms of the key development of these institutions as well as our obtaining an international worldview.

Question: How have the cultural institutions that you have built influenced African American World History?

HAKI: Well, we felt the two ways we could contribute were to educate and to publish. We felt early on that Third World Press would be a publisher for major writers. One of the first major writers we published was Chancellor Williams, who wrote *The Destruction of Black Civilization,* a book that continues to be a mainstay for the Press today. By that time I was teaching at Howard University, and Dr. Billingsley gave me a book by this historian. He was teaching in the history department at Howard. I read the book in one setting over an eight to ten-hour period. The next day after I had finished reading the book, I went to speak to Chancellor Williams, and I asked if he would consider publishing it through Third World Press. He said he would consider it, but he had to rewrite and expand the book. I said, of course, and that's what happened. That started our long and very fruitful association with Dr. Chancellor Williams. We published two of his books: *The Destruction of Black Civilization* (1974) and *The Rebirth of African Civilization* (1993).

We were publishing poetry, non–fiction, Black history, psychology, and sociology. By that time we also began publishing "The Black Pages" out of the Institute of Positive Education. "The Black Pages" were a series of very short pamphlets, usually between 8 and 16 pages, on ideas from African architecture to health to a Black philosophy of life. We knew Black people were reading, but sometimes they didn't always have the money to pay for a book; however, they could come up with fifty cents or a dollar to pay for a pamphlet. In conjunction with the pamphlets, we then would have forums and debates at IPE. These forums were constructive and important because they started to bring people into the Institute, which became a meeting and gathering place for all kinds of people and all kinds of organizations.

SAFISHA: I'd like to add a few things, in terms of the influence between Third World Press, the Institute and the school, and the kind of impact they had. I gave a PowerPoint presentation on the history of the three institutions at an Nguzo Saba Conference that Maulana Karenga had several years ago. It became evident when I started listing some of the major books published by Third World Press, these were materials that people were reading to fuel their ideas and to support African–centered, Pan African, and Black revolutionary organizations across the country and in other parts of the world. A book like *The Destruction of Black Civilization* was almost like the bible of the era. The novel, *2000 Seasons* by Ayi Kwe Armah, was one of the most important pieces of literature. The *Isis Papers*, by Frances Cress Welsing, later became a staple of what people were reading. I think the books, themselves, had a very strong impact in terms of institutional development

in other places and in terms of the evolution of Black Studies programs and the ideological development of individuals. In addition, I think that our work as one of the earliest African–centered, independent schools to start in that era, in conjunction with our work with Black institutions, became a model for a cultural orientation to education that still has an impact today. You will find public schools in cities across the country that have adopted an African–centered approach to education. I think that is a direct impact of the work that we did at New Concept and continue to do, along with lots of other people around the country.
A third area of impact actually has been the growing emphasis on issues related to health. Many of the early seminars that we had in the community, along with "Black Pages," as well as some of Haki's work, emphasized diet, exercise and health. Another local impact that we almost take for granted was the introduction of Kwanzaa.

HAKI: In fact, we brought Kwanzaa to Chicago back in 1968 and 1969. And of course I did that pamphlet on the principles of Kwanzaa in the 1970s. I would like to go back to what Safisha said about the things we did in terms of health. In the 1970s, we sponsored the first ten–mile run for the city of Chicago. We did this for about three or four years out on Lakeshore Drive. We worked with the city, and actually had hundreds of Black people come out to run ten miles for health. We also bought an eighty–acre farm in Michigan, because we wanted to have land to take our children to from the school, and to have some space outside of Chicago. Also we felt that there might indeed be a need to get out of the city, if necessary, so we wanted a place of our own.

It's really too much too tell in one setting, but we had IPE and TWP. We also had another journal that grew out of the impact of IPE's "Black Pages." The *Black Books Bulletin* magazine became another organ for getting ideas out to a wider audience and gave young scholars and activists an outlet for publishing their work. We published a whole list of thinkers and gave some their first national vehicle in which to share their scholarship. Among the many voices that we published were John Henrik Clarke, Frances Cress Welsing, Fred Hord and James Turner. We published interviews from Cheikh Anta Diop and Hoyt Fuller, Lerone Bennett Jr. book reviews and more.

These institutions served as a foundation for the development of not only these ideas, but also as a showcase of what could be done when serious Black people come together. People from all over the country would come to visit, study, work, and see how we did things. These intuitions became not only a part of our lives; they became our lives.

SAFISHA: A point I'd like to make about influence, specifically in terms of the schools, is that we have been extraordinarily effective in socializing young people. We have now been in existence long enough that we have people in their mid–thirties who would have gone through the school. I have not yet met a young person that came through that school who I am not really extraordinarily proud of. Our young people are politically conscious, politically active, and they are well educated. They understand that their education—that the proof of that education—is not just for the individual but also for their family and for the Black community. If we didn't do anything else right, we did a good job with them, and I think we are poised to see the continued impact they will have on our communities.

Question: What has been the most significant impact of each of you on the other in respect to the reality of institution building?

HAKI: One of things that Safisha and I have always felt was critical was that we continue to grow and develop. The world is changing, and we have to be aware of those changes. We have to change ourselves in order to be current and effective. If you make mistakes, admit your mistakes, and do not make excuses for those mistakes. Learn from them and keep on going. That has allowed us to not only grow and develop, but to maintain a sense of competitiveness about the larger world. We have to stay on top of things. This is all a part of how we have been able to continue to grow. We respected each other's work. We were always reading and sharing the works of other men and women. We never thought we had all of the answers. We thought we had an answer, and we felt that our answer was important, but it was not necessarily the most important.

SAFISHA: I want to share two other points that I think are crucial, specifically, to the Institute and the schools. We have always had a philosophy around the collective decision–making process. For example, people often tend to look at Haki—or Haki and me—as the "head" of the Institute. In reality the decision–making was always collectively structured. Back in the early 1970s, we had Baraza ya Kati, which was sort of an executive board, if you will, that was selected from the general membership. Haki and I were members, but we had no more say in that decision making than anybody else. We never allowed the organization to revolve around him or either of us in terms of leadership. I think that has been one quality that is different between our and other institutions. This has allowed us to make transitions of leadership. Right now, Anthony Taifa Daniels is the executive director of IPE. We have had other directors and principals at NCS and, of course, now at Betty Shabazz, the leadership is very effective.

We have to really look critically at how we think about leadership. That is particularly important in the Black community. We have had such a history with the Black church or the Black political leadership. Even if you look on the continent, there is this implicit assumption that there is some head, some special authority vested in that head, and that person sort of has that position for life.

The other thing that relates to the question and the struggle to maintain the institution is survival. We have had many points where these institutions really could have died, without a doubt. I think this point relates to the point Haki was making about change. In the very early days, we were able to do what we did because of the kind of energy, sacrifice and commitment from so many people who gave of themselves in such deep ways. We needed that. We continue to need that. But at the same time, as the institution grew—in terms of the complexity and the kinds of work we were trying to do—we needed more and more to sustain that institution. That leads to this whole notion of independence and the ability to financially sustain ourselves. This has been an ongoing struggle. We had a period where we got into very serious debt with the IRS. We called upon the expertise of key people who had the technical knowledge related to fiscal management. Without their technical expertise, there is not much question in my mind that, several times, we could have died.

I'd also like to mention Soyini Walton who, in addition to Haki and me, is the person who has the longest affiliation with IPE and the schools. She started before I did with Third World Press, and she has had several stints. She left for a short while when she went back to school and became an engineer. Again, I think it's very important to mention her as part of the history.

HAKI: Yes, there are a lot of people we could mention: Rufaro Din, Janet Sankey, Kofi Moyo, Kimya Moyo, Hilary Godfrey, Chaga Walton, Johari Amini, Jabari Mahiri, and Sterling Plumpp. We obviously may have missed many people, but in any case, the point is that it's been a very collective group and, in many cases, a very democratic one. It's also been non–dogmatic, so that once we found something that worked, we just clearly talked it through and moved it to a level that could work and continue to develop.

Our goal has always been to grow and to move to a productive space where we could be a model for the Black community. We knew we had outgrown the Cottage Grove facility almost three or four years after we arrived there. But we had kept the idea of moving on the back burner until about 1993 or 1994 when we learned that the property that we now occupy was for sale. This was very important because this was the property we would run by everyday, and think "what we would do if we had this property." As soon as I found out it was available, I went immediately to the Catholic Archdiocese and began to inquire about bidding on it. Initially, we were told that the bidding process was closed. And of course, coming out of the 60s, I wasn't going to accept "no" for an answer. So I wanted to find out who was the person of authority that we should contact. That man was Bishop Winston Gregory, a Black bishop on Chicago's South Side. By that time I had changed my name to Haki Madhubuti, and, when I left that name, I did not get a call back. So I called him back as Don L. Lee. Within a day or two, his office called and asked if I was the poet. I said, "Yes, I need to speak with Bishop Gregory; it's an emergency." They set up an appointment. We prepared a huge document about our school, along with a package of books from the Press and went out to South Holland, Illinois, and sat down to talk to him. A fifteen–minute appointment turned into two hours. I left his office with his letter to Cardinal Bernadine stating that not only should we be on the list to bid on the property, but we should be at the top of the list. Without going into a lot of details, that's how we got the property. The buildings needed major improvements, and we had to make a lot of changes. But my point is that we have our school. And TWP bought the rectory for its headquarters.

SAFISHA: I think this also speaks to one of the biggest lessons that I certainly have gotten out of this thirty–odd–year experience. To me, it relates directly to how the work we are doing fits in the broader scheme of the history of our people: the ability to develop an indomitable will. To take a position—that under no circumstances are you going to give up. As I said, there have been many instances over the years where we have faced challenges from which we could have fallen down. Not only was there the challenge to get the building that we are in right now but when we applied for the charter school in 1998, we were originally denied. But that initial denial did not deter our going to the next step. And it's because of Haki's unwillingness to accept "no" as the final word that we have our charter school, a very successful school. These are the three areas, I think, in which Haki has been most influential in this institutional development. First, he's probably financially given out of his own pocket more than anybody else. Second, he has been probably the biggest generator of new ideas. But third is his unwillingness to give up.

HAKI: I think it speaks to the development of our whole philosophy in life. We are not out here by ourselves. One reason Chicago is such an important city in terms of our struggle is that it's one of the few cities in the United States that has Black independent institutions in almost every area of Black life.

SAFISHA: I also think that this notion of never giving up is the spirit; in fact, this is the lesson of our history. This is the lesson of Mary McCleod Bethune and her last will and testament, that we are inspired by a woman who felt that cooking and catering was the way to start college. So, in many respects, the history has been a lesson to us. And we have a responsibility to continue to teach that history, so that this new generation coming up is in a better position to navigate a world that is very different from the world we inherited back in the 60s and 70s. I don't think that the lessons for the future are to totally replicate what we've done. For I think that the conditions are different. Each generation has got to figure out how to maintain a continuity with the past, but, at the same time, transform itself to meet the particular challenges of that generation.

HAKI: I agree with that, but what can be replicated is that we have always felt that the truth is what we must move toward. We don't teach lies at our school. We don't publish lies at Third World Press. I think that the important thing is we have always tried to move toward is truth, that which is real, correct, that which is in the best interest for not only Black people but for all people.

SAFISHA: But the point is each generation really does have to negotiate that.

HAKI: Each generation builds upon that. That's why the study of history is so important that you build upon what preceded you. So you're talking about Mary McLeod Bethune; we stand on her shoulders. We stand on the shoulders of W.E.B. Dubois; we stand on the shoulders of Paul Robeson, Marcus Garvey, Malcolm X, Shirley Graham Dubois, Margaret Burroughs, Gwendolyn Brooks, Dudley Randall, Hoyt W. Fuller, and so many others.

That brings us to: What's your vision of the future for the institution?

HAKI: Well, I think it's growing. I think, in terms of Third World Press, we are going to truly become not only a national publishing house but also a world–publishing house. And we do that by continuously seeking and moving to find the best writers and poets, to publish while continuing to struggle for economic development. As far as the school is concerned, we surely hope to continue to improve what we are doing and most certainly look at the growth to move beyond the elementary school to develop a high school. We've been thinking about that for many years. (In September 2005, we will start the city of Chicago's first and only African–centered High School.)

SAFISHA: We are going to do it. We just are trying to work on the mechanics right now. I think that the biggest challenge that we have for the future, in terms of our growth, is thinking about what it means in terms of the transition to new leadership. This is very important because of the length of our history in this organization and the age of Haki and me. I think that is a central challenge that all independently–minded, particularly African–centered organizations face, so that there will be a Third World Press, there will be a Betty Shabazz and there will be a New Concept or an Institute of Positive Education when we are elders or when we are no longer physically here. I think it is incumbent upon us now to think about those challenges, institutionally. I think that has to do, both with development of new leadership, and the development of financial endowment.

HAKI: I agree with that.

Which leads us to this last question: What implications does your struggle have for institutional members of the ABCC that are serious about becoming independent?

HAKI: Over the last twenty years, I've been teaching at Chicago State University, and soon as I arrived there, the idea was how could I become more involved in the institutional life of the school? Shortly after arriving, I started the Gwendolyn Brooks Center for Creative Writing and Black Literature. A year after that we brought Gwendolyn Brooks to our faculty, and the following year, we started the Gwendolyn Brooks Writers' Conference. Two years after that we started the Hall of Fame for writers of African descent. My point is I think that wherever independent people and independent–thinking people go, they have to be involved in the life of the institution with the work they are doing, if at all possible. Chicago State is ninety–seven to ninety–eight percent Black. So, I have used the expertise I had in terms of working in higher institutions with the men and women I've met over the last thirty–five or forty years in the area of culture. Certainly my experience was to bring that same kind of vision and wealth to Chicago State. The English department is now becoming nationally known, and the writers now have the MFA program in Creative Writing.

I'm just stating that the development of "independent" structures at public institutions or private institutions really depends upon the type of creative spirit and the willingness to fight wherever you find yourself. I see our future as a bright one. I'm what is called a realistic optimist and, at the same time, I am progressive enough to realize we don't own very much in this country. So I see us, at all levels, moving toward ownership; moving toward wealth creation, not for individuals to go out and buy more cars, but wealth creation that will develop cultural institutions that will impact the lives of our children.

How do we keep millions and millions of young boys and girls out of the streets? You have to have institutions at every level of involvement in their lives, and so, therefore, we have to develop men and women who are not afraid of our own people and who are dedicated enough to go into Black communities as well as live in these communities and continue to build for our tomorrow.

SAFISHA: Two other comments. One is in terms of the future of the Institute of Positive Education. We would like to be able to re–invigorate the idea of rites of passage programs for kids who are not in our school. We need to try to push that as a national model, such that we can imagine a point in time where every neighborhood that has large concentrations of people of African descent will have some sort of institution that is specifically focused on socializing young people. This is one of the necessary prerequisites to keeping so many of our kids from falling into the prison system, drugs, and that whole thing. That is a challenge that is bigger than [the ones] we faced back in the 70s because issues that have to do with the infestation of drugs, along with gang violence in the Black community, were not anything like they are today.

The other broad issue about independence is one that we have grappled with and evolved with over the years. In the 70s our position was that, independently, we decided that you didn't accept money from White people. I don't think that that's where we are right now. That's part of my point about each generation trying to negotiate what these core principles mean at a given point of time. I think independence at this point of time has to do with the independence of ideas and the ability to have enough resources—ideological, political, and economic—such that what you do is not dependent on some single external source to determine whether you live or die. But I think that this is a complex issue, depending upon the kinds of institutions and where the institutions are located.

HAKI: I think that Safisha is correct on this. I think that the major point is, though there is continued debate on this, we cannot accept money from any source that is going to demand that we change our fundamental role or our direction for the good of African people. Obviously we realize that we are in America. Most of our people don't make any major money and, for the most part, the money that most Black people earn is really small change. We understand that the competition and most certainly those who are against our development are thinking of ways every day to thwart Black development. We cannot function in this country without resources. But independently we are able to say no as well as yes, and can stand on our decisions.

SAFISHA: This is what I said to Taifa when we first started talking to him about coming on to work with the Institute. It's a wonderful opportunity at some point in time to be able to look back on your life and know that you contributed to the development of something that is truly important and bigger than yourself. I think that it's both a wonderful gift that you give and a wonderful opportunity that you have.

FROM BEHIND THE WALLS:
PONTIAC HOLDS COMMUNITY IN-MATE CONFERENCE

John Shaka Parker

Pontiac Prison hosted over 50 community people at that rural maximum security institution recently.

Grace Holt, who heads the Black Studies Department at Chicago Circle Campus, was excited to see so many "together" young Black men who were planning and structuring alternatives, while creatively speaking to the issue of "Corrections in Illinois."

The participants in the all-day-long Inmate-Community gathering toured all of the prison's facilities.

Warden John J. Petrilli and his talented Black Assistant Warden, Donald Harvey, escorted community members and inmates through various cells and housing units.

Surprisingly, visitors were allowed into the Segregation and Isolation Units.

Petrilli explained, "We have nothing to hide here at Pontiac. We are always open to examination."

Inmates accompanying the community tour pointed out the glaring inconsistencies of modern treatment programs and the doubtful need for antiquated punishments, such as isolation confinement.

Among the many inmate guides, "Che" McCarry and Earl Mimms enlightened the visiting group to Pontiac's strong potential for becoming the Illinois educational Mecca for young imprisoned Blacks to gain viable educational and vocational training and skills while confined.

Having taken a panoramic view of the prison, community persons and inmates retired to the Prison Chapel for a briefing on the Workshop Agenda that would later in the day have all participants applying Black Brain Power in the search for solutions to specific problem areas.

Black Brain power there was!

Many community representatives were asked to attend this conference, but only a few actually did. Those who made the journey contributed their multi-talents and expertise in a way that more than compensated for the glaring lack of response displayed by those major Black organizations who are merely vocal x-ponents of prison reform measures.

Positive Gains Cited

Acting Minister of Muhammad's Temple at Pontiac, Yaree X Walton, gave a penetrating and moving opening address wherein he evaluated the positive gains of this first conference saying, "The success of this conference was unbelievable!"

Selects On-Going Chairman

Having traversed many areas concerning the prevention of Black-on Black crime, issues relating to the abuses of the Illinois Pardon and Parole Board against inmates, the unrealistic furlough policy of the Department of Corrections, and other troubles common to all prisons, the community representatives unanimously selected Eugene Perkins, long time advocate of prison reform, as Chairman of an ongoing committee for continuance of community involvement.

What was begun at Pontiac will certainly be felt across the country as inmates tackle the root causes of their oppression.

(This article reprinted from The Black X-Press *Collection of the Vivian Harsh Archives at the Carter G. Woodson Library)*

SECTION FIVE

"LES ENFANTS" OF CHICAGO'S BLACK STRUGGLE

" What will be our generations contributions to the centurieslong African American struggle for liberation, and how do we redefine the struggle for our time Our parents achievements the Civil Rights and Black Power Movements continue to overshadow our lives, as we continue to answer these questions and define our generations own identity and distinctiveness."

The Hip Hop Generations
by Bakari Kitwana

GROWING UP IN THE SIXTIES

Ellis Cose

When 1960 arrived I was eight years old. When 1975 ended I was three years out of college. So my memories of that era are largely those of a kid growing up on Chicago's West Side, struggling to understand what was happening just outside my window and in the world beyond.

I was five when my family moved to Henry Horner Homes, a fourth floor apartment at Washington Boulevard and Wolcott Avenue. For me, my parents, my two brothers and two sisters, that apartment in the housing projects was a huge step up from our cramped quarters on Roosevelt Road. In summer 1966 I was fifteen years old and still in Henry Horner. It was the 12th of July, a sweltering Tuesday evening, when I witnessed my first community uprising.

The uprising, or riot, began with the police turning off a fire hydrant. That act led to a confrontation with angry residents and set off three nights of violence that left two people dead. I retain two strong memories from that summer. One is of sitting in my apartment and hearing shots being fired from a building across the way. The other is walking through the neighborhood after the third night of hostility and seeing soldiers—actually National Guardsmen—on the streets in battle gear.

Had I been better informed, I would have been aware that tensions had been building for some time and that several months before the violence broke out, Martin Luther King, Jr. had brought the Civil Rights battle to Chicago's West Side. Only two days before the riot started, King had led a rally in Soldier's Field that had culminated with a march to City Hall. There, King had posted 12 demands—for open housing and jobs, among other things.

As a fifteen-year-old with no great interest in current affairs, I was only vaguely aware of the significance of the Chicago campaign and of the fact that 1966 was a critical moment in the history of the larger Civil Rights Movement. But I did understand that something unusual was going on, that huge currents of emotional energy were surging through the city, and I felt there had to be some connection between the violence in the streets and the demands for equality that were sweeping the nation. Mayor Richard Daley had blamed Civil Rights workers (exempting King for responsibility) for creating that atmosphere in which the rioting broke out. I knew enough not to believe that. But I also knew that there was something that united the demands for freedom and opportunity that King and his movement represented and the frustration that had violently erupted in the streets.

In 1968 when King was assassinated and my community again exploded, I had much clearer understanding of the context. Impelled in large part by the events of 1966, I had done a lot of reading, particularly of the works of Black authors. I had been particularly moved by James Baldwin's *The Fire Next Time* and by his vision, both apocalyptic and hopeful, of America and its future. I felt that the first part of his book, "Letter to My Nephew on the One-Hundredth Anniversary of the Emancipation," spoke directly to me:

> "This innocent country set you down in a ghetto in which, in fact, it intended that you should perish...You were born where you were born and faced the future that you faced because you were Black and for no other reason. You were born into a society which spelled out with brutal clarity and in as many ways as possible that you were a worthless human being. You were not expected to aspire to excellence, you were expected to make peace with mediocrity."

When I read those words my early experiences in the neighborhood schools took on a whole new meaning. I began to understand how it had come to pass that my friends and I had been left behind so many times in the care of teachers who had essentially told us they had no intention of teaching—because they judged us incapable of or uninterested in learning. I came to see the housing projects, which as a five-year-old I had thought to be some kind of paradise (which they no doubt were compared to our previous apartment) in an altogether different light: as compounds designed to isolate us from the greater Chicago—and, in a sense, contain us.

After King was killed and the community erupted—as did many communities across the nation—a curfew was imposed, federal troops were sent in, and eventually eleven Black people ended up dead. I remember walking down Madison Street, which had been the commercial hub of the community, passing one store after another. They were now burned out shells. What impressed me particularly about those structures was the heat that emanated from them long after the fire had burned out. I also recall military tanks parked in a huge field. I no longer remember exactly where that field was located, but I recall having a strong negative reaction to the fact that my neighborhood was under federal occupation.

What I remember most strongly; however, is my reaction to the news coverage. What I read in the newspapers and saw on television bore no resemblance to the community I knew. There was little nuance and virtually no humanity in that reporting. There was little sense the neighborhood was occupied by real people. I thought I could tell the story better. And out of that conviction my decision to become a writer was born. Not that I had any real sense of what it meant to be a writer. At the time I didn't even know any writers, but I did know that my story and the story of the people I knew could be told better.

Shortly thereafter, I convinced my high school English teacher to exempt me from the usual class work. I promised instead to write an essay about riots and race in America. That essay became a manuscript of well over a hundred pages, which my teacher encouraged me to send to Gwendolyn Brooks, then the poet laureate of Illinois.

Weeks passed. Though I had no real notion of what poet laureates did, I assumed that they were very busy people. Eventually I gave up hope of getting Ms. Brooks' appraisal of my work. Nevertheless, one day the phone rang and Ms. Brooks was on the line. She insisted that I come down to visit her at Northeastern Illinois University where she was teaching. When I arrived she told me, in effect, that I was a born writer and invited me to join her writers group.

I later learned that such gestures were characteristics of Gwendolyn Brooks, who was possessed of a truly generous soul and loved to nurture young talent. I was too young to be properly appreciative and dropped out of the writers group after attending a few meetings, but by then I had become obsessed with the idea of making writing my profession.

It was not too long after that, during my first year as a student at the University of Illinois in Chicago, that I got it into my head to send a letter and several writing samples to Ralph Otwell, the managing editor of the *Chicago Sun Times*. That correspondence led to an invitation to meet him, which led to my writing a weekly column for a publication the *Sun-Times* circulated in high schools as part of a reading program. That job led to me being appointed at age nineteen as an op-ed columnist for the newspaper.

I took few lessons away form those early experiences. One was the importance of trying to understand the larger context for one's anger. As a young Black man growing up in an impoverished community, I had often fumed at the way I and those like me were routinely treated by teachers and others in authority. I had sometimes felt as if I was being smothered by others' assumptions and their low expectations—of me, and of themselves. But only after my community literally exploded did I take it upon myself to try to understand the origins of those assumptions. My studies did not liberate me from anger, but they did help me to put it in a political and historical context. That was perhaps an easier task in the 1960s than it is today, but in an age when one in three young Black men are projected to spend some time in prison, in an era where much of this next generation can envision no productive future, we need young people who can see past the anger to a path of deliverance.

I also learned that success can come from taking an unconventional approach and seeking help from friends—or potential friends—that you don't know you have. Gwendolyn Brooks, the poet, and Ralph Otwell, the editor, taught me much and truly transformed my life. They could not have done that had I not sought their assistance and trusted their wisdom.

HOW MY CAREER WAS INFLUENCED BY THE SIXTIES

Patricia Hill

The factors that influenced the fifteen-year period of my life between 1960 and 1975 began in a time so long ago that it cannot be measured. However, 1960 is personally significant because that is the year my immediate family moved from an apartment in my grandfather's house to where I would live until I left home on my own. It is also the year that America elected its first Catholic president and Blacks pronounced their loyalty to the Democratic Party.

African Americans in the northern part of the United States had overwhelmingly made the decision to vote in the general election of 1960, which became the deciding factor that got John F. Kennedy elected. I recall my parents actively engaging in numerous conversations about the situation. A very visible sign of that effect was the *Chicago Tribune* newspaper. It was delivered daily and my parents read it thoroughly. I don't really know why, but when Kennedy won, our family felt a personal victory.

December 1961 proved to be a very uneasy month for our family, both immediate and extended. My maternal grandmother, who was definitely the matriarch of the family, was stricken by and eventually succumbed to heart disease. I was ten years old and never before experienced the passing of a close family member. She died at the end of December and she was buried in the next year. One could get the impression that she was buried a year after she died. What an unusual phenomenon.

More than forty years later, her descendants continue to recall one of her often-declared wishes whenever we attend family gatherings. Grandma Trennie often stated that she wanted at least one of her family members to attend Spelman College. She and Grandpa Tomie had migrated to Chicago from Georgia in 1923. Spelman represented then, as it does today, the most prestigious all-female African American college in the United States, and she wanted to be able to claim some part of that prestige. Unfortunately, four generations after her birth, none of her descendants have been able to fulfill Grandma's dream. The closest we have come to that is my youngest daughter having attended Clark University in the 1990s, which is a part of the Atlanta University complex that also includes Spelman.

The assassination of President John F. Kennedy in 1963 turned this country on its head. The Black community was not exempt from the impact of that event, for no love was greater for Kennedy than the one demonstrated by African Americans. In the opinion of some, President Barack Obama has resurrected the hope and aspirations of the neophyte voters and some veterans, just as Kennedy did for his generation. I was a twelve-year-old eighth grader returning to school from lunch when the report of President Kennedy's death was made. That day and many others that followed felt like the world had come to a standstill. We were all glued to our television sets and transistor radios daily, hoping not to miss a single detail. I believe that the history books of this country will always perpetuate the distinction of the Kennedys.

June 1964 marks a rite of passage; that was the year I graduated from elementary school and participated in my first track meet. It represents when and where I would spend the next four years getting prepared for many of the challenges I would encounter throughout my life.

I graduated from Frank Lehman Gillespie Elementary School, located at 9301 S. State Street. It is one of the few institutions of learning in Chicago named after an African American during that time. It was built in 1933 and is where my mother, aunts, uncles and many cousins attended school. Some of my teachers taught them as well as me. Several who immediately come to mind are Mrs. Umbles (gym), Mrs. Crutchfield-Marshall (math), Mrs. Benford (disciplinarian) and Mrs. Towels (eighth grade). They all lived in the neighborhood, oftentimes seen walking to school in the morning and walking home after the school day had ended. It is where my siblings, many lifelong friends and I would experience everlasting memories and learn valuable life lessons. It is also where I came to realize that I had what is commonly called "natural ability" in athletics. Finally, it is where I was when the entire world got word of the assassination of President John F. Kennedy, which directly influenced my perspective of the country where I was born but always felt a sense of not fully belonging.

In 1963 I won the first track and field meet that I participated in at Robert S. Abbott Park, also named for a Black man, several blocks from Gillespie and adjacent to where I would receive my high school education at John Marshal Harlan. I brought home three first-place ribbons after running the hundred yard dash, two hundred twenty yard dash and the broad jump. At that time, I only knew of one other girl personally involved in athletics. We all had heard of Wilma Rudolph, who was an icon equivalent to Florence Griffith-Joyner or Marion Jones of today (without the steroids). Francine Dudley was the person who introduced me to the world of track and field. She was my neighbor in Princeton Park where we lived and the daughter of a Chicago firefighter who had died by the time I met Francine. She was six feet tall and had many other physical characteristics that always reminded me of Nina Simone, being very dark-complexioned with short hair worn naturally. This was before it became fashionable for Black women to stop straightening their hair. I didn't begin wearing a natural until 1968, at the age of seventeen.

When Malcolm X was assassinated in Harlem in 1965, I was a thirteen-year-old freshman in high school. Initially, I didn't comprehend all of what he meant to the progress of our struggle for liberation, but as time went on, the philosophy he preached and lived was one I would adopt as my own—with one exception. I never accepted his faith as a Muslim nor became a member of the Nation of Islam. It marked a time when I began to challenge many of the things I had been taught up to that point. It was also during this time that I began voluntarily reading books. Those books were exclusively about Black people and political in nature.

Fortunately for me, Harlan High School during that period was truly reflective of the community it was situated in. It was clear that the teachers understood the expectations of our community and attempted to fulfill them.

Our community was comprised of all socio-economic levels and races, including whites who were transitioning into other neighborhoods (termed "white flight"). Chatham, West Chesterfield and Roseland are three of the approximately six contributing communities to Harlan. My neighborhood at that time was called Lilydale, which was predominately Black and self-contained. My grandfather built a home for his family in 1923 and it continues to stand at 93rd and Wentworth. He was a mason and subsequently passed the trade on to my uncle, who built four houses, one for each of his children. 95th Street between State Street and Halsted was a commercial strip where virtually every business was Black-owned. There were various outlets for entertainment, but there was no movie theater. That is when we, as children, encountered the hostility of whites face-to-face.

The movie theaters we commonly frequented were the State and Roseland. Both were in the Roseland community. The other theater in close proximity to our community was the Beverly, which was in the Beverly community. The State and Roseland theaters have been demolished and the Beverly now houses Third Baptist Church at 95th and Ashland. A very vivid memory I recall when attending the Beverly was when my mother took my brother and I to see *To Kill a Mockingbird*. I don't know if there were any other Black people in the theater, but I do know we were the focus of attention to at least one of the white male patrons. He kept staring in our direction and mumbling something. At one point another white male sat next to him momentarily, whispered something to him, then returned to where he had come from. The man ceased staring at us. What I didn't know was that my mother kept in her purse a pearl-handled revolver when she was out alone with her two small children. Thank God for the whisperer. I shudder at the thought of how things may have turned out had the staring white man been perceived as a threat by my mother.

1968 was not only a highly eventful year socially and politically for this country with the assassinations of Dr. Martin Luther King, Jr. and former attorney general Robert F. Kennedy; it was for me personally as well. It was the year I graduated from Harlan, the year I qualified for the U.S. Olympic trials and the year I first engaged in civil disobedience as a part of the movement. By this time, I had become informed about the Black Power movement and gravitated towards it rather than the Civil Rights Movement. Most of my information was acquired via television, radio and music of the time (movement music). My direct contact with older college students, soldiers in the Vietnam conflict, and members of various street gangs, and my athletic peers were major sources for my social conscious development that still greatly impact my psyche. Being a part of the national and international track and field circuit from 1964 to 1968 provided me with a very conducive environment to absorb the information being thrust upon me.

The most outstanding group of politically conscious athletes I encountered was the team from San Jose State in California. Whenever there was down time during track meets, they would congregate and talk about the roles and responsibilities of Black athletes in all sports. Somewhere around late 1966 or 1967, I began hearing them talk about a humanitarian Olympic project. They were educating and organizing track athletes politically and socially. Spearheading the group were John Carlos, Tommy Smith, Lee Evans, Denise Paschal and others whose names I either didn't know or can't recall. They always mentioned their professor, Dr. Harry Edwards. Being around them, I thought, was like being in Heaven. My coach, Joseph Robichaux, and older teammates, such as Willye White, were placed in charge of us younger members and were always discouraging me from spending time with the "militants." They told us all explicitly to stay away from them. For me, it added to the mystique of the athletes from the West Coast. Although O.J. Simpson was also a part of the same track circuit and was from Cali, he distanced himself from what I called the "real" brothers and sisters. Maybe he did so because he was a football star at University of Southern California at that time.

Some of what I learned from the "militants" led me to participate in a food boycott of the cafeteria in my last year of high school. While I was receiving a social justice education, many of my childhood playmates, especially the males, were becoming active in the street gang culture. Although I lost many of my male counterparts to street crime violence, I also missed the opportunity to grow into adulthood with others because they were killed in Vietnam—a major bone of social contention during the 1960s. Even today, for many of those who did return, they never returned emotionally and psychologically. These phenomena had a direct impact on the dating pool of available Black men in my generation.

When I got word that Dr. Martin Luther King, Jr. had been assassinated on April 4, 1968, I was sitting in the front seat of the car belonging to my track coach, Joseph Robichaux. If my memory serves me correctly, some of my teammates who were also in the car had just asked me to turn the radio station. This was something we would often do when the adult would leave the vehicle, because they usually listened to news stations while we preferred "hip" music radio stations. Shortly after finding the right program, a commentator broke into the music with the announcement. Being older than I was when both Kennedy and Malcolm were killed in 1963 and 1965 respectively, I had a better understanding of what the killing of Dr. King would mean. It was a jolt to my teammates and me. I was the one who broke the news to Mr. Robichaux when he returned. To date, although I understand why he said what he said, his response to the news was the second jolt related to hearing of Dr. King's death. Mr. Robichaux responded by saying, "I'm not surprised." My interpretation at that time was, "How cold-blooded."

As fate would have it, the track team I represented was scheduled to host a track and field meet at the University of Chicago's Stagg Field the weekend after Dr. King had been assassinated. Much debate took place among the organizers to determine if in fact the meet would go on as scheduled. They decided to proceed with the original plans.

The meet itself took place on Saturday but the Friday prior to the meet, Chicago, as well as many other cities around the country, literally was on fire. Teams participating in the meet began to cancel for fear of being harmed or stranded away from home. Of the teams invited, only four showed. The meet went on but there were many tense moments. Great measures were taken to insulate us from the outside world. We were housed at the Windemire and Shoreland Hotels in Hyde Park. We were instructed to not go anywhere alone. Some events were cancelled due to not enough participants. Our team won the meet with the most points, but I personally think that was a result of us having more team members, although we had an outstanding team. I did not do my best, although I won my event, because it was difficult concentrating. I really wanted to be home with my family in my own community.

By the time I got to college in 1969, campuses all across the country were actively involved in changing the social and political paradigm in America. At Northern Illinois University, we attempted to make statements along the same lines. On more than one occasion, campus was closed at a moment's notice due to the eruption of disturbances usually rooted in racial tensions between the Black and white students. My father worked nearby in Lombard, Illinois and I can remember having to call him a couple of times in an emergency to come get me and some of my dorm mates. I remember once being part of orchestrating the takeover of the president's office, Rhodent Smith, because some of our demands were not met. I was very disappointed when I witnessed how the other participants failed to take what we did seriously. Some of them raided the refrigerator while one of the males found the purse of a clerk who left in haste and stole her money. He has been a practicing physician for the past thirty years. That takeover lasted approximately six hours before we conceded. Another one of our demands was for a Black Student Center. We got that, and one of the early directors of the Center was Professor Robert Starks, now at Northeastern Illinois University. I recently heard that Northern is still having racial problems. However, unlike us, the students today are not fighting back.

I participated in the 1968 Olympic trials in Pomona, California on the campus of California Polytechnic College just before my seventeenth birthday. After not qualifying for the games held in Mexico City in October, I officially ended my track career. It was at those Olympic Games that John Carlos and Tommy Smith stood on the victory stand wearing a black glove on one hand each, with their heads bowed in protest, symbolizing the inequitable treatment that people of color and of low economic status experience in the United States. Today, that image is shown somewhere in the world every single day. I am thrilled and remain optimistic that even after all Carlos went through after that event, he is still in the fight for social justice. I am also honored that we have become close friends. Although my track career ended in 1968, that didn't conclude my athletic career.

During my sophomore year at Northern, I became the first African American female to play varsity volleyball. I continued to play when I transferred to Chicago State University in 1971 and became a starter on the women's basketball team. I played basketball until 1975 just before the birth of my third child. Our teams, the Chicago Aces and Chicago Debs, were two of several women's teams in the Midwest that were regarded as semi-professional. One of my former teammates and coach is Dorothy Gaters, currently the "winningest" girls' high school coach in the United States, from Marshall High School. Another is the late Augustus "Nick" Seabrook, who was very active in Chicago's YMCAs.

There is no question of the significance of some of the events that took place in 1968. But the following year, 1969, had a great impact on me as well. By then I was in full Black Power mode. With this new sense of empowerment, I had just completed waging my own personal protest against the status quo in my household (my parents) after graduating from high school in June 1968. Two universities had expressed an interest in several of my teammates and me and had offered us athletic scholarships. They were Tennessee State University in Nashville and Lincoln University in Jefferson City, Missouri. I had ruled out Tennessee State because I was somewhat afraid of the track coach, Ed Temple. But I really wanted to attend Lincoln, because I was very comfortable with Coach Reed. Little did I know at the time that my parents had absolutely no intention of allowing their first-born to go "down south" to anybody's school. My mother especially was extremely fearful for me. She kept reminding me of Emmett Till and the horrible manner in which he was murdered by white racists in Mississippi. I felt at the time that I had no reason to consider that I might meet such a fate. After all, this was 1969, not 1955, and Black people were scaring the crap out of white people. They knew we weren't taking any more of their racist bullshit. The Southern Christian Leadership Conference was still strong, we had Jesse Jackson with Operation Breadbasket. Some of the Black street gangs were political and, if all else failed, nobody was badder than the Black Panther Party. We even had our own chapter in Illinois with Brother Fred Hampton in charge. Well, none of that convinced my folks that I should go to Lincoln, so I refused to enroll for college when I graduated. They didn't press me on it because I was sixteen, having skipped a grade, and I think they figured I had time to come to my senses. They were right, but I had some help.

When my coach, Mr. Robichaux, found out in November 1968 that I was not in school, he became furious and extremely concerned. After having an extended telephone conversation with my mother one day, a few days later we were filling out applications and other documents preparing me to attend Northern Illinois University in DeKalb, Illinois for the upcoming spring semester beginning in January 1969.

By the end of summer break in August 1969, I had become involved in forming a chapter of the Black Panther Party on campus at Northern. I can't say that we were very organized, because many people didn't know what we were attempting to do. But for the few of us who were committed, we stayed the course. By November, someone had contacted the Illinois Chairman Fred Hampton and invited him to speak to the group. I still have vivid memories of his visit, which was two months before he was assassinated on December 4, 1969 in Chicago. With that tragic turn of events I acquired a true sense of how this system works and how we as a people of African descent are perceived by it.

In August 1971, at twenty years old, I got married. Shortly afterward, I discovered I would soon become a mother for the first time. My husband had become eligible for the draft several years earlier but had managed to receive a deferment due to being required to assist in the care of his mother, whose health was impaired. At some point, confusion about his draft status became an issue and we began to have serious talks about fleeing to Canada. Escaping to Canada had become a common practice during that time to avoid the draft. Things got worked out, and we never had to make the trip under those circumstances.

All three of my children were born between 1972 and 1975 with twenty-eight months between each one. I began teaching school in 1974 and that is when I discovered that not all Black people had been a part of the Black Power or even the Civil Rights Movements. Up until that time, I had been so absorbed in the struggle that it never dawned on me that the majority of African Americans of my generation were ambivalent about getting involved. They were primarily focused with getting a job and making money. They never connected the dots that politics is a major influence in whether or not you get a job, a decent salary, etc. Personally, the 1970s represented a time where many people in America became more accepting of the status quo. Resistance rapidly was becoming a thing of the past. Even if I thought for a moment that I was going to turn in my dashiki for a three-piece suit, fate had other plans for me.

In September 1975, I received my first assigned teaching position. I had taught during the 1974 school year, but tenure in Chicago Public Schools didn't begin until one had been "assigned." However, upon taking the test to become a teacher, I had also taken the entry level exam to become a Chicago police officer. When the police department informed me that I had met the requirements to become an officer at the same time the Chicago Public Schools gave me my assignment, I was forced to make a very serious career decision. If I accepted the job with the Chicago Police Department, I would become one of a few female officers with a college degree and I would be among the first females to wear the title of police officer. Up until that time women were relegated to the title of youth officer or matron.

My reasons for considering becoming a police officer were both political and practical. From a political perspective, I had witnessed during the insurrections that occurred during the aftermath of the assassination of Dr. King that the police were taking advantage of the authority given them by society. They had constantly abused that authority against Black people. I was going to change all of that. From a practical perspective, I knew that being a police officer was a physically rigorous profession, and being in top physical condition, I would surpass the standards. My final decision resulted in me going into the teaching profession. That decision was greatly influence by the fact that I had two small children and my husband was totally opposed to it. Eventually, eleven years later, after the election of a Black mayor and getting a divorce, I became a Chicago police officer. I retired after twenty-one years of service to my community.

Roberto Clemente High School was my first tenured position. I was the only African American female physical education teacher in a department of twenty-four. Clemente was a relatively new school and was the result of Puerto Rican activists, primarily the FALN. The school population was eighty percent Puerto Rican; the rest of the student body was comprised of Mexicans, Cubans, other Latinos and African Americans. It was my first experience in dealing with the hierarchy of the Latin culture. For example, Cubans are higher on the food chain than Mexicans, with Puerto Ricans finding themselves on the bottom rungs. I quickly learned on of the worst things in the world is to mistake a Mexican for a Puerto Rican, or Cuban for Mexican, and so on. Teaching at Clemente afforded me to opportunity to utilize and brush up on the four years of Spanish I had taken in high school. Since most of the students were first generation born U.S. citizens, they were bilingual. They were learning English as a second language; however, the cultural exchange between us was phenomenal and I still maintain a few of the relationships I established during my two years there. Being a part of the faculty at Clemente was one of the most rewarding experiences of my twelve-year teaching career.

1975 was clearly a year of maturation for me. I was a wife, mother, and had begun my career in teaching. It was also the year I took my first trip to Jamaica, one year after attaining its independence from Great Britain. Due to our chosen vocations, my husband and I were invited to come live in Montego Bay. With me being a teacher and he in computer programming and hardware, we could have made a formable living, as well as been on the ground level of rebuilding a country. I was more than willing, while he, on the other hand, wanted no part of such an endeavor.

Though the chance of repatriating to a land closely resembling our indigenous homeland, Mother Africa, eluded me at that time, that particular experience reminds me of the possibility of such an occurrence more than thirty years later. So, all is not lost.

The decade between 1965 and 1975 symbolized an era that evolved from one of great promise to one of abuse and exploitation of the standards and values of a people that have endured centuries of degradation. For a brief time, I thought we were going to continue to be regarded as the “conscious of humanity,” but as is so evident today, we have abandoned that status. The mantra for Black people in the sixties was “I’m Black and I’m Proud.” In the seventies, it became “Superfly” and “It’s your thing, do what you wanna do. I can’t tell you who to give your thing to.” The contrast of those times is reflected in our current socio-economic and spiritual status. For now, Blacks may have more material gains, primarily “creature comforts.” However, attaining real power continues to elude us. I sincerely hope we regain our focus as a people by returning to aspiring towards the goal of self-determination.

THE BLACK PANTHER PARTY IN THE BLACK STRUGGLE FOR CIVIL RIGHTS (HUMAN RIGHTS) IN CHICAGO

W. E. Dunbar

Some Reflections and Recollections

The Illinois chapter of the Black Panther Party was formed in 1968. I attempted to join that summer, but it wasn't until the Party office opened on West Madison Street in November that my membership became a reality.

In 1968 I had choices both in education and employment. When I put on the black beret and put the "Red Book" in the pocket of my field jacket, I joined the revolution. I made a commitment to change the order of the world. I volunteered for service, service to the people. Was joining the Black Panther Party the best choice? That doesn't matter. It was the right choice.

The "Era"

I have come to understand that academia has divided our struggle into phases, periods or eras. There is a move to separate the "radical" political movement from the "Civil Rights era." Our struggle for freedom, equality and justice is centuries long. It began when they forced us into those boats in chains. There has not been a generation that did not fight to regain the human rights of our people. Our struggle is a continuum.

This era of struggle, commonly known as the sixties, is fruit born of the work and efforts of many soldiers, scholars and leaders; the human suffering of millions who preceded us. To place a few names on the time line, I note: Denmark Vessey, Nat Turner and Harriet Tubman; Martin R. Delaney, Fredrick Douglass, W. E. B. DuBois and Marcus Garvey; Medgar Evers, Elijah Muhammad, Malcolm X, Dr Martin Luther King, Jr. and in Chicago, Fred Hampton;

Black people, all radicals in their day. It took all of these people and various organizations over time, to bring about the conditions that would get Harold Washington elected mayor of Chicago. Of course there are many others worthy of mention; this struggle is over four hundred years old and not over.

Democracy and Freedom for Who?

In the fall of 1966 I turned seventeen years of age. On TV I began to watch, with more interest, two items featured on the nightly news: the war in Vietnam and coverage of the civil rights protests in the South.

American troops, American citizens, were fighting a war for democracy in Vietnam, Southeast Asia. The "conflict" in Vietnam would be the first televised war. Reporters in jungle clearings stood next to helicopters, blades spinning above their heads, while soldiers deployed and the dead and wounded were loaded on board. Body counts like box scores, troop positions and firefights would appear nightly. Bombing runs with aerial footage, in full color, were TV media firsts.

Democracy is America's greatest attribute and now the media would expose the callous, immoral practice of racism. The world would now see Black people marching in protest and the police responding violently with nightsticks, dogs and fire hoses. This struggle by America's Black citizens to change the laws that institutionalized racism and prejudice was now being documented and witnessed by millions of people, otherwise unknowing and unaffected.

Living in the South Side Chicago community of Chatham, with both of my working parents, life was good. Most of the boys I knew had part-time jobs. I got my first job at fourteen, earning about seventy-five cents an hour; minimum wage was only one dollar per hour. We were taught to pay our own way. Working a job and earning our own money gave us a sense of independence and freedom.

The "Color Line"

In the late sixties the imaginary boundary that marked the racial border between people and communities became more defined and more dangerous to cross. As Blacks sought better housing, the promise of integration was tested again and again. What occurred was not really desegregation nor was it integration because whites fled to avoid living next to Blacks. They feared living next door to "Negroes." The fear of depreciated home values was a tool used by real estate brokers to make quick profits in changing neighborhoods. I suppose my parents and most Blacks knew racism existed here in Chicago all along. While there was white flight, other whites began protecting their communities from the Negroes. Now that we were daring to go into white neighborhoods more frequently looking for housing, it got ugly; ugly just like in the South.

Whites frequently would taunt newly arrived Black residents and vandalize their homes in attempts to drive out their unwanted new neighbors. Garage burnings and firebombs were frequent. The police department, overwhelmingly white and basically patronage employees, was less than willing to protect these Blacks, who were seen as intruders. Black homeowners new on a block of all-whites sometimes had to call for a show of force. This call was for cars of family and friends, handguns and rifles visible to literally surround their homes in self-defense.

Martin Luther King's presence and demonstrations here in 1966 just made matters worse for the fearful, ignorant whites, their racist friends and the mayor at that time, Richard J. Daley.

Not Quite Segregation

Attending the still new John Marshall Harlan High School, 96th and Michigan on the recently integrated South Side, white students were in the minority. This school was one of many originally built to deal with the national surge in population, the baby boomers. The school was immediately overcrowded, so much so that mobile classroom trailers (called Willis Wagons for the then superintendent of schools) were put in the parking lot.

Black classmates would share stories about being chased out of still predominantly white neighborhoods like Roseland to the south, Marynook to the east and Evergreen Park on the west. As kids, we would explore, usually on our bicycles and on the bus. On the bus you could get to many places and back without incident. Evergreen Plaza was one of the country's first shopping malls. Racial tension was high in those years and Blacks had begun moving westward up to the Ashland Avenue de facto border, so going past there was uncharted territory in a lot of ways.

I got my second job at the Krock's & Brentano's Bookstore in the Plaza, 95th and Western. I was one of the two or three Blacks on staff. I worked alone most of the time; clean-up and stock. I did get to interact with the staff and worked there long enough to joke a bit with the teenaged white girls who were cashiers. There was curiosity on both sides, but at the end of the day we went our separate ways.

Across that Line

One weekend, leaving a house party given by a Black Calumet High School student near 85th and South Morgan, we went looking for a pay phone. This area had changed recently from white to Black residents. As my running buddy and I walked toward the hotdog restaurant at 87th Street and Morgan, we could see it was very crowded. At ten p.m. the place was filled with young white kids on a Saturday night; this was still their hang-out. Seeing this, we didn't even think about going in. We crossed to the south side of 87th Street and found a pay phone in a phone booth, less than a half block away. I was dialing the phone when my buddy alerted me that a group of whites had followed us. I hung up the phone and retrieved my dime. When I turned around there were at least six young white boys confronting us.

It went down very quickly. They didn't close in and I was actually standing in the doorway of the phone booth, so my back was protected. My buddy was outside to the right and, without a movie dialog or soundtrack; he "took on" the white boy nearest to him. The others postured or lagged, apparently one had gone somewhere and came around from the left with an aluminum milk can (think beer keg). I didn't really see it until it was coming, but when it hit me, it cut my chin, hit me in the chest and knocked me back into the phone booth. The dime dropped into my coat pocket; as I regrouped, my buddy asked if I was okay. I probably mumbled a reply; I was dazed. Stepping outside the booth, the white boys broke and ran.

I was bleeding a little. My buddy was all good, shaken, but stirred up by the attack. Just that quick, lights flashing, Chicago's finest rolled up. They gave us the "What are you guys doing over here?" talk and then listened as we explained. Details are vague, but I do know we did not get arrested. There was no written report made. We did return to the party, most likely delivered there by the police. Telling the story of our encounter at the party likely ended it early. The parents allowed me to call my ride.

My dad picked us up; our parents would often assist us in attending parties outside our immediate area because the parties would most always end after curfew. As we drove past the hotdog place we could see that a large crowd of whites had formed in the parking lot. The notion of going back to even the score passed quietly as we returned to our neighborhood just a few blocks east.

Did that encounter affect my views on race? Of course it did. It validated what I had read about and been told by others. It was just my early taste of prejudice and racism and far less severe than what Blacks were experiencing in so many American cities. I had proof racism was not only in the South.

The Machine

The presence of The Black Panther Party in Chicago was only a surprise for people who were comfortable with the status quo or for people who were content to wait for change.

At this point in the sixties, Chicago was ripe for change. Impoverished Blacks lacked efficient Black representatives. America's racist policies and segregationist laws created ghettos in nearly all of its cities. Chicago had its ghettos, parts of which were the worst slums in the country and parts that were stable middle class communities (still today). Blacks have challenged these laws and policies in every generation.

What I knew about the politics of Chicago at this time were only vague notions about "the Daley Machine" and that it controlled the city and the Black wards. My parents always seemed to be voting for the lesser of two evils because none of the candidates adequately represented their needs or offered them a voice in public policies.

Part of what I recalled from the classroom studies of the government was the president's power to end the war in Vietnam and to send the Federal troops into the South to protect the Black protesters. I couldn't understand who really controlled the laws of the land concerning segregation and/or integration.

Mayor Richard J. Daley saw himself as the king-maker, had his issues with national Democratic leadership, but still was a force in the national democratic organization. Even by 1966 Richard J. Daley had been in office so long, the press and public referred to him as Mayor Daley as if Mayor was his first name. He was also called "Da Boss." Chicago was his city, as were all of its departments, including the police.

Richard J. Daley was first elected mayor of Chicago in April 1955. He was reelected in 1959, 1963, 1967, and 1971 and in 1975 Mayor Daley was elected for a sixth four-year term as mayor of Chicago. He set a new record for serving as mayor longer than any other man in Chicago's history. He died in office on December 20, 1976.

The Draft

Being drafted into the U.S. Military was an issue closer to me than all others. Why should I be forced to go to Vietnam to fight for their freedom and right to democracy when I was not going to be assured those rights here in America?

I would consider Muhammad Ali's refusal to serve in the United States Army during the Vietnam War as a conscientious objector, but I wasn't a Muslim or religious. I considered fleeing to Canada; I didn't even know then in 1966 that Canada had been a haven for Blacks escaping from U.S. slavery. I had been taught in American history that slavery was "incidental" and as I recall, it did not get a full chapter.

I would soon have to decide. The military draft was for every male eighteen to twenty-five, fit, able and not in school. The draft was even offered as an alternative to prison for certain convictions. The draft didn't discriminate (Ha).

My parents offered no help. My dad, who had two brothers fight in WWII, was silent about my situation and left it up to me. My mom didn't want me to get into trouble by becoming a draft dodger. I thought I would get killed in Vietnam; that was probably the first time I had even considered dying.

In the spring of 1967 I chose college as a way to avoid the draft. I needed time to understand what was going on in the world beyond my obviously sheltered life. There was much activity on the Civil Rights front. There were boycotts and marches every night on the news and the Black Panther Party was getting press for the escalating police confrontations.

The Revolutionaries Have Come

The Black Panther Party for Self-Defense was formed in Oakland, California in October of 1966. It attained national prominence when the chairman/founder Bobby Seale and members were featured on TV going to the California state legislature, with rifles in hand, to assert their U.S. Constitutional right as citizens to bear arms.

There was always skepticism about the non-violent protests and their effectiveness. The Black Panther Party offered a 10 Point Program and a political platform addressing a broad range of issues. The Black Panther Party program included the request for United Nations involvement. As Malcolm X had pointed out, civil rights are a local issue while human rights are an international issue. In the spring of 1968 Dr. Martin Luther King, Jr. was killed.

In the summer of 1968, the Illinois Chapter of the Black Panther Party was organized. That November, the headquarters was opened in Chicago on West Madison Street, with Bobby Rush, Deputy Minister of Defense, now a U.S. Congressman, and Fred Hampton, deputy chairman, who was assassinated on December 4, 1969. The FBI's director, J. Edgar Hoover, ordered the elimination of the Black Panther Party as part of the COINTELPRO campaign to prevent any Black leader from becoming a new "Black Messiah."

The Black Panther Party provided alternatives to the plantation politics and patronage that denied Black and poor people of Chicago their basic rights. The Party's survival programs helped sustain the people suffering under Mayor Daley's system of clout, which required payoffs of cash, favors, and votes in order to receive city services.

Unemployment was very high and discrimination prevalent. Desegregation of the schools and housing was part of the federal government's initiative. The City of Chicago and the

Chicago Board of Education would fight against these issues in the courts for years and years.

The gains Blacks made in education, employment and economics made them a force in Chicago yet to be recognized. Social change was sweeping the world and we were soon aware that we were part of it.

The Rev. Dr. King had come to Chicago in 1966. The televised pictures I saw of the white racist response to the marches here were never as powerful to me as the now iconic images of the police dogs and fire hoses used against Blacks in the South.

Daley called the Rev. Dr. King a communist, an outsider, a troublemaker and worse. He called the Black Panther Party a gang. He was wrong in both cases.

In the summer of 1968, as Chicago hosted the Democratic Party Convention, the police rioted against the peace movement protesters in Grant Park. With TV cameras inside the convention and outside on the streets and in the park, the whole world was watching as Daley came unhinged and lost control as his tyrannical nature was exposed.

While the Illinois chapter of The Black Panther Party was still being organized at this time, seven of the peace demonstration organizers and leaders were later arrested and indicted by the federal government for conspiracy and crossing state lines to incite a riot. Also arrested and included in the case was Bobby Seales, the Chairman of The Black Panther Party. His courtroom protests for his right to defend himself resulted in Seales being bound to a chair and gagged so he could not speak during the trial.

The Black Panther Party was embraced and rebuffed in Chicago because the Black community had within it diverse social perspectives. That mixed reception had much to do with an individual's political awareness of social and economic conditions. It also had to do with age. Young people were not so heavily invested in the system; whereas our parents had toiled to give us the freedoms we now enjoyed. We felt a sense of entitlement from this country, not unlike the youth of today. However, we focused on our rights as citizens to prosper and advance. Blacks looked to the government and society to provide the same opportunities and the same protection as outlined in the U.S. Constitution. Most Blacks back then, who were on public aid and/or living in the public housing projects, were certain that they were only going to be there for a short period of time. No one could see generations of people living on welfare and becoming the underclass. Tens of thousands of Blacks lived in slum conditions on the West and South Side ghettos. These properties were usually owned by absentee landlords and rented through a few management companies. The concept of slum and ghetto was merged and referred to any area of majority Black populations.

The Black Panther Party's comprehensive Ten Point program and platform spoke to urban issues, slavery issues, and international issues. The sit-ins, marches and boycotts did not seem applicable here in Chicago. As a fast growing national organization, Black Panther Party chapters addressed local conditions. Party members initiated innovative survival programs involving the communities with actual solutions, often independent of government agencies.

Point 10 of The Black Panther Party Program

Paraphrased here is a summary of the platform:

We want land, bread, housing, education, clothing, justice, and peace.

And as our major political objective, a united nation supervised plebiscite to be held throughout the Black communities in which only Black people will be allowed to participate for the purpose of determining the will of Black people as to their national destiny.

Where are the Revolutionaries?

As members of the community, Party members were aware of the neglect and oppression. They put theory into practice, engaged community members, developed programs and initiated solutions. Party members, by their presence because of their commitment and intellect, were able to direct attention toward the needs of the community at every meeting and discussion they attended. The methodology of the Black Panther Party was to educate and organize the community into actualizing its own political power. As community organizers, the Party brokered truces between rival gangs and between political foes; in effect, stabilizing and unifying the community. Though criticized by some at the time, the Black Panther Party assisted in connecting diverse racial and ethnic groups also oppressed by the system, creating the Rainbow Coalition. That was revolutionary because it put the people in charge of their fate. That was revolutionary because it forced the politicians in government to change the status quo or be removed by political action.

Political orientation classes were a requirement for all new members. Fred Hampton was chairman of the Illinois Black Panther Party chapter and taught many of those classes. I had never heard of him before my first class. Over time I came to see in Fred Hampton, in his daily actions, the embodiment of the Black Panther Party's commitment to freedom and justice, standards I have tried to maintain throughout my life.

These revolutionaries are living and working among us today. They are present in every aspect of life as innovators and creators of real time solutions. Who are the revolutionaries in your life?

I salute my comrades, "this is a protracted struggle."

The Beat Goes On—Long Live the Spirit of Deputy Chairman Fred Hampton.

All Power to the People!

A 1960'S STORY

Michael C. Edwards

DUALITY

In 1960 my grade school English teacher assigned an essay on some aspect of what was then called Negro history. We were told that the best essays would be selected to compete in a school-wide contest. My essay won first place:

> *Long ago in a land called Africa lived a dark skinned people who looked like me. White skinned people came and took them across the Atlantic Ocean to America in slave ships. The slave ships were very large and the white men stuffed as many Africans into them as possible. Once in America the white men planned to sell the Africans as slaves and make a lot of money. The trip was very long and the living area was dark, damp, cold and unsanitary. The Africans were very uncomfortable and were treated very cruelly. Many became ill and died. However, many chose not to complete the cruel voyage and jumped overboard to their deaths. Or at least some of them did.*
>
> *Legend has it that among the dark skinned people there were those who we know very little about since the knowledge of their history is all but lost. This is a story about the dark skinned flying people who were also caught and stuffed into the slave ships, who also chose not to complete the voyage, but who simply flew away and then gathered on a remote island. You see, they avoided the certain death of the ocean plunge, but being so far away from Africa they were unsure whether to risk trying to make their way back to their homeland or to follow the slave ships to see what this new land and new people were really about. They talked it over, argued about it, but could not agree on what to do. Many of them feared they had not enough power or strength to return to Africa, while others thought they had seen enough of these strange new people and wanted nothing more to do with them—even if following would*

lead them to the place their friends and relatives were destined to end up.

They were faced with a choice. Go forward to America or try to get back to where they came from. However, after much debate some decided that they would attempt to return home, some decided to follow the slave ships and still others decided they would rather soar to the heavens as high as they could go and just see what they could see—even if it meant eventually falling to a certain death. This is where the legend ends because there is no record of what really happened to the dark skinned flying people. Did some make it to the shores of America? Did others find their way home? Did they all die?

Now, some people say they all died on that island trying to decide between American slavery, the African homeland, and uncertain flight to the heavens. Some people say that the dark skinned flying people who were stuffed into those slave ships are still dying today-everyday, trying to find their way. And others are still trying to see what they can see.

I was surprised when my essay won first place school-wide. I remember getting my paper back with a bright red "E+" on it, and a note at the bottom of the page: "Please see me after class." I was still more surprised by the questions the middle-aged white lady asked, her stern, serious face and tone of voice: "Are you okay?" "Is there something bothering you?" "Are you sure you are okay?" I was told that thoughts about death were unusual for someone my age and that she was concerned that I might be depressed. I assured her that I was not depressed and that I hadn't really thought about the paper until I wrote it, but I was glad she liked it.

I received a twenty-five dollar U.S. savings bond and a copy of the Herbert Apthteker book *Negro People in America*. I don't recall what became of the savings bond, but I was familiar with books and this one, although tedious reading, became one of my favorites. Books, magazines and newspapers were common household items in my family. There was, of course, *Ebony, Life*, and *Jet* magazines, an old set of encyclopedias, and a growing set of new subscription encyclopedias sold by A&P grocery stores. There was also the *Negro Digest*, odd copies of the *Crisis* magazine, several books by DuBois, Woodson, Langston Hughes, and nearly everything written by Baldwin. We seemed to always have a current copy of *Muhammad Speaks*. There was also a lot of notebook paper and brand new pencils. Apparently, my father would get the supplies free from some place and he always made sure we stayed well stocked with pencils and a fresh, crisp stack of paper. To this day I have an affinity for paper and the special feel of putting pencil to paper.

However, I understood nothing about self-identity. I guess, though, that I was living it, immersed in it. I was under the powerful but unspoken tutelage of my father, a "race man," who believed that we should "fight segregation with segregation" and that "black is black and white is white and ne'er the twain shall meet." I was always told that I was smart, I read a lot, and I was always at the top of my class; but I understood nothing about self-identity. Chicago is and was then a rough city. I grew up in one of the roughest neighborhoods. Outside of school I was a regular guy. I knew how to box as did all the boys in my family. We were taught early in life by my father, who boxed as an amateur at the YMCA near 47th Street and then later in his life for the army. I had an older brother who seemed to know everybody and everybody knew him, including some of the roughest guys in this roughest of neighborhoods. I had a younger brother who I would sometimes have to fight for. Overall, I was fairly well adjusted to the classroom and the streets. I was just beginning to experience the duality that would later become the full-fledged identity crisis similar to what DuBois had written about. I was immersed in it, but it was not yet a conscious dilemma or crisis. Furthermore, DuBois talked about duality in the context of what he considered biculturalism, the tension related to navigating between two ethnic or racial cultural contexts-one white and one black. What I'm talking about is structurally similar but involves the tension between conflicting aspects of the same racial-cultural context. So, it is unicultural and the content is different but its structure is similar to that which DuBois first described. My grade school essay was an abstract, symbolic expression of a not yet conscious duality.

> *The last time I had to actually physically fight someone was in 1963. Someone had stolen my pencil off my desk, a tough guy and a bully in my class. He was a year, maybe two years older. A girl said that she knew who took it and that I should go take it back. As it was now in plain sight on his desk and he was nowhere around, I took my pencil back. Needless to say, the girl wasted no time letting everybody know that I had taken the pencil back and now this bully was saying he would see me after school. I wasn't afraid. This guy was a troubled kid, a loner who liked to beat people up. I'd never had trouble with him or others like him, and so I was actually annoyed that he would push me to fight over a pencil. I had many friends and was generally cool with everyone. So, by the time school was out, several older, even tougher guys had come to me to say they had heard about my situation and that they would take care of it. I said no, confident that I could easily talk my way out of a fist fight over a pencil. It was all so very silly and so not me. You must recall that back then there were no guns and the few people who carried knives or straight razors were well known. One knew to*

> *avoid fighting with them unless you had the power to have them searched or patted down beforehand. You fought with your fists. It was not unusual to box someone just for the fun of it to see who was best. Considering age, weight, and height I was usually among the best. Even with bigger, older guys who didn't know the art of boxing, I was generally good. So, I was annoyed. I didn't want to fight him and worst of all I wasn't sure I could beat him. Here's the thing, though. Back then you fought, won or lost, and went home with the honor of having fought a good fight. There was no retaliation, no escalation, no fatal weapons or injuries. All that would soon change, though. However, on this day in 1963 I fought one of the toughest guys in the neighborhood and beat him. I never had to fight again, although I must confess to running a few times to avoid a fight I knew I couldn't win.*

So, despite my budding recognition as a scholar I was being equally drawn into the other-world of the streets. I had best friends in both worlds. I hung out at night and I won more academic contests. I got all A's but I didn't really value the learning. It was all content, simple facts. I would sometimes give the answers away because they had no value to me. Even back then, I felt strongly about my education even though I couldn't always quite articulate it. I felt the simple learning of facts without learning about he who thinks about the facts—about knowledge of the thinker—was of little value.

The duality I experienced was between different aspects of my community. It seems to me, ontologically speaking, that the duality of immersion I experienced was associated with a social-role identity. This kind of duality of immersion occurs when one grows up in an all-black community that does not define itself in opposition to mainstream white society, i.e., that loves itself in and of itself. One plays out social roles without conscious reflection on how the roles conflict or create actual choices. It may be that, ontogenetically speaking, when one experiences the duality of psychological immersion later in life one does so with conscious reflection and choice. However, the duality of social role immersion that I experienced is probably not confined to growing up during the 1960s. Although I knew intellectually about U.S. population distributions and ratios, I lived my life as though blacks were the majority or only group that really mattered. I recall childhood experiences involving racial incidents perpetrated by whites. From the standpoint of my limited worldview I saw whites as somehow inconsequential. I was taught as a child how to behave in racial encounters when I had power and vice versa.

One day after grocery shopping in the late 1950s, I was sitting at a bus stop with my mother in a nearby all-white neighborhood. A little white boy spit on me as he walked by. I was sure he had missed and so several minutes later when I noticed the spit on my pants leg, I told my mother. She said, "I know we're alone and we might not make it back, but you should have shook the shit out of him."

Growing up during the 1960s always felt to me like immersion in my community. The social role duality I experienced was between different aspects of my community and only later became a conscious conflict between my community and what is now called integration. Back then, it felt like a good fit and I could go on forever enjoying what seemed like the best that life in my community had to offer.

Transcendence, or What is it that Moves

Duality exists for the sake of transcendence. Transcendence is described as "going beyond" one's circumstances, or "rising above" the situation or somehow "deepening" one's experience. The metaphors used to describe transcendence all refer to some kind of motion or movement that results in a wider, deeper or higher experience of reality. But what is it that moves?

In my opinion, the experience of transcendence does not lend itself well to metaphor. It's not an experience that one can picture or imagine—it must be lived. My argument with the public school education I received is that it ignored the possibility of such self-awareness and, at best, was stuck in a "hole-in-the-bucket" approach. This uninformed approach ostensibly wants to fill the bucket (the student) with facts (content knowledge) until it overflows with transcendence. When there is a hole in it, however, facts and more facts will never fill the bucket. Without heed to the thinker and the underlying "I-Self" context of thought there will always be a hole in the metaphorical bucket. The fundamental flaw of public education is the assumption that all knowledge lies in things or objective events external to the inner reality of the self. The self and its interconnections with the inner realities of other selves are seen as outside of the purview of public education. This is so, although the search for knowledge of the "I-Self" can make learning an exhilaratingly meaningful experience.

In 1964 I watched on television as the country exploded with race riots from coast to coast. Harlem, Rochester, Philadelphia, Watts. Then, there were more riots in Cleveland, Detroit, Newark, and Baltimore. Malcolm was killed in 1965. King brought his Civil Rights

Movement—“live and in living color”—to Chicago in 1965-66. My friends would come to me with books and LP recordings of Malcolm’s speeches. We would listen and read intently, and then debated the merits of nationalism versus integration. I read everything by and about Malcolm.

All knowledge of self inexorably leads to the conclusion that the world is not as it appears to be. The duality was growing and intensifying. Then I discovered the power of Black Nationalistic ideology and self-determination. You might say that I had found the means to plug up the “I-Self” hole in the metaphorical bucket. In other words, I had moved beyond the small-minded circumstances of growing up poor on Chicago’s South Side. If before I was immersed in a social role identity, I had now moved into a psychological identity that was fully conscious of the internal social conflicts within my community. From my point of view, these conflicts could only be resolved (transcended) by a deeper commitment to what was liberating in the black community while moving beyond it by using the vehicle of higher education.

I left Chicago in the fall of 1967 to enroll at an elite, upper middle-class college on the east coast. I became more militant and more insistent on self-determination. Along with brothers mainly from New York, New Jersey, Chicago, Detroit and Los Angeles, I helped radicalize the campus black student organization and became involved in the black power movement all up and down the east coast.

I was surprised and also shocked that I knew nothing of Che Guevarra prior to learning of his assassination in 1967. Then, King was killed in the spring of 1968, as was Little Bobby Hutton out in Oakland. More riots erupted. Quickly thereafter, Bobby Kennedy was killed. Huey was in jail or on the run, Bobby Seale was on trial, and people were dying in shootout after shootout with police all across America’s big cities, it seemed. Fred Hampton and Mark Clark were killed in Chicago at the end of 1969.

Meanwhile, I discovered the counter cultural Hippie movement and I actively joined the protest against the Vietnam War. In the spring of 1968, during the first wave of student takeovers of university administration buildings, right around the time of the Columbia University takeover in New York, we took over the administration building at my small college and held it for three days. I was part of the black student faction on campus that negotiated first with other white student groups, and then with the administration about “issues of concern to blacks.” We insisted that not only more blacks be recruited to campus, but also that the college needed to provide supportive services that were culturally sensitive and ensured retention and academic success. We argued that the faculty and administration become more diversified. We also demanded that the college somehow begin to address local issues of poverty and racism in the city’s black neighborhoods. I became even more radical, more militant, and in 1969 I was elected president of the campus black student organization. I became part of a tri-state regional association of black student organization presidents that included New York, Connecticut and New Jersey. Through this association I met even more radical brothers and sisters. And being from Chicago seemed to command respect; people listened when a brother from Chicago had something to say. While I was determined to get a BA, I was also more and more immersed in the Black Power Movement. So, it seemed that I had again found a good fit. I could go on forever enjoying what seemed like the best that life in this new integrated community had to offer.

Back home, parts of Chicago were devastated by the 1968 riots. My childhood friends were dying in Vietnam and returning home somehow different. The Black Panthers and the Blackstone Rangers and other groups had set up in my neighborhood. The gangs were ominously present. Through it all, I never forgot where I came from, but where I came from had changed; indeed, I had changed, too. People back home looked at me differently.

DUALITY AGAIN—SOMETHING MOVES

My world had become increasingly integrated. I had good friends from places like Trinidad, Gambia, Ghana, France, and the United Kingdom. My attention had turned to the African continent and to the anti-war protests in Europe, as well. Out east I was equally respected by like-minded whites and blacks. My opinion on matters was frequently sought and my vocabulary had ballooned. My uneasiness about back home disturbed me. I could see my way out of the poverty I had grown up with and I felt that I understood the connection between black communities of poverty and my Black Power ideology. Black Power and self-determination had become the means by which I transcended the contradictions in the community I experienced as a child. I had constructed a psychological identity that was now capable of transcending internal conflicts that existed within the black community.

From my point of view these conflicts were resolved by a commitment to what was liberating in the black community while moving beyond it by using the vehicle of higher education. I was satisfied that I had moved beyond the circumstances of growing up poor on Chicago's South Side. However, I realized that power and wealth were real and that self-knowledge could be liberating and yet painful. In other words, something was beginning to move. I felt the ambivalence of moving beyond a narrowly defined community to the full embracing of this new integrated world with its allure of power and wealth. I was conscious of this ambivalence, this impending duality, and it disturbed me.

At college there was this white guy we called the Medusa Man. He had long thick dreadlocked hair and a dark full beard. He was a campus enigma—a math and philosophy major. Rumor was that he had tested out of nearly all of the first two or three years of coursework and was working on a senior's thesis that nobody, including the professors, even understood. We called him the Medusa Man not just because he looked like what we imagined the mythical Medusa would look like, but because he was also the president of the campus Medusa Society of so-called geniuses. He was a loner and never really talked to anybody. He always had an arm full of books whenever you saw him. He would show up at rallies and protest meetings and simply listen, observe. When he did talk at such meetings, he would use phrases such as "the existential impulse to freedom" or "the archetypal exchange between self and not-self falsely disguised as the rivalry of good and evil." But he was clearly sympathetic to the movement.

One night, during the time we took over the administration building, a brother from D.C. and a white guy who was the head of Students for a Democratic Society asked if I wanted to accompany them to the Medusa Man's apartment. I went and we all talked about political strategy and such things while the Medusa Man read to us from ancient philosophy texts—which was not really all that uncommon during those days. There was a young radical philosophy professor there. He had organized the "anti-war teach-ins" on campus.

Medusa Man and I got into a side conversation and he asked me was it rhythm or movement that black people referred to when talking about soul. I said yes, partially, but more fundamentally it referred to a connection people felt. Rhythm or movement served both as a manifestation of that connection and a ritualistic or stylistic way (like dancing) to sometimes manifest that connection more intensely. He seemed intrigued, and then asked was this soul connection material or immaterial. Well, I was a physics and engineering major during the first few years of college. I had been introduced to quantum physics and therefore I thought I understood the question. I replied that if it is material it must be some form of high frequency energy and if it is immaterial it must be consciousness or spirit. He appeared to become a little agitated as though there was a right answer to get to and the conversation wasn't moving to it quickly enough. I said, but then again they say that spirit is everything and everything is spirit. He smiled and said "Yes!" and "Everybody!"

The inner conflict between a segregated black community and integration disturbed me because the idea of assimilation into mainstream America was so readily accepted; even though it pits cultures and communities of people against one another on an unequal footing. It pits the black community of my childhood against its own self and so for many black people the promise of integration, power and wealth remain beyond the reach of their communities. However, the spirit had moved me and while I knew not where to, along the way I discovered the community of human beings! As I said before, all knowledge of self inexorably leads to the conclusion that the world is not as it appears to be. I had been immersed in the commitment to a black power consciousness, and then moved into an identity crisis that involved a falsely constructed choice between my so-called community and an integrated, multiracial-multicultural world. I was now moving into a more universal consciousness that was increasingly aware that the psychohistorical drama that was unfolding in the context of my life—the confluence of social justice issues related to race, moral justice issues having to do with war, and cultural values issues that point to the meaninglessness pursuit of materialism—was about more than just me and my people.

Beyond Identity

Earlier I said that duality exists for the sake of transcendence. If this is so, then transcendence must ultimately exist for the sake of the spirit and that is why no metaphor suffices to explain or describe it. Even when one fails to recognize spirit in its grosser forms (social or psychological), it is the spirit that moves. Neurocardiologists describe the biology of transcendence and how our anatomy seems to be hardwired for it. Physicists talk about quantum synaptic tunneling, nonlocal consciousness and the quantum nature of the mind. Likewise, consciousness and identity studies point to nontraditional evidence for intersubjectivity, shared consciousness and interdependent identity while challenging intellectual traditions based on the illusion of a separate self.

Universal consciousness is an imminent, higher level "going beyond" one's circumstances or "rising above" the situation or somehow "deepening" one's experience. Imminence describes movement into a powerfully shared consciousness that allows one to not only move beyond the sociocultural context, but to move also beyond the self and not-self stuff that psychological identity is made of. This higher level movement to universal consciousness is like moving beyond the time and space of one's life and what's left that moves is what has always moved. There are no words or conventions of language to adequately describe it for it must be a lived experience. The 1960s held out an elusive potential of fundamental justice and equality for all and with it an even more elusive potential for self-awareness that is often mistakenly equated with drug-induced altered consciousness. The unfulfilled potential of that era leaves one with the dilemma of somehow going back home to be alone among those who do not fly or going forward to somehow contribute to humanity as best as one can.

This is the closest I can come to retelling my experience of the 1960s. The story, however, does not end here. I believe that the sociopolitical backlash to the 1960s is lifting. The country has been at a crossroads for some time that may lead, although arduously, to an altogether new era of post partisan politics. This new politics will become increasingly colorblind while at the same time becoming increasingly irrelevant to large groups of blacks with no stake in such a society as they remain in conditions not unlike those of the 1960s. We have seen the devolution of far too many communities into concentrated poverty, senseless violence and self-destruction. Yet out of this miasma may arise again the mythical awe of human potential embodied in the cultural revolution of the 1960s.

I obtained a bachelor's degree and several other professional degrees from an even more prestigious east coast university. I work with my people in a variety of educational and mental health settings. I look into their eyes and sometimes I see myself. I feel what they feel and I think what they think. On a good day I become them and they become me. Reality becomes one and the veiled Isis reveals her truth.

> *Every now and then, when I'm alone I think about those dark skinned flying Africans who looked like me that I wrote about in 1960. I see the slave ships. I feel myself soaring along with them to see what we can see. They say to me: "Be free! What matters if one be enslaved to another man, black or white? What matters if we be enslaved to illusory things or to a set of false ideas? Why enslavement to this I-self bound by time and space?" They say: "There were others before us and there will be others after us. The conditions of one's enslavement will always exist so that we may overcome them and in doing so we may also learn to fly."*

MEMORIES OF CHICAGO'S BLACK STRUGGLE DURING THE SIXTIES AND SEVENTIES

Charles Grantham

Let me say from the onset that I doubt that I could have been called an activist by any stretch of the imagination during the sixties and seventies. However, I was an observer and occasionally a participant in events that occurred around Chicago during that historical period.

As a teenager growing up in the sixties, I was keenly aware that I lived in an all-Black community. However, I don't ever remember thinking of it as "the ghetto, nor did I think of my family as being poor. I lived in Ida B. Wells, went to Oakland Elementary School and later attended Wendell Phillips High School where outside of "us," there may have been two or three Hispanic students who attended. The only time I can remember being in class with other people besides Blacks was when I graduated from the eighth grade. This was during the summer of 1961. I attended summer school at the Wendell Phillips Elementary School. Since the Chicago Public School system was about to terminate January graduations (which was when I was scheduled to graduate), they allowed me and fellow eighth graders from nearby elementary schools to graduate from summer school as opposed to waiting until June of the following year, which would have put us all behind a year. There were both Hispanic and Chinese students from Chinatown in my class. This was my first contact with either.

At the same time that I was aware that I lived in an all-Black community, I was also aware that white people had their own communities. Two neighborhoods that stick out vividly in my mind are Bridgeport and Cicero. I also couldn't help but be aware of the tension and apprehension that sometimes existed between Black people when interacting with white people. I knew from conversations and the media that to be stopped in either one of these communities if you were Black could prove to be disadvantageous to one's well-being. My parents were from Mississippi and as far back as I can remember, we would drive south just about every summer. These trips were always an adventure. Being caught in these Chicago neighborhoods elicited the same type of apprehension and, yes, fear that must have accompanied my parents on those southern trips.

However, the thing that brought this fear of white people home for me was the murder of Emmet Till in 1955. My father took me to view his body at a funeral home on Cottage

Grove. As time went on, I became more and more conscious of the struggle of Blacks for civil rights and justice, not only in America, but right here in Chicago.

I entered Wendell Phillips High School in September of 1961. The vast majority of our teachers were Black. They were nurturing and really sincere in trying to prepare us for our future endeavors. There were a few teachers who stood out from the rest, at least for me. I had the good fortune to either have a class with or interact with teachers like Sterling Stuckey, Thomas Higginbothan, John Harwell and Donald Sykes. They were all social studies teachers and they awakened in me an interest in my African heritage. Then there was Shirley Kelso, who was an English teacher and coach of the drama club, which I eventually became a part of. It was through the drama club and regional competitions with white suburban schools that I realized the inequities that existed between black and white schools in the Chicago area. Their schools always seemed newer, larger and better equipped than ours.

Given those obvious differences, Ms. Kelso still infused in us a sense of self-awareness and pride. During a regional competition where we were the only Black school participating, Ms. Kelso refused to let us cry publicly or show any signs of defeat when we lost. Another teacher who stood out was Yvonne Pearson in business education, who would later change her name to Saruzayi Savanhu. I never had her as a teacher, but she stood out because she was the first woman I had ever seen who wore an Afro. In later years I learned that she was heavily involved in the liberation of African people on the continent as well as African peoples in the Diaspora.

Outside of the death of Emmet Till and what I saw on television, the one individual who caused me to take a serious look at what was happening here in Chicago during the sixties was a contemporary of mine who we called "Rabbi." Rabbi was not Jewish. As a matter of fact, he had gone to Holy Angels, a Catholic school a couple of blocks from my elementary school. Rabbi sometimes wore a skullcap, similar to a yarmulke, and I guess that's how he acquired the name Rabbi. It would be years before I learned that his given name was Michael Anderson. I don't know how, where, or when Rabbi became conscious of the struggle, but he definitely had an impact on me.

Rabbi also lived in Ida B. Wells. I don't remember when I first met him, but he had a persona that you couldn't ignore or forget. He was loud and brash and seemed to know everyone, even the police. It was Rabbi who was responsible for getting me to go to one of the rallies when Dr. Martin Luther King Jr. spoke at Soldier Field. I remember it because there were three of us, including Rabbi, all wearing Mexican sombreros, provided of course by Rabbi. Rabbi also introduced me to members of SNCC. I can remember going to a couple of meetings at different people's houses in Hyde Park but, unfortunately, I don't remember anything that occurred at any of these meetings or any of the people I met. We went to rallies at various churches and I participated in a couple of marches to protest housing segregation.

One event that stands out in my mind occurred around the "Wall of Respect" on 43rd and Langley just east of South Park. The mural was being painted to showcase and pay homage to Black heroes and heroines. Rabbi and I, like hundreds of other onlookers, had been going to the wall to watch the progress of the mural since its inception. There was always a festive mood at the wall. There I got an opportunity to see and meet artists like Bill Walker and Eugene Eda, who I had a chance to see paint another mural in Detroit in 1968. On this particular evening there was a heavy police presence, those in uniform as well as plain clothed. As I recall, there were even police on the rooftops of nearby buildings. To this day, I don't know what was happening or expected to happen, but the atmosphere was a lot more charged than usual. Whatever the case, Rabbi and I were there in the mix. Rabbi had been carrying a briefcase and as the evening wore on, he handed it to me to carry for a while. I thought nothing about it as we milled around the wall with the rest of the crowd. Sometime later, a white plain clothed policeman approached us and spoke to Rabbi, calling him by his nickname. As I remember, they both laughed and exchanged a few words, and then the policeman moved on. Later that evening I learned that I had been carrying a gun in the briefcase. This was in 1967.

Besides SNCC and CORE I was also aware of other organizations like the Black Panthers and the Black Muslims under the leadership of Elijah Mohammed. I knew that their approach to the struggle was somewhat different than the organizations I was more familiar with, but I don't think I ever contemplated joining either one. I agreed with some aspects of their ideologies, while others I didn't. But then, I didn't join SNCC either.

I also attended the Afro Arts Theater on 40th and Drexel, which had previously been the Oakland Theater. This all started as a result of me meeting my future wife, Carolyn J. Woolridge, in the fall of 1966. Carolyn was a dancer with the Those Who Want to Dance dance troupe, founded by Darlene Blackburn. Actually, Carolyn was more of an activist than me. She and her mother had marched in protest against plans by the Chicago Public Schools to place Willis Wagons (named after the school superintendent Benjamin Willis) on Black school grounds to alleviate overcrowding in the classrooms. Carolyn also attended civil rights rallies and participated in various marches. When the dance troupe started performing at the Afro Arts Theater, I was there to see Carolyn. It was there that I also became aware of Phil Cohran and his band, the Pharaohs, and was introduced to bean pies and papaya juice. Some of the band members went on to play with Earth, Wind and Fire. The theater was more than just a venue for entertainment, it was a place for cultural classes and political meetings. It was there that I first saw and heard Stokely Carmichael, who later changed his name to Kwame Ture. The theater was a cultural haven.

The Afro Arts Theater and those who came through it further awakened a sense of identity and an affirmation of Africaness, which was consummated when Carolyn and I went to Africa in 1973.

INVOLVEMENT IN CHICAGO'S BLACK STRUGGLE 1960-1975

Milele Cheryl Simms

In 1960 I was in grammar school, about to enter high school. The grammar school I was attending at the time was Daniel Hale Williams. The school was named for a Black physician who performed the first successful open heart surgery and founded Provident Hospital to train black health professionals and to provide health service to the black community. It is located in the housing projects of the Dearborn Homes at 29th and Federal. I lived and grew up in the infamous Harold L. Ickes housing development at 2450 South State Street, apartment 202. We were the first family to occupy that unit. I lived there with my mom Joetha Simms, one sister Patricia Beverly, and two brothers James Welden and Kevis Lynell. I am the oldest child in my family. My dad, James Welden, was a visiting parent whose financial contribution to my life was very little and very inconsistent. In an effort to have him make a more consistent and significant contribution, I lived with him briefly after high school upon entering college.

I recall having an extreme sensitivity to the criticisms of black people early in my development. I would often shed tears and begin crying whenever my mother or others would put down black people. I always wanted to defend, help and uplift us in our endeavors.

My earliest recollection of a contribution I made to Chicago's Black Struggle was during my employment at the Henry Booth House in the Ickes projects as a group worker during January 1967 until October 1969. There I worked with community residents from five-year-old children to senior citizens in groups to build a sense of leadership, responsibility, independence, self-confidence, and self-appreciation. I supervised social clubs, special interest groups, physical education classes, and teen council activities. Also, through the agency, I sponsored and coordinated local recreation tournaments.

One of my major accomplishments while there was to organize a group of young black men for the Martin Luther King Poor Peoples Campaign that took place in November of 1967 (although my philosophy was more consistent with that of Malcolm X). This was also perhaps my first introduction to organized Black movement efforts. My next tribute to black empowerment was during my graduation from the University of Illinois Circle Campus. After receiving my degree in 1969, I organized a group of black students to take a picture with raised fists in our caps and gowns. The University of Illinois at Navy Pier was a known hotbed of racism against black students. We were given lower grades and flunked out more often than our white counterparts. I had my own personal experiences with this racism. I was dropped from the University in my junior year for poor academic performance. That was a traumatic experience. It challenged my resolve. I was the oldest child in my immediate family, one of the few to have graduated from high school. I was setting the tone for the achievement of a college degree for my family. I would have been only second in my entire family to have graduated from college. Ironically, being dropped from Circle inspired a greater commitment in me to graduate from college and more confidence in my ability to do so. I went on to get accepted at the prestigious Illinois Institute of Technology, which was in my neighborhood at 35th and Federal. I spent one year there achieving an A average. After having accomplished that my self-confidence soared, I went back to the University of Illinois and graduated.

I attended Circle along with Carol Moseley Braun and Iva Carruthers. My relationship with Carol did not go beyond that of speaking. At that time we had little in common. I did, however, support her in her political endeavors. I studied with Iva as we shared a commitment to the uplifting of black people at home and abroad. Our interest in the black struggle and commitment to black people was further developed with our first trip to East Africa (Uganda, Kenya, Tanzania, Ethiopia, and Egypt). I went with her and her husband (at that time) Jake Carruthers. It was a historic trip; it was the day after Idi Amin expelled the Europeans from Uganda. We experienced firsthand the aftermath of his proclamation. I went on to establish a lasting friendship with Iva and Jake. Through an institutional program called the Communiversity, we continued to support one another in our activist endeavors over the years.

From the University of Illinois Circle Campus I went on to graduate school at the University of Chicago School of Social Service Administration. It was there and shortly after that I became more entrenched in the struggle for Black liberation. It was during my two year attendance (1969-1971) at the University that I was further indoctrinated into the struggle, and I met and worked with many people who have gone on to champion our causes, such as: Abena Joan Brown, Arnita Boswell, Earl Durham, Conrad Worrill, Julius Gaillard, (Muwasa) Charles Ross of Gary, Indiana (congressman candidate), Joan Massaquoi, Lillie Patterson, Harry Singletary (former Florida Department of Corrections Secretary), and Yaw Nyanin, who was born in Ghana. Some of these people served as mentors to me in developing a deep and endearing commitment to the struggles of our race throughout the Diaspora.

Conrad Worrill and I, along with some other noted students, formed the first Black Student Union at the University of Chicago. While it was based at SSA, we extended ourselves across campus and throughout the University for undergraduate involvement. We used the organization to raise the awareness of issues impacting the black community and adversely affecting the professional growth and development of black U of C students. We brought in speakers, planned retreats and social gatherings, and advocated for curriculum and admission policy changes. It was during these activities that I met Abena Joan Brown, established a lasting relationship with her, and supported her in her development of ETA, a Black cultural institution. The goals of the Black Student organization were the same as those employed in my group work experience: to build leadership, responsibility, black independence, self-confidence, and self-appreciation.

During graduate school, I had an internship at the Southwest Community Organization and the West Side Organization. These organizations provided me with my exposure to and experience in Civil Rights advocacy. We marched, boycotted, and rallied around issues regarding the disenfranchisement of black people in housing, education, and economics. My experience at The West Side Organization under the leadership of Chester Robinson, William Darden, John Crawford and Robert (whose last name I don't remember) was invaluable. It introduced me to the poor health, low socio-economic status, impoverished and addicted conditions of black people in America, and our ability to triumph over powerlessness. It truly demonstrated to me that power concedes to nothing but a demand. The leadership of the West Side Organization ingeniously inverted and used the resources of the University of Illinois to benefit the endeavors of the near West Side community.

I did some of my graduate field work at the West Side Organization and was later hired to develop the mental health center in a highly volatile environment. Guns were frequently seen, and drinking and the taking of drugs took place on the premises. Also, the staff of the mental health center was literally afraid of and running away from the patients they were there to help. I eventually overcame my fears of the social elements that contributed to the conditions that spawned poverty, teen pregnancy, etc. to train and educate the staff to provide professional service to our clients.

During my work at the West Side Organization, I was fortunate to have made the acquaintance of noteworthy persons, such as Congressman Danny Davis and Dr. Carl Bell. Their support of the efforts of the organization assisted in providing me with a sense of resolve in my continued efforts to better serve my people.

After graduate school, as a result of my association with Arnita Boswell and Joan Massaquoi, I became a member of and helped develop the initial League of Black Women. I was an executive board member of the League and chaired the Black Family Life committee. The League of Black Women at that time was comprised of affluent black women and served to politicize female and family issues of the Black Community. I met Gloria Wailes, a Civil Rights trooper, and Georgia Palmer, the wife of community activist Lu Palmer. I was later involved with them in their endeavors to publish and maintain the *Black X-Press*, a weekly newspaper edited by Mr. Palmer. I became the editor of youth news and issues for the paper.

My exposure to Black Nationalism was casual or vicarious at best until I enrolled in graduate school. I was introduced to writings, books, materials, and involved in the study of various doctrines. One of the first pieces of literature by which I was overwhelmed was Maulana Ron Karenga's *Kitabu on the Black Value System*. However, my involvement with the Black Nationalist community and organizations occurred after graduating from the University of Chicago. Another expression of black power was made at graduation when my cap was placed on top of my gelee for the graduation processional.

In 1971-72 my commitment to and involvement in Black Nationalist and African Center endeavors exploded. I became entrenched in activities of the struggle through the Northeastern Illinois University Communiversity program and the Institute of Positive Education. I recruited my family's participation in Kwanzaa Celebrations, African Liberation Day, Saba Saba, Black Folks Us and other activities. I also convinced my family to give up the celebration of Christmas in favor of Kwanzaa, to become vegetarian, and practice survivalism for the impending revolution. During a trip to Grenada in 1973, as a result of my familiarity with liberation struggles, I arranged to sit in on a meeting with a revolutionary leader, Morris Bishop. My traveling companion was very concerned about my safety in regards to that meeting. I did not have enough sense at that time to fully understand the danger that I had placed myself in. We discussed how we in the United States could best support their liberation struggle. Popularizing their struggle and fundraising for them is what they requested. I brought this information back and shared it at various organizational meetings.

Between 1971 and 1975 I participated in activities, such as the development of organizations like The Institute of Positive Education, a volunteer organization that sponsored African centered community programs: training, reviving African traditions, and popularizing the vegetarian diet and African names among black people. This is when I was given and accepted the African name of Milele (steadfast and everlasting) Nuru (in the sunlight). The Institute also fostered two other institutions, Third World Press and New Concept Development Center. Third World Press is a black publishing company that has remained independent for over forty years; New Concept Development Center is an independent African-centered educational institution. Additionally, the Institute was a cadre of the Congress of African People under the leadership of Amiri Baraka. It was a neo-socialist organization that espoused a combination of Karenga's black nationalistic doctrine and socialism to further the organization and development of Black people.

It was at the Institute of Positive Education where I met and established lasting relationships with Don L. Lee (Haki Madhubuti), Safisha Madhubuti, Jewel Latimore (Johari Amini), Steve Cobb (Jabari Mahari), Jawanza Kunjufu, and other persons who continued to make significant contributions to the Black struggle in Chicago.

I became acquainted with Northeastern Illinois University's Communiversity in 1972. I began attending, studying, and participating in many of the programs from organizing forums, conferences, and field trips to hosting visitors and fundraising for African Liberation organizations, such as the African National Congress. It was at Communiversity where I met and developed lasting friendships with many people involved in the movement locally and nationally. Some of those people were: Jacob Carruthers, Anderson Thompson, Bobby Wright, Harold Pates, Bernetta Bush, and Lorenzo Martin. There were many, many others. As a result of my association with these people and others, I became fanatical about the struggles of black people and African liberation and involved myself in any and almost every program or organization that professed to be about building independent black institutions or nations.

In the early seventies a group of dynamic black professionals formed an activist organization called Catalyst. This was a closed organization unlike other organizations that served the Black movement. You had to be recruited to join and you were inducted into the organization in a secret ceremony. It served to sponsor programs, infiltrate established institutions such as the Young Men's Christian Association, and develop others to advocate for the interest of Black people. The Woodson-Delaney Educational Fund was one of the programs that were organized by Catalyst. I was recruited by Catalyst to serve on the Board of Directors of Woodson-Delany. In the Woodson-Delaney Educational Fund we raised money and gave scholarships to support the educational endeavors of deserving young black people. Imani Drew, former State Attorney General for Kankakee, Illinois, was one of the recipients.

I was also an active and passionate supporter of other organizations and programs from 1960-1975, such as Shule ya Watoto, Black Theater Groups (Kuumba Workshop and ETA), Ahrura Sherri Institute, Blyden School, and Camp Jianda (a camp that taught survival skills for the impending revolution and reinforced an African-centered education). I was also very supportive of our developing Black artists like Babatunde. Afro-centric jewelry was very popular and sold during most activities. Through these organizations, I established lasting relationships with people like Harold Charles (Hannibal Afrik), Val Gray-Ward, Francis Ward, and Yvonne Pearson (Sarudzayi). While I met Stokely Carmichael (Kwame Toure) and Bob Brown on several occasions, I did not become involved with SNCC or the All

African Peoples Revolutionary Party. Those occasions were mostly social.

I made my most significant contribution to the Chicago Black struggle after I obtained my master's degree at the University of Chicago. This was the time when many professionally trained individuals from such a prestigious educational institution would lose their choice of lucrative jobs in traditional institutions and corporate America. The choice of my discipline was Community Organizing within the School of Social Service Administration program at the University. This choice emanated from my innate commitment to serve the interest of my people. I sought and maintained gainful employment to be used for my people, by my people, with my people. I feel honored and blessed to have had the opportunity to do so.

The lesson and principle that I would like young people to learn from my development during the Black struggle in Chicago from 1960-1975 are: The Lesson is that there is the opportunity to serve the interest of our people irrespective of the conditions in which we are born and the circumstances (good, bad, or ugly) that surround our lives. The principle happens to be that of my chosen namesake, to become steadfast and everlasting in our commitment to serving the best interest of our race. Where there seems to be no opportunity to serve our people, create one. There can be no greater purpose to living life and no greater contribution to mankind in general and our people in particular than to improve the condition of life and living for Black people in generations to come. It is the legacy of our ancestors upon whose shoulders we stand, and they are truly the winds beneath our wings.

A Luta Continua!

COMING OF AGE: CIVIL RIGHTS MOVEMENT 1960-1975

Dwight McKee

In 1960 I was in fourth grade at the Arthur Dixon Elementary School in the Chicago district known as Chatham. Chatham was an all-Black community in the heart of the South Side. It was comprised of upper-middle class Blacks, west of South Park (now Martin Luther King Drive), between 79th and 87th Streets, and the more modest income Blacks, east of South Park. My parents, sister, Martita, newly born brother, Donnie, and I lived on the east side. It was my fourth year in Chicago, having come up from Memphis, Tennessee with my family. I was born in Memphis, a child of segregation, but living in Chicago was in many ways very similar to living in Memphis.

The biggest difference between Chicago and Memphis for me was seeing white people. In Memphis I saw few; in Chicago I saw almost none. In Memphis we would sometimes see white people when we rode the bus. And we *always* had to sit behind them. We would see them when we went downtown to the Malco Theater. We had to, of course, sit in the balcony. We would watch them in the Easter or Christmas parade going by on the excessively decorated floats, looking like refugees from *Gone With The Wind,* trying to hold on to a bygone era of plantation grandeur and King Cotton hype.

The West Side was a different world. Amazingly, most of us never went on the West Side. For some reason, there was an unspoken veil that separated the South Side from the West Side that few people crossed. Roosevelt Road was likened unto the 38th parallel in Korea, which you never crossed. Downtown and Riverview (an amusement park) were the demilitarized zones where West Side Negros and South Side Negroes could come together, though most never went to either.

When I returned to school in 1961, in the fifth grade, many things had changed. The schools were severely overcrowded. At Dixon, there were almost fifty of us in my classroom and the school had been divided into double shifts. Half of the students went to class from eight a.m. to twelve p.m. and went home, and the other half came in from twelve p.m. to four p.m. There was no lunch, but a four-hour class with fifty students and a fifteen-minute recess. For those kids who didn't have a parent at home, it meant that if you got out of school at twelve o'clock and if your parents got home a six p.m. the whole day was yours, unsupervised. Not only did this profoundly affect our academic development, it gave those that were so inclined a portal into a life of gangs and delinquency.

Jeff Fort was the Hannibal of my generation. Cunning and deadly, he possessed the military mind of Julius Caesar; brilliant and calculating, but in a cold, macho way. He was a combination of Fidel Castro and Lucky Luciano. He consolidated twenty-one other gangs under the umbrella of his own gang called the Blackstone Rangers. He set up a ruling council called "The Main 21". To counter the threat, David Barksdale and Larry Hoover organized the Devil's Disciples in Englewood. Only the Conservative Vice Lords on the West Side could function as rivals. Black Chicago had had a tradition of gangster culture as a carryover from the Policy Kings, but it was nothing like this. The city divided into war zones and between red lining, class division, and gang turfs. Even the Black community began to function with another degree of segregation. To top it off, the police organized a special task force called the Red Squad in order to control these groups, by targeting young Black males. The criterion of suspicion was to be young, Black, and male, so all of us qualified and were placed on the endangered species list.

By 1962, in order to relieve overcrowding, the Board of Education brought to many schools mobile classrooms, which were labeled "Willis Wagons" after the superintendent of schools, Benjamin Willis. They were mobile trailers; the same kind that the government used for disaster relief. Negroes, weary and violated, had finally had enough. Al Raby, a teacher activist, organized the Coordinating Council of Community Organizations (CCCO), a coalition of organizations that involved the Urban League, the National Association for the Advancement of Colored People (NAACP), the Woodlawn Organization (TWO), the Chicago Catholic Council, the American Friends and Service Committee, and Chatham-Avalon Park Community Council (CAPCC). The parents at Burnside School had staged a sit-in against the over-crowed conditions, and CAPCC filed a lawsuit against Chicago Public Schools (CPS). In 1961, the NAACP had issued a devastating report on segregation, but this was the first time that direct confrontation on a massive level had been initiated. Now the key player in CCCO, Raby kicked off a massive boycott of Chicago Public Schools. The students that were affected, were sent to what were called Freedom Schools at the local churches. There, volunteer teachers taught us Black history and concepts involving civil rights. For many of us, this was our first systematic exposure to both.

Al Raby, Bill Barry, and CCCO were turning up the heat on the city, and started leading demonstrations. Dr. King had sent Bernard La Fayette up from the Southern Christian Leadership Conference (SCLC) in order to organize on the West Side. As I moved into the eighth grade, the summer got hotter, with anger and disenchantment raising the social temperature. By the time I graduated in June, CCCO was having daily marches against school segregation.

In July, Dr. King toured Chicago, invited in by local activists like Rev. John Porter, Al Raby, Charlie Hayes, and Addie and Claude Wyatt from the labor movement. Things were hotter around the country as well. Lyndon B. Johnson escalated the war in Vietnam fought by an army, now disproportionately poor and Black, primarily because of a military draft that afforded white students the loophole luxury of student deferments. Because more of them were in higher educational institutions, they could better take advantage of those deferments, and not be required to enlist. The sweltering heat of the summer added to the tension. Riots in Los Angeles shut down the city of dreams. The whole country was a powder keg. President Johnson responded to the racial tension by declaring war on poverty. Dr. King used it to expand in to the north. More confident after victories in Birmingham and Selma, he decided to target Chicago and invited CCCO to form the Chicago Freedom Movement, sending movement strategist James Bevels to the West Side to organize.

Things were changing in my life as well. Now a freshman at Hirsch High School, it was a summer of increased gang violence. Herb Kent, a local disc jockey, tempered the tough aspect of gang life by adding a cultural dimension (Ivy League, gouster, and conservative) based on style of dress and social orientation. The Comprehensive Employment and Training Act (CETA) had a small jobs program for the youth, but decades of neglect, oppression, poverty and mis-education were taking its toll.

In January of 1966, Dr. King moved to the West Side of Chicago to bring attention to the slum conditions in housing. In February, Dr. King would organize the Chicago Chapter of Operation Breadbasket, which was the economic development arm of SCLC. He would put in charge of it a young charismatic leader Rev. Jesse Jackson, from Greenville, North Carolina. Jackson went to Chicago Theology Seminary to study under Paul Tillich, considered by many to be the leading liberal Theologian of his time.

Jackson, along with another young seminary student, Henry Hardy, attracted by the charismatic leadership of Reverend Clay Evans, decided to make their home base Fellowship M.B. Church. Jackson would become the youth pastor, and Hardy an associate pastor. Dr. King could not have made the move soon enough. Nationally, his leadership was being challenged, and the effectiveness of the tactics of nonviolence were being questioned. The assassination of Malcolm X in New York, and the emergence of Stokely Carmichael had inflamed a new wave of militancy and cries of Black Power from a new generation. To some, the slogans "Freedom Now" and "We Shall Overcome" began to sound reactionary and antiquated. Dr. King and Stokely Carmichael of Student Nonviolent Coordinating Committee (SNCC) wrestled for the soul of the movement in Mississippi, marching against fear after James Meredith got shot, while trying to integrate the University of Mississippi.

Civil unrest was on the rise, and Pan-Africanism and African Nationalism redefined the Negro self-concept from "If you're brown, stick around" to "Be Black and proud". The fear that this new assertion of Black defiance would alienate white allies that were important to the Civil Rights Movement was unsettling to Dr. King.

Dr. King countered by focusing on Chicago. By July he held a mass rally in Soldier's Field, and announced that he would lead demonstrations through the lily white area of Gage Park. The marches would focus on open housing and discrimination. Dr. King was totally unprepared for what he would encounter. During the march, angry whites who had cheered Ernie Banks, Billy Williams, and Gale Sayers, now cursed him and hurled stones and bricks, striking him in the head. Lucky to escape with his life, Dr. King said that he had never in his thirty-six years seen such hatred and venom. Not in Mississippi, not in Georgia, not even in Alabama where his house had been bombed. Chicago was the most venomous experience he had ever had, and he was shocked by the hatred. If he didn't know, he should have asked somebody. We would have told him! Dr. King called a truce, declaring the Chicago Freedom Movement over, and got out of town. Mayor Daley had a press conference, and announced that an agreement had been reached, and project Good Neighbor was born. We were "good neighbors" as long as we stayed in our part of town. Bob Lucas, in protest, organized demonstrations in Cicero, once headquarters of Al Capone and his crowd.

In April 1967, Dr. King was the guest speaker at the Arie Crown Theater for Willa Saunders Jones' Passion play, an all-Black rendition of the last days of Christ. It was an uplifting and intense charge to a life of social justice and spiritual relevance. It was the only time that I heard Dr. King live. Little did we know that it would also be Dr. King's last days.

My pastor, Reverend Clay Evans, now a mentor and father figure to Rev. Jackson, used the church as a base for Operation Breadbasket, assigning his members to become the axis around which Jackson could build a wheel. Lucille Conway, Billy Jones, Delores Scott, Royal "Mickey" Warren, and Freddie Young, all Fellowship staff, took on the responsibility of administration and music for Breadbasket. A few years earlier when Dr. King had come to town to meet with some Negro preachers, they pulled a gun on him and forced him out of the meeting, afraid that it would impair their cozy and beneficial relationship with Mayor Daley. Dr. Joseph Jackson, president of the National Baptist Convention, and Pastor of Olivet, the largest church in America at the time, had run Dr. King out of the National Baptist Convention, some say at the behest of the race-hating J. Edgar Hoover and the FBI. Now Rev. Clay Evans was using his church as the fulcrum of the Chicago Civil Rights Movement. It was a courageous and costly decision. Daley would repay him by blocking Evans' dream of building a new church.

At Fenger, I had formalized my demonstrations into a student group called SOUL (Student Organization for Unification and Liberation). There was now a white backlash against our activities at Fenger, particularly when we forced them to remove the mural and to hire more Black staff, including an assistant principal. We also started an Afro American Club. There had been some beatings, a few riots, and I had even been sent to the hospital because it was thought that someone had put glass in my food. The administration said they could not guarantee my safety, and had me meet with a psychologist to find out my "real problem," after they offered me a sell-out type of deal that I refused to accept. My sister, Martita, who had also gone to Fenger, now very concerned, introduced me to Jackie Jackson (the wife of Rev. Jesse Jackson), who encouraged me to bring my activities inside the structure of the movement. The move would bring discipline and historical context to what I was doing with SOUL, and would also give me cover. I brought some of my students to Breadbasket, then meeting on Saturday mornings in a community forum.

Breadbasket was restructured to deal with broader based community issues. Now divided into auxiliaries, everything from a teachers division headed by Harold "Hannibal" Charles, dealing with education, to a health division headed by Dr. Andrew Thomas, focusing on health issues, the organization used its Saturday morning forum to address almost every issue that affected the Chicago Black community. Jackson put on a dashiki and grew an afro to appeal to a more nationalist crowd enamored with the rhetoric of H. Rap Brown and Stokely Carmichael, now Kwame Toure. Ideology was now an issue. Everyone was trying to choose the philosophic frame work in which he or she would operate. Cultural nationalism, Pan-Africanism, Afro Centricity, Maoist, Communism, Marxism, Islam, Black Capitalism, Liberation Theology—everyone was trying to find a theoretical launching pad. Some wanted to drop all labels and become simply patriotic Americans. The pursuit of freedom became an esoteric as well as civil pursuit. Camps lined up as people made choices.

At Fenger, I was just trying to survive. In November of 1968, I was arrested for a sit-in in the auditorium and put in jail. Ed Riddick and Charles Bevel, brother of movement strategist James Bevel, bailed me out. I was suspended from school until January of 1969, long enough to prevent me from graduating in June. Some of the most militant students responded by setting fires to the office and the lunchroom. I would be barred from the graduation ceremony, and transferred to Harlan High in order to graduate from summer school. But the good part was that we got all of our demands met, and the slavery mural on the wall came tumbling down.

Reverend Jackson targeted A & P (Atlantic and Pacific, the largest grocery store chain in the Midwest), forcing it to accommodate Black interests, bringing the powerful company to its knees. They were compelled to sign a covenant committing itself to hire Blacks in management positions and to do business with Black companies. That victory, plus some major victories on the political front (such as Carl Stokes becoming mayor of Cleveland, Ohio; Richard Hatcher in Gary, Indiana; and Kenneth Gibson in Newark, New Jersey), gave Blacks a new source of power. It was a profound experience watching people transform themselves in front of the whole world. "If you're Black, get back" gave way to "We're a Winner/Movin' on Up" by Curtis Mayfield and "Respect" by Aretha Franklin.

Even the gangs transformed their self-concepts. The Devil's Disciples added a community service dimension and adopted the six-pointed star in honor of their slain leader, David Barksdale. The Blackstone Rangers became the Black P. Stone Nation, and then the El Rukins. The Vice Lords, under Bobby Gore, created a job and vocational training program. Part of the gangs' change was rooted in social consciousness, but part of it was the need to compete with the Black Panther Party, led by Fred Hampton and Bobby Rush, and the Black Muslims—for the hearts and minds of young Blacks excited by the Panther's breakfast program, self-defense programs, and the Elijah Muhammad philosophy of "Do for Self." Rev. Jackson, convinced that he could redirect the energy of the gangs, reached out his hand and got his fingers bitten. White liberals, driven by a combination of guilt and misappropriated grace, invested huge sums of money into the gangs. W. Clement Stone gave a million dollars. President Nixon funneled in grant money. Even entertainers like Sammy Davis, Jr. and Oscar Brown, Jr. invested time and money. The new credibility gave the gang leaders an even greater sense of power and invincibility.

In the summer of 1969, we had the SCLC convention in Memphis in memory of Dr. King. Dr. Abernathy keynoted with a speech titled "I'm Not Lost. I Just Don't Know Where I Am." I was impressed. Rev. Jackson was disappointed. For the first time I started to notice a level of tension between Rev. Abernathy and Rev. Jackson. That summer, I went on staff full-time as the national youth director and traveled with Rev. Jackson as we moved to build a national organization. My role was to bring the Civil Rights Movement to my generation.

Now housed in our own building, the Capital Theater on 79th and Halsted, Operation Breadbasket was a national phenomenon anchored by Jesse Jackson, Calvin Morris, Attorney Tom Todd, Ed Riddick, and Willie Barrow. The organization was attracting thousands of members, volunteers, and visitors. On any given Saturday, any major Black personality in America—Bill Cosby, Flip Wilson, Aretha Franklin, Isaac Hayes, Jim Brown, or Roberta Flack—would stop by. Most Black stars had climbed the rough side of the mountain and felt obligated to give something back. We also had a full orchestra run by Ben Branch and Gene "Daddy G" Barge. Talent in the choir could compete with any talent on the world stage, and they toured to raise money in the tradition of the Fisk Jubilee Singers. My youth division was impacting not only the organization, but learning how to challenge the young people in their own churches, schools, and communities to a higher standard. Information, inspiration and speaking truth to power was the common goal of the young and the old.

In September 1969, I enrolled in Southeast Junior College, a small liberal arts college that shared a building with CVS High School on the South Side. The school revolved around debates on cultural nationalism and bid whist tournaments. By December 1, Cap Manuel, "Brother Ike," and a few other activists began to lead demonstrations to change the name of the school to Hampton Clark, in memory of our slain brothers. We closed the school and started negotiations with Oscar Shabbat, then Chancellor of City Colleges. The school reopened under the name Olive-Harvey, named after a young Black soldier named Milton Oliver III, who dove on top of a bomb in Vietnam to save his white comrades; and Carmel Harvey, a young white soldier also killed in the war. Under the circumstances, it was a legitimate compromise, but we maintained the appendix Olive Harvey-Hampton Clark College in the hood.

By then, Reverend Jackson and I were together nearly every day trying to turn Dr. King's dream of a national organization that could make an economic impact a reality. My responsibility as the national youth director of Breadbasket was trying to pull the next generation into a movement of civil, but nonviolent disobedience, and away from apathy on one hand, and violent confrontation on the other. The FBI had implemented its program of Counter Intelligence (COINTELPRO), and it was strategically and methodically liquidating the groups that they viewed as a military threat, including the Black Panthers, some Pan-African groups, and paramilitary and anti-war organizations.

In September, Reverend Evans and Reverend Jackson shipped me off to Trinity College in Deerfield, Illinois, an evangelical college that Reverend Evans was affiliated with. He had already sent some promising young people from Fellowship church, including two of his own children, Diane and Ralph. It was unlike any world that we had ever seen before. The school was conservative republican and vanilla white. It was the only school in the country to have a pro-Nixon march, and the year before, it had forced Dick Gregory to speak off campus. Some of the students had never seen Black people, and with no dancing or parties allowed, it was truly a culture shock.

The theme of the 1972 PUSH Black Expo was "Save the Children", a star-studded production that was turned into a movie. But the reality was that before we save the children, who was going to save us? The next line in Marvin Gaye's song was: "Panic is spreading, only God knows where we're headed." Marvin was right. Good thing God knew, because we certainly didn't. Battered, bruised, and bloodied, we didn't know who to be. A people who controlled no means of production or distribution, that lived in a land where their adversaries face was on the money; a place where their grandparent's grandparents were slaves, struggled to find a collective direction. Ideology gave way to survival. There was no clear strategy for our social progress. We could not decide whether to go inside the American system or remain outside and build our own institutions. Should we refine the white man's religion and generate a new Black Liberation theology; or should we reject the white man's religion and convert to Islam, Yoruba, Buddhism, or Judaism? Do we become revolutionary and unite with the third world, or do we become Black capitalists and go for the American dream? With no clear social theory, it became every man for himself.

The Black politicians, led by poet Amiri Baraka and Mayor Richard Hatcher, met in Gary, Indiana in a Black political convention, and pondered a third political party. Black Republicans put on their business suits and joined President Nixon's Black Capitalism program. Black Hebrews moved to Israel while Black Pan Africanists moved to Africa. Black Catholics went "charismatic," while many Black Protestants went evangelical. Some Blacks, in a spirit of reverse migration moved back south to the family farms. The Black farmers, squeezed by the racist lending practices of the Department of Agriculture, were losing millions of acres of land, and many had no home left to go back to.

Jesse tried the political route. Guided by political strategists Leon Davis and Alice Tregay, Jesse, along with independent Chicago alderman William Singer, led a charge to challenge the legitimacy of Mayor Richard J. Daley's selection process at the 1972 Democratic National Convention. For years, delegates had been selected by Mayor Daley behind closed doors, with back slaps, cigars, and handshakes. In 1964, Fannie Lou Hamer had challenged the process of selection in Atlantic City, New Jersey with her Mississippi Freedom Party. In 1968, Mayor Daley had dominated and traumatized the Democratic National Convention in Chicago. Four years later in Miami, the legitimacy of his selection process was formally being challenged before the Rules Committee. Daley lost. His delegation was unseated and replaced by the Jackson/Singer delegation. This opened up the selection process in the Democratic Party, and gave Blacks and women a voice in the party that they never before had. It was a devastating blow to Mayor Daley, and a major victory for Jackson and Singer. It was a victory out of a tradition of Black and Jewish coalitions that had stretched through the life of the Civil Rights Movement. It was a coalition that was coming apart at the seams.

In that same year of 1972, I received a scholarship from the family of Whitney Young, presented by his sister, Dr. Anita Boswell. The year before, Whitney Young had died in Africa while attending the Pan-African conferences. Now with "The Big Three," King, Wilkins, and Young gone from the national scene, a leadership void was created. Reverend Jackson, now national and bridging generations, emerged to fill that void. With chapters in the major urban areas, he focused on "Silver" rights and economic parity, forcing white companies and municipalities to do business with Black companies.

In June 1973, my senior year, I left Trinity College to help disc jockey Cecil Hale restructure the National Association of Television and Radio Artists (NATRA). This was the trade group for all Afro-Americans who were involved in the entertainment industry. Black music by then was setting the standard for the world and was a billion dollar industry. It was basically self-contained and run by a few major Black controlled music companies like Stax, Motown, Philly International, Chi-Town, V-Jay, and T-Neck. Black messages were transported by the music, and Black images transmitted by Soul Train were replacing the mundane images of American Bandstand as the face of American culture. I had helped Cecil Hale win the election as president of NATRA, and we thought that it would be a wonderful opportunity to add a political dimension to the entertainment world. The decision to leave college and focus on NATRA created a breech between Reverend Jackson and myself that never quite resolved. It was not the only unresolved issue in the movement.

Only equals can negotiate, and integration was a great triumph for white America. But for us, it may have been a net loss, coming at the expense of the sacrifice of many Black traditions and Black institutions. And as the ultimate slap in the face, the state even took over policy (the numbers racket), and changed its name to the lottery. In the summer of 1975, at the NATRA convention in Baltimore, I sat with a young Al Sharpton in the suite of James Brown, and we pondered the future of Black America. Elijah Muhammad had just died, and we wondered if we would ever be able to "do for self," or if we would forever be unequally yoked to a system that would forever regard us as second-class citizens and inferior human beings. We also pondered the profundity of the title of Dr. King's last book, *Where Do We Go From Here; A Community or Chaos.*

EVERYTHING MUST CHANGE

Runako Jahi

The evolution of Black social consciousness that took place during the Black arts movement of the sixties truly laid the groundwork for where Black art is today. Its strengths have influenced all media—from literature, cinema, theater, music, painting to dance. There was a great passion for being Black. Such a love was a great appreciation and respect for heritage. It was very exciting watching everyone celebrate Africentric-ness. It manifested itself in clothing, music, jewelry, art, poetry, and dance. Suddenly, conscious-minded Black folk allowed *color* to seep in. It was hip to be Black. My mother even gave up straightened hair and wigs! Those days are now bronzed in memory. Archival treasures, the great yesterday.

The sixties were a great period of discovery for me. I remember being a teenager in the then integrated Austin High School on Chicago's West Side. I became fascinated with the theater, but during that time all the plays in school were white and I could never get a role. I laugh at it now as I remember auditioning for *You Can't Take it With You,* written by George S. Kaufman and Moss Hart. In 1968 that was a real dilemma for a Black student who was interested in a theater career. It was as though we did not exist. There were certainly plays written by Black playwrights during that time, works by Amiri Baraka (the LeRoi Jones), Ossie Davis, and Lorraine Hansberry amongst them. For some reason the teachers did not feel that our works were appropriate or legitimate theater for that matter. They certainly did not view our plays as classic, something to be taught in schools. At that young age I was devastated, blatantly aware that as a Black student interested in acting and who did not want to carry a tray, there were no roles for me of any merit. However, if you could sing or dribble a basketball, you were in! Neither singing nor sports were my thing, so stage work consisted of emceeing school talent shows because the teachers felt I had a good speaking voice and a charismatic personality. I was not deterred by them. They did not break my spirit. I always believed in the power of having patience. However, it did bother me a great deal. It provoked me to start protesting. I had a best friend in school who later became a Black Panther. I had protest signs for just about everything, including the Vietnam War, during a rally atop the base of the newly unveiled Picasso sculpture in

Chicago's Loop. I had a cousin who was killed in the war and I did not understand how we could be drafted to fight for a country that did not respect us, that did not allow us to even walk through certain neighborhoods without being harassed or attacked with baseball bats.

Needless to say, at Austin High School I found my niche in the art department. There, I sketched and painted pictures in my art class after lunch. Even then I found myself confronted with racism. One afternoon my art teacher, Miss Cohen, was demonstrating a technique and said to us, "Let's render this one in white and black." That struck me. "White and black?" I asked respectfully. She retorted, "Yes, that's what I said." I asked her, "But Miss Cohen, isn't it black and white? Like in black and white televisions, black and white movies, black and white pictures?" I remember her simply staring at me without answering, without saying a word, as though I had never said anything.

My grandfather was a race man. I remember him giving me a book for my birthday one November called *Great Negroes Past and Present*. In this book there were remarkable Black people who achieved greatness in various fields. This inspired me! Granddad told me that I should be proud of being a Negro and to fully embrace my heritage. I listened to him say that, but I was not sure I believed it because I seldom saw us on television, with exception of maybe on Ed Sullivan or some other variety show.

I remember my mother having a copy of *Jet* magazine. In it was that horrific photo of Emmitt Till. One look at that picture terrified me. That wasn't a Hollywood movie photo. It was very real. It really *happened*. I used to avoid even looking at the cover of that magazine because I knew what was inside of it. My mother explained that he was murdered because they said he was "whistling at a white girl." Here I was at an integrated high school, with white girls hitting on me, and that certainly put an end to that! No white girls! I didn't want to meet the same fate as Emmitt Till. My mother also explained to me that Billie Holiday's song "Strange Fruit" was definitely not about rotten apples and oranges, but about "Black bodies swinging in the Southern breeze."

When Martin Luther King, Jr. was assassinated in1968, I remember the rioting in the streets and the aftermath, the destruction of neighborhoods and businesses. It was shocking. I remember getting off the L and having to walk amongst hostile white people to get to school, praying that I would not have to stay late after school and perhaps never make it home. I remember how everything was divided. Everything was black and white. To stay on the safe side, it was best to stay with your own people. In the school cafeteria, there was the Black section and the white section. I remember the Mexicans and Puerto Ricans stayed in the Black section, too.

Through it all, during this tumultuous but exciting time, I began to really embrace my heritage and truly feel what my grandfather was trying to tell me. I realized that Black was beautiful, Black was *hip,* Black was *creative* and *alive*! We had strong, proud hair and chocolate skin; we had our own way of speaking and walking and dancing! We wore bright colors and had exotic looks. We were what's going on! I have always appreciated the Blackness of me.

My mother was a big fan of Sidney Poitier. Every Poitier picture that ever came out, she wanted me to see: *To Sir with Love, A Patch of Blue, The Long Ships, Guess Who's Coming to Dinner*—I saw them all. Poitier represented the positive Black man: noble, intelligent, the good Negro. I think she was concerned about me seeing Black actors who were not in demeaning roles. One film she introduced me to resonates with me to this day. On her small black and white television I sat up with her one night and we watched *Black Orpheus* together. I was enthralled with the characters, the music, the story, the beauty of Brazil and Mardi Gras! Today, I still find *Black Orpheus* a hauntingly beautiful film. And to think, my own mother brought this bit of magic into my life.

Oscar Brown, Jr. Wow. In my youth *nobody* was cooler than Oscar Brown, Jr. He wrote plays and sang songs about the people I could relate to: the watermelon man, the rag man, the community folks—incredible. I'd collect all of his articles and pictures and keep them in a folder. I had newspaper clippings from *Slave Story, Opportunity Please Knock, Mr. Kicks*—plus his press photos for club gigs. I was a fan! I loved Oscar because he was brilliant and talented and political and always spoke on behalf of the social liberation of Black people. He was a great inspiration for me. When I grew up I wanted to be just like him. I wanted to create art that reflected our community, as we coexist in this tapestry of many cultures called the United States of America. Oscar told his stories through the venues of music and musical theater. He was thoroughly non-apologetic about his ideas, his truth, his art, and refused to compromise his integrity. How can you not love and admire someone with convictions as strong as his?

Nina Simone is another artist I put on a pedestal. She was a storyteller like Billie Holiday, but had more of the contemporary angst of the times. Billie's wounded sound was universal in its appeal; the lovelorn ballads, the heartache, the grim life experiences clouded her work in ways that affected everyone who listened. Nina Simone's songs spoke directly to Black people: "Four Women" and "Mississippi Goddam" are quintessential examples of where she came from. Nina did not coax, nor seduce—she smacked you in the face with her declarations of rage and freedom. She challenged audiences. Billie's version of "Love Me or Leave Me" reasoned with the listener, almost begging not to be abandoned. Nina's version had a finite quality. Hers said to listeners, "Go on. I will live without you." She was deliciously Black. Everything about her resonated Blackness. Her appearance was the natural look of Africa. She was bold and articulate, what Gwendolyn Brooks would refer to in a poem as "the real thing."

The sixties were also a great time for Black poetry. Gwendolyn Brooks, Haki Madhubuti, Carolyn Rogers and many other great voices raged and shouted and screamed of injustices, love, politics, racism, etc. up front and center, directly in your face. It was the Black Power movement and it was beautiful. Yet I often heard people say to me, "So, you're into that Black stuff, huh?" Black stuff? This was coming from Black people. How can you be Black and *not* be into that "Black stuff?"

Diana Sands was another artist who I loved. There she was with this attitude. I wouldn't call her an angry Black woman so much as a no-nonsense one. Her performances in films like *A Raisin in the Sun, Willie Dynamite, The Landlord*, and *Georgia. Georgia* all depicted women with flaws who were not victims and knew how to navigate through whatever situations they encountered. They were beautifully human characters who were real. With a sometimes icy exterior, her women always bore a vulnerability, a softness, just below the surface of all the toughness. Because of the truth she brought to her work, we remember her name today. Diana Sands was one of the great icons of the sixties.

This period was great for soul music. James Brown wailing "Say it Loud! I'm Black and I'm Proud," Aretha Franklin's demand of "Respect" to the Motown empire with Berry Gordy bringing the world Marvin Gaye, Diana Ross and the Supremes, Stevie Wonder, The Temptations, Martha and the Vandellas, Mary Wells, Tami Tarrell, Smokey Robinson and the Miracles, and Junior Walker and the All-Stars were all legendary acts that continue to inspire the entertainers of today. Hip hop also benefited from those early voices. Perhaps the strongest influence was the voice of Gil Scott-Heron. He once said, "The Revolution Will Not be Televised," but the election of President Barack Obama has clearly changed that.

I appreciated Melvin Van Peebles in an Oscar Brown, Jr. kind of way. They were different in approach, but they told the same story: the stories of Black communities. Oscar's community was clearly Chicago. Melvin Van Peebles' community was New York City (though he was, in fact, born in Chicago). "Ain't Supposed to Die a Natural Death" was a brilliant work. It was ugly yet lyrically beautiful in its sad, provocative realities, its tender poetry of souls connecting and disconnecting, fascinating from top to bottom, ending with a blazing crescendo, "I put a CURSE on you!" That piece depicted all of the pathos that came out of the sixties. The play opened up on Broadway in 1971 and was a Tony-nominated triumph. Melvin Van Peebles is acclaimed for making *Sweet Sweetback's Badass Song,* a controversial, groundbreaking film that not only made ten million dollars in national release, but was also significant in heralding a new wave of Black American films. To this end, Black faces began to rise up on movie screens across the nation, Black directors were visible, Black writers were writing screenplays and found work in television. History was being made.

The Black arts movement of the sixties had a profound effect on me in my choice of work as an artist and mentor. In 1972 I was introduced to ETA Creative Arts Foundation by Oscar Brown, Jr. and my life was no longer the same. At ETA everything was about Black culture. I studied drama with Okoro Harold Johnson and was introduced to the life of Malcolm X. Before ETA all I knew about Malcolm was the mean-spirited, false journalism of newspaper articles and television news segments. My first show was "El Hajj Malik," a musical about the life of Malcolm X. In my pursuit of knowledge and the construction of my character, I visited the Chicago Public Library. I read articles, watched documentary footage, and purchased albums of his speeches. It was an amazing journey. To this day I appreciate the things I learned from Okoro Harold Johnson. He taught me that it was important to "do the best work that you can do and not put emphasis on being a star—that we should all strive to be dynamic artists." That resonated with me because I had met many people whose primary interest was just to be a star, to make it big, to go to Hollywood or Broadway. There is nothing wrong with that if that is what you want. But it is important to "bring something of substance to one's creativity." It is important to have one's talent developed before you embark upon the yellow brick road of fame and fortune.

When I met president, cofounder and producer, Abena Joan Brown, I believed in the philosophy of ETA Creative Arts Foundation, of the importance of "telling our stories in the first voice." Our stories are important to tell and we have many of them in the Diaspora. Abena's steadfast persistence and drive, along with a committed board of directors and a loyal staff, has been instrumental in ETA's presence as one of the nation's leading cultural arts institutions. It has been an exhilarating journey. The ETA model grew out of the Black arts movement. Through this glorious venture came Useni Eugene Perkins, Dr. Margaret Burroughs, Etta Moten Barnett, Woodie King, Jr., Ron Milner, Haki Madhubuti, Bea Winde; my peers, Darryl Goodman, Anthony Llorens, Pemon Rami, Dee Alexander, Kemati J. Porter, Kevin McIlvaine, as well as Angela Jackson, Paul Carter Harrison, Vantile Whitfield, Julian Swain, Rob Penny, Don Evans, Jaye Stewart, Afaa Michael Weaver, Charles Michael Moore, and a host of brilliant talents who have contributed to the success of the ETA Creative Arts Foundation. This institution has allowed me to grow into the artist and individual that I am today. I am most grateful for that opportunity. When one is young, there is a crossroad. One must decide which path to take. I believe I chose the right one.

If the Black arts movement of the sixties had not occurred at the time that it did, many Black institutions, artists and the like would probably not have been. It takes a strong movement to make a difference, to create a paradigm. We all benefited from it and were inspired by it. It was a catalyst for change, for awakening, to be bold and present.

Today, there seems to be a kind of cultural backlash. Artists do not seem very committed to the aesthetics of Blackness in their pursuits of not only their images, but of the content of their work. Even during the Black arts movement there were those who appeared to shun their Blackness, but they were cognizant of the fact that it existed. Saddest of all is the message to the people. The current messages that we hear in contemporary music are mostly degrading to women and children and frequently depict an astonishing lack of cultural pride by constantly portraying deviant role models. These images, unfortunately, are embraced and win the highest accolades in their fields. Today the social emphasis appears to be primarily about making money. Very few people in positions to make a difference seem to care to do so.

There is a new generation of strong young Black voices in the theater. One of those belongs to Tarrell McCraney, who like a bolt of lightning, is thrilling audiences across the nation with his trio of searing, provocative "Brother/Sister Plays." The ball is rolling again and more and more writers are speaking for a contemporary generation. The work, like almost everything that occurs now, is more raw and blatant, with liberal usage of the word "nigger." There is power in storytelling and every artist is entitled to tell his or her story in their own unique way. At this very minute the seeds of a new movement are growing. After all, like the song says, "Everything Must Change."

SECTION SIX

EPILOGUE

" In order for us to survive and transcend the terrible days ahead of us, the country will have to turn and take me in its arms. Now, this may sound mystical , but at bottom that is what has got to happen, because it is not a matter of giving me this or that it is not yours to give me. Let us be clear about that. It is not a question of whether they are going to give me my freedom. I am going to take my freedom."

The Cross of Redemption
UncollectedWritings
by James Baldwin

Margaret Goss Burroughs

The term renaissance when attributed to some people is often overstated and becomes a hallowed cliché. Renaissance as defined by Webster Dictionary states "the great revival of art, literature and learning." When we apply this term to Dr. Margaret G. Burroughs we can be assured that is it being properly used. As an artist of many genres; lithograph, oil paintings, sculpture, literature, and dramatist, she was the Cultural Mother to many artists of the Chicago's Black Arts Movement. She was also an institution builder and co-founded the Du Sable Museum of African American History and was one of the principle organizers of the South Side Community Art Center.

Her achievements as an artist were recognized by other nationally known artists and scholars. She became a friend of Paul Robeson, Langston Hughes, Arna Bontemps, Margaret Walker, Elizabeth Catlett, Eta Moten Barnett, Katherine Dunham, Gwendolyn Brooks, Dudley Randall and W. E. B. DuBois. Dr. Burroughs was also a passionate supporter of the incarcerated and made many visits to the prisons to teach art and history. Her iconic poem, What Shall I Tell My Children Who Are Black , has gained international recognition as a poem to educate and inspire Black children. Indeed, Dr. Burroughs' contributions to Chicago's Black Struggle are immeasurable and will be forever enshrined in our Ancestral Garden of Black Liberation.

Useni Eugene Perkins

WHAT WILL YOUR LEGACY BE?

Margaret G. Burroughs

Do you know what the word "Legacy" means? Well, if you don't know, let me tell you what the dictionary says it means.

Legacy: property or money left to someone by a will; something handed down from those who have gone before; a legacy of honor, our legacy, of freedom.

In this poem I'm not referring to material things like property or money, either of honor or of freedom. I am referring to what a person has done with this life that God has given to him or her.

Yes, I want to know what will your legacy be? This is a question that I would like to put to each and every one of you.

What will your legacy be?
When you have finally cast off these mortal coils?
When you have crossed the great divide?
What will your legacy be?
When you can no longer run life's race.
When you no longer have a place; when you have at last completed the circle round and when an escape is no longer to be found.
What will your legacy be?
When you walk into the unknown all by yourself and alone,
What will your legacy be?
Stop for a moment and listen to me and answer this question if you can.
What will your legacy be?
When you must cross that great divide into an area from which none can hide. When you, alone, with no one by your side with no friend to lead you or to hold your hand?
What will your legacy be?
What deeds have you done in your lifetime which will be left for you to be remembered by?
Will it be just a gray decaying tombstone standing alone in a cemetery or will it be, as

it should be some act, some service or some deed that will insure that you will be remembered on and into the eternity of life's game?
I ask you. What will your legacy be?
Will it be the fact that you helped somebody along the way, during the time while you were here on earth?
What will your legacy be?
Will it be similar to the legacies left to our generation by people like Harriet Tubman, Sojourner Truth, Frederick Douglass, John Brown, Ida B. Wells, Mary Bethune and so many others who made of their lives a bridge for us to cross over on and whose lives were an inspiration for us of today to make of our lives bridges for future generations to cross over on?
What will your legacy be?
Legacy! Legacy!

Let us stop for a moment and recall some of our people who left their lives as legacies to us and who always will be honored and remembered.

They were people like:

Harriet Tubman's legacy was the work that she did on the underground railroad in which she brought hundreds of our ancestors out of the bonds of slavery. Frederick Douglass's legacy was the work that he did to help abolish slavery. Ida B. Wells's legacy was the fact that she fought against the evil of black men being lynched in this country. Mary McLeod Bethune's legacy was that she worked for the education of our youth by starting on faith a small school, which grew to be a great university. Dr. Martin Luther King, Jr.'s legacy was that he devoted his life to fighting for full equality for our people. Sojourner Truth's legacy was her fight for the liberation of and full equality for all women in our country. John Brown's legacy was that he sacrificed his life for an end to slavery and for the freedom of our people. Bessie Coleman's legacy was that she became the first woman in America, black or white, to acquire a pilot's license. Paul Robeson's legacy was that he was a renaissance man. He was a concert and folk singer, an athlete, linguist, and he fought for the liberation of all oppressed people all over the world. Poets Langston Hughes and Margaret Walker's legacies were the many inspirational poems that they wrote, which expressed the soul of our people. Dr. W.E.B. DuBois's legacy was his life-long struggle for the liberation of our people in his actions, speeches and writings. Dr. Carter G. Woodson's legacy was that he brought attention to the numerous and significant contributions of people of Africa and African descent to the world. Booker T. Washington's legacy was the fact he worked for the education of our people when he founded and opened Tuskegee Institute in Alabama. George Washington Carver's legacy was his significant and important accomplishments in the field of science. Jean Baptiste Pointe DuSable's legacy was the fact he, a black man, was the first person to settle in the area that became Chicago and grew into a great trading center from the little post that DuSable of African blood started over 100 years ago. Last but not least, Charles Gordon Burroughs's legacy was the first black history museum in the world, which he, as co-founder, started in his living room at 3806 South Michigan Avenue in Chicago. This act inspired many who were interested in the recognition and preservation of black history to the point that today there are over 100 black history museums in our country.

There are many, many others who were like these and left, through their contributions in their lifetime, their legacies as bridges for us to cross over on. So, I ask you, what will you leave as your legacy, as a bridge for those now and those coming on to cross over on? What will your legacy be?

I ask you, what will your legacy be? Do you know? Have you thought about it? Do you have an answer? What will you leave as your legacy? If you have no answer at this point, you cannot say, hearken! Listen to me! This is the moment. This is the prime moment for you to think and to get to work and identify what you will leave as your legacy for you to be remembered by. You are here. You are still here, alive and quick, and you have time. You have time on your side. You have time to begin even now, so get busy and do something to help somebody improve the conditions of life for people now and for those who come after. To build institutions to educate and broaden the minds for people now and for those who came after and to make your life a contribution, that will be your legacy. Do this and your name will be remembered from now on and into eternity.

What will your legacy be? Hopefully, it will not be just a gray and decaying tombstone.

Think now! Act now! To insure that your legacy will be a positive contribution to humanity and you will be remembered, yes, you will be remembered on and on and into eternity as God wills it.

What will your legacy be?

RISE OF THE PHOENIX

EPILOGUE

Bennett Johnson, Jr.

The modern Civil Rights Movement was resurrected in 1954 with the horrendous murder of a fourteen year old Chicago boy in Mississippi. The photograph of his mutilated body was taken by Lester Davis, a leader in the Chicago Teachers' Union. The picture of the corpse of Emmett Till was first displayed on the front page of the news magazine, "American Negro", which was published by Gus Savage. Johnson Publishing Company's Jet Magazine initially rejected the photo; however, after the huge public interest and the record sales by its competitor, the photo made the front page of *Jet*.

A local community activist, Arlene Brigham (who was a friend of Mamie Till), Emmett's mother, had urged Mrs. Till to have an open casket funeral service in Chicago. The funeral drew thousands of Black people and the line to view the body was more than three blocks long. The story received national attention in large part because of the publicity, but also due to the role of Dr. T.R.M. Howard, who went with Mamie Till to hundreds of cities, in order to tell the story of her son, Emmett.

Rosa Parks, a board member of the NAACP, was motivated not to move to the back of the bus in Montgomery, Alabama in large part because of this evil event. The organizing of the Montgomery bus boycott began with E.D. Nixon, President of the Montgomery NAACP and a member of the Brotherhood of Sleeping Car Porters. Two leaders emerged from the boycott, Rev. Ralph Abernathy and Rev. Martin Luther King. The Civil Rights Movement emerged from these two incidents.

One must understand that a "movement" is not like a campaign. In some churches you have fundraising campaigns to raise funds to build an addition to the church. There are political campaigns which are well organized and planned to elect an individual to public office. Military campaigns are well planned and executed in order to achieve control of a section of land or to conquer an enemy. A movement is usually not well organized. The movement is characterized by a poorly structured organization and a charismatic leader who has limited control over the people in the movement. The fact that the movement is made up of individuals and groups with a common goal, is what makes it a movement. The common goal of the Civil Rights Movement was "Freedom Now." Many of the people in the Movement defined freedom differently. The stories and essays in this book reveal the various tactics which were used to make a difference.

The cumulative effect of the Movement was a change in the socio-political conditions in the United States of America. The white only signs have disappeared. Black people vote in those Southern states which used intimidation, violence and various techniques to prevent them from voting. Today the Mayor of Columbia, South Carolina is African American as well as the Mayor of Selma, Alabama, James Perkins. There are thousands of public officials who have been elected to public office in those states that outlawed registration and voting by Black people.

The Movement had different characteristics in the North because segregation was not legal. There were no signs, but there traditions and practices. The legal struggles that were won had to do with housing discrimination and excusive from some restaurants and public places. The landmark case of Hansberry v. Lee in 1948 was critical in the end of restrictive covenants that limited the ownership of homes in certain areas. The 1954 Brown v. the Board of Education case in the U.S. Supreme Court began the end of legal school segregation. This was the same year that witnessed the murder of Emmett Till and beginning of the Montgomery Bus Boycott. Six years later in 1960, the NAACP launched the March on Conventions Movement. The goal of the demonstrations was to demand a Civil Rights plank in the platform of both parties. The National Republican Convention was held in Chicago at the International Amphitheater. A march was held and all of the leaders of the national civil rights group were together for the first time: Roy Wilkins of the NAACP; A. Philip Randolph of the Brotherhood of Sleeping Car Porters; Dr. Martin Luther King of the Southern Christian Leadership Conference; Whitney Young of the National Urban League; James Farmer of the Congress on Racial Equality. This was the dress rehearsal for the 1963 March on Washington.

There are many stories about the Movement. There were thousands of people who were in the Movement. Each person was a critical part of the giant juggernaut, the Civil Rights Movement. This volume chronicles some of these stories. Some readers may complain by asking where is the victory over racism and repression of Black citizens, Native American people, the people of Hispanic lineage, Asian Americans and other ethnic minorities. The struggle continues, but the essence of that struggle for Freedom Now is in itself victory.

AN INTERPRETIVE CHRONOLOGY OF SOME ACTIVITIES THAT TOOK PLACE DURING CHICAGO'S BLACK STRUGGLE FROM 1960-1975

1960

- In an unprecedented effort to challenge the Democratic and Republican Parties to approve a progressive Civil Rights Plank, national and local civil rights leaders met in Chicago to plan a march on the Republican National Convention, which was to be held at Chicago's International Amphitheater. This march was to follow a similar march held six days earlier in Los Angeles at the Democratic National Convention. The main organizers of this march were A. Phillip Randolph, his assistant Bayard Rustin and several Black leaders from Chicago which included Dempsey Travis, Timuel D. Black, Bennett Johnson and Diane Nash. On July 25th the march took place led by Randolph, Roy Wilkens, Whitney Young, Dr. Martin Luther King Jr., and other prominent civil rights leaders. By all accounts, this was the largest civil rights march in the history of Chicago.

- On August 29th, members from the NAACP Youth Council went to challenge the covert discrimination policy at Rainbow Beach. For decades this policy had been used by whites to intimidate Blacks from using this scenic beach located at 75th Street. Although their challenge was rebuffed by hundreds of angry whites, the group, with other Black activists, continued to challenge this policy on a daily basis until it was discontinued several months later.

- Chicago Committee of Racial Equality (CORE): a long-standing civil rights group in Chicago was one of many organizations to address the Chicago Public Schools pending double shift schedule and proposed mobile units, known as Willis Wagons, after its school superintendent, Benjamin C. Willis. These activities were to be implemented to keep Black students in predominantly Black schools.

- The South Side Art Center opened an important federal arts program (FAP) in the Bronzeville community. It quickly became a major cultural institution and resource to the Black Chicago Renaissance. Margaret Burroughs was one of the principle founders.

1961

- The Coordinating Council of Community Organizations (CCCO), comprised of leaders from many community organizations and religious institutions, became a formidable coalition to address school reform and other problems relevant to the Black community. However, none of the six Black aldermen, known as the "Silent Six," participated or supported its activities. Charles Davis, secretary of the Chicago Chapter of the NAACP, Ed Berry, president of the Chicago Urban League and the League of Negro Voters, were among its founders. Al Raby, an activist and school teacher, became its first spokesperson.

- The Woodlawn Organization, (TWO) was organized by Saul Alinsky, Rev. Arthur Brazier, Squire Lance, Ed Chambers and Nicholas von Hoffman to address the social problems in the Woodlawn community.

- On March 6th, TWO mobilized over 1,000 residents of Woodlawn to march down 63rd Street to protest credit abuses by local merchants.

- On August 26th, TWO organized 2,500 residents to take forty buses downtown for voter registration.

- Rev. Archibald Hargraves founded the West Side Organization (WSO) to address the myriad of problems that festered on Chicago's West Side. Chester Robinson was its director and William Darden, his assistant.

- DuSable Museum (originally called the Ebony Museum) received its charter on October 21st as the first community-based African American Museum in America. Its principle founders were Dr. Margaret G. Burroughs, Charlie Burroughs, Gerald N. Lew, Ralph Turner, Marian Hadley and Eugene Fieldman.

1962

- On May 18th, CCCO and other civil rights and community organizations plan its first city-wide school boycott to protest the "Willis Wagons." In doing so, they called for Freedom Schools to accommodate students during the boycott. The first school boycott took place at Carnegie School. Approximately 224,770 students did not attend school and the boycott was considered to be a success.

- On June 2nd, Al Raby and Dick Gregory were arrested for refusing to surrender their 24-hour vigil at the Board of Education.

- In their determination to meet with Mayor Daley, regarding Chicago's segregated school system, the Federation of Civil Rights Organization led hundreds of marchers to City Hall on July 10th, but they were denied a meeting with the mayor.

- On July 11th, Al Raby and 250 marchers staged a sit-down at Balboa Drive. The police demanded that the marchers remain in one line, which violated an earlier agreement that they be allowed to march in two lines. Twenty-eight of the marchers were arrested.

- Chicago's de facto segregated (aka Jim Crow) school system continued to be the prime target of Civil Rights groups. In September, during its Chicago Convention, the NAACP led a rally against the "Willis Wagons" and marched down State

Street with Mayor Richard J. Daley walking beside its national president, Roy Wilkins.

1963

- In January, the Chicago Area Friends of the Student Nonviolent Coordinating Committee (CAFSNCC) was formed. Lawrence Landry, Sylvia Fisher, Diane Nash and Rose Jennings were the principle organizers.

- Lawrence Landry is selected to be the spokesperson for CCCO.

- On February 28th, Alderman Benjamin Lewis of the 24th Ward in Lawndale was mysteriously slain, gangland style, in his office at Roosevelt Road and Homan. Many speculated that he was killed because he had defected from the Daley Machine and was beginning to confront Chicago's long-time crime syndicate.

- On November 22nd, President John F. Kennedy was assassinated in Dallas, Texas.

- Civil Rights leaders protested the appointment of Mrs. Wendell Green to the school board, who many believe to be a puppet of the Daley Machine.

1964

- To counter plans for a second school boycott, Alderman Kenneth H. Campbell and Congressman William H Dawson championed a new organization called the Assembly to End Prejudice, Injustice and Poverty. This ad-hoc committee was linked with the Daley Machine and failed to diffuse the momentum that helped the first school boycott to be successful.

- On October 29th, Rev. John H. Porter, pastor of the Christ United Methodist Church in Englewood and SCLC organizer, recruited 10,000 community residents to hear Dr. King speak at the Ogden Park Field House.

- Dr. Phillip Hauser, University of Chicago professor, released his study that confirmed the Chicago Public Schools were segregated. In particular, he cites the Washburne Trade School as an example of how Black students are denied admission due to the discriminatory policies of the American Federation of Labor.

1965

- On February 21st, Malcolm X was assassinated in the Audubon Ballroom in Harlem as he was beginning to make a speech.

- In May the Association for the Advancement of Creative Musicians (AACM) was founded as an organization "to expose and showcase original music of its members and to conduct free training programs for aspiring musicians. Principle founders were Muhah Richard Abrams, Kelan Phil Cohran, Jodie Christian and Steve McCall.

- A cadre of ministers and priests organized the Kenwood-Oakwood Community Organization (KOCO) and selected Rev. Jesse Jackson as its first director, who served in this capacity for only a couple of months. Later James McGowan became the director and was followed by Rev. Curtis E. Burrell, Jr. and Robert Lucas, director of CORE: Lucas eventually assumed the position of director after a court injunction had ruled that Rev. Burrell be removed.

- On July 25th, Dr. King led 30,000 demonstrators on a march to City Hall to bring a litany of social, educational and economic grievances, to the attention of Mayor Daley. In a speech at City Hall, he declared "Chicago as the North's most segregated city."

- Rev. James Bevel, a veteran civil rights organizer and aide to Dr. King, arrived in Chicago to garner support from the Black clergy in preparation for Dr. King's pending Freedom Movement campaign in Chicago. However, many Black clergy failed to support Dr. King's new initiative for fear the movement would disrupt the status quo. Among the most prominent of these clergymen was Rev. John Jackson, perennial president of the National Black Baptist Convention and pastor of the Mt. Olivet Baptist Church.

- Jerome Huey, a fifteen year old Black youth, was beaten to death by white thugs while looking for a job in Cicero, Illinois, an all-white suburb near the far west side of Chicago.

1966

- Dr. Donald Smith founded the Center of Inner City Studies, a branch of Northeastern Illinois University. It was located at Oakwood Boulevard and Langley. The Center's primary purpose was to improve the skills of perspective teachers to be more effective in teaching disadvantaged students.

- On January 26th, Dr. King and his wife Coretta moved into a three-story walk-up apartment at 1550 South Hamlin in the Lawndale community. The move symbolized his commitment to eliminate slums and improve housing on Chicago's West Side.

- On February 24, Dr. King and the Honorable Elijah Muhammad, head of the Nation of Islam, met in Chicago for their first and only public recorded meeting.

- Dr. King selects Rev. Jesse Jackson to head Operation Breadbasket, a new program of SCLC to address the economic problems in the Black community.

- On March 12th, the Chicago Freedom Movement, with the support of some unions, held a large Freedom Festival at the International Amphitheater. Celebrities participating included: Harry Belafonte, Sidney Poitier, Dick Gregory and Mahalia Jackson.

- The shooting of a 20-year-old Puerto Rican, Arceilis Cruz, by a Chicago policeman sparked a rebellion by members of the Puerto Rican community on June 12th. This incident was the catalyst that helped the Puerto Rican community acknowledge it shared a common struggle with the Black community. As a result of this acknowledgement, many members of the Puerto Rican community supported the Chicago Freedom Movement.

- Dr. King addressed over 50,000 supporters at a Freedom Rally at Soldiers Field on July 10th. This rally was supported by a broad cross-section of religious, ethnic, civic, labor and civil rights organizations. After the rally, Dr. King led 38,000 followers of the Non-Violent Freedom Fighters to City Hall where they nailed a list of 24 demands on the door. (See Documents)

- Due to the sweltering weather and closing of beaches on July 12th, on the corner of 13th and Throop, an adult opened a fire hydrant so the youth could gain some relief from the heat. Earlier, two policemen had closed the hydrant in accordance with city policy, but the adult who reopened it was arrested. His arrest drew a large crowd of disenchanted people who demanded he be set free. When the policemen refused, a brief conflict ensued and the police called for additional support to help diffuse the conflict. That evening, the conflict spread to other West Side communities and by morning, had erupted into the burning of some stores and looting. To suppress the rebellion, Mayor Daley asked support from the Illinois National Guard's 33rd Infantry Division which was located on the West Side. The Guard responded with 200 guardsmen who began to patrol the streets in jeeps and trucks carrying thirty caliber machine guns. The rebellion spread throughout most of the West Side and for approximately 24 hours it was under martial law.

- After the rebellion, Dr. King met with several leaders of street gangs in his apartment and spoke to them about the futility of violence and that non-violence was a better way to achieve equality and self-reliance. At this meeting, Dr. King encouraged gang members to serve as marshals for the non-violent marchers being plan to protest housing discrimination.

- On July 30th at the Friendship Missionary Baptist Church, Dr. King announced he would address the problems of open housing with a series of non-violent marches in predominantly white segregated communities. (The three communities targeted for the marches were Marquette Park, Gage Park and Bowen Park)

- On July 31st, the first march was at Marquette Park where marchers were met by hundreds of hostile whites who threatened and intimidated the marchers with obscenities and a barrage of rocks, stones, and bottles to show their contempt and anger. Dr. King was hit by a stone on his head but continued to march. Gang members who served as marshals demonstrated considerable restrain during the incident.

- On August 3rd, 500 marchers participated in a second march in Gage Park where they were met with similar acts of hostility. Due to previous commitment, Dr. King did not participate in this march.
- On August 8th at the Warren Avenue Congregational Church, it was announced that the third march, scheduled for Bogan Park, would be cancelled due to the lack of assurances that the marchers would have adequate police protection because of increased anger and hostility that resonated in the white communities.

- A march planned for Cicero, Illinois, an all-white suburb next to Chicago's West Side, was met with mixed feelings from members of the action committee of CCCO and the key organizers of SCLC. On August 26th, the issue was temporarily resolved when Dr. King declared that the march would be cancelled. However, contrary to Dr. King's announcement, Robert Lucas of CORE and Chester Robinson of the WSO agreed to go on with the march. Later, Chester Robinson chose not to participate and Robert Lucas led 250 marchers to Cicero where they encountered greater hostilities than any of the earlier marches, despite the presence of police and guardsmen.

- Walli Saddique (previously known as Lou House), a well-known radio commentator and activist, organized several busloads of Chicagoans to travel to Jackson, Mississippi to join thousands of other marchers to protest the shooting of James Meredith, the first Black student to attend the University of Mississippi. Mr. Meredith was shot during his "March Against Fear" from Memphis to Jackson, Mississippi.

1967

- The YMCA helped to fund the On the Beach Program, held at the 63rd Street Beach Field House, to quell the anticipated violence during the summer. The program, which offered workshops in creative writing, dancing, art and music, was conceived by Betty Conda. Some of the artists who participated weekly were Kelan Phil Cohran and the Pharaohs, Rev. Spencer Jackson and Family and the Darlene Blackburn dancers. A publication from the writer's workshop titled "Black Expression: An Anthology of New Black Poets," featured the works of poets who had never before been published.

- Some of the Blackstone Rangers participated in Oscar Brown, Jr.'s musical revue entitled, "Opportunity Please Knock," which premiered on May 19th at the First Presbyterian Church in Woodlawn. Later, it received some funding from Sammy Davis, Jr. Afterwards, a brief national tour was cancelled due to internal conflict between some members.

- Chicago's emerging young Black artists began to demonstrate in their works an acknowledgement of the Black Arts Movement which had been defined by poet and critic Larry Neal as "the aesthetic and spiritual sister to the Black Power concept."

- At the end of December the Pan-Afrikan community of Chicago began to host an annual city-wide seven day Kwanzaa celebration.

1968

- On March 2nd, the National Advisory Commission on Civil Disorders made public its report, also known as the Kerner Report (named after Governor Otto Kerner). It most poignant finding was that "Our nation is moving toward two societies, one black, one white—separate and unequal."

- On April 4th, Dr. King was assassinated in Memphis, Tennessee. When it was reported, Blacks throughout America began to show their grief and anger. In Chicago these feelings were expressed by Black students from Harrison and Farragut high schools, who combined to begin a peaceful march to Garfield Park where they listened to various speakers lament about what Dr. King stood for and his belief in non-violence. The students then decided to march to Austin High School and join other students to express their spontaneous feelings of grief and anger. Joining the students in their march was Warner Saunders, executive director of the Better Boys Foundation, and John Root, president of the YMCA. En route to Austin High School, the students were met by policemen who ordered them to disperse. Although Saunders and Root informed the policemen that the students meant no harm and were not a threat to public safety, the policemen interpreted the student group as being a mob and aggressively began to disperse them. This set off a negative reaction from the students and put in motion an outcry of police harassment that quickly spread to other West Side communities. Once again, the West Side was in a state of turmoil as the burning and looting of businesses and stores sparked a rebellion that far surpassed the one of 1967.

  As he had done in 1967, Mayor Daley called for the National Guard, who this time responded with over 600 guardsmen accompanied with jeeps and trucks with thirty caliber machine guns. It was also during this time that Mayor Daley gave his infamous order to "shoot to kill!" and for the next two days Black Chicagoans were once again placed under martial law and in a state of war. Although the South Side also experienced similar acts of rebellion, it was the West Side which bore the brunt of its devastating and crippling outcome.

- On May 8th, one hundred Black students, predominantly undergrads, took over the Bursar's Office on the campus of Northwestern University in Evanston, Illinois. The take-over lasted for thirty-eight hours and was a response to the administration's insensitive and paternalistic treatment of Black students who were exposed to a white cultural and educational environment. The leaders of this take-over were Kathy Ogletree, an undergrad student from Chicago's West Side who headed the For Members Only (FMO) organization, and James Turner, a graduate student from New York, who headed the Afro-American Student Union (AASU). Both organizations worked in concert and issued fifteen demands to the administration that represented the central concerns of the Black students. (See Documents in Appendix)

- Concomitantly, a similar outcry for greater student involvement was occurring at Crane Junior College in Chicago which had a predominantly Black student body. Under the leadership of Henry English, a member of the Black Panther Party, Stan Willis, an Air Force veteran, and Edward "Buzz" Palmer, co-founder of the Afro-American Patrolmen's League with Renault Robinson, began a broad community-based activist campaign that demanded a comprehensive Black Studies Program and eventually were primarily responsible for changing its name to Malcolm X Junior College.

- The Chicago Area Association of Black Psychologists was formed under the leadership of Dr. Bobby Wright and Dr. Maisha Bennett. However, it did not form a legal and structural relationship with the National Association of Black Psychologists until the fall of 1968. (See Documents)

- Edward "Buzz" Palmer and Renault Robinson co-founded the Afro-American Patrolman's League to ensure that the Black community was receiving fair treatment and equal protection from the Chicago Police Department. (See Documents)

- The Lawndale People Planning Committee (LPPC), Lawndale Union to End Slums, and West Side Federation merged to form the Lawndale People Planning and Action Conference (LPPAC) to address the poor economic and housing conditions in Lawndale.

- Earnest Thomas from Bogalusa, Louisiana, one of the organizers for the Deacons For Defense, a group committed to protecting Civil Rights organizations, formed a Chicago Chapter with John Harris and Edward "Fats" Crawford.

- The Catalyst, an activists' organization of social workers, human service practitioners and other professionals, was founded to change their traditional roles as gatekeepers for the oppressor to advocates for the oppressed. Charles Ross was its first convener. Later, the Catalyst became aligned with the national movement that was developing cadres of Black social workers to start their own organizations independent from the established white-dominated national association for social workers. In September the Catalyst held an important conference at the Center for Inner City Studies which featured Charles Hamilton, co-author of *Black Power* with Stokely Carmichael, and Lerone Bennett, Jr., senior editor at Johnson Publications and author of *Before the Mayflower*. This conference eventually became the template for the first national Black Social Workers conference, held in Philadelphia in 1969. (See Documents in Appendix)

- The Chicago Chapter of the Illinois Black Panther Party was founded by Fred Hampton, Billy "Che" Brooks, Bobby Rush and Jewell Cook. The chapter quickly became an outspoken advocate of social, economic and political justice. As a member of the National Black Panther Party, headed by Huey Newton in Oakland, California, the Chicago chapter adopted its Ten Point Plan. (See Documents in Appendix)

- Although Blacks played a minor role in the political debacle and confrontations that mired the Democratic National Convention, when thousands of anti-war protestors came to Chicago, the Black community did experience an increase in police surveillance due to rumors that some gang members had aligned themselves with the protestors.

1969

- The new Malcolm X College (formerly Crane Junior College) was becoming the educational hub for Black nationalists, socialists, Marxists and community activists to dialogue and debate over what ideologies and strategies would best achieve Black liberation.

- *The Spook Who Sat By The Door,* Sam Greenlee's controversial but plausible story of a Black CIA agent who organizes members of a Black street gang on Chicago's West Side to fight the white establishment, was first published in March. Later, it was made into a movie, which premiered at the Maryland Theater on 63rd Street in 1973.

- In the spring, the Chicago Chapter of the National Association of Black Social Workers was organized to join other Black social workers' chapters that were also emerging in other cities to establish an agenda that was more relevant to the needs of Black people. Its founding members were Audrey Johnson, James Craigen, Karim Childs, Jerome C. Stevenson, and Barbara Bacon. (See Documents)

- In September Bobby Seale, co-founder of the Black Panther Party, was in Chicago's U.S. District Court to face charges for his alleged role in instigating the rebellion that took place between anti-war protestors and the police at the Democratic National Convention. During the trial he was identified as one of the Chicago Eight who conspired to disrupt the convention. Seale was adamant about his innocence and Judge Julius Hoffman ordered that he be handcuffed to a chair. Seale continued to defy Judge Hoffman and was sentenced to four years for contempt of court. Later, in an appeal upheld by a higher court, he was exonerated.

- On a cold, wintry December 4th night, nine Chicago policemen under the clandestine orders of states attorney Edward V. Hanrahan, initiated a pre-dawn raid on the apartment of Fred Hampton at 2337 South Monroe that left Fred (and Mark Clark, Chairman of the Illinois Black Panther Party) slain from a barrage of gunfire. Verleria Brewer, a sixteen-year-old, was shot in the leg. In this nefarious incident, it was first reported that the policemen encountered resistance from the occupants of the apartment who fired at them first. Days later, after careful examination of the apartment, it was discovered that no one inside had fired a shot and Chairman Fred Hampton had been shot several times while he was asleep.

- On December 15th, the Catalyst and the Black United Front held a press conference at the Pick-Congress Hotel and announced that white people should be under a curfew and not be present in the Black community from 6 pm to 6 am. The announcement was read by Rev. C. T. Vivian, spokesman for the Coalition for United Action, and drew mixed reactions from other Black leaders.

1970 – 1971

- *Bird of the Iron Feather* premiered in January on WTTW television as the first Black dramatic series on Chicago television, based in part on the career of Edward "Buzz" Palmer and created by Richard Durham. Okoro Harold Johnson, veteran director of many plays, was its director.

- Robert Butler, aka Hannibal Barcar Shabazz, organized the All African Peoples Alliance which was located at 3316 West Roosevelt Road. The alliance provided educational and cultural activities for youth that embodied traditional African traditions. It also advocated community control of schools and economic development.

- United Afrikans for One Motherland (UFOMI) was formed and elected James Robinson as its director. Ruwa Chiri, an activist born in Zimbabwe, was his assistant, Sarudzayi Scuanhu as secretary and Kanzetta Howell as treasurer. From UFOMI, the Konakri Institute (AKI) was established and it also published *Akrika Must Unite*, a magazine that featured national and international news about the struggles of African people.

- The Chicago Plan, a program designed to provide jobs for minorities in the building and trade unions, failed to achieve its goals because of resistance from the predominantly white controlled unions. In an effort to contest their control, some street gangs attempted to close down the construction site at the University of Illinois Chicago campus. Several gang leaders were arrested for their involvement in the demonstrations.

1972 – 1973

- As the result of the Black community's ongoing campaign to dethrone State Attorney Hanrahan for his role in the execution of Fred Hampton and Mark Clark, Haranhan was defeated in his bid for reelection by Republican Bernard Carey.

- State Representative Harold Washington's bill, to make Dr. Martin Luther King, Jr., an official holiday in Illinois, was signed by Governor Daniel Walker.

- The Chicago Chapter of the National Black Nurses was formed. (See Documents)

- In March 1972, approximately 8,000 delegates from across the country attended the National Black Political Convention, held in Gary, Indiana at West Side High School. The convention was conceived by Amiri Baraka and its delegates ranged from Julian Bond to Minister Louis Farrakhan and focused on a myriad of social, education and economic issues that were crucial to Black empowerment.

- The Black Theater Alliance was formed to bring Black Theater groups together and to challenge the predominantly white controlled Illinois Arts Council and Chicago Arts Council to provide greater Black representation on their various review, funding, and proposal committees. It also published a newsletter, held several theater festivals and later became the template for the development of the Midwest Black Theater Alliance, which involved theater groups from Missouri, Michigan and Indiana.

- The Rev. Dr. Jeremiah Wright was appointed pastor of the United Trinity Church of Christ and was one of the first clergy to vehemently criticize South Africa's dehumanizing system of apartheid.

- Although the Second International Festival of the Arts and Culture (FESTAC) was scheduled to take place in Nigeria in 1975, it was postponed until 1977. However, the preparation for this prestigious event began in 1973. Chicagoans played a major role in its organization and implementation. Dr. Jeff Donaldson served as chairman of the North American Zone and was assisted by Hoyt Fuller, editor of *Black World*, Abena Joan Brown, president of eta Creative Arts Foundation, and Haki R. Madhubuti, founder of Third World Press.

- In May 1973, the first African Liberation Day parade in Chicago was supported by thousands and began at 31st and Dr. Martin Luther King Drive. It proceeded south on State Street and ended at Washington Park, where an all day program of speeches, music and other festivities were celebrated. African Liberation Day was founded by Ghandian president, Osegyefo Kwame Nkrumah, as a call for African Unity and Liberation.

1974 – 1975

- To break Mayor Daley's ironclad control of the Black community, several Black leaders began to seek a strong independent Black candidate to oppose Daley in 1975. Candidates considered to challenge Daley were eventually narrowed down to State Senator Richard Newhouse and one-time Daley loyalist Congressmen Ralph Metcalfe. Metcalfe declined to be a candidate, but Newhouse did not. However, Metcalfe's endorsement of Alderman William Singer helped to split the Black vote and Daley easily was reelected for a fifth term.

APPENDIX

Catalyst

THIS IS OUR BAG!

CODE OF ETHICS FOR BLACK PEOPLE

The following items are take-off points to help develop awareness about our current state of Blackness and to look at the relevance of what it may take to improve our total participation in the Black Revolution. They are designed to help us confront ourselves, respect the various methods and shades of opinion projected, be open-minded, develop possibilities for coalitions of opinion, provide bases for causes of action and provide the groundwork necessary to effect linkages between Black People.

WE MUST recognize that the traditional role of the Black Leaders has been to act as a buffer between a hostile and unsympathetic white community and our oppressed Black Brothers and Sisters. As Black People, we must determine that this is a condition that we cannot and will not tolerate any longer.

WE MUST make it absolutely clear that we are totally committed to the Revolution.

WE MUST view all issues only from the vantage point of what is best for Black People.

WE MUST be responsible for using our acquired skills to wipe out the obstacles which prevent Black People from achieving maximum realization of their innate potential for social, economic and political growth.

WE MUST demand excellence from anyone serving the Black Community.

WE MUST take advantage of our unique relationship to the system and "TELL IT LIKE IT IS" at every opportunity.

WE MUST demand that the same level of excellence in service be extended to Black People that is extended to whites.

WE MUST stop trying to maintain our status by "PUTTING OTHER BLACK PEOPLE DOWN."

WE MUST demand that the same level of goods and services be placed into Black Communities that is taken out.

WE MUST take appropriate action to exploit all means and ways of establishing and maintaining the human dignity and worth of Black People as a group.

WE MUST give the Black Community and especially the younger generation a sense of the past as a foundation for approaching the future.

WE MUST be totally committed to our individual ongoing learning as well as assuming maximum responsibility for the education of Black People as a group.

WE MUST use our skills to initiate programs for the Black Community based only on information collected and interpreted by Black Researchers.

WE MUST take advantage of every opportunity to use the system in whatever fashion that is beneficial to Black People.

Finally, because the foregoing is essential to the success of the Revolution —

WE MUST PLEDGE to do all that we can to bring these things about BY ANY MEANS NECESSARY.

THE CATALYSTS

GOALS OF AFRO-AMERICAN PATROLMEN'S LEAGUE

1. That the Afro-American Patrolmen's League pledge itself to the support of all community efforts devoted to establishing respect for black manhood, black womanhood and black pride within the law.
2. That the black community and will accept and support the efforts of the Afro-American Patrolmen's League to reverse the distrust and hostility towards black police officers.
3. That the black community and the Afro-American Patrolmen's League dedicate themselves to the proposition that law enforcement may be practiced by black officers with compassion, understanding and efficiency.
4. That the goal of the law enforcement officers will become the employment of courtesy and compassion rather than the mere absence of brutality.
5. That the black community and the black police officers will be mutually supportive of efforts to bring about a new community where unity of purpose and recognition of the nobility of the black heritage will be a deterrent to crime; where moral authority imposed from within will govern human relationships rather than technical legalism; and where those of us who are black will be able to live lives of beautiful fulfillment.[5]

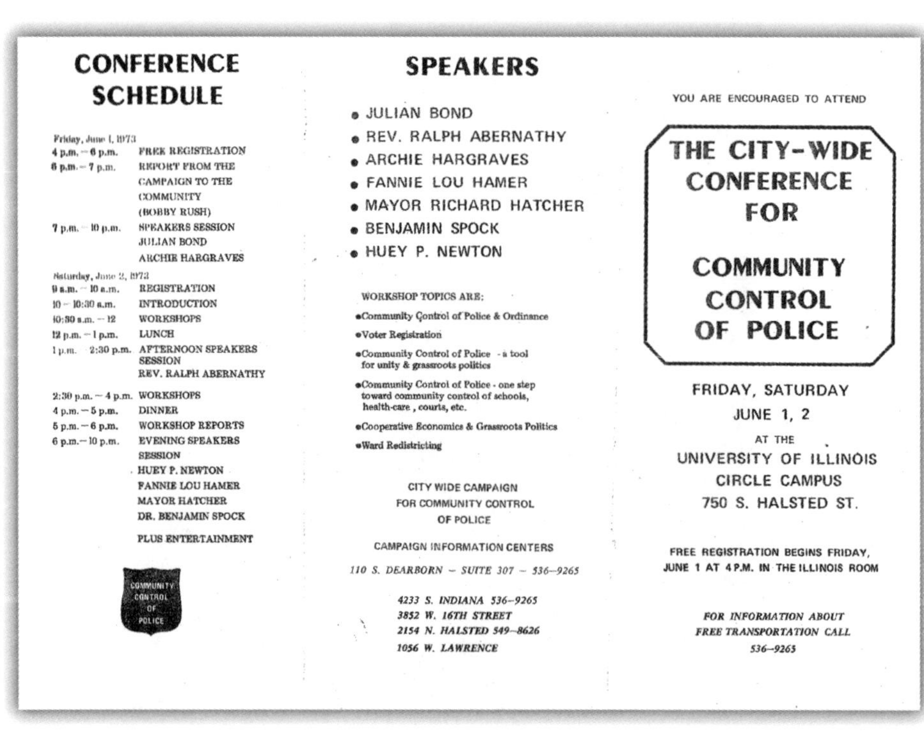

CONFERENCE SCHEDULE

Friday, June 1, 1973

4 p.m. – 6 p.m.	FREE REGISTRATION
6 p.m. – 7 p.m.	REPORT FROM THE CAMPAIGN TO THE COMMUNITY (BOBBY RUSH)
7 p.m. – 10 p.m.	SPEAKERS SESSION JULIAN BOND ARCHIE HARGRAVES

Saturday, June 2, 1973

9 a.m. – 10 a.m.	REGISTRATION
10 – 10:30 a.m.	INTRODUCTION
10:30 a.m. – 12	WORKSHOPS
12 p.m. – 1 p.m.	LUNCH
1 p.m. – 2:30 p.m.	AFTERNOON SPEAKERS SESSION REV. RALPH ABERNATHY
2:30 p.m. – 4 p.m.	WORKSHOPS
4 p.m. – 5 p.m.	DINNER
5 p.m. – 6 p.m.	WORKSHOP REPORTS
6 p.m. – 10 p.m.	EVENING SPEAKERS SESSION HUEY P. NEWTON FANNIE LOU HAMER MAYOR HATCHER DR. BENJAMIN SPOCK

PLUS ENTERTAINMENT

COMMUNITY CONTROL OF POLICE

SPEAKERS

- JULIAN BOND
- REV. RALPH ABERNATHY
- ARCHIE HARGRAVES
- FANNIE LOU HAMER
- MAYOR RICHARD HATCHER
- BENJAMIN SPOCK
- HUEY P. NEWTON

WORKSHOP TOPICS ARE:

- Community Control of Police & Ordinance
- Voter Registration
- Community Control of Police - a tool for unity & grassroots politics
- Community Control of Police - one step toward community control of schools, health-care, courts, etc.
- Cooperative Economics & Grassroots Politics
- Ward Redistricting

CITY WIDE CAMPAIGN
FOR COMMUNITY CONTROL
OF POLICE

CAMPAIGN INFORMATION CENTERS

110 S. DEARBORN – SUITE 307 – 536–9265

4233 S. INDIANA 536–9265
3852 W. 16TH STREET
2154 N. HALSTED 549–8626
1056 W. LAWRENCE

YOU ARE ENCOURAGED TO ATTEND

THE CITY-WIDE CONFERENCE FOR COMMUNITY CONTROL OF POLICE

FRIDAY, SATURDAY
JUNE 1, 2
AT THE
UNIVERSITY OF ILLINOIS
CIRCLE CAMPUS
750 S. HALSTED ST.

FREE REGISTRATION BEGINS FRIDAY, JUNE 1 AT 4 P.M. IN THE ILLINOIS ROOM

FOR INFORMATION ABOUT FREE TRANSPORTATION CALL 536–9265

BLACK STUDENT STATEMENT AND PETITION TO NORTHWESTERN UNIVERSITY ADMINISTRATORS,

Received Monday, April 22, 1968

We, the Black Students at Northwestern University have found the academic cultural and social conditions for us on the campus deplorably limited. In order to counteract the physical, emotional and spiritual strains we have been subjugated to. In order to find some menaing and purpose in our being here, we demand that the following conditions be immediately met.

I. Policy Statement

We demand, firstly, that a policy statement be issued from the administration deploring the viciousness of "white racism: and insuring that all conscious or unconscious racist policies, practices, and institutions existing now on campus will no longer be tolerated. This statement should make clear that Northwestern is willing to go to any extent to enforce such a policy and also to protect the interests of the Black students on campus who have been negatively affected by such racist attitudes and practices. Furthermore, this statement should express Northwestern's readiness to exert its influences (both political and financial, in uprooting racism in the city of Evanston.)

II. Admission

Considering that Black people account for 12% of the total American population, we demand that Northwestern initiate a project which guarantees the gradual increase of the number of Black students to a more "realistic" figure which we shall decide. We dean also that we have some say in the development and initiation of such a project with Black student of our own choosing on the sterring committee. We further demand that at least half (1/2) of each year's incoming Black students are from the inner school system.

As for now, we demand a complete list containing the names of all Black student enrolled at Northwestern as of Fall Quarter 1967.

III. Scholarships

We demand that our scholarships be increased to cover what is now included in our "required jobs" and to include funds for those who want or need to attend summer school. We have found that students who work because they want to, and not because they have to perform much better academically and with less mental tension and frustration. Furthermore, we have found it a contradiction that in view of the fact that we adequately prepare for the type of competition we encountered at Northwestern. We were still expected to keep up and hold a job a mutinously. We strongly fell, as well, that those Black students who want to continue their intellectual pursuits through the summer should have the same opportunity to do so as any other Northwestern student. The University should not deny them that opportunity by requiring that they work instead. In order to substantiate their scholarships for the other three quarters.

IV. Housing

We demand that the University provide a living unit(s) for those Black students who want to live together. We demand that immediate action be taken to provide such a unit(s) by Fall Quarter 1968.

In as much as that Black freshman women do not usually room with each other, we demand that they receive the same treatment as their white roommates. In the past upon receiving room assignments, a white girl or her parents have been allowed to object to having a Negro for a roommate and upon either of their requests a shift in room assignments took place. We contend that if girl or her parents wanted to be assured that she would not be rooming with a Negro, she should have stated on her housing form her preference of a Caucasian roommate to a Negro one. Black students did not even have the option to request another Black student for a roommate. We were told from the start that it was the University's intention to split us up and that we would not be allowed to room with each other.

Due to contradictory (racist) housing policies and practices, to be the definite differences in social and cultural differences between us and our white roommates, and to the general tenseness of the racial situation, we demand that this Black living unit be made available to us by Fall quarter to help alleviate some of the tension of being "a Black student at a white university."

V. Curriculum

We demand that a Black Studies Course be added to the curriculum including studies in Black history, literature, and art in view of the fact that Black accomplishments have been underplayed and Black history misconstrued, we demand to have the ultimate decision in the choice of professors to be hired to teach these courses. There is no doubt that since they inevitably must be "Black" professors no one on the administration is capable of adequately judging their qualification.

VI. Counselling

We demand that a Black Counselor be provided by the University in order to help us properly cope with the psychological, mental, and academic tensions resulting from the dualism of our existence as "black college students." There is a definite need for Black students seeking to overcome the contradictions of the demands placed on us by this white community, which offers little for us to identify with, and the demands of our own people and out native communities which look to us for some kind of inspiration, guidance, and instruction in the struggle to overcome white oppression, to have someone who can relate to us and understand us out of a common experience. The "Great White Father" image the university has been projecting must be destroyed If any real communication is to develop.

VII. Facilities

We demand a Black Student Union, a place to be used for social and recreational activities, as well as a place to office F.M.D. and all other Black organizations on campus. Black students have nothing at Northwestern to call our own. We need a place where we will feel free to come and to go as we please, a place which will substitute for the lack of fraternity and sorority houses and provide us with necessary facilities to function as independently as the Student Senate office.

VIII. Open Occupancy

We are aware that Northwestern University has taken a stand in favor of Open Occupancy. However, what good, we ask, in such a stand when Northwestern is in effect the main promoter of segregation in the City of Evanston? We demand that the University immediately cease with the hypocrisy and take the necessary steps to desegregate all of its real estate holdings. We further demand that evidence be presented to us, verifying that Northwestern is doing more than taking "a stand," on Open Occupancy and that monthly reports be turned over to the president of F.M.O. indicating N.U.'s subsequent progressive measures.

There has been how to solve too much idle talk about some of the problems facing Black students here at Northwestern. Indeed, there has been too much talk and little action in regard to the general racial situation. We are not about to solve America's race problems. If there is in fact a solution, however, we are concerned about the problem as it affects us on campus and in the City of Evanston.

Northwestern was wrong to assume that in bringing us here, we would be able to disassociate ourselves from the injustices, sufferings, and mounting frustration of our people. Like them, we too, are tired of being talked about and we are weary of talking to people who cannot or refuse to do anything else but talk.

It would be useless to engage in further discussion—there are some things which will never be understood, and even if they were understood, it would make little difference anyway. These are our demands of the University. We are willing to confer with the administration, but we have no intention of debating or conceding our stand. We have been to the administration before but with little consequence. We want tangible results, not excuses or even promises. The University either responds to our demands or we have no other alternative but to respond to its lack of response. The University had until 5:00 p.m., Friday, April 26, to notify us of its decision.

CONTACT: Kathryn Ogletree (F.M.O.) James Turner (A.A.S.U.)

DEMANDS LEFT ON THE DOOR OF CITY HALL BY DR. MARTIN LUTHER KING, JR.

Real Estate Boards and Brokers

1. Public statements that all listing will be available on a nondiscriminatory basis.

Banks and Savings Institutions

1. Publication of headcounts of whites, Negroes and Latin Americans for all city departments and for all firms from which city purchases are made.
2. Revocation of contracts with forms that do not have a full scale fair employment practice.
3. Creation of a citizens review board for grievance against police brutality and false arrests or stops and seizures.
4. Ordinance giving ready access to the name of owners and investors for all slum properties.
5. A saturation program of increased garbage collection street cleaning and building inspection services in the slum properties

Political Parties

1. The requirement that precinct captains be residents of the precincts.

Chicago Housing Authority and the Chicago Dwelling Association

1. Program to rehabilitate present public housing including such items as looked lobbies, restrooms in recreation areas, increased police protection and child care on every third floor.
2. Program to increase vastly the supply of low-cost housing on a scattered basis for both low and middle income families.

Business

1. Basic headcounts, including white, Negro and Latin American, by job classification and income level, made public.
2. Racial steps to upgrade and to integrate all department, all levels of employment.

Unions

1. Headcounts in unions for apprentices, journeymen and union staff and officials by job classification. A crash program to remedy any inequities discovered by the head-count.
2. Indenture of at least 400 Negro and Latin apprentices in craft unions.

Governor

1. Prepare legislative proposals for a $2.00 state minimum wage law and for credit reform, including the abolition of garnishment and wage assignment.

Illinois Public Aid Commission and the Cook County Department of Public Aid

1. Encouragement of grievance procedures for the welfare recipients so that recipients know that they can be members of and represented by welfare union or a community organization.
2. Institution of a declaration of income system to replace the degrading investigation and means test for welfare eligibility.

Federal Government

1. Executive enforcement of Title I of the 1984 Civil Rights Act regarding the complaint against the Chicago Board of Education.
2. An executive order for Federal supervision of the nondiscriminatory granting of loans by banks and savings institutions that are members of the Federal Deposit Insurance Corporationor the Federal Deposit Insurance Corporation.
3. Passage of the 1968 Civil Rights Act without any deletions or crippling amendments.
4. Direct funding of Chicago community organizations by the Office of Economic Opportunity.

People

1. Financial support of the freedom movement.
2. Selective buying campaigns against business that boycott the products of Negro-owned companies.
3. Participation in the Freedom Movement target campaigns for the summer, including volunteer services and membership in one of the Freedom Movement Organizations.

"DR. KING'S GET OUT THE VOTE RALLY!"

October 29, 1964

Chicago's Englewood Community

On picture from right to left

Dr. John R. Porter (white trench coat), Dr. Martin Luther King, Jr. (Black coat standing) Dr. Bayard Rustin (with microphone), Rev. Bernard Lee (bending over the stage)

Photo taken by Dr. Porter's photographer
The late George Murphy

PURPOSE OF THE CHICAGO CHAPTER OF THE NATIONAL ASSOCIATION OF BLACK PSYCHOLOGISTS

(Founded by Dr. Bobby Wright and Dr. Maisha Bennett)

Objectives:

1. To access the psychological needs of the Black community.
2. To identity existing psychological services in the Black community.
3. To identify the personnel involved in those services.
4. To create a directory of Black mental health personnel and services in the Black community.
5. To provide psychological services to the Black community.
6. To provide service and counseling to Black students.
7. To create clinical, school, and other internships for Black psychologists and students.
8. To establish permanent offices in the Chicago area that can be utilized by CAABP members and the Black community for the purpose of delivering community psychological services.
9. To cooperate with the Association of Black Psychologists in making it a viable organization in order to implement the above goals for the national Black community.

Organizational Structure

1. Steering Committee
2. Education Committee
3. Counseling Committee
4. Community Services Committee

NATIONAL ASSOCIATION OF BLACK SOCIAL WORKERS CODE OF ETHICS

In America today, no Black person, except the selfish or irrational, can claim neutrality in the quest for Black liberation nor fail to consideration the implication of the events taking place in our society. Given the necessity for committing ourselves to the struggle for freedom, we as Black Americans practicing in the field of social welfare, set forth this state of ideas and guiding principles.

If a sense of community awareness is a precondition to humanitarian acts, then we as Black social workers must use our knowledge of the Black community, our commitments to its determination, and our helping skills for the benefit of Black people as we marshal our expertise to improve the quality of life of Black people. Our activities will be guided by our Black consciousness, our determination to protect the security of the Black community, and to serve as advocates to relieve suffering of Black people by any means necessary.

Therefore, as Black social workers we commit ourselves, collectively, to the interest of our Black brethren and as individuals subscribe to the following statements:

- I regard as my primary obligation the welfare of the Black individual, Black family and Black community and will engage in action for improving social conditions.
- I give precedence to this mission over my personal interest
- I adopt the concept of a Black extended family and embrace all Black people as my brothers and sisters, making no distinction between their destiny and my own.
- I hold myself responsible for the quality and extent of service I perform and the quality and extent of service performed by the agency or organization in which I am employed, as it relates to the Black community.
- I accept the responsibility to protect the Black community against unethical and hypocritical practice by an individual or organizations engaged in social welfare activities.
- I stand ready to supplement my paid or professional advocacy with voluntary service in the Black public interest.
- I will consciously use my skills and my whole being as an instrument for social change, with particular attention directed to the establishment of Black social institutions.

BLACK LAW RIGHTS OF ALL BLACK PEOPLE

BL

RIGHTS X

NO.	BLACK LAW SOCIETY	FROM	TO	MALE	FEMALE	FOOD	CLOTHES	SHELTER	SAFETY	WORKER	WARRIORS	B.L.D.	AS MANY WIVES AS HE CAN AFFORD
1	Rights of Babies	0	6	X	X	X	X	X	X			X	
2	Rights of Children	6	12	X	X	X	X	X	X			X	
3	Rights of Young Men	13	30	X							X	X	X
4	Rights of Young Women	13	30		X	X	X	X	X			X	
5	Rights of Full Men	30	60	X						X		X	X
6	Rights of Full Women	30	60		X	X	X	X	X	X		X	
7	Rights of Elders	60	X	X	X	X	X	X	X			X	X

GIVE ETERNAL THANKS TO:

1. OUR ANCESTORS FOR NOT GIVING UP.
2. OUR ANCESTORS FOR NOT DEVELOPING A GENOCIDAL ATTITUDE AND DYING.
3. OUR ANCESTORS FOR NOT BECOMING DEPRESSED TO THE DEGREE OF A HOPELESS STATE OF MIND.
4. OUR ANCESTORS FOR THEIR GREAT STRENGTH AND ENDURANCE.
5. OUR ANCESTORS FOR MAKING IT POSSIBLE FOR US ALL, BEING HERE.

BLACK MASSES CLASS - NATIONAL HOLIDAY

Calendar Seasons

ASSES	BABIES	CHILDREN	WARRIORS	WORKERS	ELDERS
	MALE AND FEMALE	MALE AND FEMALE	NEW LIFE — Challenging, Alertness, responsiveness, physical strength, searching, unpredictable, daring, courageous, ferocious, bold, brave, unsettled, temperamental, protective.	MALE AND FEMALE	MALE AND FEMALE
	NEW LIFE — THE POSITIVE BEGINNING OF A SINGLE PERSON ON EARTH. THE MOST TENDER, INNOCENT, INTRIGUING, HELPLESS AND ONE OF THE MOST BEAUTIFUL SEASONS IN EXISTENCE.	NEW LIFE — AMAZEMENT, HAPPY, PLAYFUL, CAREFREE, INNOCENT, HONEST, PERSISTENT, POSSESSIVE, CURIOUS, DEMANDING, ENERGETIC.	**SISTERS** NEW LIFE — Radiant, charming, graceful, feminine brave, loyal to their love, beautiful, dependable, patient, motivating, inspirationing, aggressive, determined, relentless of desire, alluring, tender, loving, soft, sentimental, subtil, temperamental.	NEW LIFE — SOCIAL MATURITY, POLITICALLY CONSISTENT, DEPENDABLE, PREDICTABLE, MAXIMUM MENTAL, STABILITY PLANNERS AND FORMULATERS OF THE FUTURE, HEIGHT OF KNOWLEDGE.	NEW LIFE — BLESSED, STEADY, HUMAN HISTORIANS, ENCOURAGERS OF TRADITION AND CULTURE, WISDOM, BEAUTIFUL, MYSTERIOUS, UNDERSTANDING. — THE MIND FROM THE PAST AND THE EYES INTO THE FUTURE.
	0 3.12-4 6.12	Young Middle Age Elder	Young Middle Age Elder	Young Middle Age Elder	61 90.12 91 Death—
	Young Middle Age Elder	7 9.12-10 12.12	13 21.12-22 30.12	31 45.12-46 60.12	Young Middle Age Elder
	APRIL MAY	JUNE JULY	AUG SEPT	OCT NOV	DE JA FE MA

KUUMBA THEATER
12 PRINCIPLES OF ART

1. We are an African people, bound together as a world-wide family by race, ancestry, culture and common oppression
2. Black art and Black life are inseparable
3. Black art is functional
4. Black art must deal honestly and fully with every aspect of the Black condition, past and present
5. Black art must provide positive images of African people, and if not, say something relevant to hem about their condition while presenting negative images
6. Black art must clearly define the social, political, economic and cultural context of any realities it treats
7. Black art must relate to all Black people, and not just the middle class or intellectuals
8. We reject the sterile Western concept of "art for art's sake"
9. There is a lasting relationship between Black art and politics
10. Black artists not only owe an equitable portion of their time and talent to the Black community but also their earnings
11. Black art and artist must be fully supported and judged by Black people
12. Black artist must be rooted in the Black community and totally involved in its activities and struggle

History of CCNBNA

In the fall of 1973 in Chicago, Illinois the Chicago Chapter of the National Black Nurses' Association, Inc., was formed. Having been inspired by the First National Convention in Cleveland, Ohio, this group of nurses set out to establish a chapter dedicated to the ideals of unity, sisterhood, brotherhood, and fostering the ideals of honesty, integrity, understanding, and love.

Membership is open to R.N.'s, L.P.N.'s and Student Nurses regardless of race, creed, color, national origin, sex or age.

Philosophy

Provision for the enjoyment of optimal health is the birthright of every American. Major health interest groups and governmental agencies believe this and act upon it.

Yet Black Americans, along with other minority groups in our society, are by design neglected/excluded from the means to achieve access to the health mainstream of America.

Therefore, we as Black Nurses have established a national organization to investigate, define, and determine what the health care needs of Black Americans are, to implement changes, to make available to Black Americans and other minorities health care commensurate to that of the larger society.

Black Nurses have the understanding, knowledge, interest, concern, and experience to make a significant difference in the health care status of the Black Community.

Purposes and Objectives

In order to implement our belief we find it mandatory for Black Nurses to:

Define and determine nursing care for Black consumers for optimum quality of care by acting as their advocates.

Act as change agents in reconstructing existing institutions and/or helping to establish institutions to suit our needs.

Serve as the national nursing body to influence legislation and policies that affect Black people; and work cooperatively and collaboratively with other health workers to this end.

Conduct, analyze, and publish to increase the body of knowledge about health needs of Blacks.

Compile and maintain a National Directory of Black Nurses on all levels, by providing consultation to nursing faculties and by monitoring for proper utilization and placement of Black Nurses.

Recruit, counsel and assist Black persons interested in nursing to insure a constant procession of Blacks into the field.

Be the vehicle for unification of Black Nurses of varied age groups, educational levels, and geographic locations to insure continuity and flow of our common heritage.

Collaborate with other Black groups to compile archives relevant to historical, current and future activities of Black Nurses.

Provide the impetus and means for Black Nurses to write and publish on an individual or collaborative basis.

Meetings held second Saturday.

If you wish to become a member, please return t[illegible] application accompanied by your check or mone[illegible] der to:

CHICAGO CHAPTER
NATIONAL BLACK NURSE[illegible]
ASSOCIATION
P.O. BOX 4612
CHICAGO, ILLINOIS [illegible]
(773) 792-722[illegible]

MEMBERSHIP INFORMATION

Name ________________ (Last) (First) (M.I.)

Address ________________

City ________ State ________ Zip ________

Home Tel. ( ) ________ D.O.B ________

S. S. # ________________

State(s) Licensed In ________________

EDUCATION (HIGHEST LEVEL OF EDUCATION)

Licensed Vocational/ Prac. Nurse ______ Baccalaureate ______ Other ______

Diploma ________ Masters ________

Associate ________ Doctorate ________

PRACTICE AREA

Hospital ________ Home Main. Org. ________

N[illegible]ing Home ________ Industry ________

[illegible] Svc ________ Private Office ________

[illegible]ify) ________

CHICAGO CHAPTER NATIONAL BLACK NURSES ASSOCIATION, INC.

Contributors

(A) Ancestor (H) History Makers

Dr. Afi Samella B. Abdullah—Past President of the Association of Black Psychologists and a founding member of the National Association of Black Social Workers. She is the owner and lead Mental Health consultant for Abdullah and Associates.

Dr. Damali Carol L. Adams—Founder and CEO of Urban Prescriptives Inc., a consulting firm that specializes in program and organizational development for enterprises engaged in educational, social, political and cultural practice. She is a founding member of the Catalyst, Association of Black Sociologists, Ujima Learning Center, and the Council on Black Studies. Dr. Adams is the past Executive Director of Northeastern Illinois University's Jacob Carruthers Center for Inner City Studies, a former Director of African American Studies at Loyola University, and a past President of DuSable Museum of African American History. (H)

Dr. Abdul Alkalimat aka Gerald McWorter—Professor Emeritus of African-American Studies and Information Science, University of Illinois, Urbana-Champaign. He is co-author with Dr. Douglas Gill of *Harold Washington and the Crisis of Black Power in Chicago*. He moderates the largest African-American Studies discussion list and edits Malcolm X: A Research Site.

Monroe Anderson—Former journalist for *Chicago Tribune*, reporter for National Observer, assistant editor for *Ebony* Magazine, correspondent for *Newsweek* and press secretary of former Mayor Eugene Sawyer of Chicago. (H)

Hannibal Tirus Afrik aka Harold Charles—Founding member of Council of Independent Black Institutions, Afrikan National Rites of Passage Kollective, National Coalition of Blacks for Reparations in America, Republic of New Afrika and Malcolm X College Annual Kwanzaa Celebration. He is the co-founder of Shule Ya Wototo, an independent school. (A) (H)

Dr. Donn F. Bailey—Past Director of the Center for Inner City Studies (CICS), Northeastern University, Ebonics scholar and Chairman on Desegregation of Public Schools. (A)

Brenetta Howell Barrett—President and CEO, Pathfinders Preventions Education Fund, and Founder of African American Women for Access and Reproductive Education. She served in the cabinet of Governor Dan Walker, Vice-president of Chicago Committee to Defend the Bill of Rights and Co-founder Chicago's Westside NAACP Branch. In addition, she served as Mayor Harold Washington's Private Industry County Commissioner of Consumer Services. (H)

Lerone Bennett, Jr.—Former Senior Editor for Ebony Magazine, imminent historian and author of Before the Mayflower and Forced into Glory: Abraham Lincoln's White Dream. (H)

Timuel D. Black Jr.—Distinguished elder, civil rights activist, Professor Emeritus of Social Sciences, City College of Chicago and author of *Bridges of Memory: Chicago's First Wave of Black Migration*. (H)

Abena Joan Brown—Co-founder Ebony Talent Performing Arts (eta) and Catalyst. Board member Chicago Fine Arts Commission and Queen Mother to Chicago's Black Arts Movement. (A) (H)

Rev. Curtis Burrell—Pastor of Woodlawn Mennonite Church and former Executive Director of Kenwood-Oakland Community Organization (KOCO).

Margaret G. Burroughs—An African American artist, educator, institution builder and art activist. An exceptional printmaker, she worked with linoleum block prints to create evocative images of African American culture. Burroughs was a co-founder of the DuSable Museum of African American History. (A) (H)

Hannibal Barcar Shabazz aka Robert C. Butler—Is a retired Race and Economic Inequality and Gender Inequality professor from the University of Memphis. Presently, he serves as a consultant in Higher Education and Innovative Solutions in Nashville. He can be contacted at: butlernshvll@aol.com.

Dr. Iva E. Carruthers—General Secretary, Samuel DeWitt Proctor Conference, Kemetic scholar and author of The Church and Reparations: An African American Perspective. (H)

Kelan Phil Cohran—Was a jazz musician. He was best known for playing trumpet in the Sun Ra Arkestra in Chicago from 1959 to 1961, and for his involvement in the foundation of the Association for the Advancement of Creative Musicians (AACM). (A) (H)

James Compton—Retired President of the Chicago Urban League. Served on boards of Com Ed, De Paul University and Ariel Mutual Funds and eta Creative Arts Foundation. He served as Board President of the Chicago Public Library and was a member of the Chicago Broad of Education. (H)

Dr. Nyala Joan Smith Cooper—Founder of Afri-Psych Consultants. She remains active in community and is a Licensed Psychologist in 3 states (CA, IL and NV). Her years of treatment-related training, research mentoring and grant development span more than four decades. Her thirty-five years of marriage to Ernest C. Cooper (d. 2016) has given her loving generational descendants.

Ellis Cose is the author of a dozen books on issues of national and international concern, including the best-selling non-fiction book, *The Rage of a Privileged Class,* a novel, *The Best Defense*, and is currently completing his memoir, *Fighting to be Heard.* (H)

Arlene Crawford—Visual artist, curator, educator, muralist and cultural activist. She served on the Executive Board of the National Conference of Artists as the Youth Initiatives, co-chair, Executive Board Secretary for the African American Arts Alliance, co-founded the Sutherland Community Arts Initiative and is a member of AfriCOBRA.

Dr. Amira Millicent Davis—Independent scholar, activist, artist, educator, consultant and founder of AmiRa Enterprise.

Charles A. Davis— A noted civic leader and former Secretary of the South Side Branch, NAACP. He is a Commercial real estate developer and founder of Chicago's first African American public relations agency. (A) (H)

Congressman Danny Davis—U. S. Representative for Illinois 7th Congressional District. He is a member of the Congressional Black Caucus and Chairman of the Congressional Postal Caucus. (H)

W.E. Dunbar—Was a member of the Chicago Illinois Chapter of the Black Panther Party for Self-Defense (BPP). He is a founding member of the Illinois BPP History Project, which is currently conducting oral histories to document the Chicago Chapter.

Dr. Michael C. Edwards—Is the former Chairperson and Director of Counseling and Psychological Services at Chicago State University. He now serves as Co-Director of the Institute for Youth and Community Engagement.

Dorothy Odell Foster—Director, Government Affairs and Board member, Ebony Talent Performing Arts (eta).

Charles A. Grantham—Retired Special Education Teacher and former U. S. Peace Corps Volunteer. He is the author of The Battle for Kemet and lecturer on national and international topics pertaining to Africa and Ancient Egypt (Kemet).

Eric E. Graham—Practicing attorney. Appointments include Assistant Attorney, State of Illinois and Hearing Officer, Fair Employment Practice Commission. He served as council to Black Legislative Clearing House and Illinois Senate Committee on Economic Development. Graham represented not-for-profit groups such as Garfield Organization, Evanston Community Hospital, Afro-American Patrolmen's League and Trinity United Church of Christ. (H)

Dr. Douglas Gill—Retired professor, University of Illinois Circle Campus, KOCO administrator and co-author with Dr. Abdul Alkalimat, Harold Washington and the Crisis of Black Power.

Patricia L. Hill—Educator, law enforcement officer and community activist, served as both president and executive director of the African-American Police League. (H)

Runako Jahi—Is a theater director, playwright, performer, acting coach, poet, set designer, scenic painter, and portrait painter. He is the former Artistic Director of eta Creative Arts Foundation.

Bennett Johnson—Book Publishing Executive and co-founder of Path Press Inc., with Herman E. Gilbert and Frank London Brown. Johnson was vice-president and editorial support for Third World Press. (H)

Okoro Harold Johnson—Is an actor, producer, director and playwright. He served as Artistic Director at ETA Creative Arts Foundation for 17 years and was director of South Shore Cultural Center. (A) (H).

Lawrence E. Kennon—Civil Rights Attorney who represented the NAACP, ACLC, Black Panthers Party and the African American Patrolmen's League. He served as Vice President, Cook County Bar Association, Board member, South Side Community Arts Center and, as a member of the National Lawyers Guild, worked in the Mississippi Summer Project. Kennon, with Attorney Stan Willis, initiated legal proceedings against Jon Burge for police brutality.

Benneth Lee—Founder and CEO, National Alliance for the Empowerment of the Formerly Incarcerated, assistant professor, Jacob H. Carruthers Center for Inner City Studies and Community Liaison and Reentry Specialist to TASC.

Roy Lewis—Renowned international photographer and recipient of the Maurice Sorrell Lifetime Achievement Award. His photographic exhibit titled "EVERYWHERE" has been shown at the Essence Music Festival in New Orleans, DuSable Museum of African American history in Chicago and Blackburn University Center Gallery at Howard University. (H)

Theodis R. Leonard Sr.—Served as principal of Paderewski School in Chicago and was a lifetime member of the NAACP. He was an informal advisor to Congressman Danny Davis and retired State Representative Arthur L. Turner. (A)

Dr. Antonio R. Lopez—Senior Advisor for the Little Village Environmental Justice Organization and member of St. Charles Juvenile Correctional Center Mentors.

Robert Lucas—Former Executive Director, Kenwood Oakland Community Organization and member of CORE. (A) (H)

Dr. D. Soyini Madison—Professor of Performing Studies and Anthropology at Northwestern University. She is the author of Critical Ethnography: Method, Performance and Ethics and Acts of Activism Human Rights as Radical Performance.

Dr. Haki R. Madhubuti—Is an award-winning poet, essayist, educator, founder and publisher of Third World Press. He is the author of over thirty books. A long-time community activist and institution builder, Madhubuti is a co-founder of the Institute of Positive Education and the co-founder of four schools in Chicago. He retired in 2011 after a distinguished teaching career that included Chicago State University and DePaul University where he served as the Ida B. Wells-Barnett University Professor. (H)

Dr. Safisha Madhubuti—Is the Edwina S. Tarry Professor of Education in the School of Education and Social Policy and in African-American Studies at Northwestern University. She is a past president of the American Educational Research Association (AERA). She is a co-founder of four African-centered schools and is the chair of the Board of Directors for the Betty Shabazz International Charter Schools.

Dwight McKee—Serves as a South Side Community Advisor to Chicago Votes Action Fund and is a manager with Urban Strategies Solution.

Edward L. "Buzz" Palmer—A former member of the Chicago Police department and founder of the African American Patrolman's League. With his wife Alice, he co-developed the People Programme, which is dedicated to analyzing and sharing international policy. (H)

Lu Palmer—Served as a journalist for the Chicago Defender and Chicago Daily News. Radio commentator for "Lu's Notebook" and noted for his famous saying "It's enough to make a Negro turn Black." (A) (H)

John Shaka Parker—Freelance writer and poet.

Dr. Harold Pates—Former president of Kennedy-King College and founding member of the Chicago Communiversity, Northeastern State University, Association of African Educators, Kemetic Institute and the Study of Classical African Civilizations. (H)

Rev. Kwame John R. Porter—Retired pastor of the Christ United Methodist Church. Founded first SCLC Chapter in Chicago and first Black Student Body President at Garrett Theologian Seminary. Also, is author of several books which include the Autobiography of Black Male Violence and Rev. Jeremiah A. Wright Jr., and President Barack H. Obama: Role Models for Excellence in Leadership. (H)

Nahaz Rogers—Activist, lecturer and historian. (A)

Dr. Fannie Rushing—Associate professor, Department of History, Benedictine University, Coordinator, Southern Africa Program of the American Friends Service Committee, Director of Minority Services, Rosary College and Specialist in history and culture of African people in Latin American and the Caribbean. (H)

Rev. Al Sampson—Ordained by Dr. Martin Luther King Jr., retired pastor, Fernwood United Methodist Church, Assistant Director of Affiliates, SCLC and Founder and President of Agricultural Improvement Project. (H)

Warner Saunders—Retired co-anchor WMAQ –TV. Member of Chicago Journalism Hall of Fame and the Chicago Academy of Television Arts land Science Silver Circle. Recipient of 19 Emmy Awards and honored by Museum of Broadcast Communications (2009). (H)

Sarudzayi Chapupu Sevanhu—Co-founder for United Africans for One Motherland International (UFOMI), organizer of All-People's Revolutionary Party, Pan-Africanist and grandmother to six children and great grandmother to three children. Currently writing her memoirs of her political journey.

Milele Cheryl Simms—Organizer for the Westside Organization (WSO) and cadre member of the Institute of Positive Education (IPE). She was co-convener of the National Black Political Convention in Chicago (1981), and economic developer in the South Shore community and owner of "A Natural Harvest," food and health store.

Dr. Barbara Sizemore—First Black woman to be elected superintendent of the District of Columbia Public Schools. She served as District Superintendent of the Woodlawn Experimental School in Chicago, Professor Emerita at De Paul University and Scholar in Residence at the National Alliance of Black Educators. Sizemore was a recipient of Lifetime Achievement Award from Research Focus on Black Education and a Chicago Charter School, Barbara Sizemore Academy, bears her name. (A) (H)

Dr. Robert Starks—Educator, political consultant and activist professor. He served as Director of Black Studies, Northern Illinois University and Associate professor of political science at Jacob Carruthers Center for Inner City Studies. He served as Chairman, Illinois Black United Fund and contributing editor to Urban Affairs Quarterly. (H)

Thomas N. Todd—Civil Rights attorney, president of Operation PUSH, law professor, Northwestern University. (H)

William Walker—Graduate of the Columbia College of Art and Design is considered by many to be the "father of the Black Arts Mural Movement" and one of the architects of Chicago's famed Wall of Respect. (A)

Soyini Walton—Founding member of New Concept Developmental Center and Betty Shabazz International Charter School. She was the founding principal of the Barbara A. Sizemore Academy. She is the president of her own company Asset E3 which provides mechanical and environmental engineering services for corporate and government clients.

Judge Mitchell Ware—Former Justice of the Circuit Court of Cook Count and Illinois first African American State Trooper. He served as Superintendent of the Illinois Division of Narcotic Control, Deputy Superintendent of the Chicago Police Department Bureau of Inspectional Services and appointed by the president as a Commissioner on the National Commission on Marijuana and Drug Abuse.

Francis Ward—Former professor of journalism, Syracuse University, journalist for Los Angeles Times and co-founder Kuumba Workshop.

Harold Lee Washington—Was an American lawyer and politician from the state of Illinois who was elected as the 41st Mayor of Chicago. Washington was noted as the first African-American to be elected as mayor of Chicago in February 1983. Washington was also a member of the U.S. House of Representatives representing the Illinois First District. Prior to his time as a member of the House of Representatives, Washington served in the Illinois State Senate and the Illinois House of Representatives. (A)

Dr. Conrad Worrill—Professor Emeritus and former Director, Jacob H. Carruthers Center for Inner City Studies. Has been an activist/scholar for over fifty years and is currently writing his memoirs on his participation in the African Liberation Movement. (H)

About the Editor

Useni Eugene Perkins has been truly blessed to have had two successful careers. As a Human Service Administrator, he has been the President of the Better Boys Foundation Family Center in Chicago, President of the Portland Urban League, President of the DuSable Museum of African American History and Director of the Chicago State University Family Life Center. As a poet , playwright and author, he served as the Chairman for the Artists for Harold Washington, a city-wide coalition of artists that campaigned on behalf of Chicago's first Black mayor. He also is the publisher of *Black Child Journal* and the Presiding Elder for the National Rites of Passage Institute. In 2002 he was honored with the National Black Network Playwright Award for his play "If We Must Die". Also, in 2016 he was awarded the Black Ensemble Theater Playwright Award. In 1999, he was inducted into the Gwendolyn Brooks National Literary Hall of Fame for Writers of African Descent. He also is a History Maker and his iconic poem "Hey Black Child", with illustrations by Bryan Collier, will be released by Little Brown and Company in the fall of 2017.

Foreword by

Julieanna L. Richardson, Public Historian and Founder & Executive Director of *The HistoryMakers,* has a unique and diverse background in theatre, television production and the cable television industry. She is a magna cum laude graduate of Brandeis University, where she double-majored in Theatre Arts and American Studies. After conducting oral histories on the Harlem Renaissance and Langston Hughes, Richardson attended Harvard Law School. She was driven to start *The HistoryMakers* out of a strong desire to make a difference and to leave a living legacy. The University of Illinois at Chicago's Great Cities Institute named Julieanna Richardson its Vernon D. Jarrett Fellow. In 2002, she served on the board of The Henry Hampton Collection at Washington University. She currently sits on the Honors Council of Lawyers for the Creative Arts and was appointed in 2011 to the Comcast NBCUniversal African American Diversity Council. In 2012, she was awarded an Honorary Doctorate in the Humanities by Howard University; and in 2014, she served as the commencement speaker for Dominican University who also awarded her an Honorary Doctorate in the Humanities. In 2014, *Black Enterprise Magazine* awarded Richardson its 2014 Legacy Award, its highest recognition of women's achievement.